New Perspectives on

The Internet

8th Edition

Comprehensive

New Perspectives on

The Internet

8th Edition

Comprehensive

Gary P. Schneider
Quinnipiac University

Jessica Evans

COURSE TECHNOLOGY
CENGAGE Learning™

Australia • Brazil • Japan • Korea • Mexico • Singapore • Spain • United Kingdom • United States

COURSE TECHNOLOGY
CENGAGE Learning™

New Perspectives on The Internet, 8th Edition—Comprehensive

Vice President, Publisher: Nicole Jones Pinard

Executive Editor: Marie L. Lee

Associate Acquisitions Editor: Brandi Shailer

Senior Product Manager: Kathy Finnegan

Product Manager: Leigh Hefferon

Associate Product Manager: Julia Leroux-Lindsey

Editorial Assistant: Zina Kresin

Director of Marketing: Cheryl Costantini

Marketing Manager: Ryan DeGrote

Marketing Coordinator: Kristen Panciocco

Developmental Editors: Amanda Brodkin,
    Kim T. M. Crowley

Senior Content Project Manager:
    Catherine G. DiMassa

Composition: GEX Publishing Services

Text Designer: Steve Deschene

Art Director: Marissa Falco

Cover Designer: Elizabeth Paquin

Cover Art: Bill Brown

For product information and technology assistance, contact us at
Cengage Learning Customer & Sales Support, 1-800-354-9706

For permission to use material from this text or product,
submit all requests online at **cengage.com/permissions**
Further permissions questions can be emailed to
permissionrequest@cengage.com

Some of the product names and company names used in this book have been used for identification purposes only and may be trademarks or registered trademarks of their respective manufacturers and sellers.

Microsoft and the Office logo are either registered trademarks or trademarks of Microsoft Corporation in the United States and/or other countries. Course Technology, Cengage Learning is an independent entity from the Microsoft Corporation, and not affiliated with Microsoft in any manner.

Disclaimer: Any fictional data related to persons or companies or URLs used throughout this book is intended for instructional purposes only. At the time this book was printed, any such data was fictional and not belonging to any real persons or companies.

ISBN-13: 978-0-538-74495-9

ISBN-10: 0-538-74495-2

Course Technology
20 Channel Center Street
Boston, Massachusetts 02210
USA

Cengage Learning is a leading provider of customized learning solutions with office locations around the globe, including Singapore, the United Kingdom, Australia, Mexico, Brazil, and Japan. Locate your local office at:
international.cengage.com/region

Cengage Learning products are represented in Canada by Nelson Education, Ltd.

To learn more about Course Technology, visit **www.cengage.com/coursetechnology**

To learn more about Cengage Learning, visit **www.cengage.com.**

Purchase any of our products at your local college store or at our preferred online store **www.ichapters.com**

Printed in the United States of America
1 2 3 4 5 6 7 8 9 13 12 11 10 09

Preface

The New Perspectives Series' critical-thinking, problem-solving approach is the ideal way to prepare students to transcend point-and-click skills and take advantage of all that the Internet has to offer.

Our goal in developing the New Perspectives Series was to create books that give students the software concepts and practical skills they need to succeed beyond the classroom. With this new edition, we've updated our proven case-based pedagogy with more practical content to make learning skills more meaningful to students.

With the New Perspectives Series, students understand *why* they are learning *what* they are learning, and are fully prepared to apply their skills to real-life situations.

About This Book

This book provides complete coverage of the Internet, and includes the following:
- Up-to-date coverage of the most popular browsers and email tools, highlighting new features such as tabbed browsing
- Instruction on how to use Microsoft Internet Explorer 8, Mozilla Firefox 3, Google Chrome, Microsoft Outlook Express, Windows Mail, and Webmail
- A comprehensive presentation of searching the Web and downloading data, including search engines, digital rights management, online storage providers, and Web-based collaboration services
- Expanded and in-depth coverage of user-generated content on the Web, wireless networks, protecting privacy and avoiding identity theft, and successful online businesses
- Interactive Student Edition Labs on using a browser, working with email, protecting a computer from viruses, wireless networking, creating Web pages, Web design principles, protecting privacy online, and electronic commerce
- An Online Companion, which is a centralized and constantly updated launching pad for students to find all the links they will use and explore in conjunction with this text
- Updated business case scenarios throughout, which provide a rich and realistic context for students to apply the concepts and skills presented
- Complete compatibility with Windows XP, Windows Vista, and Windows 7

System Requirements

This book assumes that either Microsoft Internet Explorer 8 (or higher) or Mozilla Firefox 3.5 (or higher), and Windows Vista or Windows 7 are installed. (Students using Internet Explorer 7 (or lower) or Firefox 3.0 (or lower) and Windows XP can still complete the steps in this book, but they might encounter some differences.) Note that the figures and steps in this edition were written using Windows 7; therefore, Windows Vista users might notice minor differences in the figures and steps. This book assumes that students have a complete installation of the Web browser and its components, an Internet connection, and the ability to create an email account. Because the Web browser or email program students use might be different from those used in the figures in this book, students' screens might differ slightly; this difference does not present any problems for students completing the tutorials.

"I really love the Margin Tips, which add 'tricks of the trade' to students' skills package. In addition, the Reality Check exercises provide for practical application of students' knowledge. I can't wait to use them in the classroom."
—Terry Morse Colucci
Institute of Technology, Inc.

www.cengage.com/ct/newperspectives

The New Perspectives Approach

Context
Each tutorial begins with a problem presented in a "real-world" case that is meaningful to students. The case sets the scene to help students understand what they will do in the tutorial.

Hands-on Approach
Each tutorial is divided into manageable sessions that combine reading and hands-on, step-by-step work. Colorful screenshots help guide students through the steps. **Trouble?** tips anticipate common mistakes or problems to help students stay on track and continue with the tutorial.

InSight

InSight Boxes
InSight boxes offer expert advice and best practices to help students better understand how to work with the Internet. With the information provided in the InSight boxes, students achieve a deeper understanding of the concepts behind the features and skills presented.

Tip

Margin Tips
Margin Tips provide helpful hints and shortcuts for more efficient use of the Internet. The Tips appear in the margin at key points throughout each tutorial, giving students extra information when and where they need it.

Reality Check

Reality Checks
Comprehensive, open-ended Reality Check exercises allow students to practice skills by completing practical, real-world tasks, such as hosting a Web site, evaluating Internet resources, searching for information of personal interest, and shopping online.

Review

In New Perspectives, retention is a key component to learning. At the end of each session, a series of Quick Check questions helps students test their understanding of the concepts before moving on. Each tutorial also contains an end-of-tutorial summary and a list of key terms for further reinforcement.

Apply

Assessment
Engaging and challenging Review Assignments and Case Problems have always been a hallmark feature of the New Perspectives Series. Colorful icons and brief descriptions accompany the exercises, making it easy to understand, at a glance, both the goal and level of challenge a particular assignment holds.

Reference Window

Task Reference

Reference
While contextual learning is excellent for retention, there are times when students will want a high-level understanding of how to accomplish a task. Within each tutorial, Reference Windows appear before a set of steps to provide a succinct summary and preview of how to perform a task. In addition, a complete Task Reference at the back of the book provides quick access to information on how to carry out common tasks. Finally, each book includes a combination Glossary/Index to promote easy reference of material.

Our Complete System of Instruction

Coverage To Meet Your Needs

Whether you're looking for just a small amount of coverage or enough to fill a semester-long class, we can provide you with a textbook that meets your needs.

- Brief books typically cover the essential skills in just 2 to 4 tutorials.
- Introductory books build and expand on those skills and contain an average of 5 to 8 tutorials.
- Comprehensive books are great for a full-semester class, and contain 9 to 12+ tutorials.

So if the book you're holding does not provide the right amount of coverage for you, there's probably another offering available. Visit our Web site or contact your Course Technology sales representative to find out what else we offer.

Online Companion

This book has an accompanying Online Companion Web site designed to enhance learning. This Web site includes:

- All the links necessary for completing the tutorials and end-of-tutorial exercises
- Student Data Files
- Additional resources for topics in each tutorial
- Links to the Student Edition Labs for hands-on reinforcement of selected topics

Student Edition Labs

These interactive labs help students review and extend their knowledge of Internet concepts through observation, step-by-step practice, and review questions. The Student Edition Labs are tied to individual tutorials and cover various subject areas, such as using a browser, working with email, and protecting a computer from viruses.

CourseCasts – Learning on the Go. Always available...always relevant.

Want to keep up with the latest technology trends relevant to you? Visit our site to find a library of podcasts, CourseCasts, featuring a "CourseCast of the Week," and download them to your mp3 player at http://coursecasts.course.com.

Ken Baldauf, host of CourseCasts, is a faculty member of the Florida State University Computer Science Department where he is responsible for teaching technology classes to thousands of FSU students each year. Ken is an expert in the latest technology trends; he gathers and sorts through the most pertinent news and information for CourseCasts so your students can spend their time enjoying technology, rather than trying to figure it out. Open or close your lecture with a discussion based on the latest CourseCast.

Visit us at http://coursecasts.course.com to learn on the go!

Instructor Resources

We offer more than just a book. We have all the tools you need to enhance your lectures, check students' work, and generate exams in a new, easier-to-use and completely revised package. This book's Instructor's Manual, ExamView testbank, PowerPoint presentations, data files, solution files, figure files, and a sample syllabus are all available on a single CD-ROM or for downloading at www.cengage.com/coursetechnology.

Brief
Introductory
Comprehensive

Student Edition Labs

COURSECASTS

Instructor Resources

Blackboard

Skills Assessment and Training

SAM 2007 helps bridge the gap between the classroom and the real world by allowing students to train and test on important computer skills in an active, hands-on environment. SAM 2007's easy-to-use system includes powerful interactive exams, training or projects on critical applications such as Word, Excel, Access, PowerPoint, Outlook, Windows, the Internet, and much more. SAM simulates the application environment, allowing students to demonstrate their knowledge and think through the skills by performing real-world tasks. Powerful administrative options allow instructors to schedule exams and assignments, secure tests, and run reports with almost limitless flexibility.

Online Content

Blackboard is the leading distance learning solution provider and class-management platform today. Course Technology has partnered with Blackboard to bring you premium online content. Content for use with *New Perspectives on The Internet, 8th Edition, Comprehensive* is available in a Blackboard Course Cartridge and may include topic reviews, case projects, review questions, test banks, practice tests, custom syllabi, and more. Course Technology also has solutions for several other learning management systems. Please visit http://www.course.com today to see what's available for this title.

Acknowledgments

Creating a textbook is a collaborative effort in which authors and publisher work as a team to provide the highest quality book possible. We want to acknowledge the major contributions of the Course Technology editorial team members: Marie Lee, Executive Editor; Brandi Shailer, Associate Acquisitions Editor; Kathy Finnegan, Senior Product Manager; Leigh Hefferon, Product Manager; Julia Leroux-Lindsey, Associate Product Manager; Zina Kresin, Editorial Assistant; and Cathie DiMassa, Senior Content Project Manager. We also appreciate the expert management of Karen McCutcheon and the Online Development Group for their creation of the Online Companion for this book. We thank Christian Kunciw and his team of Quality Assurance testers for their work as well. We offer our heartfelt thanks to the Course Technology organization as a whole. The people at Course Technology have been, by far, the best publishing team with which we have ever worked. We also thank our Developmental Editors, Kim Crowley and Amanda Brodkin. Their sharp eyes caught many mistakes and they contributed excellent ideas for making the manuscript more readable. Our thanks to Katherine Pinard, who has contributed to this book in the past and also authored the book's adaptation for other markets; and to Janice Jutras, for her diligent efforts in securing permissions for this text.

Finally, we want to express our deep appreciation for the continuous support and encouragement of our spouses, Cathy Cosby and Richard Evans. They demonstrated remarkable patience as we worked to complete this book on a very tight schedule. We also thank our children for tolerating our absences while we were busy writing.

– Gary P. Schneider
– Jessica Evans

Dedication

To the memory of my brother, Bruce. – G.P.S.
To Hannah and Richard. – J.E.

Brief Contents

Table of Contents

Tutorial 2 Basic Communication on the Internet: Email

Internet—Level II Tutorials

Tutorial 3 Using Web-Based Services for Communication and Collaboration

Exploring Web-Based Email and File Sharing Sites . . . .*WEB 135*

Tutorial 5 Information Resources on the Web

Finding, Evaluating, and Using Online

Tutorial 9 Creating Effective Web Pages

Creating HTML Documents and Understanding Browser Extensions . . . .*WEB 441*

Tutorial 10 Electronic Commerce

Doing Business on the Internet . . . .*WEB 497*

Appendix A The Internet and the World Wide Web

History, Structure, and Technologies ....WEB A1

Credits

Tutorial 1

Figures 1-3 and 1-4: Courtesy of Copyright © 1994–2009 W3C

Figures 1-7, 1-12 through 1-15, and 1-18 through 1-25: Courtesy of © 2009 Microsoft Corporation. All rights reserved. Microsoft product screenshot(s) reprinted with permission from Microsoft Corporation.

Figures 1-8 and 1-9, 1-29 through 1-31, 1-34 through 1-41, and 1-43: Courtesy of Copyright © 2005–2009 Mozilla. All rights reserved.

Figure 1-10: Courtesy of Copyright © 2009 Opera Software ASA. All rights reserved.

Figure 1-11: Courtesy of © 2009 Google

Tutorial 2

Figures 2-1 and 2-2, 2-4, and 2-17 through 2-30: Courtesy of © 2009 Microsoft Corporation. All rights reserved. Microsoft product screenshot(s) reprinted with permission from Microsoft Corporation.

Figures 2-5 through 2-11: Courtesy of Copyright © 2005–2009 Mozilla. All rights reserved.

Figures 2-12 through 2-15: Courtesy of Copyright © 2009 Opera Software ASA. All rights reserved.

Tutorial 3

Figures 3-1 through 3-19: Courtesy of © 2009 Microsoft Corporation. All rights reserved. Microsoft product screenshot(s) reprinted with permission from Microsoft Corporation.

Figures 3-20 through 3-37: Courtesy of © 2009 Google

Tutorial 4

Figure 4-4: Courtesy of © 2009 Microsoft Corporation. All rights reserved. Microsoft product screenshot(s) reprinted with permission from Microsoft Corporation.

Figures 4-5 and 4-6, 4-15, 4-19, and 4-20: Courtesy of © 2009 Google

Figures 4-7, 4-10, and 4-12: Courtesy of Yahoo! Inc. ® 2009 by Yahoo! Inc. YAHOO! and the YAHOO! logo are trademarks of Yahoo! Inc.

Figure 4-9: Courtesy of Wolfram Alpha LLC, a Wolfram Research Company (www.wolframalpha.com)

Figure 4-11: Courtesy of © 2009 AOL LLC. All Rights Reserved and Courtesy of Copyright © 1998–2009 Netscape.

Figure 4-13: Courtesy of © 2009 InfoSpace, Inc. All rights reserved.

Figure 4-14: Courtesy of ©1999–2009 KARTOO S.A.

Figure 4-18: Courtesy of © 2008 Exalead S.A. All rights reserved.

Figure 4-21: Courtesy of © 2009 Vivísimo, Inc. All rights reserved.

Figure 4-22: Courtesy of the National Science Foundation and the University of Utah

Figure 4-23: Courtesy of © 1995–2009 by Jakob Nielsen. ISSN 1548-5552 (http:// www.useit.com/alertbox/children.html)

Tutorial 5

Figures 5-1 through 5-3: Courtesy of Yahoo! Inc. ® 2009 by Yahoo! Inc. YAHOO! and the YAHOO! logo are trademarks of Yahoo! Inc.

Figures 5-4, 5-6, 5-9a, and 5-17: Courtesy of © 2009 Google

Figure 5-5: Reproduced with permission from the Internet Public Library Consortium, Copyright 2009 by the Internet Public Library Consortium (http://www.ipl.org). All rights reserved.

Figure 5-9b: Courtesy of © 2009 Microsoft Corporation. All rights reserved. Microsoft product screenshot(s) reprinted with permission from Microsoft Corporation.

Figure 8-4: Courtesy of © 2009 Verizon Wireless

Figures 8-6 and 8-16: Courtesy of © 2009 Bluetooth

Figure 8-10: Courtesy of © 1999–2009 Towerstream Corp. All Rights Reserved.

Figure 8-11: Courtesy of Copyright © 2009 Research In Motion and © 2009 PRNewsFoto/Verizon Wireless

Figure 8-12: Courtesy of Copyright © 2001–2009 Boingo Wireless, Inc. All rights reserved.

Figure 8-15: Courtesy of Copyright © 2002–2009, AirMagnet, Inc.

Tutorial 9

Figure 9-3: Courtesy of Copyright © 2005–2009 Mozilla. All rights reserved.

Figures 9-6, 9-10, 9-13, 9-16 and 9-17, 9-20, 9-22 and 9-23, and 9-28: Courtesy of © 2009 Microsoft Corporation. All rights reserved. Microsoft product screenshot(s) reprinted with permission from Microsoft Corporation.

Figures 9-18 and 9-19, 9-21, and 9-29: Courtesy of Copyright © 2009 Adobe Systems Incorporated. All rights reserved.

Figure 9-22: Courtesy of script author Peter Ghiringhelli, B.A. (Hons.), M.A, www.petergh.f2s.com and Courtesy of Copyright 2009 WebMediaBrands Inc. All Rights Reserved.

Figure 9-23: Courtesy of script author Peter Ghiringhelli, B.A. (Hons.), M.A, www.petergh.f2s.com

Figure 9-24: Courtesy of Copyright 2009 WebMediaBrands Inc. All Rights Reserved.

Figure 9-25: Courtesy of © JSMadeEasy.com. All Rights Reserved.

Figure 9-27: Courtesy of Copyright © 2006 IconNicholson, LLC. All rights reserved.

Figure 9-31: Courtesy of © 1995–2009 Register.com®

Figure 9-32: Courtesy of © 2003–2008 ePowHost.com. All Rights Reserved.

Figure 9-34: Courtesy of Incisive Interactive Marketing LLC. 2009 All rights reserved.

Appendix A

Figure A-1: Courtesy of AAGAMIA/Getty Images

Figure A-4: Courtesy of BBN Technologies

Figure A-5: Image Courtesy of © Computer History Museum

Figure A-7: Courtesy of http://www.nitrd.gov/fnc/Internet_res.html

Figure A-8: Source: Adapted from Internet Systems Consortium (http://www.isc.org/) and other sources

Figure A-9: Courtesy of MIT museum; Courtesy of Ted Nelson/Project Xanadu; Courtesy of Doug Engelbart Institute

Figure A-10: Courtesy of Yahoo! Inc. ® 2009 by Yahoo! Inc. YAHOO! and the YAHOO! logo are trademarks of Yahoo! Inc.

Figure A-11: Courtesy of Pär Lannerö; Source: http://www.dejavu.org/emulator.htm

Figure A-12: Source: Adapted from Netcraft Web Survey (http://www.netcraft.com/survey/Reports)

Appendix C

Figures C1 through C13: Courtesy of © 2009 Microsoft Corporation. All rights reserved. Microsoft product screenshot(s) reprinted with permission from Microsoft Corporation.

Browser Basics

Introduction to the Web and Web Browser Software

Case | Danville Animal Shelter

The Danville Animal Shelter is an organization devoted to helping improve the welfare of animals, particularly unwanted pets, in the local Danville area. Trinity Andrews is the director of the shelter, and she is always looking for ways to improve the services it offers to the community.

The shelter is a charitable organization that is supported mainly by contributions from the local community. Trinity budgets the limited funds that the shelter receives to do the most good for the animals. One of the critical needs of the shelter is to let people in the community know about the pets available for adoption. Trinity has placed some advertising in local newspapers and television stations, but advertising is very expensive, even when the local media outlets provide reduced rates or offer to run stories about the shelter.

The problem with using newspapers and television is that the pets available for adoption change from day to day and, by the time a news story or ad runs, the pet that is featured often has been adopted. Trinity realizes that although newspaper and television advertising and promotion can be a good way for the shelter to get its general message out to the community, these outlets are not the best way to let people know about specific pets that are available for adoption.

You have served as a volunteer at the shelter for several years, and Trinity heard that you were learning to use the Internet. Trinity would like you to help identify ways to use the Internet to let the community know about the shelter and, in particular, about specific pets that are available for adoption. Your college friend, Maggie Beeler, earned her degree in library science. You meet with Maggie at the local public library, where she is working at the reference desk, to discuss how you might use the Web to help the shelter.

Starting Data Files

There are no starting Data Files needed for this tutorial.

Session 1.1

Understanding the Internet and the World Wide Web

Computers can be connected to each other in a configuration called a **network**. If the computers are near each other (usually in the same building), the network is called a **local area network** or a **LAN**. Networked computers that are not located near each other form a **wide area network**, or a **WAN**. When networks are connected to each other, the system is called an **interconnected network** or **internet** (with a lowercase "i"). The **Internet** (with an uppercase "i") is a specific interconnected network that connects computers all over the world using a common set of interconnection standards. Although it began as a large science project sponsored by the U.S. military, the Internet today allows people and businesses all over the world to communicate with each other in a variety of ways.

The part of the Internet known as the **World Wide Web** (or the **Web**) is a subset of the computers on the Internet that use software to make their contents easily accessible to each other. The Web has helped to make information on the Internet easily accessible by people who are not computer scientists. The Internet and the Web give people around the world new ways to communicate with each other, obtain information resources and software, conduct business transactions, and find entertainment. You can read Appendix A to learn more about the history of the Internet and about the technologies that make it work.

The Web is a collection of files that reside on computers, called **Web servers**, that are located all over the world and are connected to each other through the Internet. Most files on computers, including computers that are connected to the Internet, are private; that is, only the computer's users can access those files. The owners of the computer files that make up the Web have made the files publicly available by placing them on the Web servers. Anyone who has a computer connected to the Internet can obtain access to the files.

When you use your Internet connection to become part of the Web, your computer becomes a **Web client** in a worldwide client/server network. A **Web browser** is the software that you run on your computer to make it work as a Web client. The Internet connects many different types of computers running different operating system software. Web browser software lets your computer communicate with all of these different types of computers easily and effectively. Figure 1-1 shows how this client/server structure uses the Internet to provide multiple interconnections among the various kinds of client and server computers.

Client/server structure of the World Wide Web ◀ **Figure 1-1**

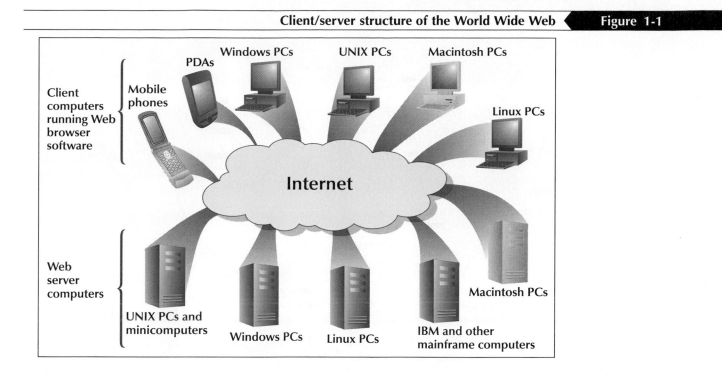

Hypertext, Links, and Hypermedia

The public files on Web servers are ordinary text files, much like the files created and used by word-processing software. To enable Web browser software to read these files, however, the text must be formatted according to a generally accepted standard. The standard used on the Web is **Hypertext Markup Language (HTML)**. HTML uses codes, or **tags**, that tell the Web browser software how to display the text contained in the text file. For example, a Web browser reading the following line of text

```
<B>A Review of the Book <I>Wind Instruments</I></B>
```

recognizes the <B> and </B> tags as instructions to display the entire line of text in bold and the <I> and </I> tags as instructions to display the text enclosed by those tags in italics. Different Web clients that connect to this Web server might display the tagged text differently. For example, one Web browser might display text enclosed by bold tags in a blue color instead of displaying the text in bold. A text file that contains HTML tags is called an **HTML document**.

   HTML provides a variety of text formatting tags that can be used to indicate headings, paragraphs, bulleted lists, numbered lists, and other text enhancements in an HTML document. The real power of HTML, however, lies in its anchor tag. The **HTML anchor tag** enables Web designers to link HTML documents to each other. Anchor tags in HTML documents create **hypertext links**, which are instructions that point to other HTML documents or to another section of the same document. Hypertext links also are called **hyperlinks** or **links**. Figure 1-2 shows how these hyperlinks can join multiple HTML documents to create a web of HTML documents across computers on the Internet. The HTML documents shown in the figure can be on the same computer or on different computers. The computers can be in the same room or an ocean away from each other.

Figure 1-2
Hyperlinks create a web of HTML text across multiple files

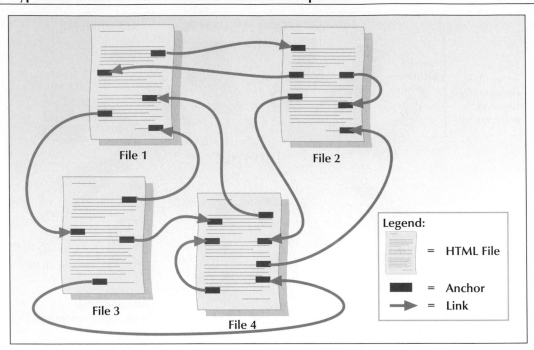

Most Web browsers display hyperlinks in a color that is different from other text in an HTML document and also underline the hyperlinks so they are easy to distinguish. When a Web browser displays an HTML document, it is often referred to as a **Web page**. Maggie shows you a Web page at the World Wide Web Consortium (W3C) Web site. See Figure 1-3. The hyperlinks on this Web page are easy to identify, because the Web browser software that displayed this page shows the hyperlinks as blue, underlined text.

Figure 1-3
W3C Web page

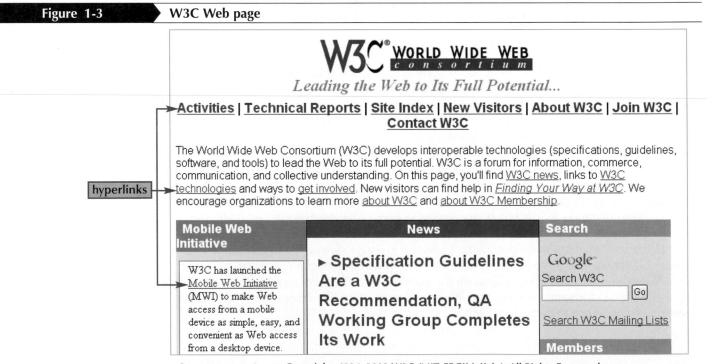

Source: www.w3.org Copyright 1994–2009 W3C (MIT, ERCIM, Keio), All Rights Reserved

Each of the hyperlinks on the Web page shown in Figure 1-3 enables the user to connect to another Web page. In turn, each of those linked Web pages contains hyperlinks to other pages, including one hyperlink that leads back to the original Web page. Hyperlinks can also lead to computer files that contain pictures, graphics, and media objects such as sound and video clips. Hyperlinks that connect to these types of files often are called **hypermedia links**. You are especially interested in learning more about hypermedia links, but Maggie suggests you first need to understand a little more about how people organize Web pages on their Web servers.

The easiest way to move from one Web page to another is to use the hyperlinks that the authors of Web pages have embedded in their HTML documents. Web page authors often use a graphic image as a hyperlink. Sometimes, it is difficult to identify which objects and text are hyperlinks just by looking at a Web page displayed on your computer.

Figure 1-4 shows the pointing index finger icon on a Web page at the World Wide Web Consortium (W3C) site. The mouse pointer was positioned over the Finding Your Way at W3C hyperlink, and the shape of the pointer indicates that if you click the Finding Your Way at W3C text, the Web browser will open the Web page to which that hyperlink points.

Mouse pointer hovering over a hyperlink | **Figure 1-4**

Source: www.w3c.org Copyright 1994–2009 W3C (MIT, ERCIM, Keio), All Rights Reserved

Web Site Organization

People who create Web pages usually have a collection of related pages stored on one computer that they use as their Web server. A collection of linked Web pages that has a common theme or focus is called a **Web site**. Most Web sites store all of the site's pages in a single location, either on one computer or on one LAN. Large organizations with Web sites that serve pages to thousands, or even millions, of visitors each month use many computers linked to function as one Web server. In fact, it can be difficult to determine where one Web site ends and another begins. One common definition of a Web site is any group of Web pages that relates to one specific topic or organization, regardless of where the HTML documents are located.

The main page that all of the other pages on a particular Web site are organized around and link back to is called the site's **home page**. The term *home page* is used at least three different ways on the Web, and it is sometimes difficult to tell which meaning people intend when they use the term. The first definition of home page indicates the main page for a particular site. This home page is the first page that opens when you visit a particular Web site. The second definition of home page is the first page that opens when you start your Web browser. This type of home page might be an HTML document on your own computer. Some people create such home pages and include hyperlinks to Web sites that they frequently visit. If you are using a computer on your school's or employer's network, its Web browser might be configured to open the main page for the school or firm. The third definition of home page is the Web page that a particular Web browser loads the first time you use it. This page usually is stored at the Web site of the firm or other organization that created the Web browser software. Home pages that meet the second or third definitions are sometimes called **start pages**.

Addresses on the Web

The Internet has no centralized control point or centralized control mechanism. Therefore, no central starting point exists for the Web, which is a part of the Internet. However, there is a system for locating a specific computer on the Web.

Domain Name Addressing

Each computer on the Internet has a unique identification number, called an **IP (Internet Protocol) address**. IP addressing is a way of identifying each unique computer on the Web, just like your home address is a way of identifying your home in a city. (You can learn more about IP addressing by reading Appendix A.) Most people do not use the IP address to locate Web sites and individual pages. Instead, the browsers use domain name addressing. A **domain name** is a unique name associated with a specific IP address by a program that runs on an Internet host computer. This program, which coordinates the IP addresses and domain names for all computers attached to it, is called **DNS (domain name system) software**, and the host computer that runs this software is called a **domain name server**. Domain names can include any number of parts separated by periods; however, most domain names currently in use have only three or four parts. For example, the domain name gradsch.psu.edu is the computer connected to the Internet at the Graduate School (gradsch), which is an academic unit of Pennsylvania State University (psu), which is an educational institution (edu). No other computer on the Internet has the same domain name.

Domain names have a hierarchical structure that you can follow from top to bottom if you read the domain names from right to left. The last part of a domain name is called its **top-level domain (TLD)**. For example, DNS software on the Internet host computer that is responsible for the "edu" domain keeps track of the IP addresses for all of the educational institutions in its domain, including "psu." Similar DNS software on the "psu" Internet host computer would keep track of the academic units' computers in its domain, including the "gradsch" computer.

Since 1998, the **Internet Corporation for Assigned Names and Numbers (ICANN)** has had responsibility for managing domain names. In the United States, the six most common TLDs are .com, .edu, .gov, .mil, .net, and .org. Although a seventh TLD, the "us" domain, is approved for general use by any person within the United States, it is most frequently used by state and local government organizations in the United States and by U.S. primary and secondary schools (because the "edu" domain is reserved for post-secondary educational institutions). Internet host computers outside the United States often use two-letter country domain names instead of, or in addition to, the six general TLDs. For example, the domain name uq.edu.au is the domain name for the University of Queensland (uq), which is an educational institution (edu) in Australia (au).

In 2000, ICANN added seven TLDs. Some of these TLDs are like the original TLDs, which are **general TLDs** (or **gTLDs**). A general TLD is maintained by ICANN. Other TLDs that were introduced in 2000 are **sponsored TLDs** (**sTLDs**), which are maintained by a sponsoring organization other than ICANN.

The four gTLDs introduced in 2000 included .biz (for business organizations), .info (for any person or organization that wanted to provide an informational Web site), .name (for individual persons), and .pro (for licensed professionals, such as accountants, lawyers, and physicians).

The three sTLDs introduced in 2000 that are sponsored by various industry organizations are .aero (for airlines, airports, and the air transport industry), .coop (for cooperative organizations), and .museum (for museums). Each of these domains is maintained by its sponsoring organization, not by ICANN. For example, the .aero domain is maintained by SITA, an air transport industry association.

Although ICANN chose these new domain names after much deliberation and considering more than 100 possible new names, a number of people were highly critical of the selections. In 2005, ICANN again undertook the process of considering new TLDs. One of the proposed domains, an .xxx domain for Web sites with adult content, raised quite a bit of controversy. You can learn more about these criticisms and controversies by going to the Online Companion Web page for this tutorial at www.cengage.com/internet/np/internet8. After logging in, you can click the Tutorial 1 link, and then follow the links in the Additional Information section under the heading ICANN and Controversy Over Its Rulings. Figure 1-5 presents a list of the general TLDs, including those added since 2000, and some of the country TLDs.

Common top-level domains (TLDs) **Figure 1-5**

Original TLDs		Country TLDs		General TLDs Added Since 2000	
TLD	**Use**	**TLD**	**Country**	**TLD**	**Use**
.com	U.S. Commercial	.au	Australia	.uk	United Kingdom
.edu	U.S. Post-secondary educational institution	.ca	Canada	.asia	Companies, individuals, and organizations based in Asian-Pacific regions
.gov	U.S. Federal government	.de	Germany	.biz	Businesses
.mil	U.S. Military	.fi	Finland	.info	General use
.net	U.S. General use	.fr	France	.int	International organizations and programs endorsed by a treaty between or among nations
.org	U.S. Not-for-profit organization	.jp	Japan	.name	Individual persons
.us	U.S. General use	.se	Sweden	.pro	Professionals (such as accountants, lawyers, physicians)

Source: Internet Assigned Numbers Authority Root Zone Database, http://www.iana.org/domains/root/db/

Uniform Resource Locators

The IP address and the domain name each identify a particular computer on the Internet, but they do not indicate where a Web page's HTML document resides on that computer. To identify a Web page's exact location, Web browsers rely on Uniform Resource Locators. A **Uniform Resource Locator (URL)** is a four-part addressing scheme that tells the Web browser:

- The transfer protocol to use when transporting the file
- The domain name of the computer on which the file resides
- The pathname of the folder or directory on the computer on which the file resides
- The name of the file

The **transfer protocol** is the set of rules that the computers use to move files from one computer to another on an internet. The most common transfer protocol used on the Internet is the **hypertext transfer protocol (HTTP)**. You can indicate the use of this protocol by typing http:// as the first part of the URL. People do use other protocols to transfer files on the Internet, but most of these protocols were used more frequently before the Web became part of the Internet. Two protocols that you still might see on the Internet are the **file transfer protocol (FTP)**, which is indicated in a URL as ftp://, and the **Telnet protocol**, which is indicated in a URL as telnet://. FTP is just another way to transfer files, and Telnet is a set of rules for establishing a connection between two computers over the Internet that allows a person at one computer to control the other computer.

The domain name was described in the preceding section. The pathname describes the hierarchical directory or folder structure on the computer that stores the file. Most people are familiar with the structure used on Windows and DOS PCs, which uses the backslash character (\) to separate the structure levels. URLs follow the conventions established in the UNIX operating system that use the forward slash character (/) to separate the structure levels. The forward slash character works properly in a URL, even when it is pointing to a file on a Windows or DOS computer.

The filename is the name that the computer uses to identify the Web page's HTML document. On most computers, the filename extension of an HTML document is either .html or .htm. Although many PC operating systems are not case-sensitive, computers that use the UNIX operating system *are* case-sensitive. Therefore, if you are entering a URL that includes mixed-case and you do not know the type of computer on which the file resides, it is safer to retain the mixed-case format of the URL.

Tip

Not all URLs include a filename, so when this is the case, most Web browsers will load the file named index.html, which is the default name for a Web site's home page on most Web servers.

InSight | Filename Extensions for HTML files

Computer engineers have long used the part of a filename that follows the period, called the filename extension, to identify the contents of files. The operating systems of some computers (including Windows PCs) use the filename extension to determine which software program is used with which files. HTML was first created on large computers, and its filename extension was always .html. When Web browsers were developed for PCs, a problem arose. Most operating systems used on PCs at that time limited filename extensions to three characters. Thus, many HTML files were created with the shortened filename extension, .htm, so that they could be used on PCs. Since then, PC operating systems have become able to handle longer filename extensions, but the practice of using both .htm and .html for HTML files has become entrenched, and both are commonly used today.

Figure 1-6 shows an example of a URL annotated to show its four parts.

Structure of a Uniform Resource Locator (URL) | **Figure 1-6**

protocol   pathname

http://www.nytimes.com/pages/sports/index.htm

domain name   filename

The URL shown in Figure 1-6 uses the HTTP protocol and points to a computer that is connected to the Web (www) at the *New York Times* newspaper (nytimes), which is a commercial entity (com). The *New York Times* Web site contains many different kinds of information about the newspaper, including stories that are included in the pages of the printed newspaper each day. The path shown in Figure 1-6 includes two levels. The first level indicates that the information is a story from the pages of the newspaper (pages), and the second level indicates that the page is from the sports section (sports) of the newspaper. The filename (index.html) indicates that this page is the home page in the sports section.

Encountering Error Messages on Web Pages | InSight

You might encounter an error message when you enter a URL in a Web browser. Two common messages that you might see are "server busy" and "DNS entry not found." Either of these messages means that your browser was unable to communicate successfully with the Web server that stores the page you requested. The cause for this inability might be temporary—in which case, you might be able to try the URL later—or the cause might be permanent. The browser has no way of determining the cause of the connection failure, so the browser provides the same types of error messages in either case. Another error message that you might receive appears as a Web page and includes the text "Error 404: File not Found." This error message usually means that the Web page's location has changed permanently or that the Web page no longer exists. You should also keep in mind that if you type a URL incorrectly, you could see either of these error messages, so always double-check your typing before considering other reasons that you were unable to load a particular Web page.

Now that you understand the importance of Internet addressing and URLs, you will notice that you can find URLs in many places; for example, newspapers and magazines often publish URLs of Web sites that might interest their readers. Friends who know about the subject area in which you are interested also are good sources. The best source, however, is the Web itself.

You are eager to begin learning how to use a Web browser. Common elements and similar functionality among most Web browsers make it easy to use any Web browser after you have learned how to use one.

Main Elements of Web Browsers

Having gained some familiarity with Web site organization and addressing, you start to wonder how a particular computer can communicate with other computers over the Internet. Maggie tells you that there are a number of different Web browsers. By running Web browser software, your computer becomes a Web client that can communicate through an Internet service provider (ISP) or a network connection with Web servers all over the world. The two most popular browsers in use today are **Microsoft Internet Explorer**, or simply **Internet Explorer**, and **Mozilla Firefox**, or simply **Firefox**. You will learn more about these and other Web browsers later in this tutorial.

Most Windows programs use a standard graphical user interface (GUI) design that includes a number of common screen elements. Figures 1-7 and 1-8 show the main elements of the Internet Explorer and Firefox program windows, respectively. These two Web browsers share many common Windows elements, such as a title bar at the top of the window, a scroll bar on the right side of the window, and a status bar at the bottom of the window.

Figure 1-7 ▶ **Main elements of the Internet Explorer program window**

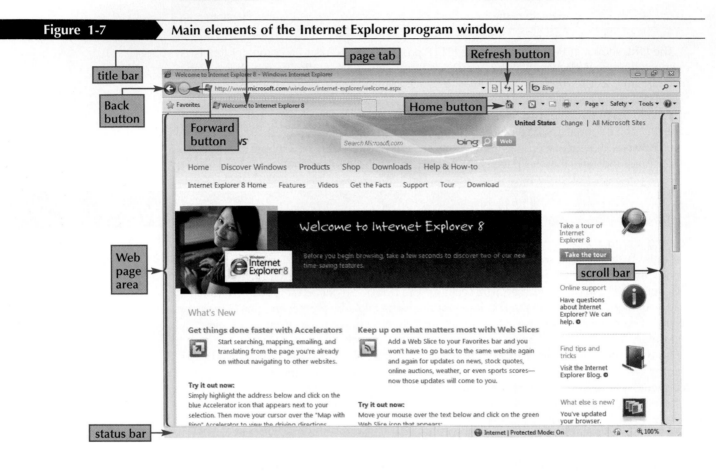

Main elements of the Firefox program window   Figure 1-8

The next section describes the common browser window elements.

Title Bar

A Web browser's **title bar** shows the name of the open Web page and the Web browser's program name. As in all Windows programs, you can double-click the title bar to resize the window quickly. The right side of the title bar contains the **Minimize**, **Restore Down**, and **Close buttons** when the window is maximized to fill the screen. When the window is not maximized, the Restore Down button is replaced by a **Maximize button**; to expand a browser window so it fills the screen, you click the Maximize button.

Scroll Bars

A Web page can be much longer than a Web browser window, so you often need to use the **scroll bar** at the right side of the program window to move the page up or down through the document window. You can use the mouse to click the Up scroll button or the Down scroll button to move the Web page up or down through the window's **Web page area**. You can also use the mouse to click and drag the scroll box up and down in the scroll bar to move the page accordingly.

Status Bar

The **status bar** at the bottom of the browser window includes information about the browser's operations. Each browser uses the status bar to deliver different information, but generally, the status bar indicates the name of the Web page that is loading, the load status (partial or complete), and important messages, such as "Document: Done." Some Web sites send messages as part of their Web pages that are displayed in the status bar as well. You will learn more about the specific functions of the status bar in Internet Explorer and Firefox in Sessions 1.2 and 1.3, respectively.

Menu Bar

The browser's **menu bar** provides a convenient way for you to execute typical File, Edit, View, and Help commands. In addition to these common Windows command sets, the menu bar also provides specialized commands for the browser that enable you to navigate the Web. The menu bar appears just below the title bar in Firefox. The menu bar is hidden by default in Internet Explorer, but some of the common menu options are available from the Page button and the Tools button located on the **Command bar** in Internet Explorer. You will learn more about the options available from these buttons in Session 1.2 as well as how to show the menu bar in Internet Explorer.

Page Tab

Most Web browsers can show multiple Web pages within the Web page area. These Web browsers display a **page tab** for each Web page that shows the title of the Web page. This feature allows you to open multiple Web pages within a single browser window and switch among the open Web pages by clicking the page tabs, rather than opening multiple browser windows. Some users prefer to open multiple Web pages in one browser window and switch among them using the page tabs rather than opening each Web page in its own browser window. This method of using one browser window for all open pages is called **tabbed browsing**.

Home Button

Clicking the **Home button** in Internet Explorer or in Firefox displays the home (or start) page for the browser. Most Web browsers let you specify a page that loads automatically every time you start the program. You might not be able to do this if you are in your school's computer lab because schools often set the start page for all browsers on campus and then lock that setting. Similarly, some companies set a start page for the computers their employees use, so you might not be able to set your own start page if you are using a computer at work. If you are using your own computer, you can choose your own start page. Some people like to use a Web page that someone else has created and made available for others to use. One example of a start page that many people use as their start page is the Refdesk.com Web page.

Pages such as the Refdesk.com home page offer links to pages that many Web users frequently visit. The people and organizations that create these pages often sell advertising space on their pages to pay the cost of maintaining their sites. Refdesk.com sells advertising and also accepts donations from users to help defray the cost of operating the site.

Finding Information on the Web Using Search Engines and Web Directories

Web search engines are Web pages that conduct searches of the Web to find the words or expressions that you enter. The result of such a search is a Web page that contains hyperlinks to Web pages that contain matching text or expressions. These pages can give new users an easy way to find information on the Web. Internet Explorer and Firefox each include a toolbar button that opens search engines and Web directories chosen by the companies that wrote the browser software. However, many people prefer to select their own tools for searching the Internet.

Sometimes the number of results from a search conducted using a search engine is overwhelming, and you find that you need to sort through links to pages that only vaguely match your criteria. You can use a **Web directory**, a Web page that contains a list of Web page categories, such as education or recreation, to narrow the results returned for a particular search. The hyperlinks on a Web directory page lead to other pages that contain lists of subcategories leading to other related category lists and Web pages. Instead of relying on a computer to categorize the pages, Web directories employ Web directory editors to categorize Web pages. These editors can weed out the pages that do not fit in a particular category.

Returning to Web Pages Previously Visited

Web addresses can be long and hard to remember. You can store the addresses of specific Web pages in most browsers, and then open the pages by clicking the stored address. You can also return to a page you have visited in the past by using the browser's history feature.

You realize that using the browser to remember important pages will be a terrific asset as you start collecting information for the shelter, so you ask Maggie to explain more about how to return to a Web page.

Using Favorites and Bookmarks

In Internet Explorer, you can save the URL of a site you would like to revisit as a **favorite** in the Favorites folder. In Firefox, you can use a **bookmark** to save the URL of a specific page so you can return to it. Using the Internet Explorer's Favorites feature or a Firefox bookmark lets you store and organize a list of Web pages that you have visited, making it easier to return to them without having to remember the URL or search for the page again. Internet Explorer favorites and Firefox bookmarks serve the same purpose as a bookmark you might use in a printed book: They mark the page and help you find the location again quickly.

You can save as many Internet Explorer favorites or Firefox bookmarks as you want. You can mark all of your favorite Web pages, so you can return to pages that you frequently use or pages that are important to your research or tasks.

InSight | **How Web Browsers Store Favorites and Bookmarks**

All Web browsers let you store favorites or bookmarks on your computer, but different browsers store them in different ways. Internet Explorer stores each favorite as a separate file on your computer. Firefox stores all bookmarks in one file on your computer. The Internet Explorer approach of storing each favorite separately offers more flexibility but uses more disk space and can make it hard to find a specific favorite. The Firefox approach of storing all bookmarks in one file uses less disk space and makes the bookmarks easier to find.

Navigating Web Pages Using the History List

As you click hyperlinks to go to new Web pages, the browser stores the location of each page you visit during a single session in a **history list**. You click the **Back button** and the **Forward button** in either Internet Explorer or Firefox to move through the history list.

When you start your browser, both buttons are inactive (dimmed) because no history list for your new session exists yet. After you follow one or more hyperlinks, the Back button becomes active and lets you retrace your path through the hyperlinks you have followed. Once you use the Back button, the Forward button becomes active and lets you move forward through the session's history list.

In most Web browsers, you can right-click either the Back or Forward button to display a portion of the history list. You can reload any page on the list by clicking its name in the list. The Back and Forward buttons duplicate the functions of commands on the browser's menu. You will learn more about the history list for Internet Explorer in Session 1.2 and for Firefox in Session1.3.

Navigating Web Pages Using Page Tabs

If you use the tabbed browsing approach and open Web pages in tabs within one browser window instead of in separate browser windows, you can navigate from page to page by clicking the page tab for the page you want to display. This approach has its limits, however. Depending on the size of the monitor you are viewing, you will only be able to read the titles in the page tabs for a few pages. But if you are doing work that requires frequent back and forth browsing between three or four pages, the page tabs can provide a very handy way to navigate among those pages. You will learn more about how tabbed browsing works in Sessions 1.2 and 1.3.

Reloading a Web Page

When you use your browser to access a Web page, your browser downloads the page to your computer from the Web server on which it is stored. The browser stores a copy of every displayed Web page on your computer's hard drive in a **cache** folder, which increases the speed at which the browser can display pages as you navigate the history list. The cache folder lets the browser reload pages from the cache instead of from the remote Web server. On Windows computers, the cache folder is named Temporary Internet Files.

Clicking the **Refresh button** in Internet Explorer or the **Reload button** in Firefox loads the same Web page that appears in the browser window again. When you click the Refresh or the Reload button, the browser contacts the Web server to see if the Web page has changed since it was stored in the cache folder. If it has changed, the browser gets the new page from the Web server; otherwise, the browser loads the cache folder copy.

Tip

If you want to force the browser to load the most current version of the page from the Web server, hold down the Shift key as you click the Refresh or Reload button.

Stopping a Web Page Transfer

The amount of time it takes for a Web page to arrive from a Web server depends on the size of the page's files (the HTML file, graphics elements, and any active content that is included in the page) and the bandwidth of the Internet connection. Sometimes a Web page takes a long time to load, especially if you are using a low bandwidth connection and the page contains a number of graphics or active content files. When this occurs, you can click the Stop button in Internet Explorer or Firefox to halt the Web page transfer from the server. You can then click the hyperlink again; a second attempt may connect and transfer the page more quickly. You also might want to click the Stop button to abort a transfer when you accidentally click a hyperlink that you do not want to follow.

Cookies

Another issue that Web users should know about is the use of cookies. A **cookie** is a small file that a Web server writes to the disk drive of the client computer (the computer on which the Web browser is running). Cookies can contain information about the user, such as login names and passwords. By storing this information on the user's computer, the Web server can perform functions such as automatic login, which makes it easier to quickly return to favorite Web pages. However, the user often is unaware that these files are being written to the computer's disk drive. Most Web browsers allow the user to prohibit the writing of cookies or specify general categories of cookies that will be allowed or not allowed to be written. Internet Explorer, which stores each cookie in a separate file, allows users to delete the individual cookie files if the user can identify the files to delete, which can be difficult. Other browsers, such as Firefox, store all cookies in one file and give users more comprehensive tools for managing the cookies that have been stored on their computers. You will learn more about cookies and managing them in Internet Explorer in Session 1.2 and in Firefox in Session 1.3.

Printing and Saving Web Pages

As you use your browser to view Web pages, you might find some pages that you want to print or store for future use. You can use a Web browser to print a Web page or to save either an entire Web page or just parts of the page, such as selections of text or graphics.

Printing a Web Page

When you execute a print command, the current page (or part of a page, called a **frame**) that appears in the Web page area of the browser is sent to the printer. Most browsers also provide a print preview command that lets you see how the printed page will look. If the page contains light colors or many graphics, you might consider changing the printing options so the page prints without the background or with all black text. You will learn how to change the print settings for Internet Explorer and Firefox in Sessions 1.2 and 1.3, respectively.

Saving a Web Page

Although printing an entire Web page is often useful, there are times when you will want to save all or part of the page to disk. All Web browsers allow you to save copies of most Web pages as files that you can store on your computer's hard disk, a USB flash drive, or other storage medium. Some Web pages are written in ways that make copying difficult; these pages cannot be saved easily. Internet Explorer and Firefox each perform the save operation somewhat differently, thus you will learn more about saving a Web page and its graphics in Sessions 1.2 and 1.3.

Other Web Browser Choices

After many years as the dominant Web browser, Internet Explorer, which was used by more than 90 percent of all Web users in 2004, saw other browsers gain in popularity. The media reported security issues with Internet Explorer, and users became concerned that the browser was becoming a way for criminals and others with ill intent to attack and take control of their computers. Many organizations and individuals began to doubt whether relying on a single browser was a good idea. In recent years, many users have installed Firefox. Industry experts estimate that about 32 percent of skilled Web users rely on Firefox as their default browser. Most of the remaining 68 percent still use Internet Explorer, and a small but growing number of users employ other Web browsers. Beginning Web users tend to use whatever is installed on their computers. Most computer manufacturers still install Internet Explorer, so many people start using that browser and never consider using anything else. In the next section, you will learn about other Web browsers that people are now using instead of or in addition to Internet Explorer and Firefox.

Mozilla Project

Mosaic was one of the first Web browsers developed in the early 1990s. A group of researchers who had helped develop Mosaic left their jobs at the University of Illinois Supercomputing Center to form a new company called Netscape and launched the first commercially successful Web browser, **Netscape Navigator**. Because they wanted to replace Mosaic, they named their development project Mozilla, which was short for "Mosaic Killer." When Navigator was first introduced in 1994, Netscape charged a small license fee for corporate users, but the fee was waived for individuals and academic institutions. During this time, Microsoft began distributing Internet Explorer with its Windows operating system at no additional cost, therefore Netscape was forced to drop its license fee in response and was no longer able to earn a profit on its browser business. AOL bought Netscape's other business assets in 1999, but donated the Netscape browser software to a nonprofit organization that continued developing the browser software and distributing it to users at no cost. The nonprofit group named the browser software development project "Mozilla" in a revival of the browser's original name, and the nonprofit group that took over development of this browser software became known as the **Mozilla Project**.

When the Mozilla Project started work in 1999, the team focused on a complete rebuild of the internal workings of the browser, called the **browser rendering engine**. In the Mozilla Project, the browser rendering engine, which is named the **Gecko engine**, is used in Netscape Navigator, the Mozilla browser, and the Mozilla Firefox browser.

The Mozilla Project has been operated on a volunteer basis by programmers working in their spare time since its inception in 1999. In 2003, the Mozilla Foundation was created to support the Mozilla Project with an initial contribution of $2 million from Time Warner's AOL division. AOL also contributed equipment, domain names, trademarks, and employees to help with the foundation's initial organization activities. Other corporate supporters of the foundation include Nokia, Sun Microsystems, and Red Hat Software. The foundation will help ensure that the Mozilla Project continues into the future.

Today, the development of the Firefox browser (and related projects, such as the Thunderbird email client that you will learn about in the next tutorial) is carried on by the Mozilla Corporation, an entity formed for that purpose. The original Mozilla Foundation continues to develop the Gecko browser engine, new interfaces for Web browsers based on that engine, and a number of related technologies. You can learn more about the Mozilla Foundation's current projects by going to the Online Companion Web page for this tutorial at www.cegage.com/internet/np/internet8. After logging in, click the Tutorial 1 link, and then follow the links in the Additional Information section under the heading Current Mozilla Projects.

SeaMonkey Project

Originally, the main focus of the Mozilla Foundation was the continuing development of the **Mozilla Suite**, a combination of Web-related software applications that were created by the Mozilla open source project. This development continues today as the **SeaMonkey Project**, an all-in-one software suite that includes a Web browser that runs on the Gecko engine, an email client, a newsgroup client, an HTML editor, and an instant messaging chat client. The software that Time Warner's AOL division distributes as Netscape Navigator is based on the SeaMonkey software.

The SeaMonkey's Web browser offers tabbed windows (including an option to make your start page a set of multiple tabbed windows), a pop-up ad blocker, an image manager that lets you set the browser so it does not load images until you click the Images button on the toolbar, and a "find as you type" page navigation option. Figure 1-9 shows the SeaMonkey browser displaying the home page for the SeaMonkey Project.

SeaMonkey Web browser   Figure 1-9

Opera

Opera started out in 1994 as a research project at Telenor, which is Norway's state telecommunications company. One year later, an independent development company (Opera Software ASA) was formed to continue work on the Opera project. This company continues to develop and sell the Opera Web browser and related software.

Because Opera's program code was written independently and does not use any elements of the Gecko engine or Internet Explorer, Opera is not affected by any security flaws that might be exploited by those attacking any of the Gecko-based browsers or Internet Explorer. Figure 1-10 shows the Opera browser main screen.

Figure 1-10 **Opera Web browser**

When Opera was first introduced, it was only available as a licensed software product; that is, users had to pay a fee of $39 to use the software. In 2000, Opera began offering a free version of its browser that was supported by advertising. The advertising messages were displayed in the toolbar area of the screen. In 2005, the company decided to make the browser free to all users. Opera still offers a premium support program for an annual fee, but most Opera users today do not enroll in that program. Today, Opera devotes most of its corporate resources to the development of Web browsers for mobile phones and other handheld devices.

Opera was the first Web browser to offer tabbed browsing and a search window that the user could configure to run searches in specific search engines automatically. These and other Opera features have proven to be popular and are now available in most major browsers.

Google Chrome and the Chromium Project

Google is an Internet-based business that operates a number of Web sites and earns much of its revenue by selling advertising on the Web. Since its beginnings, Google has encouraged its employees to work on independent technology projects on company time that offer some promise of improving the online world. One of these projects, the **Chromium Project**, is devoted to developing new technologies for Web browsing.

The first major product to come out of the Chromium Project is a browser that was released in 2008 named **Google Chrome**. Google Chrome uses its own browser rendering engine to implement many of the features developed by other brower creators (most notably, Opera) combined in an uncluttered window. When Google Chrome was introduced, several computer industry magazines conducted test that found it to be the fastest browser available. Figure 1-11 shows the Google Chrome browser displaying its welcome page.

Google Chrome Web browser — Figure 1-11

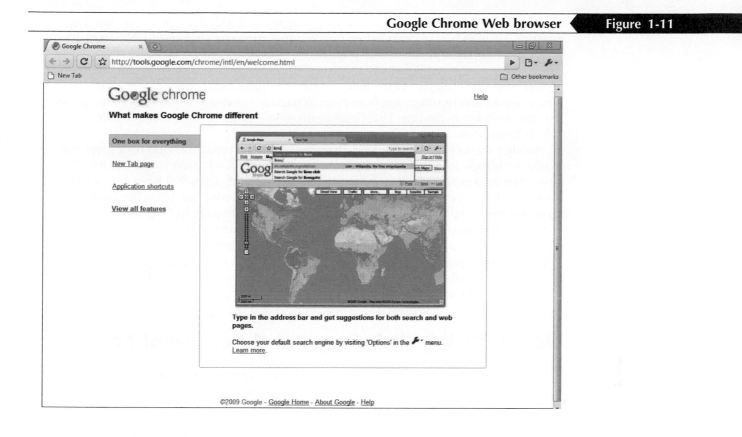

Browser for Hire: iRider

Internet Explorer, Firefox, Google Chrome, SeaMonkey, and Opera are all available at no cost. Several other browsers available today charge a license fee. The most widely used is **iRider**, a browser designed for power users. A power user is a person who is especially knowledgeable about a specific technology and has a high level of skill in using that technology. A power user of Web browsers might regularly have six browsers open at once while shopping for the best deals on airfares, comparing products being auctioned on eBay, or looking up a series of different addresses on a maps and directions Web site.

The current licensing fee for iRider is $20. The iRider browser allows power users to open and manage multiple Web pages at once. Other browsers do provide this functionality, but they either open the Web pages in separate windows or in separate tabs within a window. Either way, the user only sees a tiny icon and (perhaps) a part of each Web page name. With iRider, the user can view thumbnail images of all open Web pages displayed in a hierarchical map called a Page List.

More important, iRider keeps all open Web pages in memory until the user deletes them, allowing the user to click any thumbnail image in the Page List to open a Web page and review its contents. Most power users find using the Page List to be much easier than using the Back and Forward buttons or a history list because the page thumbnails are displayed as a hierarchy (all Web pages that are linked from a single Web page are shown indented under that page's thumbnail image) instead of being listed in the order in which they were opened (as they would be in a history list).

Many experienced Web surfers open pages in new windows as a matter of course, but the Web site does not always allow new windows to open, or in some cases, to stay open. In iRider, any window that is opened in the browser remains in the Page List (and thus it is available to be opened again) until the user closes it.

Most airline and travel sites take a few moments to search through all possible flights (or car rentals or hotel rooms) before they return a page of search results. When the search results page appears, a user might decide to try a flight leaving a day earlier or later. Travel sites generally require the user to run the search again, which removes the results of the first search. With iRider, the user can run several searches simultaneously and compare the results, going from page to page as necessary because all of the pages remain available in the Page List. Once again, iRider gives the user more control over which pages remain available and which are closed.

Another useful feature of iRider is that users can select multiple links on a page and iRider will begin to download the pages simultaneously. Each page appears in the Page List when its download is complete so the user can select pages that have downloaded more quickly, rather than waiting for a specific page to download, using the Back button to revisit the search page, clicking and waiting for another page to download, and so on.

The Web provides users with a vast quantity of information and makes it easy for them to view, store, and print the information. However, the ability to access information using a Web browser does not give the user an unfettered right to possess or use that information. These rights are controlled by copyright laws, which exist to protect the owners of the information.

Reproducing Web Pages and Copyright Law

A **copyright** is the legal right of the author or other owner of an original work to control the reproduction, distribution, and sale of that work. A copyright comes into existence as soon as the work is placed into a tangible form, such as a printed copy, an electronic file, or a Web page. Copyright laws can place significant restrictions on the way that you can use information or images that you copy from another entity's Web site. Because of the way a Web browser works, it copies the HTML code and the graphics and media files to your computer before it can display them in the browser. Just because copies of these files are stored temporarily on your computer does not mean that you have the right to use them in any way other than having your computer display them in the browser window. The United States and most other countries have copyright laws that govern the use of photocopies, audio or video recordings, and other reproductions of authors' original work. The copyright exists even if the work does not contain a copyright notice. If you do not know whether material that you find on the Web is copyrighted, the safest course of action is to assume that it is.

U.S. copyright law has a fair use provision that allows students to use limited amounts of copyrighted information in term papers and other reports prepared for academic purposes. The source of the material used should always be cited. Commercial use of copyrighted material is much more restricted. You should obtain permission from the copyright holder before using anything you copy from a Web page. The copyright holder can require you to pay a fee for permission to use the material from the Web page.

InSight | **Identifying the Owner of Copyrighted Material**

Although it is important to gain permission to use copyrighted material acquired from the Web, it can be difficult to determine the owner of a source's copyright if no notice appears on the Web page. However, many Web pages provide a hyperlink to the email address of the person responsible for maintaining the page. That person, sometimes called a **Webmaster**, usually can provide information about the copyright status of material on the page. Many Web sites also include the address and telephone number of the company or organization that owns the site.

Now that you understand the basic functions of a browser, you are ready to start using your browser to find information for the Danville Animal Shelter. If you are using Internet Explorer, your instructor will assign Session 1.2; if you are using Firefox, your instructor will assign Session 1.3. The authors recommend, however, that you read both sessions because you might encounter a different browser on a public or employer's computer in the future.

Session 1.1 Quick Check | Review

1. True or False: Web browser software runs on a Web server computer.
2. True or False: You can format text using HTML tags.
3. The Web page that opens when you start your browser is called a(n) _____ or a(n) _____ .
4. The general term for links to graphic images, sound clips, or video clips that appear in a Web page is _____ .
5. A local political candidate is creating a Web site to help in her campaign for office. Describe three things she might want to include in her Web site.
6. What is the difference between IP addressing and domain name addressing?
7. Identify and interpret the meaning of each part of the following URL: http://www.savethetrees.org/main.html.
8. What is the difference between a Web directory and a Web search engine?

Session 1.2

Starting Microsoft Internet Explorer

Microsoft Internet Explorer is Microsoft's Web browser; it is installed with all recent versions of Windows operating system software. In this session, you will use Internet Explorer to begin research work for the Danville Animal Shelter. This introduction assumes that you have Internet Explorer installed on your computer. You should have your computer turned on so the Windows desktop is displayed.

To start Internet Explorer:

▶ 1. Click the **Start** button on the taskbar, point to **All Programs**, and then click **Internet Explorer**. After a moment, Internet Explorer opens.

   Trouble? If you cannot find Internet Explorer on the All Programs menu, check to see if an Internet Explorer shortcut icon appears on the desktop, and then double-click it. If you do not see the shortcut icon, ask your instructor or technical support person for help. The program might be installed in a different location on your computer.

▶ 2. If the program does not fill the screen entirely, click the **Maximize** button on the Internet Explorer program's title bar. Your screen should look like Figure 1-12.

Figure 1-12   **Internet Explorer main program window**

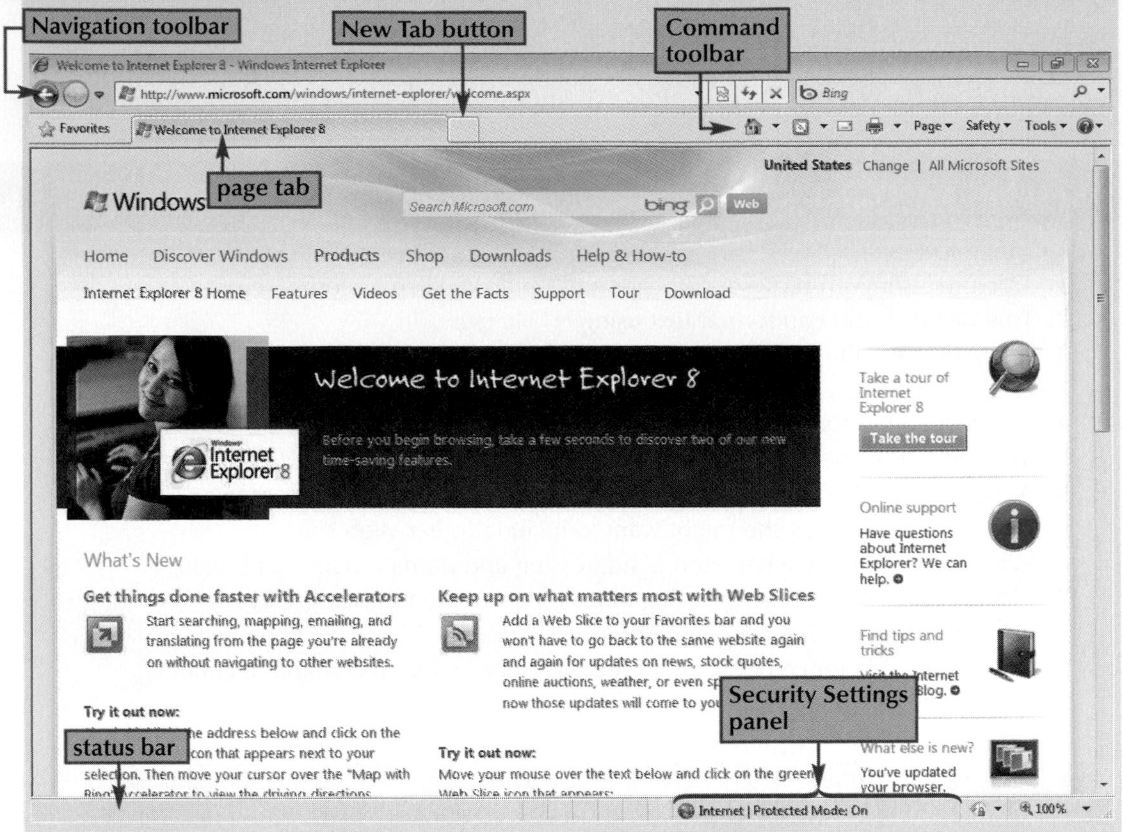

Navigation toolbar

New Tab button

Command toolbar

page tab

Security Settings panel

status bar

Trouble? Figure 1-12 shows the Internet Explorer welcome page, which is the page that Internet Explorer opens the first time it starts. Your computer will be configured to open to a different Web page or no page at all.

Trouble? Figure 1-12 shows the Internet Explorer program window as it appears when it is first installed on a new computer. Many programs add icons and even entire toolbars to the program window, so if you are using a computer that has been used by other people, the program window might include icons and toolbars that are not shown in the figure.

Internet Explorer includes two main toolbars, a Navigation toolbar and a Command toolbar. These toolbars are shown in Figure 1-13. Many of the buttons on these toolbars execute frequently used commands for browsing the Web. You will learn about the functions of the most commonly used toolbar buttons in this session. The toolbars on your Internet Explorer browser might contain icons not shown in Figure 1-13 because the Command toolbar can be customized, which means that icons can be deleted and new icons can be added. Other software programs installed on your computer can place icons on your toolbar so that these programs can be used from within Internet Explorer.

Internet Explorer Navigation toolbar and Command toolbar ◄ **Figure 1-13**

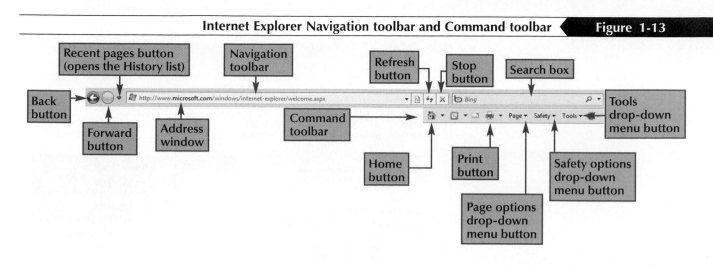

Now that you understand how to start Internet Explorer, you want to learn more about components of the Internet Explorer program window.

Status Bar

The status bar at the bottom of the window includes several panels that give you information about Internet Explorer's operations. The first panel—the **transfer progress report**—presents status messages that show, for example, the URL of a page while it is loading. When a page is completely loaded, this panel displays the text "Done" until you move the mouse over a hyperlink, at which time this panel displays the URL of the hyperlink. While Internet Explorer is loading a Web page from a Web server, a second panel opens and displays a blue **graphical transfer progress indicator** that moves from left to right to indicate how much of a Web page has been loaded. This indicator is especially useful for monitoring progress when the browser is loading large Web pages.

The last (rightmost) element on the status bar is a tool that allows you to adjust the magnification of a Web page. Some Web pages display printed text in a font that is too small for some users to see. Other Web pages have pictures or graphic elements, such as drawings or maps, that users might want to see in a larger or smaller form. This tool lets you increase or decrease the magnification level of a Web page.

Just to the left of the screen magnification tool is a panel that displays the **security settings** for the page you are viewing. As part of its security features, Internet Explorer lets you classify Web pages by the security risk you believe they present. You can open the Security tab in the Internet Options dialog box shown in Figure 1-14 by double-clicking the Security Settings panel.

Figure 1-14 ▶ **Internet Security dialog box**

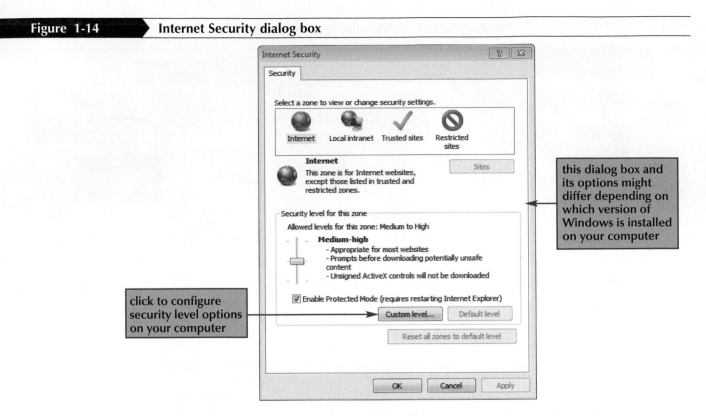

This dialog box lets you set five levels of security-enforcing procedures: High, Medium-High, Medium, Medium-Low, and Low (although not all five options are available for all types of sites; for example, sites in the "Restricted sites" category can only be assigned a level of "High"). In general, the higher the level of security you set for your browser, the slower it will operate. Higher security settings also disable some browser features.

Menu Bar

The menu bar is not displayed by default in recent versions of Internet Explorer. The menu bar gives you access to list menus that contain all of the menu commands available in Internet Explorer. You can display the menu bar by clicking the Tools button arrow, clicking Toolbars on the menu that appears, then clicking Menu Bar to select it.

Expanding the Web Page Area

Internet Explorer lets you hide its menu bar and toolbars to show more of the Web page area. As stated earlier, the menu bar is hidden by default; however, if you have it displayed, you can click the Tools button arrow and deselect the Menu Bar option to hide the menu bar, or you can select the Full Screen option on the Tools menu. When the window is in **Full Screen**, the toolbars and menu bar are no longer visible. You can display the hidden toolbars by moving the mouse pointer to the top of the screen and holding it there for a few seconds. When you move the mouse pointer away from the toolbars, they will become hidden again. To exit Full Screen mode, move the mouse pointer to the top of the screen until the toolbars appear, click the Tools button arrow, and then click Full Screen to remove the checkmark and deselect this option.

Hiding and Restoring Toolbars in Internet Explorer | Reference Window

- To hide the toolbars, click the Tools button arrow, then click Full Screen to check this option.
- To restore the toolbars, click the Tools button arrow, then click Full Screen to uncheck this option.
- To temporarily restore the toolbars in Full Screen, move the mouse cursor to the top of the screen until the toolbars appear.

To use the Full Screen command:

▶ 1. Click the **Tools button arrow** on the Command toolbar, and then click **Full Screen**. Now, you can see more of the Web page area.

▶ 2. If the toolbars do not immediately roll up out of view, move the mouse pointer away from the top of the screen for a moment.

▶ 3. Move the mouse pointer to the top of the screen. The toolbars scroll back down into view.

▶ 4. Click the **Tools button arrow** on the Command toolbar, and then click **Full Screen** to redisplay the toolbars.

You can add (or delete) buttons that appear on the Command toolbar by clicking the Tools button arrow, pointing to Toolbars, and then clicking Customize to open the Customize Toolbar dialog box.

Entering a URL in the Address Window

You can use the **Address window**, which is located on the Navigation toolbar, to enter URLs directly into Internet Explorer. As you learned in Session 1.1, you must enter the URL to identify a Web page's exact location. Although a complete URL includes the name of a file, entering just the IP address or the domain name will usually be enough information to find the home page of the site.

Internet Explorer will try to add standard URL elements to complete partial URLs that you type in the Address window. For example, if you type cnn.com, Internet Explorer will convert it to http://www.cnn.com and load the home page at that URL.

Entering a URL in the Address Window | Reference Window

- Click at the end of the current text in the Address window, and then delete any unnecessary or unwanted text from the displayed URL.
- Type the URL of the location that you want to view.
- Press the Enter key to load the URL's Web page in the browser window.

Trinity has asked you to start your research by examining the home page for the Midland Pet Adoption Agency's Web site. She has given you the URL so that you can find it.

To load the Midland Pet Adoption Agency's Web page:

▶ **1.** Click at the end of the text in the Address window to position the cursor at that point, and then delete any unnecessary or unwanted text by pressing the **Backspace** key as necessary.

Trouble? Make sure that you delete all of the text in the Address window so the text you type in Step 2 will be correct.

▶ **2.** Type **www.midlandpet.com** in the Address window. This is the URL for the Midland Pet Adoption Agency Web site.

▶ **3.** Press the **Enter** key. The home page of the Midland Pet Adoption Agency Web site loads, as shown in Figure 1-15.

Figure 1-15	Midland Pet Adoption Agency Web page

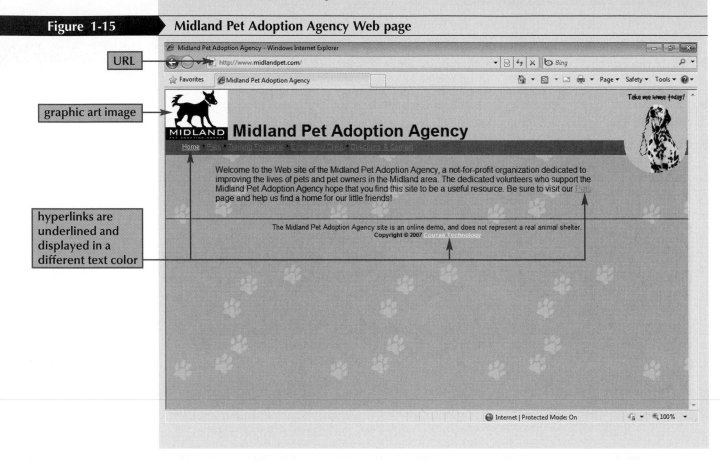

Navigating Web Pages Using the Mouse

The easiest way to move from one Web page to another is to use the mouse to click hyperlinks that the authors of Web pages include in their HTML documents. You can also right-click the mouse on the background of a Web page to open a shortcut menu that includes navigation options.

Navigating Between Web Pages Using Hyperlinks and the Mouse | Reference Window

- Click the hyperlink.
- After the new Web page has loaded, right-click on the Web page's background.
- Click Back on the shortcut menu.

To follow a hyperlink to another Web page and return using the mouse:

▶ **1.** With the Midland Pet Adoption Agency home page open in your browser, move the mouse pointer to position it over the **Training Programs** hyperlink, as shown in Figure 1-16. Note that your pointer changes to the shape of a hand with a pointing index finger, and the status bar displays the URL to which the hyperlink points.

Midland Pet Adoption Agency home page ◀ **Figure 1-16**

▶ **2.** Click the **Training Programs** hyperlink and move the mouse pointer away from the hyperlink. Watch the left-hand panel in the status bar—when it displays the text "Done," you know that Internet Explorer has loaded the full page. If you do not move the mouse pointer away from the hyperlink, the status bar will continue to display the URL to which the hyperlink points.

Trouble? The status bar only briefly displays the "Done" message. Do not worry if you do not see it.

▶ **3.** Right-click anywhere in the Web page area that is not a hyperlink to display the shortcut menu, as shown in Figure 1-17.

Figure 1-17 **Using the shortcut menu to go back to the previous page**

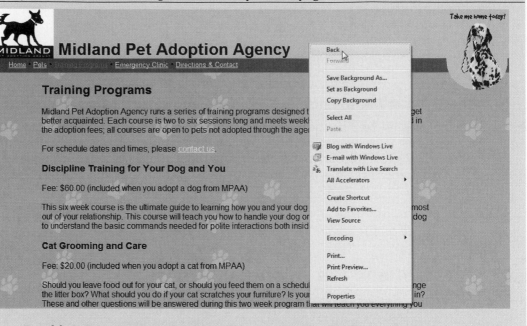

Trouble? If you right-click a hyperlink or a graphic Web page element, your shortcut menu will display a list that differs from the one shown in Figure 1-17; therefore the Back item might not appear in the same position on the menu or it might not appear at all. If you do not see the shortcut menu shown in Figure 1-17, click anywhere outside of the shortcut menu to close it, and then repeat Step 3.

Trouble? Some programs add options to the shortcut menu, so the shortcut menu you see might include items that do not appear on the shortcut menu shown in Figure 1-17.

▶ **4.** Click **Back** on the shortcut menu to return to the Midland Pet Adoption Agency home page.

Returning to Previously Viewed Web Pages

You like the format of the Midland Pet Adoption Agency's home page, so you want to make sure that you can go back to that page later if you need to review its contents. You can write down the URL so you can refer to it later, but an easier way is to store the URL in the Favorites list for future use. You can also use the History list and Back button to return to the pages you have previously visited, and the Home button to return to your browser's start page.

Navigating Web Pages Using the Favorites Center

Internet Explorer's Favorites Center lets you store and organize a list of Web pages that you have visited so you can return to them easily. The Favorites Center button opens the Favorites Center, as shown in Figure 1-18. You can use the Favorites Center to open URLs you have stored as favorites.

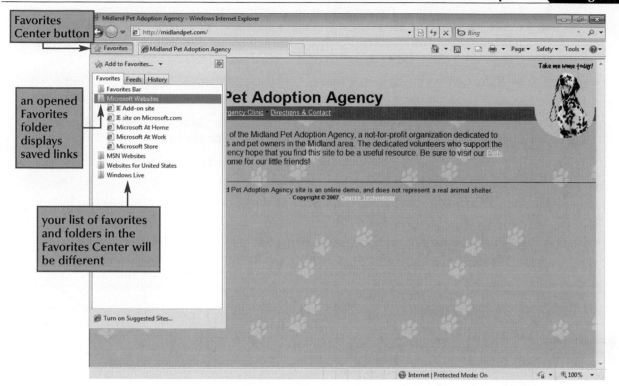

Figure 1-18 shows the hierarchical structure of the Favorites Center. For example, the figure shows five links to Web pages maintained by Microsoft stored in a folder named "Microsoft Websites." You can organize your favorites in whatever way best suits your needs and working style.

Creating a New Favorite in its Own Folder | Reference Window

- Open the Web page in Internet Explorer.
- Click the Favorites button, then click Add to Favorites.
- Type the title you would like to use for this Favorite in the Name text box (most Web pages will place text that describes the page in the Name text box; you can edit or replace that text).
- Click the New Folder button.
- Type the name of the new folder in the Folder Name text box, and then click the Create button.
- Click the Add button.

As you use the Web to find information about pet adoption agencies and other sites of interest, you might find yourself creating many favorites so you can return to sites of interest. When you start accumulating favorites, it is helpful to keep them organized so that you can quickly locate the site you need. Using folders within the Favorites Center, Internet Explorer helps you keep your favorites organized.

You will save the URL for the Midland Pet Adoption Agency Web page as a favorite in a Pet Adoption Agencies folder, which you will create in the process.

To create a new Favorite in its own folder:

▶ **1.** Before continuing, close the Favorites Bar. To do this, click **Tools** on the Command Bar, point to Toolbar in the menu that appears, and then click **Favorites Bar**. With the Midland Pet Adoption Agency's home page open, click the **Favorites** button, and then click Add to Favorites. The Add a Favorite dialog box opens.

▶ **2.** If the text in the Name text box is not "Midland Pet Adoption Agency" (without the quotation marks), delete the text, and then type **Midland Pet Adoption Agency**.

▶ **3.** Click the **New Folder** button. The Create a Folder dialog box opens. The new folder will be stored as a subfolder within the Favorites folder.

▶ **4.** Type **Pet Adoption Agencies** in the Folder Name text box, and then click the **Create** button.

▶ **5.** Click the **Add** button to close the dialog box. The favorite is now saved in Internet Explorer. You can test the favorite by opening it from the Favorites Center.

▶ **6.** Click the **Back** button on the Navigation toolbar as many times as necessary to return to the page that had been open in the browser before you opened the Midland Pet Adoption Agency home page, and then click the **Favorites** button to open the Favorites Center.

▶ **7.** Click the **Pet Adoption Agencies** folder to open it, as shown in Figure 1-19.

| Figure 1-19 | Favorites Center with the new favorite and folder |

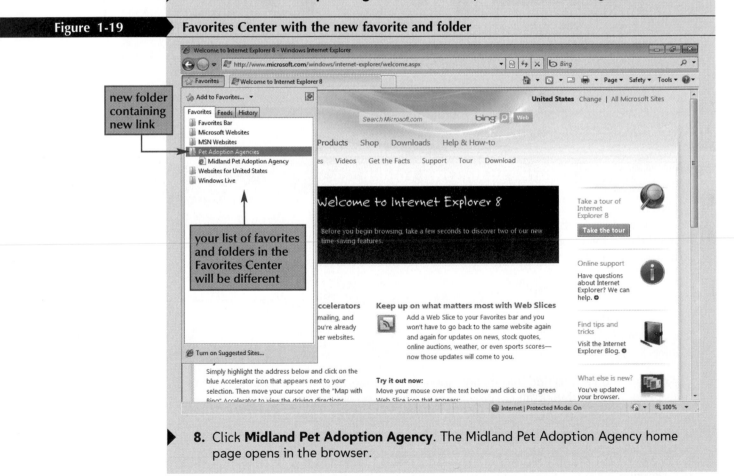

▶ **8.** Click **Midland Pet Adoption Agency**. The Midland Pet Adoption Agency home page opens in the browser.

Organizing Favorites

Internet Explorer offers an easy way to organize your folders in a hierarchical structure—even after you have stored them. You can rearrange URLs or even folders within folders in the Favorites Center.

Moving an Existing Favorite into a New Folder	Reference Window

- Click the Favorites button.
- Right-click the folder in which you want to add the new folder and click the Create New Folder command to display a new folder in the Favorites Center window.
- Type the name of the new folder, and then press the Enter key.
- Drag the favorite that you want to move into the new folder.

You explain to Maggie that you have created a new folder for Pet Adoption Agencies in the Internet Explorer Favorites Center and stored the Midland Pet Adoption Agency's URL in that folder. Because you might be collecting information about adoption agencies in different states as you conduct your research, Maggie suggests that you organize the information about adoption agencies by state. The Midland Pet Adoption Agency is located in Minnesota, so you decide to put information about the Midland Pet Adoption Agency in a separate folder named MN (which is the two-letter abbreviation for Minnesota) under the Pet Adoption Agencies folder. As you collect information about other agencies, you will add folders for the states in which they are located, too.

To move an existing favorite into a new folder:

▶ 1. Click the **Favorites** button to open the Favorites Center.

▶ 2. Right-click the **Pet Adoption Agencies** folder and then click the **Create New Folder** command on the shortcut menu. A new folder appears in the Favorites Center.

▶ 3. Type **MN** to replace the New Folder text, and then press the **Enter** key to rename the folder.

▶ 4. If necessary, click the **Pet Adoption Agencies** folder to open it, click and drag the **Midland Pet Adoption Agency** favorite to the new MN folder, and then release the mouse button.

▶ 5. Click the new **MN** folder to see the favorite now stored there, as shown in Figure 1-20.

Figure 1-20 Moving a favorite to a new folder

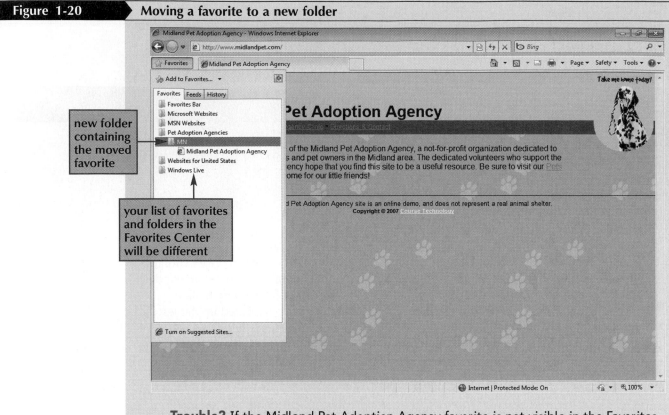

new folder containing the moved favorite

your list of favorites and folders in the Favorites Center will be different

Trouble? If the Midland Pet Adoption Agency favorite is not visible in the Favorites Center, click the MN folder to open that folder and display its contents.

6. Click the **Favorites** button to close the Favorites Center.

Navigating Web Pages Using the History List

The Back and Forward buttons on the Navigation toolbar and the Back and Forward options on the shortcut menu (which you can access by right-clicking a blank area of a Web page) enable you to move to and from previously visited pages. As you move back and forth between pages, Internet Explorer records these visited sites in the History list. To see where you have been during a session, you can open the history list by clicking the Recent Pages button (to the right of the Back and Forward buttons on the Navigation toolbar) or by clicking the Favorites button, and then clicking the History button at the top of the Favorites Center window.

To view the History list for this session:

1. Click the **Favorites** button, and then click the **History** tab in the Favorites Center window. The history list appears in a hierarchical structure in a separate window on the left side of the screen. The pages that you have visited are grouped by date of visit, so the last icon in the list will be labeled "Today" and will include Web sites you visited today. The other icons will be labeled with the names of days of the week (Monday, Tuesday, and so on) if Internet Explorer has been used regularly. If not, the icons will be labeled with week names (Last Week, Two Weeks Ago, and so on).

▶ **2.** Click the **Today** icon to open a list of Web sites you visited today. Each page you visited is stored in this list. To return to a particular page, click that page's entry in the list. You can see the full URL of any item in the History list by moving the mouse pointer over the history list item.

▶ **3.** Click the **Favorites** button to close the History list.

Erasing Your History | InSight

In some situations, such as when you are finishing a work session in a school computer lab, you might want to remove the list of Web sites that you visited from the History list of the computer on which you had been working. Erasing your browser history helps protect your personal information and guard your privacy when working on a shared computer. You can do this in Internet Explorer by clicking the Tools button, selecting Internet Options, and then clicking the General tab in the Internet Options dialog box. In the Browsing history section, click the Delete button, and then click the History check box to select it (unless it is already selected). If any other check boxes are selected, click each of them to clear the selections. Click the Delete button and your History will be erased.

Refreshing a Web Page

The Refresh button on the Navigation toolbar loads a new copy of the Web page that currently appears in the browser window. Internet Explorer stores a copy of every Web page it displays on your computer's hard drive in a **Temporary Internet Files folder** in the Windows folder. Storing this information increases the speed at which Internet Explorer can display pages as you move back and forth through the history list, because the browser can load the pages from a local disk drive instead of reloading the page from the remote Web server. When you click the Refresh button, Internet Explorer contacts the Web server to see if the Web page has changed since it was stored in the Temporary Internet Files folder. If it has changed, Internet Explorer gets the new page from the Web server; otherwise, it loads the copy stored on your computer.

Returning to the Home Page

The Home button on the Command bar displays the home (or start) page for your installation of Internet Explorer. You can set the Home button to display the page you want to use as the default home page.

Changing the Default Home Page in Internet Explorer | Reference Window

- Click the Tools button on the Command toolbar, and then click Internet Options.
- Click the General tab in the Internet Options dialog box.
- Select whether you want Internet Explorer to open with the current page, its default page, or a blank page by clicking the corresponding button in the Home page section of the Internet Options dialog box.
- To specify a home page, type the URL of that Web page in the Home page list box. If you want multiple home pages to open on separate tabs, type the URL for each home page on separate lines in the Home Page list box.
- Click the OK button.

To view the settings for the home page:

▶ **1.** Click **Tools** on the Command toolbar, and then click **Internet Options**. The Internet Options dialog box opens, as shown in Figure 1-21. To use the currently loaded Web page as your home page, you would click the Use current button. To use the default home page that was installed with your copy of Internet Explorer, you would click the Use default button. If you don't want a page to open when you start your browser, you would click the Use blank button. If you want to specify a home page other than the current, default, or blank page, you would type the URL for that page in the Home page list box.

| Figure 1-21 | Home page setting in Internet Explorer |

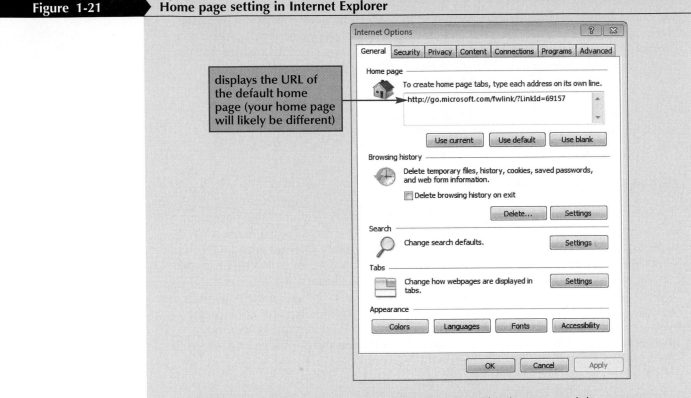

displays the URL of the default home page (your home page will likely be different)

Trouble? If you are working on a computer in a school computer lab or at your employer's place of business, do not change any settings unless you are given permission to do so by your instructor, employer, or lab supervisor. Many schools and businesses set the home page defaults on all of their computers and then lock those settings.

▶ **2.** Click the **Cancel** button to close the dialog box without making any changes.

Navigating Web Pages Using Page Tabs

Like most other Web browsers, Internet Explorer offers page tabs in its program window. This feature allows users to navigate from one page to another by opening new Web pages in tabs instead of separate browser windows. This tabbed browsing technique is especially useful when you need to move frequently back and forth between multiple Web pages. You can click the New Tab button and type a URL in the address window or select a favorite from the Favorites Center, but the most common use of tabbed browsing is to navigate from a page that is already open.

Using Page Tabs to Navigate in Internet Explorer | Reference Window

- Open pages by right-clicking hyperlinks and selecting Open in New Tab on the short-cut menu.
- Click the page tabs to move among open Web pages.

To use page tabs to navigate in Internet Explorer:

▶ **1.** Using the Back and Forward buttons (or the Recent Pages button, or the History list in the Favorites Center), open the Midland Pet Adoption Agency home page in the browser window.

▶ **2.** Right-click the **Pets** hyperlink, and then select **Open in New Tab** on the shortcut menu. Note that the Pets page will not appear until you click the tab (as you will in Step 4).

▶ **3.** Right-click the **Training Programs** hyperlink, and then select **Open in New Tab**. Note that the Training Programs page will not appear until you click the tab (as you will in Step 4).

▶ **4.** Click each visible tab to open its Web page in the browser. The browser with these three tabs open is shown in Figure 1-22.

Internet Explorer with three tabs open | **Figure 1-22**

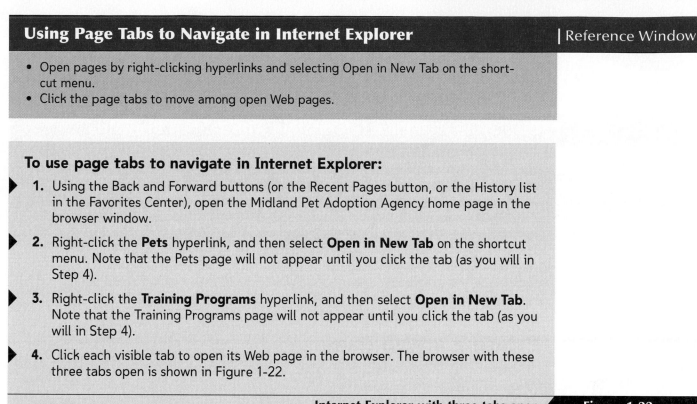

> **5.** Close the two tabs you opened by clicking each tab and then clicking the Close Tab button on the tab. The Midland Pet Adoption Agency home page appears again in the browser window.

| InSight | **Displaying Web Page Information with Tabbed Browsing** |

If you are using tabbed browsing, the page tabs can become rather small as you open more and more tabs. When the page tabs get smaller, the amount of text that is displayed on the tab might not be enough to identify the page. To see the entire Web page title and URL, move the mouse pointer over a page tab and hold it there for a second or two. The information will appear in a screentip near the mouse pointer. Another way to navigate a large number of open tabs is to use the Quick Tabs button. This button appears to the left of the original tab when a second tab is opened. Clicking the Quick Tabs button opens a page in the browser window that displays small pictures of each Web page that is opened in a tab. Clicking on a picture opens the represented page in the main browser window.

Printing a Web Page

Tip

If you encounter a page that is difficult to print, be sure to look on the Web page for a link to a version of the page that is designed to be printed.

Clicking the Print button arrow on the Command bar opens a menu that gives you choices for printing the current Web page, viewing the page as it will appear when printed (Print Preview), or accessing the Page Setup dialog box, which provides options for adjusting the margins, header, footer, and other attributes of the pages you print.

| Reference Window | **Printing the Current Web Page** |

- Click the Print button on the Command bar, and then click Print to print the current Web page with the default print settings.
  or
- Click the Print Button arrow on the Command bar, and then click Print to open the Print dialog box.
- In the Print dialog box, select the printer you want to use, and then indicate the pages you want to print and the number of copies you want to make of each page.
- To print a range of pages, click the Pages option button, type the first page of the range, type a hyphen, and then type the last page of the range.
- Click the Print button.

To print a Web page:

> **1.** Click the **Print button arrow** on the Command bar, and then click **Print**.

> **2.** Make sure that the printer selected (highlighted) in the Select Printer list box is the printer you want to use; if not, click the icon of the printer you want to use to change the selection.

> **3.** Click the **Pages** option button in the Page Range section of the Print dialog box, and then type **1** in the text box to specify that you only want to print the first page. (If the text box already contains a "1" you do not need to change it.)

▶ **4.** Make sure that the Number of copies text box displays **1**.

▶ **5.** Click the **Print** button to print the Web page and close the Print dialog box.

Changing the Page Setup Settings

Usually, the default settings in the Print dialog box are fine for printing a Web page, but you can use the Page Setup dialog box to change aspects of a Web page printout, such as margins and print orientation. Figure 1-23 shows the Page Setup dialog box with the default print settings.

Page Setup dialog box ◀ **Figure 1-23**

The Paper Options and Margin settings are similar to those used in word-processing software. The Headers and Footers section allows you to choose up to three items to print in each section. The default settings for Header are to print the Web page title in the left of the header, leave the center of the header empty, and print the page number and the total number of pages in the right portion of the header. You can click the drop-down boxes to change the left, middle, and right sections of both the header and footer on Web pages you print.

Using Print Preview in Internet Explorer | InSight

You can open the Print Preview window by clicking the Print button arrow on the Command bar, and then clicking Print Preview. The Print Preview window lets you change the page from portrait to landscape orientation with a single click, which can be helpful when printing certain graphic images, such as maps. The Print Preview window also lets you change the magnification level of the page. This can help you save a significant amount of paper when printing Web pages. The Print Preview window lets you set the magnification and see the result before you print, so you avoid reducing the magnification to the point that text is unreadable. The Print Preview window also lets you toggle headers and footers on and off with one click.

Checking Web Page Security

Most Web pages are sent from the Web server to the Web browser as plain text and image files. Anyone who intercepts the transmission can read the text and see the images. For most Web pages, which are designed to be viewed by anyone, this is not really a problem. In some cases, however, the Web site and the user would like to have a private interaction. For example, you might not want anyone to know what book titles or what size clothes you are ordering from an online store. You certainly wouldn't want an unauthorized person to intercept your interactions with your bank or stockbroker. To prevent unauthorized persons from reading intercepted transmissions, Web servers can use encryption.

Encryption is a way of scrambling and encoding data transmissions that reduces the risk that a person who intercepts the Web page as it travels across the Internet will be able to decode and read the page's contents. Web sites use encrypted transmission to send and receive information, such as credit card numbers, to ensure privacy. You can determine whether a Web page has been encrypted by examining the page's properties. To open the Properties dialog box for a Web page, right-click the Web page and select Properties from the shortcut menu. If the Web page is not encrypted, the Connection property in the Properties dialog box will appear as "Not Encrypted." If the Web page is encrypted, the Connection property will display information about the type and level of encryption used to transmit the page from the Web server.

Another protection used by Web sites is to register with a third-party certification authority. A **certification authority** is a company that attests to a Web site's identity. A Web site that has obtained the attestation of a certificate authority has the right to display information about the certification authority when you load its Web page. Most Web sites display this information when you enter a secure area of the site such as the checkout page of an online store or your account page at a banking or financial services Web site. A few Web sites do display their certificate authority's information.

Reference Window | **Reviewing a Web Site's Certificate Information**

- Open the Web page in Internet Explorer.
- Click the Web site owner's name (or the name of the certificate authority) that appears to the right of the padlock icon on the Address Bar to open the Website Identification window.
- Click the View certificates link near the bottom of the Website Identification window to open the Certificates window.
- Review the information in the General tab, and then click the Details tab and the Certification Path tab to review additional information.
- Click the OK button.

To review information about a Web site's certificate:

▶ 1. Type **www.cengage.com/internet/np/internet8** in the address window of Internet Explorer to open the Online Companion page, log on to your account (if necessary), click the **Tutorial 1** link, and then click the **Session 1.2** link.

▶ 2. Click one of the company names listed under the heading **Web Site Home Pages That Display Certificate Information** to open that company's home page. The address window will display the URL of the Web page, a padlock icon, and the name of the company slowly alternating with the name of the certificate authority.

Trouble? If the address window does not display the padlock icon with the name of the company slowly alternating with the name of the certificate authority, click the **Back** button and select a different company name from the list.

▶ 3. Click either the name of the company or the name of the certificate authority (whichever is displayed) to open the Website Identification window.

▶ 4. Click the View certificates link near the bottom of the Website Identification window to open the Certificates window. Figure 1-24 shows a Certificate window displaying information about the certificate issued by VeriSign (a certificate authority) that attests to the identity of the computer hosting the Web site of USAA, a company that provides financial services to members of the U.S. military and their families.

Certificate information for USAA home page ◀ Figure 1-24

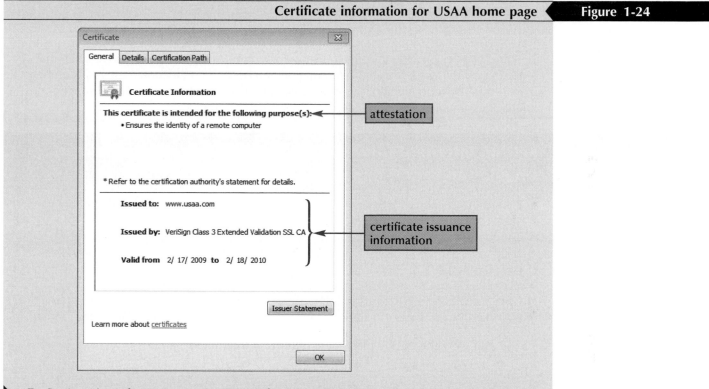

▶ 5. Review the information in the **General** tab, which will include a statement of the certificate's purpose, the domain name of the Web site to which the certificate is issued, the name of the certificate authority, and the dates within which the certificate is valid.

▶ 6. Click the **Details** tab and then click the **Certificate** tab to view more details about this certificate.

▶ 7. When you are finished reviewing information about the certificate for this Web site, click the **OK** button to close the Certificate window.

Managing Cookies

Many Web users are concerned about cookies, the small files you learned about in Session 1.1 that some Web servers write to the disk drives of client computers. Unlike most other Web browsers, Internet Explorer stores each cookie in an individual file and does not provide any advanced tools for examining or deleting specific cookies. It does, however, allow you to delete all cookies and set options that control the writing of cookies to your computer's disk drive.

Reference Window | **Deleting All Cookies in Internet Explorer**

- Click the Tools button arrow on the Command bar, and then click Internet Options.
- Click the Delete button in the Browsing history section, and then click the Cookies check box to select it (unless it is already selected). Clear any other check boxes for items you do not want to delete, and then click the Delete button.
- Click the OK button.

Some cookies provide benefits to users. For example, if you regularly visit a site that requires you to log in, that login information can be stored in a cookie on your computer so you don't have to type your username each time you visit the site. Therefore, you might not want to delete all of the cookies on your computer.

Reference Window | **Setting Internet Explorer Options that Control Placement of Cookies on Your Computer**

- Click the Tools button arrow on the Command bar, and then click Internet Options.
- Click the Privacy tab in the Internet Options dialog box.
- Use the Settings slider control to set the way cookies are handled by Internet Explorer.
- Click the Sites button to specify sites that are allowed (or not allowed) to place cookies on your computer.
- Click the OK button to close the Per Site Privacy Actions dialog box.
- Click the OK button to close the Internet Options dialog box.

You will view the cookie placement options in Internet Explorer.

To view cookie placement options in Internet Explorer:

▶ 1. Click **Tools** on the Command bar, and then click **Internet Options**. The Internet Options dialog box opens.

▶ 2. Click the **Privacy** tab to display these options.

▶ 3. Click and drag the slider control in the Settings section on the Privacy tab to examine the various settings available that control placement of cookies on your computer.

▶ 4. Click the **Cancel** button to close the Internet Options dialog box without saving any of the changes you might have made to the privacy settings.

Advertising Cookies | InSight

You might notice that many of the cookies on your computer are placed there by companies that sell banner advertising on Web pages (AdRevolver or DoubleClick). These companies use cookies to record which ads have appeared on pages you have viewed so that they can present different ads the next time you open a Web page. This can be beneficial because it prevents sites from showing you the same ads over and over again. On the other hand, many people believe that this sort of user tracking is an offensive invasion of privacy.

Private Web Browsing

As you have learned, Internet Explorer stores a considerable amount of information about your Web browsing activity. It stores a list of all the Web pages you have viewed in History and stores cookies that can contain information about your logins, passwords, and even which ads have been displayed on the Web pages you have viewed. It also stores copies of all or part of the Web pages you visit on whatever computer you are using. If you do not wish to have this information stored, you can use Internet Explorer in private browsing mode. When in **private browsing mode**, Internet Explorer does not store History, cookies, or copies of the Web pages you visit. When you are using a computer other than your own (such as a friend's computer or a computer at work, school, or another public location), private browsing mode can help protect your privacy and security. The private browsing mode in Internet Explorer is called InPrivate Browsing.

Opening Internet Explorer in Private Browsing Mode | Reference Window

- Open Internet Explorer.
- Click the Safety button on the Command toolbar.
- Click InPrivate Browsing.
- Use Internet Explorer to visit Web pages.
- When you have finished browsing in private mode, click the browser's Close button.

To use Internet Explorer in private browsing mode:

▶ 1. Open Internet Explorer if necessary.

▶ 2. Click the **Safety** button on the Command toolbar, and then click **InPrivate Browsing**.

▶ 3. Type **www.midlandpet.com** in the Address window and then press the **Enter** key. The left area of the Address window will display "InPrivate" with a blue background.

▶ 4. Click any link on the Web page to visit another part of the Midland Pets Web site, and then click other links to visit several other pages on the site.

▶ 5. Click the Internet Explorer **Close** button.

   If you examine the browser's History, you will find that it includes no record of the Web pages you just visited. Although the browser does not record the pages you have visited (or other information, such as cookies), the network server that connects the computer to the Internet might have software that does. Therefore, it is best not to rely on private browsing mode to keep secret the Web pages you visit while using a computer at work or another public location.

Getting Help in Internet Explorer

Internet Explorer includes an online Help system. Internet Explorer Help includes information about how to use the browser and how it is different from previous versions of the browser, and provides some tips for exploring the Internet.

Reference Window | **Opening Internet Explorer Help**

- Press the F1 key to open the Windows Help and Support window.
- Click the Browse Help button near the top of the Windows Help and Support window.
- Click a hyperlink to open a specific Help topic.
- Click the Close button.

To open Internet Explorer Help:

▶ **1.** Press the **F1** key. The Windows Help and Support window opens, as shown in Figure 1-25.

Figure 1-25 ▶ **Internet Explorer help window**

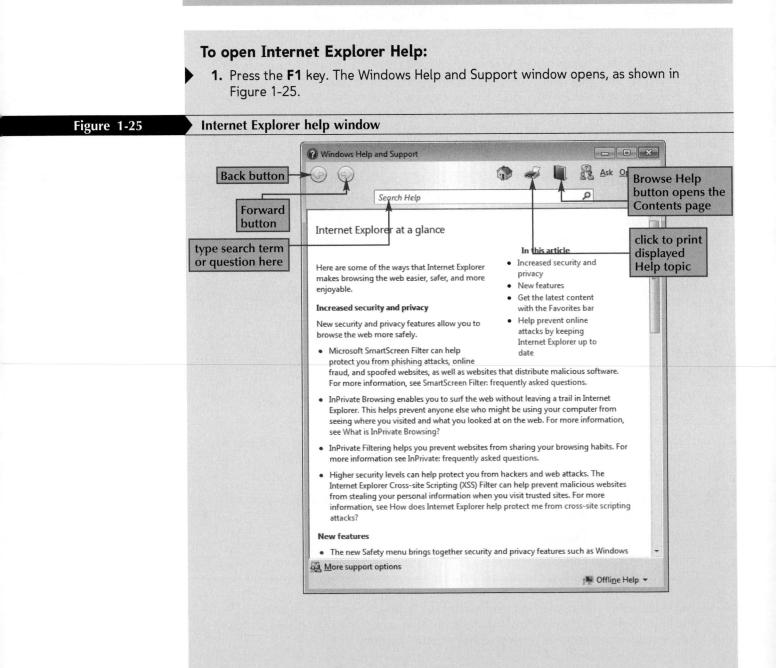

▶ **2.** Click the **Browse Help** button to open the Windows Help and Support Contents page. You can explore any of the items in the Help system by clicking the topics displayed as hyperlinks in this window. You can also type terms or questions into the Search Help box to find information in the Help system.

▶ **3.** When you are finished exploring the Help system, click the **Close** button.

You want to show Trinity the Midland Pet Adoption Agency Web page, but you are concerned that the Web site might change before she has a chance to visit it on the Web. You can save the Web page as a file on a computer or another storage medium. She will then be able to open the Web page on her own computer using her Web browser.

Using Internet Explorer to Save Web Page Content

There will be times when you will want to refer to the information that you have found on a Web page without having to return to the site. In Internet Explorer you can store entire Web pages, selected portions of Web page text, or particular graphics from a Web page to a disk.

Saving a Web Page

You like the Midland Pet Adoption Agency's Web site and want to save a copy of the page to a disk so you can show the Web page to Trinity. To save a Web page, you must have the page open in Internet Explorer.

Saving a Web Page | Reference Window

- Open the Web page in Internet Explorer.
- Click the Page button arrow on the Command bar, and then click Save As.
- Navigate to the desired location for your saved Web page.
- Accept the default filename, or change the filename in the File name text box, but retain the file extension .mht.
- Click the Save button.

You will save the Midland Pet Adoption Agency home page so you can show it to Trinity later.

To save the Web page:

▶ **1.** If necessary, use the Back and Forward buttons or the Favorites Center to return to the Midland Pet Adoption Agency home page if it is not already displayed in your browser.

▶ **2.** Click the **Page button arrow** on the Command bar, and then click **Save As**. The Save Webpage dialog box opens.

▶ **3.** Navigate to the location where you will save the Web page.

▶ **4.** Type **MidlandHomePageMSIE.mht** in the File name text box.

▶ **5.** Click the **Save** button. Now the Web page for the Midland Pet Adoption Agency's home page is saved in the location you specified. When you send it to Trinity, she can open her Web browser and type the file location and name in the browser's Address window to open the Web page.

InSight | **Understanding Web Page File Formats**

Internet Explorer by default saves Web pages in a proprietary archive format (the .mht format) that can be read by Internet Explorer Web browsers. Not all Web browsers, however, can read this file format. You can change the format in the Save As dialog box by choosing either Webpage, complete (which saves the graphic page elements along with the HTML text), Webpage, HTML only (which saves the Web page's text with the HTML markup codes), or Text File (which saves the Web page's text without the HTML markup codes) in the Save as type list box. Avoiding the Internet Explorer proprietary format will ensure that the page you save can be read by users who are using other Web browsers.

Saving Web Page Text to a File

You can save portions of a Web page's text to a file, so that you can use the text in other programs. You will use WordPad to save text that you will copy from a Web page; however, any word processor or text editor will work.

Reference Window | **Copying Text from a Web Page to a WordPad Document**

- Open the Web page in Internet Explorer.
- Use the mouse pointer to select the text you want to copy.
- Right-click the selected text to open the shortcut menu, and then click Copy.
- Open WordPad (or another word processor or text editor if WordPad is not available).
- Click Edit on the WordPad menu bar, and then click Paste (or click the Paste button).
- Click the Save button, select the location in which you want to store the file, and then enter a new filename, if necessary.
- Click the Save button.

Trinity will be traveling in Minnesota next week, and she would like to visit the Midland Pet Adoption Agency while she is in the area. She will meet with the director there to learn more about how the agency developed its Web site. You will visit the Midland Pet Adoption Agency's Web site and get the agency's address and telephone number so Trinity can contact the director and schedule a meeting.

To copy text from a Web page and save it as a WordPad document:

▶ **1.** Return to the Midland Pet Adoption Agency home page if it is not already displayed in your browser.

▶ **2.** Click the **Directions & Contact** hyperlink to open the Web page that has the address and phone number you want to copy.

▶ **3.** Click and drag the mouse pointer over the address and telephone number to select it, as shown in Figure 1-26, right-click the selected text, and then click **Copy** on the shortcut menu to copy the selected text to the Clipboard.

Selecting and copying text on a Web page in Internet Explorer ◄ Figure 1-26

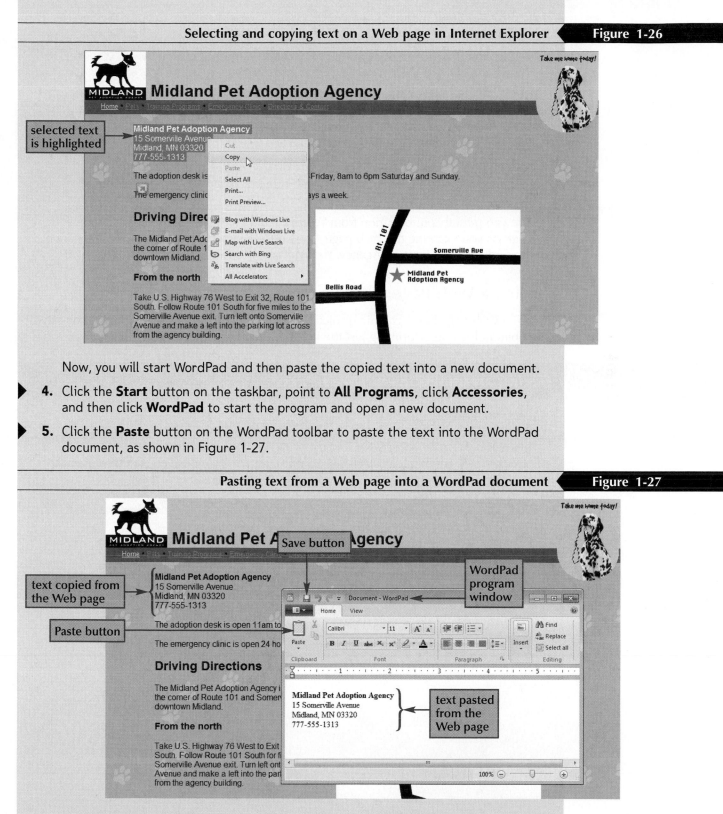

Now, you will start WordPad and then paste the copied text into a new document.

▶ **4.** Click the **Start** button on the taskbar, point to **All Programs**, click **Accessories**, and then click **WordPad** to start the program and open a new document.

▶ **5.** Click the **Paste** button on the WordPad toolbar to paste the text into the WordPad document, as shown in Figure 1-27.

Pasting text from a Web page into a WordPad document ◄ Figure 1-27

Trouble? If the WordPad toolbar does not appear, click View on the menu bar, click Toolbar, and then repeat Step 5. Your WordPad program window might be a different size from the one shown in Figure 1-27, which does not affect the steps.

▶ **6.** Click the **Save** button on the WordPad Quick Access toolbar to open the Save As dialog box.

▶ **7.** Click the **Browse Folders** button to navigate to the location in which you want to save the file.

▶ **8.** Click the **Save as type** button, and then click **Text document (*.txt)**. Delete the text in the File name text box, type **MidlandAddressPhoneMSIE**, and then click the **Save** button. Now, the address and phone number of the agency are saved in a text file for future reference. If a dialog box appears that warns about loss of formatting, click the Yes button.

▶ **9.** Click the **Close** button on the WordPad title bar to close it.

You can print this information from WordPad and give it to Trinity the next time you see her. As you examine the Web page, you notice a street map that shows the location of the Midland Pet Adoption Agency. You will save this map to give to Trinity as well.

Saving a Web Page Graphic

When a Web page has a graphic or picture that you would like to save or print, you have the option of saving or printing just the image, instead of the entire Web page.

Reference Window | **Saving an Image from a Web Page**

- Open the Web page in Internet Explorer.
- Right-click the image you want to copy, and then click Save Picture As on the shortcut menu.
- Navigate to the location in which you want to save the image and change the default filename, if necessary.
- Click the Save button.

Now you will save the image of the street map for Trinity.

To save the street map image:

▶ **1.** Right-click the map image to open its shortcut menu, as shown in Figure 1-28.

Saving the map image ◀ **Figure 1-28**

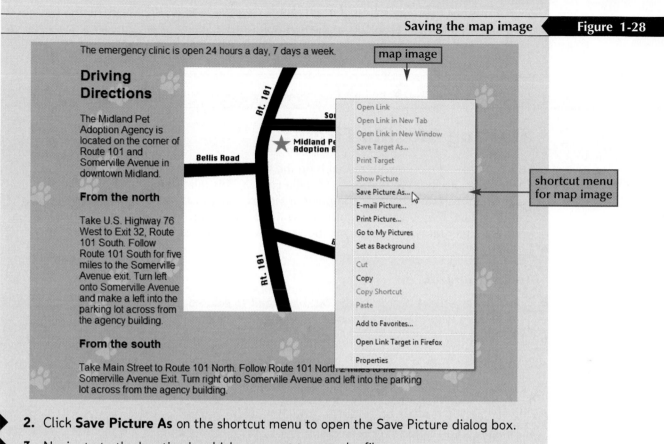

2. Click **Save Picture As** on the shortcut menu to open the Save Picture dialog box.

3. Navigate to the location in which you want to save the file.

4. Delete the text in the File name text box, type **MidlandMapMSIE.gif**, and then click the **Save** button to save the file.

5. Close your Web browser.

Now, you have copies of the Midland Pet Adoption Agency home page and map that will show Trinity how to get there during her trip to Minnesota. She will be able to use her Web browser to open the files and print them.

Session 1.2 Quick Check | Review

1. Describe two ways to increase the Web page area in Internet Explorer.
2. You can use the _____ button in Internet Explorer to visit previously visited sites during your Web session.
3. Clicking the _____ button on the Command bar opens the page that the browser is configured to display when it first starts.
4. List the names of two Favorites folders (in addition to your Pet Adoption Agencies folder) that you might want to add as you continue to gather information for Trinity.
5. To ensure that Internet Explorer loads a Web page from the server rather than from its cache, you can hold down the _____ key as you click the Refresh button.
6. Explain how you can identify encrypted Web pages when viewing them in Internet Explorer.
7. To obtain help in Internet Explorer, press the _____ key.

If your instructor assigned Session 1.3, continue reading. Otherwise complete the Review Assignments and Case Problems at the end of this tutorial.

Session 1.3

Starting Mozilla Firefox

You could decide to do your research on the Web for Trinity and the Danville Animal Shelter with a major Web browser, Mozilla Firefox. This introduction assumes that you have Firefox installed on your computer. If Firefox is not installed on your computer, you can download the program and install it without paying any license fee. You should have your computer turned on so the Windows desktop is displayed.

To start Firefox:

▶ **1.** Click the **Start** button on the taskbar, point to **All Programs**, click **Mozilla Firefox**, and then click **Mozilla Firefox**. After a moment, Firefox opens.

Trouble? If you cannot find Mozilla Firefox on the All Programs menu, check to see if a Mozilla or Firefox shortcut icon appears on the desktop, and then double-click it. If you do not see the shortcut icon, ask your instructor or technical support person for help. The program might be installed in a different location on the computer you are using.

▶ **2.** If the program does not fill the screen entirely, click the **Maximize** button on the Firefox program's title bar. Your screen should look like Figure 1-29.

Figure 1-29 | **Firefox main program window**

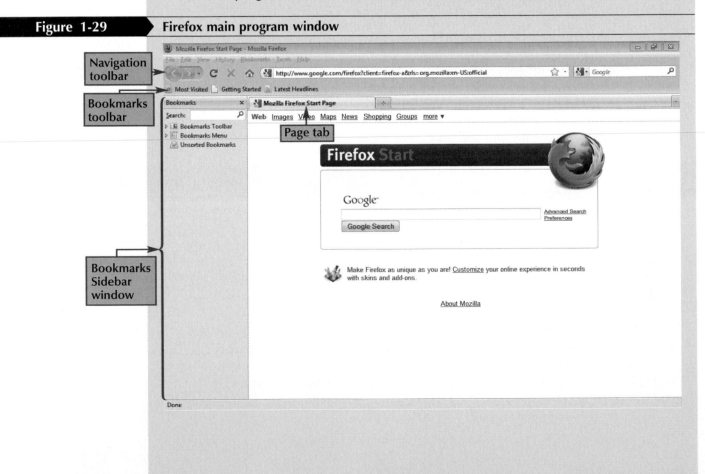

Trouble? Figure 1-29 shows the Firefox Start page, which is the page that Firefox opens the first time the program is started after its initial installation on a computer. Your computer might be configured to open to a different Web page, or no page at all.

Trouble? If you don't see a page tab on your screen, then your browser is set to hide page tabs when only one Web site is open. Click Tools on the menu bar, click Options, click Tabs in the Options dialog box, and then click the Always show the tab bar check box to select it. Click OK to close the dialog box.

Trouble? If the Bookmarks toolbar is not displayed on your screen, click View on the menu bar, point to Toolbars, and then click Bookmarks Toolbar to display the toolbar, as shown in Figure 1-29.

Trouble? If the Bookmarks Sidebar window shown in Figure 1-29 is not visible in your browser window, skip Step 3.

▶ 3. Click **View** on the menu bar, point to **Sidebar**, and then click **Bookmarks** to close the Bookmarks Sidebar. This will give you more room to view Web pages when using the Firefox browser. You can reopen the Bookmarks Sidebar by selecting View, Sidebar, Bookmarks on the menu bar.

Now that you understand how to start Firefox, you want to learn more about the components of the Firefox program window.

Firefox Toolbars

The **Navigation toolbar** includes buttons that execute frequently used commands for browsing the Web. Figure 1-30 shows the Navigation toolbar. This toolbar contains buttons that perform basic Web browsing functions, a Location bar, and a Search bar. In Firefox, the formal names of the Forward button and Back button are the Go forward one page button and Go back one page button, respectively. This text refers to the navigation buttons as the Forward and Back buttons.

Firefox Navigation toolbar ◀ Figure 1-30

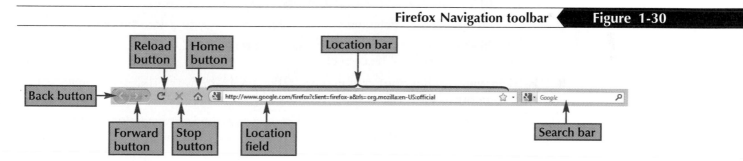

The **Location bar** includes a **location field** that allows users to type the URL of the site they wish to visit. The Navigation toolbar also has a search bar that allows users to type a search term that Firefox sends to the user's choice of search engines and Web directories.

You can use the View menu to hide or show the Firefox toolbars. This is useful when you want to expand the Web browser window to show more of the Web pages you are viewing. The View menu commands are toggles—meaning you click the command once to activate it, and you click it again to turn it off. You will hide the Bookmarks toolbar.

To hide the Bookmarks toolbar using the View menu:

▶ 1. Click **View** on the menu bar, point to **Toolbars**, and then click **Bookmarks Toolbar** to remove its check mark. The Bookmarks toolbar is hidden in the browser window. To redisplay the Bookmarks toolbar, you will repeat the same steps.

> **Trouble?** If the Bookmarks Toolbar command does not have a check mark next to it, then the Bookmarks toolbar already is hidden.
>
> ▶ **2.** Click **View** on the menu bar, point to **Toolbars**, and then click **Bookmarks Toolbar** to check this command. The toolbar is displayed again.

Firefox will try to add standard URL elements to complete partial URLs that you type in the Address bar. For example, if you type cnn.com, Firefox will convert it to http://www.cnn.com and load the home page at that URL.

Navigating Web Pages Using the Location Field

You can use the Location field to enter URLs directly into Firefox. As you learned in Session 1.1, you must enter the URL to identify a Web page's exact location. Although a complete URL includes the name of a file, entering just the IP address or the domain name will usually be sufficient to take you to the home page of the site.

Reference Window | **Entering a URL in the Location Field**

- Click in the location field, and then delete any unnecessary or unwanted text from the displayed URL.
- Type the URL of the site you want to view.
- Press the Enter key to load the URL's Web page in the browser window.

Trinity has asked you to start your research by examining the home page for the Midland Pet Adoption Agency's Web site. She has given you the URL so that you can find it.

To load the Midland Pet Adoption Agency's Web page:

▶ **1.** Click in the Location field and press the **Backspace** key to delete any existing text.

   Trouble? Make sure that you delete all of the text in the Location field so the text you type in Step 2 will be correct.

▶ **2.** Type **www.midlandpet.com** in the Location field. This is the URL of the Midland Pet Adoption Agency Web site.

   Trouble? Depending on how Firefox is configured, the Location field might display a list of suggested URLs as you type. You should ignore these suggestions and continue typing.

▶ **3.** Press the **Enter** key. The home page of the Midland Pet Adoption Agency Web site loads, as shown in Figure 1-31.

Midland Pet Adoption Agency Web page ◄ Figure 1-31

Navigating Web Pages Using the Mouse

The easiest way to move from one Web page to another is to use the mouse to click hyperlinks that the authors of Web pages embed in their HTML documents. You can also right-click the mouse on the background of a Web page to open a shortcut menu that includes navigation options.

Navigating Between Web Pages Using Hyperlinks and the Mouse	Reference Window

- Click the hyperlink.
- After the new Web page has loaded, right-click the Web page's background.
- Click Back on the shortcut menu.

To follow a hyperlink to a Web page and return using the mouse:

▶ 1. Point to the **Training Programs** hyperlink, shown in Figure 1-32, so your pointer changes to an icon of a hand with a pointing index finger.

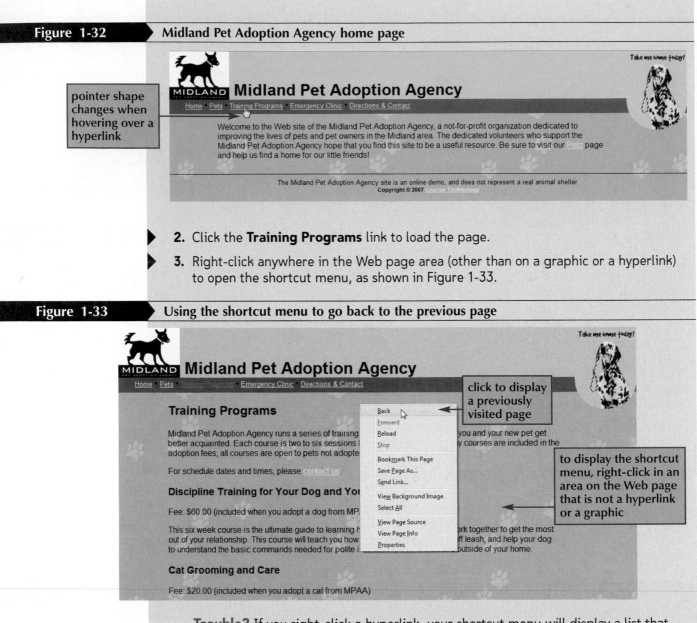

Figure 1-32 Midland Pet Adoption Agency home page

2. Click the **Training Programs** link to load the page.

3. Right-click anywhere in the Web page area (other than on a graphic or a hyperlink) to open the shortcut menu, as shown in Figure 1-33.

Figure 1-33 Using the shortcut menu to go back to the previous page

Trouble? If you right-click a hyperlink, your shortcut menu will display a list that differs from the one shown in Figure 1-33; therefore, the Back option might not appear in the same position on the menu. If you don't see the shortcut menu shown in Figure 1-33, click anywhere outside of the shortcut menu to close it, and then repeat Step 3.

4. Click **Back** on the shortcut menu to go back to the Midland Pet Adoption Agency home page.

Returning to Web Pages Previously Visited

You like the format of the Midland Pet Adoption Agency's home page, so you want to make sure that you can go back to that page later if you need to review its contents. You can write down the URL so you can refer to it later, but an easier way is to store the URL as a bookmark for future use. You can also use the History list and the Back and Forward buttons to return to Web pages you have already visited, and the Home button to return to your browser's start page.

Navigating Web Pages Using Bookmarks

Earlier in this chapter, you learned that Web browsers have a feature that allows you to store and organize Web pages you have visited before. In Firefox, the implementation of this feature uses **bookmarks**. Bookmarks in Firefox are stored, along with the History list, in the Firefox **Library**. The Library includes tools for managing and organizing the bookmarks you collect. Figure 1-34 shows an open Firefox Library window, showing some bookmarks stored in a folder named "Mozilla Firefox."

Bookmarks sorted into categories ◄ **Figure 1-34**

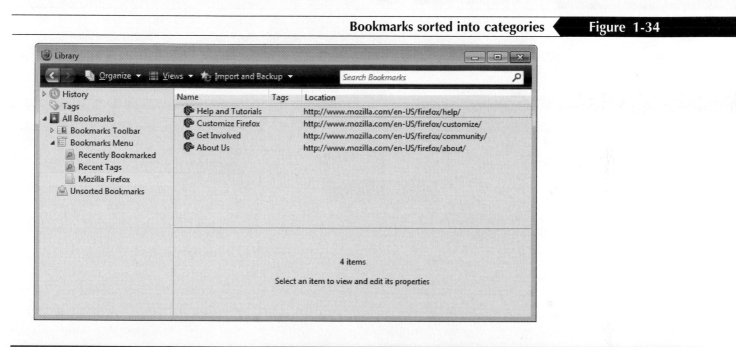

Creating a New Bookmarks Folder | Reference Window

- Click Bookmarks on the menu bar, and then click Organize Bookmarks to open the Firefox Library.
- If the Bookmarks Menu entry in the left pane of the Library window is not highlighted, click it, click the Organize button near the top of the Library window, and then click New Folder.
- Delete the default text in the Name text box, and then type a new folder name.
- Click the Add button.

You will create a bookmark for the Midland Pet Adoption Agency Web page, but first, you need to create a folder in which to store your bookmarks. You will then save your bookmark in that folder. Because you might not work on the same computer again, you will save a copy of the bookmark file to a USB flash drive or another storage device for future use.

To create a new Bookmarks folder:

▶ 1. Click **Bookmarks** on the menu bar, and then click **Organize Bookmarks**. The Library window opens.

▶ 2. If Bookmarks Menu in the left pane of the Library window is not highlighted, click it, and then click the **Organize** button near the top of the Library window.

▶ 3. Click **New Folder** to open the New Folder dialog box.

▶ 4. Delete the default text in the Name text box, type **Pet Adoption Agencies**, and then click the **Add** button. The Pet Adoption Agencies folder is added to the Bookmarks Menu, as shown in Figure 1-35.

Figure 1-35 ▶ **Pet Adoption Agencies folder**

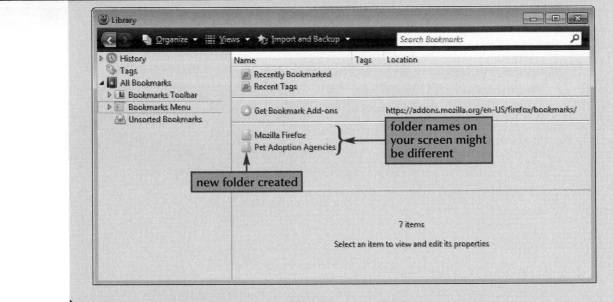

▶ 5. Click the **Close** button in the Library window to close it.

Now that you have created a folder, you can save your bookmark for the Midland Pet Adoption Agency Web page in the new folder.

Reference Window | **Saving a Bookmark in a Bookmarks Folder**

- Open the page that you want to bookmark in Firefox.
- Click Bookmarks on the menu bar, and then click Bookmark This Page.
- Type a descriptive name in the Name box (or leave the default name for the page as is).
- Select the folder in which you want to save the bookmark.
- Click the Done button.

To save a bookmark for the Midland Pet Adoption Agency Web page in the Pet Adoption Agencies folder:

▶ 1. With the Midland Pet Adoption Agency Web home page open, click **Bookmarks** on the menu bar, and then click **Bookmark This Page**. The Page Bookmarked dialog box shown in Figure 1-36 opens.

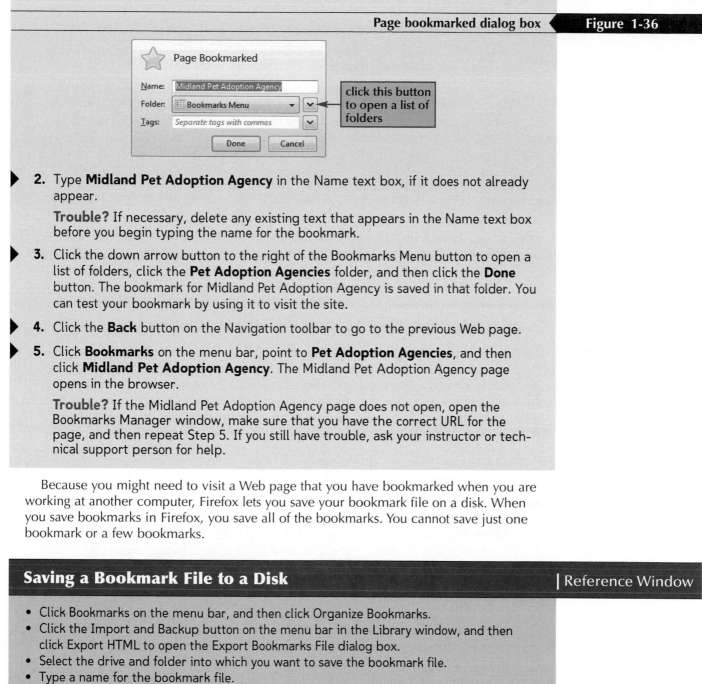

Page bookmarked dialog box ◀ **Figure 1-36**

2. Type **Midland Pet Adoption Agency** in the Name text box, if it does not already appear.

Trouble? If necessary, delete any existing text that appears in the Name text box before you begin typing the name for the bookmark.

3. Click the down arrow button to the right of the Bookmarks Menu button to open a list of folders, click the **Pet Adoption Agencies** folder, and then click the **Done** button. The bookmark for Midland Pet Adoption Agency is saved in that folder. You can test your bookmark by using it to visit the site.

4. Click the **Back** button on the Navigation toolbar to go to the previous Web page.

5. Click **Bookmarks** on the menu bar, point to **Pet Adoption Agencies**, and then click **Midland Pet Adoption Agency**. The Midland Pet Adoption Agency page opens in the browser.

Trouble? If the Midland Pet Adoption Agency page does not open, open the Bookmarks Manager window, make sure that you have the correct URL for the page, and then repeat Step 5. If you still have trouble, ask your instructor or technical support person for help.

Because you might need to visit a Web page that you have bookmarked when you are working at another computer, Firefox lets you save your bookmark file on a disk. When you save bookmarks in Firefox, you save all of the bookmarks. You cannot save just one bookmark or a few bookmarks.

Saving a Bookmark File to a Disk | Reference Window

- Click Bookmarks on the menu bar, and then click Organize Bookmarks.
- Click the Import and Backup button on the menu bar in the Library window, and then click Export HTML to open the Export Bookmarks File dialog box.
- Select the drive and folder into which you want to save the bookmark file.
- Type a name for the bookmark file.
- Click the Save button.

Because you might need to visit the Midland Pet Adoption Agency page when you are working at another computer, you will save your bookmark file on a disk.

To store the Midland Pet Adoption Agency bookmark file to a disk:

1. Click **Bookmarks** on the menu bar, and then click **Organize Bookmarks**. The Library window opens.

2. Click the **Import and Backup** button on the menu bar in the Library window, and then click **Export HTML**. The Export Bookmarks File dialog box opens.

Trouble? If prompted, insert a disk in the appropriate drive on your computer.

3. Select the location to which you want to save the bookmarks file.

Trouble? If you were prompted to insert a disk in Step 2, then the correct drive and disk should automatically appear in the Save in list box.

The filename that you give the bookmark file should indicate the Web page you have marked. The file extension must be .htm or .html so the browser into which you load this file will recognize it as an HTML file. Most browsers will recognize either file extension; however, some do not.

4. Type **MyFirefoxBookmarks.html** in the File name text box.

5. Click the **Save** button, and then close the Library window.

When you use another computer, you can open the bookmark file from your disk (or other storage device) by starting Firefox, clicking Bookmarks on the menu bar, and clicking Organize Bookmarks to open the Library. You can then click the Import and Backup button near the top of the Library window. Click Import HTML to open the Import Wizard and follow the instructions to import your bookmarks file.

Navigating Web Pages Using the History List

The History menu commands enable you to move back and forward through a portion of the history list and allow you to choose a specific Web page from the list. To see where you have been during a session, you also can open the history list for your current session. The Back and Forward buttons on the Navigation toolbar and the Back and Forward on the shortcut menu allow you to move to and from recently viewed pages; these buttons duplicate the functions of the History menu commands.

To view the history list for this session:

1. Click **View** on the menu bar, point to **Sidebar**, and then click **History** to open the history list in the sidebar window. You will see that the history list is organized into folders that each contain lists of sites that you visited by day (or groups of days). For example, your history list might show folders titled Today, Yesterday, 2 Days Ago, and so on.

2. Click the **arrow icon** next to the Today folder to open the list of Web sites visited today. You can click the file icon next to any entry to return to that specific Web page.

3. Click the **Close** button (the small "x" near the top-right corner of the sidebar window) on the History sidebar to close it.

Tip

If you are using a computer in a computer lab or an Internet café, the History list will include sites visited by anyone who has used the computer, not just you.

You can change the way that pages are organized in the History list by using the View button in the sidebar window. For example, you can list the pages by Web page title or in the order in which you visited them.

Erasing Your History | InSight

In some situations, such as when you are finishing a work session in a school computer lab, you might want to remove the list of Web sites that you visited from the History list of the computer on which you had been working. Erasing your browser history helps protect your personal information and guard your privacy when working on a shared computer. You can do this in Firefox by clicking Tools on the menu bar, selecting Options, and clicking the Privacy icon at the top of the Options dialog box. Click the clear your recent history link (near the middle of the dialog box), choose how much of your browsing history you want to delete, then click the Clear Now button in the Clear Recent History dialog box. Click the OK button in the Options dialog box to close it.

Reloading a Web Page

The Reload button on the Firefox toolbar loads a new copy of the Web page that currently appears in the browser window. Firefox stores a copy of every Web page it displays on your computer's hard drive in a **Temporary Internet Files folder** in the Windows folder. Storing this information increases the speed at which Firefox can display pages as you move back and forth through the History list, because the browser can load the pages from a local disk drive instead of reloading the page from the remote Web server. When you click the Reload button, Firefox contacts the Web server to see if the Web page has changed since it was stored in the Temporary Internet Files folder. If it has changed, Firefox gets the new page from the Web server; otherwise, it loads the copy stored on your computer.

Returning to the Home Page

The Home button on the Navigation toolbar displays the home (or start) page for your installation of Firefox. You can set the Home button to display the page you want to use as the default home page by using the Options dialog box, which is accessible from the Tools menu.

Changing the Default Home Page in Firefox | Reference Window

- Click Tools on the menu bar, and then click Options.
- Click the Main icon in the Options dialog box, if it is not already selected.
- In the Startup section of the dialog box, type the URL or filename of the page you want to use as your default home page in the Home Page text box.
- Click the OK button.

To view the settings for the default home page:

▶ **1.** Click **Tools** on the menu bar, and then click **Options**. The Options dialog box opens, as shown in Figure 1-37.

Figure 1-37 ▶ Firefox Options dialog box

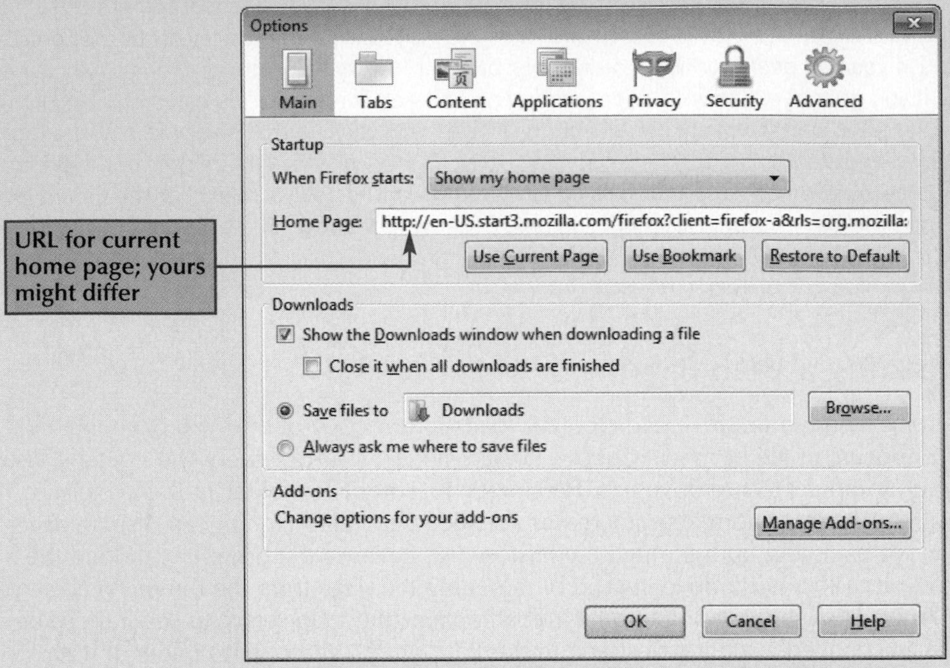

URL for current home page; yours might differ

Trouble? If the dialog box does not look like Figure 1-37, make sure that the Main icon near the top of the dialog box is selected.

▶ 2. To set the page currently displayed in the browser as your home page, you can click the Use Current Page button in the Startup section of the Options dialog box. To specify a different home page than the one displayed, you would select the text in the Home Page text box and then enter the URL of the Web page you want to use. If you load the Web page that you want as your new home page before beginning these steps, you can click the Use Current Page button to place the page's URL in the Home page text box. You can also choose to use one of your bookmarks as your home page by clicking the Use Bookmark button.

Trouble? If you are using a computer in a school computer lab or at your employer's place of business, do not change any settings unless you are given permission by your instructor, employer, or lab supervisor. Many organizations set the home page defaults on all of their computers and lock those settings.

▶ 3. Click the **Cancel** button to close the dialog box without making any changes.

Navigating Web Pages Using Page Tabs

Firefox was one of the first Web browsers to follow the lead of Opera and introduce tabbed browsing, which allows users to navigate from one page to another by opening new Web pages in tabs instead of separate browser windows. This tabbed browsing technique is especially useful when you need to move frequently back and forth between five or six Web pages. You can right-click in any existing tab or the area to the right of the page tabs to open a Web page in a new tab, but the most common use of tabbed browsing is to navigate from a page that is already open.

Using Page Tabs to Navigate in Firefox | Reference Window

- Open pages by right-clicking hyperlinks and selecting Open Link in New Tab on the shortcut menu.
- Click the page tabs to move among open Web pages.

To use page tabs to navigate in Firefox:

▶ **1.** Using the Back and Forward buttons or the History list, open the Midland Pet Adoption Agency home page in the browser window.

▶ **2.** Right-click the **Pets** hyperlink, and then select **Open Link in New Tab** on the shortcut menu. Note that the Pets page will not appear until you click the tab (as you will in Step 4).

▶ **3.** Right-click the **Training Programs** hyperlink, and then select **Open Link in New Tab**. Note that the Training Programs page will not appear until you click the tab (as you will in Step 4).

▶ **4.** Click each visible tab to open its Web page in the browser. The browser with these three tabs open is shown in Figure 1-38.

Firefox with three tabs open ◀ Figure 1-38

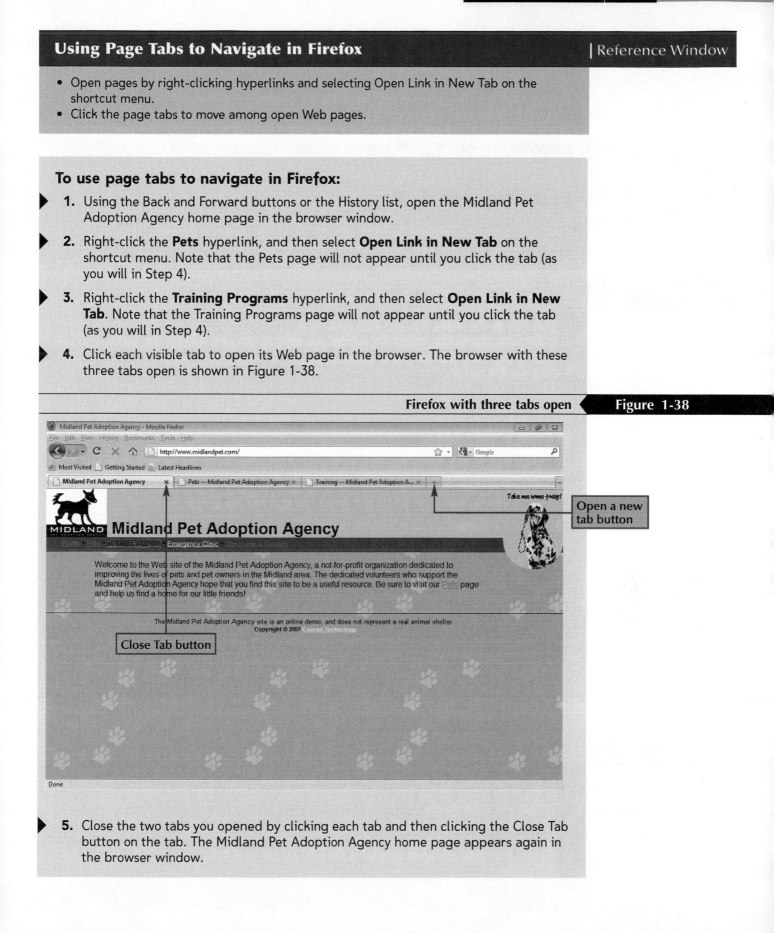

▶ **5.** Close the two tabs you opened by clicking each tab and then clicking the Close Tab button on the tab. The Midland Pet Adoption Agency home page appears again in the browser window.

InSight | **Displaying Web Page Information with Tabbed Browsing**

If you are using tabbed browsing, the page tabs can become rather small as you open more and more tabs. When the page tabs get smaller, the amount of text that is displayed on the tab might not be enough to identify the page. To see the entire Web page title, move the mouse pointer over a page tab and hold it there for a second or two. The Web page title will appear in a box near the mouse pointer.

Printing a Web Page

The Print command on the File menu lets you print the current Web page. You can use this command to make a printed copy of most Web pages.

Reference Window | **Printing the Current Web Page**

- Click File on the menu bar, and then click Print.
- In the Print dialog box, select the printer you want to use and indicate the pages you want to print and the number of copies you want to make of each page.
- Click the OK button.

To print a Web page:

▶ 1. Click **File** on the menu bar, and then click **Print**. The Print dialog box opens.

▶ 2. Make sure that the printer in the Name list box displays the printer you want to use; if not, click the Name list arrow and select the appropriate printer from the list.

▶ 3. Click the **Pages** option button in the Print range section of the Print dialog box, type **1** in the from text box, press the **Tab** key, and then, if necessary, type **1** in the to text box to specify that you want to print only the first page.

▶ 4. Make sure that the Number of copies text box displays **1**.

▶ 5. Click the **OK** button to print the Web page and close the Print dialog box.

Firefox provides a number of useful print options that allow you to customize the printed format of Web pages. You can use the Page Setup dialog box to create custom formats for printing Web pages in Firefox.

Tip

If you encounter a page that is difficult to print, be sure to look on the Web page for a link to a version of the page that is designed to be printed.

Reference Window | **Using Page Setup to Create a Custom Format for Printing a Web Page**

- Click File on the menu bar, and then click Page Setup.
- In the Page Setup dialog box, select the orientation, scaling, and print background options you want to use.
- Click the Margins & Header/Footer tab.
- Type the margin settings you want to use.
- Choose elements you want to print in the left, center, and right areas of the page header and footer.
- Click the OK button.

To create a custom format for printing a Web page:

▶ 1. Click **File** on the menu bar, and then click **Page Setup** to open the Page Setup dialog box. On the Format & Options tab of this dialog box, you can change settings for page orientation, scale, and background print options. The default settings are good for printing most Web pages, but you can customize any of these settings if you wish.

▶ 2. Click the **Margins & Header/Footer** tab in the Page Setup dialog box. See Figure 1-39. In this part of the dialog box you can change the page margins and specify elements of the header and footer that will print with each page. The default settings are good for printing most Web pages, but you can customize any of these settings if you wish.

Tip

The scale settings are especially helpful for saving paper when printing long Web pages.

Margins & Header/Footer tab in the Page Setup dialog box ◀ Figure 1-39

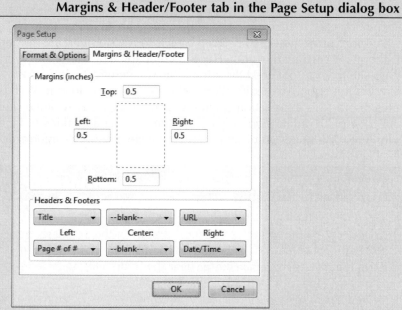

▶ 3. After you make any changes you wish to the page layout, click the **OK** button to close the dialog box.

You can also set these page print options in the Print Preview window. You can click File on the menu bar, and then click Print Preview to open this window. Some of the page print options are available at the top of the window; all options are available by clicking the Page Setup button, which will open the Page Setup dialog box you worked with in the previous steps. Once you have set the formatting options you want for printing a Web page, you can use the Print button to print the page.

Checking Web Page Security

Most Web pages are sent from the Web server to the Web browser as plain text and image files. Anyone who intercepts the transmission can read the text and see the images. For most Web pages, which are designed to be viewed by anyone, this is not really a problem. In some cases, however, the Web site and the user would like to have a private interaction. For example, you might not want anyone to know what book titles or what size clothes you are ordering from an online store. You certainly wouldn't want an unauthorized person to intercept your interactions with your bank or stockbroker. To prevent unauthorized persons from reading intercepted transmissions, Web servers can use encryption.

Encryption is a way of scrambling and encoding data transmissions that reduces the risk that a person who intercepts the Web page as it travels across the Internet will be able to decode and read the page's contents. Web sites use encrypted transmission to send and receive information, such as credit card numbers, to ensure privacy. You can determine whether a Web page has been encrypted by examining the page's properties.

The **Security indicator button** is a small picture of a padlock that appears at the right edge of the status bar at the bottom of the Firefox browser window when a secure Web page is loaded. The button will appear when the Web page was encrypted during transmission from the Web server. When you double-click this button—or when you click Tools on the menu bar, click Page Info, and then click the Security tab in the Page Info dialog box—you can check some of the security elements of the Web page. If the Web page is not encrypted, the Security tab in the Page Info dialog box will show "Connection Not Encrypted." If the Web page is encrypted, the dialog box will display information about the type and level of encryption used to transmit the page from the Web server.

Another protection used by Web sites is to register with a third-party certification authority. A **certification authority** is a company that attests to a Web site's identity. A Web site that has obtained the attestation of a certificate authority has the right to display information about the certification authority when you load its Web page. Most Web sites display this information when you enter a secure area of the site such as the check-out page of an online store or your account page at a banking or financial services Web site. A few Web sites do display their certificate authority's information.

Reference Window	**Reviewing a Web Site's Certificate Information**

- Open the Web page in Firefox.
- Click the Web site owner's name (or the name of the certificate authority) that appears in the Location window to the left of the site's URL to open an information window.
- Click the More information button near the bottom of the information window to open the Page Info window with the Security tab selected.
- Review the information in the Page Info window, then click the View Certificate button to open the Certificate Viewer window.
- Review the information in the Certificate Viewer window, then click the Details tab to review additional information about the certificate.
- Click the Certificate Viewer window's Close button, then click the Page Info window's Close button.

To review information about a Web site's certificate:

1. Type **www.cengage.com/internet/np/internet8** in the address window of Internet Explorer to open the Online Companion page, log on to your account (if necessary), click the **Tutorial 1** link, and then click the **Session 1.3** link.

2. Click one of the company names listed under the heading **Web Site Home Pages That Display Certificate Information** to open that company's home page. The Location field will display the name of the Web site owner with a green background to the left of the URL of the Web page.

    Trouble? If the Location window does not display the Web site owner's name with a green background to the left of the URL of the Web page, click the **Back** button and select a different company name from the list.

3. Click the company name (in the green background area), and then click the **More Information** button to open the Page Info window with the Security icon selected.

4. Review the information in the Page Info window, then click the View Certificate button to open the Certificate Viewer window. Figure 1-40 shows a Certificate Viewer window displaying information about the certificate issued by VeriSign (a certificate authority) that attests to the identity of the computer hosting the Web site of USAA, a company that provides financial services to members of the U.S. military and their families.

Certificate information for USAA home page ◀ **Figure 1-40**

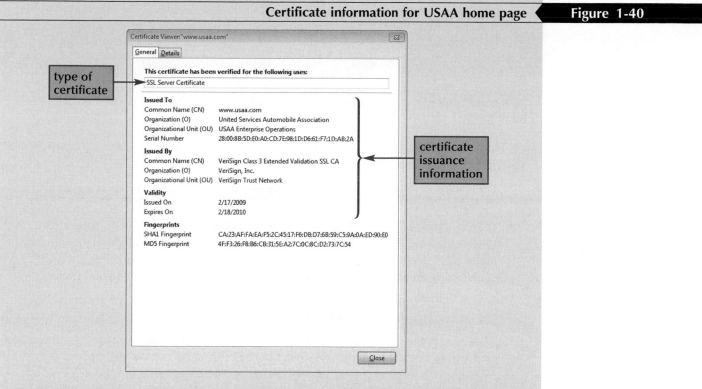

5. Review the information in the General tab, which will show the type of certificate, the domain name of the Web site to which the certificate is issued, the name of the certificate authority, the dates within which the certificate is valid, and some other technical information.

6. Click the **Details** tab to view more information about this certificate.

7. When you are finished reviewing information about the certificate for this Web site, click the **Close** button to close the Certificate Viewer window, and then click the Page Info window's **Close** button.

Managing Cookies

Many Web users are concerned about cookies, the small files you learned about in Session 1.1 that some Web servers write to the disk drives of client computers. Firefox stores all cookies in one file, sorted by the name of the Web site that placed each cookie on your computer, and gives users a way to manage the individual cookies.

Reference Window | Managing Cookies in Firefox

- Click Tools on the menu bar, and then click Options to open the Options dialog box.
- Click the Privacy icon to display options for managing privacy issues, and then click the remove individual cookies link near the middle of the Options dialog box to open the Cookies dialog box.
- Select a Web site folder, and click the arrow icon to the left of the folder. You can then click one of the cookies placed on your computer by that Web site and read the information about that cookie. The cookie information is displayed in the bottom half of the dialog box.
- Select the cookie that you want to delete, and then click the Remove Cookie button.
- Click the OK button.

You will delete a cookie stored on your computer using the Firefox cookie management tool.

To manage cookies in Firefox:

▶ **1.** Click **Tools** on the menu bar, click **Options**, and then click the **Privacy** icon in the Options dialog box.

▶ **2.** Click the **remove individual cookies** link near the middle of the Options dialog box to open the Cookies dialog box, and then examine the Web site names in the list of sites that appears in the Cookies dialog box. If your computer has many cookies stored on it, you can use the scroll bar to move up and down in the list.

▶ **3.** Select one of the Web site folders displayed in the Cookies dialog box, then click the arrow icon to the left of the folder.

▶ **4.** Click one of the cookies placed on your computer by that Web site, and read the cookie information, which is displayed in the bottom half of the dialog box. An example of a Cookies dialog box with several cookies appears in Figure 1-41. Your list of cookies will be different. Information about the selected cookie appears below the list of cookies.

Figure 1-41 ▶ **Managing cookies in Firefox**

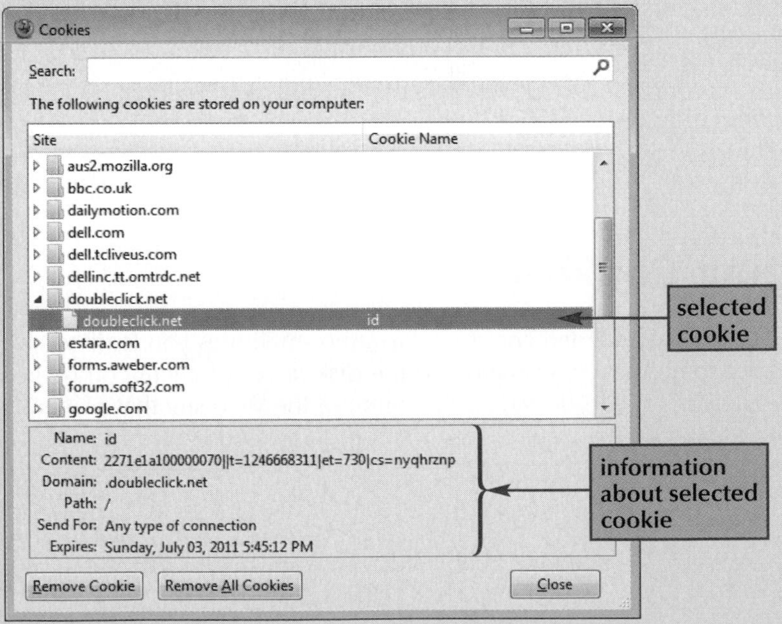

▶ **5.** Find a cookie that you want to delete, click to select it, and then click the **Remove Cookie** button.

   Trouble? You might be instructed to delete specific cookies or no cookies at all. Ask your instructor or technical support person for assistance if you are unsure which cookies can be deleted.

▶ **6.** When you are finished exploring and deleting cookies, click the **Close** button to close the Cookies dialog box.

▶ **7.** Click the **Cancel** button in the Options dialog box to end your cookie management activities.

Private Web Browsing

As you have learned, Firefox stores a considerable amount of information about your Web browsing activity. It stores a list of all the Web pages you have viewed in History and stores cookies that can contain information about your logins, passwords, and even which ads have been displayed on the Web pages you have viewed. It also stores copies of all or part of the Web pages you visit on whatever computer you are using. If you do not wish to store this information stored, you can use Firefox in private browsing mode. When in **private browsing mode**, Firefox does not store History, cookies, or copies of the Web pages you visit. When you are using a computer other than your own (such as a friend's computer or a computer at work, school, or another public location), private browsing mode can help protect your privacy and security. The private browsing mode in Firefox is called Private Browsing.

Opening Firefox in Private Browsing Mode | Reference Window

- Open Firefox.
- Click Tools on the menu.
- Click Start Private Browsing.
- Use Firefox to visit Web pages.
- When you have finished browsing in private mode, click the browser's Close button.

To use Firefox in private browsing mode:

▶ **1.** Open Firefox if necessary.

▶ **2.** Click **Tools** on the menu, and then click **Start Private Browsing**. If a Start Private Browsing dialog box appears, click the Start Private Browsing button.

▶ **3.** Type **www.midlandpet.com** in the Address window and then press the **Enter** key.

> **4.** Click any link on the Web page to visit another part of the Midland Pets Web site, then click other links to visit several other pages on the site.

> **5.** Click the Firefox **Close** button.

If you examine the browser's History, you will find that it includes no record of the Web pages you just visited. Although the browser does not record the pages you have visited (or other information, such as cookies), the network server that connects the computer to the Internet might have software that does. Therefore, it is best not to rely on private browsing mode to keep secret the Web pages you visit while using a computer at work or another public location.

Getting Help in Firefox

Firefox includes a comprehensive Help facility. You can open the Mozilla Firefox Help window to learn more about the Help options that are available.

Reference Window | **Opening Firefox Help**

- Click Help on the menu bar, and then click Help Contents.
- In the Firefox Help Web page that opens, type a question in the search box to find a relevant topic in the Firefox Knowledge Base or click a link to a Featured Tutorial or Handy Reference page.
- Close the browser tab when you are finished.

You will use Firefox Help to read about browsing the Web.

To use Firefox Help:

> **1.** Click **Help** on the menu bar, and then click **Help Contents**. The Firefox Help Web page opens.

> **2.** Under Featured Tutorials, click the **Browsing basics** link to open a list of specific help topics in that category.

> **3.** Click the **Navigating web Pages** link to view help on that subject.

> **4.** Click the **Close tab** button on the Browsing basics tab to close the Web page.

You want to show Trinity the Midland Pet Adoption Agency Web page, but you are concerned that the Web site might change before she has a chance to visit it on the Web. You can save the Web page as a file on your computer or to a disk. She will then be able to open the Web page on her own computer using her Web browser.

Using Firefox to Save Web Page Content

There will be times when you will want to refer to the information that you have found on a Web page without having to revisit the site. In Firefox, you can store entire Web pages, selected portions of Web page text, or particular graphics from a Web page on your computer or other storage device.

Saving a Web Page

You like the Midland Pet Adoption Agency's Web site and want to save a copy of the page so you can show it to Trinity. That way, she can review the page as it currently appears whenever she wishes. To save a Web page, you must have the page open in Firefox.

Saving a Web Page	Reference Window

- Open the Web page in Firefox.
- Click File on the menu bar, and then click Save Page As.
- Select the location to which you want to save the Web page file.
- Accept the default filename, or change the filename, but retain the file extension .htm or .html.
- Click the Save button.

You will save the Midland Pet Adoption Agency page so you can show it to Trinity later.

To save the Web page:

▶ **1.** Use your bookmark to return to the Midland Pet Adoption Agency page, if necessary.

▶ **2.** Click **File** on the menu bar, and then click **Save Page As**. The Save As dialog box opens.

▶ **3.** Navigate to the location in which you want to save the file, and then type the name **MidlandHomePageMF.htm** in the File name box.

▶ **4.** Select **Web page, HTML only** in the Save as type drop-down list, if necessary.

▶ **5.** Click the **Save** button. Now the HTML document for the Midland Pet Adoption Agency's home page is saved in the location you specified. When you send it to Trinity, she can start her Web browser and then use the Open File command on the File menu to open the Web page.

Trouble? If the Downloads dialog box is open on your screen after you complete this step, click the Close button on the title bar of the Downloads dialog box.

Saving Web Page Graphics	InSight

If a Web page contains graphic elements (such as photo, drawings, images), those elements are each saved in their own file and stored in a separate folder with the same name as the HTML document if the Save as type text box is set to Web Page, complete. If you use the Web Page, HTML only setting, the graphic page elements are not saved. To save a graphic, right-click it in the browser window, click Save Image As on the shortcut menu, and then save the graphic to the same location as the Web's HTML document. You will need to do this for each graphic element on the page. Graphics files are referenced in HTML documents as hyperlinks; therefore, you might need to change the HTML tags in the Web page so they point to the new location of the graphics. Copying the graphics files to the same folder as the HTML document often works, since many Web sites store their Web pages and the graphics files they reference in the same folder.

Saving Web Page Text to a File

You can save portions of Web page text to a file, so that you can use the file in other programs. You will use WordPad to save text that you will copy from a Web page; however, any word processor or text editor will work.

Reference Window | **Copying Text from a Web Page to a WordPad Document**

- Open the Web page in Firefox.
- Use the mouse pointer to select the text you want to copy.
- Click Edit on the menu bar, and then click Copy.
- Start WordPad (or another word processor or text editor if WordPad is not available).
- Click Edit on the WordPad menu bar, and then click Paste (or click the Paste button).
- Click the Save button, select the folder where you want to store the file, and then enter a new filename, if necessary.
- Click the Save button.

Trinity will be traveling in Minnesota next week, and she would like to visit the Midland Pet Adoption Agency while she is in the area. She will meet with the director there to learn more about how the agency developed its Web site. You will visit Midland Pet Adoption Agency's Web site and get the agency's address and telephone number so Trinity can contact the director and schedule a meeting.

To copy text from a Web page and save the text as a WordPad document:

▶ **1.** Make sure the Midland Pet Adoption Agency home page is open in the browser window.

▶ **2.** Click the **Directions & Contact** hyperlink to open the page with information about Midland's location.

▶ **3.** Find the address and telephone information just under the links to other pages, and then click and drag the mouse pointer over the address and telephone number to select it, as shown in Figure 1-42.

Selecting and copying text on a Web page in Firefox ◄ **Figure 1-42**

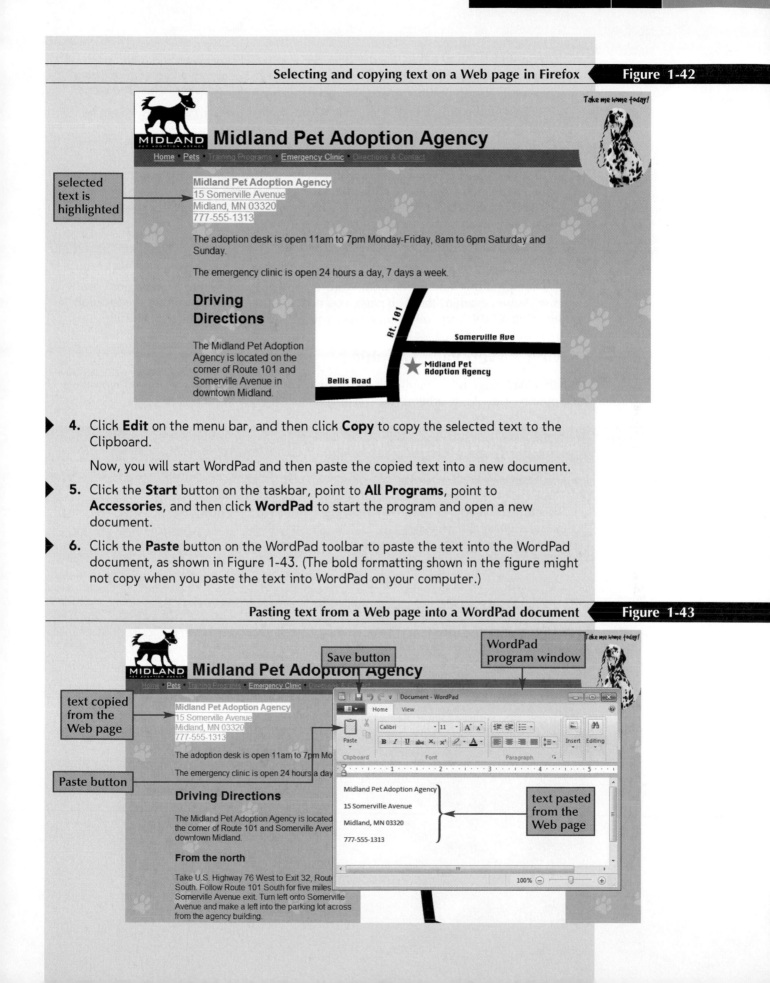

4. Click **Edit** on the menu bar, and then click **Copy** to copy the selected text to the Clipboard.

   Now, you will start WordPad and then paste the copied text into a new document.

5. Click the **Start** button on the taskbar, point to **All Programs**, point to **Accessories**, and then click **WordPad** to start the program and open a new document.

6. Click the **Paste** button on the WordPad toolbar to paste the text into the WordPad document, as shown in Figure 1-43. (The bold formatting shown in the figure might not copy when you paste the text into WordPad on your computer.)

Pasting text from a Web page into a WordPad document ◄ **Figure 1-43**

Trouble? If the WordPad toolbar does not appear, click View on the menu bar, click Toolbar, and then repeat Step 6. Your WordPad program window might be a different size from the one shown in Figure 1-43, which does not affect the steps.

▶ 7. Click the **Save** button on the WordPad Quick Access toolbar to open the Save As dialog box.

▶ 8. Select the location in which you would like to save the file.

▶ 9. Click the **Save as type** button, and then click **Text document**. Delete the text in the File name text box, type **MidlandAddressPhoneMF.txt**, and then click the **Save** button to save the file. Now, the address and phone number of the agency are saved in a text file for future reference.

▶ 10. Click the **Close** button on the WordPad title bar to close it.

You can print this information from WordPad and give it to Trinity the next time you see her. As you examine the Web page, you notice a street map that shows the location of the Midland Pet Adoption Agency. Now you will save the map image for Trinity.

Saving a Web Page Graphic

When a Web page has a graphic or picture that you would like to save or print, you have the option of saving or printing just the image, instead of the entire Web page.

Reference Window | **Saving an Image from a Web Page**

- Open the Web page in Firefox.
- Right-click the image you want to copy, and then click Save Image As.
- Select the drive and the folder in which you want to save the image, and change the default filename, if necessary.
- Click the Save button.

To save the street map image:

▶ 1. Right-click the map image to open its shortcut menu, as shown in Figure 1-44.

Saving the map image | Figure 1-44

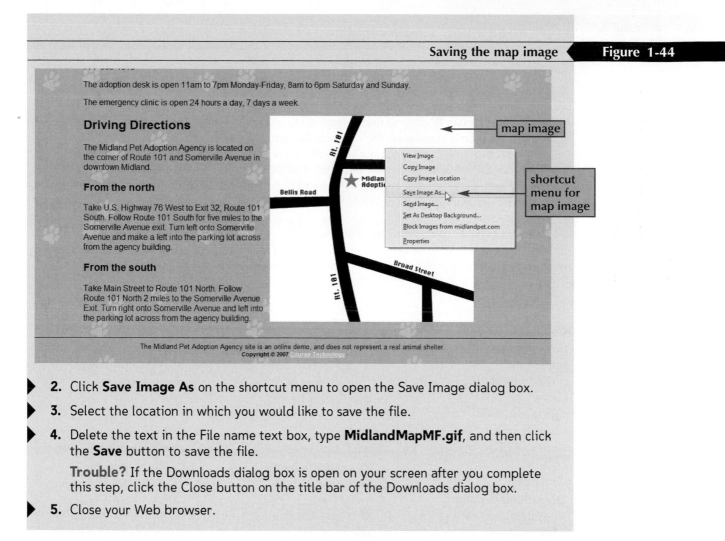

2. Click **Save Image As** on the shortcut menu to open the Save Image dialog box.

3. Select the location in which you would like to save the file.

4. Delete the text in the File name text box, type **MidlandMapMF.gif**, and then click the **Save** button to save the file.

   Trouble? If the Downloads dialog box is open on your screen after you complete this step, click the Close button on the title bar of the Downloads dialog box.

5. Close your Web browser.

Now, you have copies of the Midland Pet Adoption Agency Web home page and a map that will show Trinity how to get there during her trip to Minnesota. She will be able to use her Web browser to open the files and print them.

Session 1.3 Quick Check | Review

1. Describe three ways to load a Web page in the Firefox browser.
2. You can use the _____ in Firefox to visit sites previously visited during your Web session.
3. Why would you hold down the Shift key as you clicked the Reload button?
4. What happens when you click the Home button in the Firefox Web browser?
5. Some Web servers _____ Web page files before returning them to the client to prevent unauthorized access.
6. True or False: You can identify an encrypted Web page when viewing it in Firefox.
7. What is the purpose of the Firefox bookmark feature?

In this tutorial, you learned how Web pages and Web sites make up the World Wide Web. The Web uses a client/server structure in which Web server computers make Web page files available to Web client computers that are running Web browser software. Each server computer on the Internet has an IP address that is mapped to a domain name. The domain name plus the Web page filename make up the Uniform Resource Locator (URL) of that file.

All Web browsers have the same basic elements and can be used to explore the Web in similar ways. Web browsers display Web pages, maintain a history list that can be used to find pages previously visited, and allow users to print and save Web pages and elements of Web pages. You learned about several Web browsers that are currently available for free or at low cost.

Internet Explorer and Firefox are the two most widely used Web browsers. You learned how to navigate the Web by opening several different Web pages. You also learned how to print and save Web page elements using these two browsers.

Key Terms

Common Terms
Back button
bookmark
browser rendering engine
cache
Chromium Project
Close button
Command bar
cookie
copyright
DNS (domain name system) software
domain name
domain name server
favorite
file transfer protocol (FTP)
Firefox
Forward button
frame
general top-level domain (gTLD)
Gecko engine
Google Chrome
history list
Home button
home page
HTML anchor tag
HTML document
hyperlinks
hypermedia links
hypertext links
Hypertext Markup Language (HTML)
hypertext transfer protocol (HTTP)
interconnected network
internet

Internet
Internet Corporation for Assigned Names and Numbers (ICANN)
Internet Explorer
IP (Internet Protocol) address
iRider
links
local area network (LAN)
Maximize button
menu bar
Microsoft Internet Explorer
Minimize button
Mosaic
Mozilla Firefox
Mozilla Project
Mozilla Suite
Netscape Navigator
network
Opera
page tab
private browsing mode
Refresh button
Reload button
Restore Down button
scroll bar
SeaMonkey project
sponsored top-level domain (sTLD)
start page
status bar
tabbed browsing
tag
Telnet protocol
Temporary Internet Files folder
title bar
top-level domain (TLD)

transfer protocol
Uniform Resource Locator (URL)
Web browser
Web client
Web directory
Web page
Web page area
Web search engine
Web server
Web site
Webmaster
wide area network (WAN)
World Wide Web (Web)
Internet Explorer
Address window
certification authority
encryption
Full Screen
graphical transfer progress indicator
security settings
Temporary Internet Files folder
transfer progress report
Firefox
certification authority
encryption
Library
Location Bar
location field
Navigation toolbar
private browsing mode
Security indicator button
Temporary Internet Files folder

Practice | **Review Assignments**

Practice the skills you learned in the tutorial using the same case scenario.

There are no Data Files needed for the Review Assignments.

Trinity is pleased with the information you gathered thus far about the Midland Pet Adoption Agency's Web pages. In fact, she is thinking about having you chair a committee that will supervise the design of a Web site for the Danville Animal Shelter. Because Trinity would like you to be well prepared to direct the committee, she has asked you to compile some information about the Web pages that other animal welfare groups have created. You will examine Web sites for additional background information by completing the following steps.

1. Start your Web browser, go to www.cengage.com/internet/np/internet8 to open the Online Companion page, click the Tutorial 1 link, and then click the Review Assignments link.
2. Click the hyperlinks listed under the heading Animal Welfare Organizations to explore the Web pages for organizations that have goals and activities similar to those of the Danville Animal Shelter. The list includes a large number of links; however, Web sites change their URLs and even close from time to time. If a link does not lead you to an active site or to a site that you believe is relevant to this assignment, simply choose another link.
3. Choose three interesting home pages, print the first page of each, and then create a bookmark or favorite for each of these sites. Answer the following questions for these three sites:
   a. Which sites include a photograph of the organization's building or any of its physical facilities?
   b. Which sites have photographs of pets available for adoption on the home page?
   c. Which sites provide information about the people who work for the organization (as paid employees or as volunteers)?
   d. Which sites include information about donors who have made contributions to support the organization?
   e. Which sites provide information about their charitable purpose or tax-exempt status?
4. Choose your favorite pet photograph and save it to a file.
5. Do any of the three sites you have chosen provide contact information or directions (with or without a map) to their facilities? If so, which ones? Is this information on the home page, or did you click a hyperlink to find it? Copy the contact information and save it to a text file.
6. Which site made finding specific information (about the organization or about pets available for adoption) the easiest? What did that site do differently from the other sites that made this true?
7. Write a two-page report that summarizes your findings in a form suitable for distribution at your committee's first meeting. Include a recommendation regarding specific elements the Danville Animal Shelter should consider including in its Web site.
8. Close your Web browser.

Apply | Case Problem 1

Use the skills you learned in the tutorial to find and evaluate Web pages that present business information.

There are no Data Files needed for this Case Problem.

Value City Central Business Web sites range from very simple informational sites to comprehensive sites that offer information about the firm's products or services, history, current employment openings, and financial information. An increasing number of business sites offer products or services for sale using their Web sites. You just started a position in the marketing department of Value City Central, a large retail chain of television and appliance stores. Your first assignment is to research and report on the types of information that competing businesses offer on their Web sites, which you will do by completing the following steps.

1. Start your Web browser, go to www.cengage.com/internet/np/internet8 to open the Online Companion page, click the Tutorial 1 link, and then click the Case Problem 1 link.
2. Use the Value City Central hyperlinks to open each business site.

✧ EXPLORE

3. Review the contents of these sites and choose three sites that you believe would be most relevant to your assignment. (*Hint*: Keep in mind that you are looking to identify different *types* of information, not just different information.)
4. Print the home page for each Web site that you have chosen.
5. Select one site that you feel does the best job in each of the following five categories:
   a. overall presentation of the company's brand or image
   b. description of products offered
   c. ease of use
   d. description of employment opportunities with the company
   e. presentation of financial statements or other financial information about the company
6. Prepare a report that includes one paragraph describing why you believe each of the sites you identified in the preceding step best achieved its goal.
7. Close your Web browser.

Research | Case Problem 2

Compare four Web browsers, identify features that could be included in future browsers, and recommend a specific browser for a college.

There are no Data Files needed for this Case Problem.

Northwest Community College Your employer, Northwest Community College, is a school with an enrollment of about 7,000 that prepares students for direct entry into the workforce and for future academic studies at four-year schools. The school has increased its use of computers in all of its office operations. Many of Northwest's computers currently run either Microsoft Internet Explorer or Firefox; however, the administrative vice president (AVP) has decided that the school should support only one browser to save money on user training and computer support personnel costs. The AVP has heard some good things about two other browsers: iRider and Opera. The AVP is wondering whether one of these browsers might be the right product for the school. As the AVP's special assistant, you have been asked to recommend which of these four Web browsers the school should choose to support. You will research the browsers for your report by completing the following steps.

1. Start your Web browser, go to www.cengage.com/internet/np/internet8 to open the Online Companion page, click the Tutorial 1 link, and then click the Case Problem 2 link.

2. Use the Northwest Community College hyperlinks to learn more about these four Web browsers.

3. Write a two-page memo to the AVP (to submit to your instructor) that outlines the strengths and weaknesses of each product. Recommend one Web browser program and support your decision using the information you collected. Remember that the AVP is concerned about overall cost; not just the cost to license the browser, but the cost of training users and supporting them with technical help. However, the AVP is also concerned about making the school's employees more productive, so if a more expensive browser could increase employee productivity, the AVP would be willing to pay more to install and maintain the software.

EXPLORE

4. Prepare a list of features that you would like to see in a new Web browser software package that would overcome any limitations you see in Firefox, Internet Explorer, iRider, or Opera. (*Hint*: If you do not have access to a computer that runs one or more of these Web browsers, you can develop your list of features by reading what others have written about those browsers.)

5. Close your Web browser.

Research | **Case Problem 3**

Read Web pages to learn more about cookies and the risks they pose, and compare cookies' risks to their benefits.

There are no Data Files needed for this Case Problem.

Citizens Central Bank You are a new staff auditor at the Citizens Central Bank. You have had more recent computer training than other audit staff members at Citizens, so Sally DeYoung, the audit manager, asks you to review the bank's policy on Web browser cookie settings. Some of the bank's board members expressed concerns to Sally about the security of the bank's computers. Specifically, they are concerned about the PCs on its networks that are connected to the Internet. One of the board members learned about browser cookies and was afraid that a bank employee might open a Web site that would write a dangerous cookie file that could do damage to the bank's computer network. Not all Web servers write cookies, but those that do can read the cookie file the next time the Web browser on that computer connects to the Web server. The Web server can then retrieve information about the Web browser's last connection to the server. None of the bank's board members knows very much about the detailed technical workings of computers, but all of them became concerned that a virus-laden cookie could significantly damage the bank's computer system. Sally asks you to help her inform the board of directors about cookies and to establish a policy on using them. You will accomplish these tasks by completing the following steps.

1. Start your Web browser, go to www.cengage.com/internet/np/internet8 to open the Online Companion page, click the Tutorial 1 link, and then click the Case Problem 3 link.

EXPLORE

2. Use the Citizens Central Bank hyperlinks to learn more about cookie files.

3. Choose the three most helpful sites you have visited, and prepare a brief outline of the content on each site.

4. Write a one-page memo in which you list the risks that Citizens Central Bank might face by allowing cookie files to be written to their computers.

5. Write a one-page memo in which you list the benefits that individual users obtain by allowing Web servers to write cookies to the computers that they are using at the bank to access the Web.

6. Close your Web browser.

| Create | **Case Problem 4** |

Select a model charitable organization Web site and explain why it would be a good example on which to base your organization's site.

There are no Data Files needed for this Case Problem.

Columbus Suburban Area Council   The Columbus Suburban Area Council is a charitable organization devoted to maintaining and improving the general welfare of people living in Columbus suburbs. As the director of the council, you are interested in encouraging donations and other support from area citizens and would like to stay informed of grant opportunities that might benefit the council. You are especially interested in developing an informative and attractive presence on the Web and will pursue that goal by completing the following steps.

1. Start your Web browser, go to www.cengage.com/internet/np/internet8 to open the Online Companion page, click the Tutorial 1 link, and then click the Case Problem 4 link.

✦ EXPLORE
2. Follow the Columbus Suburban Area Council hyperlinks to charitable organizations to find out more about what other organizations are doing with their Web sites.

3. Select three of the Web sites you visited and, for each, prepare a list of the site's contents. Note whether each site included financial information and whether the site disclosed how much the organization spent on administrative or nonprogram-related activities.

✦ EXPLORE
4. Identify which Web site you believe would be a good model for the Columbus Suburban Area Council's new Web site. Prepare a presentation in which you explain to the council why you think your chosen site would be the best example to follow.

5. Close your Web browser.

| Create | **Case Problem 5** |

Examine the structure of several Web directory pages and use your findings to design a personal start page.

There are no Data Files needed for this Case Problem.

Emma Inkster   Your neighbor, Emma Inkster, was an elementary schoolteacher for many years. She is now retired and has just purchased her first personal computer. Emma is excited about getting on the Web and exploring its resources. She has asked for your help. After you introduce her to what you have learned in this tutorial about Web browsers, she is eager to spend more time gathering information on the Web. Although she is retired, Emma continues to be very active. She is an avid bridge player, enjoys golf, and is one of the neighborhood's best gardeners. Although she is somewhat limited by her schoolteacher's pension, Emma loves to travel to foreign countries and especially likes to learn the languages of her destinations. She would like to have a start page for her computer that would include hyperlinks that would help her easily visit and regularly return to Web pages related to her interests. Her nephew knows HTML and can create the page, but Emma would like you to help her design the layout of her start page. You know that Web directory sites are designed to help people find interesting Web sites, so you begin your search by completing the following steps.

1. Start your Web browser, go to www.cengage.com/internet/np/internet8 to open the Online Companion page, click the Tutorial 1 link, and then click the Case Problem 5 link.

✦ EXPLORE
2. Use the Emma Inkster hyperlinks to Web directories to learn what kind of organization they use for their hyperlinks. (*Hint*: Links in Web sites can be organized in a linear fashion, in a hierarchy, or in some other logical structure.)

3. You note that many of the Web directories use a similar organizational structure for their hyperlinks and categories; however, you are not sure if this organization structure would be ideal for Emma. You decide to create categories that suit Emma's specific interests. List five general categories around which you would organize Emma's start page. For each category, list three subcategories that would help Emma find and return to Web sites she would find interesting.

4. Write a report of 100 words in which you explain why the start page you designed for Emma would be more useful to her than a publicly available Web directory.

5. Close your Web browser.

| Reinforce | **Lab Assignments** |

Student Edition Labs

The interactive Student Edition Lab on **Getting the Most Out of the Internet** is designed to help you master some of the key concepts and skills presented in this tutorial, including:

• using a browser to view Web pages
• saving Web pages as favorites
• deleting the files in the Temporary Internet Files folder

This lab is available online and can be accessed from the Tutorial 1 Web page on the Online Companion at www.cengage.com/internet/np/internet8.

| Review | **Quick Check Answers** |

Session 1.1

1. False
2. True
3. home page; start page
4. hypermedia links
5. Any three of these: candidate's name and party affiliation; list of qualifications; biography of the candidate; position statements on campaign issues; list of endorsements with hyperlinks to the Web pages of individuals and organizations that support her candidacy; audio or video clips of speeches, interviews and ads for the candidate that have run on radio or television; address and telephone number of the campaign office, a page that allows supporters to make a donation to the campaign fund.
6. A computer's IP address is a unique identifying number; its domain name is a unique name associated with the IP address on the Internet host computer responsible for that computer's domain.
7. "http://" indicates use of the hypertext transfer protocol; "www.savethetrees.org" is the domain name and includes three parts: the ".org" suggests a charitable or not-for-profit organization, "savethetrees" indicates that the organization is probably devoted to forest ecology; and the "www" indicates that it is the address of a site on the World Wide Web. The "main.html" that follows the domain name is the name of the HTML file on the Web server that hosts the Web pages for this site.
8. A Web directory contains a hierarchical list of Web page categories; each category contains hyperlinks to individual Web pages. A Web search engine is a Web site that accepts words or phrases you enter and finds Web pages that include those words or expressions.

Session 1.2

1. You can hide its toolbars or click the Full Screen command on the View menu. Two other possible answers (assuming that the window is not maximized already) are to maximize the window or to use the mouse to pull the edges of the browser window out to make the entire browser larger.
2. Recent Pages, History, the History list, or the History button
3. Home
4. Animal Shelters, Humane Societies, Animal Welfare Organizations, Veterinary Offices
5. Shift
6. Right-click a blank area of the Web page and select Properties. Information about any encryption used to send the Web page will appear next to the word "Connection."
7. F1

Session 1.3

1. Any three of these: Type the URL in the location field; click a hyperlink on a Web page; click the Back button; click the Forward button; click the Bookmarks button and select a page; click Go on the menu bar, click History, and then click the entry for the site you want to visit.
2. history list (or the Back or Forward buttons)
3. when you wanted to make sure that the browser reloads the page from the Web server instead of from the local cache on your computer
4. Firefox loads the page that is specified as the Home page in the Startup section under the Main tab of the Options dialog box (which you can open from the Tools menu).
5. encrypt
6. True
7. a Firefox feature that enables you to store and organize a list of Web pages that you have visited

Objectives

Basic Communication on the Internet: Email

Evaluating Email Options and Programs

Case | Kikukawa Air

Since 1994, Sharon and Don Kikukawa have operated an air charter service in Maui, Hawaii. At first, Kikukawa Air employed only Sharon, who managed the office, reservations, and the company's financial records, and her husband Don, who flew their twin-engine, six-passenger plane between Maui and Oahu. After many successful years in business, Sharon and Don expanded their business to include scenic tours and charter service to all of the Hawaiian Islands. As a result of their expansion, Kikukawa Air now has six twin-engine planes, two turboprop planes, and a growing staff of more than 30 people.

Because Kikukawa Air has a ticket counter at airports on all of the Hawaiian Islands, many miles now separate the company's employees. Originally, employees used telephone and conference calling to coordinate the business's day-to-day operations, such as schedule and reservation changes, new airport procedures, and maintenance requests. Sharon soon realized that these forms of communication were difficult to coordinate with the growing number of busy ground-service agents and pilots. Most employees already use email to communicate with each other and with outside vendors and clients, but they are not all using the same email program. Sharon believes that Kikukawa Air could benefit from organizing the company's employees so that everyone uses the same email program. This coordination will make it easier to manage the accounts and computers, and will streamline the company's operations.

Sharon has hired you to train the staff members of the Kikukawa Air offices and ticket counter facilities to use Windows Live Mail.

Starting Data Files

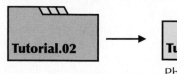 →

Tutorial.02

Tutorial
Physicals.pdf

Review
KAir.gif

Cases
Recycle.pdf

Session 2.1

What Is Email and How Does It Work?

Electronic mail, or **email**, is a form of communication in which electronic messages are created and transferred between two or more devices connected to a network. Email is one of the most popular forms of business communication, and for many people it is their primary use of the Internet. Email travels to its destination and is deposited in the recipient's electronic mailbox. Although similar to other forms of correspondence, including letters and memos, email has the added advantage of being fast and inexpensive. Instead of traveling through a complicated, expensive, and often slow mail delivery service, such as a postal system, email travels quickly, efficiently, and inexpensively to its destination down the hall or around the world. You can send a message any time you want, without worrying about when the mail is collected and delivered or adding any postage. For many personal and business reasons, people rely on email as an indispensable form of communication.

Email travels across the Internet like other forms of information—that is, in small packets that are reassembled at the destination and delivered to the recipient, whose address you specify in the message. When you send an email message, the message is sent to a **mail server**, which is a hardware and software system that determines from the recipient's address one of several electronic routes on which to send the message. The message is routed from one computer to another and is passed through several mail servers. Each mail server determines the next leg of the message's journey until it finally arrives at the recipient's electronic mailbox.

Sending email uses one of many Internet technologies. Special **protocols**, or rules that determine how the Internet handles message packets flowing on it, are used to interpret and transmit email. **SMTP (Simple Mail Transfer Protocol)** determines which paths an email message takes on the Internet. SMTP handles outgoing messages; another protocol called **POP (Post Office Protocol)** handles incoming messages. POP is a standard, extensively used protocol that is part of the Internet suite of recognized protocols. Other protocols used to deliver mail include IMAP and MIME. **IMAP (Internet Message Access Protocol)** is a protocol for retrieving mail messages from a remote server or messages that are stored on a large local network. The **MIME (Multipurpose Internet Mail Extensions)** protocol specifies how to encode nontext data, such as graphics and sound, so it can travel over the Internet.

When an email message arrives at its destination mail server, the mail server's software handles the details of distributing the message locally, in the same way that a mailroom worker opens a mailbag and places letters and packages into individual mail slots. When the server receives a new message, it is not saved on the recipient's Internet device, but rather, the message is held on the mail server. To check for new email messages, you use a program stored on your Internet device—which might be a personal computer, cellular phone, or other wireless device—to request the mail server to deliver any stored mail to your device. The software that requests mail delivery from the mail server to an Internet device is known as **mail client software**, or an **email program**.

An **email address** uniquely identifies an individual or organization that is connected to the Internet. To route an email message to an individual, you must identify that person by his or her account name, or **user name**, and also by the name of the mail server that manages email sent to the domain. The two parts of an email address—the user name and the domain name—are separated by an "at" sign (@). Sharon Kikukawa, for example, selected the user name *Sharon* for her email account. Kikukawa Air purchased the domain name KikukawaAir.com to use as both its Internet address (URL) and in the email addresses for its employees. Therefore, Sharon's email address is Sharon@KikukawaAir.com.

Tip

Most organizations have a single mail server to manage the email sent to and from the domain. For very large organizations, the domain might use multiple mail servers to manage the organization's email.

A user name usually identifies one person's email account on a mail server. When you are given an email address from an organization, such as your school or an employer, the organization might have standards for assigning user names. Some organizations set standards so user names consist of a person's first initial followed by up to seven characters of the person's last name. Other organizations assign user names that contain a person's first and last names separated by an underscore character (for example, Sharon_Kikukawa). When you are given the opportunity to select your own user name, you might use a nickname or some other name to identify yourself. On a mail server, all user names must be unique.

The domain name is the second part of an email address. The domain name specifies the server to which the mail is to be delivered on the Internet. Domain names contain periods, which are usually pronounced "dot," to divide the domain name. The most specific part of the domain name appears first in the address, followed by the top-level domain name. Sharon's Web site address, KikukawaAir.com (and pronounced "Kikukawa Air dot com"), contains only two names separated by a period. The *com* in the domain name indicates that this company falls into the large, general class of commercial locations. The *KikukawaAir* indicates the unique computer name (domain name) associated with the IP address for KikukawaAir.com.

Most email addresses aren't case-sensitive; in other words, the addresses sharon@kikukawaair.com and Sharon@KikukawaAir.com are the same. It is important for you to type a recipient's address carefully; if you omit or mistype even one character, your message could be undeliverable or sent to the wrong recipient. When a message cannot be delivered, the receiving mail server might send the message back to you and indicate that the addressee is unknown. Sometimes mail that cannot be delivered is deleted on the receiving mail server and no notice is sent to the sender.

Managing More than One Email Address | InSight

Most people have more than one email address to manage their correspondence. It is very common for people to have a primary email address that they use for personal or business correspondence, and a secondary email address that they use for online subscriptions, online purchases, and mailing lists. If you are careful about how you distribute your primary email address, you might reduce the amount of unsolicited mail that you receive. When your secondary email address starts getting a lot of unwanted messages, you can discard it and create a new one. If you keep track of who has your secondary email address, it will be easy to update them if you need to change your secondary email address.

Keep in mind that an email account that you have from your school or employer is subject to the rules of use that the organization has established. Some schools and most employers have policies that dictate the permitted use of their equipment and email accounts. You should not use your employer's email address for personal correspondence unless your employer specifies that your personal use of the email account and your workplace computer is acceptable. In some cases, an employer might terminate employees who abuse the company's resources for personal use.

Common Features of an Email Message

An email message consists of three parts: the message header, the message body, and the signature. The **message header** contains information about the message, and the **message body** contains the actual message content. An optional **signature** might appear at the bottom of an email message and contain standard information about the sender, which the recipient can use to contact the sender in a variety of ways.

Figure 2-1 shows a message that Sharon Kikukawa wrote to Bob Merrell, Kikukawa Air ticket agents, and Don Kikukawa. The message contains an attached file named MaintenanceSchedule.xlsx. Sharon created this file using a spreadsheet program, saved it, and then attached it to the message. Each of the message parts is described in the next sections.

Figure 2-1	Common features of an email message

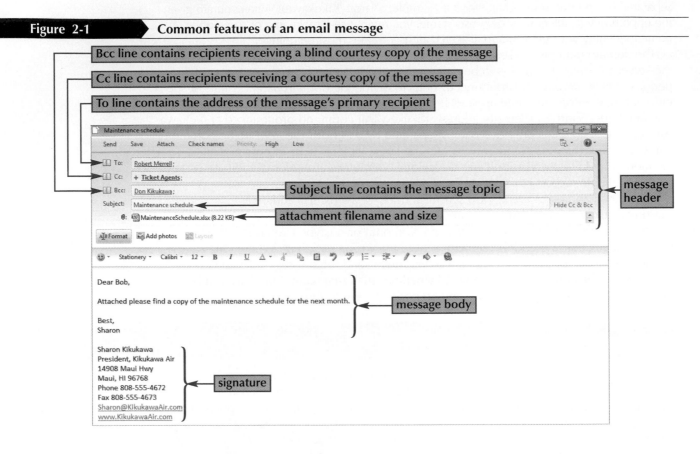

Bcc line contains recipients receiving a blind courtesy copy of the message

Cc line contains recipients receiving a courtesy copy of the message

To line contains the address of the message's primary recipient

Subject line contains the message topic

attachment filename and size

message header

message body

signature

To, Cc, and Bcc

You type the recipient's full email address in the **To line** of a message header. You can send the same message to multiple recipients by typing a comma or semicolon between the recipients' email addresses in the To line. If you have saved a recipient's email address, the email program might display the address using the person's name, as shown in Figure 2-1, instead of the recipient's actual email address. The number of addresses you can type in the To line or in the other parts of the message header that require an address is not limited, but some mail servers will reject messages with too many recipients (usually 50 or more) as a way of controlling unsolicited mail. In Figure 2-1, Sharon used the To line to address her message to one recipient.

You can use the optional **courtesy copy (Cc)** and the **blind courtesy copy (Bcc)** lines to send mail to people who should be aware of the email message, but are not the message's main recipients. When an email message is delivered, every recipient can see the addresses of other recipients, except for those recipients who receive a blind courtesy copy. Because Bcc addresses are excluded from messages sent to addresses in the To and Cc lines, neither the primary recipient (in the To line) nor the Cc recipients can view the list of Bcc recipients. Bcc recipients are unaware of other Bcc recipients, as well. For example, if you send a thank-you message to a salesperson for performing a task especially well, you might consider sending a blind courtesy copy to that person's supervisor. That way, the supervisor knows a customer is happy and that the praise was unsolicited. In Figure 2-1, Sharon sent a blind courtesy copy of her email message to Don Kikukawa so he could monitor the maintenance schedule without Bob or the ticket agents at Kikukawa Air being aware of his involvement.

Sometimes an email address is not one person's address, but rather, a special address called a **group** or a **category**. In a group, a single email address can represent several or many individual email addresses. In Figure 2-1, the "Ticket Agents" address in the Cc line represents the three email addresses of people who work as ticket agents at Kikukawa Air; there is no "Ticket Agents" user name. Clicking the plus sign in the "Ticket Agents" user name displays the individual user names in the group or category.

From

The **From line** of an email message includes the sender's name, the sender's email address, or both. Most email programs automatically insert the sender's name and email address in the From line of all outgoing messages. You usually do not see the From line in messages that you are composing, but you can see it in messages that you receive. Figure 2-1 does not show a From line because this is a message that Sharon is composing.

Subject

The content of the **Subject line** is very important. Often the recipient will scan an abbreviated display of incoming messages, looking for the most interesting or important message based on the content in the Subject line. If the Subject line is blank, then the recipient might not read the associated message immediately or at all. Including an appropriate subject in your message helps the reader determine its content and importance. For example, a Subject line such as "Just checking" is less informative and less interesting than "Urgent: new staff meeting time." The email message shown in Figure 2-1, for example, contains the subject "Maintenance schedule" and thus indicates that the message concerns maintenance.

Attachments

Because of the way the messaging system is set up, you can send only text messages using SMTP, the protocol that handles outgoing email. When you need to send a more complex document, such as a Word document or an Excel workbook, you send it along as an attachment. An **attachment** provides a simple and convenient way of transmitting files to one or more people. An attachment is encoded so that it can be carried safely over the Internet, to "tag along" with the message. Frequently, the attached file is the most important part of the email message, and the message body contains only a brief statement, such as "Here's the file that you requested." Sharon's email message (see Figure 2-1) contains an attached file, whose filename and size in kilobytes appear in the Attach line in the message header. (A **kilobyte (KB)** is approximately 1,000 characters.) You can attach more than one file to an email message; if you include multiple recipients in the To, Cc, and Bcc lines of

Tip

If you need to send a large attachment to a recipient, ask for the recipient's preferences in how to send it.

the message header, each recipient will receive the message and the attached file(s). However, keep in mind that an email message with many attachments quickly becomes very large in size, and it might take some recipients with slower Internet connections a long time to download your message. In addition, some Internet service providers (ISPs) place limits on the size of messages that they will accept; in some cases, an email message with file attachments over two megabytes in size might be rejected and returned to the sender.

Email programs differ in how they handle and display attachments. Some email programs identify an attached file with an icon that represents a program associated with the attachment's file type. In addition to an icon, some programs also display an attached file's size and filename. Other email programs display an attached file in a preview window when they recognize the attached file's format, and can start a program on the user's device to open the file. Double-clicking an attached file usually opens the file using a program on the user's device that is associated with the file type of the attachment. For example, if a workbook is attached to an email message, double-clicking the icon for the workbook attachment might start a spreadsheet program and open the workbook. Similarly, a Word document opens in the Word program window when you double-click the icon representing the attached document.

Viewing an attachment by double-clicking it lets you open a read-only copy of the file, but it does not save the file on your device. (A **read-only** file is one that you can view but that you cannot change.) To save an attached file on your computer or other device, you need to perform a series of steps to save the file in a specific location, such as on a hard drive. Some programs refer to the process of saving an email attachment as **detaching** the file. When you detach a file, you must indicate the drive and folder in which to save it. You won't always need to save an email attachment; sometimes you can view it and then delete it. You will learn how to attach and detach files using your email program later in this tutorial.

Message Body and Signature Files

Tip

Most mail servers do not allow you to retract mail after you send it, so you should examine your messages carefully before sending them, and always exercise politeness and courtesy in your messages.

Most often, people use email to write short, quick messages. However, email messages can be many pages in length, although the term "pages" has little meaning in the email world. Few people using email think of a message in terms of page-sized chunks; email is more like an unbroken scroll with no physical page boundaries. An email message is often less formal than a business letter that you might write, but it's still important to follow the rules of formal letter writing when composing an email message. You should begin your messages with a salutation, such as "Dear Sharon," use proper spelling and grammar, and close your correspondence with a signature. After typing the content of your message—even a short message—you should check your spelling and grammar. You can sign a message by typing your name and other information at the end of each message you send, or you can create a signature file.

If you are using email for business communication, a **signature file** usually contains your name, title, and your company's name. Signature files might also contain a mailing address, voice and fax telephone numbers, a Web site address, and a company's logo. If you are using email for personal communication, signatures can be more informal. Informal signatures can include nicknames and graphics or quotations that express a more casual style found in correspondence between friends and acquaintances.

You can set your email program to insert a signature automatically into every message you send so you don't have to repeatedly type its contents. You can modify your signature easily or choose not to include it in selected messages. Most email programs allow you to create multiple signature files so you can choose which one to include when sending a message.

When you create a signature, don't overdo it—it is best to keep a signature to a few lines that identify ways to contact you. Figure 2-2 shows two examples of signatures. The first signature, which Sharon might use in her business correspondence to Kikukawa Air employees, is informal. Sharon uses the second, more formal signature for all other business correspondence to identify her name, title, and contact information to make it easy for people outside of the organization to reach her.

Sample signatures ◀ **Figure 2-2**

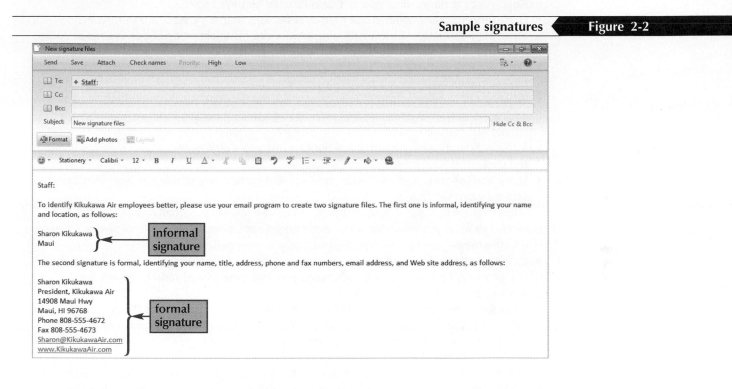

Internet Etiquette (Netiquette)

Netiquette, a term coined from the phrase "Internet etiquette," is the set of commonly accepted rules that represent proper behavior on a network. Just as there are rules of proper conduct on networks that are owned or operated by schools and businesses, the Internet has its own set of acceptable rules. Unlike business networks on which administrators and webmasters set guidelines for acceptable use, and moderators are authorized to restrict usage of that network by users who don't follow those rules, the Internet is self-policing. Email has its own set of rules, which have evolved over time and will continue to evolve as it gains new users.

When composing email messages, keep the following generally accepted rules in mind, especially for business correspondence:

- Avoid writing your messages in ALL CAPITAL LETTERS BECAUSE IT LOOKS LIKE YOU ARE SHOUTING.
- Keep your messages simple, short, and focused on their topics.
- Don't forward information about viruses or hoaxes. In many cases, you're forwarding incorrect information. Check with a reputable site for information about viruses or hoaxes.
- Don't use the "Reply All" feature when only the sender needs to know your response.
- Don't assume that everyone you know likes to receive jokes or family pictures. Check with the recipients first.
- When sending messages to a large group, use the Bcc field for the recipients' email addresses to protect them from receiving additional responses from people who use the "Reply All" feature to respond.
- Include a descriptive subject in the Subject line and a signature, so the recipient knows the content of your message and how to get in touch with you.
- Use a spell checker and read your message and correct any spelling or grammatical errors before sending it.
- Don't overuse formatting and graphics, which can make your email message difficult to read. The fonts you select on your device might not be available on the recipient's device and the message might not be displayed as you intended.
- Email is not private—don't divulge private or sensitive information in an email message. It's very easy for the recipient to forward your message to everyone he or she knows, even if it's by accident.
- Use caution when attempting sarcasm or humor in your messages, as the recipient might not appreciate the attempt at humor and might actually misunderstand your intentions. Without the sender's body language and tone of voice, some written statements are subject to misinterpretation.
- Use common courtesy, politeness, and respect in all of your written correspondence.
- When specifying a user name for your email address, select something that is appropriate for both professional and personal correspondence, and that clearly identifies you to recipients.

Because it sometimes takes so little time and effort to compose an email message, you might be tempted to take some shortcuts in your writing, such as omitting the salutation and using acronyms for commonly used phrases, such as the ones shown in Figure 2-3. These shortcuts are fine for informal messages that you might send to your friends and family members but they are not acceptable in business communication. An email message is a business document, just like a memo or letter, and you should treat it with the same formality. Sending a message containing spelling and grammatical errors to a colleague or to an employer at which you are seeking a job is a poor reflection on you and your work. Many employers seeking to fill open positions automatically disregard email messages that do not contain a subject line or information in the message body describing the contents of the attachment and the applicant's intention to apply for the position. In addition, some employers will not seriously consider applications that are sent with email messages that contain typos or demonstrate poor communication skills.

Commonly used email acronyms ◄ Figure 2-3

Acronym	Meaning
atm	At the moment
b/c	Because
btw	By the way
iac	In any case
iae	In any event
imho	In my humble opinion
imo	In my opinion
iow	In other words
jk	Just kidding
thx	Thanks

Email can be an impersonal form of communication, and as a result some writers use emoticons to express emotion. An **emoticon** is a group of keyboard characters that when viewed together represent a human expression. For example, a smiley :-) looks like a smiling face when you turn your head to the left. Other emoticons are a frown :-(a smiley with a wink ;-) and fear or surprise :-o . Some writers use emoticons to show their readers a form of electronic body language. Just like acronyms, emoticons are appropriate in informal correspondence but not in business correspondence.

You can learn more about Netiquette by following the links in the Netiquette section of the Online Companion page for Tutorial 2.

Tip

Some email programs let you insert emoticons as pictures instead of typing keyboard combinations.

Common Features of Email Programs

Although there are many different ways to send and receive email messages, most email programs have common features for managing mail. Fortunately, once you learn the process for sending, receiving, and managing email with one program, it's easy to use another program to accomplish the same tasks.

Sending Messages

After you finish addressing and composing a message, it might not be sent to the mail server immediately, depending on how the email program or service is configured. A message can be **queued**, or temporarily held with other messages, and then sent when you either exit the program, connect to your ISP or network, or check to see if you have received any new email. Most email programs and services include a "Drafts" folder in which you can store email messages that you are composing but that you aren't ready to send yet. These messages are saved until you finish and send them.

Receiving and Storing Messages

The mail server is always ready to process mail; in theory, the mail server never sleeps. When you receive email, it is held on the mail server until you use your email program to ask the server to retrieve your mail. Most email programs allow you to save delivered mail in any of several standard or custom mailboxes or folders on your Internet device. However, the mail server is a completely different story. Once the mail is delivered to your Internet device, one of two things can happen to it on the server: either the server's copy of your mail is deleted, or it is preserved and marked as delivered or read. Marking mail as delivered or read is the server's way of distinguishing new mail from mail that you have read. For example, when Sharon receives mail on the Kikukawa Air mail server, she might decide to save her accumulated mail on the server—even after she reads it—so she can access her email messages again from another device. On the other hand, Sharon might want to delete old mail to save space on the mail server. Both methods have advantages. Saving old mail on the server lets you access your mail from any device that can connect to your mail server. However, if you automatically delete mail after reading it, you don't have to worry about storing and organizing messages that you don't need, which requires less effort. Some ISPs and email providers impose limits on the amount of material you can store so that you must occasionally delete mail from your mailbox to avoid interruption of service. In some cases, once you exceed your storage space limit, you cannot receive any additional messages until you delete existing messages from the server, or the service deletes your messages without warning to free up space in your mailbox.

Printing a Message

Reading mail on a computer or an Internet device is fine, but there are times when you will need to print some of your messages. Most email programs let you print a message you are composing or that you have received. The Print command usually appears on the File menu, or as a Print button on the toolbar.

Filing a Message

Most email programs let you create folders in which to store related messages in your mailbox. You can create new folders when needed, rename existing folders, or delete folders and their contents when you no longer need them. You can move mail from the incoming folder to any other folder to file it. Some programs let you define and use a **filter** to move incoming mail into a specific folder or to delete it automatically based on the content of the message. Filters are especially useful for moving messages from certain senders into designated folders, and for moving **junk mail** (or **spam**), which is unsolicited mail usually advertising or selling an item or service, to a trash folder. If your email program does not provide filters, you can filter the messages manually by reading them and filing them in the appropriate folders.

> **Tip**
>
> Filters aren't perfect. When using filters to move mail to specific folders or to the trash, it's a good idea to check your messages occasionally to make sure that your incoming messages are not moved to the wrong folder.

Forwarding a Message

You can forward any message that you receive to one or more recipients. When you **forward** a message to another recipient, a copy of the original message is sent to the new recipient you specify without the original sender's knowledge. You might forward a misdirected message to another recipient or to someone who was not included in the original message routing list.

For example, suppose you receive a message intended for someone else, or the message requests information that only a colleague can provide. In either case, you can forward the message you received to the person who can best deal with the request. When you forward a message, your email address and name appear automatically in the From line; most email programs amend the Subject line with the text "Fw," "Fwd," or something similar to indicate that the message has been forwarded. You simply add the recipient's address to the To line and send the message. Depending on your email program and the preferences you set for forwarding messages, a forwarded message might be sent as an attached file or as quoted text. A **quoted message** is a copy of the sender's original message with your inserted comments. A special mark (a > symbol or a solid vertical line) sometimes precedes each line of the quoted message. Figure 2-4 shows a quoted message; the quoted message appears at the bottom of the message and the "Fw:" text in the Subject line indicates a forwarded message.

Sample forwarded message Figure 2-4

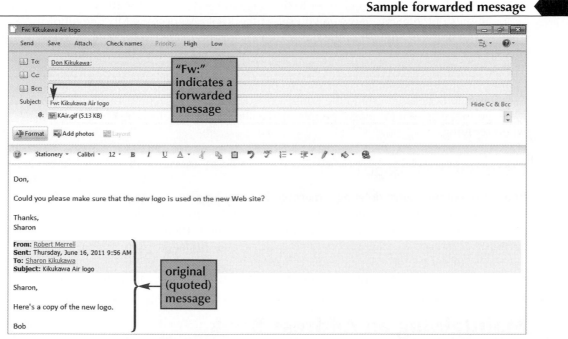

Forwarding Messages Appropriately | InSight

When forwarding a message to a new recipient, and especially when forwarding a message that was forwarded originally to you, keep in mind that a forwarded message includes the email addresses of all the message's previous recipients and senders. Some people might not want to have their addresses sent to other users, who might in turn send them unwanted email messages. If you need to send something you received to a new recipient, and it's not important that the new recipient know who sent you the original message, you should use the Copy and Paste commands in your email program to paste the content of the forwarded message into a new message, thus protecting the privacy of the message's original recipients and making the message easier to read for its new recipients.

Some people routinely send information about Internet viruses and hoaxes or about emotional causes, such as cancer research, to everyone they know in an attempt to "spread the word." Often, these messages contain incorrect information. Before being alarmed by information about viruses or hoaxes, contributing to any charity that you learn about in this way, or forwarding the message to other users, be sure to check one of the many reputable Internet resources for more information. The Virus Protection section of the Online Companion page for Tutorial 2 contains links to sites that contain information about viruses, hoaxes, and fraudulent schemes.

Replying to a Message

Replying to a message is a quick way of sending a response to someone who sent a message to you. Most email programs provide two options for replying to a message that you have received. You can reply to only the original sender using the Reply option, or you can reply to the original sender and all other To and Cc recipients of the original message by using the Reply All option. When you **reply** to a message that you received, the email program creates a new message and automatically addresses it to the original sender (when you select the Reply option) or to the original sender and all of the original To and Cc recipients of the message (when you select the Reply All option). Most email programs will copy the contents of the original message and place it in the message body of the reply. Like forwarded messages, a special mark might appear at the beginning of each line to indicate the text of the original message. When you are responding to more than one question, you might type your responses below the original questions so the recipient can better understand the context of your responses. When you respond to a message that was sent to several people, make sure that you select the correct option when replying.

Deleting a Message

In most email programs, deleting a message is a two-step process to prevent you from accidentally deleting important messages. First, you temporarily delete a message by placing it in a "trash" folder or by marking it for deletion. Then you permanently delete the trash or marked messages by emptying the trash or indicating to the email program to delete the messages. It is a good idea to delete mail you no longer need because it takes up a lot of space on the drive or server on which your email messages are stored.

Maintaining an Address Book

You use an **address book** to save email addresses and other optional contact information about the people and organizations with which you correspond. The features of an email address book vary by email program. Usually, you can organize information about individuals and groups. Each entry in the address book can contain an individual's full email address (or a group email address or category to represent several individual addresses), full name, and complete contact information. In addition, most email programs allow you to include notes for each contact. You can assign a unique nickname to each entry so it is easier to address your email messages. A **nickname** might be "Mom" for your mother or "Maintenance Department" to represent all the employees working in a certain part of an organization.

After saving entries in your address book, you can refer to them at any point while you are composing, replying to, or forwarding a message. You can review your address book and sort the entries in many ways.

Email Programs

Tip

Some domains, such as Yahoo.com, let you send and receive email messages using its Web site. However, you must pay an additional fee to send and receive Yahoo email using an email program.

Different software companies that produce Web browsers might also produce companion email programs that you can use to manage your email. For example, when you install Microsoft Internet Explorer for Windows XP, the Outlook Express email program is also installed. Windows Vista and Windows 7 users might choose to install Windows Live Mail, and Mozilla Firefox users might choose to install the companion Thunderbird email program to manage their email messages. You can use these types of email programs to manage messages that are routed through a domain that sends email messages using the POP protocol. Messages that are routed through a domain in this way are called **POP messages** or **POP3 messages** because of the protocol used to send them. You might also have multiple email programs installed on your computer; in this case, the choice of which email program to use is up to you.

Before you can use an email program to send and receive your email messages, you must configure it to work with your email accounts. Before you decide which email program to use, you should be familiar with the different ones available. In Session 2.2, you will learn how to configure and use Windows Live Mail. Because you might end up using different email programs in the future, it is important to know about two other popular email programs, Mozilla Thunderbird and Opera's M2 email client, which are free email programs available for download.

Tip

Two other email programs, Outlook Express and Windows Mail, are covered in this book in Appendices B and C.

Mozilla Thunderbird

Mozilla Thunderbird is part of the Mozilla open source project. Although Thunderbird complements the Mozilla Firefox Web browser, Thunderbird is available only as a separate download from the Mozilla Web site. A link to Thunderbird's Web site is provided on the Online Companion page for Tutorial 2.

Starting Thunderbird

When you start Thunderbird for the first time, you might have the option of importing items from other email programs on your computer. If you choose this option, the address book entries and other settings from the email program on your computer that you select will be imported into Thunderbird. You'll also see the Account Wizard, which lets you set up mail and other types of accounts. Figure 2-5 shows the Thunderbird Account Wizard dialog box.

Thunderbird Account Wizard dialog box | **Figure 2-5**

The first thing you need to set up is your email account so you can send and receive email messages through your ISP. You need to enter your name and email address, your incoming and outgoing mail server information and user name, and the account name you'd like to use to identify your email account. After setting up your email account, you can use Thunderbird to send and receive email messages. Figure 2-6 shows the Thunderbird Inbox window.

Figure 2-6   **Thunderbird Inbox window**

Thunderbird uses a Folders pane, a Message pane, and a Preview pane to organize your email messages.

Sending and Receiving Mail in Thunderbird

To write a message, click the Write button on the toolbar. The Compose window opens, in which you enter the email address of the message's recipient in the To text box. You can send the message to multiple recipients by separating their email addresses with commas. To send Cc or Bcc messages to additional recipients, press the Enter key to move to the next line in the message header, click the To button, select the message recipient type, and then type the recipient's email address. You can also click the Contacts button to open the Contacts pane and view the email addresses you have saved in your Thunderbird address book. You can use the Attach button to attach files, Web pages, or personal cards to your message. Figure 2-7 shows the Compose window after writing a message to Don Kikukawa and attaching a file named Physicals.pdf.

Thunderbird Compose window   **Figure 2-7**

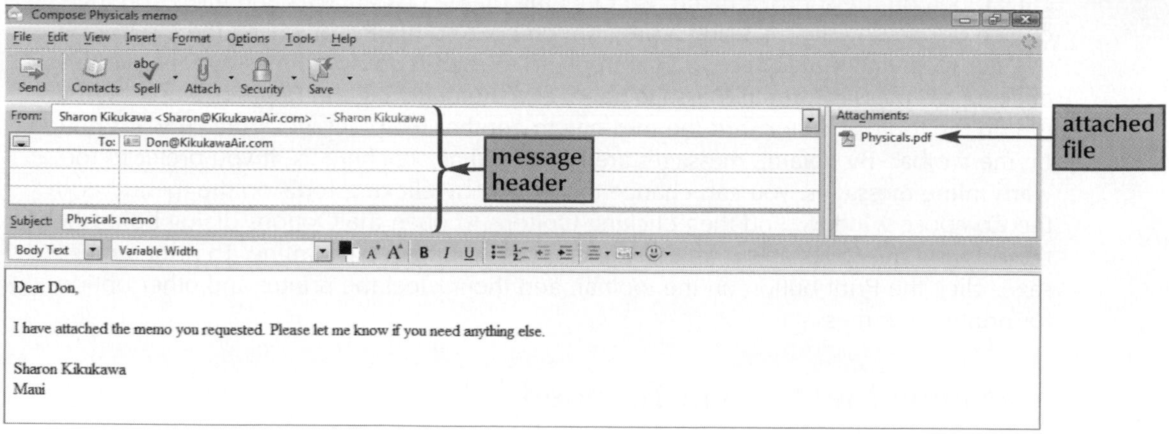

Before sending the message, you can check the document for spelling errors by clicking the Spell button on the toolbar. If you don't want to send the message right away, you can use the options on the Save button menu to save the message as a file, as a draft in the Drafts folder, or as a template. To send the message, click the Send button on the toolbar. By default, messages are sent immediately when you click the Send button, and copies of your sent messages are saved in the Sent folder in the Folders pane.

When you receive a message, the message header appears in the Message pane. Clicking the message opens it in the Preview pane, as shown in Figure 2-8.

Receiving a message in Thunderbird   **Figure 2-8**

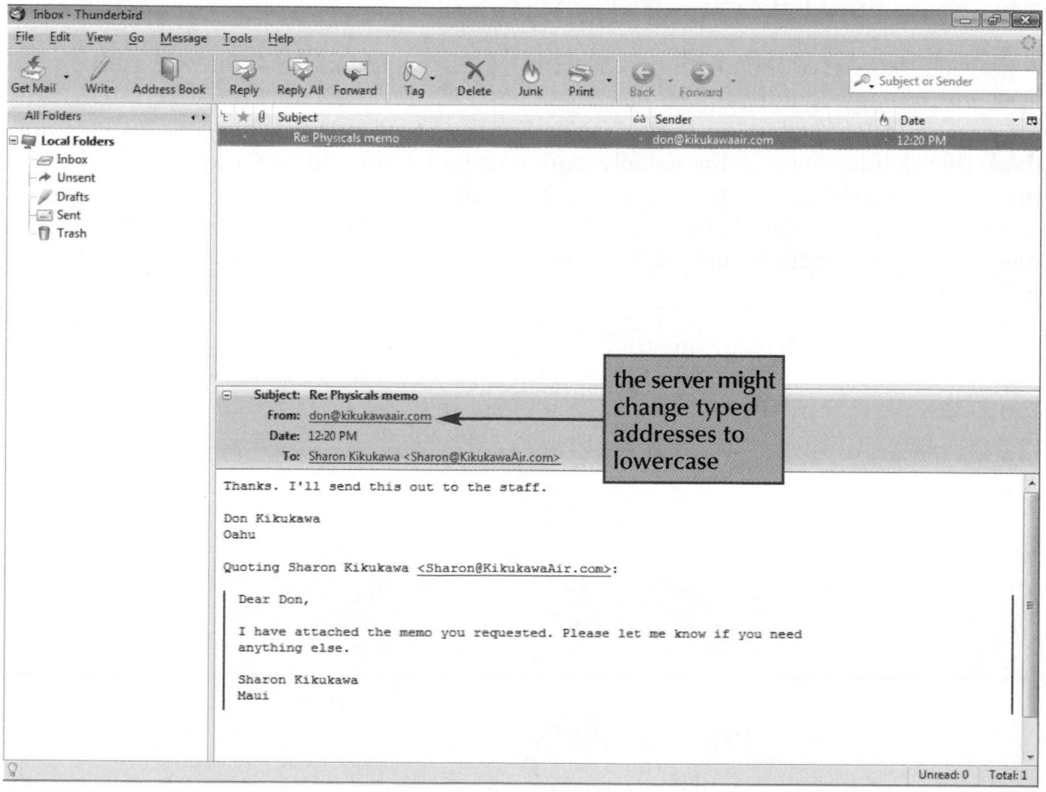

To view an attached file, right-click the filename in the Attachments box, and then click Open on the shortcut menu. An Opening dialog box appears and gives you the choice of opening the file using a program on your computer, or saving the file to disk.

After receiving a message, you can reply to the sender or to all message recipients by clicking the message in the Message pane, and then clicking the Reply or Reply All button on the toolbar. To forward the message to another recipient, click the Forward button on the toolbar. By default, messages are forwarded as attachments. If you prefer to forward inline messages, you can change this setting by clicking Tools on the menu bar in the Compose window, and then clicking Options to open the Options dialog box. Click the Forward messages arrow on the General tab, and then click Inline. To print a message, click the Print button on the toolbar, and then select the printer and other options for printing the message.

Managing Messages in Thunderbird

Just like in other email programs, Thunderbird lets you create folders to manage your messages. To create a new folder in the Folders pane, right-click Local Folders (or your mailbox account name) at the top of the Folders pane to open the shortcut menu, and then click New Folder. In the New Folder dialog box, type the name of the folder, specify where to create it (if necessary), and then click the OK button. To file a message in a folder, drag it from the Message pane to the folder in which you want to save it. To delete a message, select the message in the Message pane, and then click the Delete button on the toolbar. Messages are not permanently deleted until you empty the trash by right-clicking the Trash folder in the Folders pane, and then clicking Empty Trash on the shortcut menu.

Managing Junk Mail in Thunderbird

Tip

If Thunderbird treats a message as junk mail but should not, click the Not Junk button so Thunderbird won't categorize mail from that sender as junk in the future.

A powerful feature of Thunderbird is its adaptive spam and junk mail filters. Based on how you manage your incoming mail, these filters "learn" how to manage your messages for you—with the goal of displaying less junk mail in your Inbox. When you receive junk mail, Thunderbird might automatically mark it as junk mail. You can also click the Junk button on the toolbar, which changes to a Not Junk button after you click it, to designate a message as junk. After clicking the Junk button on the toolbar, Thunderbird changes the message and its sender to junk mail and displays a junk mail icon and notice, as shown in Figure 2-9.

Junk mail identification in Thunderbird | **Figure 2-9**

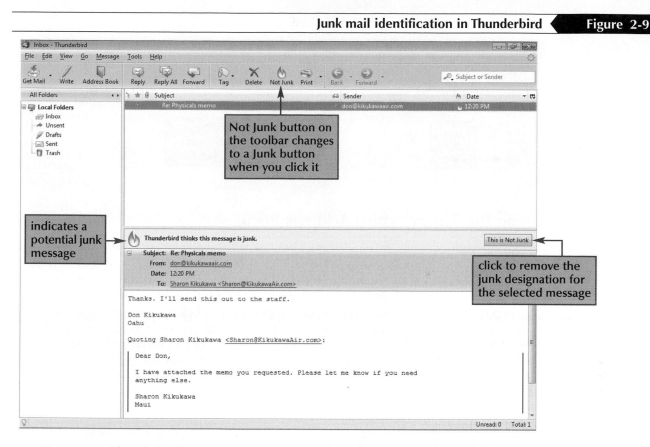

You can set Thunderbird to move messages into a junk folder so it's easy for you to identify and delete unwanted messages later. You can use the "Run Junk Mail Controls on Folder" option located on the Tools menu to set up the junk mail filter so it learns how to identify your incoming mail.

Creating a Saved Search Folder in Thunderbird

To make it easy to find messages based on criteria that you specify, Thunderbird lets you create Saved Search folders. A **Saved Search folder** looks like a regular mail folder, but when you click it, it searches every folder and message for matches using criteria that you specify. To create a Saved Search folder, click File on the menu bar, point to New, and then click Saved Search. The New Saved Search Folder dialog box opens, in which you must specify a Saved Search folder name, location, and the criteria that define the search. For example, you might create a Saved Search folder that finds all messages sent by a specific person, or messages that are older than 60 days. When you run the search, matching messages will appear in the Message pane. Figure 2-10 shows a Saved Search folder named "Don" in the Folders pane. Double-clicking the Don Saved Search folder finds all messages in which Don Kikukawa is the sender.

Figure 2-10 Using a Saved Search folder in Thunderbird

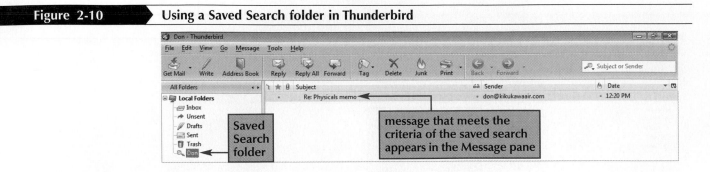

Using the Thunderbird Address Book

To manage your contacts in Thunderbird, click the Address Book button on the toolbar. The Address Book window shown in Figure 2-11 opens and displays the contacts in your Personal Address Book and in the Collected Addresses Book. You can add new email addresses using the New Card button or manage mailing lists using the New List button. To compose a message to someone in your address book, click the person's name, and then click the Write button on the toolbar. Thunderbird lets you store more than just a person's name and email address; if you double-click the contact name in the address book, you can enter a person's phone number, address, and other information, such as a cell phone number.

Figure 2-11 Thunderbird Address Book window

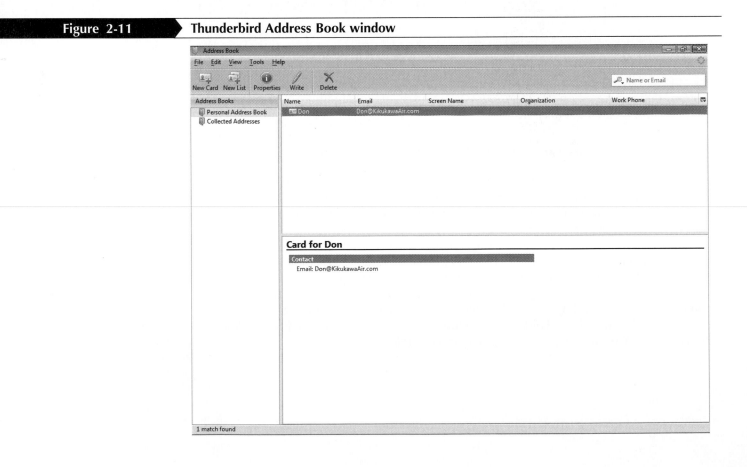

Opera Mail

Another popular email program is the **Opera Mail** built-in email client, which is installed with the Opera Web browser. You can download the Opera browser by following the link on the Online Companion page for Tutorial 2.

Starting Opera Mail

When you start the Opera Web browser for the first time, you can use the New account wizard to create an email or other type of account. You can also import information from other email programs.

   The first thing you need to set up is your email account so you can send and receive email messages through your ISP. You need to enter your name and email address, your incoming and outgoing mail server information and user name, and the account name you'd like to use to identify your email account. After setting up your email account, you can use Opera to send and receive email messages.

   To send and receive messages using Opera, start the Opera browser, and then click the Mail button on the Panels toolbar to open the Mail panel, as shown in Figure 2-12.

Opera Mail panel   **Figure 2-12**

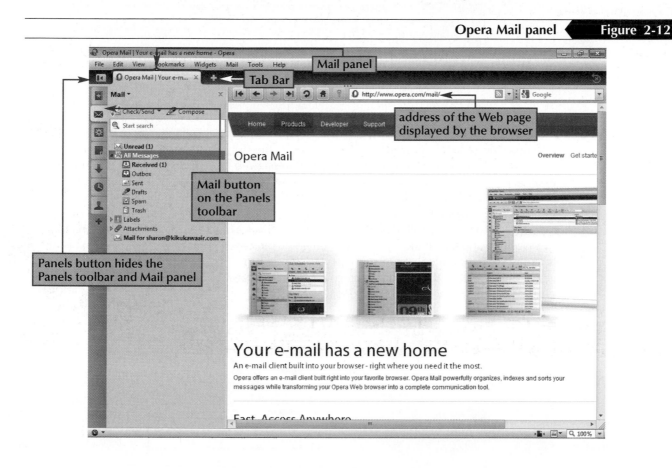

The Mail panel includes buttons to check (receive) and send email, and a Compose button to create new messages. You can close the Mail panel and the Panels bar by pressing the F4 key. Most people use the Mail panel to check for new messages quickly without closing the current page being displayed by the browser. To read a message, click the Received folder on the Mail panel to open the Received tab, which displays the message list and a preview pane, a shown in Figure 2-13.

| Figure 2-13 | Mail received using Opera Mail |

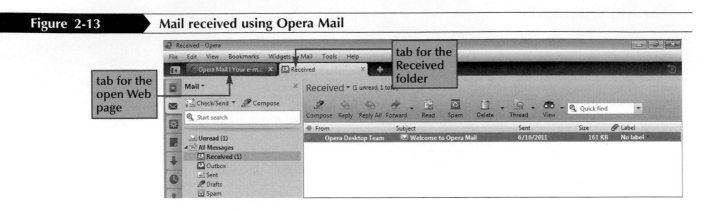

Sending and Receiving Email in Opera

To write a message, click the Compose button on the Mail panel. The Compose Message tab opens and displays a new message. You can type email addresses in the To, Cc, and Bcc text boxes to add them to your message. To view contacts saved in your address book, click the Contacts button on the Panels toolbar, which opens the Contacts panel to the left of the Compose Message tab. Clicking the Add button on the Contacts panel opens a dialog box in which you can enter a person's name, email address, Web site address, and other contact information. To attach a file to your message, click the Attach button on the Compose Message toolbar, and then browse to and select the file. After attaching the file, it appears in the Attachment window. Figure 2-14 shows the Compose Message tab after writing a message to Don Kikukawa and attaching a file named Physicals.pdf. Notice the promotional message that appears at the bottom of all outgoing messages sent from Opera. This text is actually a signature file that Opera inserts by default into all outgoing messages. If you don't want to include this message in an outgoing email message, you can select the text and delete it from your message before sending it.

| Figure 2-14 | Composing a message in Opera Mail |

Clicking the View button on the Compose Message toolbar lets you show and hide the different parts of the message header, such as the email account name and the Cc and Bcc text boxes. To send the message, click the Send button on the Compose Message toolbar. A ScreenTip opens in the lower-left corner of the browser window to indicate that your message is being sent. By default, messages are sent immediately when you click the Send button, and copies of your sent messages are saved in the Sent folder.

To download new messages, click the Check/Send button on the Mail panel. Figure 2-15 shows that one new message was received.

Receiving a message in Opera   **Figure 2-15**

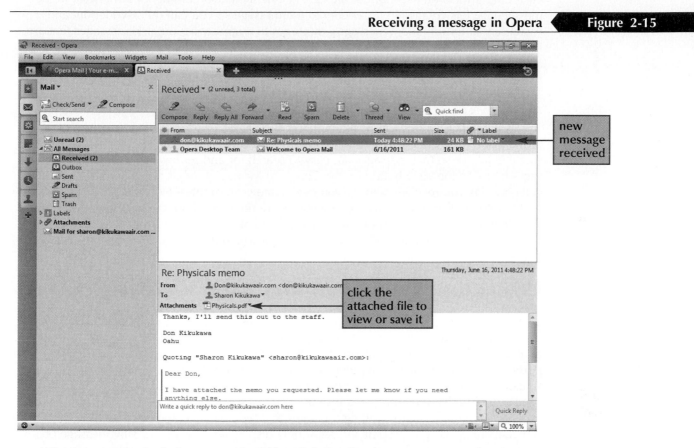

When a message includes an attached file, click the attachment to open a shortcut menu. Click the Open command to open the attachment using a program on your computer, click the "Save to Download Folder" option to save it to the default download location for Opera files, or click the Save As option to save it in a specific folder or drive on your computer.

After receiving a message, you can reply to the sender or to all recipients by clicking the Reply or Reply All button on the Compose Message toolbar. To forward a message to another recipient, click the Forward button on the Compose Message toolbar. By default, Opera sends forwarded messages as inline text. To redirect a message to a new recipient, click the Forward button arrow on the Compose Message toolbar, and then click Redirect. This option makes it easy to send a message to a new recipient without adding the "Fwd:" prefix to the Subject line. To print a message, click File on the menu bar, and then click Print.

Managing Messages in Opera

After reading a message, you can mark it as read by clicking the Read button on the Compose Message toolbar. Clicking the Spam button on the Compose Message toolbar flags the sender of the selected message so that future messages sent to you by this sender are automatically saved in the Spam folder. Clicking the Delete button on the Compose Message toolbar deletes the message and moves it to the Trash folder. To permanently delete the message, right-click the Trash folder on the Mail panel, and then click Empty Trash on the shortcut menu. Clicking the Label column for a message in the message list lets you assign a category to the message so you can quickly identify and easily search for important messages, messages that require action, and messages that are funny or valuable. Clicking Labels on the Mail panel lists messages that you have assigned to categories so you can identify and sort them easily. The View button above the message list contains options for displaying relevant information about all of your messages, such as only the message headers or messages received during predefined time periods (such as "Today" or "Three Months").

A unique feature of Opera's email client is how it stores its messages. In other email programs, messages are stored in folders in a mailbox. Opera's messages are stored in a single database so that messages are easy to search for and retrieve. You can sort messages by using the View button on the Compose Message toolbar to assign messages to categories as you receive them, or you can create custom filters to sort messages based on their content or sender. Because messages are not saved into folders, viewing messages based on their content or category results in all messages matching your search criteria being selected, regardless of the folder in which they are stored.

Protecting Your Computer from Viruses

Email attachments, just like any other computer files, can contain malicious programs called **viruses** that can harm your computer and its files. Some users send attachments containing viruses without realizing that they are doing so; other users send viruses on purpose to infect as many computers as possible. If you receive an email message from a sender that you don't recognize and the message contains an attached file, you should avoid opening that file until you are sure that it doesn't contain a virus.

People create viruses by coding programs that hide by attaching themselves to other programs on a computer. Some viruses simply display an annoying or silly message on your screen and then go away, whereas others can cause real harm by reformatting your hard drive, changing all of your computer's file extensions and their associations, or sending a copy of the virus to everyone in your email program's address book. You must know how to detect and eradicate viruses if you plan to download anything, including data, programs, instant messages, or email attachments, from any Internet server.

Software that only detects viruses and eliminates them is called an **antivirus program**. The category of software that detects viruses and other common security threats on the Internet is called **Internet security software**. This software usually includes tools that eradicate specific Internet threats, including viruses. Internet security software and antivirus programs start automatically when you start the computer and regularly scan the files on your computer and the files being downloaded to your computer and compare them to a signature that known viruses carry. A **virus signature** (also called a **virus pattern** or a **virus definition**) is a sequence (string) of characters that is always present in a particular virus. An antivirus program can scan a single file or folder or your entire computer to search for infected files. When the antivirus program finds a virus signature, it warns you. You can either delete the file containing the virus or ask the antivirus program to remove the virus. Most antivirus programs can clean infected files by removing the virus. If your computer does not have an antivirus program or security suite installed on it, you can follow the links in the Virus Protection and Internet Security Software sections of the Online Companion page for Tutorial 2 to find

---

Tip

An antivirus program might be part of an Internet security suite of programs that also scans files for other security threats and does other things such as blocking unwanted pop-up ads.

resources on Internet security, viruses, and antivirus programs. The Online Companion is located at www.cengage.com/internet/np/internet8. (After logging in, click the Tutorial 2 link to access the information and links for this tutorial.)

Using Antivirus Software Effectively | InSight

Dell Inc., Hewlett-Packard, Apple, and other computer manufacturers preload most new computers with an antivirus program or Internet security suite. Three popular choices for protecting computers are produced by Symantec (Norton), McAfee, and ZoneAlarm. Security and antivirus programs protect your computer from viruses, but only when they are turned on, properly configured, and include current virus patterns. When you first start your antivirus program, it will ask you to make a connection to its server, from which the program will download the most recent virus patterns. You must regularly download virus patterns from the server to keep your computer safe. Some programs include features that automatically download the patterns for you on a weekly or bi-weekly basis; other programs require you to connect to the server and initiate the download. When you purchase and install an antivirus program, you usually receive a free trial subscription—usually up to 12 months—for downloading current virus patterns. After this initial period ends, you must pay the software producer a fee to continue downloading current virus patterns. In either case, your antivirus software can protect you only from viruses that it recognizes. If you install an antivirus program and do not regularly download new patterns, your computer isn't protected from dozens of new virus threats each month. In addition, if your antivirus software isn't turned on or set to scan downloaded files, it cannot protect your computer.

And, finally, keep in mind that you usually have to open or execute a file to unleash any virus it contains. By regularly scanning your computer for viruses, keeping your virus patterns current, configuring your antivirus program to work automatically, and scanning all downloaded files, you can protect your computer from viruses.

"You've Got Spam!"

Spam, also known as **unsolicited commercial email (UCE)** or **bulk mail**, includes unwanted solicitations, advertisements, or email chain letters sent to an email address. For most Internet users, spam represents waste in terms of the time it takes to download, manage, and delete. Besides wasting people's time and their computers' disk space, spam can consume large amounts of network capacity. If one person sends a useless email message to hundreds of thousands of people, that unsolicited message consumes Internet resources for a few moments that would otherwise be available to users with legitimate communication needs. Although spam has always been an annoyance, companies are increasingly finding it to be a major problem. In addition to consuming bandwidth on company networks and space on email servers, spam distracts employees who are trying to do their jobs and requires them to spend time deleting unwanted messages. In addition, a considerable number of spam messages include content that is offensive or misleading to its recipients. According to the Messaging Anti-Abuse Working Group (MAAWG), approximately 80% of all email messages sent every day are abusive. In real numbers, this is billions of email messages a day.

Many grassroots and corporate organizations have decided to fight spam aggressively. AOL, for example, has taken an active role in limiting spam through legal channels. Many companies now offer software that organizations can run on their email servers to limit the amount of spam that is delivered to the organization's email addresses. Although individual users can install client-based spam-filtering programs on their computers or set filters that might be available within their email client software, most companies find it more effective and less costly to eliminate spam before it reaches users.

As spam continues to be a serious problem for all email users and providers, an increasing number of approaches have been devised or proposed to combat it. Some of these approaches require new laws, and some require technical changes in the mail handling systems of the Internet. Other approaches can be implemented under existing laws and with current technologies, but only with the cooperation of many organizations and businesses.

One way to limit the amount of spam an organization or individual receives is to reduce the likelihood that a spammer can automatically generate their email addresses. Many organizations create email addresses for their employees by combining elements of each employee's first and last names. For example, small companies often combine the first letter of an employee's first name with the entire last name to generate email addresses for all employees. Any spam sender able to obtain an employee list can generate long lists of potential email addresses using the names on the list. If no employee list is available, the spammer can simply generate logical combinations of first initials and common names. The cost of sending email messages is so low that a spammer can afford to send thousands of messages to randomly generated addresses in the hope that a few of them are valid.

Another way to reduce spam is to control the exposure of your email address in places where spammers look for them. Spammers use software robots to search the Internet for character strings that include the "@" character that appears in every email address. These robots search Web pages, discussion boards, chat rooms, and other online sources that might contain email addresses. If you don't provide your email address to these sources, you reduce the risk of a spammer getting it. A spammer can afford to send thousands of messages to email addresses gathered in this way. Even if only one or two people respond, the spammer can earn a profit because the cost of sending email messages is so low.

Some individuals use multiple email addresses to thwart spam. They use one address for display on a Web site, another to register for access to Web sites, another for shopping accounts, and so on. If a spammer starts using one of these addresses, the individual can stop using it and switch to another. Many Web hosting services include a large number of email addresses—often up to 10,000—as part of their service, so this is a good tactic for people or small businesses with their own Web sites.

The strategies previously described focus on limiting spammer's access to, or use of, an email address. Other approaches use one or more techniques that filter email messages based on their contents. Many U.S. jurisdictions have passed laws that provide penalties for sending spam. In January 2004, the U.S. CAN-SPAM law (the law's name is an acronym for "Controlling the Assault of Non-Solicited Pornography and Marketing") went into effect. Researchers who track the amount of spam noted a drop in the percentage of spam messages in February and March 2004. A MessageLabs study tracked the spam message rate from 62% of all Internet messages sent in January to 59% in February and 53% in March. However, by April, the rate was back up to a new high—68% of all messages sent. It appears that spammers slowed down their activities immediately after the effective date of CAN-SPAM to see if a broad federal prosecution effort would occur. When the threat did not materialize, the spammers went right back to work.

The CAN-SPAM law was the first U.S. federal government effort to legislate controls on spam, as shown in Figure 2-16. It regulates all email messages sent for the primary purpose of advertising or promoting a commercial product or service, including messages that promote the content displayed at a Web site. The law's main provisions are that unsolicited email messages must identify the sender, contain an accurate message subject and a notice that the message is an advertisement or solicitation, make it possible for the recipient to "opt out" of future mailings within 10 days of receipt of the request, include the sender's physical postal address, and prohibit the sender from selling or transferring an email address with an opt out request to any other entity. Each violation of a provision of the law is subject to a fine of up to $11,000. Additional fines are assessed for those who violate one of these provisions and also harvest email addresses from Web sites, send messages to randomly generated addresses, use automated tools to register for email accounts that are subsequently used to send spam, and relay email messages through a computer or network without the permission of the computer's or network's owner.

CAN-SPAM Act requirements for commercial emailers Figure 2-16

Few industry experts expect CAN-SPAM or similar laws to be effective in preventing spam on the Internet. After all, spammers have been violating existing deceptive advertising laws for years. Many spammers use email servers located in countries that do not have (and that are unlikely to adopt) antispam laws. Enforcement is a problem, too. Spammers can move their operations from one server to another in minutes.

Some critics argue that any legal solution to the spam problem is likely to fail until the prosecution of spammers becomes cost-effective for governments. To become cost-effective, prosecutors must be able to identify spammers easily (to reduce the cost of bringing an action against them) and must have a greater likelihood of winning the cases they file (or must see a greater social benefit to winning). The best way to make spammers easier to find is to make changes in the email transport mechanism in the Internet's infrastructure. To learn more about legislation geared to prevent spam, follow the links in the Email section on the Online Companion page for Tutorial 2.

Now that you understand some basic information about email and email software, you are ready to start using Windows Live Mail.

1. The special rules governing how information is handled on the Internet are collectively called _____ .
2. What are the three parts of an email message?
3. True or False: On receipt, Bcc recipients of an email message are aware of other Bcc recipients who received the same email message.
4. Can you send a Word document over the Internet? If so, how?
5. What are the two parts of an email address and what information do they provide?
6. Why is it important to delete email messages that you no longer need?
7. What is a Saved Search folder and in which program is this feature available?

Session 2.2

Windows Live Mail

Windows Live Mail is an email program that you use to send and receive email. You start Windows Live Mail by using the Start button. Figure 2-17 shows the Windows Live Mail Inbox window. You can customize Windows Live Mail in many ways by resizing, hiding, and displaying different windows and their individual elements, so your screen might look different from Figure 2-17.

Windows Live Mail Inbox window ◄ Figure 2-17

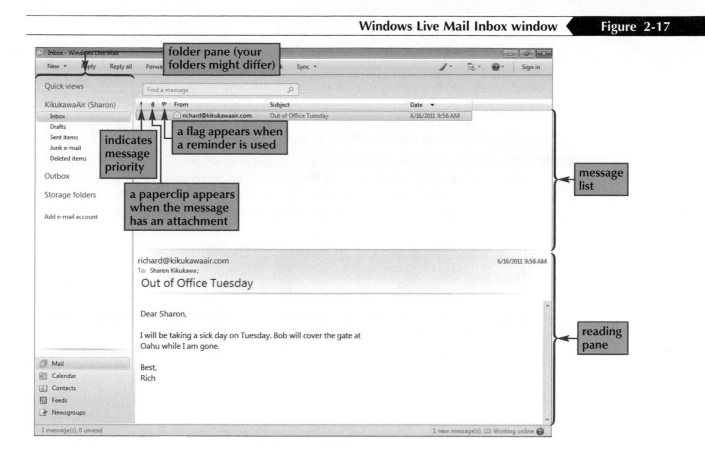

The Inbox window contains three panes: the folder pane, the message list, and the reading pane. The **folder pane** displays a list of folders for receiving, saving, and deleting mail messages. You might see more folders than those shown in Figure 2-17, but you should see the five default folders. The **Inbox folder** stores messages you have received, the **Sent items folder** stores copies of messages you have sent, the **Deleted items folder** stores messages you have deleted, the **Drafts folder** stores messages that you have written but have not sent, and the **Junk e-mail folder** stores messages that Windows Live Mail has tagged as junk and unsolicited mail. The **Outbox** stores outgoing messages that have not been sent. Your copy of Windows Live Mail might also contain folders you have created, such as a folder in which you store all messages from a certain recipient.

The **message list** contains summary information for each message that you receive. The first three columns on the left might display icons indicating information about the email message. The first column indicates the message's priority: You might see an exclamation point to indicate a message with high priority; a blue arrow icon to indicate a message with low priority; or nothing, which indicates normal priority. The sender indicates a message's priority before sending it; most messages have no specified priority, in which case no icon will appear in the column. The second column displays a paperclip icon when a message includes an attachment. Finally, if you click the third column for a message you have received, a red flag will appear. You can use a flag to remind yourself to follow up on the message later.

The message list also displays the sender's name in the From column, the message's subject in the Subject column, and the date and time the message was received in the Date column. You can sort messages by clicking any column in the message list.

The message that is selected in the message list appears in the reading pane. The **reading pane** appears below the message list and displays the content of the selected message in the message list. You can use the horizontal scroll bar to scroll the message.

Tip

The first time you start Windows Live Mail, you will not see the Inbox window until you create your mail account.

Creating an Email Account

You are ready to get started using Windows Live Mail. These steps assume that Windows Live Mail is already installed on your computer. First, you need to configure Windows Live Mail so it will retrieve your mail from your ISP.

To configure Windows Live Mail to manage your email:

▶ 1. Click the **Start** button on the Windows taskbar, click **All Programs**, click **Windows Live**, and then click **Windows Live Mail** to start the program. Normally, you do not need to be connected to the Internet to configure Windows Live Mail; however, your system might be configured differently. If necessary, connect to the Internet.

   Trouble? If you do not see a Windows Live folder on your Start menu, Windows Live Mail might not be installed on your computer. Ask your instructor or technical support person for help.

   Trouble? If your computer runs Windows XP or earlier, you should complete Appendix B on Outlook Express.

   Trouble? If you see a Windows Mail folder on the All Programs menu, instead of a Windows Live Mail folder, complete Appendix C on Windows Mail.

   Trouble? If a dialog box opens and asks to make Windows Live Mail your default email program, click the No button.

   Trouble? If a dialog box opens and asks to import information from another email program installed on your computer, click the Cancel button.

▶ 2. Click the **Add e-mail account** link on the left side of the Windows Live Mail window. The Add an E-mail Account dialog box opens, as shown in Figure 2-18. The first step in creating an email account is to the enter your email address, password, and the name that you want to appear in the From line of your messages.

   Trouble? If you have already set up your mail account (or if someone has set up an account for you), click the Cancel button in the Add an E-mail Account dialog box and skip this set of steps. If you are unsure about any existing account, ask your instructor or technical support person for help.

| Figure 2-18 | Add an E-mail Account dialog box |

▶ **3.** Type your full email address (such as student@university.edu) in the E-mail address text box, and then press the **Tab** key twice to move the insertion point to the Password text box. To protect your password's identity, Windows Live Mail displays dots or asterisks in this text box instead of the characters you type. To prevent other users from being able to access your mail account, you will not enter your password and you will clear the Remember password check box. When you access your mail account, Windows Live Mail will prompt you to enter your password. If you are working on a computer to which you have sole access, you might want to set Windows Live Mail to remember your password, so you don't need to type it every time you access your account.

▶ **4.** If necessary, click the **Remember password** check box to clear it.

▶ **5.** Press the **Tab** key to move the insertion point to the Display Name text box, type your first and last names as you would like them to be displayed in the From line of your messages, if necessary, click the **Manually configure server settings for e-mail account** check box to select it, and then click the **Next** button. The next dialog box asks you to specify your incoming and outgoing server information.

▶ **6.** Type the names of your incoming and outgoing mail servers in the Incoming server and Outgoing server text boxes. Your instructor, technical support person, or ISP will provide this information to you. Usually, an incoming mail server name is POP, POP3, or IMAP followed by a domain name. An outgoing mail server name usually is SMTP or MAIL followed by a domain name.

▶ **7.** If necessary, type your Login ID as supplied by your instructor, technical support person, or ISP in the Login ID text box. Make sure that you type your user name and not your domain name (some ISPs require both a user name and a domain name). When you are finished, click the **Next** button to continue.

▶ **8.** In the final dialog box, click the **Finish** button to save the mail account information, close the dialog box, and display your mail account in the folder pane. Figure 2-19 shows the Windows Live Mail window after creating an account for Sharon Kikukawa.

  Trouble? The Windows Live Mail window can be configured differently, so your window might look different from the one shown in Figure 2-19.

Figure 2-19   **Mail account created for Sharon Kikukawa**

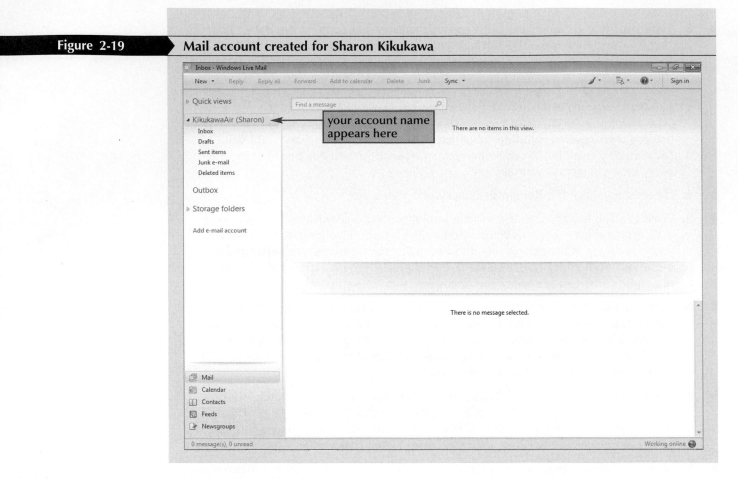

Now Windows Live Mail is configured to send and receive messages, so you are ready to send a message to Don Kikukawa.

Sending a Message Using Windows Live Mail

You are ready to use Windows Live Mail to send a message with an attached file to Don Kikukawa. You will also send a courtesy copy of the message to your own email address to simulate receiving a message.

Sending a Message Using Windows Live Mail

- Click the New button on the toolbar to open the New Message window.
- In the To text box, type the recipient's email address. To send the message to more than one recipient, separate additional email addresses with commas or semicolons.
- If necessary, click the Show Cc & Bcc link to the right of the Subject text box to display the Cc and Bcc text boxes, and then type the email address of any Cc or Bcc recipients in the appropriate boxes. Separate multiple recipients' email addresses with commas or semicolons.
- If necessary, click the Attach button on the toolbar, in the Open dialog box browse to and select a file to attach to the message, and then click the Open button.
- In the message body, type your message.
- Check your message for spelling and grammatical errors.
- Click the Send button on the toolbar.

To send a message with an attachment:

▶ 1. If necessary, click your mail account in the folder pane, and then click the **New** button on the toolbar to open the New Message window. If necessary, click the **Maximize** button on the New Message window. See Figure 2-20. The New Message window contains a toolbar for working with the message options. It also contains the message display area, a toolbar for formatting and composing the message content, and boxes in which you enter address and subject information. The insertion point is positioned in the To text box when you open a new message.

Trouble? If you do not see the Cc and Bcc text boxes in the message header, click the Show Cc & Bcc link to the right of the Subject text box.

Trouble? If you don't have the starting Data Files, you need to get them before you can proceed. Your instructor will either give you the Data Files or ask you to obtain them from a specified location (such as a network drive). In either case, make a backup copy of the Data Files before you start so that you will have the original files available in case you need to start over. If you have any questions about the Data Files, see your instructor or technical support person for assistance.

Figure 2-20 New Message window

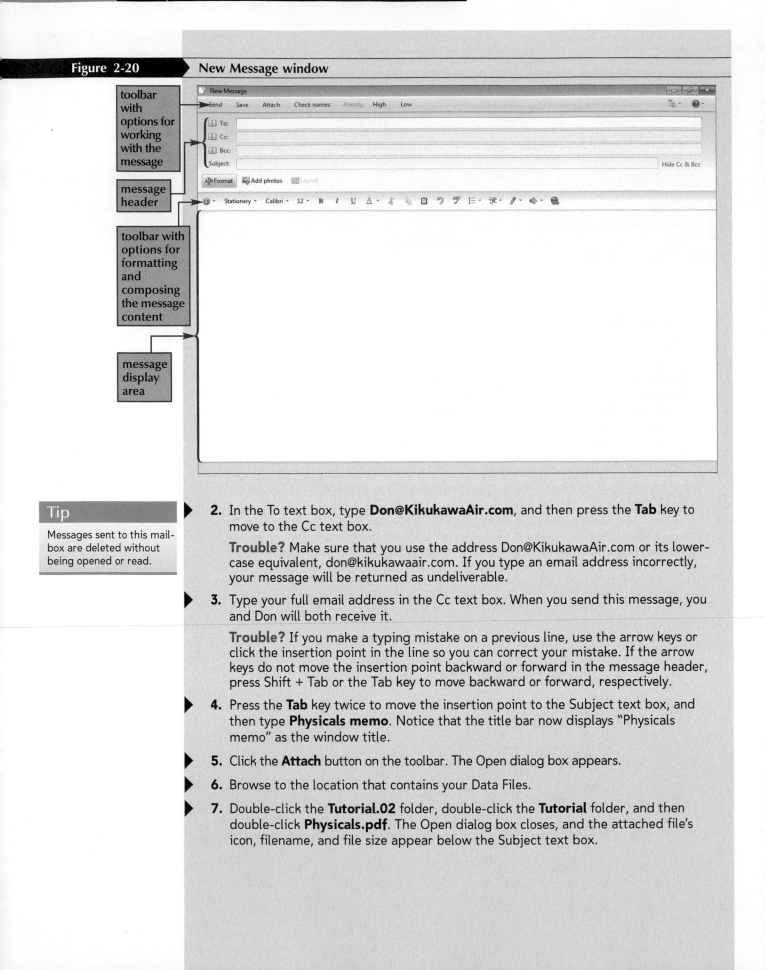

toolbar with options for working with the message

message header

toolbar with options for formatting and composing the message content

message display area

► **2.** In the To text box, type **Don@KikukawaAir.com**, and then press the **Tab** key to move to the Cc text box.

Trouble? Make sure that you use the address Don@KikukawaAir.com or its lowercase equivalent, don@kikukawaair.com. If you type an email address incorrectly, your message will be returned as undeliverable.

► **3.** Type your full email address in the Cc text box. When you send this message, you and Don will both receive it.

Trouble? If you make a typing mistake on a previous line, use the arrow keys or click the insertion point in the line so you can correct your mistake. If the arrow keys do not move the insertion point backward or forward in the message header, press Shift + Tab or the Tab key to move backward or forward, respectively.

► **4.** Press the **Tab** key twice to move the insertion point to the Subject text box, and then type **Physicals memo**. Notice that the title bar now displays "Physicals memo" as the window title.

► **5.** Click the **Attach** button on the toolbar. The Open dialog box appears.

► **6.** Browse to the location that contains your Data Files.

► **7.** Double-click the **Tutorial.02** folder, double-click the **Tutorial** folder, and then double-click **Physicals.pdf**. The Open dialog box closes, and the attached file's icon, filename, and file size appear below the Subject text box.

8. Click in the message display area, type **Dear Don,** (including the comma), and then press the **Enter** key twice to insert a blank line.

9. In the message display area, type **I have attached the memo you requested. Please let me know if you need anything else.**

10. Press the **Enter** key twice, type **Sincerely,** (including the comma), press the **Enter** key, and then type your first name to sign your message. See Figure 2-21.

Composing an email message | Figure 2-21

11. Click the **Check spelling** button on the toolbar above the message display area to check your spelling before sending the message. If necessary, correct any typing errors. When you are finished, click the **OK** button to close the Spelling dialog box.

12. Click the **Send** button on the toolbar to mail the message. The Physicals memo window closes and the message is sent.

Trouble? If a Send Mail dialog box opens and tells you that the message will be sent the next time you choose the Sync command, click the OK button to continue.

Trouble? If Windows Live Mail is configured to queue messages, the message will be stored in the Outbox, as indicated by a "(1)" in the Outbox. This difference causes no problems.

Depending on your system configuration, Windows Live Mail might not send your messages immediately. It might queue (hold) messages until you connect to your ISP or click the Sync button on the toolbar. If you want to examine the setting and change it, click the Menus button on the toolbar, click Options, and then click the Send tab in the Options dialog box. If the Send messages immediately check box contains a check mark, then Windows Live Mail sends messages when you click the Sync button on the toolbar. Otherwise, Windows Live Mail holds messages until you click the Sync button.

Receiving and Reading a Message

When you receive new mail, messages that you haven't opened yet are displayed with a closed envelope icon next to them in the message list; messages that you have opened are displayed with an open envelope icon next to them. You check for new mail next.

Reference Window | **Using Windows Live Mail to Send and Receive Messages**

- If necessary, connect to your ISP.
- Click the Sync button on the toolbar.

To check for incoming mail:

▶ **1.** Click the **Sync** button on the toolbar, type your password in the Password text box of the Logon dialog box (if necessary), and then click the **OK** button. Depending on your system configuration, you might not need to connect to your ISP and type your password to retrieve your messages. Within a few moments, your mail server transfers all new mail to your Inbox. The Physicals memo message was sent to Don and also to your email address, which you typed in the Cc text box. Notice that the Inbox folder in the folder pane is bold, but other folders are not. A bold folder indicates that it contains unread mail; the number in parentheses next to the Inbox folder indicates the number of unread messages in that folder.

Trouble? If a message box opens and indicates that it could not find your host, click the Hide button to close the message box, right-click your mail account in the folder pane, and then click Properties on the shortcut menu. Verify that your incoming and outgoing server names are correct, make any necessary changes, click the OK button, and then repeat Step 1. If you still have problems, ask your instructor or technical support person for help.

Trouble? If you do not see any messages in your Inbox, then you either did not receive any new mail or you might be looking in the wrong folder. If necessary, click the Inbox folder for your mail account in the folder pane. If you still don't have any mail messages, wait a few moments, and then repeat Step 1 until you receive a message.

▶ **2.** If necessary, click the **Physicals memo** message in the message list to open the message in the reading pane. See Figure 2-22.

Receiving an email message | Figure 2-22

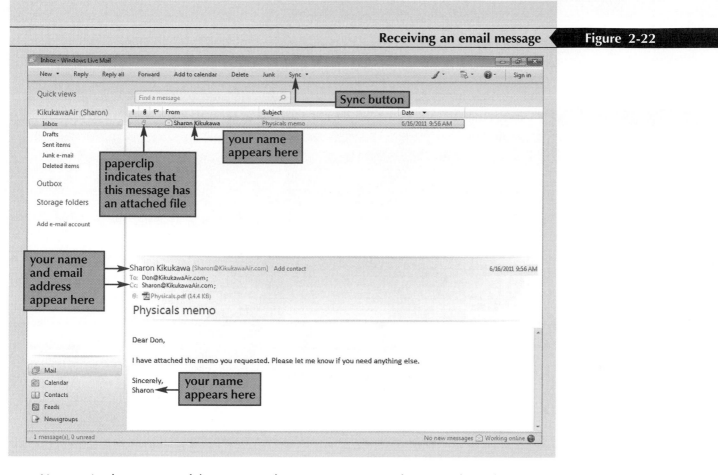

You received your copy of the message that you sent to Don. The paperclip indicates that the message has an attachment. When you receive a message with one or more attachments, you can open the attachment or save it.

Viewing and Saving an Attached File

You want to make sure that your attached file was sent properly, so you decide to open it. Then you will save the file.

Viewing and Saving an Attached File in Windows Live Mail | Reference Window

- If necessary, click the message that contains the attached file in the message list to display its contents in the reading pane.
- To view an attached file, double-click it, and then click the Open button in the Mail Attachment dialog box. Close the program window that opens after viewing the file.
- To save an attached file, right-click the file to open the shortcut menu, click Save as, navigate to the drive and folder in which to save the attached file, and then click the Save button.

To view and save the attached file:

▶ **1.** Make sure that the **Physicals memo** message is selected in the message list.

▶ **2.** Double-click the **Physicals.pdf** file in the reading pane. The Mail Attachment dialog box opens, as shown in Figure 2-23.

| Figure 2-23 | Mail Attachment dialog box |

The Mail Attachment dialog box identifies the name of the attached file and the program that Windows Live Mail will use to open it.

▶ **3.** Click the **Open** button. Adobe Reader or another program on your computer starts and opens the attached file. If necessary, maximize the program window that opens.

▶ **4.** Click the **Close** button on the program window displaying the Physicals memo document. Now that you have viewed the attachment, you can save it.

▶ **5.** Right-click the **Physicals.pdf** file in the reading pane, and then click **Save as** on the shortcut menu. The Save Attachment As dialog box opens. The Physicals.pdf file is already selected for you.

▶ **6.** Navigate to the drive or folder that contains your Data Files, open the **Tutorial.02** folder, and then open the **Tutorial** folder.

▶ **7.** Click the **Save** button to save the attached file, and then click the **Yes** button to overwrite the file with the same name.

When you receive a message with an attached file, you can view and save the attachment for as long as you store the message. When you delete the message, you also delete the file attached to the message. When you detach a file from an email message and save it on a disk or drive, it is just like any other file that you save. Be sure to save any important attachments soon after receiving them, so you do not inadvertently delete the messages containing them.

Replying to and Forwarding Messages

You can forward any message you receive to one or more email addresses. Similarly, you can respond to the sender of a message quickly and efficiently by replying to a message.

Replying to an Email Message

To reply to a message, select the message in the message list, and then click the Reply button on the toolbar to reply only to the sender, or click the Reply All button to reply to the sender and other people who received the original message (those email addresses listed in the To and Cc text boxes). Windows Live Mail will open a new "Re:" message window and place the original sender's address in the To text box; if you clicked the Reply All button, then other email addresses that received the original message will appear in the To and Cc text boxes as appropriate. You can leave the Subject text box as is or modify it. Most email programs, including Windows Live Mail, will copy the original message and place it in the message body. A special mark might appear to the left of the response, indicating a quote from the text of the original message. Figure 2-24 shows a reply to the Physicals memo message.

Replying to a message ◄ **Figure 2-24**

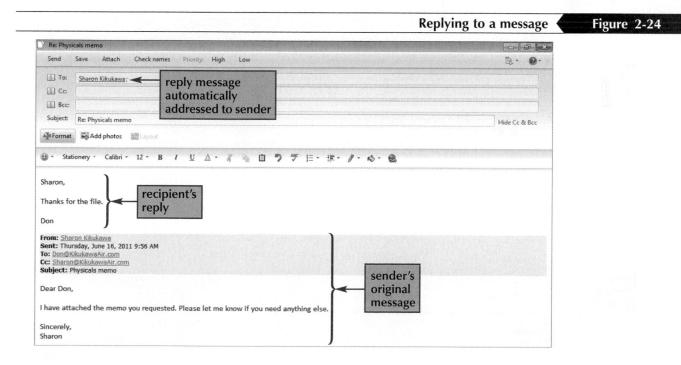

Reference Window | **Replying to a Message Using Windows Live Mail**

- Click the message in the message list to which you want to reply.
- Click the Reply button on the toolbar to reply only to the sender, or click the Reply all button on the toolbar to reply to the sender and other "To" and "Cc" recipients of the original message.
- Type other recipients' email addresses in the message header as needed.
- Change the text in the Subject text box as necessary.
- Edit the message body as necessary.
- Click the Send button on the toolbar.

Forwarding an Email Message

When you forward a message, you are sending a copy of your message, including any attachments, to one or more recipients who may not have been included in the original message. (If you do not want to forward the original sender's attached file to the new recipients, select the attachment filename in the message header, and then press the Delete key.) To forward an existing mail message to another user, open the folder containing the message you want to forward, select it in the message list, and then click the Forward button on the toolbar. The "Fw:" window opens, where you can type the address of the recipient in the To text box. If you want to forward the message to several people, type their addresses, separated by commas (or semicolons), in the To text box (or Cc or Bcc text boxes). Windows Live Mail inserts a copy of the original message in the message display area (as it does when you reply to a message). Figure 2-25 shows a forwarded copy of the Physicals memo message.

Figure 2-25 ▸ **Forwarding a message**

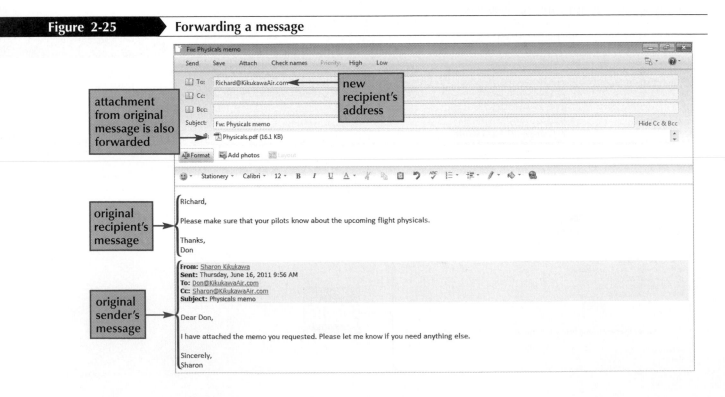

- Click the message in the message list that you want to forward.
- Click the Forward button on the toolbar to open the "Fw:" window, which contains a copy of the original message.
- Click the To text box, and then type one or more email addresses, separated by commas or semicolons.
- Click the blank line above the quoted message, and then type an optional message to add a context for the recipient(s).
- Click the Send button on the toolbar.

Occasionally, you receive important messages, so you want to make sure that you can file and print them as needed.

Filing and Printing an Email Message

You can use the Windows Live Mail folders to file your email messages by topic or category. When you file a message, you move it from the Inbox to another folder. You can also make a *copy* of a message in the Inbox and save it in another folder by right-clicking the message in the message list, clicking Copy to folder on the shortcut menu, and then selecting the folder in which to store the copy. You will file your message in a new folder named "FAA" for safekeeping. Later, you can create other folders to suit your needs.

To create a new folder:

▶ 1. Right-click the **Inbox** folder in the folder pane to open the shortcut menu, and then click **New folder**. The Create Folder dialog box opens. When you create a new folder, first you must select the folder at the level above which to create the new folder. Because the Inbox folder is selected, the new folder that you create is a subfolder of the Inbox folder.

▶ 2. Type **FAA** in the Folder name text box. See Figure 2-26.

Creating a new folder ◄ Figure 2-26

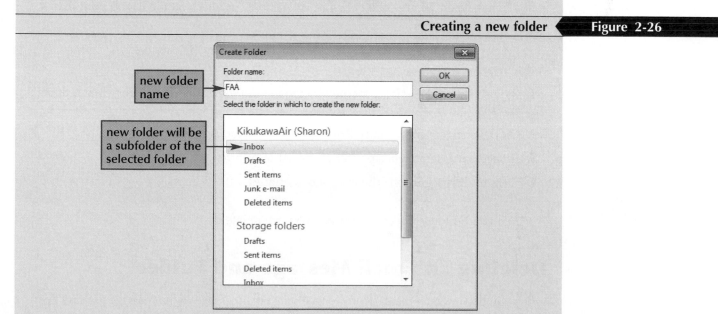

> **3.** Click the **OK** button to create the new folder and close the Create Folder dialog box. The FAA folder appears in the folder pane as a subfolder of the Inbox folder.

After you create the FAA folder, you can transfer messages to it. Besides copying or transferring mail from the Inbox folder, you can select messages in any other folder and then transfer them to another folder.

To file the Physicals memo message:

> **1.** If necessary, click the **Physicals memo** message in the message list to select it.

> **2.** Drag the **Physicals memo** message from the message list to the FAA folder in the folder pane. See Figure 2-27.

Figure 2-27	Filing a message

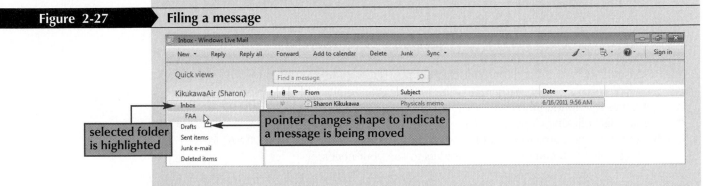

> **3.** When the FAA folder is selected, release the mouse button. The Physicals memo message is now stored in the FAA folder.

> **4.** Click the **FAA** folder in the folder pane to display its contents. The Physicals memo message appears in the FAA folder, and its contents (the Physicals memo message) appear in the message list.

You might want to print certain messages for future reference. You can print a message at any time—when you receive it, before you send it, or after you file it. You print the message next.

To print the email message:

> **1.** Right-click the **Physicals memo** message in the message list to select it and open the shortcut menu.

> **2.** On the shortcut menu, click **Print**. The Print dialog box opens.

> **3.** If necessary, select your printer in the list of printers.

> **4.** Click the **Print** button. The message is printed.

When you no longer need a message, you can delete it.

Deleting an Email Message and Folder

When you don't need a message any longer, select the message in the message list, and then click the Delete button on the toolbar. You can select multiple messages by pressing and holding the Ctrl key, clicking each message in the message list, and then releasing the Ctrl key. When you click the Delete button on the toolbar, each selected message is deleted. You can select folders and delete them using the same process. When you delete a message or a folder, you are really moving it to the Deleted items folder. To remove items permanently, use the same process to delete the items from the Deleted items folder.

Deleting Messages on a Public Computer | InSight

If you are using a public computer in a university computer lab, it is always a good idea to delete all of your messages from the Inbox and then to delete them again from the Deleted items folder when you finish your session. Otherwise, the next person who uses Windows Live Mail will be able to access and read your messages.

Deleting an Email Message or a Folder in Windows Live Mail | Reference Window

- Click the message you want to delete in the message list. If you are deleting a folder, click the folder in the folder pane that you want to delete.
- Click the Delete button on the toolbar. If you are deleting a folder, click the Yes button.
- To delete items permanently, click the Deleted items folder to open it, select the message(s) or folder(s) that you want to delete permanently, click the Delete button on the toolbar, and then click the Yes button.
  or
- Right-click the Deleted items folder to open the shortcut menu, click Empty 'Deleted items' folder, and then click the Yes button.

To delete the message:

▶ 1. If necessary, select the **Physicals memo** message in the message list.

▶ 2. Click the **Delete** button on the toolbar. The message is deleted from the FAA folder and is moved to the Deleted items folder.

▶ 3. Click the **Deleted items** folder in the folder pane to display its contents.

▶ 4. Click the **Physicals memo** message to select it, and then click the **Delete** button on the toolbar. A dialog box opens and asks you to confirm the deletion. See Figure 2-28.

Deleting a message ◀ Figure 2-28

Windows Live Mail

Are you sure you want to permanently delete the selected message(s)?

Yes   No

▶ 5. Click the **Yes** button. The Physicals memo message is deleted from the Deleted items folder.

To delete the FAA folder, you follow the same process.

To delete the FAA folder:

▶ **1.** Click the **FAA** folder in the folder pane to select it. Because this folder doesn't contain any messages, the message list is empty.

▶ **2.** Click the **Delete** button on the toolbar. A dialog box opens and asks you to confirm moving the folder to the Deleted items folder.

▶ **3.** Click the **Yes** button. The FAA folder moves to the Deleted items folder. The Deleted items folder has an arrow to its left, indicating that this folder contains another folder.

▶ **4.** Click the **arrow** to the left of the Deleted items folder, and then click the **FAA** folder to select it.

▶ **5.** Click the **Delete** button on the toolbar, and then click the **Yes** button in the message box to delete the FAA folder permanently.

▶ **6.** Click the **Inbox** folder in the folder pane to return to the Inbox.

Maintaining Your Windows Live Contacts

As you use email to communicate with business associates and friends, you can save their addresses in an address book to make it easier to enter addresses into the header of your email messages. In Windows Live Mail, the address book is called **Windows Live Contacts**.

Adding a Contact to Windows Live Contacts

Tip

Windows Live Mail also includes a calendar, which you can use to enter information about your appointments and reminders. To open Windows Calendar, click the Calendar shortcut in the folder pane.

You can open the Windows Live Contacts window by clicking the Contacts shortcut in the folder pane. To create a new address, click the New button arrow on the toolbar to open the Add a Contact dialog box, in which you can enter information about the new contact. On the Quick add page, you can enter a contact's name, email address, phone number, and company name; you can use the other pages to enter optional address, business, personal, and other information about that contact. If you enter a short name in the Nickname text box on the Contact page, you can type the nickname instead of a person's full name when you address a new message.

Reference Window | **Adding a Contact to Windows Live Contacts**

- Click the New button arrow on the toolbar, and then click Contact.
- On the Quick add page of the Add a Contact dialog box, enter the contact's name and email address. Use the other pages in the Add a Contact dialog box as necessary to enter other information about the contact.
- Click the Add contact button to add the contact.

You will start by adding Jenny Mahala's contact information to Windows Live Contacts.

To add a contact to Windows Live Contacts:

▶ **1.** Click the **Contacts** shortcut in the folder pane. If necessary, maximize the Windows Live Contacts window that opens.

▶ **2.** On the toolbar, click the **New** button arrow, and then click **Contact**. The Add a Contact dialog box opens with the insertion point positioned in the First name text box on the Quick add page.

▶ **3.** Type **Jenny** in the First name text box.

▶ **4.** Press the **Tab** key to move the insertion point to the Last name text box, and then type **Mahala**.

▶ **5.** Press the **Tab** key to move the insertion point to the Personal e-mail text box, and then type **Jenny@KikukawaAir.com**. Jenny's contact is complete. See Figure 2-29.

Tip

As you send messages, Windows Live Mail might add the addresses of the recipients to Windows Live Contacts automatically. So you might see contacts listed, even if you didn't add them.

Adding a contact to Windows Live Contacts **Figure 2-29**

▶ **6.** Click the **Add contact** button. The Add a Contact dialog box closes and you return to the Windows Live Contacts window. Jenny's contact now appears in the contacts list.

▶ **7.** Repeat Steps 2 through 6 to create two new contacts for the following Kikukawa Air employees:

First	Last	Email Address
Zane	Norcia	Zane@KikukawaAir.com
Richard	Forrester	Richard@KikukawaAir.com

▶ **8.** When you are finished entering the contacts, click the **Close** button on the Windows Live Contacts window title bar to close it.

Now that these email addresses are stored in Windows Live Contacts, when you create a new message and start typing the first few letters of a nickname or first name in a text box in the message header, Windows Live Mail will complete the entry for you. Clicking the Check names button on the toolbar in the New Message window changes the names you typed to their matching entries in Windows Live Contacts.

When you receive mail from someone who is not in your Windows Live Contacts, double-click the message to open it, right-click the "From" name to open the shortcut menu, and then click Add to contacts. This process adds the sender's email address to Windows Live Contacts, where you can open his or her information as a contact and edit and add information as necessary.

Using Windows Live Contacts to Create a Category

You can use Windows Live Contacts to create a group of email addresses, called a category. Usually, you create a category when you regularly send messages to a group of people.

For example, Sharon frequently sends messages to Zane, Jen, and Rich as a group because they have the same positions at the Kikukawa Air ticket counters. She asks you to create a category so she can type one category name for the group of email addresses, instead of having to type each address separately.

Reference Window | **Using Windows Live Contacts to Create a Category**

- Click the Contacts shortcut in the folder pane to open Windows Live Contacts.
- In the Windows Live Contacts window, click the New button arrow on the toolbar, and then click Category.
- In the Create a new category dialog box, type a category name for the group in the Enter a category name text box.
- Click the contacts that you want to add to the category.
- Click the Save button.

To create a category in Windows Live Contacts:

1. Click the **Contacts** shortcut in the folder pane, and then, if necessary, maximize the Windows Live Contacts window.

2. Click the **New** button arrow on the toolbar, and then click **Category**. The Create a new category dialog box opens and displays a list of your contacts.

3. With the insertion point positioned in the Enter a category name text box, type **Ticket Agents**. This category name will represent the individual email addresses for employees working in this position.

4. Click **Jenny Mahala** in the list. Jenny's contact is added to the text box as the first member of the category.

5. Click **Richard Forrester** and **Zane Norcia** to add them to the category. Figure 2-30 shows the completed Ticket Agents category, which contains three contacts.

Creating a category   **Figure 2-30**

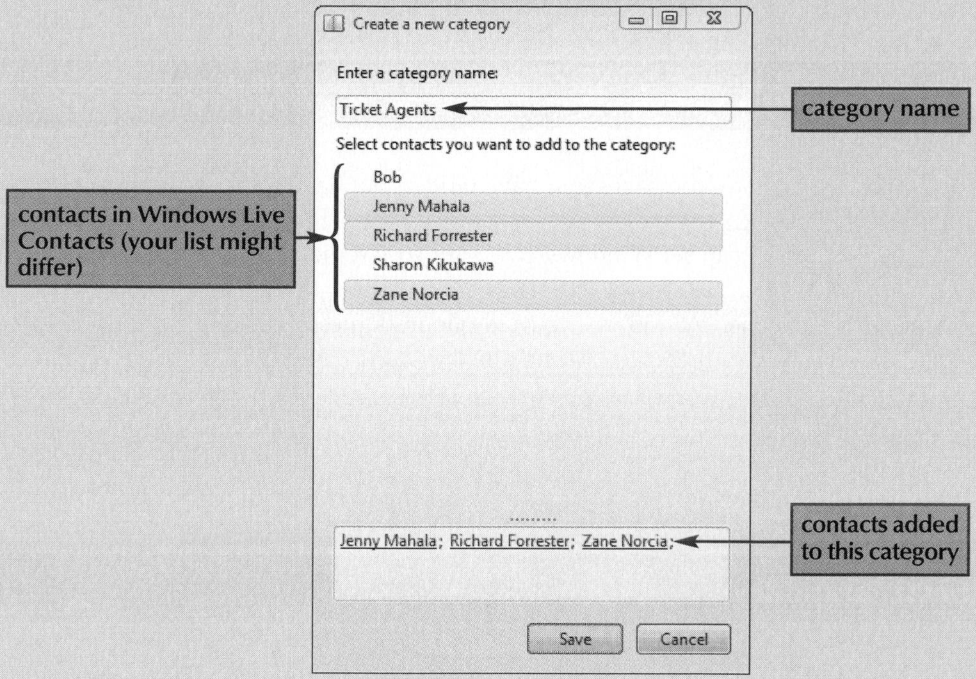

Create a new category

Enter a category name:

Ticket Agents ◄——— category name

Select contacts you want to add to the category:

Bob

contacts in Windows Live
Contacts (your list might
differ) }——►
Jenny Mahala

Richard Forrester

Sharon Kikukawa

Zane Norcia

Jenny Mahala; Richard Forrester; Zane Norcia; ◄——— contacts added
to this category

Save   Cancel

▶ **6.** Click the **Save** button to close the Create a new category dialog box. The name of the new category, appears in the Contacts pane.

▶ **7.** Click the **Close** button on the Windows Live Contacts window to close it.

Now, test the new category by creating a new message.

To address a message to a category and close Windows Live Mail:

▶ **1.** Click the **New** button on the toolbar. The New Message window opens.

▶ **2.** Type **Ticket Agents** in the To text box. As you type the first two or three letters, Windows Live Mail might complete your entry for you by selecting the Ticket Agents category. As soon as you see the Ticket Agents category in the menu, stop typing.

▶ **3.** Press the **Tab** key. The Ticket Agents category changes to bold and underlined, indicating that Windows Live Mail recognizes it as a category. A plus sign appears to the left of the category name to indicate that the category might contain more than one email address. Clicking the plus sign expands the category and lists the individual email addresses in the category, so you can see who will receive the message, and delete any recipients as necessary.

▶ **4.** Click the **Close** button on the New Message window title bar, and then click the **No** button to close the message without saving it.

▶ **5.** Click the **Close** button on the Windows Live Mail title bar to close the program.

When you need to modify a category's members, you can delete one or more members from the category by opening Windows Live Contacts, clicking the category name in the Contacts pane, clicking the contact to remove, clicking the Delete button on the toolbar. Similarly, you can add members by clicking the category, clicking the contacts to add to it, and then clicking the Save button.

In this session, you have learned how to use Windows Live Mail to create, send, receive, and manage email messages. You have also learned how to use Windows Live Contacts to manage email addresses.

| Review | **Session 2.2 Quick Check** |

1. The folder that stores messages you have written but have not yet sent is the _____ folder.
2. True or False: You can set Windows Live Mail so it remembers your Internet account password.
3. What happens when Windows Live Mail queues a message?
4. When you receive a message with an attachment, what two options are available for the attached file?
5. When you delete a message from the Inbox folder, can you recover it? Why or why not?
6. What information can you store about a person you have added as a contact?

| Review | **Tutorial Summary** |

In this tutorial, you learned how to use email as a form of communication and how to send and receive email messages using Windows Live Mail. You also learned how to print, file, save, delete, respond to, and forward email messages. You used Windows Live Contacts to store the name, email address, and other important details about a person or a group of people. Now that you have learned these important skills, you can use Windows Live Mail or the email program of your choice to send and receive your own email messages. As you use your email program, expand your skills by using its Help system to explore the many other features that it includes.

Key Terms

address book
antivirus program
attachment
blind courtesy copy (Bcc)
bulk mail
category
courtesy copy (Cc)
Deleted items folder
detaching
Drafts folder
electronic mail
email
email address
email program
emoticon
filter
folder pane
forward
From line
group
IMAP (Internet Message
    Access Protocol)
Inbox folder

Internet security software
Junk e-mail folder
junk mail
kilobyte (KB)
mail client software
mail server
message body
message header
message list
MIME (Multipurpose
    Internet Mail
    Extensions)
Mozilla Thunderbird
netiquette
nickname
Opera Mail
Outbox
POP (Post Office Protocol)
POP message
POP3 message
protocol
queued
quoted message

read-only
reading pane
reply
Saved Search folder
Sent items folder
signature
SMTP (Simple Mail
    Transfer Protocol)
spam
Subject line
To line
unsolicited commercial
    email (UCE)
user name
virus
virus definition
virus pattern
virus signature
Windows Live Contacts
Windows Live Mail

| Practice | **Review Assignments** |

Practice the skills you learned in the tutorial using the same case scenario.

Data File needed for the Review Assignments: KAir.gif

Now that you have learned how to use Windows Live Mail to manage your email messages, Sharon asks you to submit a review of your experience using the program and a recommendation about whether Kikukawa Air should continue using it. Sharon also wants to see how graphics are sent over the Internet, so she asks you to send her the Kikukawa Air logo to simulate how it will appear when sent by Kikukawa Air employees. To evaluate the Windows Live Mail program for Sharon, complete the following steps.

1. Start Windows Live Mail.
2. Add your instructor's full name and email address and Sharon Kikukawa's full name and email address (Sharon@KikukawaAir.com) to Windows Live Contacts.
3. Create a category named **Classmates** in Windows Live Contacts using the full names and email addresses of three of your classmates.
4. Create a new message. Address the message to Sharon and to your instructor. Send a courtesy copy of the message to yourself, and send a blind courtesy copy of the message to the Classmates category. Use the subject **Email Recommendation** for the message.
5. In the message body, type three or more sentences describing your overall impressions about Windows Live Mail. Be sure to evaluate the program's features, ease of use, and other important considerations that you determine. Conclude your message with a recommendation of whether Kikukawa Air employees should continue using Windows Live Mail.
6. In the message body, press the Enter key twice, and then type your full name and email address on separate lines.
7. Attach the file named **KAir.gif**, from the Tutorial.02\Review folder included with your Data Files, to the message.
8. Check the spelling in your message before you send the message and correct any mistakes. Proofread your message and verify that you have created it correctly, and then send the message.
9. Wait about one minute, check for new mail (enter your password, if necessary), and then open the message you sent to Sharon and your instructor. Print the message.
10. Forward the message and the attached file to only your instructor. In the message body, describe the appearance of the file you attached to the message and explain your findings in terms of attaching a graphic to an email message. Send the message.
11. Exit Windows Live Mail.

| Apply | **Case Problem 1** |

Apply the skills you learned to send and file an email message.

There are no Data Files needed for this Case Problem.

Worldwide Golf Resorts   Worldwide Golf Resorts is a corporation based in Kansas City, Missouri that owns and operates golf resorts in 22 countries worldwide. These resorts are popular destinations for people on vacation, and two of them host annual professional golf tournaments. You work for the regional vice president, Michael Pedersen, and handle all of his business correspondence. The Information Technology department just installed Michael's new computer, and now you need to send a test message to make sure that Michael's email account is working correctly. You will create and send the message by completing the following steps.

1. Start Windows Live Mail.
2. Use Windows Live Contacts to create individual contacts with the full name and email address of your instructor and two classmates.
3. Use Windows Live Contacts to create a category named **Managers** using the two classmates you added in Step 2.
4. Create a new message addressed to your instructor. Send a courtesy copy of the message to the Managers group and a blind copy of the message to yourself. Use the subject **Worldwide Golf Resorts test message**.
5. In the message display area, type a short note telling the recipients that you are sending a message for Michael and ask them to respond to you when they receive your message. Sign your message with your first and last names.
6. Send the message, wait a minute, and then retrieve your messages from the server. Print the message you sent to your instructor.
7. Create a folder named **Golf**, and then file the message you received in the Golf folder.
8. Exit Windows Live Mail.

Challenge | Case Problem 2

Use Windows Live Help to learn how to manage unsolicited email messages.

There are no Data File needed for this Case Problem.

Estancia Ridge Estate Bridget Estancia owns and operates the Estancia Ridge Estate, a small, private, family-owned olive grove specializing in locally grown olives that are pressed into olive oil on the premises. Bridget manages the gardens, historic estate where she also lives, tours of the home and grove, and a gift shop. Olive oil sales are Bridget's largest income item, but she has seen a rise in tourism over the past year at her unique estate. Because of this rise in tourism, Bridget is advertising in local tourism publications and in other publications that might attract people to visit the estate. As part of the advertisements, she includes the estate's phone number, Web site address, and her email address. Although she receives many email messages from interested tourists, she has also started receiving many unsolicited messages as her email address is added to different mailing lists distributing information that she does not want to receive. Bridget asks you to research how she can use Windows Live Mail to manage the email messages she receives by blocking senders from which she does not want to receive mail, deleting junk mail, and filtering messages into categories or different views so she receives fewer messages in her Inbox. You will conduct this research for Bridget by completing the following steps.

1. Start Windows Live Mail.
2. Create a new message addressed to your instructor. Enter your email address on the Cc line. Use the subject **Junk Mail and Filter Options**.
3. Click the Help button on the toolbar, and then click Get help with Mail. Your browser will start and open the Help page for Windows Live Mail.

⊕ EXPLORE
4. Use the Search text box to search Windows Live Mail Help using the word **filter**. Explore the links provided to learn about how to set the junk email filtering level, how to block unwanted messages, and how to create a custom view. As you read each topic, consider how Bridget might use each feature to block mail from senders from which she does not want to receive any mail, filter mail into categories, and delete junk mail. If necessary, explore the Help topics further to conduct additional research.

EXPLORE

5. In the message display area for the message addressed to your instructor, type a short memo of two to three paragraphs explaining your recommendations about how Bridget can use Windows Live Mail to better manage the mail she receives. Use information from Windows Live Mail Help in your response and cite specific features and steps for your recommendations. Sign your message with your first and last names.

6. Send the message to your instructor.

7. Exit Windows Live Mail.

| Challenge | **Case Problem 3** |

Create a signature for your outgoing email messages.

Data File needed for this Case Problem: Recycle.pdf

Recycling Awareness Campaign You are an assistant in the Mayor's office in Cleveland, Ohio. The mayor has asked you to help with the recycling awareness campaign. Your job is to use email to increase awareness of the recycling centers throughout the city and to encourage Cleveland's citizens and businesses to participate in the program. You will send an email message to members of the city's chamber of commerce with an invitation to help increase awareness of the program by forwarding your message and its attached file to their employees and colleagues by completing the following steps.

1. Start Windows Live Mail.

2. Add the full names and email addresses of five classmates to Windows Live Contacts to act as chamber of commerce members. After creating the contacts for your classmates, use Windows Live Contacts to create a category named **Chamber**. Then add the full name and email address of your instructor to Windows Live Contacts.

3. Create a new message and address it to the Chamber category. Add your instructor's email address to the Cc line and your email address to the Bcc line. Use the subject **Recycling campaign for businesses**.

EXPLORE

4. Write a two- or three-line message urging the chamber members to promote the city's new business recycling campaign by forwarding your message and the attached file to local businesses. Make sure to thank them for their efforts on behalf of the Mayor's office.

5. Attach the file named **Recycle.pdf**, located in the Tutorial.02\Cases folder included with your Data Files, to the message.

EXPLORE

6. Create a signature file with your full name on the first line, the title **Assistant to the Mayor** on the second line, and your email address on the third line. (*Hint:* In Windows Live Mail, click the Menus button on the toolbar, and then click Show menu bar. Click Tools on the menu bar, click Options, and then click the Signatures tab in the Options dialog box. Click the New button and then type your signature in the Text text box in the Edit Signature section.)

EXPLORE

7. Include your signature file in the new message. If necessary, insert one blank line between your memo and your signature. (*Hint:* In Windows Live Mail, click Insert on the menu bar, and then click Signature.)

8. Proofread and spell check your message, and then send your message. After a few moments, retrieve your email message from the server and print it.

9. Forward the message to one of the classmates you added to Windows Live Contacts in Step 2. Add a short message to the forwarded message that asks the recipient to forward the message to appropriate business leaders per your program objectives.

EXPLORE

10. Save a *copy* of your message in a new subfolder of the Inbox named **Recycling**, and then delete the message from the Inbox.

✦ **EXPLORE**   11. Delete your signature file. (*Hint:* In Windows Live Mail, select your signature on the Signatures tab in the Options dialog box, and then click the Remove button.)

12. Exit Windows Live Mail.

| Apply | **Case Problem 4** |

Apply the skills you learned in this tutorial to create a category for a group of students.

There are no Data Files needed for this Case Problem.

Student Study Group   In two weeks, you have a final exam, and you want to organize a study group with your classmates. Everyone in your class has an email account provided by your school. You want to contact some classmates to find out when they might be available to get together in the next week to study for the exam. To create a study group, you will complete the following steps.

1. Start Windows Live Mail.
2. Obtain the email addresses of at least four classmates, and then enter them in the To line of a new message. In the Cc line, enter your email address, and then in the Bcc line, enter your instructor's email address. Do *not* add these names to Windows Live Contacts.
3. Use the subject **Study group** for the message. In the message body, tell your classmates about the study group by providing possible meeting times and locations. Ask recipients to respond to you through email by a specified date if they are interested. Sign the message with your full name and email address.
4. Proofread and spell check your message, and then send your message. After a few moments, retrieve your email message from the server and open it.
5. Add each address in the To and Cc lines to Windows Live Contacts.
6. Create a new category named **Study Group** using the addresses you added to Windows Live Contacts in Step 5. Then forward a copy of your message to the study group.
7. Send your message. After a few moments, retrieve your email message from the server and print it.
8. Exit Windows Live Mail.

| Create | **Case Problem 5** |

Expand the skills you learned in this tutorial to create a document that you can send to a group of recipients as an email attachment.

There are no Data Files needed for this Case Problem.

Murphy's Market Research Services   You work part-time for Murphy's Market Research Services, a company that surveys students about various topics of interest to college students. A local music store, CD Rocks, wants you to send a short survey via email to students at your university to learn more about student-buying habits for music CDs. You need to find out the names of three of their favorite music CDs, where they prefer to shop for music CDs, and how much time they spend each day listening to music. You will create the survey using any word-processing program, such as Microsoft Word, WordPad, or WordPerfect, and then you will attach the survey to your email message. You need to receive the survey results within three weeks, so you will ask the respondents to return the survey via email within that time period. You will create and send the survey by completing the following steps.

1. Using any word-processing program, create a new document named **Survey** and save it with the program's default filename extension in the Tutorial.02\Cases folder included with your Data Files.

2. Create the survey by typing the following questions (separate each question with two blank lines) in the new document:
   a. What are the titles of your three favorite music CDs?
   b. Where is the best place (online or retail) to shop for music CDs?
   c. Approximately how much time per day do you spend listening to music?
3. At the bottom of the document, type a sentence that thanks respondents for their time, and then on a new line, type your first and last names. Save the document, and then close your word-processing program.
4. Start Windows Live Mail.
5. Obtain the email addresses of three classmates, and then enter them in the To line of a new message. In the Cc line, enter your email address, and then in the Bcc line, enter your instructor's email address. Do *not* add these names to Windows Live Contacts.
6. Use the subject **Music survey** for the message. In the message body, ask recipients to open the attached file and to complete the survey by typing their responses into the document. Make sure that recipients understand that you need them to return the survey within three weeks. As an incentive for completing the survey, ask recipients to return the survey via email, and also to print their completed survey and bring it to their local CD Rocks outlet for a $2 discount on any purchase. Sign the message with your full name, the company name (Murphy's Market Research Services), and your email address.
7. Attach the survey to your email message, and then send the message. After a few moments, retrieve your email message from the server.

⊕ EXPLORE
8. Open the attached file, and then complete the survey. Before saving the file, use your word-processing program's Print command to print the document.

⊕ EXPLORE
9. In your word-processing program, click File on the menu bar, and then click Save As. Browse to the Tutorial.02\Cases folder included with your Data Files and then save the file as **Completed Survey**, using the program's default filename extension. Close your word-processing program.
10. Forward the message to your instructor, attach the **Completed Survey** file to the message, make sure that the original message text appears in the message body, type a short introduction (such as "Here is my completed survey."), sign your message with your full name and email address, and then send the message.
11. Exit Windows Live Mail.

| Reinforce | **Lab Assignments** |

Student Edition Labs

The interactive Student Edition Lab **Email** is designed to help you master some of the key concepts and skills presented in this tutorial, including:

- sending and receiving email messages
- replying to email messages
- storing and deleting email messages

This lab is available online and can be accessed from the Tutorial 2 Web page on the Online Companion at www.cengage.com/internet/np/internet8.

Review | Quick Check Answers

Session 2.1

1. protocols
2. message header, message body, signature
3. False
4. Yes; you can attach the Word document file to an email message.
5. The user name identifies a specific individual, and the domain name identifies the computer on which that individual's account is stored.
6. By deleting unnecessary messages, you clear space on the drive or server on which your email messages are stored.
7. A folder that contains a saved search; clicking the folder runs the search and finds all messages that match the search criteria. This feature is available in Thunderbird.

Session 2.2

1. Drafts
2. True
3. Windows Live Mail holds messages that are queued until you connect to your ISP and click the Sync button on the toolbar.
4. You can view the attached file if your computer has a program that can open it, or you can save the attached file on your computer.
5. Yes, you can recover the message because it is stored in the Deleted items folder.
6. name, email address, nickname, address, business information, personal information, and so on

Reality Check

In Tutorials 1 and 2, you learned that every computer on the Internet has a unique IP address, and that this IP address is more commonly called a domain name. When you use a Web browser to load a Web page or an email program to send and receive email messages, you use the domain name as a way of identifying the Web site or email address that you need.

In Tutorial 1, you learned that the not-for-profit organization that coordinates and ensures unique domain names and IP addresses on the Internet is ICANN. ICANN is also responsible for accrediting domain name registrars. A **registrar** is a for-profit organization that collects information about new or renewed domains and submits information about it to a database of all Internet domain names, called the **registry**. The registry contains the necessary information to associate a specific domain name with an IP address, and to connect this information to a specific computer. The registry also contains information that delivers email messages sent to a domain to the correct computer.

Some registrars simply register a domain for a yearly fee; other registrars register the domain and offer additional services, such as Web site hosting and creation or email forwarding. Because registrars often provide different services, the amount that you pay to register a domain differs. Some registrars will provide a free yearly domain name when you use the registrar to host a Web site. When you purchase a domain name, you might choose to purchase it for one year. Some registrars offer discounted annual fees when you purchase a domain for longer than one year. However, ICANN does not permit registrars to sell domain names for longer than a period of 10 years at a time.

When you use a registrar to register a domain, you must provide your contact information. This information is stored in the registry; some registrars offer additional services so that your information is held private in the registry for an additional fee. The domain is registered for you for the duration of the registration term. At the end of the registration term, the domain will expire. Before a domain expires, most registrars will contact the domain name owner using the information that was collected during registration. When the domain expires, you have the choice of renewing it or relinquishing it. Some registrars provide additional services to prevent the loss of a domain name when it expires. If you fail to renew a domain name, the Web site you host at that domain and all email accounts associated with it might be deleted from the Internet. In some cases, another person or organization might purchase the domain and associate it with its Web site, causing you to lose access to your site and all email sent to it.

ICANN maintains a list of accredited registrars on its Web site. When you purchase a domain through an accredited registrar, you are protected by certain legal rights about how your domain name will be registered and protected. ICANN has accredited over 800 registrars that can register a domain name. Some registrars are not accredited directly by ICANN because they are resellers of domain names from accredited registrars. ICANN suggests working with accredited registrars for maximum consumer protection.

In this exercise, you'll use the Internet to learn more about how to register a domain name that you can use for a Web site and email accounts. You will send an email to your instructor summarizing your findings.

1. Start your Web browser, open the Online Companion page at www.cengage.com/internet/np/internet8 and log in to your account, click the Tutorial 2 link, and then click the Reality Check link.

2. Click the ICANN FAQs link and wait while your browser opens the Web page. Read the information on the page to learn more about what it means to register a domain and how to register a domain. In an email message addressed to your instructor, describe how to register a domain.

3. Return to the Online Companion page for Tutorial 2, and then click the Network Solutions Registry Whois link to open the Web page. Read the information provided on this page to learn about the Whois service. In your email message to your instructor, describe the Whois service.

4. Click in the Search text box on the page, enter the domain name **course.com**, make sure the Domain Name option button is selected, and then click the Search button. In your email message to your instructor, note the name of the registrant for this domain and when the domain record expires.

5. Near the bottom of the page, click the Email link in the "by Category" section to open a page that contains information about email hosting services. In your email message to your instructor, describe the features that are provided with email hosting services.

6. Use your browser's Back button to return to the WHOIS page, clear the Search text box if necessary, and then enter your full name, followed by a period and the top-level domain **com** in the Search text box. Make sure that the Domain Name option button is selected, and then click the Search button. Is the domain name available? If not, who owns it and when does it expire? Add this information to your email message to your instructor.

7. Add your full email address to the Cc line of your message and an appropriate subject, and then send the message.

8. Close your Web browser.

Objectives

Session 3.1
- Create a Windows Live ID
- Configure and use Windows Live Hotmail to send, receive, and print email messages
- Create and maintain contacts using Windows Live Contacts
- Explore Windows Live Web-based services

Session 3.2
- Create a Google account
- Configure and use Gmail to send, receive, and print email messages
- Create and maintain contacts using the Gmail Contact Manager
- Explore Google Web-based services

Using Web-Based Services for Communication and Collaboration

Exploring Web-Based Email and File Sharing Sites

Case | Kikukawa Air

Since 1994, Sharon and Don Kikukawa have operated an air charter service in Maui, Hawaii. At first, Kikukawa Air employed only Sharon, who managed the office, reservations, and financial records, and her husband Don, who flew their twin-engine, six-passenger plane between Maui and Oahu. After many successful years, Sharon and Don expanded their business to include scenic tours and charter service to all of the Hawaiian Islands. Kikukawa Air now has six twin-engine planes, two turboprop planes, and a growing staff of more than 30 people.

Because Kikukawa Air has a ticket counter at airports on all of the Hawaiian Islands, many miles now separate the company's employees. Originally, employees used telephone and conference calling to coordinate the business's day-to-day operations, such as schedule changes, new airport procedures, and maintenance requests. Sharon soon realized that these forms of communication were difficult to coordinate with the growing number of busy ground-service agents and pilots. The employees use email to exchange important files as well as files such as pictures from company events. However, they do not have a central place to share and collaborate on files, nor do they all use the same email program.

Sharon asks you to investigate an Internet-based solution for her employees to use Web-based email accounts to exchange email messages and share business documents and other files. She wants you to investigate the different Web-based services for email and other online collaboration services that might benefit Kikukawa Air.

Starting Data Files

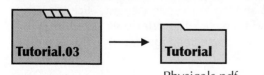

Tutorial.03 → Tutorial

Physicals.pdf

Review

KAir.gif

Cases

Bales.jpg   Maple.jpg   Rocky.jpg
Chance.jpg   Paper.jpg   Scout.jpg
Mangietti.rtf

Session 3.1

Windows Live Hotmail

Tip

If you need to review basic email concepts, read Session 2.1 in Tutorial 2.

Windows Live Hotmail is a Webmail provider from Microsoft that you use to send and receive email. A **Webmail provider** is an Internet Web site that provides free email addresses and other Web-based services, such as online file sharing, to registered users as well as the capability to use any Web browser with Internet access to send and receive email messages. Some Webmail providers also include options to let you use your free email address with an email program such as Windows Live Mail or Thunderbird. To use Windows Live Hotmail, you must use a Web browser to connect to the Windows Live Web site, where you create and sign in to an account to retrieve and send email messages. An email account that you have with a Webmail provider is also called **Webmail** because you access the email account through the Webmail provider's Web site.

The Windows Live service is free, but you must have a way to access it using a Web browser and an existing Internet connection, which someone else might supply for you. Most people who use Windows Live and other Webmail providers have Internet access from their employer, school, public library, or a friend. Many public and school libraries provide free Internet access that you can use to access your Windows Live account. No matter where you are in the world, if you can connect to the Internet, you can access your Windows Live account. This portability makes Webmail a valuable resource for people who travel or do not have a computer or other device on which to send and receive email.

You might wonder how these companies can provide free services such as Webmail—after all, nothing is free. The answer is advertising. When you use a Webmail provider or any Web-based service, you might see advertising, such as a banner ad on the page or links to services sponsored by businesses that pay to display their information on your screen, or insert their information into the email messages you send from your Webmail account. Users must decide whether they are willing to endure this level of advertising in exchange for using the service. Most users of these free services agree that seeing some ads is a small price to pay for the convenience the free services provide.

To begin using Windows Live Hotmail, you need to use your Web browser to connect to the Windows Live Web site. Then you can create a Windows Live ID, which also serves as your Windows Live Hotmail email address, so you can send and receive messages.

Creating a Windows Live ID

The steps in this session assume that you have a Web browser and can connect to the Internet. Before you can use Windows Live Hotmail, you need to create a Windows Live ID. If you have an existing Hotmail email address or a Passport, you can use them as your Windows Live ID.

To create a Windows Live ID:

▶ 1. Start your Web browser, open the Online Companion page at **www.cengage.com/internet/np/internet8** and log in to your account, click the **Tutorial 3** link, click the **Session 3.1** link, and then click the **Windows Live** link. The Windows Live Sign In page opens in your browser. See Figure 3-1.

Windows Live·

One Windows Live ID gets you into **Hotmail**, **Messenger**, **Xbox LIVE** — and other places you see

Hotmail

🔒 Powerful Microsoft technology helps fight spam and improve security.

⚡ Get more done thanks to greater ease and speed.

📁 Enjoy 5 GB of storage that grows when you need it. More cool stuff on the way.

Learn more

Don't have a Windows Live ID?

Sign up

More about Windows Live ID

Privacy Policy

Sign in

Windows Live ID: [   ]
(example555@hotmail.com)

Password: [   ]
Forgot your password?

☑ Remember me on this computer (?)
☐ Remember my password (?)

Sign in

Use enhanced security

[callout: Sign up button]

[callout: if you already have an account, type your Windows Live ID and password here]

[callout: Sign in button (for users with existing Windows Live ID accounts)]

©2009 Microsoft Corporation   About   Privacy   Trademarks   Account | Help Central | Feedba

Trouble? The Windows Live Sign In page and other Windows Live Hotmail pages might change over time. Check the Online Companion page for Tutorial 3 for notes about any differences you might encounter.

Trouble? If you already have a Windows Live ID, Windows Live Hotmail account, Passport, or Messenger account, use the Sign in section to enter your Windows Live ID and password, click the Sign in button, and then skip this set of steps.

▶ 2. Click the **Sign up** button. (If you do not see a Sign up button, Windows Live may have redesigned the Web site. Examine the page carefully until you find the button or tab that lets you create a Windows Live ID or Hotmail account.)

The Create your Windows Live ID page shown in Figure 3-2 opens.

Figure 3-2 **Create your Windows Live ID page**

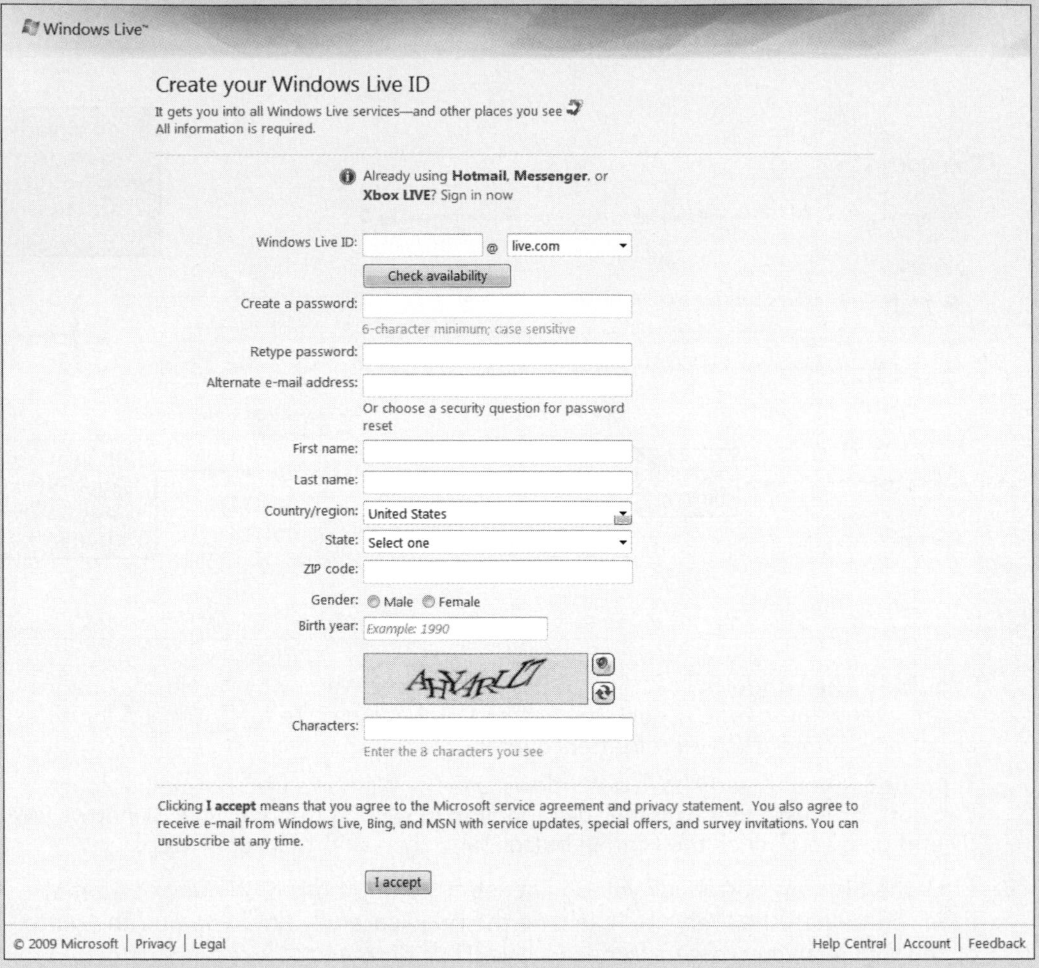

Trouble? The Create your Windows Live ID page might change over time. If your page looks different, follow the on-screen instructions to create a Windows Live account.

The first step in creating a free email account is to create a **Windows Live ID** (Windows Live also calls this a sign-in name, an email address, or a Passport), which you will also use as your Windows Live Hotmail email address. A Windows Live ID can contain letters, numbers, or underscore characters (_), but it cannot contain any spaces. After creating a Windows Live ID, you must create a password containing letters and/or numbers, but no spaces. You type your password twice to ensure that you entered it correctly. Finally, to help remember your password in the event that you forget it, you enter a question and its secret answer so Windows Live can verify your identity in the future, as necessary.

► **3.** Click in the **Windows Live ID** text box, and then type a user name, which you will use in both your Windows Live ID and your Windows Live Hotmail address. Your user name must be unique. You can try your first and last names, separated by an underscore character, followed optionally by your birth date or year of birth, such as sharon_kikukawa0616. A Windows Live ID can contain only letters, numbers, periods, hyphens, and underscores.

Trouble? If you need help creating a user name, click the More about Windows Live ID link on the page to get help. This link appears to the right of the Windows Live ID text box after you click in the Windows Live ID text box.

4. Click the **arrow** on the list box to the right of the Windows Live ID text box, and then click **hotmail.com**. (If the menu closes, click the arrow on the list box to open the menu again.) A message appears above the Windows Live ID text box telling you whether the Windows Live ID you selected is available. If it is not, try a different Windows Live ID until you find one that is available.

   Trouble? If the Windows Live ID you entered is already in use, a menu might open with suggestions for available IDs. Click a suggestion to enter it into the Windows Live ID text box, or type a new Windows Live ID in the Windows Live ID text box.

5. Click in the **Create a password** text box, and then type a password with at least six characters. See Figure 3-3. The most effective passwords are ones that are not easily guessed and that contain letters and numbers. As you type your password, dots or asterisks appear in the Create a password text box to protect your password from being seen by other users. In addition, the Password strength indicator analyzes the password you typed to identify its strength. A weak password is one that contains only letters, such as "pencil." A stronger password includes letters and numbers, such as "pencil87." The strongest password is one that does not form a word and that includes mixed-case letters, numbers, and special characters, such as "p2nc1L%."

Windows Live ID selected ◄ **Figure 3-3**

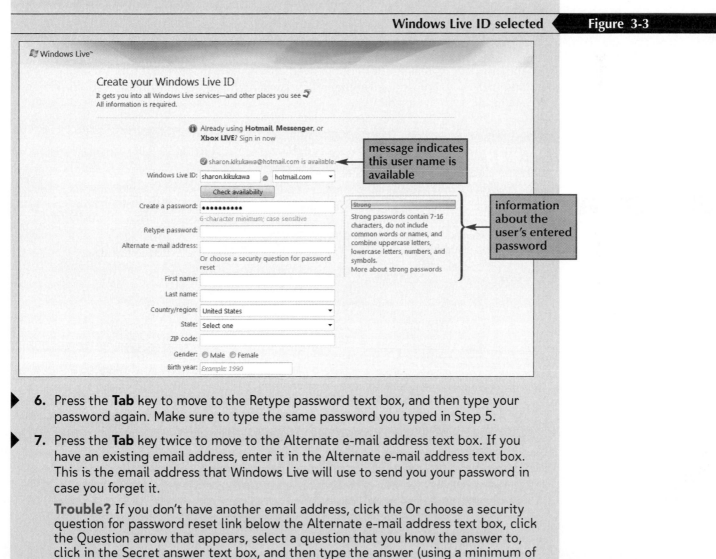

6. Press the **Tab** key to move to the Retype password text box, and then type your password again. Make sure to type the same password you typed in Step 5.

7. Press the **Tab** key twice to move to the Alternate e-mail address text box. If you have an existing email address, enter it in the Alternate e-mail address text box. This is the email address that Windows Live will use to send you your password in case you forget it.

   Trouble? If you don't have another email address, click the Or choose a security question for password reset link below the Alternate e-mail address text box, click the Question arrow that appears, select a question that you know the answer to, click in the Secret answer text box, and then type the answer (using a minimum of five characters) to your question.

Now that you have entered a Windows Live ID and a password, you need to provide your account information.

To enter your account information:

1. Click in the **First name** text box, type your first name, press the **Tab** key to move to the Last name text box, and then type your last name. Your first and last names will appear in all email messages that you send.

2. If necessary, click the **Country/region** arrow, and then click the country or region where you live.

3. If necessary, click the **State** arrow (or **Province** arrow, depending on the country you selected in Step 2), and then click the state or province where you live.

4. If necessary, click in the **ZIP code** (or **Province**) text box, and then type your zip code or postal code. Windows Live will use this information to provide you with additional services, such as local weather forecasts, that you might request in the future.

5. Click the appropriate **option** button in the Gender section to indicate your gender.

6. Click in the **Birth year** text box, and then type the four-digit year of your birth.

The last part of creating a Windows Live ID is to verify that you are a person and not an automated program, and also to read and accept the agreements that govern the use of a Windows Live ID account.

To finish creating a Windows Live ID:

1. Scroll down the page as necessary so you see characters in a box. See Figure 3-4.

Figure 3-4 | **Required character entry to prevent abuse**

the characters you see will differ

Refresh button

Characters:

Enter the 8 characters you see

Clicking **I accept** means that you agree to the Microsoft service agreement and privacy statement. You also agree to receive e-mail from Windows Live, Bing, and MSN with service updates, special offers, and survey invitations. You can unsubscribe at any time.

I accept

© 2009 Microsoft | Privacy | Legal   Help Central | Account | Feedback

Trouble? If you can't read the characters in the box, click the Refresh button to the right of the box to display a different collection of characters.

2. Click in the **Characters** text box, and then type the characters you see in the box. Make sure to type the characters shown in the box on your screen; do not type the characters you see in Figure 3-4. This process ensures that a person is creating a Windows Live ID account, instead of an automated program. This registration check protects Windows Live users from service delays and from receiving junk email messages.

3. Read the agreements, which appear as hyperlinks in the last paragraph on the page. After reading these agreements, click the **I accept** button. Your registration is complete when the page shown in Figure 3-5 (or a similar page) opens.

Windows Live Hotmail Inbox | Figure 3-5

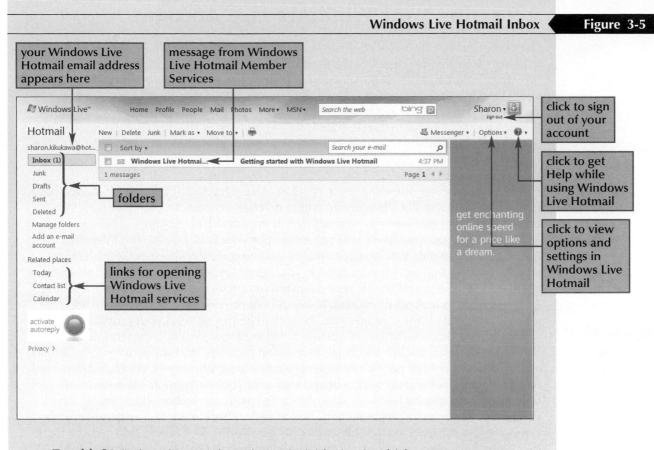

Trouble? Windows Live might redesign its Web site, in which case your screen might not match the one shown in Figure 3-5. If your page indicates that you did not successfully create a Windows Live ID, follow the on-screen instructions to correct any identified problems.

Now that you have created a Windows Live ID, Windows Live opens the Inbox for your Windows Live Hotmail address. So that you can practice signing in to your Windows Live account, you'll sign out. Signing out closes your account and logs you out of the system. You should always sign out of your account when you have finished working so that other users cannot access your email or send messages using your email address.

To sign out of your account:

▶ **1.** In the upper-right corner of the window, click the **sign out** link. The MSN home page (or another page) appears in your browser.

▶ **2.** Return to the Online Companion page for Tutorial 3, and then click the **Windows Live** link. The Windows Live Sign In page opens.

Accessing Your Windows Live Account

Depending on your browser configuration, you might see your Windows Live ID on the Windows Live Sign In page. If you see your Windows Live ID, clicking it opens a text box where you can enter your password and then click the Sign in button to sign into your Windows Live account. If you will be accessing your Windows Live account from your own computer, you might decide to click the Save my password check box to select this option after entering your password, so you don't have to enter it in the future. This option does present some security risk as anyone with access to your computer can sign in to your account because your Windows Live ID and password appear automatically in the Sign In page.

You might also see someone else's Windows Live ID account information on the page; in this case, you can click the Sign in with a different account link to enter your Windows Live ID and password so you can sign in to your own account.

If you forget your password, you can enter your Windows Live ID and then click the Forgot your password? link. The system asks you the question you specified when you created your account so you can provide your secret answer. If you provided an alternate email address, the system sends your password information or instructions for resetting your password to that email address. If you did not provide an alternate email address when you signed up for your account, the system helps you reset your password.

Finally, you can use the Forget me link to tell the browser not to display your Windows Live ID when it loads this page. This option provides the best security for users who access their email from public computers, because your Windows Live ID and password information are never displayed until you sign in to your account. If you select this option, you can specify how you want the computer to remember you. Clicking the Remember me on this computer check box to add a check mark to it remembers your Windows Live ID; clicking the Remember my password check box to add a check mark to it remembers your password. If you clear both check boxes, the computer won't remember your Windows Live ID or your password.

Next, you'll sign in to your Windows Live account and open your Inbox.

Tip

The privacy you expect on the computer you are using to access your Windows Live account should help you decide which sign in method to choose. Always choose the method that provides the most security, so you won't risk having your account accessed by unauthorized users.

To sign in to your Windows Live account:

▶ **1.** If necessary, click your Windows Live ID or enter it as instructed, type your password, and then click the **Sign in** button. A Today page opens and displays your Windows Live account.

   Trouble? If you receive a message that your Windows Live ID or password is not found, clear the Windows Live ID and Password text boxes, and then reenter your information. If you are still having problems, you may have entered your password incorrectly. Click the Forgot your password? link and follow the on-screen directions to retrieve your password, and then try logging in to your Windows Live account again. If you are still having problems, ask your instructor or technical support person for help.

▶ **2.** Click the **Inbox** on the left side of the page to open your Inbox. You might see one new message from Windows Live Hotmail, welcoming you to the service. (You might see other messages, as well.)

   Trouble? If you don't see a message in the Inbox, skip Step 3.

▶ **3.** Click the sender's name to open the message. Depending on your browser's security settings, you might see advertisements when you view your email messages. See Figure 3-6.

Message from Windows Live Hotmail | **Figure 3-6**

Trouble? Your message might look different from the one shown in Figure 3-6. This difference causes no problems.

Figure 3-6 displays the default mail folders for your account. The **Inbox** stores messages you have received, the **Junk folder** stores messages that Windows Live Hotmail thinks are unsolicited, the **Drafts folder** stores messages that you have written but have not sent, the **Sent folder** stores copies of messages that you have sent, and the **Deleted folder** stores messages you have deleted. Clicking a folder opens it and displays its contents.

Figure 3-6 also displays the Today, Contact list, and Calendar links in the Related places section. Clicking the Today link opens the **Today page,** which also opens when you log in to your Windows Live account. It includes the latest information about the day's current events, your mailbox, and appointments that you have scheduled using your calendar. Clicking the Contact list link opens the **Contact list page**, which contains options for managing information about your contacts. Clicking the Calendar link opens the **Calendar page**, which contains options for organizing your scheduled appointments and daily calendar using **Windows Live Calendar**, another Windows Live service. You can click the Options or the Help buttons in the upper-right corner of the page to open pages containing program options and help for Windows Live Hotmail users, respectively.

Now that you have created a Windows Live ID and a Hotmail email address, you are ready to send a message to Don.

Sending a Message Using Windows Live Hotmail

When you use Windows Live Hotmail to send a message with an attached file to Don, you will also send a courtesy copy of the message to your own email address to simulate receiving a message.

Reference Window | **Sending a Message Using Windows Live Hotmail**

- Click the Inbox, and then click the New link.
- In the To text box, type the recipient's email address. To send the message to more than one recipient, separate additional email addresses with commas or semicolons.
- If you need to address the message to Cc and Bcc recipients, click the Show Cc & Bcc link on the right side of the message header, and then type the email address of any Cc or Bcc recipients in the appropriate text boxes. Separate multiple recipients' email addresses with commas or semicolons.
- If necessary, click the Attach link, click File, browse to and select the file to attach, and then click the Open button.
- Click in the message body, and then type your message.
- Check your message for spelling and grammatical errors.
- Click the Send link.

To send a message with an attachment:

▶ **1.** Click the **Inbox**.

▶ **2.** Click the **New** link. The New Message page opens, and the insertion point appears in the To text box in the message header. See Figure 3-7.

Figure 3-7 | Creating a new message

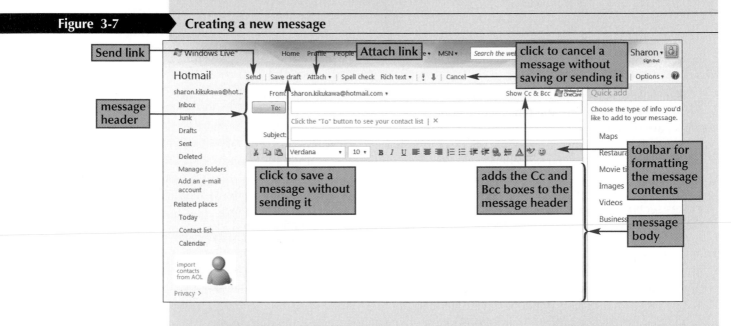

Trouble? Your screen might look slightly different, depending on your computer's operating system, the browser you are using to access your email, and future changes to the Windows Live site. These differences should not affect how Windows Live Hotmail functions.

Trouble? If you don't have the starting Data Files, you need to get them before you can proceed. Your instructor will either give you the Data Files or ask you to obtain them from a specified location (such as a network drive). In either case, make a backup copy of the Data Files before you start so that you will have the original files available in case you need to start over. If you have any questions about the Data Files, see your instructor or technical support person for assistance.

3. In the To text box, type **Don@KikukawaAir.com**.

Trouble? Make sure that you use the address Don@KikukawaAir.com or its lower-case equivalent, don@kikukawaair.com. If you type an email address incorrectly, your message will be returned as undeliverable.

4. In the upper-right corner of the message header, click the **Show Cc & Bcc** link to add the Cc and Bcc text boxes to the message header.

5. Click in the **Cc** text box, and then type your full email address. When you send this message, you and Don will both receive it.

Trouble? If you make a typing mistake on a previous line, use the arrow keys or click the insertion point to return to a previous line so you can correct your mistake. If the arrow keys do not move the insertion point backward or forward in the message header, press Shift +Tab or the Tab key to move backward or forward, respectively.

6. Click in the **Subject** text box, and then type **Physicals memo**.

7. Click the **Attach** link. The Choose File to Upload dialog box opens.

Trouble? If you are using Firefox, click the Attach link, and then click the Browse button that appears below the Subject text box to open the File Upload dialog box, and then continue with Step 8.

8. Browse to the location of your Data Files, double-click the **Tutorial.03** folder, double-click the **Tutorial** folder, click **Physicals**, and then click the **Open** button. The message header now shows the attached file's name and size below the Subject text box.

9. Click in the message display area, type **Dear Don,** (including the comma), and then press the **Enter** key twice to insert a blank line.

10. In the message display area, type **I have attached the memo you requested. Please let me know if you need anything else.**

11. Press the **Enter** key twice, type **Sincerely,** (including the comma), press the **Enter** key, and then type your first name to sign your message. See Figure 3-8.

Tip

As you begin typing your email address, Windows Live Hotmail might open a menu with your complete email address in it. Pressing the Enter key adds the full email address to the Cc text box and closes the menu.

Completed message | **Figure 3-8**

Tip

Even when you use the spell checker to find spelling errors, it is still important to read your message and make any necessary corrections before sending it.

Before sending your message, you can click the Spell check link to check the message for spelling errors. Misspelled words and words not in the dictionary (such as proper names) will appear with a red, wavy underline. When you right-click one of these words, you have the choice of selecting a word from a menu, ignoring the word, or adding it to the dictionary. If you don't see the correct word in the menu, you can correct the misspelled word directly.

▶ **12.** Click the **Spell check** link, review your message for typing or grammatical errors, and if necessary, correct any errors.

Trouble? If you are using Firefox, a dialog box might open and tell you that the browser is checking the spelling automatically. Click the OK button, and then check the message for spelling errors by looking for words with red, wavy lines under them. Make any necessary corrections, and then continue with Step 13.

▶ **13.** Click the **Send** link to mail the message. A message confirmation page opens and shows that your message has been sent. See Figure 3-9.

| Figure 3-9 | Message confirmation page |

Trouble? If you see a message asking you to verify your account, click the verify your account link in the message, enter the characters shown in the Help us fight junk e-mail page that opens, click the Continue button, and then click the Close button. Repeat Step 13 to send the message.

If the email addresses in your message are not already saved in your Contact list, Windows Live Hotmail provides an option for you to add new contacts to your account by selecting the email address and clicking the Add to contacts button. If the contact already exists, you'll see an "Already a contact" note. You will add contacts to your account later, so no action is necessary now.

Receiving and Opening a Message

When you receive new mail, messages that you have not opened are displayed with closed envelope icons, and messages that you have opened are displayed with open envelope icons. You check for new mail next.

To check for incoming mail:

▶ **1.** Click the **Inbox**. The Physicals memo message appears in the Inbox. To read the message, you click it.

▶ **2.** Click the **Physicals memo** message. The message opens and displays the message header and content. See Figure 3-10.

Message received   Figure 3-10

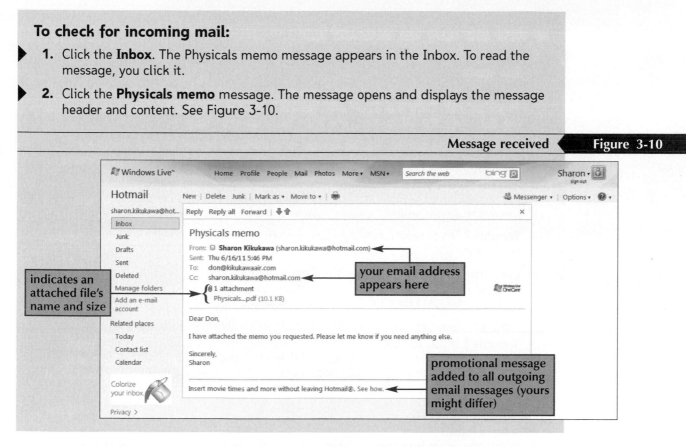

You received your copy of the Physicals memo message that you sent to Don. The filename in the message header indicates that you received an attached file with the message. When you receive a message with one or more attachments, you can open the attachment or save it.

Viewing and Saving an Attached File

You want to make sure that your attached file was sent properly, so you decide to open it. Then you will save the file.

Viewing and Saving an Attached File in Windows Live Hotmail | Reference Window

- In the Inbox, click the message that contains the attachment.
- To open the file using a program on your computer, click the attached file's name in the message header, and then click the Open button in the File Download dialog box (or click the Open with option button and then click the OK button in the dialog box).
- To save the file, click the attached file's name in the message header, click the Save button in the File Download dialog box (or click the Save File option button in the Opening dialog box and then click the OK button), browse to the drive and folder where you want to save the attached file, click the Save button, and then click the Close button.

To view and save the attached file:

▶ 1. Click the **Physicals.pdf** link in the message header. The File Download dialog box opens.

   Trouble? If you are using Firefox, the dialog box that opens is named Opening Physicals.pdf. Click the Open with option button in the Opening Physicals.pdf dialog box, click the OK button, and then continue with Step 3.

▶ 2. Click the **Open** button. Adobe Reader or another program on your computer starts and opens the attached file. If necessary, maximize the program window that opens.

▶ 3. Click the **Close** button on the program window's title bar. Now that you have viewed the attachment, you can save it.

   Trouble? If a Downloads dialog box is open, click the Close button on its title bar to close it.

▶ 4. Click the **Physicals.pdf** link in the Attachment section, click the **Save** button in the File Download dialog box, browse to the drive or folder containing your Data Files, open the **Tutorial.03** folder, open the **Tutorial** folder, click the **Save** button, and then click the **Yes** button to replace the existing file with the same name.

   Trouble? If you are using Firefox, the Opening Physicals.pdf dialog box opens. Click the Save File option button, and then click the OK button. Browse to and select the Tutorial.03\Tutorial folder, click the Save button, click the Yes button to overwrite the existing file with the same name, and then skip Step 5.

   Trouble? If a Downloads dialog box is open, click the Close button on its title bar to close it.

▶ 5. If you are using Internet Explorer, click the **Close** button to close the Download Complete dialog box and return to the message.

When you receive a message with an attached file, you can view and save the attachment for as long as you store the message. When you delete the message, you delete the file attached to the message. When you detach a file from an email message and save it on a disk or drive, it is just like any other file that you save. Be sure to save any important attachments soon after receiving them, so you do not inadvertently delete the messages containing them.

Replying to and Forwarding Messages

Replying to and forwarding messages are common tasks for email users. You can forward any message you receive to one or more email addresses. Similarly, you can respond to the sender of a message quickly and efficiently by replying to a message.

Replying to an Email Message

To reply to a message, click the Reply link to reply only to the sender, or click the Reply all link to reply to the sender and other people who received the original message (those email addresses listed in the To and Cc text boxes). Windows Live Hotmail opens a reply message and places the original sender's address in the To text box; other email addresses that received the original message appear in the To and Cc text boxes as appropriate. You can leave the Subject text box as is or modify it. Most programs, including Windows Live Hotmail, copies the original message and places it in the reply window. Figure 3-11 shows a reply to the Physicals memo message.

Replying to a message | Figure 3-11

recipient's reply

sender's original message

Replying to a Message Using Windows Live Hotmail | Reference Window

- Open the message you want to reply to.
- Click the Reply link to reply only to the sender, or click the Reply all link to reply to the sender and other To and Cc recipients of the original message.
- Type other recipients' email addresses in the message header as needed.
- Change the text in the Subject text box if necessary.
- Edit the message body as necessary.
- Click the Send link.

Forwarding an Email Message

When you forward a message, you are sending a copy of your message, including any attachments, to one or more recipients who were not included in the original message. (If you do not want to forward the original sender's attached file to the new recipients, click the Remove file link for the message.) To forward an existing mail message to another user, open the message you want to forward, and then click the Forward link. A Forward message opens, where you can type the address of the recipient in the To text box. If you want to forward the message to several people, type their addresses, separated by commas, in the To text box (or Cc or Bcc text boxes). Windows Live Hotmail includes the original message in the message display area and adds a blank line above it in which you can add an optional message to provide context for the recipient. Figure 3-12 shows a forwarded copy of the Physicals memo message.

Figure 3-12 ▶ **Forwarding a message**

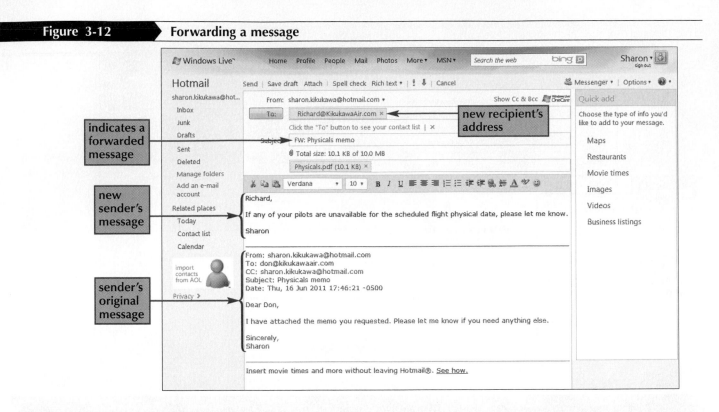

Reference Window | Forwarding an Email Message Using Windows Live Hotmail

- Open the message that you want to forward.
- Click the Forward link.
- Click the To text box, and then type one or more email addresses, separated by commas. Add Cc and Bcc email addresses as necessary.
- Click the blank line above the quoted message, and then type an optional message to add a context for the recipient(s).
- Click the Send link.

Occasionally, you receive important messages, so you want to make sure that you can file and print them as needed.

Filing and Printing an Email Message

You can use the Windows Live Hotmail folders to file your email messages by category. When you file a message, you move it to another folder. You file your message in a new folder named "FAA" for safekeeping. Later, you can create other folders to suit your needs.

To create the new folder:

▶ **1.** Click the **Inbox,** click the **Manage folders** link on the left side of the page, and then click the **New** link. The New folder page opens, and the insertion point appears in the Folder name text box. See Figure 3-13.

Creating a new folder ◄ **Figure 3-13**

▶ **2.** With the insertion point in the Folder name text box, type **FAA.**

▶ **3.** Click the **Save** link. The FAA folder appears in the list of folders.

After you create the FAA folder, you can transfer messages to it. Besides transferring mail from the Inbox, you can select messages in any other folder and then transfer them to a different folder.

To file the Physicals memo message:

▶ **1.** Click the **Inbox**.

▶ **2.** Click the **check box** to the left of the Physicals memo message to add a check mark to it.

▶ **3.** Click the **Move to** link, and then click **FAA** in the list. The message is transferred to the FAA folder.

▶ **4.** Click the **FAA** folder on the left side of the page. The Physicals memo message appears in the FAA folder.

You might want to print certain messages for future reference. You can print a message at any time—when you receive it, before you send it, or after you file it. You print the message next.

To print the email message:

▶ **1.** Click the **Physicals memo** message to open it.

▶ **2.** Click the **Print** button above the message header. A new window opens and displays a "printer-friendly" version of the message, and the Print dialog box opens.

▶ **3.** If necessary, select your printer in the list, and then click the **Print** button (or the **OK** button). The message is printed.

▶ **4.** Close the window with the printer-friendly version of the message, and then click the **Inbox**.

> **Tip**
>
> A printer-friendly version of a message excludes ads and other content on the page, such as links.

When you no longer need a message, you can delete it.

Deleting an Email Message and Folder

When you don't need a message any longer, you can delete it by opening the message or selecting the message in the Inbox, and then clicking the Delete link. You can delete a folder by selecting it and then clicking the Delete link. When you delete a message or folder, you are simply moving it to the Deleted folder. The default setting for Windows Live Hotmail accounts is for the system to periodically delete all messages in the Deleted folder. However, if you want to remove items permanently, you can delete them from the Deleted folder.

| Reference Window | **Deleting an Email Message in Windows Live Hotmail** |

- Open the folder that contains the message you want to delete, click the check box to the left of the message you want to delete to add a check mark to it, and then click the Delete link.
- To delete items permanently, click the Deleted folder on the left side of the page, click the Empty link, and then click the OK button.

To delete the message:

▶ 1. Click the **FAA** folder on the left side of the page.

▶ 2. Click the **check box** that appears to the left of the Physicals memo message to add a check mark to it and select the message.

▶ 3. Click the **Delete** link. The message is deleted from the FAA folder and is moved to the Deleted folder.

▶ 4. Click the **Deleted** folder on the left side of the page. The Physicals memo message appears in the folder.

▶ 5. Click the **check box** to the left of the Physicals memo message to add a check mark to it, and then click the **Delete** link. The Physicals memo message is permanently deleted from your Windows Live Hotmail account.

You delete the FAA folder using the Manage folders link.

| Reference Window | **Deleting a Windows Live Hotmail Folder** |

- Click the Manage folders link on the left side of the page.
- Click the check box to the left of the folder you want to delete.
- Click the Delete link.
- Click the OK button.

To delete the FAA folder:

▶ 1. Click the **Manage folders** link on the left side of the page.

▶ 2. Click the **check box** to the left of the **FAA** folder to select it.

▶ 3. Click the **Delete** link. A dialog box opens and warns that deleting the folder also deletes any messages stored in the folder.

▶ **4.** Click the **OK** button. The FAA folder is deleted.

▶ **5.** Click the **Inbox**.

Maintaining Your Windows Live Contacts

As you use email to communicate with business associates and friends, you might want to save their contact information in **Windows Live Contacts** to make it easier to enter addresses into the header of your email messages.

Adding a Contact to Windows Live Contacts

You can open Windows Live Contacts by clicking the Contact list link on the left side of the page. To create a new contact, click the New link, and then enter the contact's information in the appropriate text boxes.

Adding a Contact to Windows Live Contacts	Reference Window

- Click the Contact list link.
- Click the New link.
- Enter the contact's information in the appropriate text boxes on the Edit contact details page.
- Click the Save link.

Now you can add contacts to Windows Live Contacts. You begin by adding Jenny Mahala's contact information.

To add a contact to Windows Live Contacts:

▶ **1.** On the left side of the page, click the **Contact list** link. The All contacts page opens.

▶ **2.** Click the **New** link. The Edit contact details page opens and displays text boxes for entering a contact's first name, last name, nickname, personal email address, Windows Live ID, and other information. The insertion point appears in the First name text box.

▶ **3.** In the First name text box, type **Jenny**.

▶ **4.** Press the **Tab** key to move the insertion point to the Last name text box, and then type **Mahala** in the Last name text box.

▶ **5.** Press the **Tab** key twice to move the insertion point to the Personal e-mail text box, and then type **Jenny@KikukawaAir.com**. See Figure 3-14.

| Figure 3-14 | Adding a contact to Windows Live Contacts |

6. Click the **Save** link. Jenny's name and email address are stored in Windows Live Contacts.

7. Repeat Steps 2 through 6 to create contacts for the following Kikukawa Air employees:

First name	Last name	Personal email
Zane	Norcia	Zane@KikukawaAir.com
Richard	Forrester	Richard@KikukawaAir.com

8. Click the **Inbox**.

Now that you have stored the names and email addresses for Jenny, Zane, and Richard in Windows Live Contacts, you can click the To, Cc, or Bcc button that appears to the left of a To, Cc, or Bcc text box in a new message, and then click one of their names on the People tab in the Contact list to enter that person's email address in the message header.

Using Windows Live Contacts to Create a Category

You can use Windows Live Contacts to create a group of contacts, called a **category**. Usually, you create a category when you regularly send messages to a specific group of people. For example, Sharon frequently sends messages to Zane, Jenny, and Richard as a group because they have the same positions at the Kikukawa Air ticket counters. She asks you to create a category in Windows Live Contacts so she can type one nickname for the group of email addresses, instead of having to type each address separately.

Creating a Category in Windows Live Contacts | Reference Window

- Click the Contact list link.
- Click the Categories link, and then click New category.
- Type a name for the category in the Name text box.
- In the Members text box, type the contacts you want to include in the category, either by typing names stored in Windows Live Contacts or by typing email addresses. Continue adding contacts to the category until you have entered all of the desired contacts.
- Click the Save link.

To create a category in Windows Live Contacts:

▶ 1. Click the **Contact list** link, click the **Categories link**, and then click **New category**. The New category page opens. The insertion point appears in the Name text box.

▶ 2. In the Name text box, type **Ticket Agents**.

▶ 3. Click in the **Members** text box, and then type **Richard**. As you type Richard's first name, his name appears in a box that opens. Press the **Enter** key to add Richard's name to the category.

▶ 4. With the insertion point in the Members text box, type **Jenny**. When Jenny's name appears in the box, press the **Enter** key to add Jenny's name to the category.

▶ 5. With the insertion point in the Members text box, type **Zane**. When Zane's name appears in the box, press the **Enter** key to add Zane's name to the category. The category contains three contacts. See Figure 3-15.

Tip

To remove a contact from the category, click the "x" on the contact name.

Category added to Windows Live Contacts ◀ Figure 3-15

▶ 6. Click the **Save** link to save the category.

Now, test the category by creating a new message.

To address a message to a category:

▶ 1. Click the **Inbox**, and then click the **New** link.

▶ 2. Click the **To** button to the left of the To text box. A pop-up window opens and displays your individual contacts on the People tab. To see the Ticket Agents category, you need to display the Categories tab.

3. Click the **Categories** tab. The Ticket Agents category appears in the list. The notation "3 people" indicates the number of individual contacts stored in the category.

4. Click the **check box** to the left of the Ticket Agents category to add a check mark to it. The Ticket Agents category name is added to the To text box. The pop-up window stays open until you close it, so you can add additional recipients to the message if necessary.

5. Click the **Close** link on the pop-up window to close it. The Ticket Agents category appears in the To text box.

6. Click the **Show Cc & Bcc** link to add the Cc and Bcc text boxes to the message header.

7. Click the **Cc** button in the message header, click the **People** tab, click the **check box** for your email address, and then click the **Close** link. Your email address is added to the Cc text box. See Figure 3-16.

Tip

Clicking the plus sign to the left of the Ticket Agents category displays the individual email addresses in the category, so you can delete any contact that you do not want to send the message to.

Figure 3-16 | **Using Windows Live Contacts to address a message**

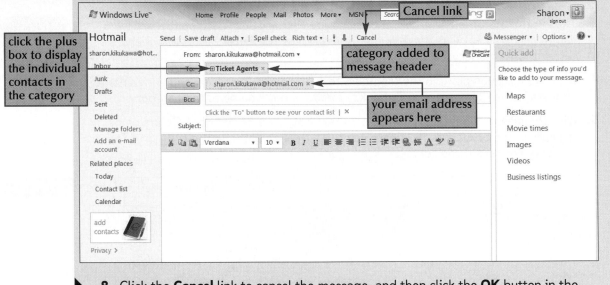

8. Click the **Cancel** link to cancel the message, and then click the **OK** button in the message box asking you to confirm discarding the message. You return to the Inbox.

When you need to modify a category's contacts, you can do so by clicking the Contact list link, clicking the Manage categories link, clicking the category's name, and then using the Edit link to change details about the category, remove individual contacts from the category, or add new contacts to the category. To delete the category (but not the individual contacts), you click the Delete link.

Exploring Other Windows Live Web-Based Services

In addition to a free Hotmail account, Windows Live also provides account holders with other free Web-based services that they can use to create a network of friends or share files and photos, for example. These services might be useful to Kikukawa Air employees, so you decide to explore them next. All of these services are available after you sign in to Windows Live using your Windows Live ID. Because you are already signed in, you won't need to provide your sign in information again.

Managing Your Online Profile

When you create your Windows Live account, your first and last names automatically become part of your profile. You can edit your profile to include as little or as much personal information as you want to share and specify with whom you want to share your information. Your profile might contain information about your favorite books or music, your title or position at your place of employment, your address or email address, your educational background, or general information about your hobbies and interests. Windows Live has built-in controls that let you specify how to display and share your information. Because privacy is an important consideration for Kikukawa Air employees, Sharon asks you to explore the information that employees can post in their profiles and the settings they can use to control who views their profiles.

To view the Profile page and set your account permissions:

▶ **1.** At the top of the page, click the **Profile** link. Your profile page opens.

▶ **2.** On the left side of the page, click the **Details** link. The page shown in Figure 3-17 opens.

Details page for Sharon Kikukawa ◀ Figure 3-17

The default setting for your profile is to share your first name with everyone, which makes it public. By default, your last name is shared only with people you add to your network, unless you change the settings to share it with everyone. You view these settings next.

▶ 3. Below your name, click the **Edit** link. The Edit Profile page opens and displays the first and last names you entered when you created your Windows Live ID. Below the Last name text box, there is a check box that allows everyone to see your last name. If this check box is empty, then only people in your network can see your last name.

▶ 4. Click the **Go to contact info** link to the right of the Last name text box. The Your contact info page opens and displays text boxes for information that you can add to your profile, such as your birth date, home phone, and personal email address. Notice that the "Shared with" link at the top of the page is set to My network, indicating that only people in your network can view this information. Clicking the My network link lets you change the way that other users can access your profile.

▶ 5. Click the **My network** link to open the page that lets you examine the various options and change the way other users access your profile.

▶ 6. Click the **Cancel** button to return to the previous page, and then click the **Cancel** button again. You return to the Details page.

▶ 7. Click some of the links on the page to explore the different information that you can add to your profile. As you explore the site, you can update your information if you would like to do so, but this is not required.

Trouble? Be careful what you post about yourself on the Windows Live or any other Web site. Information posted on Windows Live is public.

▶ 8. Near the top of the page, click the **Profile** link to return to the main page for your profile, and then click the **Permissions** link. The Permissions page shown in Figure 3-18 opens and describes the different permissions available for Windows Live services. Read the information in this page carefully, so you understand how to set the permissions in your Windows Live account. As you explore the different sections, be sure to change your profile settings to provide the level of security that you want.

Windows Live Permissions page **Figure 3-18**

Windows Live™   Home Profile People Mail Photos More▾ MSN▾   Search people or web   bing 🔎   Sharon ▾ 🔲
                                                                                                          sign out

Permissions
Sharon ► Permissions

- Windows Live
- Mail
- Spaces
- **Permissions**

Concerned about privacy and what you're sharing with who? As you get familiar with your new Windows Live profile, here are a few tips:

When you visit your Profile, you see **your view** of **your Profile** - which will always include all of the information you've entered about yourself, and all of your activities.

You decide who is allowed to see each piece of information on your Profile (and when they visit it, they'll only see what you've given them permission to see).

To **manage permissions**, see all of the links below:

Profile details

Name
Choose whether to make your last name public. Permissions

Contact info
Choose who can see your e-mail address, mobile number, and more. Permissions

Profile picture
Choose who can see your profile picture. This is different than your Messenger picture. Permissions

About you
Choose who can see your age, occupation, interests, and more. Permissions

Your network
Choose who can see the people in your network. (Your network includes your Messenger contacts, but no one can see them or other people in your network that you haven't explicitly added to your profile.) Permissions

Personal message
Choose who can see your personal status message. (This also appears in Messenger.) Permissions

Social
Choose who can see your favorite quote, sense of humor, and more. Permissions

Favorite things
Choose who can see your favorite books, music, and movies. Permissions

Work info
Choose who can see what company you work for, your title, and more. Permissions

Education info
Choose who can see your school, major, and more. Permissions

Invitations and Communication preferences

Communication preferences
Choose who can invite you to their network, and if you want to get email notifications when they invite you. Permissions

Notes
Choose who can post and view notes on your profile. Permissions

Photo and file comments
Choose if you want to allow comments on your shared photos and files. Permissions

Blog comments
Choose if you want to allow comments on your blog posts. Permissions

Guestbook comments
Choose whether to allow guestbook comments on your space, and the settings for those comments. Permissions

People tagging
Choose who can tag people in your photos and who can tag you in other people's photos. Permissions

Your stuff

Space
Choose who can see your space (including your blog). Permissions

Photos
Choose who can see the photos in each of your albums. Permissions

Files
Choose who can see the files in each of your folders. Permissions

Shared favorites
Choose who can see the links to web pages you've saved as shared favorites. To start sharing favorites, download the Windows Live Toolbar. Permissions

What's New

What's New with you
Choose which of your activities (like posting photos or adding people to your network) that you want others to see. You can remove individual items and/or remove all future items for each type of activity. Permissions

Web activities
Choose who will see your activities from other web services you can add to your profile like Flickr and Twitter. Permissions

© 2009 Microsoft | Privacy | Terms of use   Code of Conduct | Report Abuse | Account | Feedback

If you choose to use your Windows Live account to connect with friends, family, or business associates, you will receive messages from other users who want to connect to your profile. If you choose to accept messages from only those users who are in your network, you will need to add these people to your Windows Live Contacts and then specify that they can view your online profile. The safest way to make online connections is to restrict access to your profile to only people you know.

Sharing Photos and Files

A popular way of creating online communities, especially among friends, family members, or colleagues who are separated by geographical distances, is to post pictures. Windows Live includes a photo-sharing service and provides a large amount of storage space to upload photos.

| InSight | **Protecting Your Privacy When Sharing Photos** |

When you post photos to your Windows Live account, keep in mind that your photos become public. Don't post anything that you wouldn't want other people to see, even if you restricted who can view your photos. In addition, be careful that photos don't inadvertently disclose more information than you want to share. For example, don't post a picture of yourself standing in front of a geographical marker such as an address or street sign, or post a picture of yourself wearing clothes that identify your school or other information if you do not want to disclose where you live.

Sharon might want to post pictures of company-wide events or pictures of the remodeled terminal in Maui, so she asks you to explore the options for posting photos on Windows Live.

To view the Photos page:

▶ **1.** At the top of the page, click the **Photos** link. The Photos page opens. An indicator on the right side of the page shows how much storage space you have to post photos.

▶ **2.** Click the **Create album** link to open the Create a photo album page. Notice that you can assign a name to the album and change the settings to control how to share the album. The default setting is to share the album with everyone, which makes the album public.

▶ **3.** Click the **Share with** arrow to open a menu and view the other options for sharing information. Notice that you can select several options to restrict who views your album. For example, you might choose to share your album only with people that you select from Windows Live Contacts.

▶ **4.** Click the **Share with** arrow to close the menu.

Sharon might also like to post files, such as Word documents and PowerPoint presentations, in the future. She asks you to explore the file-sharing service provided by Windows. This service is called SkyDrive.

To view the SkyDrive page:

▶ **1.** At the top of the page, click the **More** link, and then click **SkyDrive** in the list. The SkyDrive page shown in Figure 3-19 opens. An indicator on the right side of the page shows how much storage space you have to post files.

SkyDrive page | **Figure 3-19**

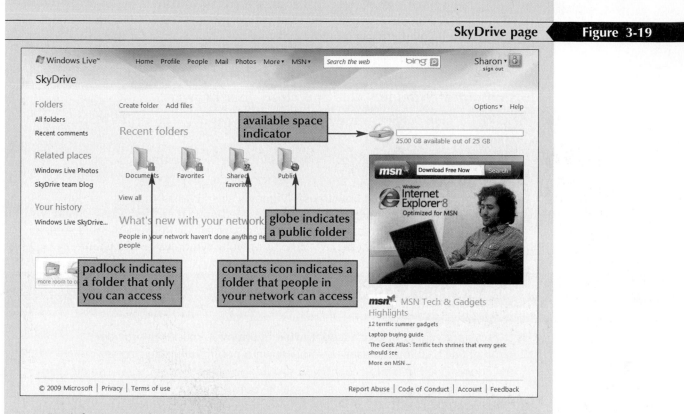

By default, two of the folders, Documents and Favorites, include a padlock in them to indicate that these folders are restricted and that only you can access them initially. The Shared favorites folder includes a contacts icon to indicate that these files are shared only with people you add to your Windows Live network. The Public folder is just that—it is public, and its files are available to anyone who accesses the folder.

2. Click the **Documents** folder, and then click the **Add files** link. The Add files to Documents page opens. You can use the options on this page to upload files from your computer.

After uploading a file to SkyDrive, you can click the file and add comments to it, rename it, or move it into a folder that you create. You can also change the way the file is shared. By default, files are uploaded so that only you can access them. You can change a file's permission by selecting it and then clicking the default permission level.

As with most file-sharing sites, part of the user and terms of service agreements that you must accept when creating a Windows Live account prohibit you from uploading copyrighted material to the Windows Live site without authorization from the copyright's owner. SkyDrive also puts other restrictions on files uploads; for example, you cannot upload a file that is larger than 50 megabytes or a file that has the same name as a file that you already uploaded to SkyDrive.

Signing Out of Your Windows Live Account

You are finished evaluating Windows Live, so you need to sign out of your Windows Live account and close your browser. It is important that you sign out before closing the browser to ensure the security of your email and to prevent unauthorized access. If you do not sign into your Windows Live Hotmail account within 10 days after creating it, or for 270 days at any point after that, Microsoft will inactivate your email address and might delete it. If you do not sign in to your Windows Live account for more than a year, Microsoft will inactivate it and possibly delete it.

To sign out of Windows Live and close your browser:

▶ **1.** Click the **sign out** link near the upper-right corner of the page. The MSN.com home page (or another Web page) opens.

▶ **2.** Click the **Close** button on your browser's title bar to close the browser.

In this session, you learned how to use Windows Live Hotmail to create, send, receive, and manage email messages. You also learned how to create and use Windows Live Contacts to manage information about contacts. Finally, you learned about some of the Windows Live services that are available using your Windows Live account.

Review | **Session 3.1 Quick Check**

1. To set up a Windows Live account, what information must you provide?
2. True or False: If you are using a computer in a public library to access your Windows Live Hotmail account, you should log off your account when you are finished viewing your messages to protect your privacy.
3. When you receive a message with an attachment in Windows Live Hotmail, what two options are available for the attached file?
4. When you delete a message from the Inbox, can you recover it? Why or why not?
5. What information can you store about a person using Windows Live Contacts?
6. What are three types of permissions that you can use to secure files that you upload to Windows Live SkyDrive?

Session 3.2

Tip

If you need to review basic email concepts, read Session 2.1 in Tutorial 2.

Gmail is a Webmail provider from Google that you can use to send and receive email. A **Webmail provider** is an Internet Web site that provides free email addresses and other Web-based services, such as online file sharing, to registered users as well as the capability to use any Web browser with Internet access to send and receive email messages. Some Webmail providers also include options to let you use your free email address with an email program such as Windows Live Mail or Thunderbird. To use Gmail, you must use a Web browser to connect to the Google Web site, where you create and sign in to an account to retrieve and send email messages. An email account that you have with a Webmail provider is also called **Webmail** because you access the email account through the Webmail provider's Web site.

The Gmail service is free, but you must have a way to access it using a Web browser and an existing Internet connection, which someone else might supply for you. Most people who use Gmail and other Webmail providers have Internet access from their employer, school, public library, or a friend. Many public and school libraries provide free Internet access that you can use to access your Gmail account. No matter where you are in the world, if you can connect to the Internet, you can access your Gmail account. This portability makes Webmail a valuable resource for people who travel or do not have a computer or other device to send and receive email with.

You might wonder how these companies can provide free services such as Webmail—after all, nothing is free. The answer is advertising. When you use a Webmail provider or any Web-based service, you might see advertising, such as a banner ad on the page or links to services sponsored by businesses that pay to display their information on your screen, or you might see advertising information inserted into the email messages you send from your Webmail account.

Targeted Advertisements in Gmail | InSight

One of the initial concerns about Gmail was how Google planned to support it. The service is paid for by adding advertisements to email messages based on searches of those messages. Ads are added to the user's messages based on predefined keywords included in the messages. For example, when your email message includes a discussion of meeting friends for Chinese food later, ads for local Chinese restaurants might automatically appear in your message. Although there is no human intervention to produce the advertisements, some users have concerns about the privacy of the email messages they receive because they are scanned and read by computers. Some people do not like the idea of seeing advertisements based on the content of the messages they send and receive because they see it as an invasion of privacy. Gmail has made efforts to make sure that its advertising appears only as targeted text ads. This strategy is different from other Webmail providers that include untargeted advertising in the form of banners and pop-up windows, which some users find to be more invasive. Just like any other free service, it is up to the user to determine the level of advertising they are willing to endure in exchange for the free service provided.

To begin using Gmail, you need to use your Web browser to connect to the Gmail Web site. Then you can create a Google account and a Gmail email address so you can send and receive messages.

Creating a Google Account

The steps in this session assume that you have a Web browser and can connect to the Internet. Before you can use Gmail, you need to create a Google account. If you have an existing Google account or Gmail email address, you can use these user names as your Google account.

To create a Google account:

1. Start your Web browser, open the Online Companion page at **www.cengage.com/internet/np/internet8** and log in to your account, click the **Tutorial 3** link, click the **Session 3.2** link, and then click the **Gmail** link. The Welcome to Gmail page opens in your browser. See Figure 3-20.

Figure 3-20 | **Welcome to Gmail page**

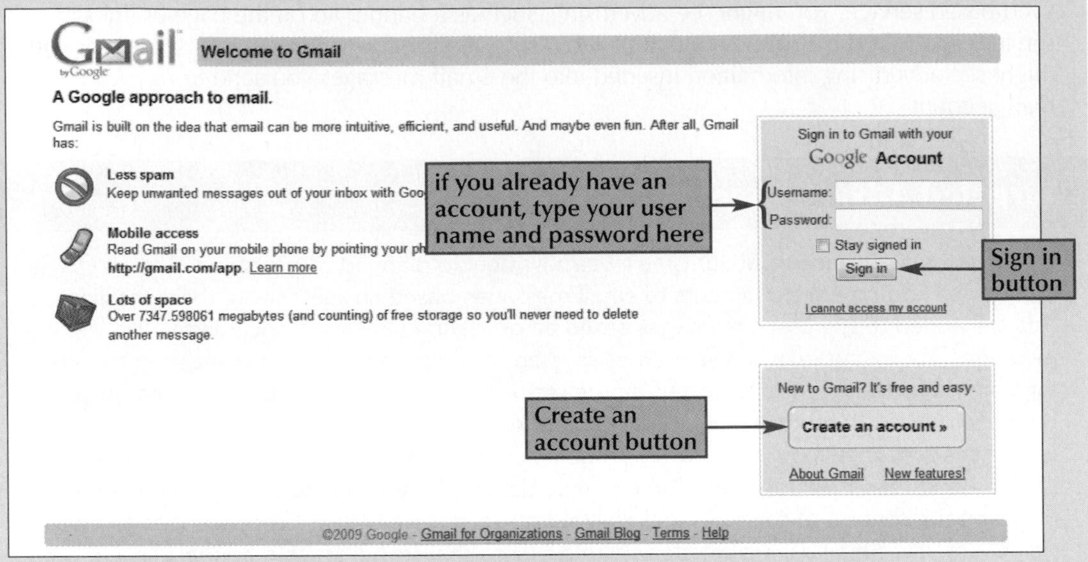

Trouble? The Welcome to Gmail page and other Google pages might change over time. Check the Online Companion page for Tutorial 3 for notes about any differences you might encounter.

Trouble? If you already have a Google account, use the Sign in section to enter your user name and password, click the Sign in button, and then skip this set of steps.

2. Click the **Create an account** button. (If you do not see a Create an account button, Google may have redesigned the Web site. Examine the page carefully until you find the button or tab that lets you create a Gmail or Google account.) The Create a Google Account – Gmail page shown in Figure 3-21 opens.

Figure 3-21 | **Google Account – Gmail page**

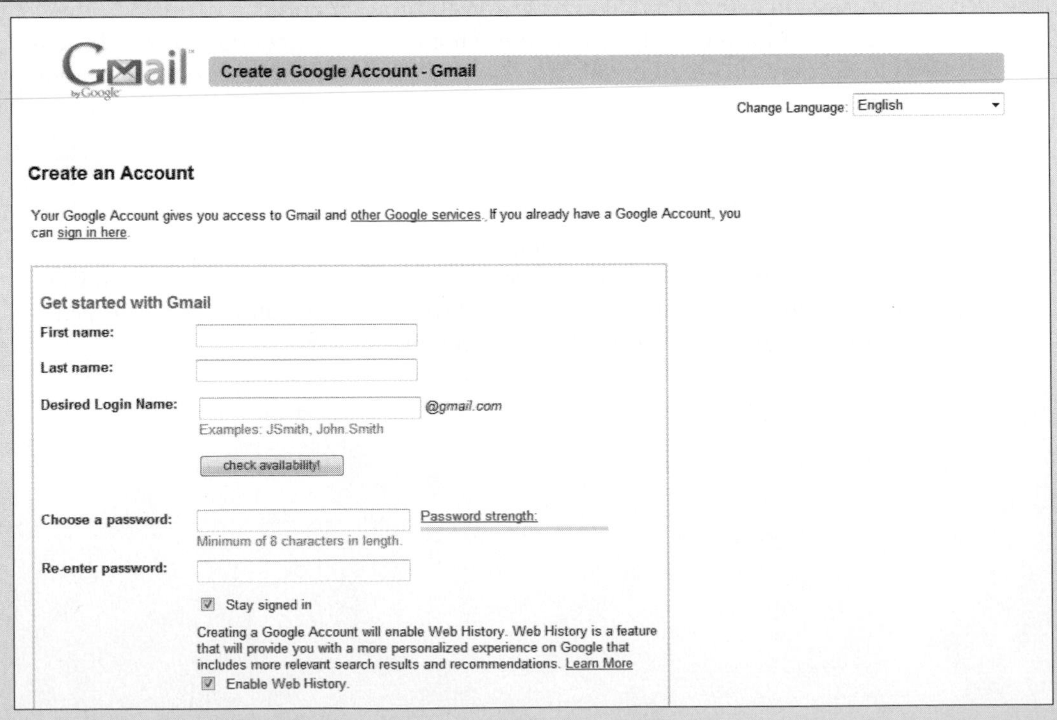

Trouble? The Create a Google Account - Gmail page might change over time. If your page looks different, follow the on-screen instructions to create a Google account.

The first step in creating a free email account is to enter your first and last names, and then to create a Google account login name, which will have the same user name as your email address. A login name can contain letters, numbers, or periods, but it cannot contain any spaces. After selecting a login name, you must create a password containing at least eight characters. You type your password twice to ensure that you entered it correctly. Finally, to help you remember your password in the event that you forget it, you select a security question and answer so Google can verify your identity in the future, if necessary.

▶ 3. Click in the **First name** text box, type your first name, and then press the **Tab** key to move the insertion point to the Last name text box.

▶ 4. In the Last name text box, type your last name, and then press the **Tab** key to move the insertion point to the Desired Login Name text box.

▶ 5. In the Desired Login Name text box, type a user name. Your user name must be unique. You can try your first and last names, separated by a period, followed optionally by your birth date or year of birth, such as sharon.kikukawa0616. Gmail addresses can contain only letters, numbers, and periods.

▶ 6. Click the **check availability!** button. A message appears below the Desired Login Name text box to tell you whether the login name you selected is available. See Figure 3-22.

Figure 3-22	Message that appears when you locate an available login name

Trouble? If you see a message that your login name is not available, select an option in the list that appears and continue with Step 7, or repeat Steps 5 and 6 until you find one.

7. In the Choose a password text box, type a password that has at least eight characters. The most effective passwords are ones that are not easily guessed and that contain letters and numbers. As you type your password, dots or asterisks appear in the Choose a password text box to protect your password from being seen by others. In addition, the Password strength indicator analyzes the password as you type it to identify its strength. A weak password is one that contains only letters, such as "pencil." A stronger password includes letters and numbers, such as "pencil87." The strongest password is one that does not form a word and that includes mixed-case letters, numbers, and special characters, such as "p2nc1L%."

8. Press the **Tab** key to move to the Re-enter password text box, and then type your password again. Make sure to type the same password you typed in Step 7.

Now that you have created a Google login and a password, you need to select a security question and finish creating your account. Google will use the security question and answer you select to identify you if you forget your password. When you create your Google account, the default settings keep you signed in and enable Web history, a feature that tracks your Internet usage to make it easier to return to and track previous searches. You will disable both of these features.

To finish creating your account:

▶ **1.** Click the **Stay signed in** check box to clear it, so that you are not always signed in to your Google account on the computer you are using. You should always sign out of your Google account after you use it, especially when you are working on a public computer.

▶ **2.** Click the **Enable Web History** check box to clear it, so Google will not activate this feature.

▶ **3.** Click the **arrow** on the Security Question text box, and then click a question to which you know the answer.

Trouble? If you'd rather write your own question, click the Write my own question option in the list, and then type the question in the text box that opens.

▶ **4.** Click in the **Answer** text box, and then type the answer to the question you selected or created in Step 3.

▶ **5.** Press the **Tab** key to move the insertion point to the Secondary email text box. If you have an existing email address, enter it in the Secondary email text box. This is the email address that Google will use to send you your account information to in case you forget it.

Trouble? If you don't have another email address, leave the Secondary email text box blank.

▶ **6.** If necessary, click the **arrow** on the Location text box, and then click the country or region where you live.

The last part of creating a Google account is to verify that you are a person and not an automated program and also to read and accept the agreements that govern the use of a Google account.

▶ **7.** Scroll down the page as necessary so you see characters in a box. See Figure 3-23.

Required character entry to prevent abuse | Figure 3-23

Word Verification: Type the characters you see in the picture below.

harmen ← the characters you see will differ

Letters are not case-sensitive

Terms of Service: Please check the Google Account information you've entered above (feel free to change anything you like), and review the Terms of Service below.

With Gmail, you won't see blinking banner ads. Instead, we display ads you might find useful that are relevant to the content of your messages. Learn more

Printable Version

Google Terms of Service

Welcome to Google!

1. Your relationship with Google

By clicking on 'I accept' below you are agreeing to the Terms of Service above and both the Program Policy and the Privacy Policy.

I accept. Create my account.

©2009 Google - Gmail for Organizations - Gmail Blog - Terms - Help

8. Click in the **Word Verification** text box, and then type the characters you see in the box. Make sure to type the characters shown in the box on your screen; do not type the characters you see in Figure 3-23. This process ensures that a person, instead of an automated program, is creating a Google account. This registration check protects Google users from service delays and from receiving junk email messages.

9. Read the terms of service agreement that appears in a text box, and then click the **I accept. Create my account.** button. Your registration is complete when the page shown in Figure 3-24 (or a similar page) opens.

Figure 3-24	Page that opens when you create a Google account

Trouble? Google might redesign its Web site, in which case your screen might not match the one shown in Figure 3-24. If your page indicates that you did not successfully create a Google account, follow the on-screen instructions to correct any identified problems.

Now that you have created a Google account, you can open your Gmail Inbox.

10. Click the **Show me my account** button. Google opens your Inbox and might send you one or more messages to welcome you to Gmail.

So that you can practice signing in to your Google account, you'll sign out. Signing out closes your account and logs you out of the system. You should always sign out of your account when you have finished working so that other users cannot access your email or send messages using your email address.

To sign out of your account:

1. In the upper-right corner of the window, click the **Sign out** link. The Welcome to Gmail page appears in your browser.

Trouble? If you don't see the Welcome to Gmail page, return to the Online Companion for Tutorial 3, and then click the Gmail link in the Session 3.2 section.

Accessing Your Gmail Account

If you will access your Gmail account from your own computer, you might decide to enter your user name and password and then click the Stay signed in check box to select this option so you don't need to enter your account information from this computer in the future. This option does present some security risk because anyone with access to your computer can sign in to your account when your user name and password appear automatically in the Sign in section.

If you forget your user name or password, or experience problems when trying to log in, you can click the I cannot access my account link. Google asks you to select the problem you are having from a list, and then Google helps you solve the problem. Google might ask you the security question you specified when you created your account so you can provide your answer. If you provided an alternate email address, Google sends your account information or instructions for resetting your password to that email address. If you did not provide an alternate email address when you signed up for your account, Google helps you reset your password.

Next, you'll sign in to your Google account and open your Inbox.

Tip

The privacy you expect on the computer you are using to access your Gmail account should help you decide which login method to choose. Always choose the method that provides the most security, so you won't risk having your account accessed by unauthorized users.

To sign in to your Google account:

▶ **1.** If necessary, click in the **Username** text box, and then type your login name.

▶ **2.** Press the **Tab** key, and then type your password in the Password text box.

▶ **3.** If the Stay signed in check box contains a check mark, click the **check box** to clear it.

▶ **4.** Click the **Sign in** button. Gmail opens your Inbox. You might see one or more messages from the Gmail Team, welcoming you to the service. (You might see other messages, as well.)

   Trouble? If your browser opens a dialog box and asks if you want the browser to remember your password, click the No button.

   Trouble? If you receive a message that your user name or password is incorrect, clear the Username and Password text boxes, and then reenter your information. If you are still having problems, you may have entered your password incorrectly. Click the I cannot access my account link and follow the on-screen directions to retrieve your password, and then try logging into your Google account again. If you are still having problems, ask your instructor or technical support person for help.

▶ **5.** Click the sender's name ("Gmail Team") in any new message to open the message. See Figure 3-25.

Figure 3-25 ▶ **Message from the Gmail Team**

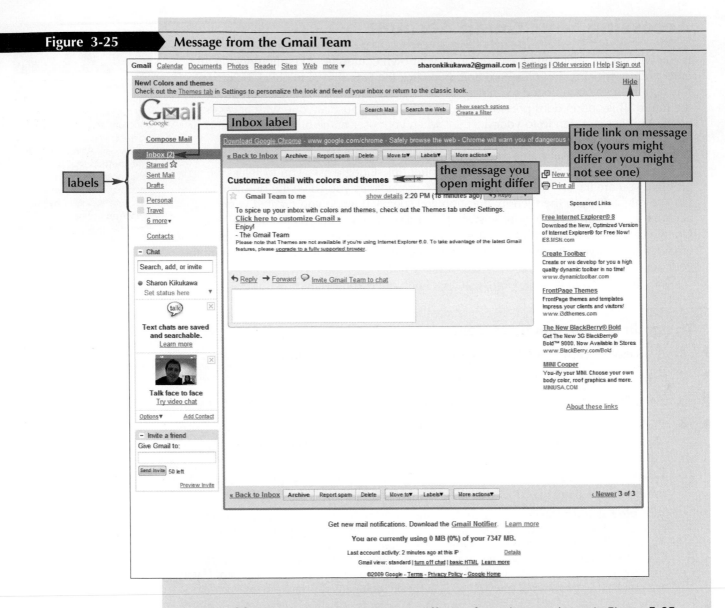

Trouble? Your message might look different from the one shown in Figure 3-25. This difference causes no problems.

Trouble? If you see a message box at the top of the page, like the one shown in Figure 3-25, click the Hide link to remove it.

Figure 3-25 displays the default mail folders, which Gmail calls **labels**, for your account. The **Inbox label** is assigned to messages you have received, and is generally referred to as the Inbox. The **Starred label** is assigned to messages that you have flagged by clicking the star next to the message sender. The **Sent Mail label** is assigned to messages that you have sent, and the **Drafts label** is assigned to messages that you have written but have not yet sent. Two other labels that are common to most email programs and Webmail providers, which store deleted messages and junk email, are visible when you click the "6 more" link. Gmail uses the **Spam label** to mark messages that it identifies as unsolicited, and it uses the **Trash label** to mark messages that you have deleted. You can use the Personal and Travel labels to mark messages that are personal in nature or related to travel. You can click the Contacts link to open the Contact Manager, which is the address book in Gmail. (You will learn more about the Contact Manager later in this session.)

When a number appears in parentheses to the right of a label, the number indicates how many unread or total messages are assigned to that label. Clicking a label displays the messages assigned to the label.

Now that you have opened your Inbox, you are ready to send a message to Don.

Sending a Message Using Gmail

When you use Gmail to send a message with an attached file to Don, you will also send a courtesy copy of the message to your own email address to simulate receiving a message.

Sending a Message Using Gmail | Reference Window

- Click the Compose Mail link on the left side of the screen.
- In the To text box, type the recipient's email address. To send the message to more than one recipient, separate additional email addresses with commas or semicolons.
- If you need to address the message to Cc and Bcc recipients, click the Add Cc and Add Bcc links below the To text box as necessary, and then type the email address of any Cc or Bcc recipients in the appropriate text boxes. Separate multiple recipients' email addresses with commas or semicolons.
- If necessary, click the Attach a file link, browse to and select the file to attach, and then click the Open button.
- Click in the message body, and type your message.
- Check your message for spelling and grammatical errors.
- Click the Send button.

To send a message with an attachment:

▶ **1.** Click the **Compose Mail** link on the left side of the screen, below the Gmail logo. The Compose Mail page opens. See Figure 3-26.

Figure 3-26 **Compose Mail page**

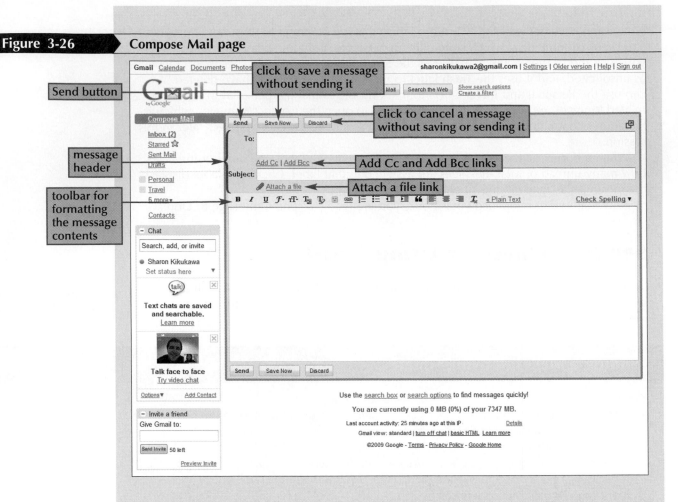

Trouble? Your screen might look slightly different, depending on your computer's operating system, the browser you are using to access your email, and future changes to the Gmail site. These differences should not affect how Gmail functions.

Trouble? If you don't have the starting Data Files, you need to get them before you can proceed. Your instructor will either give you the Data Files or ask you to obtain them from a specified location (such as a network drive). In either case, make a backup copy of the Data Files before you start so that you will have the original files available in case you need to start over. If you have any questions about the Data Files, see your instructor or technical support person for assistance.

2. In the To text box, type **Don@KikukawaAir.com**.

   Trouble? Make sure that you use the address Don@KikukawaAir.com or its lower-case equivalent, don@kikukawaair.com. If you type an email address incorrectly, your message will be returned as undeliverable.

3. Below the To text box, click the **Add Cc** link to add the Cc text box to the message header.

4. In the Cc text box, type your full email address. When you send this message, you and Don will both receive it.

   Trouble? If you make a typing mistake on a previous line, use the arrow keys or click the insertion point to return to a previous line so you can correct your mistake. If the arrow keys do not move the insertion point backward or forward in the message header, press Shift +Tab or the Tab key to move backward or forward, respectively.

Tip

As you begin typing your email address, Gmail might open a menu with your complete email address in it. Pressing the Enter key adds the full email address to the Cc text box and closes the menu.

5. Click in the **Subject** text box, and then type **Physicals memo**.

6. Click the **Attach a file** link. The Select file(s) to upload by mail.google.com dialog box opens.

   Trouble? If you are using Firefox, click the Browse button that appears below the Subject text box to open the File Upload dialog box, and then continue with Step 7.

7. Browse to the location of your Data Files, double-click the **Tutorial.03** folder, double-click the **Tutorial** folder, click **Physicals**, and then click the **Open** button. The message header now shows the attached file's name and size below the Subject text box.

8. Click in the message display area, type **Dear Don,** (including the comma), and then press the **Enter** key twice to insert a blank line.

9. In the message display area, type **I have attached the memo you requested. Please let me know if you need anything else.**

10. Press the **Enter** key twice, type **Sincerely,** (including the comma), press the **Enter** key, and then type your first name to sign your message. See Figure 3-27.

Completed message ◄ Figure 3-27

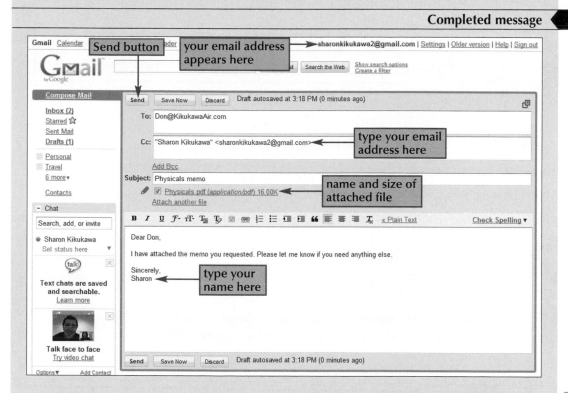

Before sending your message, you can click the Check Spelling link to check the message for spelling errors. Misspelled words and words not in the dictionary (such as proper names) will appear with a yellow highlight. To correct spelling errors, click the highlighted word, and then click the correct word in the menu that opens, or type the correction directly. Click the Recheck link if necessary to check your message for spelling errors again. When you are finished, click the Done link.

11. Click the **Check Spelling** link, review your message for typing or grammatical errors, and if necessary, correct any errors. Click the **Done** link when you are finished.

Tip

Even when you use the spell checker to find spelling errors, it is still important to read your message and make any necessary corrections before sending it.

> **12.** Click the **Send** button to mail the message. A confirmation message opens at the top of the Inbox indicating that your message has been sent. Depending on the speed of your Internet connection, you might also see the copy of the message you sent to yourself in your Inbox, with the sender name "me." See Figure 3-28.

| Figure 3-28 | Message sent |

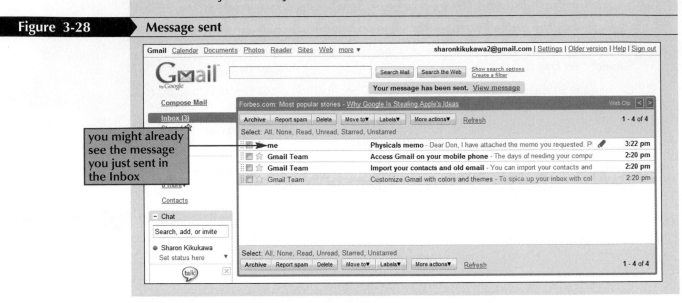

Receiving and Opening a Message

When you receive new mail, messages that you have not opened are displayed in bold, and messages that you have opened are displayed in regular font. You check for new mail next.

To check for incoming mail:

> **1.** Click the **Inbox**. The Physicals memo message appears in the Inbox. To read the message, you click it.

> **2.** Click the **Physicals memo** message. The message opens and displays part of the message header and the message content. See Figure 3-29.

Message opened in Gmail ◀ **Figure 3-29**

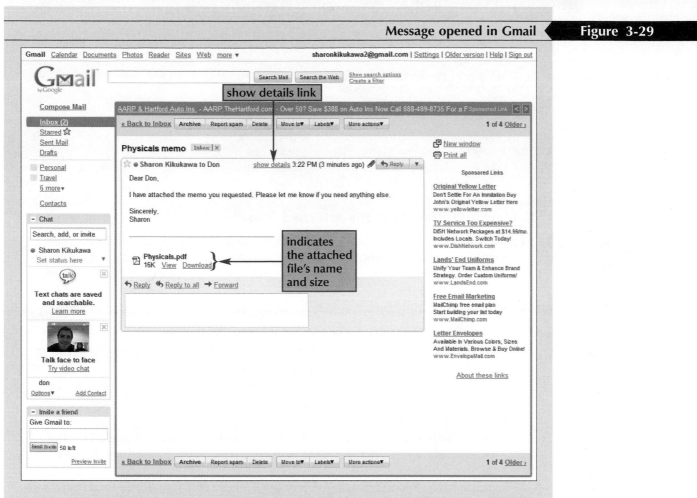

By default, Gmail hides most of the message header. You can view the full message header by clicking the show details link.

▶ **3.** Click the **show details** link. Gmail displays the message sender and email address, the message recipient and email address, the Cc message recipient and email address, the date and time the message was sent, the message subject, and the service that mailed the message (in this case, gmail.com).

▶ **4.** Click the **hide details** link to hide most of the message header.

You received your copy of the Physicals memo message that you sent to Don. The filename at the bottom of the message body indicates that you received an attached file with the message. When you receive a message with one or more attachments, you can view the attachment or download (save) it.

Viewing and Downloading an Attached File

You want to make sure that your attached file was sent properly, so you decide to view it. Then you will download the file and save it with your Data Files.

Reference Window | **Viewing and Downloading an Attached File in Gmail**

- In the Inbox, click the subject for the message that contains the attachment to open the message.
- To open the file, click the View link for the attached file. Google Docs opens a viewer for the file based on its file extension and displays the document. Click the Close button in the window that displays the document to close it.
- To download the file, click the Download link for the attached file, click the Save button in the File Download dialog box, browse to the drive and folder where you want to save the attached file, click the Save button, and then click the Close button.

Tip

You can also download the attachment by clicking the Download link at the top of the window that opened the viewer.

To view and download the attached file:

▶ 1. Click the **View** link for the Physicals.pdf file. Google Docs opens a new browser window and starts a program that can open and display the attachment. When an attachment contains multiple pages, you can use the pane on the right to scroll through the pages.

▶ 2. Click the **Close** button on the title bar or tab for the browser window that opened. Now that you have viewed the attachment, you can download it.

▶ 3. Click the **Download** link for the Physicals.pdf file, click the **Save** button in the File Download dialog box, browse to the drive or folder containing your Data Files, open the **Tutorial.03** folder, open the **Tutorial** folder, click the **Save** button, and then click the **Yes** button to replace the existing file with the same name.

   Trouble? If you are using Firefox, the Opening Physicals.pdf dialog box opens. Click the Save File option button, click the OK button, browse to and select the Tutorial.03/Tutorial folder, click the Save button, click the Yes button, and then skip Step 4.

   Trouble? If a Downloads dialog box is open, click the Close button on its title bar to close it.

▶ 4. If you are using Internet Explorer, click the **Close** button in the Download complete dialog box.

When you receive a message with an attached file, you can view and download the attachment for as long as you store the message. When you delete the message, you delete the file attached to the message. When you detach a file from an email message and save it on a disk or drive, it is just like any other file that you save. Be sure to download any important attachments soon after receiving them, so you do not inadvertently delete the messages containing them.

Replying to and Forwarding Messages

Replying to and forwarding messages are common tasks for email users. You can forward any message you receive to one or more email addresses. Similarly, you can respond to the sender of a message quickly and efficiently by replying to a message.

Replying to an Email Message

To reply to a message, click the Reply link at the bottom of the message body to reply only to the sender, or click the Reply to all link to reply to the sender and other people who received the original message (those email addresses listed in the To and Cc text boxes). Gmail opens a reply message below the original message and places the original sender's address in the To text box; other email addresses that received the original message appear in the To and Cc text boxes as appropriate. You can edit the message subject by clicking the Edit Subject link, and you can edit or add Cc and Bcc recipients by clicking the Add Cc and Add Bcc links. Figure 3-30 shows a reply to the Physicals memo message.

Replying to a message   Figure 3-30

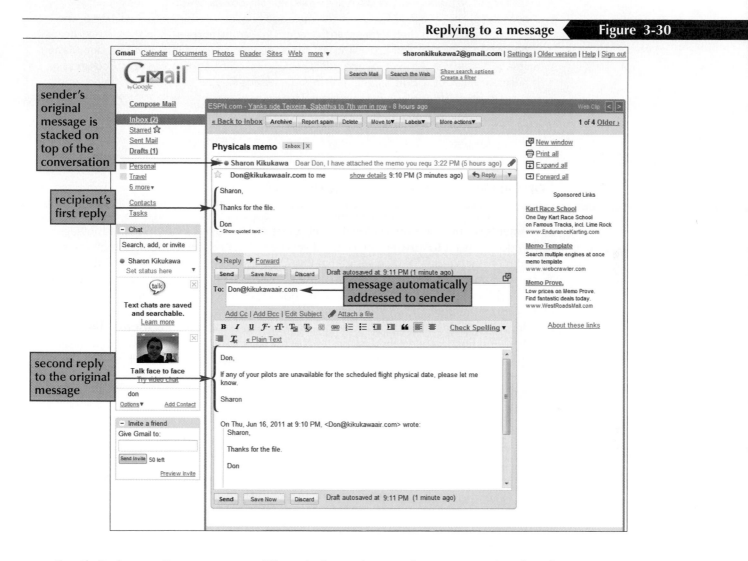

Gmail displays replies to messages differently from other email programs and Webmail providers. When you receive an email message, it appears in your Inbox on a single line. If you reply to the original message, the reply is appended to the bottom of the original message. As you send messages back and forth with the original sender, each subsequent reply from the original sender or from you is stacked with the original message. In Gmail, this organization of messages is called a **conversation**, or a **thread**. Instead of needing to find and open multiple messages from different recipients, all of the messages related to a single original message are stacked on top of each other. To expand one of the previous replies, click the sender's name.

Reference Window | **Replying to a Message Using Gmail**

- Open the message you want to reply to.
- Click the Reply link at the bottom of the message body to reply only to the sender, or click the Reply to all link to reply to the sender and other To and Cc recipients of the original message.
- Type other recipients' email addresses in the To text box as needed.
- If necessary, click the Add Cc link in the message header to add the Cc text box to the message header, and then type other Cc recipients' email addresses in the Cc text box.
- If necessary, click the Add Bcc link in the message header to add the Bcc text box to the message header, and then type other Bcc recipients' email addresses in the Bcc text box.
- If necessary, click the Edit Subject link in the message header to open the Subject text box so you can edit the original message subject.
- Edit the message body as necessary.
- Click the Send button.

Forwarding an Email Message

When you forward a message, you are sending a copy of your message, including any attachments, to one or more recipients who were not included in the original message. (If you do not want to forward the original sender's attached file to the new recipients, click the check box next to the attachment to clear the check box and remove the file.) To forward an existing mail message to another user, open the message you want to forward, and then click the Forward link at the bottom of the message body. Type the address of the recipient in the To text box. If you want to forward the message to several people, type their addresses, separated by commas, in the To text box (or use the Add Cc and Add Bcc links to open the Cc and Bcc text boxes). Gmail stacks the original message on top of the new message. Figure 3-31 shows a forwarded copy of the Physicals memo message, along with the stacked conversations since the original message.

Forwarding a message | Figure 3-31

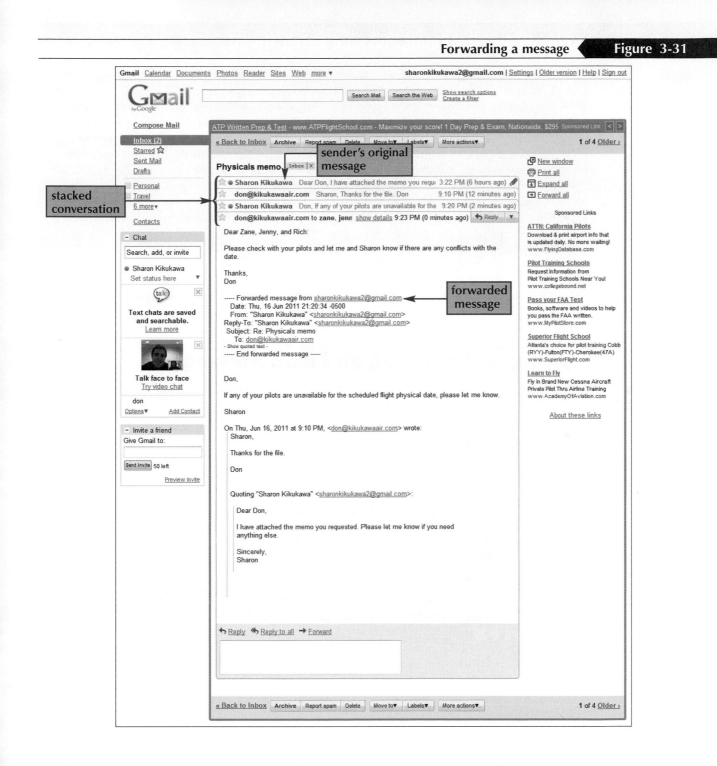

Forwarding an Email Message Using Gmail

- Open the message that you want to forward.
- Click the Forward link at the bottom of the message body.
- Click the To text box, and then type one or more email addresses, separated by commas.
- If necessary, click the Add Cc link in the message header to add the Cc text box to the message header, and then type other Cc recipients' email addresses in the Cc text box.
- If necessary, click the Add Bcc link in the message header to add the Bcc text box to the message header, and then type other Bcc recipients' email addresses in the Bcc text box.
- If necessary, click the Edit Subject link in the message header to open the Subject text box so you can edit the original message subject.
- Click in the message body of the message you are forwarding, and then type an optional message to add a context for the recipient(s).
- Click the Send button.

Occasionally, you receive important messages, so you want to make sure that you can file and print them as needed.

Filing and Printing an Email Message

You can use Gmail to file your email messages by category by using the default Gmail labels or labels that you create. Instead of moving a message into a folder, you apply a label to the message. You assign your message to a new label named "FAA" for safekeeping. Later, you can create other labels to suit your needs.

To create the new label:

1. Click the **Inbox** on the left side of the screen.

2. In the upper-right corner of the Gmail page, click the **Settings** link. The Settings page opens.

3. Click the **Labels** link on the Settings page.

4. Scroll down the page as necessary so you can see the Labels section, click in the text box that contains the text "Create a new label," and then type **FAA**. See Figure 3-32.

Creating a new label | Figure 3-32

5. Click the **Create** button. The FAA label is created and appears in the Labels section on the Settings page, and also on the left side of the screen in the list of labels.

After you create the FAA label, you can apply it to messages. When you need to see all messages for a label, you click the label on the left side of the screen.

To apply the FAA label to the Physicals memo message:

1. Click the **Inbox**.

2. Click the **check box** to the left of the Physicals memo message to add a check mark to it.

3. Click the **Labels** button, click the **check box** to the left of the FAA label, and then click **Apply**. The message is assigned to the FAA label. See Figure 3-33.

Trouble? If you click the label name instead of the check box, you won't need to click the Apply command because the menu will close automatically. Continue with Step 4.

Figure 3-33 FAA label assigned to Physicals memo message

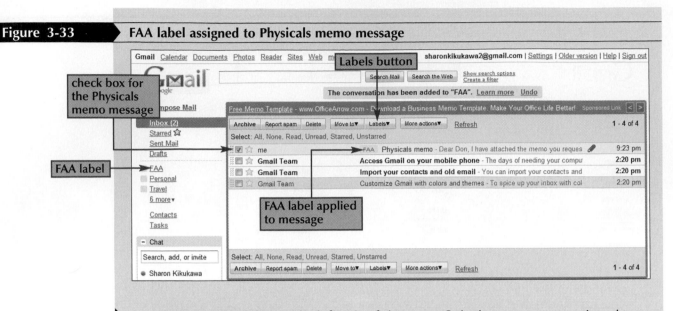

4. Click the **FAA** label on the left side of the page. Only those messages assigned to the FAA label appear in the list.

You might want to print certain messages for future reference. You can print a message at any time—when you receive it, before you send it, or after you file it. You print the message next.

To print the email message:

1. Click the **Physicals memo** message to open it.

2. Click the **Print all** link on the right side of the window. A new browser window or tab opens and displays a "printer-friendly" version of the message, and the Print dialog box opens.

3. If necessary, select your printer in the list, and then click the **Print** button (or the **OK** button). The message is printed.

4. Close the browser window or tab with the printer-friendly version of the message, and then click the **Inbox**.

Tip

A printer-friendly version of a message excludes ads and other content on the page, such as links.

When you no longer need a message, you can delete it.

Deleting an Email Message and Label

When you don't need a message any longer, you can delete it by selecting the check box to the left of the message in the Inbox, and then clicking the Delete button. You can delete a label by clicking the Settings link, clicking the Labels link, and then clicking the remove link for the label. When you delete a message or label, you are marking it with the Trash label. The default setting for Gmail accounts is for the system to delete all messages marked with the Trash label after 30 days. However, if you want to delete items permanently and right away, you can delete messages marked with the Trash label manually.

Deleting an Email Message in Gmail | Reference Window

- Click the label for the message in the list of labels on the left side of the screen, click the check box to the left of the message that you want to delete to add a check mark to it, and then click the Delete button.
- To delete items permanently, click the Trash label, click the check box to the left of the message you want to delete to add a check mark to it, and then click Delete forever.

To delete the message:

▶ 1. Click the **FAA** label in the list of labels on the left side of the screen.

▶ 2. If necessary, click the **check box** to the left of the Physicals memo message to add a check mark to it and select the message.

▶ 3. Click the **Delete** button. The message is marked with the Trash label.

▶ 4. Click the **6 more** link on the left side of the page, and then click **Trash** in the menu that opens. The Trash page opens and displays the Physicals memo message.

   Trouble? If you or another user has customized Gmail, the "6 more" link name might contain a different number. Click the link you see to open the menu that contains the Trash label.

▶ 5. Click the **check box** to the left of the Physicals memo message to add a check mark to it, and then click the **Delete forever** button. The Physicals memo message is deleted permanently from your Gmail account.

You delete the FAA label by using the Settings link to access the Labels page.

Deleting a Label | Reference Window

- Click the Settings link near the top of the Gmail page.
- Click the Labels link.
- Scroll down the page as necessary, and click the remove link for the label you want to delete.
- Click the OK button.

To delete the FAA label:

▶ 1. Click the **Settings** link near the top of the Gmail page.

▶ 2. Click the **Labels** link.

▶ 3. If necessary, scroll down the page so you can see the FAA label, and then click the **remove** link for the FAA label. A dialog box opens asking you to confirm deleting the label from any conversations and deleting the label.

▶ 4. Click the **OK** button. The FAA label is deleted.

▶ 5. Click the **Inbox**.

InSight | **Gmail's Free Storage Space**

When Google launched the test program for Gmail, it received a lot of publicity from the media. At the time, other Webmail providers such as Yahoo! and MSN Hotmail (now Windows Live Hotmail) had been gradually reducing the free storage space allotted to individual subscribers for email messages from 50 megabytes to two to four megabytes in favor of "premium" services that included additional features and storage capacity for a monthly fee. After Gmail began testing its free Webmail service, which at the time promised more than two gigabytes of storage space for every user, other Webmail providers had to change their offerings quickly to avoid losing their subscribers. With substantial storage space, you can save virtually every message you receive—in fact, Google actually encourages you to do so. Because Google performs routine maintenance on its servers, such as backups and archives, your messages might be stored forever in these files. Even if you delete your messages, they still might exist in these files, making your private messages part of a permanent archive. This same scenario applies to most Webmail accounts, regardless of the provider.

Maintaining Your Gmail Contacts

As you use email to communicate with business associates and friends, you might want to save their contact information in the **Contact Manager** to make it easier to enter addresses into the header of your email messages.

Adding a Contact to the Contact Manager

You can open the Contact Manager by clicking the Contacts link on the left side of the screen. To create a new contact, click the New Contact button, and then use the text boxes to enter the contact's information.

Reference Window | **Adding a Contact to the Contact Manager**

- On the left side of the screen, click the Contacts link.
- Click the New Contact button.
- Enter the contact's information in the appropriate text boxes.
- Click the Save button.

You will begin by adding Jenny Mahala's contact information to the Contact Manager.

To add a contact to the Contact Manager:

▶ 1. On the left side of the screen, click the **Contacts** link. The Contact Manager opens.

▶ 2. In the upper-left corner of the Contact Manager, click the **New Contact** button (the button has one person on it to represent an individual contact). The page displays text boxes for entering a contact's name, title, company, email address, and other information.

▶ 3. Click the **Name** text box, and then type **Jenny Mahala**.

Tip

To add additional email addresses for a contact, click the "add" link above the Email text box.

▶ **4.** Click in the **Email** text box, and then type **Jenny@KikukawaAir.com**. As you are typing the email address, the background color of the text box changes color to red. When you have entered an email address in the correct format (username@domainname.com), the background color of the text box changes color back to white. See Figure 3-34.

Adding a contact to the Contact Manager ◀ Figure 3-34

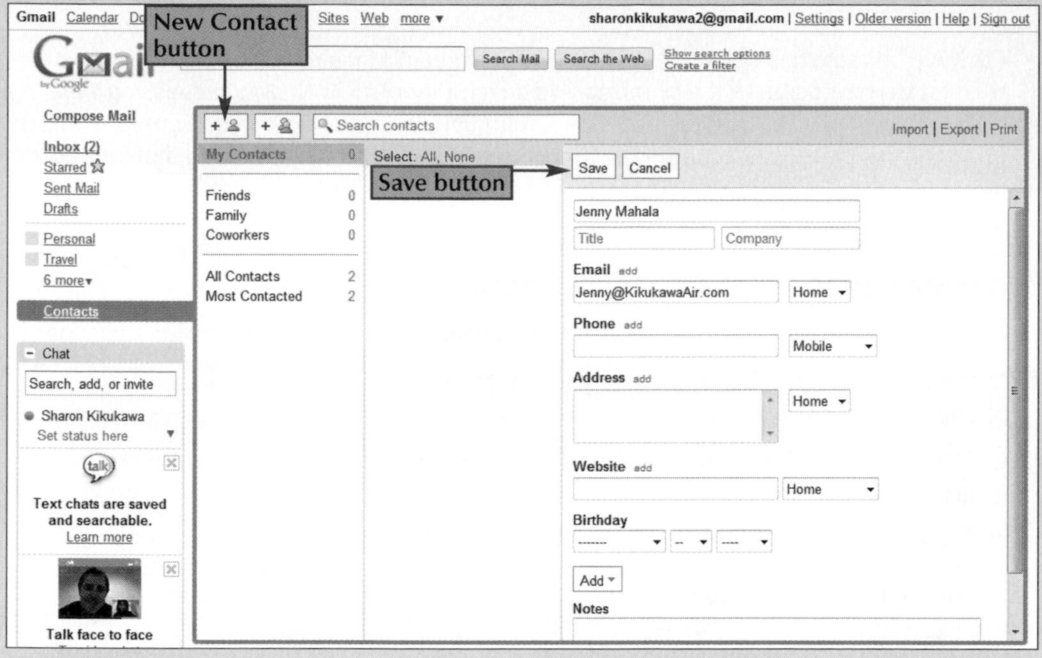

▶ **5.** Click the **Save** button. Jenny's name and email address are stored in the Contact Manager.

▶ **6.** Repeat Steps 2 through 5 to create contacts for the following Kikukawa Air employees:

Name	Email
Zane Norcia	Zane@KikukawaAir.com
Richard Forrester	Richard@KikukawaAir.com

▶ **7.** Click the **Inbox** on the left side of the screen.

Now that you have stored the names and email addresses for Jenny, Zane, and Richard in the Contact Manager, you can address a new message to a contact by displaying the contact in the Contact Manager, and then clicking the contact's email address. Or, just start typing the contact's name in the To text box of a new message to display the contact's email address in a list, where you can select it to enter it into the text box.

Using the Contact Manager to Create a Group

You can use the Contact Manager to create a group of contacts. Usually, you create a group when you regularly send messages to a specific group of people. For example, Sharon frequently sends messages to Zane, Jenny, and Richard as a group because they have the same positions at the Kikukawa Air ticket counters. She asks you to create a group in the Contact Manager so she can use the group to address her messages, instead of having to type each contact separately.

Reference Window | **Creating a Group in the Contact Manager**

- On the left side of the screen, click the Contacts link.
- In the Contact Manager, make sure that none of the check boxes for your contacts contain a check mark.
- Click the New Group button. If necessary, click the Information Bar and select the option to temporarily allow scripted windows.
- Type the group's name in the What would you like to name this group? text box, and then click the OK button.
- Click All Contacts to display the contacts in the Contact Manager. Click the check box for the first person to add to the group to add a check mark to it. Continue checking the check boxes for the people to add to the group until you've selected each group member.
- Click the Groups button, and then click the group name to add the selected people to.

To create a group in the Contact Manager:

▶ **1.** On the left side of the screen, click the **Contacts** link. The Contact Manager opens.

▶ **2.** If any of the check boxes next to your contacts contain check marks, click the check boxes to clear them.

▶ **3.** Click the **New Group** button. A dialog box opens and asks you to enter the group name.

Trouble? If you are using Internet Explorer, the Information Bar might open and display a message about the Web site using a scripted window. Right-click the Information Bar, click Temporarily Allow Scripted Windows, and then repeat Step 3.

▶ **4.** In the dialog box, type **Ticket Agents**, and then click the **OK** button. The Ticket Agents group is created. Next, you add contacts to it.

▶ **5.** Click the **All Contacts** link to display your Gmail contacts.

▶ **6.** Click the **check boxes** for Jenny Mahala, Richard Forrester, and Zane Norcia to add check marks to them, which also selects them for the group. See Figure 3-35.

Figure 3-35 | Selecting the members for a group

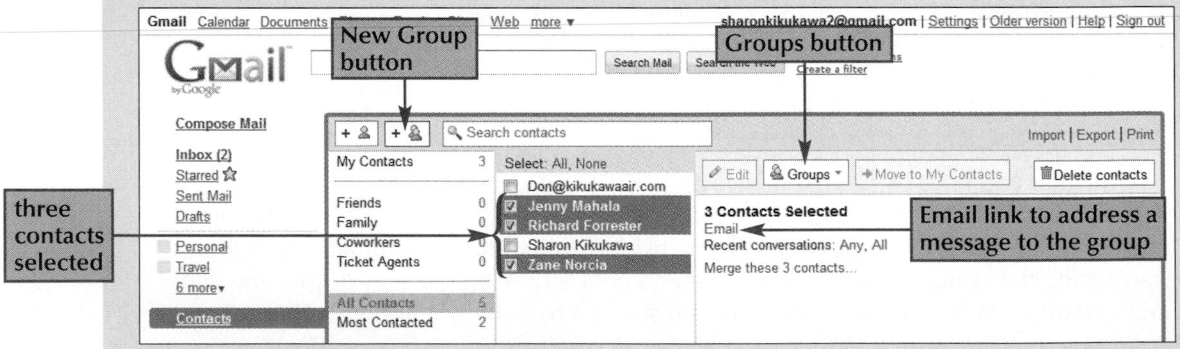

▶ **7.** Click the **Groups** button to open a list of options for the group.

▶ **8.** In the list, click **Ticket Agents**. A message appears and tells you that the three selected contacts have been added to the Ticket Agents group.

Now, test the group by creating a new message. In Gmail, you address messages to a group by clicking the Email link for the group in the Contact Manager, or by typing the group name in the To text box of a new message. Because the Contact Manager is already open, you'll use the first method.

▶ **9.** With the Ticket Agents group displayed in the Contact Manager, click the **Email** link (see Figure 3-35). A new message opens in the Compose Mail page, and the names and email addresses for the three contacts in the group appear in the To text box.

▶ **10.** Click the **Discard** button to cancel the message. Gmail displays the Inbox.

When you need to modify a group's members, you can do so by clicking the Contacts link, clicking the group name, and then using the Edit button to edit the group members. To delete a contact from the group, click the check box for the contact to add a check mark to it, click the Groups button, and then click the group name below the "Remove from" entry on the list that opens. To add a member to a group, click All Contacts, click the check box for the person to add to the group to add a check mark to it, click the Groups button, and then click the group name in the list that opens.

Exploring Other Google Services

In addition to providing you with a free Gmail email address, your Google account also provides you with other free Web-based services that you can use to share and edit documents and photos. These services might be useful to Kikukawa Air employees, so you decide to explore them next.

Using Google Docs to Share and Edit Documents

Sharon occasionally uses email attachments to circulate documents, spreadsheets, and presentations that different Kikukawa Air employees work on for meetings and promotional items such as direct mail pieces. Occasionally, the group working on a file gets confused about which person has the master copy, and sometimes two people work on the file at the same time.

You think that Google's file-sharing service, Google Docs, might be an excellent tool for collaborating on files, because one copy of the file is posted to Google Docs, and then the file's author can invite other people to access it. Because the author can secure the file and choose who can view and edit it, this might be a useful tool for Kikukawa Air.

Sharon asks you to explore Google Docs next.

To view the Google Docs tour:

▶ **1.** At the top of the page, click the **Documents** link. Depending on your browser, Google Docs might open in a new browser window or in a new tab. If your browser opens a new window, click the **Maximize** button on its title bar to maximize it. Figure 3-36 shows the Google Docs home page.

Figure 3-36	Google Docs page

As you create and upload documents in Google Docs, they appear in the file system shown in Figure 3-36. When you create a new document, you can use the tools in Google Docs to specify who can edit your document and who can view your document. If you want to invite other people to collaborate on your document, you give them permission to open and edit the file. This collaboration makes it possible for users to update a single master document, spreadsheet, or presentation from any computer with an Internet connection.

2. At the top of the page, click the **Help** link. Depending on your browser, the Help page might open in a new browser window or in a new tab. If your browser opens a new window, maximize it.

3. On the left side of the Help page, click the **Take a Tour** link. The Tour page opens.

   Trouble? If you cannot find the Take a Tour link, return to the Online Companion page for Tutorial 3, and click the Google Docs Take a Tour link in Session 3.2.

4. Read the information on the Tour page, and then click the **arrow** to the right of the Start now button to start the tour. Read each page that opens, and click the arrow button to open each page.

   Trouble? Clicking the Start now button returns you to the Google Docs home page so you can immediately begin using the service. Click the arrow button next to the Start now button to begin the tour.

5. When you have finished the tour, close the browser window or tab that contains it.

6. Close the browser window or tab that contains the Google Docs home page. If necessary, activate the browser window or tab that displays the Gmail Inbox.

As with most file-sharing sites, part of the user and terms of service agreements that you must accept when creating a Google account prohibit you from uploading copyrighted material to the Google Docs site without authorization from the copyright's owner. Google Docs also puts other restrictions on files uploads; for example, you cannot upload a document file that is larger than 500 kilobytes or more than 5,000 documents total.

After viewing the tour, Sharon agrees that Google Docs might be a good solution for Kikukawa Air. She also likes the feature that lets authors create new files, spreadsheets, and presentations, because this makes it possible for employees to work on files even when they are traveling on business and don't have immediate access to the applications on their computers.

Sharing Photos

A popular way of creating online communities, especially among friends, family members, or colleagues who are separated by geographical distances, is to post pictures. Google's photo sharing service, called Picasa, provides a large amount of storage space to upload photos.

Protecting Your Privacy when Sharing Photos | InSight

When you post photos to your Google account, keep in mind that your photos become public. Don't post anything that you wouldn't want other people to see, even if you restricted who can view your photos. In addition, be careful that photos don't inadvertently disclose more information than you want to share. For example, don't post a picture of yourself standing in front of a geographical marker such as an address or street sign, or post a picture of yourself wearing clothes that identify your school or other information if you do not want to disclose where you live.

Sharon might want to post pictures of company-wide events or pictures of the remodeled terminal in Maui, so she asks you to explore the options for posting photos using Picasa.

To view the Picasa page:

▶ 1. At the top of the page, click the **Photos** link. Depending on your browser, Picasa Web Albums might open in a new browser window or in a new tab. If your browser opens a new window, click the **Maximize** button on its title bar to maximize it.

Before you can post pictures to your Google account, you need to download the Picasa program to your computer. Then you use the Picasa Web Albums page to launch Picasa and upload pictures.

Trouble? You do not need the Picasa program installed to complete the steps in this book. Unless you are working on your own computer, you should not download the Picasa program at this time.

Instead of downloading the Picasa program, you view a page that describes more about Picasa's features.

▶ 2. Return to the Online Companion page for Session 3.2, and then click the **Picasa** link.

▶ 3. On the Picasa home page, click the **Learn more about Picasa and Picasa Web Albums** link to open the page shown in Figure 3-37.

Figure 3-37 **About Picasa & Picasa Web Albums page**

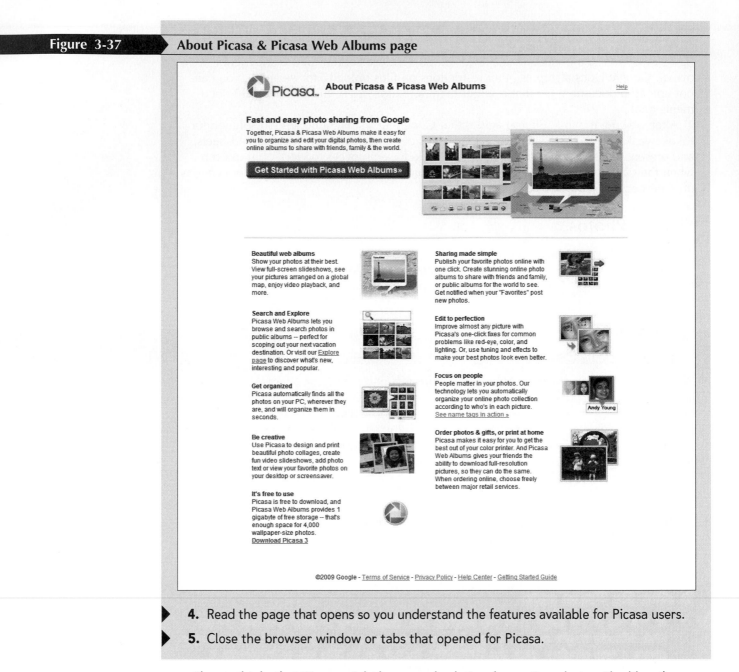

▶ **4.** Read the page that opens so you understand the features available for Picasa users.

▶ **5.** Close the browser window or tabs that opened for Picasa.

Sharon thinks that Picasa might be a good solution for posting photos. She likes the built-in features Picasa has for photo editing.

You are finished evaluating Gmail and the Google Web-based services, so you need to log off your Google account and close your browser. It is important that you sign out before closing the browser to ensure the security of your email and to prevent unauthorized access. If you do not sign in to your Google account after a year, Google might delete your account.

To sign out of Google and close your browser:

▶ **1.** Click the **Sign out** link near the upper-right corner of the page. The Welcome to Gmail page (or another Web page) opens.

▶ **2.** Click the **Close** button on your browser's title bar to close the browser.

Trouble? If any other browser windows are open, close them.

In this session, you learned how to use Gmail to create, send, receive, and manage email messages. You also learned how to create and use the Contact Manager to manage information about contacts. Finally, you learned about some of the services that are available using your Google account.

Session 3.2 Quick Check | Review

1. To set up a Google account, what information must you provide?
2. True or False: If you are using a computer in a public library to access your Gmail account, you should sign out of your account when you are finished viewing your messages to protect your privacy.
3. When you receive a message with an attachment in Gmail, what two options are available for the attached file?
4. When you delete a message that is in the Inbox in Gmail, can you recover it? Why or why not?
5. What information can you store about a person using the Contact Manager?
6. What kinds of files can you share using Google Docs?

Tutorial Summary | Review

In this tutorial, you learned how to use Webmail to send, receive, print, file, save, delete, respond to, and forward email messages. You created an address book where you stored the name, email address, and other important details about a person or a group of people. You also learned about other Web-based services that you can use to collaborate on documents and share photos. Now that you have learned these important skills, you can use the Webmail provider of your choice to send and receive your own email messages. As you use your Webmail provider, expand your skills by using its Help system to explore the many other features that it includes.

Key Terms

Calendar page	Inbox	Today page
category	Inbox label	Trash label
Contact list page	Junk folder	Webmail
Contact Manager	label	Webmail provider
conversation	Sent folder	Windows Live Calendar
Deleted folder	Sent Mail label	Windows Live Contacts
Drafts folder	Spam label	Windows Live Hotmail
Drafts label	Starred label	Windows Live ID
Gmail	thread	

Practice | **Review Assignments**

Practice the skills you learned in the tutorial using the same case scenario.

Data File needed for the Review Assignments: KAir.gif

Now that you have learned how to use Windows Live Hotmail or Gmail to manage your email messages, Sharon asks you to submit a review of your experience using the Web-mail provider and a recommendation about whether Kikukawa Air should continue using it. Sharon also wants to see how graphics are sent over the Internet, so she asks you to send her the Kikukawa Air logo to simulate how it appears when sent by Kikukawa Air employees.

1. Sign in to your Webmail provider.
2. Add your instructor's full name and email address and Sharon Kikukawa's full name and email address (Sharon@KikukawaAir.com) to Windows Live Contacts or the Contact Manager.
3. Create a category or group named **Classmates** in Windows Live Contacts or the Contact Manager using the full names and email addresses of three of your classmates.
4. Create a new message. Address the message to Sharon and to your instructor. Send a courtesy copy of the message to yourself, and send a blind courtesy copy of the message to the Classmates category or group. Use the subject **Email Recommendation** for the message.
5. In the message body, type three or more sentences describing your overall impressions about Windows Live Hotmail or Gmail, depending on which Webmail provider you used. If you used both Webmail providers, recommend the Webmail provider that Kikukawa Air should use. Be sure to evaluate the program's features, ease of use, and other important considerations that you determine.
6. In the message body, press the Enter key twice, and then type your full name and email address on separate lines.
7. Attach the file named **KAir.gif**, from the Tutorial.03\Review folder included with your Data Files, to the message.
8. Check the spelling in your message before you send the message, and correct any mistakes. Proofread your message and verify that you have created it correctly, and then send the message.
9. Wait about one minute, check for new mail (enter your password, if necessary), and then open the message you sent to Sharon and your instructor. Print the message.
10. Forward the message and the attached file to only your instructor. In the message body, describe the appearance of the file you attached to the message and explain your findings in terms of attaching a graphic to an email message. Send the message.
11. Sign out of your Webmail provider.

| Apply | **Case Problem 1** |

Apply the skills you learned to send an email message with attached files.

Data Files needed for this Case Problem: Bales.jpg and Paper.jpg.

Greenfield County Recycling Greenfield County is one of the most environmental friendly counties in the United States, boasting 98% cooperation from residential, business, and governmental entities in the county's extensive recycling program. Separate facilities process all kinds of paper, glass, cans, plastics, and household goods. The county just opened its eighth paper facility and needs you to send some pictures to the media liaison and to two managers in the county's technology office for an upcoming press release. You will create and send the message by completing the following steps.

1. Sign in to your Webmail provider.
2. Use Windows Live Contacts or the Contact Manager to create individual contacts using the full name and email address of your instructor and two classmates.
3. Use Windows Live Contacts or the Contact Manager to create a category or group named **Managers** using the two classmates you added in Step 2.
4. Create a new message addressed to your instructor. Send a courtesy copy of the message to the Managers category or group, and send a blind courtesy copy of the message to yourself. Use the subject **New Paper Facility Pictures**.
5. In the message display area, type a short note telling the recipients that you are attaching two pictures of the new recycling facility, and ask them to respond to you when they receive your message. Sign your message with your first and last names.
6. Attach the files named **Bales.jpg and Paper.jpg**, from the Tutorial.03\Cases folder included with your Data Files, to the message.
7. Send the message, wait a minute, and then check your Inbox for new messages. Print the message you sent to your instructor.
8. Create a new folder or label named **Paper Facility**, and then file the message you received in the Paper Facility folder or apply the Paper Facility label to it.
9. Sign out of your Webmail provider.

| Challenge | **Case Problem 2** |

Use Windows Live Hotmail Help or Gmail Help to learn how to manage unsolicited messages.

There are no Data Files needed for this Case Problem.

Estancia Ridge Estate Bridget Estancia owns and operates the Estancia Ridge Estate, a small, private, family-owned olive grove specializing in locally grown olives that are pressed into olive oil on the premises. Bridget manages the gardens, the historic estate where she also lives, tours of the home and grove, and a gift shop. Olive oil sales are Bridget's largest income item, but she has seen a rise in tourism over the past year at her unique estate. Because of this rise in tourism, Bridget is advertising in local tourism publications and in other publications that might attract people to visit the estate. As part of the advertisements, she includes the estate's phone number, Web site address, and her email address. Although she receives many email messages from interested tourists, she has also started receiving many unsolicited messages as her email address is added to different mailing lists distributing information that she does not want to receive. Bridget asks you to research how she can use Windows Live Hotmail or Gmail to manage the email messages she receives by blocking senders from whom she does not want to receive mail, deleting junk mail, and filtering messages into categories or different views so she receives fewer messages in her Inbox. You conduct this research for Bridget by completing the following steps.

1. Sign in to your Webmail provider.

2. Create a new message addressed to your instructor. Enter your email address in the Cc text box. Use the subject **Junk Mail and Filter Options**.

3. Click the Help button in Windows Live Hotmail or the Help link in Gmail to open the Help page for your Webmail provider.

⊕ EXPLORE

4. Use the Help page for your Webmail provider to learn how to set the junk email filtering level, how to block unwanted messages, and how to deal with spam messages. You can find this information by searching for key words such as "filter," "junk mail," and "spam," or you can display the table of contents and look for similar topics. As you read each topic, consider how Bridget might use each feature to block mail from senders from whom she does not want to receive any mail, filter mail into categories, and delete junk mail. If necessary, explore the Help topics further to conduct additional research.

⊕ EXPLORE

5. In the message display area for the message addressed to your instructor, type a short memo of two to three paragraphs explaining your recommendations about how Bridget can use Windows Live Hotmail or Gmail (depending on which Webmail provider you are using) to better manage the mail she receives. Use information from Help in your response, and cite specific features and steps for your recommendations. Sign your message with your first and last names.

6. Send the message to your instructor.

7. Sign out of your Webmail provider.

Challenge | **Case Problem 3**

Use Windows Live Hotmail Help or Gmail Help to learn how to create a signature for your outgoing email messages.

There are no Data Files needed for this Case Problem.

Trinity Cablevision You have just been hired as an installation contractor for Trinity Cablevision, which provides digital cable television, digital phone service, and high-speed Internet connections to residential and business customers. Because you are a contractor, you will need to use your Windows Live Hotmail or Gmail account for your business correspondence. To identify yourself to email recipients, you decide to create a signature file to attach to your messages that identifies your name, city, email address, and contractor license number by completing the following steps.

1. Sign in to your Webmail provider.

2. Use Windows Live Contacts or the Contact Manager to create an individual contact using the full name and email address of your instructor.

⊕ EXPLORE

3. Use the Help page for your Webmail provider to learn how to create a signature file with your first and last names on the first line, your city and state on the second line, your email address on the third line, and Contractor number plus any six-digit number on the fourth line. (*Hint*: If you are using Windows Live Hotmail, click the Options button, and then click More options in the list. Click the option in the Customize your mail section for creating a signature. If you are using Gmail, click the Settings link at the top of the page, and then examine the options on the General tab.)

4. Return to the Inbox.

5. Create a new message addressed to your instructor. Send a courtesy copy of the message to yourself. Use the subject **Contractor Services**.

⊕ EXPLORE

6. Use the toolbar to change your name in your signature for the current message to blue, bold font.

7. Send the message, wait a minute, and then retrieve your messages from the server. Print the message you sent to your instructor.

EXPLORE 8. Disable your signature file from all outgoing messages. (*Hint*: Return to your Webmail provider's Help page if you need to learn how to do this.)

9. Sign out of your Webmail provider.

| Challenge | Case Problem 4 |

Use Windows Live to create a photo album.

Data Files needed for this Case Problem: Chance.jpg, Maple.jpg, Rocky.jpg, and Scout.jpg.

Rescue Me Canine Amy Brask works as a volunteer for Rescue Me Canine, an agency that places healthy puppies and dogs that have been picked up by animal control officers with people who agree to care for these pets either as foster or adoptive families. Amy receives many email messages from local vets and community leaders who refer potential foster and adoptive families to her. Amy had been sending pictures of dogs to prospective families, but she would rather post them in one place. She decides to investigate using a Windows Live photo album to see if this might make distributing photos of pets easier and more efficient.

Note: You must have a Windows Live ID account to complete this Case Problem.

1. Start your Web browser, open the Online Companion page at www.cengage.com/internet/np/internet8 and log on to your account, click the Tutorial 3 link, and then click the Case Problem 4 link. Click the Windows Live link, and wait while the browser loads the page.

2. Sign in to your Windows Live account.

3. Create individual contacts in Windows Live Contacts using the full name and email address of your instructor and two classmates.

4. At the top the page, click the Photos link.

EXPLORE 5. Click the link to create a new album named **Dogs**, and choose the option to share the album with people you select. Use the link to select people from your contact list, and then add your instructor and the two classmates you added to Windows Live Contacts in Step 3 to share the album. Type your own email address into the list so you will also receive the invitation. At the bottom of the page, click the Next button.

EXPLORE 6. Click the option to select pictures on your computer, browse to and select the Tutorial.03\Cases folder with your Data Files, press and hold the Ctrl key, click the files **Chance.jpg**, **Maple.jpg**, **Rocky.jpg**, and **Scout.jpg**, release the Ctrl key, and then click the Open button. Four files are ready to be uploaded. Click the Upload button to continue.

EXPLORE 7. After the files have been uploaded, click the link to let people know that you posted them. Type a message in the message box that describes the files you posted, and then sign the message with your first and last names. Click the Send button.

8. Sign out of your Windows Live account.

Challenge | Case Problem 5

Expand the skills you learned in this tutorial to upload and edit a document in Google Docs.

Data File needed for this Case Problem: Mangietti.rtf.

Mangietti's Pizza Garden Mangietti's Pizza Garden serves pizza and other Italian specialties. Its claim to fame is its coal-fired pizza oven and homemade, hand-tossed pizza dough. Customers are asked for their email addresses when they pay their bills so Mangietti's can send them coupons and follow-up surveys. You are working on an advertisement for the local newspaper and want to use actual customer comments in the ad, so you decide to gather these comments using a survey that you will send to customers with an email message that includes a 10 percent discount on their next meal. Because you need to coordinate the survey's questions with the owner and a few other staff members, you decide to post it on Google Docs so the group can collaborate on the document before it is finalized and sent to customers. You will create the survey by completing the following steps.

Note: You must have a Google account to complete this Case Problem.

1. Start your Web browser, open the Online Companion page at www.cengage.com/internet/np/internet8 and log on to your account, click the Tutorial 3 link, and then click the Case Problem 5 link. Click the Gmail link, and wait while the browser loads the page.
2. Sign in to your Gmail account.
3. Use the Contact Manager to create individual contacts using the full name and email address of your instructor and two classmates.
4. At the top of the page, click the Documents link to open Google Docs.
5. Locate and click the button or option to upload a file.
6. Click the button or option to browse for the file to upload. Browse to and select the location where your Data Files are stored, and then open the Tutorial.03\Cases folder. Double-click the **Mangietti.rtf** file to select it.

⊕ EXPLORE
7. Click or select the option to upload the file. (*Hint*: After selecting the file, you need to upload it. If you skip this step, the file will not appear in Google Docs.) After the file has been uploaded, Google Docs will open it in a word processor.
8. Scroll to the bottom of the document, and then type your first and last names. Click the Save & Close button to close the file.

⊕ EXPLORE
9. Click the check box for your document to add a check mark to it, and then click the Share button. Click the option to invite people to share the document, and then select the collaborators from the Contact Manager. Select your instructor and the two classmates you added to the Contact Manager in Step 2 as your collaborators, and then click the Done button.

⊕ EXPLORE
10. Type a short message in the Message text box to explain that you are attaching the survey file for Mangietti's Pizza Garden, sign the message with your first and last names, click the Send button, and then click the Save & Close button.
11. Close the browser window for Google Docs.
12. Sign out of your Google account.

Reinforce	**Lab Assignments**

The interactive Student Edition Lab **Email** is designed to help you master some of the key concepts and skills presented in this tutorial, including:

Student Edition Labs

- sending and receiving email messages
- replying to email messages
- storing and deleting email messages

This lab is available online and can be accessed from the Tutorial 3 Web page on the Online Companion at www.cengage.com/internet/np//internet8.

Review	**Quick Check Answers**

Session 3.1

1. Your name, preferred language, country, state, zip code, time zone, gender, and birth date; you must also submit a unique sign-in name, a password, and a secret question and answer.
2. True
3. You can view the attached file if your computer has a program that can open it, or you can save the attached file on your computer.
4. Yes, you can recover the message because it is stored in the Deleted folder.
5. name, email address, nickname, address, business information, personal information, and so on
6. You can choose to secure a file so that only you, only those people you choose, or anyone can access it.

Session 3.2

1. Your name and location; you must also submit a unique login name, a password, a secret question and answer, and an optional alternative email address.
2. True
3. You can view the attached file if your computer has a program that can open it, or you can save the attached file on your computer.
4. Yes, you can recover the message for up to 30 days because it is marked with the Trash label.
5. name, email address, nickname, address, business information, personal information, and so on
6. documents, spreadsheets, and presentations

Objectives

Session 4.1
- Determine whether a research question is specific or exploratory
- Learn how to formulate an effective Web search strategy to answer research questions
- Learn how to use Web search engines, Web directories, and Web metasearch engines effectively

Session 4.2
- Use Boolean logic and filtering techniques to improve your Web searches
- Use advanced search options in Web search engines
- Assess the validity and quality of Web research resources
- Learn about the future of Web search tools

Searching the Web

Using Search Engines and Directories Effectively

Case | International Executive Reports

International Executive Reports (IER) is a company that publishes a variety of weekly newsletters, monthly reports, and annual reviews of major trends in economic conditions and management developments. IER's clients are top-level managers and other people who serve on the governing boards of large companies and not-for-profit organizations. IER publications are mailed or emailed to subscribers. The subscription rates range from $300 to $900 per year.

The IER writing staff provides content for all of its publications. In some cases, content that is developed for one publication is edited and used in other publications. Anne Hill, the managing director for content at IER, has recruited an excellent staff of editors, writers, and researchers who work together to create a wide variety of content. Anne has hired you to fill an intern position on the research staff. Your job will involve conducting online research and fact-checking for two of the staff writers, Dave Burton and Ranjit Singh. Dave is an international business specialist and Ranjit is an economist who writes about current economic trends.

Anne is counting on you to become skilled in conducting Web searches. She can help you with questions you might have as you find your way around the Web.

Starting Data Files

There are no starting Data Files needed for this tutorial.

Session 4.1

Types of Search Questions

Dave and Ranjit will need different kinds of help because of their different writing goals. Dave will need quick answers to specific questions. For example, he might need to know the population of Bolivia or the languages spoken in Thailand. Ranjit will be looking for help finding new perspectives on recurring economic issues and a wide range of information on broad topics. For example, he might need you to find Web sites that contain collections of research papers that discuss the causes of the Great Depression.

Dave writes about business opportunities and developments in almost every country in the world. His writing requires background research on most major businesses and industries. To support Dave, you need to be able to "get the facts" using the Web.

Ranjit writes longer, more thought-provoking pieces about broad economic and business issues and will count on you to provide him with new ideas that he can explore in his columns. The Web is a good place to find unusual and interesting views on the economy and general business practices. Ranjit needs you to use the Web as a source of interesting concepts and new angles on old ideas, rather than as a place to find fast answers to specific questions.

You can use the Web to obtain answers to both of these question types—specific and exploratory—but each requires a different search strategy. A **specific question** is a question that you can phrase easily and one for which you will recognize the answer when you find it. In other words, you will know when to end your search. The search process for a specific question is one of narrowing the field down to the answer you seek. In contrast, an **exploratory question** is an open-ended question that can be harder to phrase; it also is difficult to determine when you find a good answer. The search process for an exploratory question requires you to fan out in a number of directions to find relevant information.

Specific questions require you to start with broad categories of information and gradually narrow the search until you find the answer to your question. Figure 4-1 shows this process of sequential, increasingly focused questions.

| Figure 4-1 | Specific research question search process |

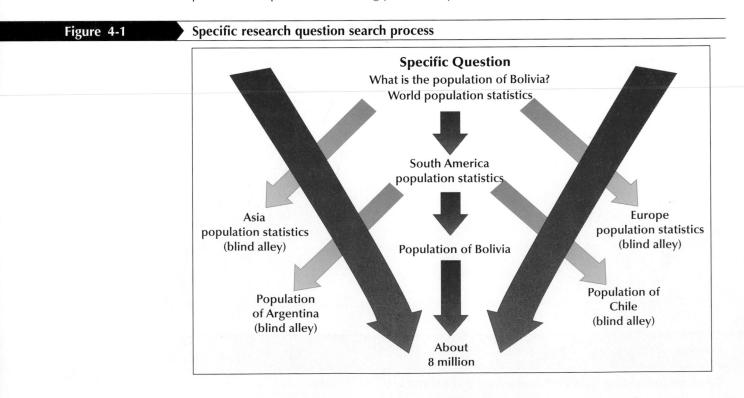

As you narrow your search, you might find that you are heading in the wrong direction or down a blind alley. In that case, you need to move back up the funnel shown in Figure 4-1 and try another path.

An exploratory search starts with general questions that lead to other, less general questions. The answers to the questions at each level should lead you to more information about the topic in which you are interested. This information then leads you to more questions. Figure 4-2 shows how this questioning process leads to a broadening scope as you gather information pertinent to the exploratory question.

Exploratory research question search process ◀ Figure 4-2

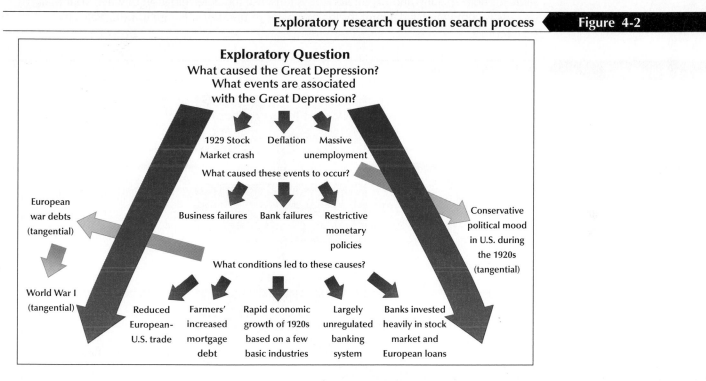

As your exploratory search expands, you might find yourself collecting tangential information. Tangential information is data that is somewhat related to your topic but does not help answer your exploratory question.

Determining Useful Information | InSight

The boundary between useful and tangential information can be difficult to identify for exploratory search questions. Sometimes, what appears to be tangential information can turn out to be useful information that leads you to expand your exploratory search in a fruitful direction. Do not be too quick to classify information as tangential. Remember, an exploratory search involves examining an increasingly wider range of information and identifying new insights in that information as you continue to search.

Web Search Process

Now that you understand the different types of questions that you will need to answer, you should learn something about searching the Web. You know the Web is a collection of interconnected HTML documents, and you know how to use Web browser software to navigate the hyperlinks that connect these documents. The search tools available on the Web are an integral part of these linked HTML documents, or Web pages.

Before you begin any Web search, you must decide whether your question is specific or exploratory. Then you can begin the actual Web search process, which includes four steps. The first step is to carefully formulate and state your question. Next, you select the appropriate tool or tools to use in your search. After obtaining your results from a Web search tool, you need to evaluate these results to determine whether they answer your question. If the results answer your question, you do not need to continue the search. If they do not answer your question, you continue the search by refining or redefining your question and then selecting a different search tool to see if you get a different result. The first three steps are the same for both specific and exploratory questions, but the determination of when your search process is completed is different for the two types of questions. Figure 4-3 illustrates the search process.

Figure 4-3 ▶ **Web search process**

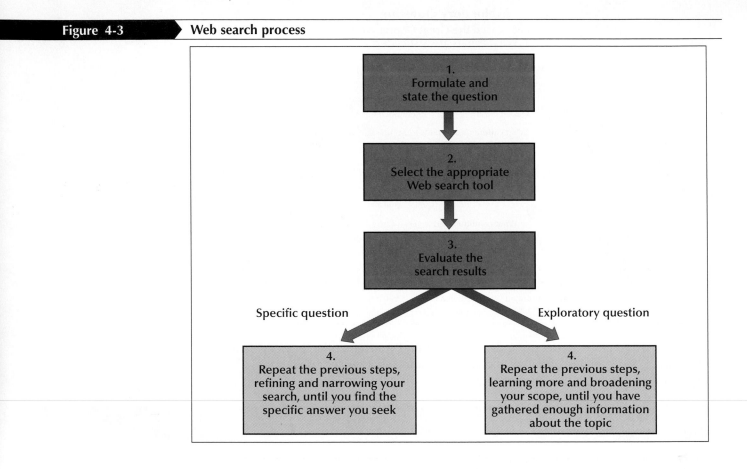

Repeating the Search Process | InSight

You can repeat the search process as many times as necessary until you obtain the specific answer you seek or a satisfactory range of information regarding your exploratory topic. Sometimes, you might find that the nature of your original question is different than you had originally thought. You also might find that you need to reformulate, or more clearly state, your question. As you restate your question, think of synonyms for each word. Unfortunately, many words in the English language have multiple meanings. For example, the word *mogul* can mean an influential businessperson, an Indian person of Mongolian or Persian descent, or a small bump in a ski run. If you use a word in your search that is common and has many meanings, you can be buried in irrelevant information or be led down many blind alleys. Identifying unique phrases that relate to your topic or question is a helpful way to avoid some of these problems. For example, if you are searching for sites that discuss ways to ski safely over a mogul, you could include the word "skiing" or "slope" in your search expression to reduce the chances of obtaining results that link to Web pages about Indians or business magnates.

An important part of any search is evaluating the search results you obtain. You will learn how to assess the validity and reliability of Web pages you find during your searches in the next session.

Using Search Engines

To implement any Web search strategy, you will use one or more Web search tools. **Web search tools** include four broad categories of sites: search engines, directories, metasearch engines, and other Web resources such as Web bibliographies. The Additional Information section of the Online Companion page for Tutorial 4 includes links to many of these Web search tools. (The Online Companion page is located at www.cengage.com/internet/np/internet8.)

In this section, you will learn the basics of using each type of search tool. Remember that searching the Web is a challenging task using any of these tools. No one knows exactly how many pages exist on the Web, but the number is now in the billions. Each of these pages might have thousands of words, images, or links to downloadable files. Thus, the content of the Web is far greater than any library. Unlike the content of a library, however, the content of the Web is not indexed in any standardized way. Fortunately, the tools you have to search the Web are powerful.

Understanding Search Engines

A Web **search engine** is a Web site (or part of a Web site) that finds other Web pages that match a word or phrase you enter. This word or phrase is called a **search expression** or a **query**. A search expression or query might also include instructions that tell the search engine how to search; you will learn how to formulate search expressions that include additional search instructions later in this tutorial. The basic search page for Bing, a popular search engine site, is shown in Figure 4-4.

| Figure 4-4 | Bing basic search page |

A basic search page includes a text box for entering a search expression and a command button to begin the search. The basic search page for Google, one of the most popular search engines, appears in Figure 4-5.

| Figure 4-5 | Google basic search page |

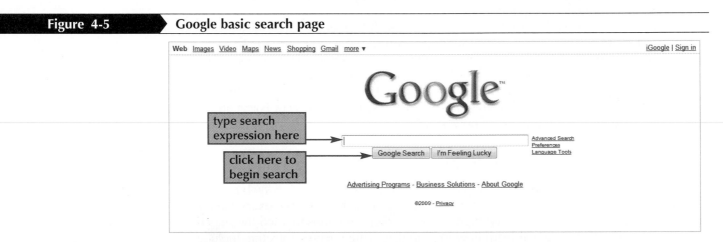

A search engine does not search the Web to find a match; it searches only its *own* database of information about Web pages that it has collected, indexed, and stored. A search engine's database includes the URL of the Web page (recall from Tutorial 1 that a Web page's URL, or uniform resource locator, is its address). If you enter the same search expression into different search engines, you will often get different results because each search engine has collected a different set of information in its database, and each search engine uses different procedures to search its database. Some search engines do not collect their own information to build their databases. These search engines buy the right to use the database of another search engine. However, because each search engine uses different procedures to retrieve information from its database, a search engine that uses another search engine's database can still yield different results even though it uses the same database. Later in this session, you will learn more about variations in how search engines work.

Most search engines report the number of hits they find. A **hit** is a Web page that is indexed in the search engine's database and that contains text that matches a specific search expression. All search engines provide a series of **results pages**, which are Web pages that list hyperlinks to the Web pages containing text that matches your search expression. An example of a search results page (for a search on the word "car") from the Google search engine appears in Figure 4-6.

Google search results for the search term "car"　　Figure 4-6

Most search engines use Web robots to build their databases of links to Web pages. A **Web robot**, also called a **bot** or a **spider**, is a program that automatically searches the Web to find new Web sites and update information about old Web sites that already are in the database. One of a Web robot's more important tasks is to delete information in the database when a Web site no longer exists. The main advantage of using an automated searching tool is that it can examine far more Web sites than an army of people ever could. However, the Web changes every day, and even the best search engine sites cannot keep their databases completely updated. When you click hyperlinks on a search engine results page, you will find that some of the Web pages no longer exist. A hyperlink to a Web page that no longer exists or has been moved to another URL is called a **dead link**.

People who create Web pages want their sites to be found by people who are interested in the content of those pages. Most search engines allow Web page creators to submit the URLs of their pages to the databases of search engines. This gives search engines another way to add Web pages to their databases. Most companies that operate search engines screen Web page submissions to prevent a Web page creator from submitting a large number of duplicate or similar Web pages. When the search engine receives a submission, it sends its Web robot out to visit the submitted URL and collect data about the site.

The organizations that operate search engines often sell advertising space on the search engine Web page and on the results pages. An increasing number of search engine operators also sell paid placement rights on results pages. A **paid placement** is the right to have a link to your Web site appear on the search results page when a user enters a specific search term. For example, Toyota might want to purchase the right to have its site listed on the search results page whenever a user enters the search term "car." When you enter a search expression that includes the word "car," the search engine creates a results page that will have a link to Toyota's Web site at or near the top of the results page. Most, but not all, search engines label these paid placement links as "sponsored," and they are usually called **sponsored links**. If the advertising appears in a box on the page (usually at the top, but sometimes along the side or at the bottom of the page), it is usually called a **banner ad**.

Search engines use the revenue from sponsored links and banner ads to generate profit after covering the costs of maintaining the computer hardware and software required to search the Web and to create and search the database. The only price a user pays for access to these excellent search tools is that you will see banner ads on many of the pages, and you might have to scroll through a few sponsored links at the top of results pages; otherwise, your usage is free. Figure 4-6 shows the sponsored links to advertisers that have paid for the placement on this page.

Your first research assignment is to find the amount of average rainfall in Belize for Dave. This search question is a specific question, not an exploratory question, because you are looking for a fact and you will know when you have found that fact. You can use the four steps from Figure 4-3 as follows:

1. Formulate and state the question. You have identified key search terms in the question that you can use in your search expression: *Belize*, *rainfall*, and *annual*. You use these terms because they all should appear on any Web page that includes the answer to the question. None of these terms are articles, prepositions, or other common words, and none have multiple meanings. The term *Belize* should be especially useful in narrowing the search to relevant Web pages.

2. Because the question is very specific, you decide that a basic search engine would be a good tool to use.

3. When you obtain the results, review and evaluate them and then decide whether they provide an acceptable answer to your question.

4. If the results do not answer the question to your satisfaction, you need to redefine or reformulate the question so it is more specific, and then conduct a second search using a different tool, question, or search expression until you find the fact you seek.

To find the average annual rainfall in Belize:

▶ **1.** Start your Web browser, go to **www.cengage.com/internet/np/internet8** to open the Online Companion page, log in to your account, click the **Tutorial 4** link, and then click the **Session 4.1** link.

▶ **2.** Select any one of the search engines in the Basic Search Engines section, click the link to that search engine, and then wait while the browser opens that search engine's Web page.

▶ **3.** Type **Belize annual rainfall** in the search text box.

▶ **4.** Click the appropriate button to start the search. The search results appear on a new page. This page should indicate that there are hundreds, perhaps even thousands, of Web pages that might contain the answer to your question.

▶ **5.** Scroll down the results page and examine your search results. Click some of the links until you find a page or several pages that provide annual rainfall information for Belize. If you do not find any useful links on the first page of search results, click the link to view more search results pages (usually located at the bottom of the first results page). Click the **Back** button on your Web browser to return to the results page after going to each hyperlink. You should find that Belize has several climate zones and that the annual rainfall ranges from 50 to 180 inches, or 130 to 470 centimeters.

You probably expected that you would find one rainfall amount that would be representative of the entire country, but that is not the case. Web searches often disclose information that helps you adjust the assumptions you made when you formulated the original research question.

You discuss the results of your search with Dave and explain that you obtained several different rainfall amounts for different regions within Belize. Dave finds your results interesting and will use them to expand the story he is working on. Because you are fact-checking for a story that IER will publish, Dave asks you to search again using a different search engine just to confirm what you found.

Using More Than One Search Engine

To get a confirmation of your results, you decide to search for the same information in another search engine.

To conduct the same search to confirm your results:

▶ **1.** Return to the Online Companion page for Session 4.1, and then click a link to another of the search engines in the Basic Search Engines section.

▶ **2.** Type **Belize annual rainfall** in the search text box.

▶ **3.** Click the appropriate button to start the search. You will most likely see a completely different set of links on your search results page.

▶ **4.** Scroll down the results page and examine your search results, and then click some of the links until you find a page that provides the average annual rainfall for Belize. Return to the results page after going to each hyperlink. Once again, you should find that Belize has several climate zones and that the annual rainfall ranges from 50 to 180 inches, or 130 to 470 centimeters.

Your second search returned a different set of links because each search engine includes different Web pages in its database and because different search engines use different rules to evaluate search expressions. Some search engines will return hits for pages that include *any* of the words in the search expression. Other search engines return hits only for pages that include *all* of the words in the search expression.

The best way to determine how a specific search engine interprets search expressions is to read the Help pages on the search engine Web site. As you become an experienced Web searcher, you will find that you use two or three particular search engines for most of your work. Read the Help pages on those Web sites regularly because search engines do change the way they interpret search expressions from time to time. You should also get in the habit of checking other search engines occasionally because new search engines are launched and old search engines often make changes to stay competitive. Bing, Exalead, and Wolfram Alpha are examples of search engines that were introduced in recent years to compete with established search sites such as Google. Figure 4-7 shows the Help page for the basic search function on the AltaVista search engine Web site.

AltaVista Help page for basic searches   **Figure 4-7**

altavista

Home › AltaVista Help › **Search**

Different Types of Searches

Web   Video
Image   News
Audio   Webmaster Search

AltaVista Features

AltaVista Toolbar   Settings
Advanced Web Search   Family Filter
AltaVista Shortcuts   Report offensive pages (Yahoo!)
Special search terms

Basic Web search tips

AltaVista invites you to search its digital content collection containing billions of Web pages, data resources and multimedia files by simply typing a query and clicking the Search button.

- When you type multiple words in the search box, AltaVista looks for Web pages that contain all of the words.
- Be as specific as you can. (Example: **Baltimore Ravens** instead of just **Ravens**)
- Enter words that you think will appear on the Web page you want. AltaVista indexes all of the words on each Web page.
- To search for an exact phrase, put it in quotes (Example: **"to be or not to be"**).
- Uppercase and lowercase are treated the same. To maintain a certain capitalization, put the word in quotes.
- Words with punctuation between them are treated as if they are surrounded in quotes. All punctuation marks are treated equally.
  (Example: **Ford.mustang/convertible** gives the same results as **"ford mustang convertible"**.)
- If you get results in other languages, either Translate the Web pages or select your preferred language in the search box menu.
- If you include an accent in a query word, AltaVista only matches words with that particular accent. If you do not include an accent, AltaVista will match words both with and without accents. This means you can search for French, German or Spanish words, even if you have an English-only keyboard.

To help focus your search further, use Advanced Web Search or Special search terms.

Types of Web results

Doing different types of searches

AltaVista's search tabs, located on top of the search box, allow you to instantly search in different areas: Web, Images, Audio, Video, Directory or News.

To try a different type of search, just click a tab. AltaVista takes the words that are currently in the search box and automatically perform the search for you. (Sorry, this doesn't work on all browsers.)

Features in your Web search results page

Translate: This link lets you easily translate a Web page into any of nine languages. When you translate a page, AltaVista automatically translates all of the pages you link to from that page.

More pages from [this site]: When a site contains multiple pages that closely match your query, clicking on this link lets you see all of them.If a second page is very close in relevance to the first page, AltaVista automatically shows the second page indented below the first one.

PDF files: AltaVista searches various types of files in response to your queries. When a relevant PDF file is found you will see a note saying "File Format: PDF" and a link to easily download the free Adobe Acrobat Reader software, which is required to view a PDF file.

Business Services   Submit a Site   About AltaVista   Privacy Policy   Help

© 2007 Overture Services, Inc.

information about how basic search expressions are interpreted

links to Help pages with more information about search terms and expressions

Reproduced with permission of Yahoo! Inc. ® 2007 by Yahoo! Inc. YAHOO! and the YAHOO! logo are trademarks of Yahoo! Inc.

If you found the same information after running both searches, you can confirm the information you found in your first search. If not, you should run additional searches to determine the reason your answers are not consistent, or report to Dave that you have obtained inconsistent results for your search.

You might have noticed that many of the links on the results pages led to Web sites that have no information about Belize rainfall at all. This is why most researchers routinely use several search engines; answers that are difficult to find using one search engine are often easy to find with another.

Understanding Search Engine Databases

Search engine databases store different collections of information about the pages that exist on the Web at any given time. Many search engine robots do not search all of the Web pages at a particular site. Further, each search engine database uses its own approach to index the information it has collected from the Web. Some search engine robots collect information only from a Web page's title, description, keywords, or HTML tags; others read only a certain number of words from each Web page. Figure 4-8 shows the first few lines of HTML from a Web page that contains information about electronic commerce.

Figure 4-8	Meta tags in a Web page

```
<HEAD>

<TITLE>
Current Developments in Electronic Commerce
</TITLE>

<META NAME ="description" CONTENT="Current
news and reports about electronic commerce
developments.">

<META NAME ="keywords" CONTENT ="electronic
commerce, electronic data interchange,
value added reseller, EDI, VAR, secure
socket layer, business on the internet">

</HEAD>
```

The description and keywords tags are examples of HTML meta tags. A **meta tag** is HTML code that a Web page creator places in the page header for the specific purpose of informing Web robots about the content of the page. Meta tags do not cause any text to appear on the page when a Web browser loads it; rather, they exist solely for the use of search engine robots.

The information contained in meta tags can become an important part of a search engine's database. For example, the "keywords" meta tag shown in Figure 4-8 includes the phrase "electronic data interchange." These keywords could be a very important phrase in a search engine's database because the three individual words *electronic*, *data*, and *interchange* are common terms that often are used in search expressions that have nothing to do with electronic commerce. The word *data* is so common that many search engines are programmed to ignore it. A search engine that includes the full phrase "electronic data interchange" in its database will greatly increase the chances that a user interested in that topic will find this particular page.

Some search engines store the entire content of every Web page they index; other search engines store only parts of Web pages. Search engines that store a Web page's full content are called **full text indexing** engines. If you use a search engine that is not full text indexing, and the terms you use in your search expression are not in the part of the Web page that the search engine stores in its database, the search engine will not return a hit for that page. Many search engines, even those that claim to be full text indexed search engines, omit common words such as *and*, *the*, *it*, and *by* from their databases. These common words are called **stop words**. For example, if you enter a search expression of "Law and Order" (without the quotes) while looking for pages related to the television show of that name, a search engine that omits stop words will return a large number of irrelevant links because it will search on the two words "law" and "order."

Most, but not all, search engines will include stop words if you include them as part of a phrase enclosed in quotes. You can find out how a particular search engine handles stop words by examining the search engine Web site's Help pages; many search engines include information about their search engines, robots, and databases on their Help or About pages.

Search Engine Features

Page ranking is one technique that search engines use to find Web pages that might be relevant to a specific search expression. **Page ranking** is a way of grading Web pages by the number of other Web pages that link to them. The URLs of Web pages with high rankings are presented first on the search results page. A page that has more Web pages linking into it (these connections are called **inbound links**) is given a higher ranking than a page that has fewer pages linking into it. In complex page ranking schemes, the value of each link varies with the linking page's rank.

For example, a Web page with many inbound links might have a lower ranking than another Web page that has fewer inbound links if the second page's inbound links are from Web pages that, in turn, have a large number of inbound links themselves. As you can imagine, calculating page ranks can be complex, but the rankings can effectively identify pages that are likely to meet the needs of users. Although Google was the first search engine to use page ranking, and continues to lead in the development of highly sophisticated page ranking algorithms, most other search engines now use page ranking and are constantly working to refine the effectiveness of their algorithms.

Most search engines use **stemming** to search for variants of keywords automatically. For example, if you search using the keywords *Canada travel guide*, most search engines will return hits that include the keywords "Canadian" and "Canada," as well as pages containing the plural form of the word "guide." Unfortunately, you cannot dictate which variant of your keywords the search engine will use.

Another feature that some search engines have attempted to include in their pages is natural language querying. A **natural language query interface** allows users to enter a question exactly as they would ask a person that question. For example, using a natural language query, you might phrase the Belize rainfall search as "How much rain does Belize get each year?" You could ask the same question in various ways. The search engine analyzes the question using knowledge it has been given about the grammatical structure of questions and then uses that knowledge to convert the natural language question into a search query. This procedure of converting a natural language question into a search expression is sometimes called **parsing**.

Although no major search engine has been able to make a natural language query interface that has worked consistently, mathematical software company Wolfram has a Web site that offers a natural language interface to a database of collected facts. This site, Wolfram Alpha, lets users ask questions in natural language that relate to the facts in its database. Dave is still working on the Belize article and you decide to help him by finding out what the life expectancy is for people living in Belize.

To use the Wolfram Alpha natural language interface:

▶ **1.** Return to the Online Companion page for Session 4.1, and then in the Basic Search Engines section, click the **Wolfram Alpha** link to open the Wolfram Alpha search engine page.

▶ **2.** Type **What is the life expectancy in Belize** in the box near the top of the page.

▶ **3.** Click the **compute** button to run the search. The search results should resemble the page shown in Figure 4-9.

Figure 4-9 ▶ **Wolfram Alpha natural language interface results**

▶ **4.** Examine the results and notice that the site returns a good bit of information about the population of Belize and its characteristics. Although Wolfram Alpha is a search engine, it was built by a mathematics software company and advertises itself as being a computational engine, too. When you run a search with Wolfram Alpha, it will try to identify calculations that a person entering your search expression might want to perform. It does those calculations and reports their results along with the search results.

Search engines provide a powerful tool for executing keyword searches of the Web, but they do have their limitations. Most search engine URL databases are built by computers running programs that perform the search automatically, so they can miss important classification details that a human searcher would notice instantly. For example, if a search engine's robot found a Web page with the title "Test Data: Do Not Use," it would probably not recognize the text as a warning and would include content from the page in the search engine database. If a person were to read such a warning in a Web page title, that person would know not to include the page's contents. However, with billions of Web pages on the Web, it is impossible to have people screen every Web page.

Using Directories and Hybrid Search Engine Directories

Web directories use a completely different approach from search engines to build useful indexes of information on the Web. A **Web directory** is a listing of hyperlinks to Web pages that is organized into hierarchical categories. The difference between a search engine and a Web directory is that the Web pages included in a Web directory are selected and organized into categories before visitors use the directory. In a search engine, the database is searched in response to a visitor's query, and results pages are created in response to each specific search. Most Web directories have human editors who decide which Web pages will be included in the directory and how they will be organized; however, some Web directories use computers to perform these tasks. Web directory editors, who are knowledgeable experts in one or more subject areas and skilled in various classification techniques, review candidate Web pages for inclusion in the directory. When these experts decide that a Web page is worth listing in the directory, they determine the appropriate category in which to store the hyperlink to that page. The main weakness of a directory is that users must know which category is likely to yield the information they desire. If users begin searching in the wrong category, they might follow many hyperlinks before they realize that the information they seek is not in that category. Some directories overcome this limitation by including hyperlinks in category levels that link to lower levels in other categories.

> **Tip**
>
> Most Web directories allow a Web page to be indexed in several different categories.

Paying to Submit URLs | InSight

Many Web directories, including Yahoo!, allow businesses that have Web sites to pay a fee and submit their URLs to the directory editors so they can consider including the Web site in their directory. In most cases, the fee does not guarantee that the site will be included in the directory, but it does ensure that the editors will know that the site exists. A new site on the Web that does not use a paid directory submission can wait months before a directory editor notices it and considers including it.

One of the oldest and most respected directories on the Web is Yahoo!. David Filo and Jerry Yang, two Stanford doctoral students who wanted a way to keep track of interesting sites they found on the Internet, started Yahoo! in 1994. Since then, Yahoo! has grown to become one of the most widely used resources on the Web. Yahoo! currently lists hundreds of thousands of Web pages in its categories—a sizable collection, but only a small portion of the billions of pages on the Web. Although Yahoo! does use some automated programs for checking and classifying its entries, it relies on human experts to do most of the selection and classification work. The Yahoo! Web directory home page appears in Figure 4-10.

Figure 4-10   **Yahoo! Web directory home page**

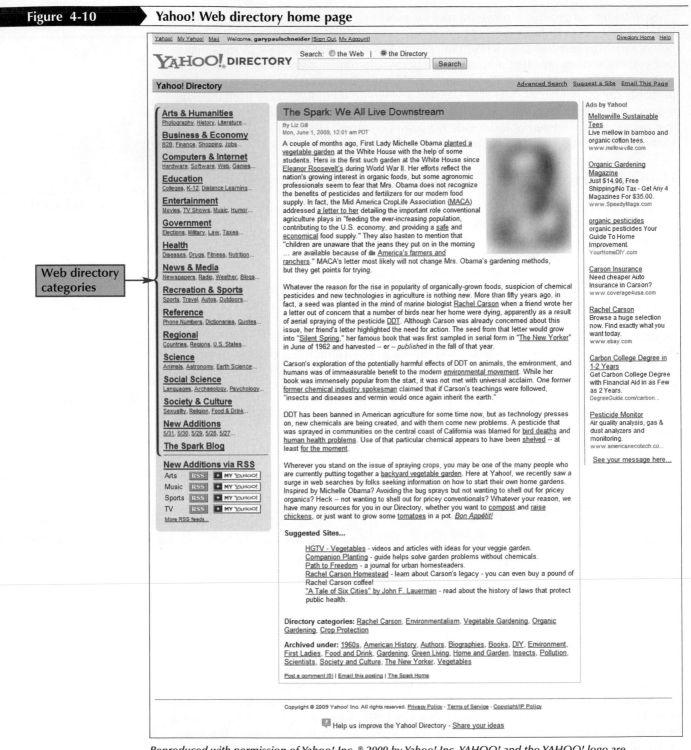

Web directory categories

The search tool that appears near the top of the page is a search engine within the Yahoo! directory. You can enter search terms into this tool, and Yahoo! will search its listings to find a match. This combination of search engine and directory is sometimes called a **hybrid search engine directory**; however, most directories today include a search engine function, so many people simply call these sites Web directories. No matter what it is called, the combination of search engine and directory provides a powerful and effective tool for searching the Web.

Using a hybrid search engine directory can help you identify which category in the directory is likely to contain the information you need. After you enter a category, the search engine is useful for narrowing a search even further; you can enter a search expression and limit the search to that category.

The Yahoo! Web directory includes 16 main categories, each with several subcategories. These are not the only subcategories; they are just a sample of those that are the largest or most used. You can click a main category hyperlink to see all of the subcategories under that category.

The Open Directory Project is different from most other Web directories because the editors volunteer their time to create the directory's entries. The home page for the Open Directory Project is shown in Figure 4-11.

Open Directory Project home page — Figure 4-11

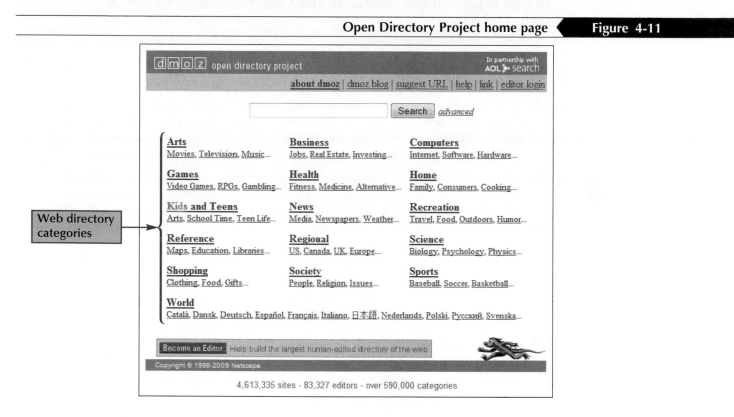

Your next assignment is from Dave. He is working on an article about current trends in corporate governance. He knows that The Conference Board is an organization that does research on business issues related to goverance. Dave would like you to give him a list of organizations similar to The Conference Board so he can do more extensive background reading before he writes the article. You decide that a Web directory might be a good tool for this type of search. You can find The Conference Board in a Web directory to learn in what category the directory has placed it. Then, you can search the other listings in that category to find similar organizations.

To find organizations similar to The Conference Board using a Web directory:

▶ **1.** Return to the Online Companion page for Session 4.1, choose one of the sites in the Web Directories section, and click the link for the site you chose.

▶ **2.** Search the directory for The Conference Board.

▶ **3.** Examine the page that loads in your browser. In the text for the link to The Conference Board, the directory will include a link to the category (or categories) in which that directory has placed The Conference Board. Click the link to open the category page and identify links to organizations' Web pages that might be helpful for Dave.

▶ **4.** If you do not find links that might be helpful to Dave, you can search another category if one was listed. You can also search similar categories or try a different Web directory. Figure 4-12 shows the category in which The Conference Board is included in the Yahoo! Directory (Organizations within Business and Economics). This category includes links to several organizations' Web sites that could be helpful to Dave.

Yahoo! Web directory search results page | Figure 4-12

link to The Conference Board Web site

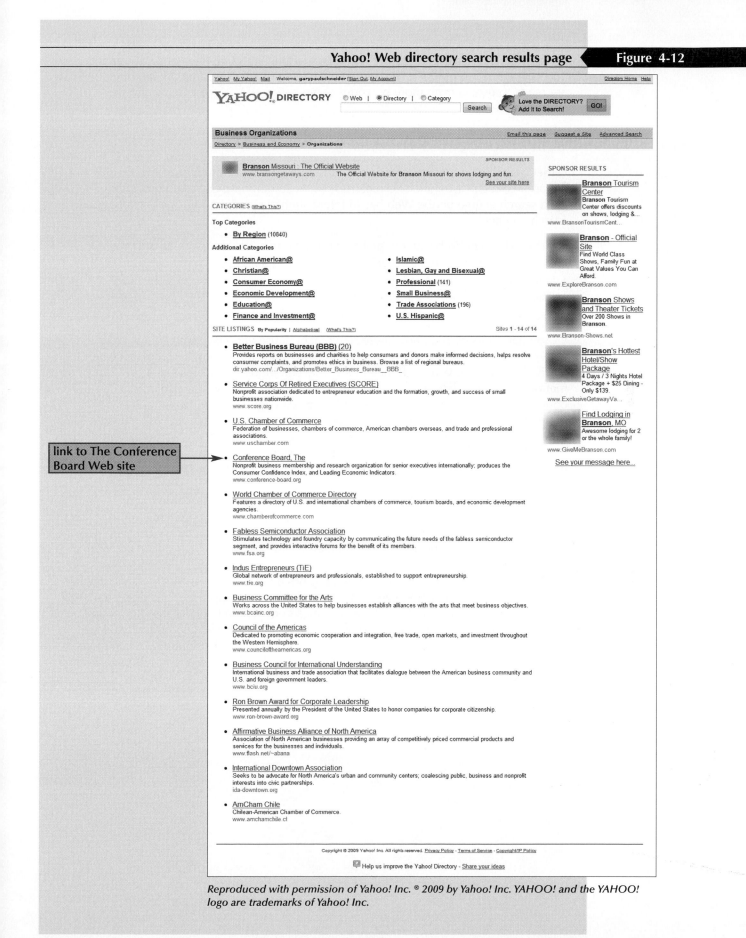

You should be able to find links to a number of organizations using one or more of the Web directories listed that you can email to Dave to complete your assignment. Now that you have seen how to use a search engine and a hybrid search engine directory, you are ready to use an even more powerful combination of Web research tools: the metasearch engine.

Using Metasearch Engines

A **metasearch engine** is a tool that combines the power of multiple search engines. Some metasearch tools also include directories. The idea behind metasearch tools is simple. Each search engine on the Web has different strengths and weaknesses because each search engine:

- Uses a different Web robot to gather information about Web pages.
- Stores a different amount of Web page text in its database.
- Selects different Web pages to index.
- Has different storage resources.
- Interprets search expressions somewhat differently.

You have already seen how these differences cause various search engines to return vastly different results for the same search expression. To perform a complete search for a particular question, you might need to use several individual search engines. Using a metasearch engine lets you search several engines at the same time, so you need not conduct the same search many times. Metasearch engines do not have their own databases of Web information; instead, a metasearch engine transmits your search expression to several search engines. These search engines run the search expression against their databases of Web page information and return results to the metasearch engine. The metasearch engine then reports consolidated results from all of the search engines it queried.

A few years ago, some Web search experts believed that metasearch engines would become unnecessary as the larger search engines expanded their coverage of the Web. But the Web continues to grow so rapidly that it outpaces the abilities of any single search engine to keep up with it. Metasearch engines still make it easier to do a complete search of the Web.

Dogpile was one of the first metasearch engines on the Web. Dogpile forwards search queries to a number of major search engines and Web directories. The specific search engines and directories that Dogpile uses change from time to time because newer and better search tools become available and older tools disappear. Each entry on the search results page is labeled to indicate the search engine or Web directory that found it. When more than one source provides the same result, that entry is labeled with all of the sources. Figure 4-13 shows the Dogpile metasearch engine home page.

Dogpile metasearch home page | Figure 4-13

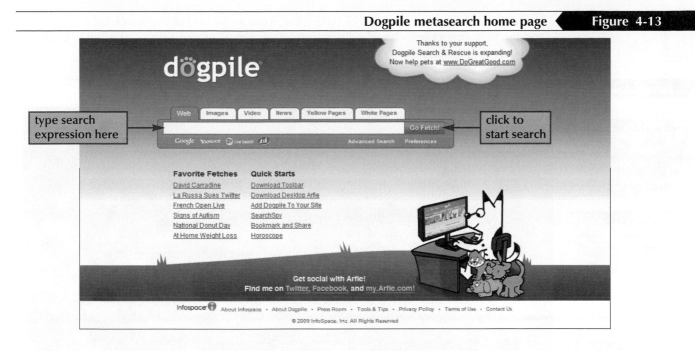

You want to learn how to use metasearch engines so that you can access information faster. You decide to test a metasearch engine using Dave's Belize rainfall question.

Using a Metasearch Engine | Reference Window

- Formulate your search question.
- Open the metasearch engine home page in your Web browser.
- Enter the search expression into the metasearch engine.
- Evaluate the results and decide whether to revise the question or your choice of search tools.

To use a metasearch engine:

▶ 1. Return to the Online Companion page for Session 4.1, choose one of the sites in the Metasearch Engines section, and click the link for the site you chose.

▶ 2. Type **Belize annual rainfall** in the search text box.

▶ 3. Execute the search by clicking the appropriate button.

▶ 4. Examine and evaluate your search results. If you did not find the information you were seeking, repeat your search using a different metasearch engine.

As you scroll through the search results pages, you can see that there is a wide variation in the number and usefulness of the results provided by each search engine and directory. You might notice a number of duplicate hits; however, most of the Web pages returned by one search tool are not returned by any other.

Figure 4-14 shows the results page from one of the more interesting metasearch engines, KartOO. KartOO presents results in a graphic format. Each image is a link and the images are clustered around words that appear in the results pages. When you move the pointer over a word, the links appear as lines between the word and the images. In the figure, the pointer is over the word "temperature," which adds that word to the end of the search expression and the clustering of links based on that term are shown as orange lines. The list of links on the left side of the page also changes to reflect the addition of the term.

Figure 4-14   KartOO metasearch graphic results

word added to end of search expression when pointer is over the word "temperature"

lines connect results pages that contain term being pointed to

pointer

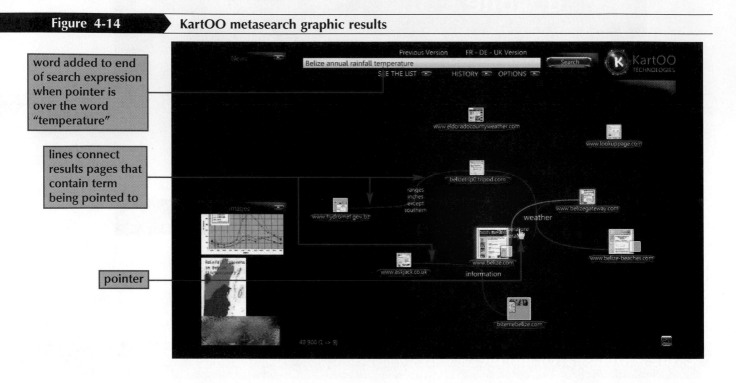

Using Web Bibliographies

In addition to search engines, Web directories, and metasearch engines, the Web includes **Web bibliographies**, another category of resource for searching the Internet. Web bibliographies can be very useful when you want to obtain a broad overview or a basic understanding of a complex subject area.

As their name suggests, Web bibliographies are similar to print bibliographies, but instead of listing books or journal articles, they contain lists of hyperlinks to Web pages. Just as some bibliographies are annotated, many of these resources include summaries or reviews of Web pages. Web bibliographies are also called **resource lists**, **subject guides**, **clearinghouses**, and **virtual libraries**. Sometimes they are called Web directories, which can be somewhat confusing. Web bibliographies are usually more focused on specific subjects than Web directories, and Web bibliographies usually do not include a tool for searching within their categories.

Using a search engine to locate broad information on a complex subject is likely to turn up a narrow list of references that are too detailed and that assume a great deal of prior knowledge. For example, using a search engine or directory to find information about quantum physics will probably give you many results that link to technical papers and Web pages devoted to current research issues in quantum physics. However, your search probably will yield very few Web pages that provide an introduction to the topic. In contrast, a Web bibliography page can offer hyperlinks to information regarding a particular subject that is presented at various levels. Many of these resources include annotations and reviews of the sites they list. This information can help you identify Web pages that fit your level of knowledge or interest.

Some Web bibliographies, such as Awesome Library and the Librarian's Internet Index, are general references. Most are more focused, such as Martindale's The Reference Desk,

Tip

You can often find useful subject guides by entering the search term along with the words "subject guide" into a regular search engine.

which emphasizes science-related links. Some Web bibliographies, such as the Internet Scout Archives, are no longer actively updated, but they are maintained on the Web as useful information resources.

Many Web bibliographies are created by librarians at university and public libraries. You can find Web bibliographies on specific subjects by entering a search term along with the words "subject guide" into a search engine. The results of an example search on the words "Native American subject guide" conducted in the Google search engine appear in Figure 4-15.

Results of a search on "Native American subject guide"   Figure 4-15

Web Images Video Maps News Shopping Gmail more ▾   Sign in

Google [Native American subject guide] [Search] Advanced Search / Preferences

Web Show options...   Results 1 - 10 of about 2,970,000 for Native American subject guide. (0.09 seconds)

ASU Libraries: **Native Americans Subject Guide**
NATIVE AMERICANS Subject Guide. The following bibliography lists reference material dealing with **Native Americans** and available in the University Libraries. ...
www.asu.edu/lib/archives/nasg.htm - 85k - Cached - Similar pages

American History and **American** Studies Research **Guide**
An author and subject index to journal articles and book reviews from English language ... **Native American** studies. Compiled by the Choice editorial staff. ...
www.library.yale.edu/rsc/native/ - 92k - Cached - Similar pages

Native American Studies Research **Guides** - HSU Library
Research Guides: **Native American** Studies ... the journal are online and there is both a subject index and a list of authors and titles for volumes 1-10. ...
library.humboldt.edu/~berman/nas.htm - 22k - Cached - Similar pages

Truman Library - **Native Americans Subject Guide**
OFFICIAL FILE - There are three major files in the Official File pertaining to **Native Americans**. OF 296 (Indians) contains general information about **Native** ...
www.trumanlibrary.org/hstpaper/nativeamericans.htm - 22k - Cached - Similar pages

Guide to **Native American** Legal Resources at the Connecticut State ...
The General Statutes of Connecticut detail the current laws pertaining to **Native Americans** in Connecticut. The statutes are indexed by subject for easy ...
www.cslib.org/indianres.htm - 33k - Cached - Similar pages

U.S. Department of the Interior Library - **Native Americans**
Alaska **Native** Claims Settlement Act Resource Center · **American** Indian Law Findlaw's subject guide to Indian Law includes summaries of law, ...
library.doi.gov/internet/subject/native.html - 46k - Cached - Similar pages

Subject Guides
The subject guides are also put together taking into account their accessibility, ... **Native American** Studies - Directory of Online Resources ...
www.academicinfo.net/subject-guides - 116k - Cached - Similar pages

Institute of **American** Indian Arts College / **SUBJECT GUIDE** - **Native** ...
SUBJECT GUIDES - **Native American** Resources on the Internet. IAIA / AIHEC Virtual Library. Information in subject areas that range from the arts and ...
www.iaia.edu/college/library/subject_guide_NAsites.php - 21k - Cached - Similar pages

USC Libraries :: **Native American** Studies **Subject Guide**
Native American Studies Subject Guide. For more information, please contact Sue Tyson, (213) 740 7044. Databases; EJournals; Websites ...
www.usc.edu/libraries/subjects/native_american/subject_guide/ - 37k -
Cached - Similar pages

University of Virginia **Subject Guides** - **Native Americans** - Home
Subject Guides. **Native Americans**. Home. Resources for **Native American** Research.
guides.lib.virginia.edu/native_americans - 36k - Cached - Similar pages

Book results for **Native American subject guide**
Twentieth Century Native American Art: Makers ... - by W Jackson Rushing - 256 pages
Handbook for Research in American History: A ... - by Francis Paul Prucha - 232 pages

Searches related to: **Native American subject guide**

native **indian tribes**   native **indians of north america**   native **pow wow**   native **peoples**

native american **animal guides**   native american **tribe chart**   native american **spirit guides**   native american **food guide pyramid**

Google Home - Advertising Programs - Business Solutions - Privacy - About Google

Search results include several links to Web bibliographies about Native Americans

Tip

If you regularly do research in a specific field, it can be helpful to ask other researchers who work in the field if they know of useful Web bibliographies that specialize in relevant subjects.

Another way to find Web bibliographies is to use a Web directory site. Many Web directories include links to subject-specific Web bibliographies within the category listings for those subjects. For example, the Yahoo! Web directory includes a link titled "Web Directories" within its Social Science category. This link leads to a list of Web bibliographies on the subject of social science. It also has similar links in many of the social science subcategories, such as Economics. Other Web directories include similar links.

Ranjit is planning a series of pieces on the business and economic effects of current trends in biotechnology, including information about the potential effects of genetic engineering research. You need to find some Web sites that Ranjit can use to learn more about biotechnology trends in general and genetic engineering research in particular. You determine that an exploratory search will locate the required information, and you decide to use a Web bibliography site for your research. Biotechnology is a branch of the biological sciences, so you will use three category terms: *biotechnology*, *genetic engineering*, and *biology* as your search categories. Many Web bibliographies contain hyperlinks to other useful sites. You can collect information from these pages by printing copies of the Web pages, sending the URLs by email, or saving the Web pages and attaching them to an email message. You can also copy and paste relevant text from the Web pages into an email or a document.

To use a Web bibliography to conduct an exploratory search:

▶ **1.** Return to the Online Companion page for Session 4.1, choose one of the sites in the Web Bibliographies section, and click its link.

▶ **2.** Use the search tool in the Web bibliography you chose to find links to general information about biotechnology, genetic engineering, or biology. Follow those links to gather information relative to your search. Make a note of any article titles that you think would be interesting to Ranjit.

▶ **3.** Examine your search results and determine whether you have gathered sufficient useful information to provide to Ranjit. If you have not, repeat the search using a different Web bibliography.

▶ **4.** Close your browser.

You have completed your search for Web sites containing information about genetic engineering and biotechnology. Because your answer to Ranjit's question involves so many pages at different sites, your best approach would be to send an email message with a list of relevant URLs.

Review	**Session 4.1 Quick Check**

1. What are the key characteristics of an exploratory search question?
2. True or False: Many Web search engine operators use advertising revenue to cover their expenses and to earn a profit.
3. The part of a search engine site that is a program that automatically searches the Web to find new Web sites is called a(n) _____ .
4. A search engine that uses page ranking will list a Web page near the top of search results pages if the page has many _____ .
5. True or False: Most search engines index all Web page contents in their databases.
6. List one advantage and one disadvantage of using a Web directory instead of a Web search engine to locate information.

7. How does a hybrid search engine directory overcome the disadvantages of using either a search engine or a directory alone?

8. How does a metasearch engine process the search expression you enter into it?

9. How can you find Web bibliographies about a specific subject area?

Session 4.2

Complex Searches with Boolean Logic and Filtering Techniques

The most important factor in obtaining good results from a search engine, a metasearch engine, or a search tool within a hybrid search engine directory is careful selection of the search terms you use. When the object of your search is straightforward, you can usually choose one or two words that will work well. More complex search questions require more complex queries, which you can use along with Boolean logic, search expression operators, wildcard operators, or filtering techniques, to broaden or narrow your search expression. In this session, you will learn how to research various topics for Dave and Ranjit using these advanced techniques.

The Boolean operators and filtering techniques you will learn to use in this session can also be helpful when you are doing searches in library databases. These databases, which can be very expensive to purchase, provide much information that cannot be found on the Internet and are often available at school libraries, company libraries, or your local public libraries. Each database has its own implementation of Boolean operators and filtering tools, but the principles you learn here will help you in formulating your searches of these library databases.

Boolean Operators

When you enter a single word into a Web search tool, it searches for matches to that word. When you enter a search expression that includes more than one word, the search tool makes assumptions about the words that you enter. You learned in Session 4.1 that some search engines assume that you want to match *any* of the keywords in your search expression, whereas other search engines assume that you want to match *all* of the keywords. These differing assumptions can result in dramatic differences in the number and quality of hits returned. Some search engines are designed to offer both options because users might want to match all of the keywords on one search and any of the keywords on a different search. One way of implementing these options is to use Boolean operators in the search expression.

George Boole was a nineteenth-century British mathematician who developed **Boolean algebra**, the branch of mathematics and logic that bears his name. In Boolean algebra, all values are reduced to one of two values. In most practical applications of Boole's work, these two values are *true* and *false*. Although Boole did his work a hundred years before computers became commonplace, his algebra is still useful to computer engineers and programmers. At the very lowest level of analysis, all computing is a manipulation of two values—a single computer circuit's on and off states. Unlike the algebra you might have learned in your math classes, Boolean algebra does not use numbers or mathematical operators. Instead, Boolean algebra uses words and logical relationships.

Some parts of Boolean algebra are useful in search expressions. **Boolean operators**, also called **logical operators**, are a key part of Boolean algebra. Boolean operators specify the logical relationship between the elements they join, just as the plus sign arithmetic operator specifies the mathematical relationship between the two elements it joins. Three basic Boolean operators—AND, OR, and NOT—are recognized by most search engines. You can use these operators in many search engines by simply including them with search terms. For example, the search expression "exports AND France" returns hits for pages that contain both words, the expression "exports OR France" returns hits for pages that contain either word, and "exports NOT France" returns hits for pages that contain the word *export* but not the word *France*. Some search engines use "AND NOT" to indicate the Boolean NOT operator.

Some search engines recognize variants of the Boolean operators, such as "must include" and "must exclude" operators. For example, a search engine that uses the plus sign to indicate "must include" and the minus sign to indicate "must exclude" would respond to the expression "exports + France - Japan" with hits that included anything about exports and France, but only if those pages did not include anything about Japan.

Figure 4-16 shows several ways to use Boolean operators in more complex search expressions that contain the words *exports*, *France*, and *Japan*. The figure shows the matches that a search engine will return if it interprets the Boolean operators correctly. Figure 4-16 also describes information-gathering tasks in which you might use these expressions.

Figure 4-16	Using Boolean operators in search expressions

Search Expression	Search Returns Pages That Include	Use to Find Information About
exports AND France AND Japan	All of the three search terms.	Exports from France to Japan or from Japan to France.
exports OR France OR Japan	Any of the three search terms.	Exports from anywhere, including France and Japan, and all kinds of information about France and Japan.
exports NOT France NOT Japan	Exports, but not if the page also includes the terms France or Japan.	Exports to and from any countries other than France or Japan.
exports AND France NOT Japan	Exports and France, but not Japan.	Exports from France to anywhere but Japan or to France from anywhere but Japan.

Other Search Expression Operators

When you join three or more search terms with Boolean operators, it is easy to become confused by the expression's complexity. To reduce the confusion, you can use precedence operators, a tool you probably learned in basic algebra, along with the Boolean operators. A **precedence operator**, also called an **inclusion operator** or a **grouping operator**, clarifies the grouping within a complex expression and is usually indicated by the parentheses symbols. Figure 4-17 shows several ways to use precedence operators with Boolean operators in search expressions.

Using Boolean and precedence operators in search expressions | Figure 4-17

Search Expression	Search Returns Pages That Include	Use to Find Information About
Exports AND (France OR Japan)	Exports and either France or Japan.	Exports from or to either France or Japan.
Exports OR (France AND Japan)	Exports or both France and Japan.	Exports from anywhere, including France and Japan, and all kinds of other information about both France and Japan.
Exports AND (France NOT Japan)	Exports and France, but not if the page also includes Japan.	Exports to and from France, except those to or from Japan.

Some search engines use double quotation marks to indicate precedence grouping; however, most search engines use double quotation marks to indicate search terms that must be matched exactly as they appear within the double quotation marks. Using an exact match search phrase can be particularly useful because most search engines ignore stop words by default. You can force most search engines to include a stop word (that they would, by default, ignore) in a search expression by enclosing it in double quotation marks (or by including it in an exact search phrase that is enclosed in double quotation marks).

Another useful search expression tool is the location operator. A **location operator**, or **proximity operator**, lets you search for terms that appear close to each other in the text of a Web page. The most common location operator offered in Web search engines is the NEAR operator. If you are interested in French exports, you might want to find only Web pages in which the terms *exports* and *France* are close to each other. Unfortunately, each search engine that implements this operator uses its own definition of "NEAR." One search engine might define NEAR to mean "within 10 words," whereas another search engine might define NEAR to mean "within 20 words." For example, the Exalead search engine interprets NEAR to mean "within 16 words," unless you enter a specific number (such as NEAR/4, which would mean "within four words"). To use the NEAR operator effectively, you must read the search engine's Help file carefully.

Wildcard Characters

A few search engines support some use of a wildcard character in their search expressions. A **wildcard character** allows you to omit part of a search term. The search engines that include this function most commonly use the asterisk (*) as the wildcard character. For example, the search expression "export*" would return pages containing the terms *exports, exporter, exporters,* and *exporting* in many search engines. Some search engines let you use a wildcard character in the middle of a search term. For example, the expression "wom*n" would return pages containing both *woman* and *women*.

Search Filters

Many search engines allow you to restrict your search by using search filters. A **search filter** eliminates Web pages from search results. The filter criteria can include such Web page attributes as language, date, domain, host, or page component (URL, hyperlink, image tag, or title tag). For example, many search engines provide a way to search for the term *exports* in Web page titles and ignore pages in which the term appears in other parts of the page.

Performing Complex Searches

Most search engines implement many of the operators and filtering techniques you have learned about in this session. The way in which various search engines apply these techniques can differ; some search engines provide separate advanced search pages for these techniques, while others allow you to use advanced techniques such as Boolean operators on their simple search pages.

This section describes how to conduct complex searches in several specific search engines. The steps are correct as this book is printed, but the Web is a changing medium. When you perform these steps, the screens you see might look different and you might need to modify the steps. If you encounter difficulties, ask your instructor for assistance or read the Help pages on the search engine site. If major changes occur, the Online Companion Web site will be updated to indicate how to make the searches work.

Using Exalead to Perform a Boolean Search

Ranjit is writing about the role that trade agreements play in limiting the flow of agricultural commodities between countries. His current project concerns the German economy. Your job is to find some Web page references that might provide useful background information. Ranjit is especially interested in learning more about the German perspective on trade issues.

You recognize this as an exploratory question and decide to use the Boolean search capabilities of the Exalead search engine to conduct a complex search for Web pages. Exalead offers very good support for Boolean and precedence operators.

To create a useful search expression, you must identify search terms that might lead you to appropriate Web pages. Some terms you might use for the search are *Germany*, *trade*, *treaty*, and *agriculture*. You want to locate a reasonable number of hyperlinks to Web pages, but you do not want to search through thousands of URLs, so you decide to combine the search terms using Boolean logic to increase the chances that the search engine will return only useful sites.

Reference Window | **Conducting a Boolean Search Using Exalead**

- Open the Exalead search engine in your Web browser.
- Formulate the Boolean search.
- Enter the search terms formatted with the Boolean and precedence operators.
- Click the Web Search button.
- Evaluate the results and, if necessary, revise your search expression.

To perform a Boolean search using Exalead:

▶ 1. Start your Web browser, go to **www.cengage.com/internet/np/internet8** to open the Online Companion page, log in to your account, click the **Tutorial 4** link, click the **Session 4.2** link, and then click the **Exalead** link.

▶ 2. Click the **Web** link on the Exalead page, if necessary.

▶ 3. Type **(Germany AND trade) AND (treaty OR agriculture)** into the text box.

▶ 4. Click the **Search** button to start the search. The results appear in Figure 4-18. The results page includes several sponsored links and links to narrowed versions of the search.

Boolean search in Exalead | Figure 4-18

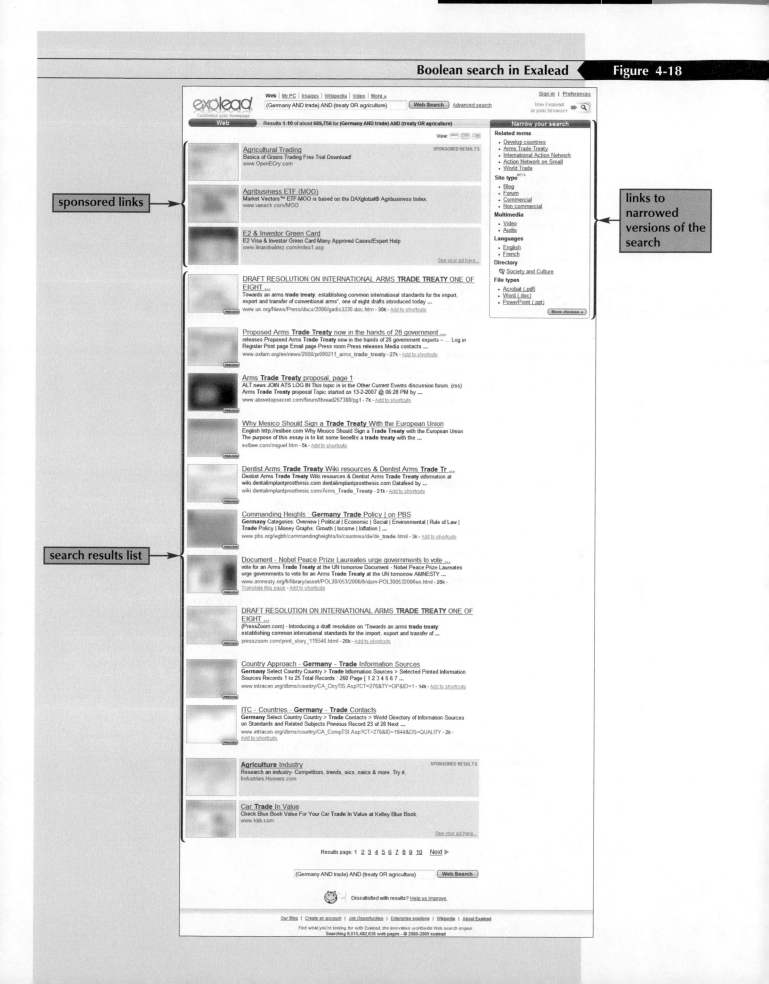

▶ **5.** After visiting several of the pages listed on the search results page, you summarize the information you found about the German perspective on agricultural trade issues and email it to Ranjit.

Filtered Search in Ask.com

Some search engines provide specific filtering options in addition to or instead of Boolean operators. The Ask.com search engine offers several such options on its Advanced Search page, including filters for date and geographic region.

Dave is writing about the upcoming corn harvest in Brazil. He wants you to check on developments that have occurred during the past six months in that country. You decide to use the Ask.com search engine to run a filtered search query.

Reference Window | **Conducting a Filtered Search Using Ask.com**

- Open the Ask.com search engine page in your Web browser.
- Click the Advanced link.
- Formulate and enter a suitable search expression.
- Set any filters you want to use for the search.
- Click the Advanced Search button.
- Evaluate the results and, if necessary, revise your search expression.

To perform a filtered search using Ask.com:

▶ **1.** Return to the Online Companion page for Session 4.2, and then click the **Ask.com** link.

▶ **2.** Click the **Advanced** link to open the Ask.com Advanced Search page.

▶ **3.** Type **corn harvest** in the Find results with all of the words text box.

▶ **4.** Click the **Country** list arrow, and then click **Brazil** to set the Country filter.

▶ **5.** Click the **Page modified** list arrow, and then click **Last 6 months** to set the date filter.

▶ **6.** Click the **Advanced Search** button to start the search. The search results page will display the search expression, the filter settings, and a list of links to related Web pages. The results also include a list of links to related searches that you can use to broaden your inquiry.

▶ **7.** Examine your search results and determine whether you have gathered sufficient useful information to complete the search. Since the search returned some links that contain information relevant to Dave's query, you can conclude the search by forwarding the URLs to Dave.

Filtered Search in Google

Dave is writing an item about Finland and would like to interview a professor he once met who taught graduate business students there. He does not remember the professor's name or the name of the university at which the professor teaches, but he does remember that the professor taught business subjects at a university in Finland. Dave is confident that he would recognize the university's name if he saw it again. He asks if you can search the Web to find the names of some Finnish universities.

You decide to use the Google search engine for this task. To create a useful search expression, you must identify search terms that might lead you to appropriate Web pages. You decide to include *Finland* as a search term. Also, Dave told you that graduate schools of business in Europe are often called Schools of Economics, so you decide to include the exact phrase *School of Economics* in your search. You know that the country code for Finland is *.fi*, so you decide to limit the search to Web pages in this top-level domain. Because Dave reads only English, you also decide to limit the search to pages that are in English.

| **Conducting a Filtered Search Using Google Advanced Search** | Reference Window |

- Open the Google search engine page in your Web browser.
- Click the Advanced Search link.
- Formulate and enter suitable search expression elements.
- Formulate and set appropriate search filters.
- Click the Advanced Search Search button.
- Evaluate the results and, if necessary, revise your search expression.

To perform a filtered search using Google Advanced Search:

1. Return to the Online Companion page for Session 4.2, and then click the **Google** link.

2. Click the **Advanced Search** link to open the Google Advanced Search page.

3. Click in the **Find web pages that have all these words** text box at the top of the page, and then type **Finland**.

4. Click in the **Find web pages that have this exact wording or phrase** text box, and then type **School of Economics**.

5. Click the arrow on the **Language** drop-down selection box, and then click **English**.

6. Click in the **Search within a site or domain** text box, and then type **.fi**. Figure 4-19 shows the Google Advanced Search page with the search expressions entered and the filters set.

> **Tip**
>
> You might need to try different combinations of filters to get a set of search results that works.

Figure 4-19 ▶ **Google Advanced Search page**

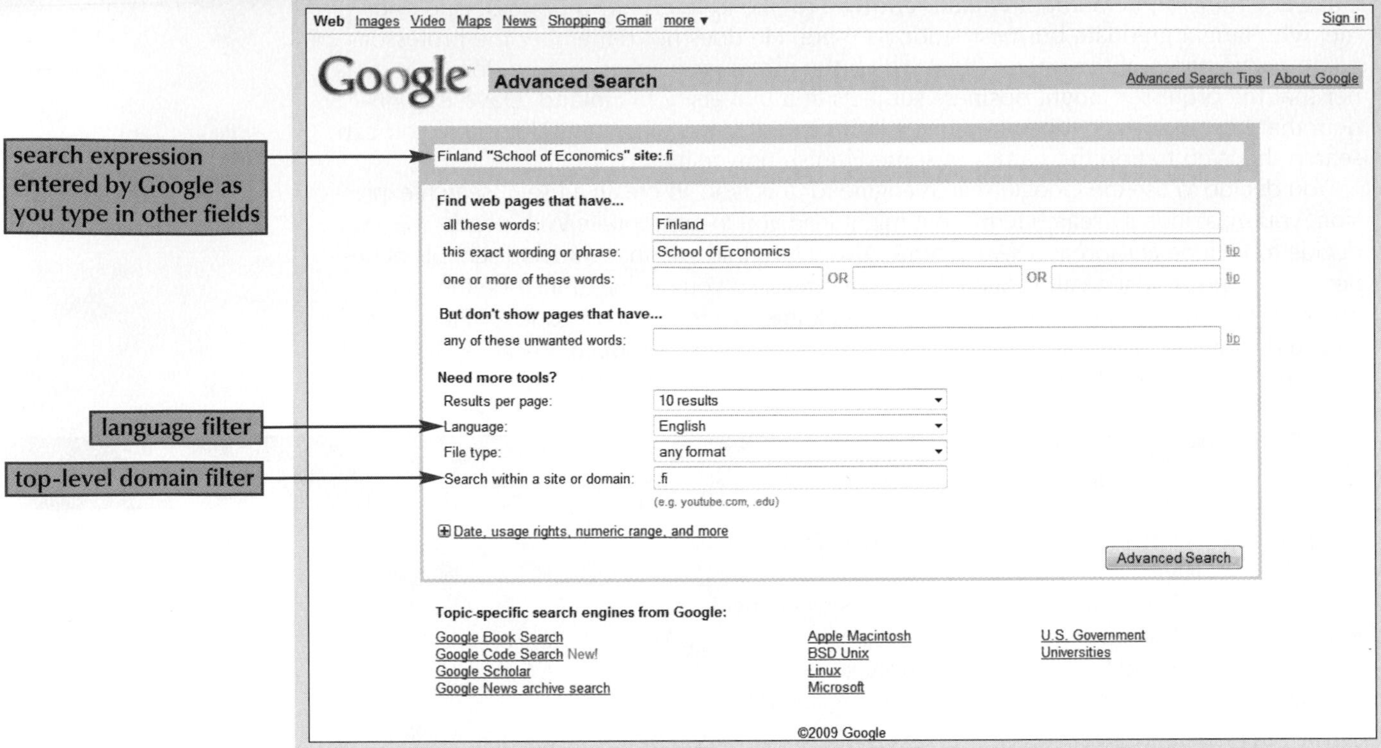

search expression entered by Google as you type in other fields

Web Images Video Maps News Shopping Gmail more ▼   Sign in

Google Advanced Search   Advanced Search Tips | About Google

Finland "School of Economics" site:.fi

Find web pages that have...

all these words: Finland

this exact wording or phrase: School of Economics   tip

one or more of these words: OR   OR   tip

But don't show pages that have...

any of these unwanted words: tip

Need more tools?

Results per page: 10 results   ▼

language filter ──▶ Language: English   ▼

File type: any format   ▼

top-level domain filter ──▶ Search within a site or domain: .fi
                                (e.g. youtube.com, .edu)

⊞ Date, usage rights, numeric range, and more

                                        [Advanced Search]

Topic-specific search engines from Google:

Google Book Search   Apple Macintosh   U.S. Government
Google Code Search New!   BSD Unix   Universities
Google Scholar   Linux
Google News archive search   Microsoft

                        ©2009 Google

▶ **7.** Click the **Advanced Search** button to start the search. The top portion of the search results page appears in Figure 4-20 and includes a number of links to Finnish universities.

Google Advanced Search results page   Figure 4-20

filters and exact
search expressions
used in this search

search results list,
your search results
will be different

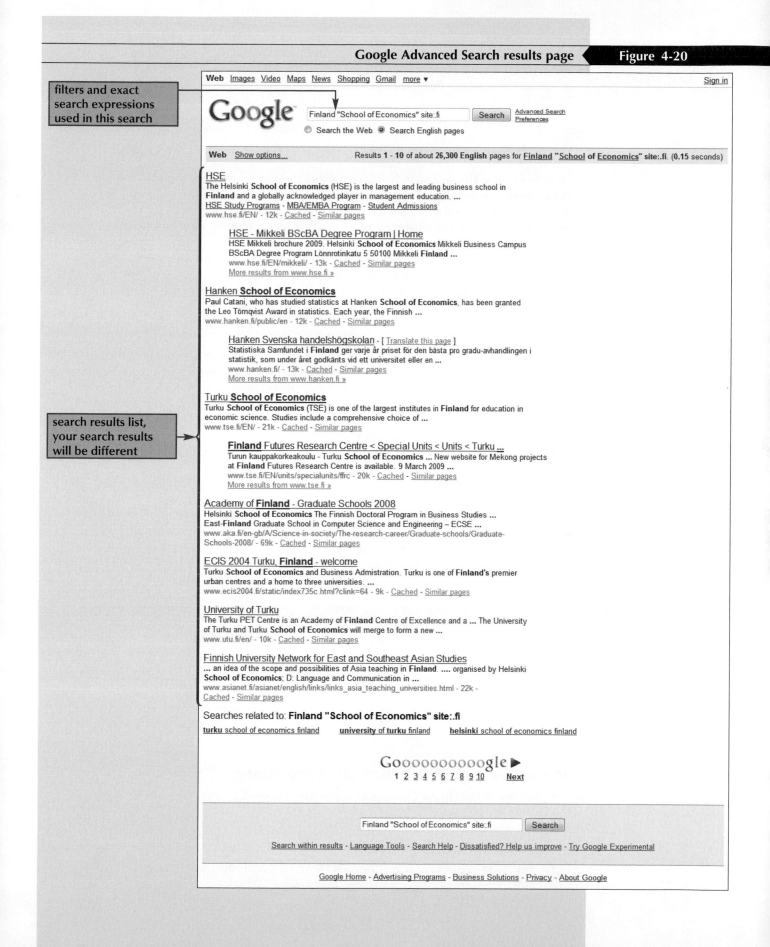

▶ **8.** Examine your search results and determine which of the hyperlinks in the search results lead to Finnish universities. You can send a list of these links to Dave in an email message. Remember that you might need to examine several pages of search results to find exactly what you need.

Search Engines with Clustering Features

One problem with using search engines is that they often generate thousands (or even millions) of hits. Scrolling through hundreds of results pages looking for useful links is not very efficient. Clusty is a search engine that uses an advanced technology to group its results into clusters. The clustering of results provides a filtering effect; however, the filtering is done automatically by the search engine after it runs the search. Clustering is especially effective when a word in the search expression has multiple meanings. For example, the word "java" can mean the name of an island, the name of a programming language, or a slang term for coffee. Clustered results place each of these meanings in separate categories.

There are two strategies used to implement search results clustering. One approach is to create categories as the search engine database is built. Each Web page that is stored in the database is placed into one or more categories. A second approach creates the categories after the search expression is run against the database. The search engine constructs the categories on the fly and uses information about all the words in the search expression (and their relations to each other and keywords in the Web pages selected). Clusty uses the second approach. You would like to try this search engine to see if its clustering feature provides results that are easier to review.

Ranjit is writing about fast-food franchises in various developing countries. He needs your help gathering information on this industry's experience in Indonesia. You decide to run this search using the Clusty search engine. To create a useful search expression, you must identify search terms that might lead you to appropriate Web pages. Some terms you might use include *Indonesia*, *fast food*, and *franchise*. You are not interested in Web pages that have the individual terms *fast* and *food*, so you will use double quotation marks to specify the phrase "fast food." The Clusty search engine uses its clustering feature as a substitute for Boolean logic, so you will enter a simple expression and let Clusty filter your results into searchable categories.

Reference Window | **Obtaining Clustered Search Results Using Clusty**

- Open the Clusty search engine page in your browser.
- Formulate and enter a suitable search expression.
- Click the Search button.
- Evaluate the results and, if necessary, revise your search expression.

To obtain clustered search results using Clusty:

▶ **1.** Return to the Online Companion page for Session 4.2, and then click the **Clusty** link.

▶ **2.** Click in the Search text box if necessary, and then type **Indonesia "fast food" franchise**. Make sure that you type the quotation marks so that you find the phrase "fast food" instead of the individual terms *fast* and *food*.

3. Click the **Search** button to start the search. Figure 4-21 shows the search results page, which includes links to a number of promising Web pages.

Clusty search results page ◄ **Figure 4-21**

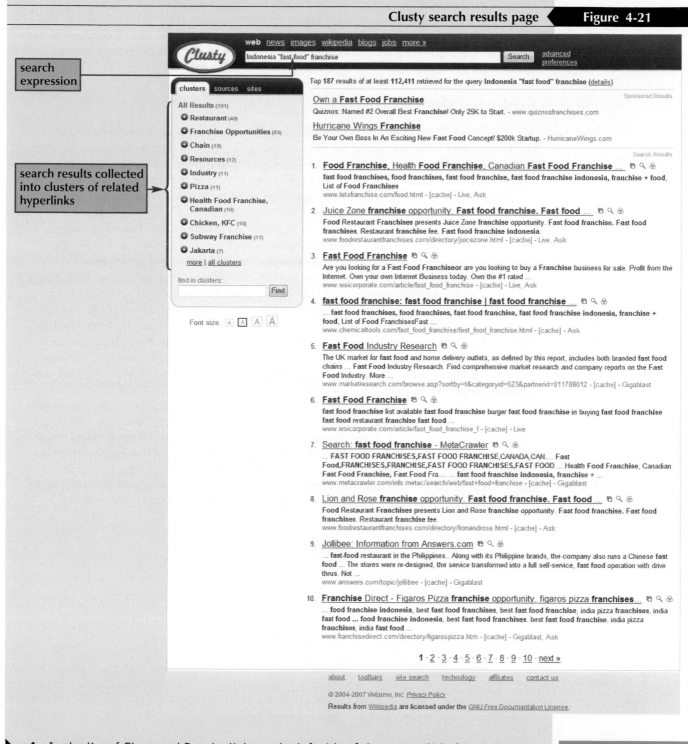

search expression

search results collected into clusters of related hyperlinks

4. In the list of Clustered Results links at the left side of the page, click the category links that look promising. Examine the search results from each cluster and determine whether you have gathered sufficient information about the fast-food industry in Indonesia.

Tip

You can click the circles that contain plus signs to reveal links to subcategories.

A unique feature of Clusty is that it collects search results into clusters and runs the clustering algorithms as the search results are returned. That is, instead of classifying Web pages into categories in its database, it creates the categories dynamically after it processes the search expression. Clusty defines its clusters using artificial intelligence. The clustering is done in real time for each search and depends on the search expression and the clustering algorithm, which is continually revised. Your search provides a number of useful links for Ranjit.

Exploring the Deep Web

Many different companies and organizations are working on ways to make searching the Web easier and more successful for the increasing numbers of people who use the Web. One weakness of most current search engines and Web directories is that they only search static Web pages. A **static Web page** is an HTML file that exists on a Web server computer. The robots used by search engines to build their databases can find and examine these files.

An increasing number of Web sites do not store information as HTML files. Instead, they store information in a database, and when a user submits a query in the search function of the site, the site's Web server searches the database and generates a Web page on the fly that includes information from the database. These generated Web pages are called **dynamic Web pages**. For example, if you visit Amazon.com and search for books about birds, the Amazon.com Web server queries a database that contains information about books and generates a dynamic Web page that includes that information. This Web page is not stored permanently on the Web server and cannot be found or examined by search engine robots. Much of the information stored in these databases can only be accessed by users who have a login and password to the Web site that generates dynamic pages from the database.

Several researchers have explored the difficulties that search engine robots face when trying to include information contained in the databases that some Web sites use to generate their dynamic pages. Some researchers call this information the **deep Web**; other researchers use the terms **hidden Web** and **invisible Web**. Many of these researchers are working at universities and research institutes. One team, working at the University of Utah, has created an experimental Web site that allows visitors to search the deep Web. The home page of this site, called DeepPeep, is shown in Figure 4-22.

DeepPeep home page ◄ Figure 4-22

A Web site that combines deep Web search with a clustering technology for results is Kosmix. A search at Kosmix is run against a database of URLs (the same approach used by most standard search engines), but it is also used to create queries that are run against databases derived from queries that Kosmix runs in the search functions of other Web sites. This provides access to parts of the deep Web. You decide to use Kosmix to find information about fast food franchising in Indonesia for Ranjit.

To obtain clustered search results from the deep Web using Kosmix:

▶ **1.** Return to the Online Companion page for Session 4.2, and then click the **Kosmix** link.

▶ **2.** Click in the text box near the top of the page if necessary, and then type **Indonesia "fast food" franchise**. Make sure that you type the quotation marks so that you find the phrase "fast food" instead of the individual terms *fast* and *food*.

▶ **3.** Click the **Explore** button to start the search. The search results page appears, which includes a number of information items with links to more details. The green links near the top of the page are the clusters into which Kosmix has categorized many of the search results. These clusters are customized results for the search expression you entered and will be different for other search expressions or for the same search expression entered at a later date (because the information in the Kosmix databases gathered from the deep Web will change over time).

> **4.** Click any of the links on the page or on the category links near the top of the page that look promising. Examine the search results and determine whether you have gathered sufficient information about the fast-food industry in Indonesia for Ranjit.

Using People to Enhance Web Directories

One company, About.com, hires people with expertise in specific subject areas to create and manage its Web directory entries in those areas. Although both Yahoo! and MSN Search use subject matter experts this way, About.com takes the idea one step further and identifies its experts. Each About.com expert, called a Guide, hosts a page with hyperlinks to related Web pages, moderates discussion areas, and provides an online newsletter. This creates a community of interested persons from around the world that can participate in maintaining the Web directory.

The Open Directory Project uses the services of more than 40,000 volunteer editors who maintain listings in their individual areas of interest. The Open Directory Project offers the information in its Web directory to other Web directories and search engines at no charge. Many of the major Web directory, search engine, and metasearch engine sites regularly download and store the Open Directory Project's information in their databases. For example, AlltheWeb, AltaVista, DogPile, and Google all include Open Directory Project information in their databases.

Evaluating Web Research Resources

One of the most important issues in conducting research on the Web is assessing the validity and quality of the information provided on the Internet. Because the Web has made publishing so easy and inexpensive, virtually anybody can create a Web page on almost any subject. Research published in scientific or literary journals is subjected to peer review. Similarly, books and research monographs are often reviewed by peers or edited by experts in the appropriate subject area. However, information on the Web is seldom subjected to the review and editing processes that have become a standard practice in print publishing.

When you search the Web for entertainment or general information, you are not likely to experience significant harm as a result of gathering inaccurate or unreliable information. When you are searching the Web for an answer to a serious research question, however, the risks of obtaining and relying on inaccurate or unreliable information can be significant.

You can reduce your risks by carefully evaluating the quality of any Web resource on which you plan to rely for information related to an important judgment or decision. To develop an opinion about the quality of the resource, you can evaluate three major components of any Web page: the Web page's authorship, content, and appearance.

Author Identity and Objectivity

The first thing you should try to do when evaluating a Web research resource is to determine who authored the page. If you cannot easily find authorship information on a Web site, you should question the validity of the information included on the site. A Web site that does not identify its author has very little credibility as a research resource. Any Web page that presents empirical research results, logical arguments, theories, or other information that purports to be the result of a research process should identify the author *and* present the author's background information and credentials. The information on the site should be sufficient to establish the author's professional qualifications. You should also check secondary sources for corroborating information. For example, if the author of a

Web page indicates that he or she is a member of a university faculty, you can find the university's Web site and see if the author is listed as a faculty member. The Web site should also provide author contact information, such as a street address, email address, or telephone number, so that you can contact the author or consult information directories to verify the addresses or telephone numbers.

You also should consider whether the qualifications presented by the author pertain to the material that appears on the Web site. For example, the author of a Web site concerned with gene-splicing technology might list a Ph.D. degree as a credential. If the author's Ph.D. is in history or sociology, it would not support the credibility of the gene-splicing technology Web site. If you cannot determine the specific areas of the author's educational background, you can look for other examples of the author's work on the Web. By searching for the author's name and terms related to the subject area, you should be able to find other sites that include the author's work. The fact that a Web site author has written extensively on a subject can provide some evidence—though not necessarily conclusive evidence—that the author has expertise in the field.

In addition to identifying the author's identity and qualifications, author information should include details about the author's affiliations—either as an employee, owner, or consultant—with organizations that might have an interest in the research results or other information included in the Web site. Information about the author's affiliations will help you determine the level of independence and objectivity that the author can bring to bear on the research questions or topics. For example, research results supporting the contention that cigarette smoke is not harmful presented in a site authored by a researcher with excellent scientific credentials might be less compelling if you learn that the researcher is the chief scientist at a major tobacco company. By reading the page content carefully, you might be able to identify potential bias in the results presented.

Determining Web Site Ownership | InSight

In some cases, it can be difficult to determine who owns a specific Web server or provides the space for the Web page. You can make a rough assessment, however, by examining the domain identifier in the URL. If the site claims affiliation with an educational or research institution, the domain should be .edu for educational institution. A not-for-profit organization would most likely have the .org domain, and a government unit or agency would have the .gov domain. These are not hard-and-fast rules, however. For example, some perfectly legitimate not-for-profit organizations have URLs with a .com domain.

Relevance and Characteristics of Content

The relevance of a site's content to your research question can be more difficult to judge than the author's identity and objectivity; after all, people often search the Web to learn about topics with which they are not familiar. However, some characteristics of the content on a Web page can help you determine whether that content will help you answer your research question. If the Web page has a clearly stated publication date, you can determine the timeliness of the content. You can read the content with a critical eye and evaluate whether the included topics are relevant to your research question. You might be able to determine whether important topics or considerations were omitted by comparing the content to what you find on other Web pages devoted to the topic. Comparisons to other Web pages can help you assess the depth of treatment the author gives to the subject. You can also search other Web sites to confirm that factual information presented is similar to factual information presented on these other sites. However, this does not guarantee that the information is correct, since it is possible for a number of sites to have incorrect information.

Another characteristic of content is whether it acknowledges its own bias. Some Web pages present a balance of viewpoints, but many are created for the specific purpose of supporting a particular position. This is especially true if the issue is contentious. The best Web sites with information on contentious issues always make clear which site they are taking in the argument and show respect for the position taken by the other side.

Form and Appearance

A Web site that is a legitimate source of accurate information usually presents its information in a professional form that helps convey its validity. Many Web pages that contain low-quality or incorrect information are poorly designed and not well edited. For example, a Web page devoted to an analysis of Shakespeare's plays that contains spelling errors is likely to be a low-quality resource. Loud colors, graphics that serve no purpose, and flashing text are all Web page design elements that often indicate that the Web page is a low-quality resource. However, these indicators are not infallible. The Web does contain pages full of misinformation and outright lies that are nicely laid out, include professionally produced graphics, and have grammatically correct and properly spelled text.

Evaluating the Quality of a Web Site

Now that you understand the principles of assessing Web page quality, Anne asks you to evaluate a Web page. Anne has been doing research on how companies can appeal to children on the Web by promoting products while not taking advantage of the children who visit their sites. Anne would like you to evaluate the quality of a URL titled "Kids' Corner."

Reference Window | **Evaluating a Web Research Resource**

- Open the Web page in your Web browser.
- Identify the author, if possible. If you can identify the author, evaluate his or her credentials and objectivity.
- Examine the content of the Web site.
- Evaluate the site's form and appearance.
- Draw a conclusion about the site's overall quality.

To evaluate the quality of the Kids' Corner Web page:

▶ **1.** Return to the Online Companion page for Session 4.2.

▶ **2.** Click the **Kids' Corner** link. The browser loads the Web page that appears in Figure 4-23. Examine the content of the Web page, read the text, examine the titles and headings, and consider the page's appearance.

Kids' Corner Web page | Figure 4-23

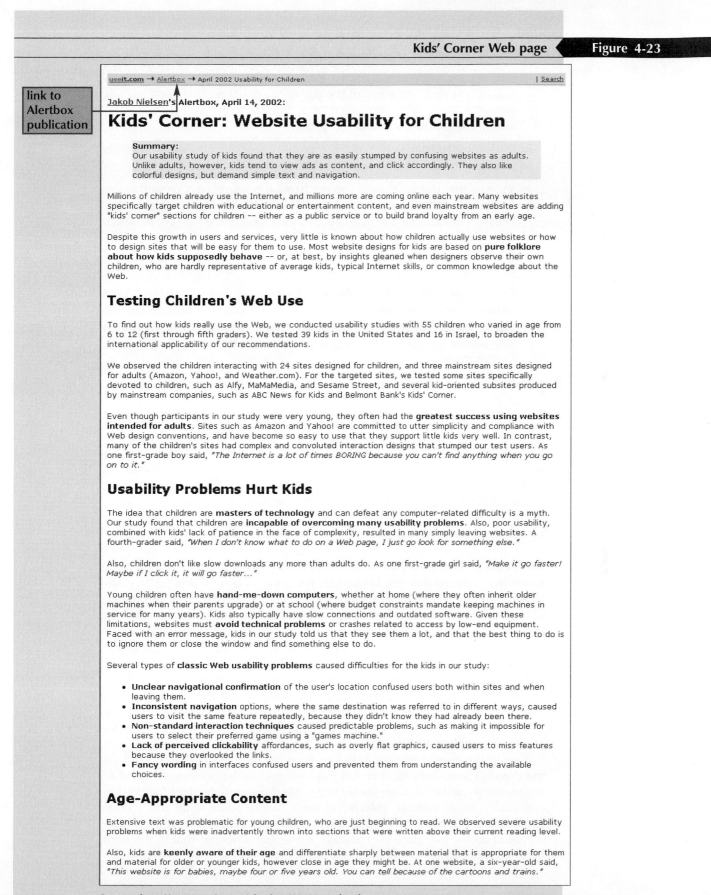

link to Alertbox publication

useit.com → Alertbox → April 2002 Usability for Children | Search

Jakob Nielsen's Alertbox, April 14, 2002:

Kids' Corner: Website Usability for Children

Summary:
Our usability study of kids found that they are as easily stumped by confusing websites as adults. Unlike adults, however, kids tend to view ads as content, and click accordingly. They also like colorful designs, but demand simple text and navigation.

Millions of children already use the Internet, and millions more are coming online each year. Many websites specifically target children with educational or entertainment content, and even mainstream websites are adding "kids' corner" sections for children -- either as a public service or to build brand loyalty from an early age.

Despite this growth in users and services, very little is known about how children actually use websites or how to design sites that will be easy for them to use. Most website designs for kids are based on **pure folklore about how kids supposedly behave** -- or, at best, by insights gleaned when designers observe their own children, who are hardly representative of average kids, typical Internet skills, or common knowledge about the Web.

Testing Children's Web Use

To find out how kids really use the Web, we conducted usability studies with 55 children who varied in age from 6 to 12 (first through fifth graders). We tested 39 kids in the United States and 16 in Israel, to broaden the international applicability of our recommendations.

We observed the children interacting with 24 sites designed for children, and three mainstream sites designed for adults (Amazon, Yahoo!, and Weather.com). For the targeted sites, we tested some sites specifically devoted to children, such as Alfy, MaMaMedia, and Sesame Street, and several kid-oriented subsites produced by mainstream companies, such as ABC News for Kids and Belmont Bank's Kids' Corner.

Even though participants in our study were very young, they often had the **greatest success using websites intended for adults**. Sites such as Amazon and Yahoo! are committed to utter simplicity and compliance with Web design conventions, and have become so easy to use that they support little kids very well. In contrast, many of the children's sites had complex and convoluted interaction designs that stumped our test users. As one first-grade boy said, *"The Internet is a lot of times BORING because you can't find anything when you go on to it."*

Usability Problems Hurt Kids

The idea that children are **masters of technology** and can defeat any computer-related difficulty is a myth. Our study found that children are **incapable of overcoming many usability problems**. Also, poor usability, combined with kids' lack of patience in the face of complexity, resulted in many simply leaving websites. A fourth-grader said, *"When I don't know what to do on a Web page, I just go look for something else."*

Also, children don't like slow downloads any more than adults do. As one first-grade girl said, *"Make it go faster! Maybe if I click it, it will go faster..."*

Young children often have **hand-me-down computers**, whether at home (where they often inherit older machines when their parents upgrade) or at school (where budget constraints mandate keeping machines in service for many years). Kids also typically have slow connections and outdated software. Given these limitations, websites must **avoid technical problems** or crashes related to access by low-end equipment. Faced with an error message, kids in our study told us that they see them a lot, and that the best thing to do is to ignore them or close the window and find something else to do.

Several types of **classic Web usability problems** caused difficulties for the kids in our study:

- **Unclear navigational confirmation** of the user's location confused users both within sites and when leaving them.
- **Inconsistent navigation** options, where the same destination was referred to in different ways, caused users to visit the same feature repeatedly, because they didn't know they had already been there.
- **Non-standard interaction techniques** caused predictable problems, such as making it impossible for users to select their preferred game using a "games machine."
- **Lack of perceived clickability** affordances, such as overly flat graphics, caused users to miss features because they overlooked the links.
- **Fancy wording** in interfaces confused users and prevented them from understanding the available choices.

Age-Appropriate Content

Extensive text was problematic for young children, who are just beginning to read. We observed severe usability problems when kids were inadvertently thrown into sections that were written above their current reading level.

Also, kids are **keenly aware of their age** and differentiate sharply between material that is appropriate for them and material for older or younger kids, however close in age they might be. At one website, a six-year-old said, *"This website is for babies, maybe four or five years old. You can tell because of the cartoons and trains."*

You can see that the author of the page is Jakob Nielsen and that the page has a clear, simple design. You note that the grammar and spelling are correct and the content is neither inflammatory nor overly argumentative, although it does reflect a strong specific viewpoint on the issue. The date on which the page was published is clearly stated at the top of the page. You note that this page appears to be a part of a Web publication called "Alertbox" by looking at the page's URL and by noting the link at the top of the page.

▶ 3. Click the **Alertbox** link near the top of the Web page to learn more about the Web publication.

You see that the full title of the publication is *Alertbox: Current Issues in Web Usability* and that it is written by Dr. Jakob Nielsen, a principal of the Nielsen Norman Group. You can also see that the site offers a free email newsletter and that it has a clearly stated privacy policy that governs use of any email addresses submitted. Although some sites state policies that they do not follow, the existence of a clearly stated policy is a good indicator of a high quality site.

▶ 4. Click the links to the **Jakob Nielsen** biography page and to the **Nielsen Norman Group** information page. These links appear under the publication title near the top of the page. Review the information on these pages and use it along with the information you gained in the previous steps to evaluate the quality of the Kids' Corner page.

▶ 5. Close your Web browser.

The information you examined should lead you to conclude that the Kid's Corner page is of high quality. Dr. Nielsen and his organization are both well respected in the field of Web site usability research. If you would like to do an additional exploration regarding this topic, you could use your favorite search engine to conduct searches on combinations of terms such as "Nielsen" and "Web usability." The determination of Web site quality is not an exact science, but with practice, you can develop your skills in this area.

Wikipedia

Wikipedia is a Web site that hosts a community-edited set of online encyclopedias in more than a dozen different languages. The concept behind Wikipedia is similar to that behind the Open Directory Project you learned about earlier in this tutorial. Instead of hiring experts to review and edit entries, which is what all print encyclopedias do, Wikipedia relies on contributions from anyone for its entries. Those entries then can be edited by anyone who reads them and thinks they should be changed in some way. The idea is that with enough people reading, editing, and re-editing the entries, the information on the site will evolve to a higher degree of accuracy.

The result of Wikipedia's open nature to date is that it contains a great deal of useful information and much of that information is valid. However, Wikipedia's content is only as good as its contributors, and consequently, some of the information on the site is inaccurate, incomplete, or biased.

One of the most important tools you have for assessing the quality of information on the Web is the author's identity. On Wikipedia, contributors may post and edit articles anonymously, in which case the author is identified only by the IP address of his or her connection to the Internet. Even when the author or editor of an article chooses to be identified, it is through a Wikipedia account name and the biographical information included on the user page is entered by the account holder. That is, the information can be limited or incorrect if the account holder so chooses.

Conducting Research Online | InSight

Although Wikipedia can be an interesting place to visit, it can be a risky place to do serious research. Very few teachers or employers would accept a research project that referenced Wikipedia as a primary source. In fact, it is always a good idea to check with your instructor for guidance before using online resources in your research.

Your research efforts have provided Dave and Ranjit with a great deal of valid information. Anne is impressed with your work.

Session 4.2 Quick Check | Review

1. The three basic Boolean operators are _____ , _____ , and _____ .

2. Write a search expression using Boolean and precedence operators that returns Web pages containing information about wild mustang horses in Wyoming but not information about the Ford Mustang automobile.

3. True or False: The NEAR location operator always returns phrases that contain all keywords within 10 words of each other in a search expression.

4. True or False: In most search engines, the wildcard character is a * symbol.

5. Name three kinds of filters you can include in a Google search run from its Advanced Search page.

6. In an advanced or Boolean search expression, parentheses are an example of a(n) _____ operator.

7. Why is the deep Web so difficult to search?

8. List three factors to consider when evaluating the quality of a Web site.

In this tutorial, you learned how to formulate specific and exploratory research questions and how to use a structured Web search process to find information on the Web. You learned how to develop search expressions, which you used in three types of Web search tools: search engines, Web directories, and metasearch engines. You learned what Boolean operators, precedence operators, and location operators are and how they work in several major search engines. You also learned how to use wildcards in search expressions and how to use several types of filtering techniques to narrow your search results. You learned how to use information about Web page author identity and objectivity along with the content, form, and appearance of the Web pages themselves to evaluate their validity and reliability.

Key Terms

banner ad
Boolean algebra
Boolean operator
bot
clearinghouse
dead link
deep Web
dynamic Web page
exploratory question
full text indexing
grouping operator
hidden Web
hit
hybrid search engine
   directory
inbound links

inclusion operator
invisible Web
location operator
logical operator
meta tag
metasearch engine
natural language query
   interface
page ranking
paid placement
parsing
precedence operator
proximity operator
query
resource list
results pages

search engine
search expression
search filter
specific question
spider
sponsored links
static Web page
stemming
stop words
subject guide
virtual library
Web bibliography
Web directory
Web robot
Web search tools
Wikipedia
wildcard character

| Practice | **Review Assignments** |

Practice the skills you learned in the tutorial using the same case scenario.

There are no Data Files needed for the Review Assignments.

Anne, Dave and Ranjit are keeping you busy at IER. You have noticed that Dave and Ranjit frequently need information about the economy and economic forecasts. Your internship will be over soon, so you would like to leave them with links to some resources that they might find useful after you leave. To create the links, complete the following steps:

1. Start your Web browser, go to www.cengage.com/internet/np/internet8 to open the Online Companion page, log in to your account, click the Tutorial 4 link, and then click the Review Assignments link. The Review Assignments section of the Tutorial 4 page contains links organized under three headings: Search Engines, Web Directories, and Metasearch Engines.
2. Choose at least one search tool from each category and conduct searches using combinations of the search terms "economy," "economics," "forecasts," "conditions," and "outlook."
3. Expand or narrow your search using each tool until you find five Web sites that you believe are good Web research resources that Anne, Dave, and Ranjit should include in their bookmarks or favorites lists to help them locate information about international business stories.
4. For each Web site, record the URL and write a paragraph that explains why you believe the site would be useful to an international business news writer. Identify each site as a guide, directory, or other resource.
5. For each Web site, conduct an evaluation of the quality of the site. Write a paragraph for each site rating the site's quality as low, medium, or high, and explain the reasons for your rating.
6. When you are finished, close your Web browser.

| Apply | **Case Problem 1** |

Apply the skills you learned in this tutorial to choose a search tool and use it to find geographic information.

There are no Data Files needed for this Case Problem.

Midland University Earth Sciences Institute You are an intern at the Midland University Earth Sciences Institute. The Institute conducts research on the primary effects of earthquakes on land stability, soil composition, and water redirection, as well as secondary effects such as changes in plant and animal life. When an earthquake strikes, the Institute sends a team of geologists, soil chemists, biologists, botanists, and civil engineers to the site to examine the damage to structures, land formations, and rivers. An earthquake can occur without warning nearly anywhere, so the Institute needs quick access to information on local conditions in various parts of the world, including temperature, money exchange rates, demographics, and local customs. In early July you receive a call that an earthquake has occurred in northern Chile. To obtain information about local mid-winter conditions there, complete the following steps:

1. Start your Web browser, go to www.cengage.com/internet/np/internet8 to open the Online Companion page, log in to your account, click the Tutorial 4 link, and then click the Case Problem 1 link. The Case Problem 1 section contains links to lists of search engines, directories, and metasearch engines.

✦ EXPLORE

2. Choose one of the search tools you learned about in this tutorial to conduct searches for information on local conditions in northern Chile. For the weather conditions information, be sure to obtain information about conditions during the month of July. (*Hint:* You might need to conduct preliminary searches to identify terms that you can use to limit your searches to northern Chile.)

3. Prepare a short report that includes the daily temperature range, average rainfall, current exchange rate for U.S. dollars to Chilean pesos, and any information you can obtain about the characteristics of the local population.

4. When you are finished, close your Web browser.

Apply	**Case Problem 2**

Apply the skills you learned in this tutorial to find information about companies that sell a specific product.

There are no Data Files needed for this Case Problem.

Lightning Electrical Generators, Inc. You work as a marketing manager for Lightning Electrical Generators, Inc. John Delaney, the firm's president, has asked you to investigate new markets for the company. One market to consider is the uninterruptible power supply (UPS) business. A UPS unit supplies continuing power to a single computer or to an entire computer system if the regular source of power fails. Most UPS units provide power only long enough for an orderly shutdown of the computer. John wants you to study the market for UPS units in the United States. He wants to know which firms make and sell UPS products. He would also like to know the power ratings and prices of individual units. To provide John the information he needs, complete the following steps:

1. Start your Web browser, go to www.cengage.com/internet/np/internet8 to open the Online Companion page, log in to your account, click the Tutorial 4 link, and then click the Case Problem 2 link. The Case Problem 2 section contains links to lists of search engines, directories, and metasearch engines.

⊕ EXPLORE
2. Use one of the search tools to conduct searches for information about specific UPS products for John. You should design your searches to find the manufacturers' names and information about the products that they offer. (*Hint*: Try searching on the full term, "uninterruptible power supply," in addition to the acronym, "UPS.")

3. Prepare a short report that includes the information you have gathered for at least five UPS products, including the manufacturer's name, model number, product features, and suggested price.

4. When you are finished, close your Web browser.

Apply	**Case Problem 3**

Apply the skills you learned in this tutorial to find and evaluate the quality of specific Web page content.

There are no Data Files needed for this Case Problem.

Eastern College English Department You are a research assistant in the Eastern College English Department. The department head, Professor Garnell, has an interest in Shakespeare. She has spent years researching whether William Shakespeare actually wrote the plays and poems attributed to him. Some scholars, including Professor Garnell, believe that most of Shakespeare's works were written by Christopher Marlowe. Professor Garnell wants to include links on the department Web page to other researchers who agree with her, but she wants only high-quality sites included. To gather the URLs, complete the following steps:

1. Start your Web browser, go to www.cengage.com/internet/np/internet8 to open the Online Companion page, log in to your account, click the Tutorial 4 link, and then click the Case Problem 3 link. The Case Problem 3 section contains links to lists of search engines, directories, and metasearch engines.

2. Use one of the search tools to find Web sites that contain information about the Shakespeare-Marlowe controversy.

⊕ **EXPLORE**

3. Use the procedures outlined in this tutorial to evaluate the quality of the sites you found in the previous step. (*Hint*: Most useful sites will have some connection to a university or research library.)

4. Choose at least five Web sites that Professor Garnell might want to include on her Web page. For each Web site, record the URL and write at least one paragraph in which you describe the evidence you have gathered about the site's quality. You should include at least one site that is low quality in your collection.

5. When you are finished, close your Web browser.

Research	**Case Problem 4**

Research the Web to find specific information, then evaluate the information.

There are no Data Files needed for this Case Problem.

Glenwood Employment Agency You work as a staff assistant at the Glenwood Employment Agency. Eric Steinberg, the agency's owner, wants you to locate Web resources for finding open positions in your geographic area. Eric would like this information to gauge whether his own efforts are keeping pace with the competition. He wants to monitor a few good pages but does not want to conduct exhaustive searches of the Web every week. To help Eric find current employment information, complete the following steps:

1. Start your Web browser, go to www.cengage.com/internet/np/internet8 to open the Online Companion page, log in to your account, click the Tutorial 4 link, and then click the Case Problem 4 link. The Case Problem 4 section contains links to lists of search engines, directories, and metasearch engines.

⊕ **EXPLORE**

2. Use one of the search tools to find Web sites containing information about job openings in your geographic area. (*Hint*: You can use search expressions that include Boolean and precedence operators to limit your searches.)

3. Prepare a list of at least five URLs of pages that you believe would be good candidates for Eric's monitoring program.

4. For each URL that you find, write a paragraph that explains why you selected it and then identify any particular strengths or weaknesses of the Web site based on Eric's intended use.

5. When you are finished, close your Web browser.

Create	**Case Problem 5**

Create a report that evaluates the effectiveness of a search tool you chose to find specific information.

There are no Data Files needed for this Case Problem.

Lynda's Fine Foods For many years, Lynda Rice has operated a small store that sells specialty foods, such as pickles and mustard, and related gift items. Lynda is thinking about selling her products on the Web because they are small, inexpensive to ship relative to their product prices, and easy to package. She believes that people who buy her products might appreciate the convenience of ordering over the Web. Lynda would like to find some specialty food store sites on the Web to learn about possible competitors and to obtain some ideas that she might use when she creates her own Web site. To research selling specialty food items on the Web, complete the following steps:

1. Start your Web browser, go to www.cengage.com/internet/np/internet8 to open the Online Companion page, log in to your account, click the Tutorial 4 link, and then click the Case Problem 5 link. The Case Problem 5 section contains links to lists of search engines, directories, and metasearch engines.

2. Use one of the search tools to find Web sites that offer gift items such as pickles or mustard. You can use search expressions that include Boolean and precedence operators to limit your searches.

3. Repeat your search using one of the Web directory tools.

4. Compare the results you obtained using a search engine and using a Web directory. Explain in a memorandum of about 100 words which search tool was more effective for this type of search. Your instructor might ask you to prepare a presentation to your class in which you summarize your conclusions.

5. When you are finished, close your Web browser.

| Review | **| Quick Check Answers** |

Session 4.1

1. open-ended, hard to phrase, difficult to determine when you have found a good answer

2. True

3. Web robot, bot, or spider

4. inbound links from other Web pages

5. False. Most search engines exclude stop words such as *and* or *the*.

6. Advantage: Experts have selected, examined, and classified the entries in a Web directory. Disadvantage: You must know which category to search to find information.

7. The power of the search engine operates on the expert-selected and classified entries in the directory.

8. It forwards the expression to a number of other search engines, and then organizes and presents the search results it receives from them.

9. Create a search expression that includes terms related to the specific topic area, then enter that search expression into a search engine or a Web directory.

Session 4.2

1. AND, OR, NOT

2. One possibility is: (mustang OR horse) AND Wyoming NOT (Ford OR automobile OR auto OR car)

3. False. The number of words will be different in different search engines.

4. True

5. Any three of these: language, file format, date, where the search terms appear on the Web page, domain, and Safe Search

6. precedence, inclusion, or grouping

7. The deep Web includes dynamic Web pages that are generated on the fly and are not stored on Web servers, so search engine robots cannot find the information they contain.

8. identity and objectivity of author(s), content characteristics, form, and appearance

Tutorial 5

Objectives

Session 5.1
- Find current news and weather information on the Web
- Obtain maps and city guides
- Find businesses and people on the Web

Session 5.2
- Find library and text resources on the Web
- Learn how to cite Web resources
- Learn how copyrights affect the use of resources found on the Web
- Find graphics and multimedia resources on the Web
- Learn about the future of online publishing

Information Resources on the Web

Finding, Evaluating, and Using Online Information Resources

Case | Cosby Promotions

You have just started a new position as the executive assistant to Marti Cosby, the president of Cosby Promotions—a growing booking agency that handles promotion and concert contract negotiations for musicians and bands. Cosby Promotions works with a wide variety of music acts. Current clients include bands that play pop, Latin, heavy metal, techno, industrial, and urban styles of music. The agency does not currently handle many country music acts, but Marti wants to expand its country music business over the next few years. The music business is dynamic because of the fluctuating popularity of musical artists; promotion and booking strategies that work best for a particular client one month might not work well the next month. Promotional tie-ins and sponsorships are also important revenue sources for music acts, and the needs of specific sponsors change with shifts in customer preferences.

Your primary job is to use your basic understanding of Web searching techniques to help Cosby Promotions' staff stay current on entertainment news and trends that might affect the agency's clients. Your other duties include updating agency executives and clients about local conditions at travel destinations and working with the agency's Web site design team to develop an effective Web presence.

In addition to working with Marti and the executive team, you will work closely with Susan Zhu, the agency's research director. Susan has worked at Cosby Promotions for six years in a variety of research jobs. The research department conducts background investigations when dealing with the agency's clients. For example, whenever Marti starts working on a booking for a concert hall or other venue that is new for the agency, she asks Susan to provide background on the venue. Susan is looking forward to having you work with her as part of the Cosby Promotions research team.

Starting Data Files

There are no starting Data Files needed for this tutorial.

Session 5.1

Current Information on the Web

In earlier tutorials, you learned how to use search engines, directories, and other resources to find information on the Web. Many of your assignments for Cosby Promotions will involve finding recent news and information about clients, potential sponsors, performance venues, and changes in the music industry. In this session, you will learn how to use search engines and directories to find recent news stories and other current information. Remember to use the techniques you learned in Tutorial 4 to assess the reliability of the information you gather in this tutorial.

To help you find current news and information, many search engines and directories include sections devoted to news items. For example, Yahoo! offers this type of information on its home page, including a "News" tab that includes general news stories. The page also includes tabs titled "World," "Local," and "Finance" that include corresponding types of news stories. The Yahoo! home page also offers links to current entertainment, sports, and weather information, as shown in Figure 5-1.

Figure 5-1 ▶ **Yahoo! home page**

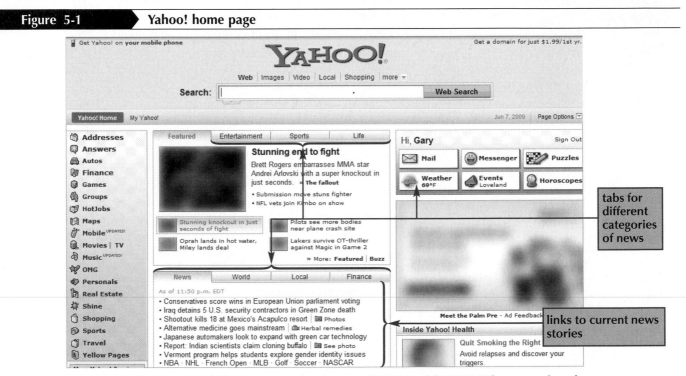

Reproduced with permission of Yahoo! Inc. ® 2009 by Yahoo! Inc. YAHOO! and the YAHOO! logo are trademarks of Yahoo! Inc.

Search engines can also be useful tools for finding news stories. Many search engines allow you to choose a date range when you enter a search expression. The AltaVista search engine allows you to set an exact "between" date range on its Advanced Search page. Figure 5-2 shows the AltaVista Advanced Web Search page with an exact date range set.

Date filters on the AltaVista Advanced Web Search page | Figure 5-2

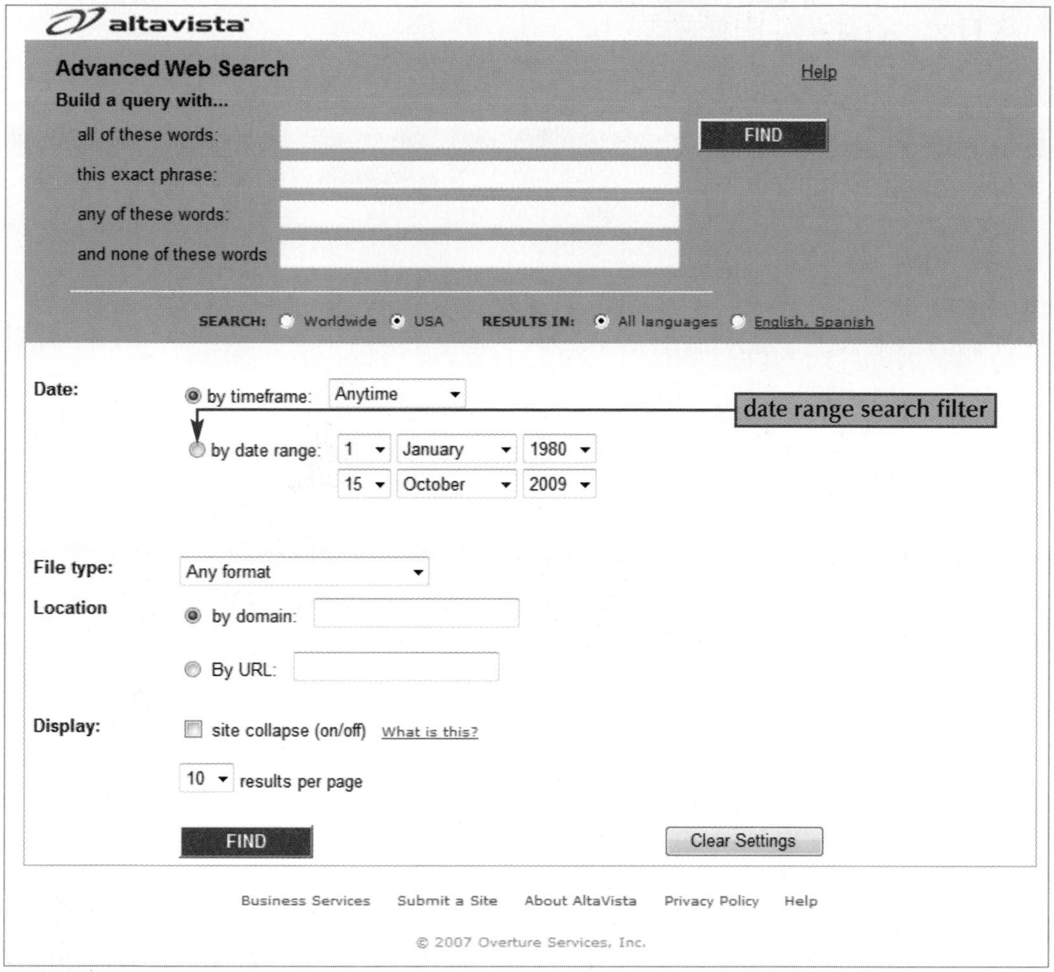

The AlltheWeb search engine uses a slightly different approach. It allows you to set separate "after" and "before" date filters. By setting both of these filters, you can construct an exact "between" date filter. Figure 5-3 shows these filters on the AlltheWeb Advanced Search page with an exact date range set.

Figure 5-3 **Date filters on the AlltheWeb Advanced Search page**

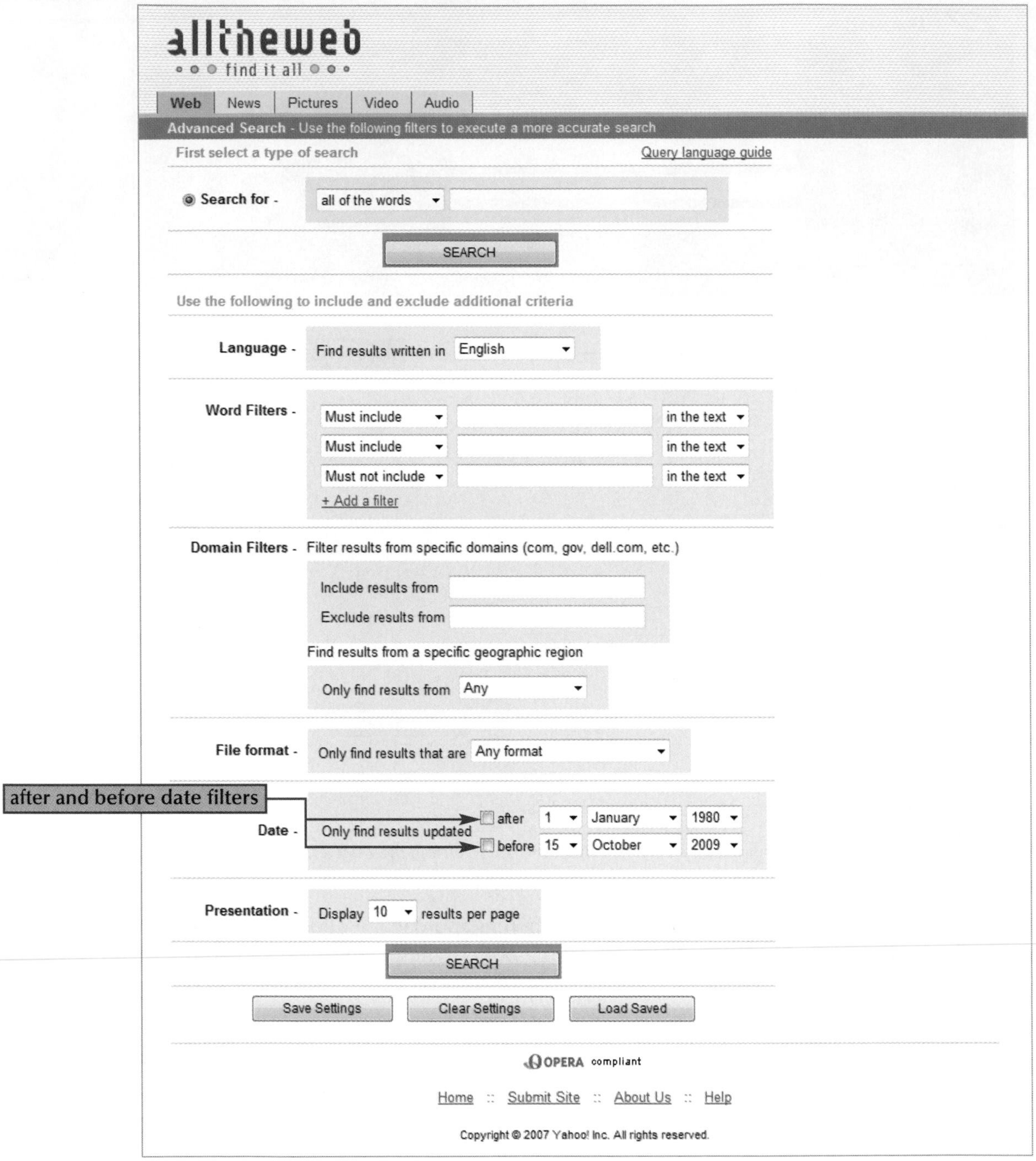

Reproduced with permission of Yahoo! Inc. ® 2007 by Yahoo! Inc. YAHOO! and the YAHOO! logo are trademarks of Yahoo! Inc.

Your first assignment for Cosby Promotions requires research on recent news about Honda. The company wants to increase its appeal to younger drivers and is looking to sponsor a band that will appeal to that market. Marti knows that other agencies will be pitching bands to Honda for this sponsorship, so she wants as much background information on Honda as possible before she meets with them next week. She would like you to search the Web and collect the URLs of sites that mention Honda; she is especially interested in learning more about the kinds of promotional activities the company is already doing. Marti needs the most recent information available, so you will search for sites that have been modified within the last month.

Finding Web Sites that Have Been Modified Recently | Reference Window

- Go to the Web site for a search engine or directory that allows date-range restrictions.
- Formulate your search expression.
- Set the date-range restriction in the search tool.
- Run the search.
- Evaluate the search results. If you do not find useful results, select an alternative search tool, and then run the search again.

Consider the search tools available. Your search term—*Honda*—is a brand name, so it is likely that Web directories will collect many useful sites that include the term in their databases. Another option is to use a search engine for this query. Search engines might include more recent listings because the editorial review process of many Web directories takes time to complete.

To find specific Web pages based on last modified dates:

▶ **1.** Start your Web browser, go to **www.cengage.com/internet/np/internet8** to open the Online Companion page, log on to your account, click the **Tutorial 5** link, and then click the **Session 5.1** link.

▶ **2.** Choose one of the search tools in the Search Engines and Web Directories with Date Filters section, and then click the link to the tool you have chosen to open its advanced search page.

▶ **3.** Formulate a search expression that will locate promotions for Honda. For most of the search tools, typing the expression **Honda promotion** in the search text box should work.

▶ **4.** Select a date filter to limit your search to the most recent month (depending on the search tool you chose, you will use either a preset filter for the last month or an exact date filter), and then click the appropriate tool's **Search** (or similar) button to start the search.

▶ **5.** Examine your search results to determine whether you have found any valuable information. If not, return to the Online Companion page for Tutorial 5, select a different search engine or Web directory from the list, and then repeat Steps 2 through 4 using that search tool.

> **Tip**
>
> Remember, if you do not find what you are looking for with one search tool, you can try your search again using different tools until you are satisfied with your results.

Figure 5-4 shows a part of the results page generated by the Google search engine for this query. The page includes several results that might be useful to Marti. Your results, even if you use Google, will be different.

Figure 5-4 ▶ **Google date-filtered search results**

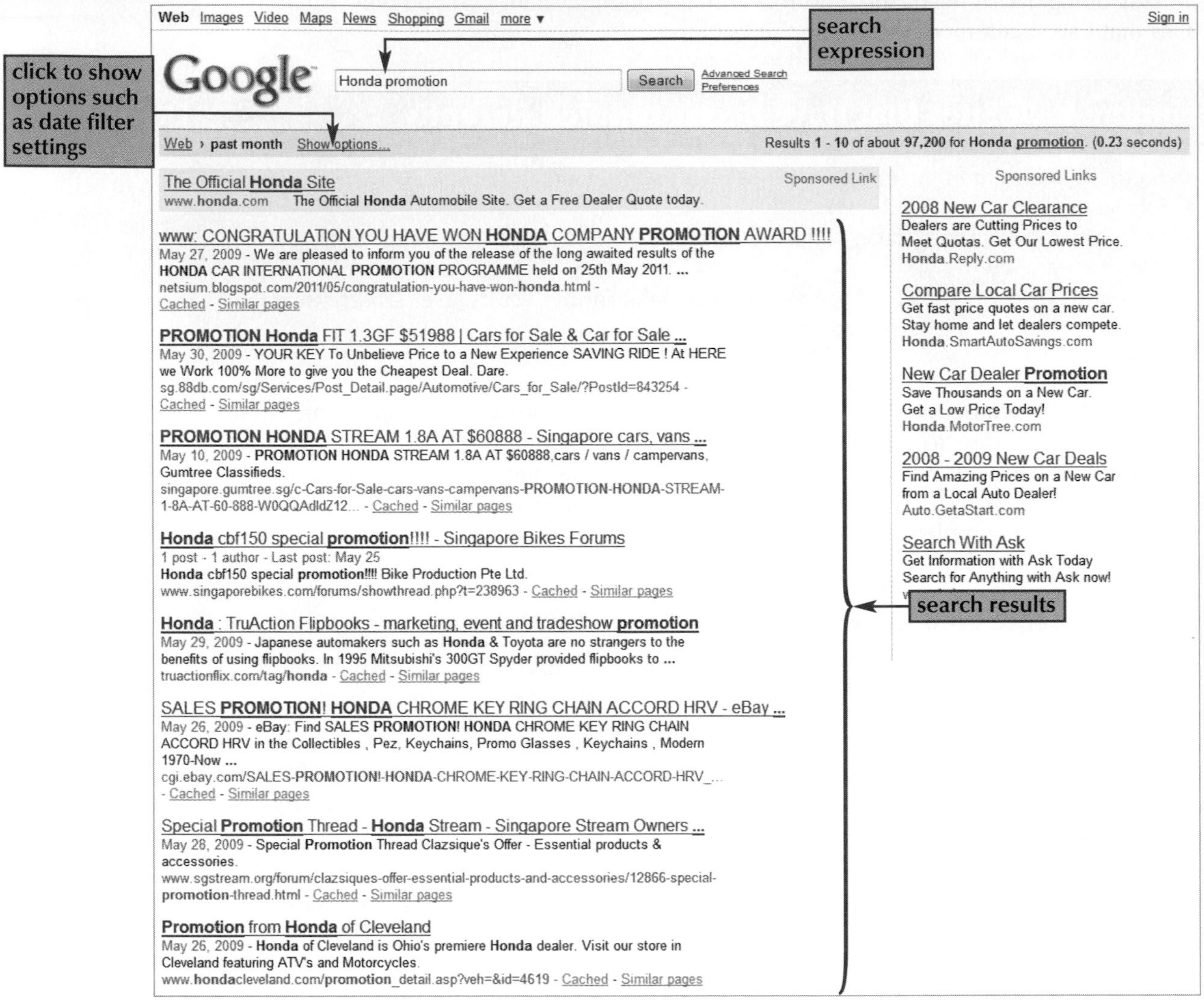

You can email the URLs to Marti or you can tell her how to obtain the same search results. For now, you decide to copy and paste the URLs that look promising and send them to her in an email message.

Getting the News

Marti is pleased with many of the recently modified Web pages you found. Now, she asks you to find current news stories about Honda that might not appear in a search of recently modified Web pages.

Finding current news stories on the Web can be easy if you know where to look. Most search engines and Web directories include links to broadcast networks, wire services, and newspapers. A **wire service** (also called a press agency or news service) is an organization that gathers and distributes news to newspapers, magazines, broadcasters, and other organizations that pay a fee to the wire service. Although there are hundreds of wire services in the world, most news comes from the four largest wire services: United Press International (UPI) and the Associated Press (AP) in the United States, Thomson Reuters in Great Britain, and Agence France-Presse (AFP) in France. In addition to selling stories to print, broadcast, and online news outlets around the world, these major wire services all display current news stories on their Web sites.

Web News Directories and News Search Engines

All of the major U.S. broadcast networks, including ABC, CBS, CNN, Fox, MSNBC, NBC, and NPR, have Web sites that carry news features. Broadcasters in other countries, such as the BBC, also provide news reports on their Web pages. Major newspapers, such as *The New York Times*, the *Washington Post*, and the *Los Angeles Times*, have Web sites that include current news and many other features from their print editions. Many of these broadcast news, wire service, and newspaper Web sites include search features that allow you to search the site for specific news stories.

The Internet Public Library's Online Newspapers site includes hyperlinks to hundreds of international and domestic newspapers. Sites like the Internet Public Library, which offer categorized links to news outlets or to specific stories on the Web pages of news outlets, are called **Web news directories**. You can explore a number of Web news directories by opening the Online Companion page, clicking the Tutorial 5 link, and then following the links in the Web News Directories section. Figure 5-5 shows the Newspapers page of the Internet Public Library Web site, which is maintained by a consortium of universities.

Figure 5-5   Internet Public Library links to newspaper Web sites

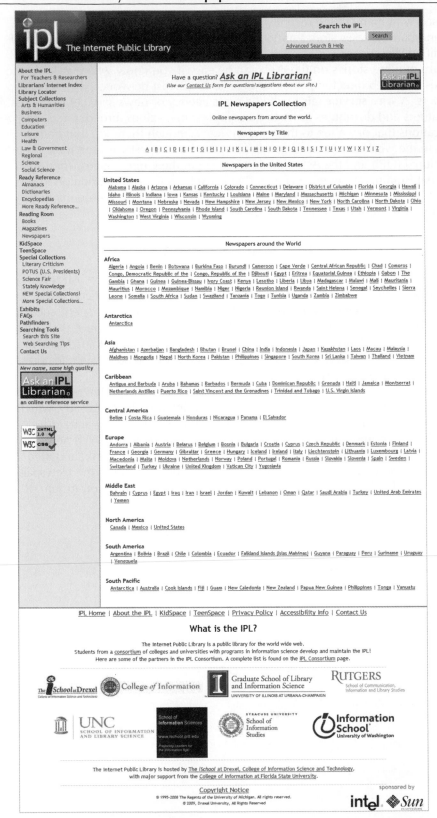

The search feature of the Internet Public Library Newspapers page searches only the title and the main entry for each newspaper and does not search the newspaper sites' contents. Therefore, you could use it to identify all of the newspapers in New Jersey or all of the newspapers that had the word Tribune in their titles, but you could not use it to find news stories that include the word Honda. You need to select a newspaper, go to the newspaper site, and conduct your search there. To search a hundred newspapers, you would need to do your search a hundred times. This drawback is shared by most Web news directory sites.

Fortunately, a number of Web sites let you search the content of current news stories in multiple publications and wire services. These sites are often called **news search engines**. In the early days of the Web, many of these sites were independently operated and offered links to specific stories on the Web sites of newspapers and other media outlets. One of these early sites, NewsHub, is still in operation, but most Web search engines today are operated by the major search engines you learned about in earlier tutorials. The databases for the news search engine components of these sites are separate from their main Web search databases, but the search mechanism is usually similar to that used on the sites' main search pages.

Yahoo! News includes stories from the major wire services along with news it purchases from newspapers and magazines. Google News and Microsoft's Bing News also include stories from those same types of news sources. Some news search engines provide ways to search **Web logs** (also called **Weblogs** or **blogs**), which are Web sites that contain commentary on current events written by individuals. You will learn more about blogs in Session 5.2.

You decide to use a news search engine to find recent news stories about Honda.

> **Tip**
>
> To obtain both breadth and currency of coverage, experienced searchers often run the same query using more than one search tool.

Searching Current News Stories | Reference Window

- Select a news search engine site.
- Open the site in your Web browser.
- Enter your search expression into the search text box.
- Set any date filters you want to use to limit your search.
- Run the search and evaluate your results.

To find recent news stories on the Web that mention Honda:

▶ **1.** Return to the Online Companion page for Session 5.1, choose one of the tools in the News Search Engines section to use in your search, and then click the link to the tool you have chosen to open its search page.

▶ **2.** Type the search term **Honda promotion** in your chosen site's search text box.

▶ **3.** Select a date filter to limit your results to the most recent few weeks or most recent month (your choices will depend on which news search engine you use) and then click the site's **Search** (or similar) button to start the search.

▶ **4.** Examine your search results to determine whether you have found any information that might be useful to Marti. If not, repeat Steps 1 through 3 using a different search tool.

Figure 5-6 shows a part of the results page generated by the Google news search engine for this query. Your results, even if you use Google News, will be different.

Figure 5-6 **Google News search results page**

search expression

date filter settings

search results

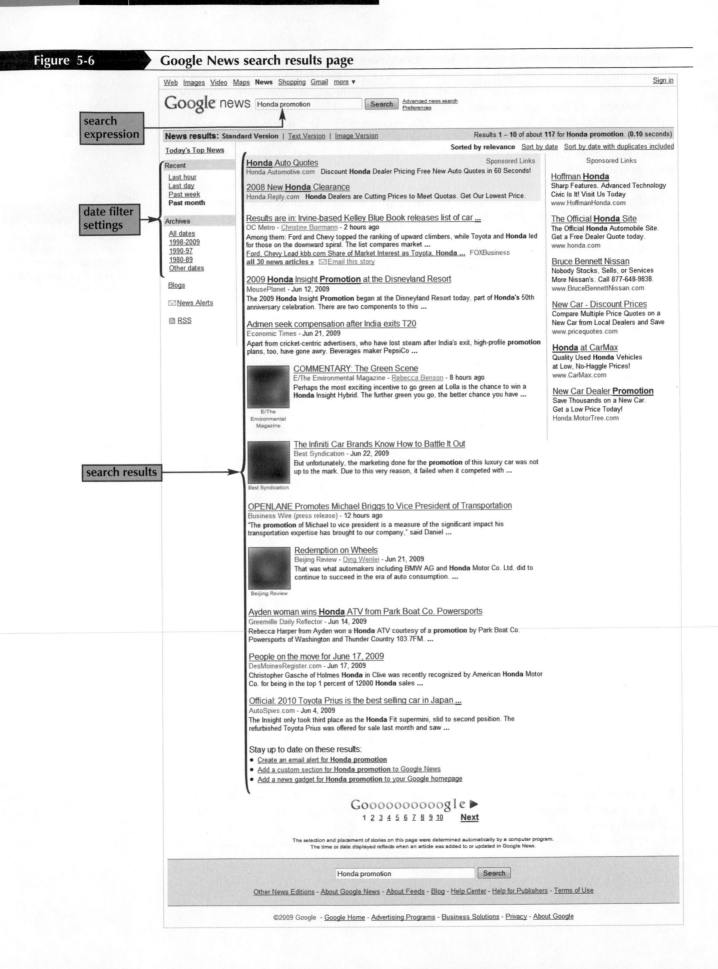

You have compiled a list of useful URLs about Honda's current promotional and sponsorship activities for Marti. You have also gained experience in searching for current topics by examining Web pages that have been modified recently and by using tools that search the Web specifically for news reports.

Republished News Stories | InSight

When you search the Web for news stories, you might find similar (or even identical) stories on different Web sites. Many newspapers and Web news outlets purchase stories from the major wire services and from leading newspapers such as *The New York Times* and the *Wall Street Journal*. Sometimes they will edit the stories to shorten them or add information that might appeal to their local readers. In other cases, they will just republish the original story without changes.

Weather Reports

Marti will travel to Nashville later in the week to meet with some new country music artists that she hopes to sign as clients for the agency. Marti is interested in the weather forecast for the area. A number of Web sites offer weather information and forecasts. The two most popular—AccuWeather and The Weather Channel—provide weather forecast information to many other Web sites, such as Excite, *USA Today*, and Yahoo!. The AccuWeather home page appears in Figure 5-7.

Figure 5-7 AccuWeather home page

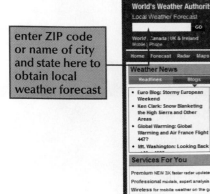

enter ZIP code or name of city and state here to obtain local weather forecast

Using Local Weather Forecasts | InSight

Local television stations offer weather information on their Web sites. Some of these sites purchase weather information from major weather Web sites such as AccuWeather or the Weather Channel, but many of them employ their own meteorologists and have their own weather prediction equipment. You might find that these local weather forecasts are more accurate and detailed than those provided by the major weather Web sites for your area. To find these sites, enter a search expression that includes your local television station's call letters into a search engine and follow the links in the search results.

You decide to check two weather sources for Marti because you know that meteorology is not an exact science.

Finding a Weather Forecast | Reference Window

- Open a weather information Web site in a Web browser.
- Locate the weather report for the city or area in which you are interested.
- Repeat the steps to find other weather forecasts in different weather information Web sites.

To find weather forecasts for the Nashville area:

▶ 1. Return to the Online Companion page for Session 5.1.

▶ 2. Choose one of the tools in the Weather Information Web Sites section to use in your search, and then click the link to the site you have chosen to open its home page. Most of these sites allow you to search on either the name of the city or its ZIP code.

▶ 3. Type the city name and state, **Nashville**, **TN**, or the ZIP code for downtown Nashville, **37201**, in your chosen site's search text box, and then click the site's **Go** (or similar) button to find the local Nashville forecast. Note the forecast for later in the week, during Marti's visit.

▶ 4. Repeat Steps 1 through 3 using a different weather information site and compare the results of your two searches.

Figure 5-8 shows a part of the Nashville local forecast page on The Weather Channel site. It includes a report on current conditions, a forecast, and a Doppler radar image. It also includes a link to a 10-day local forecast. The page you see, even if you use The Weather Channel site, will be different.

Tip

Often, various weather-forecasting sites will report slightly different (and sometimes completely different) forecasts for the same time period in the same area.

Figure 5-8 | The Weather Channel local forecast page for Nashville

type city and state or ZIP code here to obtain another weather forecast

link to 10-day local forecast

current weather

current forecast

Doppler radar image

Obtaining Maps and Destination Information

Marti would like to include a stop at Ryman Auditorium, the original home of the Grand Ole Opry, which is at 116 Fifth Avenue North. You offer to find a map of Nashville on the Web that shows the location of Ryman Auditorium. A number of Web sites provide maps and driving directions. Although the information provided by these sites is not perfect (for example, new roads and detours caused by current construction work often are not included), many people find them to be helpful travel aids.

Finding a Local Area Map on the Web | Reference Window

- Open a Web site that offers maps in your Web browser.
- Enter the location of the map you need to find.
- Zoom the map scale in or out to suit your requirements.
- Print or download the finished map.

To obtain a map of the Nashville area near Ryman Auditorium:

▶ **1.** Return to the Online Companion page for Session 5.1, choose one of the tools in the Web Sites with Maps and Directions section to use in your search, and then click the link to the site you have chosen to open its home page.

▶ **2.** Type the address, **116 Fifth Avenue North**, the city name, **Nashville**, and the state abbreviation, **TN**, in the appropriate text boxes of your chosen site's Web page. Then click the site's **Get Map** (or similar) button to open a page that includes a map of the area near Ryman Auditorium.

▶ **3.** When the page that includes the map loads, use the controls on the page to zoom in or out until you have a map image that you think will meet Marti's needs.

Downloading Maps | InSight

Some sites allow you to email the map image or download it to your computer or a handheld device such as a personal digital assistant (PDA) or a mobile phone. These sites usually include links to terms and conditions that govern your use of any maps you download, print, or email. Be sure to review those terms and conditions for your chosen site.

Figure 5-9 shows the results of this search using two Web sites, Google Maps and Bing Maps. The map you obtain, even if you use one of these sites, might look different. Each site offers a slightly different view of the area, with different features displayed. Because these differences exist, many people regularly use maps from two or three different Web sites when they are planning a trip.

Figure 5-9   **Ryman Auditorium area map in Google Maps and Bing Maps**

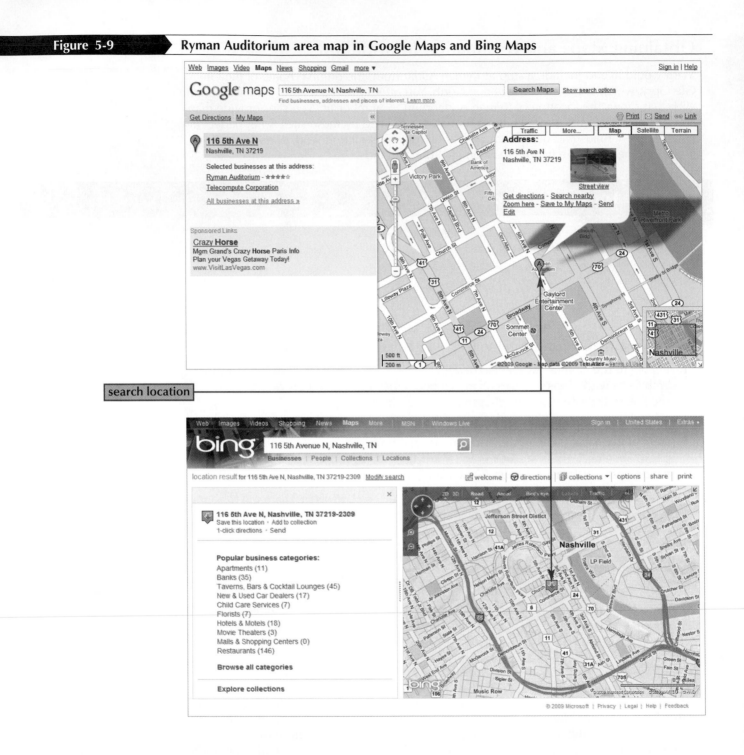

search location

You have located a map that will meet Marti's needs. To further help Marti on her Nashville trip, you want to find some information about restaurants and other points of interest in Nashville. The Web offers a number of sites with information about cities that are popular travel destinations.

Obtaining Travel Destination Information | Reference Window

- Go to a city guide Web site in your Web browser.
- Search the site for your destination city, region, or country.
- Explore the hyperlinks provided by the site for your destination.

To obtain information about Nashville restaurants and entertainment:

▶ **1.** Return to the Online Companion page for Session 5.1, choose one of the tools in the Travel Destination Guides section to use in your search, and then click the link to the site you have chosen to open its home page.

▶ **2.** Find your chosen site's page for Nashville, TN. The procedure you use will depend on which site you chose; however, most sites require you to type **Nashville** in a search text box or click a **Nashville** link. If you are unable to find an entry for Nashville on your chosen site, select a different site for your search.

▶ **3.** Examine the results page to find information about restaurants and entertainment in Nashville.

You can find a variety of useful information using city guide sites. In addition to information about entertainment and restaurants, you can often obtain useful information about specific attractions. For example, Figure 5-10 shows detailed information about the Ryman Auditorium that you might find by using the Citysearch site.

Figure 5-10 **Citysearch Ryman Auditorium page**

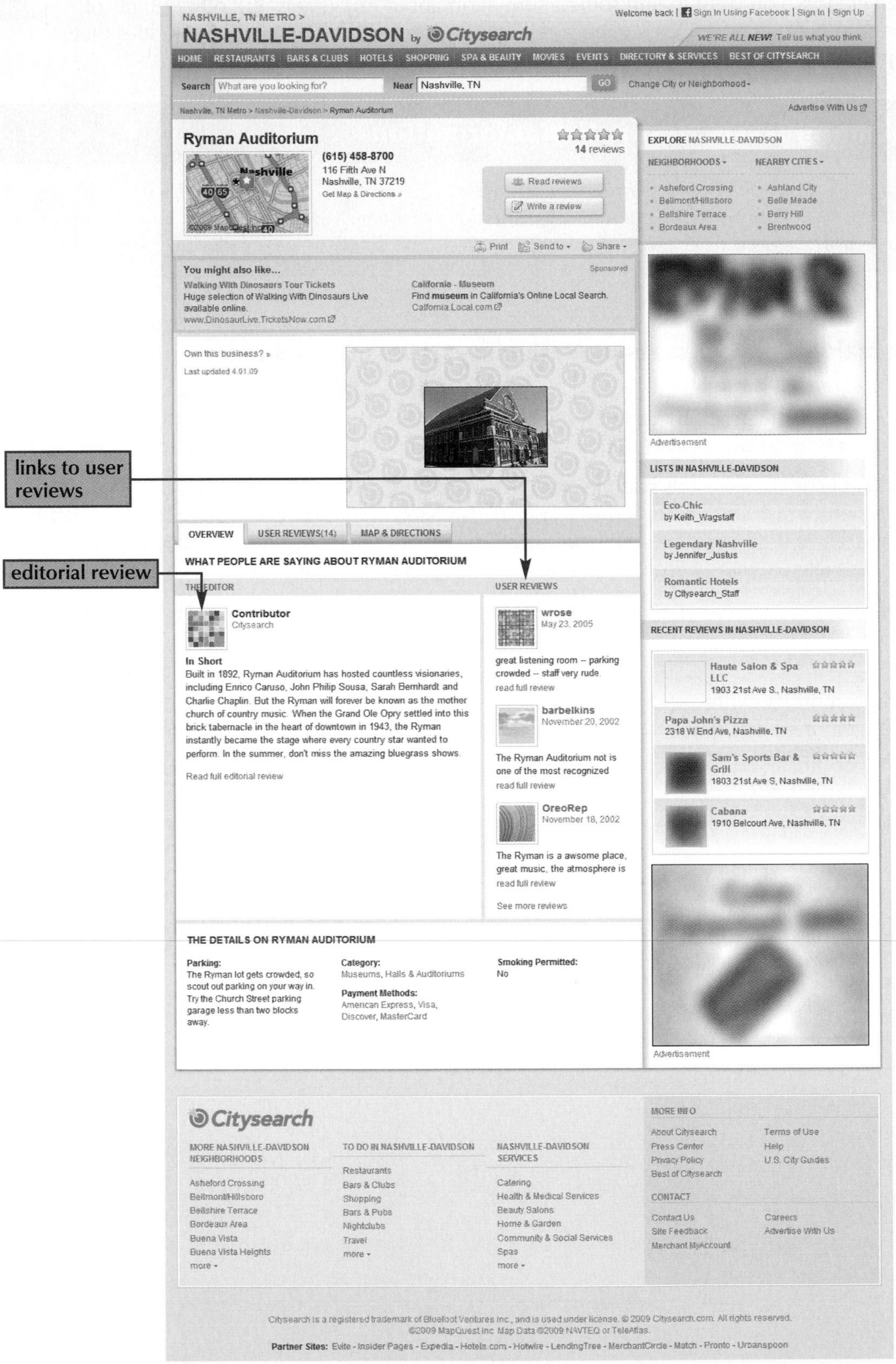

links to user reviews

editorial review

Finding Businesses and People on the Web

Some Web sites include listings of businesses and people, much like the print directories that you have probably used to find telephone numbers. These sites often include search engines that specialize in finding information about people and businesses on the Web.

Finding Businesses

Over the next few years, Marti is planning to develop reciprocal relationships with local booking agencies in Nashville. She would like to make some initial contacts during this trip and asks you to search the Web to find a list of booking agencies in Nashville. Web sites that store information about businesses only are often called **yellow pages directories**. You can use a yellow pages directory to find booking agencies located in Nashville.

Finding Business Listings on the Web	Reference Window

- Navigate to a yellow pages directory site in your Web browser.
- Enter information about the nature and geographic location of the business that you want to find.
- Run the search.
- Examine and evaluate the results to determine whether you should revise your search or try another search engine.

To find Nashville booking agencies on the Web:

▶ **1.** Return to the Online Companion page for Session 5.1, choose one of the tools in the Yellow Pages Directories section to use in your search, and then click the link to the site you have chosen to open its home page.

▶ **2.** The exact procedure you will use for your search will depend on which directory you chose. Most sites require you to enter a search term for the category of the business you want to find. For this search, you should try terms such as *agent*, *artist*, *recording artist*, or *booking agent*. Enter the location information in the appropriate field, and then click the **Search** (or similar) button. If your first search is unsuccessful, try another search with a different search term. If none of the search terms yields satisfactory results, return to the Online Companion page for Session 5.1 and try using a different yellow pages directory site.

▶ **3.** Examine your results pages to find information about booking agencies in Nashville.

This search can be challenging because there is no single category description that is universally used by companies that book performing musicians. Figure 5-11 shows the results page for a search using the term "agent" on the SuperPages.com yellow pages directory site. The search returned several categories, one of which was the category "Talent Agencies & Casting Services." This category includes a number of listings for booking agencies in Nashville. Your search will yield different categories, depending on which directory you use. In fact, your search will probably yield a different list of booking agencies, even if you use the SuperPages.com directory and click the "Talent Agencies & Casting Services" category.

Figure 5-11   SuperPages.com search results page

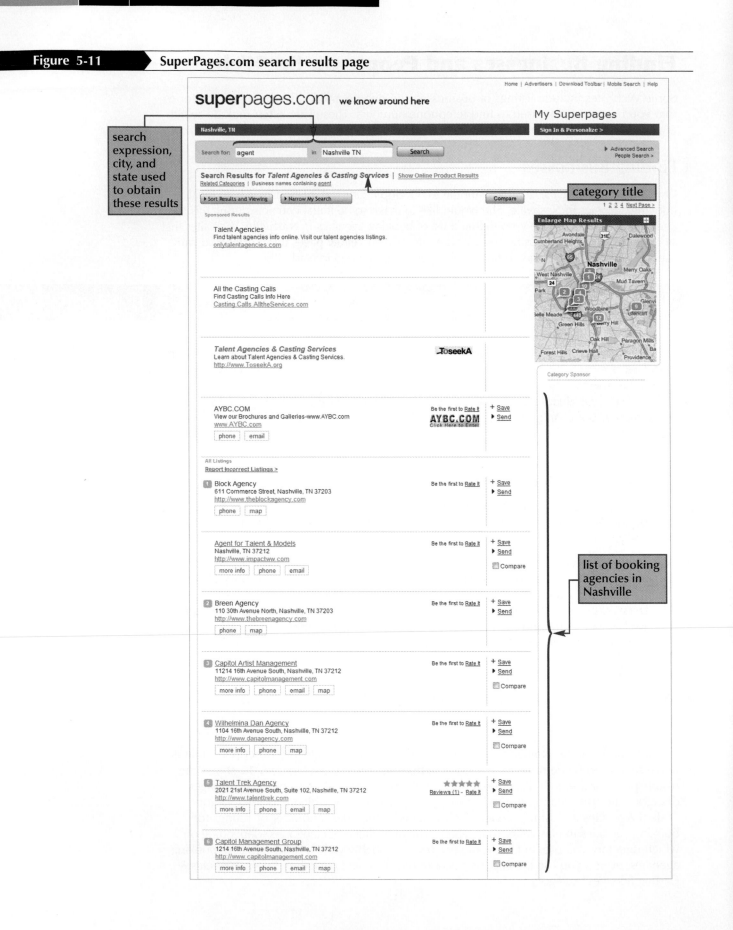

You are satisfied that you have found enough information about Nashville weather, attractions, and booking agencies.

In addition to using the Web to find businesses, you can use it to find individuals.

Finding People

Many Web sites let you search for individuals' names, addresses, and telephone numbers. These sites, often called **white pages directories**, collect information from published telephone directories and other publicly available information and index it by last name.

Some Web sites make unpublished and unlisted telephone numbers available for public use. Other sites group individual listings by categories, such as religious or political affiliation. Many people expressed concerns about privacy violations when this type of information became easily accessible on the Web. In response to these privacy concerns, most white pages sites offer people a way to remove their listings. For example, Switchboard will accept a list removal request made on its Web page or sent by email. You might want to determine whether white pages directories have a correct listing for you and whether you want your listing to appear in a white pages site.

Searching for Your White Pages Listing | Reference Window

- Open a white pages directory Web site in your Web browser.
- Enter your name and part of your address.
- Run the search, and then examine the search results.
- Consider repeating the search with various combinations of partial address information or variants of the correct spelling of your name.

To search for your listing on a white pages directory:

▶ **1.** Return to the Online Companion page for Session 5.1, choose one of the tools in the White Pages Directories section to use in your search, and then click the link to the site you have chosen to open its home page.

▶ **2.** The exact procedure you will use for your search will depend on which directory you chose; however, most sites require you to enter your first name, your last name, and a part of your address such as the city and state.

   Trouble? If your telephone number is listed under another person's name, such as a parent or roommate, use that person's name to find your listing.

   Trouble? If you do not find your listing, try searching for a friend's listing or your parents' listing. You can also try your search in a different white pages directory.

▶ **3.** Examine your listing and, if you wish, follow the site's instructions for modifying or deleting your listing.

▶ **4.** Close your Web browser and, if necessary, log off your Internet connection.

You have accomplished many tasks and helped Marti quite a bit. Next, you will learn about multimedia resources on the Web and the copyright issues that arise when you use them.

Review | **Session 5.1 Quick Check**

1. Thomson Reuters is an example of a(n) _____ .
2. When would you use a search engine with a date filter rather than a news directory or news search engine?
3. Explain why you might want to consult two or three Web resources for weather information.
4. List two advantages of using a Web map and directions site instead of a paper map or atlas.
5. Describe three types of information that you might obtain from a city guide Web page.
6. True or False: City guide Web sites are usually created by an agency of the city government.
7. A Web site that helps people find businesses by name or category is often called a(n)_____ .
8. A Web site that helps people find the telephone numbers or email addresses of other individuals is often called a(n) _____ .

Session 5.2

Online Library, Text, and Multimedia Resources

Because the Web has made publishing so easy and inexpensive, virtually anybody can create a Web page on almost any subject. These pages contain many useful items of information and form a collective online library of sorts. The resources of this vast online library include text, graphics, and multimedia files. **Multimedia** is a general term for files that contain sound, music, or video recordings. In this session you will learn how to find these resources, use them in compliance with copyright laws, and properly cite their sources.

Library Resources

Despite the proliferation of online resources, the Web has made existing libraries more accessible to more people. Traditional libraries and online collections of works that have serious research value now recognize each other as complementary rather than competing information sources, and library users have started to see many new and interesting research resources. One online collection that is both comprehensive and valuable is the LibrarySpot Web site, which is a collection of hyperlinks organized in the same general way that a physical library might arrange its collections.

To explore the LibrarySpot Web site:

▶ 1. Start your Web browser, go to **www.cengage.com/internet/np/internet8** to open the Online Companion page, log on to your account, click the **Tutorial 5** link, and then click the **Session 5.2** link. Click the **LibrarySpot** hyperlink, and then wait while your Web browser loads the Web page.

The LibrarySpot site includes many of the same materials you would expect to find in a public or school library. It lets you access reference materials, electronic texts, and other library Web sites from one central Web page. Unlike a public or school library, this library is open 24 hours a day and seven days a week.

Marti had asked you to find out how Nashville got its name.

▶ 2. Using the links listed under the heading "Reference Desk" on the LibrarySpot home page, search for information about Nashville's history. A good place to start would be the **Encyclopedias** link. Search as many sites as necessary until you find the information you seek. Make a brief note about how Nashville got its name (and be sure to include information about your source) so that you can include it in your report to Marti about Nashville.

Another useful resource is the U.S. Library of Congress Web site, which includes links to a huge array of research resources, ranging from the Thomas Legislative Information site to the Library of Congress archives. The home page of the Library of Congress Web site is shown in Figure 5-12.

Figure 5-12 ▶ **U.S. Library of Congress home page**

The Thomas Legislative Information Web site provides you with search access to the full text of bills that are before Congress, the *Congressional Record,* and Congressional Committee Reports. The American Memory link leads you to archived photographs, sound and video recordings, maps, and collections of everything from 17th century dance instruction manuals to baseball cards. The Exhibitions link leads you to information about current and past displays sponsored by the Library of Congress.

The Online Companion page for Tutorial 5 contains many other links to useful library and library-related Web sites in the Additional Information section under the Library Information Sites heading. Consider exploring the library resources on the Web the next time you need to complete a research assignment for school or your job.

Text and Other Archives on the Web

The Web contains a number of text resources, including dictionaries, thesauri, encyclopedias, glossaries, and other reference works. Many people find reference works easier to use when they have a computerized search interface. For example, when you open a dictionary to find the definition of a specific word, the structure of the bound book actually interferes with your ability to find the answer you seek. A computer interface allows you to enter a search term—in this case, the word to be defined—and saves you the trouble of scanning several pages of text to find the correct entry.

Of course, publishers sell dictionaries and encyclopedias on CDs, but the Web provides many alternatives, ranging in quality from very low to very high. Some of the best resources offered on the Web require you to pay a subscription fee. The free reference works on the Web are also worth investigating; many are good enough to provide useful answers to a wide range of questions. In addition to dictionaries and encyclopedias, the Web includes grammar checkers, rhyming dictionaries, and language-translation pages. The Online Companion page for this tutorial includes a collection of links to a number of these reference resources in the Additional Information section under the heading Reference Resources.

The Web also includes sites that offer full-text copies of works that are no longer protected by copyright. Two well-known full-text sites are the Project Gutenberg and Bartleby.com Web sites. These volunteer efforts have collected the contributions of many people throughout the world who have spent enormous amounts of time entering or converting printed text into electronic form. The Project Gutenberg site is supported by donations. The Bartleby.com site, which is named for the main character in Herman Melville's famous short story "Bartleby the Scrivener," was converted into a privately held corporate site in 1999. Since then, it has used advertising to generate revenue to support its operations. The Bartleby.com home page appears in Figure 5-13.

Figure 5-13   **Bartleby.com home page**

The Web itself has become the subject of archivists' attention. The Internet Archive's Wayback Machine provides researchers a series of snapshots of Web pages as they were at various points in the history of the Web. The Internet Archive site also stores text, moving image, audio, and other files that have been contributed to the site. The wide array of information at the Internet Archive site makes it a valuable resource for a variety of research projects. The Internet Archive home page is shown in Figure 5-14.

Internet Archive home page   Figure 5-14

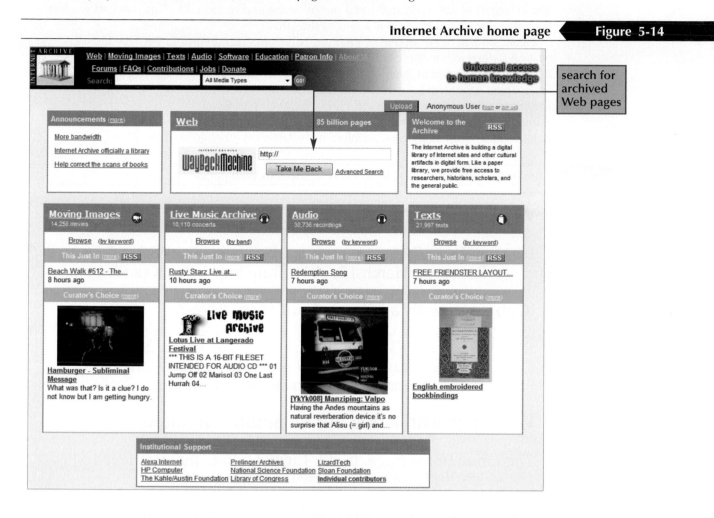

The Online Companion page for Tutorial 5 includes links to Web sites that offer electronic texts and archives in the Additional Information section under the heading Electronic Texts and Archives.

Citing Web Resources

As you search the Web for research resources, you should collect information about the sites you visit so you can include a proper reference to your sources in any research report you write based on your work. You should record the URL and name of any Web site that you use, either in a word-processor document, as a Firefox bookmark, or as an Internet Explorer favorite.

Citation formats are well-defined for print publications, but formats for electronic resources are still emerging. For academic research, the two most widely followed standards for print citations are those of the American Psychological Association (APA) and the Modern Language Association (MLA). The APA and MLA formats for Web page citations are similar and both include: name of the author or Web page creator (if known); title of the Web site in italics (if the page is untitled, provide a description of the page but do not italicize the description); name of the site's sponsoring organization (if any); date the page was retrieved; and the URL. Some authorities recommend that you enclose the URL in chevron symbols or angle brackets (< >). If you do not enclose the URL in chevron (or other) symbols, do not add a period at the end of the URL. This prevents readers from thinking that the period is a part of the URL.

Figure 5-15 shows examples of Web page citations that conform to the APA and MLA citation styles. Links to these two Web sites, and to additional sites that contain citation style and formatting resources, are listed in the Additional Information section of the Online Companion page for this tutorial under the heading Citation Style and Formatting for Web References. Be sure to check the APA and MLA Web sites for updates to these styles before using them. Also, always check to see if your instructor (for classroom work) or editor (for work you are submitting for publication) has established other guidelines.

Figure 5-15   **Commonly used formatting style for references to Web pages**

Web page with a title and an author, undated

Hinman, L.M. *Ethics Updates*. (n.d.). University of San Diego. Retrieved March 12, 2011, from http://ethics.sandiego.edu

Web page with a title and authors, dated

Rivetti, D.A. and G.P. Schneider (1998, Fall). The future of electronic cash. *AABSS Journal*. Retrieved April 19, 2011, from http://aabss.org/journal1998/rivetti.htm

Web page with a title but no author, undated

The Linux Home Page. (n.d.). Linux Online, Inc. Retrieved May 15, 2011, from http://www.linux.org/

Web page with no title and no author, undated

United States Postal Service home page. (n.d.). Retrieved June 18, 2011, from http://www.usps.com

---

The APA and MLA formats for citations to books, journal articles, and other research resources that were published in print form but are also accessible on the Web are more complex than the formats for Web pages. You should consult the APA and MLA Web sites for the latest rules.

Formatting URL Line Breaks | InSight

One of the problems that both the APA and MLA face when setting standards is the difficulty of typesetting long URLs in print documents. No clear standards have emerged specifying where or how to break long URLs at the end of a print line. Most authorities currently agree that the URL should be broken at a slash that appears in the URL and that a hyphen should not be added at the end of the line that occurs in the middle of the URL.

Any method of citing Web pages faces one serious and yet unsolved problem—moving and disappearing URLs. The Web is a dynamic medium that changes constantly. The citation systems that academics and librarians use for published books and journals work well because the printed page has a physical existence. A Web page exists only in an HTML document on a Web server computer. If the file's name or location changes, or if the Web server is disconnected from the Internet, the page is no longer accessible. Perhaps future innovations in Internet addressing technologies will solve this problem. Until then, at least one alternative is being used. Publishers of scholarly academic journals have begun assigning a unique alphanumeric identifier to journal articles and similar documents. This identifier, called a **digital object identifier (DOI)**, is issued by CrossRef.org, which is an independent registration agency. The DOI provides a uniform way to identify content and provide a persistent link to its location as long as the content continues to be located somewhere on the Internet.

Copyright Issues

Marti would like to create a Web page for each musical artist that the agency represents. Many of the agency's artists have their own Web sites, but Marti would like to have a page for each artist on the Cosby Promotions Web site and provide a standard set of information (including a link to the artist's own Web site, if one exists). She would like you to undertake a long-term assignment for her by paying close attention to the multimedia elements of the Web pages you view as you undertake searches for the agency's staff members. She asks you to note any particularly effective uses of Web page design elements and to forward any relevant URLs to her. So that you will understand how these elements work and be better able to gather this information, Marti has asked Susan to give you a tour of multimedia elements in Web pages. The first issue Susan wants to discuss with you is how copyright law governs the use of the text and multimedia elements you obtain online.

Many Web page elements and other items you can find online are a form of **intellectual property**, a general term that includes all products of the human mind, including original ideas. These products can be tangible or intangible. Intellectual property rights include the protections afforded to individuals and companies by governments through governments' granting of copyrights and patents, and through registration of trademarks and service marks.

As you learned in Tutorial 1, a copyright is, quite literally, the right of a person to make copies of his or her work. Copyright laws enforce the idea of copyright by exclusion; that is, the laws prohibit anyone other than the copyright holder from making copies of the work. Copyrights are granted by a government to the author or creator of a literary or artistic work, in other words, to those who create a tangible expression of an idea. The right is for the specific length of time provided in the copyright law and gives the author or creator the sole and exclusive right to print, publish, or sell the work. Creations that can be copyrighted include virtually all forms of artistic or intellectual expression, including books, music, artworks, recordings (audio and video), architectural drawings, choreographic works, product packaging, and computer software. In the United States, works created after 1977 are protected for the life of the author plus 70 years. Works copyrighted by corporations or not-for-profit organizations are protected for 95 years from the date of publication or 120 years from the date of creation, whichever is earlier.

In the past, many countries (including the United States) required the creator of a work to register the work to obtain copyright protection. U.S. law still allows registration, but registration is no longer required. A work that does not include the words "copyright" or "copyrighted," or the copyright symbol (©), and that was created after 1989, is copyrighted automatically by virtue of the copyright law unless the creator makes a specific statement on the work that it is not copyrighted.

Once the term of the copyright has expired, the work is in the **public domain**, which means that anyone is free to copy the files without requesting permission from the source. Older literary works, such as Dickens' *A Tale of Two Cities*, are in the public domain and may be copied and reprinted freely. An author or creator can intentionally place work into the public domain at any time. For example, some Web sites provide graphics files that you can use free of charge. You can use public domain content on a Web page that you create, in a paper that you write, or in any other form of creative expression. However, if you use the content in a paper you are writing for a school assignment, you should acknowledge the source of the material and should be careful not to represent the work as being your own.

A copyright can protect a particular expression of a creative work in addition to the work itself. For example, a Mozart symphony is in the public domain because it was written hundreds of years ago and is no longer protected by Austrian copyright law. But Mozart's creative work was writing the notes of the symphony down on paper in a particular form. If the Cleveland Orchestra makes an audio recording of that public domain Mozart symphony, its performance can be copyrighted by the Cleveland Orchestra and protected under current copyright laws.

Copyrights and Ideas

The *idea* contained in a product is not copyrightable. The particular form of expression of an idea creates a work that can be copyrighted. For example, you cannot copyright the idea to write a song about love, you can copyright only the song you end up writing. If an idea cannot be separated from its expression in a work, that work cannot be copyrighted. For example, mathematical calculations cannot be copyrighted.

A collection of facts can be copyrighted, but only if the collection is arranged, coordinated, or selected in a way that causes the resulting work to rise to the level of an original work. For example, the Yahoo! Web Directory is a collection of links to URLs. These facts existed before Yahoo! selected and arranged them into the form of its directory. However, most intellectual property lawyers would argue that the selection and arrangement of the links into categories probably makes the directory copyrightable.

Copyright Protection and Internet Technologies

When you use your Web browser to read text on a Web page, view a graphic image, listen to a sound, or watch a video clip, your Web browser downloads the multimedia element from the Web server and stores it in a temporary file on your computer's hard drive. This technological process creates a new, intermediate level of ownership that did not exist before the emergence of the Web. For example, when you go to an art gallery and view a picture, you do not take possession of the picture in any way. When you visit an online art gallery, however, your Web browser—software running on your computer—temporarily owns a copy of the file containing the image. As you have learned in earlier tutorials, it is easy to make a permanent copy of Web page images—even though your copy might infringe on the image owner's rights.

The potential for users to infringe on copyrights when viewing Web pages is much greater than when using other types of media. Web site managers who incorporate multimedia elements might infringe on copyrights when including graphics, video, and audio clips on their pages—sometimes without realizing they have done anything wrong.

Some Web site owners attempt to avoid liability under copyright laws by including on their sites hyperlinks to copyright-violating multimedia elements located on *other* Web pages. Their intent is to claim that they did not have any copyright violations on their sites because the multimedia element was located on the site to which they linked. This strategy has not yet been tested sufficiently in the courts to determine whether it is an effective shield against liability.

Using Web Search Techniques to Find Infringing Uses | InSight

Scanning a copy of a popular cartoon from a newspaper or magazine and placing it on a Web page would most likely infringe on the owner's copyright. Some cartoonists regularly search the Web using various search tools, looking for unauthorized copies of their work. They threaten or take legal action when they find Web sites that appear to infringe their copyrights.

Fair Use and Plagiarism

The U.S. copyright law allows people to use copyrighted works if their use is a fair use. The **fair use** of a copyrighted work includes copying it for use in criticism, comment, news reporting, teaching, scholarship, or research. The law's definition of fair use is intentionally broad and can be difficult to interpret.

There have been many court cases on the fair use issue. These cases usually turn on four factors: how and for what purpose the copyrighted material was used, whether the work is more factual or more fictional in nature, the amount of the copyrighted material used and how substantial a part it is of the copyrighted work, and whether the use of the copyrighted material hurts the market for the original work or impairs the ability of the copyright owner to earn income or otherwise benefit from the work. Uses of content from published works are more likely to be determined fair use than uses of content from unpublished works because the copyright owner of a published work has had a chance to benefit from the work through sales, publicity, increased reputation, or other means. The smaller the amount of the work that is used, the more likely the use will be considered fair use. However, using even a small amount of the work can be copyright infringement if it is the heart of the work. This is especially true with musical compositions. The use of even a small portion of a copyrighted song can be an infringing use. Again, there is no hard-and-fast rule that determines fair use. If a copyright holder disputes your use, the matter will be settled by the subjective assessment of a judge or jury. If you are unsure whether your use is indeed fair use, the safest course of action is to contact the copyright owner and ask for permission to use the work.

Using Free Content | InSight

Some Web sites offer text and other types of files free as samples and offer other files for sale. The free files often carry a restriction against selling or redistributing them, even though you may be able to use them without cost on your own personal Web page. You should examine carefully any site from which you download such files to determine what usage limitations apply. If you cannot find a clear statement of copyright terms or a statement that the files are in the public domain, you should not use them on your Web page or anywhere else.

Acknowledging a source can be especially important when you use public domain material in papers, reports, or other school projects. Failure to cite the source of material that you use (whether it is in the public domain or it is protected by copyright) is called **plagiarism** and can be a serious violation of your school's academic honesty policy. The Internet makes it easy to copy someone else's work and commit plagiarism. A number of companies have created sites that teachers can use to identify plagiarism in papers that students submit. One of these companies, Turnitin.com, offers tips for students who want to avoid committing plagiarism unintentionally on its Plagiarism.org page.

The Online Companion page for Tutorial 5 contains a number of links to Web sites with further information about adhering to Web copyrights in the Additional Information section under the Copyright Information Resources heading.

Images and Graphics on the Web

The Web is an excellent source of images and graphics, but you should keep in mind what you learned earlier in this tutorial about respecting the copyright interests of the owners of these types of files. In this section, you will learn about graphics file formats and how to find images and graphics on the Web.

Graphics File Formats

Most images on the Web are in one of two file formats, GIF or JPEG. **GIF**, an acronym for **Graphics Interchange Format**, is an older format that does a very good job of compressing small- or medium-sized files. Most GIF files you find on the Web have a .gif extension. This file format can store only up to 256 different colors. The GIF format is widely used on the Internet for images that have only a few distinct colors, such as line drawings, cartoons, simple icons, and screen objects. Some of the more interesting screen objects on the Web are animated GIF files. An **animated GIF** file combines several images into a single GIF file. When a Web browser that recognizes the animated GIF file type loads this type of file, it cycles through the images in the file and gives the appearance of cartoon-like animation. The size and color-depth limitations of the GIF file format prevent animated GIFs from delivering high-quality video, however.

JPEG, an acronym for **Joint Photographic Experts Group**, is a newer file format that stores many more colors than the GIF format—more than 16 million more, in fact—and more colors yields a higher-quality image. The JPEG format is particularly useful for photographs and continuous-tone art (images that do not have sharp edges). Most JPEG files that you find on the Web have a .jpg file extension.

Both of these formats offer file compression, which is important on the Web. Uncompressed graphics files containing images of significant size or complexity are too large to transmit efficiently. JPEG file compression is "lossy." A **lossy compression** procedure erases some elements of the graphic so that when it is displayed, it will not be as clear as the original image. The greater the level of compression, the more graphic detail is lost.

Although most graphic images on the Web are in either the JPEG or GIF formats, you might encounter images that use other file formats, including Windows bitmap file format (.bmp), Tagged Image File Format (or TIFF) format (.tif), PC Paintbrush format (.pcx), and the Portable Network Graphics (or PNG) format (.png). The Windows bitmap, TIFF, and PC Paintbrush formats are all uncompressed graphics formats. Web page designers usually avoid these formats because a Web browser takes too long to download them. The PNG format was designed specifically for use on the Web in the mid-1990s and has become more common in recent years.

Finding Graphics and Images on the Web

The Additional Information section of the Online Companion page for this tutorial contains links to Web pages that offer photographs and images in the Photographs and Images section. Many of these sites permit downloading of at least some of the files for personal or commercial use.

One of the best Web resources for the fine arts is the WebMuseum site, which occasionally features special exhibitions. The WebMuseum's mainstay is its Famous Paintings collection, which includes images of artwork from around the world. Susan wants you to see the museum's self-portraits of Vincent van Gogh so you can gain experience using and searching for graphics files at a museum Web site.

To view Vincent van Gogh's self-portraits at the WebMuseum site:

▶ **1.** Return to the Online Companion page for Session 5.2, and click the **WebMuseum** link.

▶ **2.** Click the **Famous Artworks** collections hyperlink.

▶ **3.** Click the **Artist Index** hyperlink.

▶ **4.** Scroll down the list of artists to find the **Gogh, Vincent van** hyperlink, and then click it.

▶ **5.** Click the **Self-Portraits** hyperlink to open the page shown in Figure 5-16.

WebMuseum Vincent van Gogh Self-Portraits page ◄ **Figure 5-16**

WebMuseum, Paris

Gogh, Vincent van: Self-Portraits

In the most limited definition of the term, Impressionism as the objective study of light did not encourage so essentially a subjective study as the self-portrait but in the later expansion of the movement this self-representation was given renewed force by Cézanne and van Gogh. The latter has often been compared with Rembrandt in the number and expressiveness of his self-portraits but while Rembrandt's were distributed through a lifetime, van Gogh produced some thirty in all in the short space of five years --- from the end of the Brabant period (1885) to the last year of his life at St Rémy and Auvers. In each there is the same extraordinary intensity of expression concentrated in the eyes but otherwise there is a considerable variety. From the Paris period onwards he used different adaptations of Impressionist and Neo-Impressionist brushwork, separate patches of colour being applied with varying thickness and direction in a way that makes each painting a fresh experience.

narrative

Self-Portrait Dedicated to Paul Gauguin
1888 (130 Kb); Oil on canvas, 60.5 x 49.4 cm (23 3/4 x 19 1/2 in); Fogg Art Museum, Harvard University, Cambridge, MA

Self-Portrait in front of the Easel
1888 (200 Kb); 65 x 50.5 cm

Self-Portrait with Bandaged Ear
1889 (250 Kb); Oil on canvas, 60 x 49 cm; Courtauld Institute Galleries, London

click thumbnail image to open a larger image

Self-Portrait
1889 (250 Kb); Oil on canvas, 65 x 54 cm (25 1/2 x 21 1/4 in); Musee d'Orsay, Paris

Self-Portrait
1889 (250 Kb); Oil on canvas, 65 x 54 cm (25 1/2 x 21 1/4 in); Musee d'Orsay, Paris

This page, devoted to van Gogh's self-portraits, includes a narrative about these works; the title, date created, file size, media, and size of the original; and information about the work's owner (if it is a public institution). You can click any of the small (or thumbnail) images to view a larger version of the image.

Some of the images included in the WebMuseum collection are in the public domain, especially those that are older. Other images are still protected by copyright. Remember, just because you see images on the WebMuseum site does not mean that you can copy them and use them without the permission of the copyright holder. Always track down the source of the image (in the case of WebMuseum exhibits, you would contact the museum or other organization that owns the artwork) and request permission to use it.

The robots that gather information for search engines cannot read graphics files to identify their attributes. Earlier search engines relied on HTML image tags that Web page builders include in their HTML documents; the tags contain terms that describe the image. This situation made finding image files on the Web difficult. Today, however, many search engine and Web directory sites have improved their image classification databases and provide separate search functions that are dedicated to finding Web pages with graphics content. A list of search engines that include image search features is included in the Online Companion Additional Information section under the heading Search Engines with Image Search Features.

Marti would like you to find some graphics and photos that include jazz-related subject matter.

To find jazz-related graphics and photos:

▶ **1.** Return to the Online Companion page for Session 5.2, and then find the list of **Search Engines with Image Search Features**.

▶ **2.** Choose one of the search engines and type **jazz** as the search term in the appropriate location on the page, and then click the site's **Search** (or similar) button to start the search.

▶ **3.** When you have found several images or photos related to jazz, examine the Web page on which they are located and attempt to determine whether the images are protected by copyright.

The results page of a Google Images search on the term "jazz" is shown in Figure 5-17. Each of the small images is a link to a page with a larger image. That page, in turn, is linked to the source of the image on the Web.

Results of a Google Images search on the term "jazz" | Figure 5-17

You can send the URLs of the pages you found that contain jazz images to Marti in an email message, along with a note about any copyright restrictions you found.

In addition to images, you can find sounds and movies on the Web. You will learn about these resources next.

Multimedia on the Web

Multimedia is a general term that includes audio, video, and moving images (such as the graphics in a computer game). In the early days of the Web, the only multimedia form available was the animated GIF file. The animated GIF format has a limited ability to present moving graphics and cannot store any audio information. Today, Web site designers can include sound or video clips to enhance the information on their pages.

The use of multimedia elements on Web sites has greatly improved the functionality and usefulness of the Web. News sites can provide video of unfolding events as they happen, audio clips let customers listen to parts of songs before they buy them, and do-it-yourself help sites can provide video that shows demonstrations, such as a master plumber installing a new sink.

Multimedia File Formats

Unlike graphics files, sound and video files appear on the Web in many different formats and can require that your Web browser have additional software extensions installed. These software extensions, or **plug-ins**, are usually available as free downloads. The firms that offer media players as free downloads earn their profits by selling encoding software to developers who want to include audio and video files in that format on their Web sites. Each firm that creates a format has an incentive to promote its use, so a variety of audio and video formats are used on the Web today.

Audio File Formats

To play any type of audio files (or the audio element of video clip), your computer must be equipped with a sound card and either a speaker or earphones. One of the first widely used audio file formats on the Web was the **Wave (WAV) format**, which was jointly developed by Microsoft and IBM. WAV files store digitized audio and can be played on any Windows computer that supports sound. WAV files can be recorded at different quality levels, which results in different size files (higher quality means a larger file). In fact, music CDs are recorded in the WAV format at a very high quality level. A standard CD has a capacity of about 650 MB and can hold about 74 minutes of high-quality stereo music. You can recognize a WAV file on the Web by its .wav file extension.

Another commonly used Web file format is the MIDI format. The **MIDI (Musical Instrument Digital Interface)** format is a standard adopted by the music industry for controlling devices that create and read musical information. The MIDI format does not digitize the sound waveform; instead, it digitally records information about each element of the sound, including its pitch, length, and volume. Most keyboard synthesizers and other electronic instruments use MIDI so that music recorded on one instrument can be played on other instruments. MIDI files can also be played on computers that have a MIDI interface or software. It is much easier to edit music recorded in the MIDI format than music recorded in the WAV format because you can manipulate the individual characteristics of the sound with precision. MIDI files are much smaller than WAV files and are used in applications where storage space is at a premium. Most mobile phone ringtones, for example, are in the MIDI format. Usually, MIDI files have either a .midi or .mid file extension.

Because much of the Internet was originally constructed on computers running the UNIX operating system, the system's audio file format still appears on the Web, although very few new audio files are created in this format today. Most Web browsers can read this audio UNIX format, which is known as the AU format. AU format files usually have a file extension of .au. The AU format can store sound at various quality levels, and the resulting files are approximately the same size as WAV files recorded at similar quality levels.

Video File Formats

As you learned earlier in this tutorial, your computer needs a sound card and some way to play the sound (speaker or headphones) for you to hear audio files. Video files do not need any special hardware. Of course, if the video file has an audio track, you will need the sound card and the speaker or headphones to hear it. High-quality audio files and video files of any significant length can be very large. A popular technique for transferring large multimedia (both sound and video) files on the Web is called streaming transmission. In a **streaming transmission**, the Web server sends the first part of the file to the Web browser, which begins playing the file. While the browser is playing the file, the server is sending the next segment of the file. Streaming transmission allows you to access large audio or video files in less time than the download-then-play procedure, because the streamed file begins playing before it finishes downloading. RealNetworks, Inc. pioneered this technology and developed the RealAudio format for audio files and the RealVideo format for video files. The RealNetworks formats are compressed to further increase the efficiency with which they can be transferred over the Internet. For example, a 1-megabyte WAV file can be compressed into a 30-kilobyte RealAudio file.

Another streaming video format that has become popular is Adobe's Flash format. Playing Flash video files requires that your Web browser have the Adobe Flash Player software plug-in installed. Flash files can include video, high-resolution moving graphics, and graphic elements that interact with the user's mouse movements. Flash files usually have an .swf extension.

Video files can be very large, so the International Standards Organization's **Moving Picture Experts Group (MPEG)** has created a series of standards for compressed file formats. The compressed files in this format usually have a file extension that identifies the version of the MPEG standard with which they were encoded. For example, a video file that uses MPEG Level 2 compression would normally have an .mp2 file extension, although you will see alternative file extensions such as .mpe, .mpeg, .mpv2, or .mpg in use on the Web. The latest release of the MPEG standard is MPEG 4, which provides DVD-quality video when it is played.

Video files are also available in older formats on the Web. Most Web browsers can play Microsoft's **AVI (Audio Video Interleaved)** format files and, with the proper software plug-in downloaded and installed, also can play Apple's **QuickTime** format files. One minute of video and sound recorded in either of these formats results in a file that is about 6 MB. AVI files usually have an .avi extension, and Apple QuickTime files usually have an .mov extension.

When you tell Marti what you have learned about online video and copyright issues, she is intrigued, and wants to make sure that the Cosby Promotions Web site adheres to applicable copyright laws. She asks you to find an online video that discusses the fair use exception in the U.S. copyright laws.

Tip

To play RealAudio files, which you can recognize by their .ra, .ram, or .rmj file extensions, you must download and install one of the Real file player plug-ins from the firm's Web site.

Tip

MPEG compression is similar to JPEG compression for graphics files in that it deletes information from the file and can thus reduce the quality of the video.

Finding Video Clips Online

- Open a video search site in your Web browser.
- Enter a search expression that includes the name or type of video you want to find.
- Run the search, and then examine the search results.
- Consider repeating the search with alternative search expressions to find a wider variety of videos that might meet your needs.

To search for videos that include a discussion of the fair use exception to U.S. copyright laws:

▶ **1.** Return to the Online Companion page for Session 5.2, choose one of the tools in the Video Search Engines section to use in your search, and then click the link to the site you have chosen to open its video search page.

▶ **2.** Enter the search expression **copyright fair use** in the search box, and then click the **Search** (or similar) button.

▶ **3.** Examine your search results and click the links to any videos that look like they might satisfy Marti's request.

   Trouble? Your computer must have a sound card and either headphones or a speaker for you to hear the audio portion of any video you play.

   Trouble? The Web browser you are using must have a plug-in installed to play video in specific formats.

▶ **4.** Make a note of the URL of the best two videos you find so you can email them to Marti.

Audio from Video: The MP3 File Format

The audio portion of the MPEG file format was responsible for the greatest revolution in online music that has occurred in the history of the Web. The MPEG format's audio track, called **MPEG Audio Layer 3 (MP3)** became wildly popular in the late 1990s as disk storage on personal computers dropped in price and CD writers (also called CD burners) became affordable for home use. Files in the MP3 format are somewhat lower in quality than WAV format files, but they are 90 percent smaller. Thus, a CD that might hold 15 popular songs in high-quality WAV format (about 40 megabytes per song) could instead hold 150 popular songs in MP3 format (about 4 megabytes per song). The MP3 file format is the most popular for music on the Web today.

Ethical and Legal Concerns: Sharing Audio Files

The smaller size of MP3 files made it easy to send them from one person to another through the Internet, and file-sharing Web sites, such as Napster and Kazaa, became popular. People began copying music from CDs that they had purchased and converting that music into MP3 files, which they then exchanged with others on the Internet through the sites. This file-sharing activity is unethical because it deprives the creators of the audio works of their rights to control distribution and to profit from their work. It is also illegal in many countries, including the United States.

   Companies in the recording industry and the recording artists themselves were not very happy with the large number of MP3 files that were being transmitted on these file-sharing networks. Recording companies and artists filed suits against Napster and other file-sharing sponsors for violating copyright laws. The recording companies were generally successful in obtaining court orders or out-of-court settlements that prevent further copyright violations in most of these suits. The case against Napster resulted in the company going out of business (the Napster of today is operated by a different company that bought the name from the failed company and sells music legally). In some of these cases, the recording companies have won hundreds of thousands of dollars in damages from individuals who illegally copied and shared music online. Many individuals, however, still violate the law and share MP3 files that contain copyrighted works.

Legal MP3 File Distribution

Since the popularity of the MP3 format became established, a number of Web sites have been created to sell digital music in MP3 and other formats. These sites, which include Napster under new management, have obtained the legal right to distribute the musical works they offer for sale. Advances in flash memory technology have made it possible to create portable digital music players (such as Apple's iPod) that can store thousands of songs downloaded from music Web sites.

Web sites such as eMusic, Rhapsody.com, and Apple's iTunes Store offer music for download in MP3 and other, lesser known, formats. Some of these sites charge per song, while others charge a monthly fee that allows subscribers to download as many songs as they wish. A small but growing group of recording artists has begun to distribute recordings that are available only as downloads from their own Web sites. Most of the sites that sell downloadable music place restrictions on the number of copies you can make of each song. Some of the sites restrict you from converting downloaded song files into other formats, or they restrict the types of devices on which you are permitted to play the song. The restrictions are implemented in the files themselves, using systems of encoding called **digital rights management (DRM)**. Because different online music vendors use different DRM systems, their files are often not compatible with each other.

Because of these differing DRM systems and because you can incur legal liability by using or copying downloaded files (even those you have purchased) in ways that the vendor prohibits, you should always check the site carefully for details about file formats and copying restrictions before you buy songs or sign up for a subscription.

Because Cosby Promotions represents a number of music artists, Marti is interested in learning more about how bands are selling their music on the Web. She asks you to do some research by finding the music of a band you like that is for sale on the Web and determining what format the music is sold in and if there are any limitations (DRM or contractual) attached to the use of the files once you buy them.

> **Tip**
>
> Make sure that the files from a particular site are compatible with your portable music player before you sign up for a download subscription.

To search for music to purchase online:

▶ **1.** Return to the Online Companion page for Session 5.2, choose one of the links in the Online Music Stores section, and then click the link to the site you have chosen to open its home page.

▶ **2.** The exact procedure you will use for your search will depend on which music store you chose. Use your chosen site's search function to find a band name or type of music.

Trouble? If the online music store you chose does not offer music by your chosen band, you can search for another band or try a different site. Not all bands sell their music online, so you might not be able to find your first choice in any online music store.

Trouble? Some online music stores require you to sign up for a trial membership before you can search for music. Many of these trial memberships are free. If you do not want to sign up for membership, try another music store.

▶ **3.** Once you find the band or type of music you want, explore the site to determine what type of files the store sells (so you will know what types of portable music devices can play the file) and to determine what (if any) restrictions the store places on the copying or use of the files.

> **4.** Make a note of the online music store name, the type of files it sells, and any restrictions on copying or use of the files so you can send this information to Marti in an email.

> **5.** Close your Web browser.

You can use the list of online music stores in the Online Companion to search for music files that you can use on your computer or on any personal music device you happen to own. The continuing developments in portable data storage technology and increasing bandwidth should ensure that digital music grows for many years.

Software on the Web

Internet users are often pleasantly surprised to discover that many programs are available for download at little or no cost, or at the same cost you would encounter if you went to a retail outlet to purchase them. The four general types of downloaded software are freeware, shareware, limited edition, and licensed (also called a full version).

Freeware

Software developers sometimes make their software available for free in exchange for user feedback as they refine their products. After collecting user feedback and improving the software, many developers provide an upgrade of the free version for a fee. Other developers do their coding as a hobby and continue to provide free software as long as they have an interest in it. Software that is available to users at no cost and with no restrictions is called **freeware**. Freeware users must accept the software as is. Although most freeware works well, it can contain errors that could cause the program to halt, malfunction or even damage the user's computer. The software's developer is rarely liable for any damage that the freeware program might cause to computers onto which it is installed. Many successful commercial software programs started as freeware. To see what kinds of successes and problems users have reported with a specific freeware program, use an Internet search engine to find reviews of the freeware program and read them carefully before you download, install, virus check, and use the program.

Shareware

Shareware is similar to freeware in that it costs nothing to download and install. However, it remains free to use only for a short evaluation period. After the evaluation period expires—after a specified number of days or a specific number of uses—shareware stops functioning. Shareware users are expected to stop using the shareware after the specified initial trial period and uninstall it from their computers. Alternatively, a user who likes the program and wants to continue using it can purchase a license to do so. Shareware developers use three methods to turn trial users into paying customers. The first way is to build a counter into the program that keeps track of the number of times they have used a program. After users have reached a usage limit, the software disables itself. The second way inserts an internal date checker that causes the shareware to stop working after a specific time period from the installation date has elapsed, such as 30 days. Third, many shareware developers use a "nag" screen that appears each time the program is started after the evaluation period ends. The screen encourages users who do not purchase a license to stop using the shareware or buy a license, although the program might continue to work. The screen usually displays a message with the developer's name and Web address and asks users to abide by the licensing agreement and to submit payment for the shareware version of the product. Shareware is generally more reliable than freeware because shareware developers are more likely to accept responsibility for the program's operation. Usually, shareware developers have an established process for users to report any problems they experience and receive free or low-cost software upgrades and patches.

Evaluation Version Software

Some developers distribute restricted versions of their software at no cost. A restricted version of a program is often called **evaluation version software**, and it provides less functionality than the full version that is available for purchase. Evaluation version software might omit one or more useful features of the full version or might only allow a limited range of storage (for example, an address book program might allow you to enter only 20 names and addresses). If you like the evaluation version, you can purchase the full version.

Regardless of which type of software you use to evaluate a product, most developers provide you with a means of contacting them to purchase a license to use the full version of the evaluation copy. Purchasing a license usually involves paying a fee to get a code to unlock the software and enable it to operate with full functionality.

Computer magazines frequently use their software testing laboratories to review software, conduct product comparisons, and report the results. They should not have a vested interest in the outcome, but always view the results with a critical eye to identify any biases. You can use the lists contained in the Software Download Web Sites and Software Review Web Sites sections of the Online Companion to find freeware, shareware, and evaluation version software downloads and reviews.

Future of Electronic Publishing

One of the key changes that the Internet and the Web have brought to the world is that information can now be disseminated more rapidly than ever and in large quantities, but with a low required investment. The impact of this change is that firms in the public relations business—which spend great amounts of time and money trying to present their clients through the major media in the best possible light—might be facing a significantly changed business environment. Many industry analysts believe that the ease of publishing electronically on the Web might help reduce the concentration of media control that has been developing over the past three decades as newspapers and publishing companies merged with each other and, along with radio and television stations, were purchased by large media companies.

Magazines and Newspapers Online

To be successful in print media publishing (such as publishing a monthly magazine or a daily newspaper), a publisher must have a large subscription or newsstand distribution. The publisher can earn a profit only if the high fixed costs of composing and creating the magazine are offset by large numbers of paid subscriptions or large numbers of readers that advertisers will pay to reach (or a combination of the two). The costs of publishing a Web page are very low compared to those for printing magazines or newspapers. Therefore, the subscription market required for a Web publication to survive can be very small or even nonexistent. If a Web-based publication can attract advertisers, it can be financially successful with no subscribers and a relatively small number of readers. Because online publications do not require a large readership, they can focus on specialized, narrow interests. An increasing number of major daily newspapers are relying on their Web site versions to bring in advertising revenue as the sale of their paper publication continues to decline. Weekly and monthly magazines are following a similar strategy. Growing numbers of publications that appear only on the Web are finding that online advertising can support enough news gathering and editorial activities to return a profit. Online publications such as Slate, Salon.com, and The Huffington Post have continued to grow in recent years.

Blogs (Web Logs) and Wikis

Most e-zines follow the general model used by print magazines for their layout, design, and structure. Also, like print magazines, e-zines are usually managed by an editor who solicits manuscripts from other writers and then publishes some of those manuscripts after editing them. However, the Web has enabled an entirely new type of individual publication, the Weblog, or blog. Blogs are usually written by a single person (called the blogger) who wishes to express a particular point of view. Some blogs allow others to add comments or reactions to the blogger's statements, which may be edited or deleted by the blogger. Although blogs exist on a wide variety of topics, most blogs focus on political, religious, or other issues about which people have strong opinions.

Blogs are usually run by one individual who writes the main commentary and decides which comments posted by readers will be included in the blog. Thus, the content and direction of the blog are controlled by its owner. Another form of interactive online writing is the wiki. A **wiki** is a Web site that is designed to allow multiple users to contribute content and edit existing content. Wiki is a Hawaiian word that means "fast," and wikis are set up to allow many different users to add and edit content quickly and easily. Most wikis are focused on facts or collaborative work. This contrasts with blogs, which are usually focused on the opinions of the blogger who controls the site. Wikipedia, the online encyclopedia that you learned about in Tutorial 4, is probably the most famous wiki in the world. The home page of Wikitravel, a wiki that invites travelers to share their experiences in a collaborative world travel guide, is shown in Figure 5-18.

Figure 5-18   **Wikitravel home page**

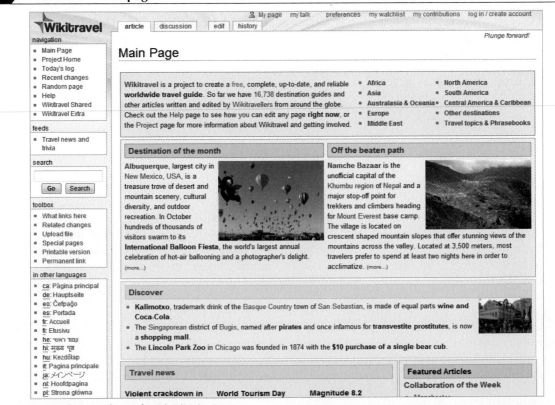

Source: http://wikitravel.org/en/Main_Page

Marti appreciates your help with travel planning and gathering information regarding clients and planned promotion ideas. When you need to use the Web to find information for your classes or your job, remember to return to the Additional Information section of the Online Companion page for Tutorial 5 for a comprehensive list of Web information resources.

Session 5.2 Quick Check | Review

1. A general term for files that contain sound, music, or video recordings is

   _____ .

2. Define the term "plagiarism."
3. Briefly describe two ways that libraries use the Web.
4. What are the advantages of using online reference works, such as dictionaries or encyclopedias, instead of print editions?
5. For how long is a work copyrighted?
6. Briefly explain the concept of "fair use."
7. True or False: Music stored in a WAV file format would be of lower quality and would result in a smaller file than the same music stored in an MP3-formatted file.
8. Briefly explain the differences between a blog and a wiki.

Tutorial Summary | Review

In this tutorial, you learned how to find current news stories, weather information, maps, and information about travel destinations on the Web by using specialized search engines and Web directories. Online library resources and other research and reference resources are also available on the Web.

You learned some basic facts about copyright protection, fair use, and avoiding plagiarism in the use of text, images, and multimedia files that you find on the Internet. You also learned how to access many of the graphics and multimedia resources on the Internet, and you learned which image, sound, and video file formats are common on the Web. Finally, you learned about software that is available for download on the Web and about the future of publishing online.

Key Terms

animated GIF
AVI (Audio Video
    Interleaved)
digital object
    identifier (DOI)
digital rights
    management (DRM)
evaluation version software
fair use
freeware
Graphics Interchange
    Format (GIF)
intellectual property

Joint Photographic Experts
    Group (JPEG)
lossy compression
MIDI (Musical Instrument
    Digital Interface)
Moving Picture Experts
    Group (MPEG)
MPEG Audio
    Layer 3 (MP3)
multimedia
news search engine
plagiarism
plug-ins

public domain
QuickTime
shareware
streaming transmission
Wave (WAV) format
Web logs (Weblogs
    or blogs)
Web news directories
white pages directory
wiki
wire service
yellow pages directory

Practice	**Review Assignments**

Get hands-on practice of the skills you learned in the tutorial using the same case scenario.

There are no Data Files needed for these Review Assignments.

Marti is preparing to visit a new techno band in Chicago, Illinois that she would like to sign. While in Chicago, she would like to visit several clubs that feature blues artists.

1. Start your Web browser, go to www.cengage.com/internet/np/internet8 to open the Online Companion page, log on to your account, click the Tutorial 5 link, and then click the Review Assignments link.

2. Obtain weather forecasts for the Chicago area from two of the weather sites included in the list of links for this assignment (or use weather sites with which you are familiar). Print the forecasts from each site.

3. The band is renting practice space in a warehouse near the corner of West 35th Street and South Morgan Street in Chicago's South Side. Print two maps from one of the map Web sites included in the list of links for this assignment. Include at least one street-level map and one higher-level map that show the surrounding area in Chicago.

4. Use one of the links to a travel destination guide site to locate information about restaurants in the Chicago area. Prepare a report that lists three restaurants you would recommend to Marti for entertaining clients while in Chicago.

5. Use one of the travel destination guide sites to locate at least two blues clubs that Marti can visit while she is in Chicago.

6. Use one or more of the links to News Search Engines in the Online Companion to find an article in a Chicago area newspaper that discusses a local band or an area club that features live music. Summarize the article in a short memo to Marti and include a citation to the article in the memo.

7. When you are finished, close your Web browser.

| Apply | Case Problem 1 |

Apply the skills you learned in this tutorial to produce a map, driving directions, and list of prospective sales clients for a business trip.

There are no Data Files needed for this Case Problem.

Portland Concrete Mixers, Inc.   You are a sales representative for Portland Concrete Mixers, Inc., a company that makes replacement parts for concrete mixing equipment. This equipment is mounted on trucks that deliver ready-mixed concrete to buildings and other job sites. You have been transferred to the Seattle area and would like to plan your first sales trip there. Because you plan to drive to Seattle, you need information about the best route as well as a map of Seattle. You hope to generate some new customers on this trip and, therefore, need to identify sales-lead prospects in the area. Companies that manufacture concrete are good prospects for you.

1. Start your Web browser, go to www.cengage.com/internet/np/internet8 to open the Online Companion page, log on to your account, click the Tutorial 5 link, and then click the Case Problem 1 link.
2. Choose one of the map sites from the list provided in the Online Companion.
3. Obtain driving directions from the site you have chosen. Your starting address is Portland, OR, and your destination address is Seattle, WA.
4. Obtain a map of Seattle from the site you have chosen. You can adjust the map to the level of detail you desire.

⊕ EXPLORE

5. To identify sales prospects in Seattle, return to the Online Companion page for Case Problem 1 in Tutorial 5, and use one or more of the directories listed under the Yellow Pages Directories heading to search for businesses in the Seattle area that sell concrete. The results pages for your searches should include contact information for a number of companies in the concrete business in Seattle. Copy the names and addresses of at least three sales prospects to a document that you will carry with you on your trip.
6. When you are finished, close your Web browser.

| Research | **Case Problem 2** |

Research specific types of MIDI files. Examine information about copyright restrictions.

There are no Data Files needed for this Case Problem.

Midland Elementary School Music Classes You are a third-grade language skills teacher at Midland Elementary School. The school has closed its music program because the state has cut the budget severely over the past several years. Although the school no longer has any music teachers on staff, you believe that it is important to expose your students to the music of the great composers, such as Beethoven and Mozart. You do not have a budget for buying CDs, but you do have a computer with an Internet connection in the classroom. You would like to find some music files to play on the computer, but you want to make sure that any use of these files complies with U.S. copyright law. You have heard that single musical instruments, particularly pianos, sound realistic when synthesized in the MIDI format and you would, therefore, like to find some music in this format to begin your collection for the class.

1. Start your Web browser, go to www.cengage.com/internet/np/internet8 to open the Online Companion page, log on to your account, click the Tutorial 5 link, and then click the Case Problem 2 link.
2. Click one or more of the MIDI music links provided for this Case Problem.

◆ EXPLORE

3. Evaluate the files offered on these Web pages or the pages to which they lead. Write a short report summarizing your experience. In your report, describe any copyright restrictions that apply to the files that you would like to use. (*Hint*: The copyright restrictions might not be on the page from which you download the files, so be sure to look for links to pages such as "Terms and Conditions" on the site's home page.)
4. When you are finished, close your Web browser.

| Create | **Case Problem 3** |

Research pending legislation about child care, evaluate a child care information Web site, and create two reports.

There are no Data Files needed for this Case Problem.

Toddle Inn Headquartered in Minneapolis, Minnesota, Toddle Inn is a chain of day-care centers operating in several Midwestern states. The directors are interested in undertaking a national expansion program that will require outside financing and an effective public relations program that integrates with their strategic marketing plans. You are an intern in the office of Joan Caruso, a public relations consultant who does work for Toddle Inn. Joan has asked you to help her with some background research as she creates a proposal for Toddle Inn to integrate a Web site into its public relations program.

1. Start your Web browser, go to www.cengage.com/internet/np/internet8 to open the Online Companion page, log on to your account, click the Tutorial 5 link, and then click the Case Problem 3 link.
2. Follow the links provided there to one or more of the news search engines and directories to find at least three current (within the past three or four months) news reports about the child-care industry. Write a memo to Joan that summarizes the major issues identified in these reports.
3. Joan would like you to conduct an evaluation of the Child Care Parent/Provider Information Network Web site. Prepare an evaluation of the site that considers the author's or publisher's identity and objectivity as well as the site's content, form, and appearance.

✛ EXPLORE

4. One issue that any public relations campaign must consider is the impact of pending legislation. Joan asks you to find out whether any bills are pending in the U.S. Congress that will affect the child-care industry. Return to the Online Companion page for Case Problem 3 in Tutorial 5, open the Thomas Legislative Information Web site, type "child care" (without quotation marks) in the Word/Phrase text box, and then click the Search button. Read one of the bills listed and prepare a one-paragraph summary for Joan of the bill's likely effects on the child-care industry in general and the Toddle Inn specifically.

5. When you are finished, close your Web browser.

| Create | **Case Problem 4** |

Identify Web sites that present arguments for and against prison privatization and create a report that summarizes findings.

There are no Data Files needed for this Case Problem.

Arnaud for Senate Campaign You work for the campaign team of Lisa Arnaud, who is running for a seat in the state senate. One issue that promises to play a prominent role in the upcoming election campaign is privatization of the state prison system. It is important for Lisa to establish a clear position on the issue early in the campaign, and she has asked you to prepare a briefing document for her to consider. Lisa tells you that she has no particular preference on the issue and that she wants you to obtain a balanced set of arguments for each side. Once the campaign takes a position, however, she will need to defend it. Therefore, Lisa wants to determine the quality of the information you gather. You decide to do part of your research on the Web.

1. Start your Web browser, go to www.cengage.com/internet/np/internet8 to open the Online Companion page, log on to your account, click the Tutorial 5 link, and then click the Case Problem 4 link.

2. Choose one of the listed search tools to conduct a search for "privatization prisons" (without the quotation marks).

✛ EXPLORE

3. Examine your search results for authoritative sites that include positions on the issue. (*Hint*: You might need to follow a number of results page hyperlinks to find suitable Web pages. In general, you should avoid current news items that appear in the results list.)

4. Find one Web page that states a clear position in favor of privatization and another that states a clear position against privatization. Print a copy of each.

5. Prepare a three-paragraph report that summarizes the content of the Web pages you chose. Include full citations for the pages along with a one or two sentence evaluation of the quality of each page.

6. When you are finished, close your Web browser.

Research | **Case Problem 5**

Find images that meet a particular need and determine the copyright limitations on their use.

There are no Data Files needed for this Case Problem.

Kim's Travel and Cruises   You are an assistant to Kim Phong, the owner of Kim's Travel and Cruises. The Web site for the firm includes pages that describe many of the destinations featured in the cruises she books for her clients. Kim would like to include images of flags that correspond to the country of each destination. She would also like to have a local artist create replicas of the flags as gifts for her regular clients. She would like you to find images of the flags from which the artist can create the replicas. You decide to do your research on the Web.

1. Start your Web browser, go to www.cengage.com/internet/np/internet8 to open the Online Companion page, log on to your account, click the Tutorial 5 link, and then click the Case Problem 5 link.

2. Select one of the sites listed for this problem and use it to conduct a search for images of flags for Thailand, Singapore, Malaysia, the People's Republic of China, South Korea, and Japan.

3. Repeat the search using another search engine.

4. Examine your list of search results for flag images that would be suitable for Kim to use on her Web site. You might need to follow a number of results page hyperlinks to find images that meet your needs.

⊕ **EXPLORE** 5. When you find a Web page or pages with suitable images, examine the Web site to determine what copyright or other restrictions exist regarding your use of the images. (*Hint*: Remember that you need to look for restrictions that could prevent the artist from creating replicas of the images you find; these restrictions might be different from restrictions on online use of the images.)

6. Prepare a one-paragraph report for each flag that describes the source you plan to use. Include the URL of the site where you found the flag image and a summary of the restrictions on Kim's use of the image. If the Web site does not include any description of restrictions, refer to the text and state your opinion regarding what restrictions might exist on Kim's use of the image.

7. Close your Web browser.

Review | **Quick Check Answers**

Session 5.1

1. a major wire service (or press agency or news service) based in Great Britain
2. when you want to find information that has been released recently but might not have been published in a newspaper or magazine
3. Different meteorologists often predict different weather conditions for the same location; gathering several forecasts provides a range of likely weather conditions.
4. You can change the map's scale, and you can email the map or save it to a hand-held computing device such as a personal digital assistant (PDA).
5. any three of: recommendations and reviews of restaurants, entertainment (or night-life), sports, shopping, landmarks, and other visitor information
6. False
7. yellow pages directory
8. white pages directory

Session 5.2

1. multimedia
2. Plagiarism is the failure to cite the source of material that you use (whether it is in the public domain or it is protected by copyright). It can be a serious violation of your school's academic honesty policy.
3. by adding online resources to their collections and by making their collections accessible to remote users and other libraries
4. available 24 hours a day, seven days a week; can be easier and faster to search
5. A work is copyrighted for the life of the author plus 70 years; works copyrighted by corporations or not-for-profit organizations are protected for 95 years from the date of publication or 120 years from the date of creation, whichever is earlier.
6. You can copy small parts of a work for use in criticism, comment, news reporting, teaching, scholarship, or research.
7. False
8. A blog is usually written by one person who uses the Web to express personal opinions on a particular subject; a wiki usually provides a place for a number of contributors to collect facts or work collaboratively on a project.

Objectives

Session 6.1
- Understand push and pull communication
- Learn about mailing lists and newsgroups
- Understand Really Simple Syndication (RSS) feeds and Web Slices
- Explore the technology used in podcasting
- Use mashup sites
- Explore a social bookmarking site

Session 6.2
- Explore the different methods of chatting, including instant messaging
- Learn about Web 2.0
- Learn about online social, political, and business networks
- Learn about blogs and microblogs
- Learn about video sharing sites
- Understand the ways to protect your privacy, identity, and reputation

User-Generated Content on the Internet

Evaluating Different Methods of Internet Communication

Case | Roberto Reyes Campaign

After being a leader in student government since grade school, Roberto Reyes knew that he wanted a career in government. While in college, he worked as an intern for State Senator Albert Frasier. After graduation, Roberto took a full-time job as Senator Frasier's legislative assistant and after two years, he was promoted to Chief of Staff. When the representative in Senator Frasier's district for the Texas House of Representatives announced his retirement, Roberto was interested in the job. After Senator Frasier encouraged Roberto to run for office and agreed to publicly support him, Roberto began putting together an election strategy.

After meeting with people who agreed to be his campaign manager and treasurer, and other people who work on grassroots campaigns, Roberto had a fundraising plan and a strategy to communicate his philosophy and experience to his audience. Because the House district is located in a metropolitan area, the group decided on a strategy that relies heavily on Internet technologies for communication with voters. As a young professional, Roberto is very knowledgeable about Internet communication. However, Roberto wants to make sure that he capitalizes on all of the technologies available to him and understands their appropriateness for a political campaign. As a communications major with a minor in information technology, he asks you to help him review different Internet communication methods to evaluate their potential use and effectiveness in the campaign.

Starting Data Files

There are no starting Data Files needed for this tutorial.

Session 6.1

Push and Pull Communications

In this text, you have learned that the Web is a collection of documents that are connected using hyperlinks. Until a few years ago, users would search the Internet for information and use links to visit a Web page or multiple Web sites to gather information. In this scenario, the Web was a resource—much like a library on a school campus—that required action on your part to get information from it. You found the sites, reviewed them, and perhaps even used your Web browser to create bookmarks so you could easily return to sites that you liked. You may have relied on a certain site for information, and as a result, your reliance on that one site may have prevented you from searching for and using new sites with more or better information. These Web sites were mostly static, with updates being posted by the Web site's developer on a regular basis. In this Web world, you found the site and used it, and later returned to the site and checked it for updates. You used these Web sites to pull the information you wanted to your computer so you could read it.

A few years ago, with new software and imaginative ways of using existing software, the way people used the Web began to change. In addition to searching for content, you could tell your browser what content you wanted and have it *sent* to you, either at your request or on a certain schedule. As more users put more information on the Web, this idea of "pushing" content to other users created a new way of using the Web for people who are "pulling" content to their computers.

You can group the Internet's many communication methods into two basic categories: push and pull. Some communication methods use **push technology** to send content to users who request to it. Some examples of push technology are chat, instant messaging, online social networks, and blogs. The other communication method, called **pull technology** because subscribers "pull" content to their computers when they want it, includes mailing lists, newsgroups, feeds, Web Slices, and podcasts. Some communication methods are both push and pull, depending on who is using them—for example, the person who writes a blog is pushing content to other users who then pull it to their computers so they can read it.

Some communication methods don't fit into neat categories based on the method they use, but you can still categorize them based on the technology they employ to present the material or on the way the information is combined. Examples of these Web sites include sites that people use to publish pictures and videos, to create online bookmarks, and to combine the data from two or more Web sites to create a single Web site.

Roberto asks you to review the different pull technologies so he can consider using them for his campaign.

Email-Based Communication on the Internet

In Tutorials 2 and 3, you learned how to use email to communicate with other people. When you use email to communicate, you must send your message and then wait for a response (or responses). In addition to providing information on the Web, the Internet stores information on a wide variety of topics that you can access using email. Two popular ways of pulling information via email are mailing lists and newsgroups.

Mailing Lists

A popular way of sharing information is to join, or **subscribe** to, a mailing list. A **mailing list** is a list of names and email addresses for a group of people who share a common interest in a subject or topic and exchange information by subscribing to the list. Each person who wants to join a mailing list is responsible for subscribing to the list. These mailing lists are not like the ones you created in Tutorials 2 and 3, in which you grouped related individuals in your email program's address book for convenience, nor are they like the email messages that you might request and receive from Web sites to learn more about a special promotion or a new product.

Mailing lists and the groups they represent (sometimes known as **discussion groups**) do not require you to enter the email addresses of people subscribed to the list into your email program's address book. Rather, you send your information and opinions to a mailing list by **posting** (or sending) an email message to the list. When you post a message to a mailing list, the **email list software** running on the server automatically forwards your message to every email address on the mailing list. The server that runs the email list software is sometimes called a **list server** because it runs the list. The list server automatically manages users' requests to join or leave a list and receives and reroutes mail messages posted to the list.

Mailing list **messages** are simply email messages that express ideas or ask questions, and these messages are forwarded to list members. **Commands** request the list server to take a prescribed action. Commands are sent as email messages that contain content that is intercepted and processed by the list server; commands are not forwarded to other list members. To subscribe to and withdraw from a mailing list, you must send the appropriate command to the list server by including the command in an email message. The **list address**, or the **list name**, is the address to which you send messages and replies. The **administrative address** is the email address to which you send commands, such as the address that you use to subscribe to a list. Figure 6-1 illustrates how the list server manages the messages it receives. In Figure 6-1, the solid arrows represent messages sent to and by the list server's administrative address. When you want to subscribe to the list, the list server processes the message and then sends a message back to you confirming your subscription. The dashed arrows represent a message that you want to send to list members. You send the message to the list server's list address, and then the list server sends your message to every member on the mailing list. When a member answers your question, the process is reversed. The list server receives a member's message and sends it to every member on the list, including you.

> **Tip**
>
> Some different types of email list software are LISTSERV, ListProc, and Majordomo; these programs usually run on large computers running the UNIX operating system.

Figure 6-1 **Information flow in a mailing list**

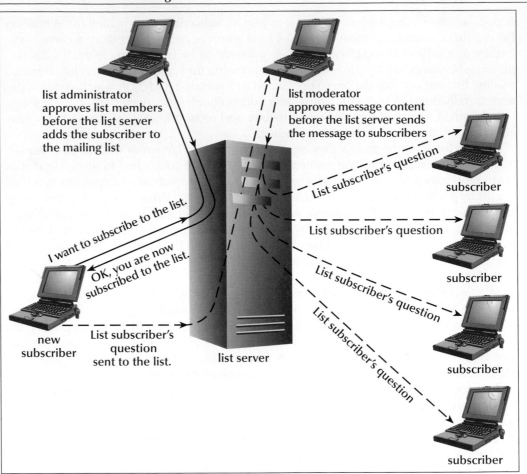

For most lists, one person, known as the **list moderator**, moderates a mailing list to ensure that the list always receives and sends appropriate and relevant information to its members. The sample mailing list shown in Figure 6-1 includes a list moderator. When a list moderator is responsible for discarding any messages that are inappropriate for or irrelevant to the list's members, the list is known as a **moderated list**. If a list receives many postings, managing it can require a lot of time, and it becomes impractical for one person to serve as a moderator. When an individual does not moderate the list and postings are sent to list members automatically, the list is an **unmoderated list**. Because of the nature of unmoderated lists, you might receive irrelevant or inappropriate messages. Most mailing lists are unmoderated because of the time it takes to read and evaluate the content of the many messages posted each day to a mailing list by its members.

Mailing lists are either closed or open. A **closed list** is one in which membership is *not* automatic. In a closed list, the **list administrator**, a person assigned to oversee one or more mailing lists, can either reject or accept your request to become a list member. The sample mailing list shown in Figure 6-1 includes a list administrator. The list administrator might reject your membership request if the list has too many members or if you are not part of the group's specified community. For example, when you try to subscribe to a list devoted to teaching accounting topics, the list might reject your subscription if you are not an accounting instructor or Certified Professional Accountant (CPA). Most lists are **open lists** that automatically accept all members, in which case the list has no administrator. However, if an open list is moderated, it will have a list moderator to oversee the content of the messages received by the mailing list. An unmoderated, open list might not have a person designated to control the list; the server does all the work of managing the list and its contents. Finally, on some open and/or moderated lists, only one person might take on the role of list administrator and list moderator.

Warnings About Mailing Lists | InSight

Mailing lists can be essential tools for receiving current and useful information in one or more subject areas, but you should be aware of some of their potential problems. Depending on the mailing list's activity, you might receive many email messages every day from the list server. If you subscribe to several mailing lists, you might find that the mail volume is more than you can read; it is not uncommon to receive hundreds of messages within a couple of weeks of joining a particularly active list.

Another potential problem occurs when new list members repeat questions and comments that have been previously posted on the mailing list. If you are new to a list, you should monitor the list's content for a few days or weeks before sending messages to it, so you do not comment on topics that other members already have discussed. Many mailing list members never post a single message, which is a completely acceptable way of using a mailing list.

Because the list server forwards the email message that you post to every person subscribed to the mailing list, you expose yourself to potential privacy problems because the message you send contains your name and email address. To protect your privacy, you might consider deleting your signature from email messages you post to the mailing list and using a free email account address for your subscriptions (such as Yahoo! or Windows Live Hotmail). This way, you protect your "real" email address and your privacy.

Finally, many unmoderated mailing lists receive postings from people who discuss topics outside the scope of the list or post spam messages that contain advertisements for unrelated products and services. Unfortunately, many postings are potentially offensive to their readers. In an unmoderated list, there is no moderator to handle the disposition of objectionable material, so you must assume that job yourself.

The Internet provides access to thousands of mailing lists on many different topics; often the difficulty is locating them. If you know of a list to which you want to subscribe, all you need to do is send an email message to the list's administrative address or visit the sponsor's Web site and use an on-screen form to submit your name and email address to the list. On high-volume lists, the list server might send you a confirmation message that you must return so it can confirm your email address before you are officially added to the list. If the list server does not receive a reply from you within a particular time period (usually within one week), then it automatically cancels your request.

Once the list server has accepted and processed your subscription request, you will receive a message confirming your membership in the list. When you want to leave a mailing list, also referred to as **unsubscribing** from or **dropping** the mailing list, follow the instructions in the confirmation message that the list server sent to you. Usually, you will send an "unsubscribe" message to the list's administrative address.

If you do not have information about a specific list, you can use your Web browser to search sites of mailing lists based on keywords or categories that you provide. There are several "lists of lists" sites that you can visit to start your search. The Mailing List Resources section of the Online Companion page for Tutorial 6 includes additional resources with lists that you can use to search for mailing lists about specific topics.

Usenet Newsgroups

The **Usenet News Service**, or **Usenet**, was founded in 1979 at Duke University as a way of collecting information and storing it by topic category. The original Usenet News Service was devoted to transmitting computing news and facilitating discussions among employees of university computing departments on topics such as operating systems and programming languages.

The topic categories on Usenet originally were called **newsgroups** or **forums**. Many people still use these terms when they refer to Usenet categories, but another popular term is **Internet discussion group**. Most of these newsgroups are available to the general public; however, some newsgroups are limited to users at a specific site or to those affiliated with a particular organization. Each site that participates in Usenet has the option of selecting which newsgroups it will carry. Therefore, not all newsgroups—even the public ones—are available on every computer that is connected to Usenet.

Usenet was one of the first large, distributed information databases in the world. A **distributed database** is stored in multiple physical locations, with portions of the database replicated in different locations. Each of these multiple physical locations does not, however, store a complete copy of the database. There are more than 90,000 newsgroups in existence, and articles that total hundreds of megabytes are added to Usenet newsgroups each day.

Newsgroups are similar to mailing lists in that they accept messages from users and make them generally available to other users. However, newsgroups do not use a list server to forward copies of submitted messages to subscribers. Instead, a newsgroup stores items on a server as **articles** or postings that are sorted by topic. Users who are interested in learning about a particular topic can connect to the network and read the posted newsgroup articles. Therefore, newsgroups are more suitable for discussions of broad topics that might interest a large audience because they do not require a list server to send a separate email message to each potential reader. Users pull the content they need to their computers and read the same copy of the posted article in the newsgroup. This subtle difference between how newsgroups and mailing lists operate was critical in the early days of Usenet because bandwidth and computing power were limited, expensive resources.

When users read Usenet articles to which they would like to respond, they can reply to them. If a Usenet article is particularly interesting to many newsgroup readers, it might generate hundreds of responses within a day or two. These responses, in turn, might generate even more responses on the same issue. Most newsgroups have discussions occurring on many different issues simultaneously. Just like in a mailing list, a series of postings on a particular issue is called a **thread**. Participants in newsgroups use various types of newsreader software to organize postings by thread within each newsgroup.

Some newsgroups have a moderator who reviews all postings before they appear in the newsgroup. These moderated newsgroups tend to focus on technical or specialized topics. Moderators provide a valuable service to Usenet by reducing the number of off-topic postings and articles sent by persons who do not have the necessary qualifications to make a contribution to advanced-level or highly technical discussions.

The server that stores a newsgroup is called a **news server**; the collection of news servers connected to the Internet make up Usenet. This network operates without any central control authority. When a user posts an article to a Usenet newsgroup, it is routed to the news server designated to maintain that newsgroup. The news server stores all the articles for that newsgroup. Periodically—daily, hourly, or even more frequently—news servers connect to other news servers and compare a list of the articles that each is currently storing. Each newsgroup article has a unique identification number that makes this comparison possible. Each news server then obtains copies of the articles it does not have. This store-and-forward process is called obtaining a **feed**. Large news servers often maintain a continuous feed connection to other large news servers to maintain the currency of their newsgroup article inventory.

Each news server site employs a **news administrator**, who specifies which other news servers will be feed providers and feed recipients. Most feeds occur over the Internet using the **Network News Transfer Protocol (NNTP)**, which is part of the TCP/IP protocol suite that is used by all computers connected to the Internet. The news administrator also chooses which newsgroups to carry. Because newsgroups are so large, computer file storage space can be a constraint. Organizations that operate news servers include most ISPs, universities, large businesses, government units, and other entities connected to the Internet. In response to the large volume of newsgroup postings, most news servers regularly delete articles after a short period of time. The news administrator is responsible for setting the deletion schedule.

Newsgroups are organized into topical hierarchies in which each newsgroup has a unique name that shows its position and classification in the hierarchy. A newsgroup's name consists of the top-level hierarchy followed by subcategories that further refine the classification. Subcategories are separated from the top-level hierarchy name and each other by periods. For example, one newsgroup that includes discussions of organic chemistry issues is named *sci.chem.organic*. This newsgroup's name shows that it is classified in the top-level category *science* (sci), the science subcategory *chemistry* (chem), and the chemistry subcategory *organic*. The original Usenet News Service included the eight main top-level categories—including one miscellaneous category for alternative topics—that appear in Figure 6-2.

Original Usenet News Service top-level categories ◀ **Figure 6-2**

Category	Includes topics related to
comp	Computers
rec	Recreation and entertainment
sci	Science
soc	Social issues and socializing
news	Operation and administration of Usenet
talk	Conversations, debates, and arguments
misc	Miscellaneous topics that do not fall within other categories
alt	Alternative and controversial topics

When the Usenet News Service began operating in 1979, the only way to read or post articles to newsgroups was to run newsreader software on your computer. **Newsreaders** were programs designed for the sole purpose of communicating with news server computers. Now, most email programs have built-in newsreaders. The most recent improvement in Usenet accessibility has been the increase in the number of Web sites that archive newsgroup articles. These Web sites offer search engines that make finding articles on specific topics much easier than was previously possible.

One such Web site that archives newsgroup articles is the Google Groups directory, which is an advertiser-supported Web site that offers many useful tools for accessing and creating Usenet newsgroups. One of the drawbacks of using newsgroup articles for serious research is that most news servers delete articles fairly frequently—often within days, and almost always within several weeks. Google Groups does not delete newsgroup articles. Google Groups has stored more than 800 million newsgroup articles dating from 1981 in its database. More important is that the Google Groups site has a search engine that allows you to query its newsgroup article database by subject, newsgroup name, or article author. You can limit your search by these criteria and by posting date.

Roberto is especially interested in the feature that lets users create new groups, as this might be a good way for him to communicate with people who share a common interest in his campaign or its issues. You decide to take a tour of the Google Groups site.

To take a tour of the Google Groups site:

▶ **1.** Start your Web browser, open the Online Companion page at **www.cengage.com/internet/np/internet8** and log on to your account, click the **Tutorial 6** link, click the **Session 6.1** link, and then click the **Google Groups** link and wait while the browser opens the page shown in Figure 6-3.

Figure 6-3 ▶ **Google Groups home page**

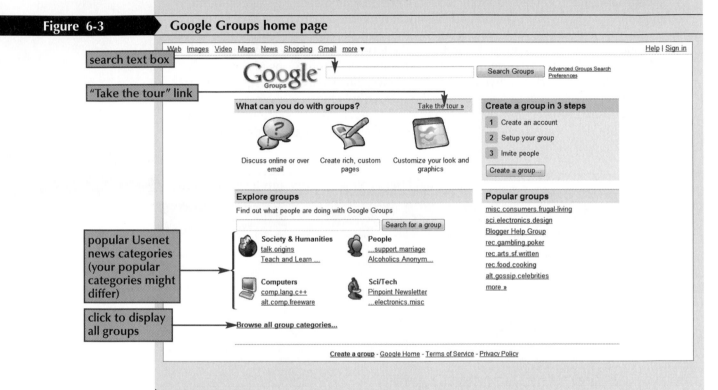

▶ **2.** On the home page, click the **Take the tour** link. A page opens and explains what you can do with Google Groups. Notice that you can search or browse for information, make your own group, or join a group.

▶ **3.** Click the **Next** link, and then read about using Google Groups to have online or email discussions.

▶ **4.** Click the **Next** link, and then read about creating Web pages inside a group.

▶ **5.** Continue clicking the **Next** link and reading the information provided to learn about Google Groups. When you get to the last page, which does not have a Next link, click the **Google Groups logo** in the upper-left corner of the page to return to the Google Groups home page (shown in Figure 6-3).

Roberto thinks the Google Groups site looks easy to use. He asks you to show him how to search the site.

Searching Google Groups for Newsgroup Articles | Reference Window

- Open the Google Groups home page in your Web browser.
- Type a search expression in the search text box, and then click the Search Groups button to run the search.
- Follow the hyperlinks to the newsgroup articles provided.
- Examine and evaluate the newsgroup articles to determine whether you should revise your search expression.

Because Google Groups lists newsgroups and individual newsgroup articles, you decide to use Google Groups to see some of the categories of information.

To search Google Groups:

▶ 1. On the Google Groups home page, type **local Texas politics** in the search text box, and then click the **Search Groups** button. After a few moments, the search engine returns a Web page with hyperlinks to information matching your search expression, similar to the page shown in Figure 6-4.

Google Groups search results for "local Texas politics" ◀ | Figure 6-4

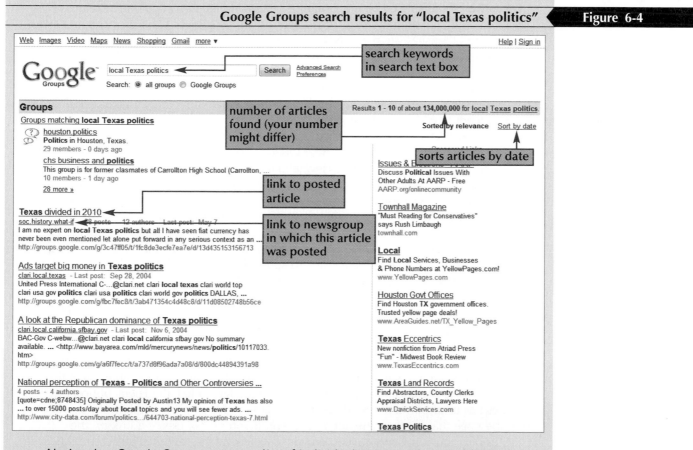

Notice that Google Groups returns a list of individual news articles in addition to the newsgroup names. The page shown in Figure 6-4 shows that Google has located about 134 million articles (your search results might differ). You can sort the hits by date to display the most recent postings at the top of the list.

▶ 2. Click the **Sort by date** link near the top of the page, and then scroll down the list of newsgroup articles and postings to view their titles and descriptions.

▶ **3.** Click a link to a posting. Notice that Google Groups displays the article's contents and information about the newsgroup in which it appeared.

▶ **4.** Return to the Online Companion page for Session 6.1.

Getting Information from RSS Feeds

Usenet is just one example of a feed (also commonly called a newsfeed or a Web feed) that uses pull technology to deliver changing content to users. This changing content might be from a blog, a Web site, or a news organization. The format that is used to syndicate (distribute) published content from one site to another is called **RSS**, an acronym for **Really Simple Syndication**; another format is **Atom**. Both RSS and Atom make it possible for computers to share updates. Feeds are similar to newsgroups in that they let you subscribe to content that you want to receive on your computer. However, feeds differ from newsgroups because of the way that content is delivered to subscribers. Newsgroup postings are delivered via email messages, whereas feeds are delivered through a program that includes a summary and a link to the published content of interest or the actual content, depending on the program you use to receive it.

Feeds were originally created for sharing news headlines and content, and as such, they were originally used by news organizations, such as Reuters, for distributing news headlines to other sites, such as CNN and ABC News. Now, feeds are also used by organizations and individuals that create and maintain blogs as a way to publish content and alert subscribers to changes in the content.

To subscribe to a feed, you need to install a program called an **aggregator** on your computer or mobile device. An aggregator is similar to an email program in that you request content from feeds to which you have subscribed and view that content like you would an email message. Most Web browsers, including Internet Explorer 8, Firefox 3, and Opera 9, and some email programs, including Microsoft Outlook 2007 and Thunderbird 2, have built-in aggregators that let you subscribe to, view, and remove feeds. Most Web sites that syndicate content also include built-in aggregators that you can use to search for, subscribe to, and view syndicated content using any Web browser.

To subscribe to a feed with content that you would like to view, you can use a feed directory to find a source, but a more common method is to use the tools provided on Web sites that sponsor feeds. Web sites that provide feeds will display a small, orange "RSS" or "Atom" icon that you can click to subscribe to the feed. Sometimes the link to subscribe to feeds is a text link with the letters "RSS" to indicate the file format of the syndicated content. Figure 6-5 shows a page from MSNBC.com, a site that includes feeds. In Internet Explorer, the Feeds button on the Command bar changes color from gray to orange when the site includes syndicated content. Clicking the orange Feeds button opens a page that contains the feed's content. To subscribe to the feed, click the Subscribe to this feed link, and then click the Subscribe button in the dialog box that opens. If you want to display the feed on the Internet Explorer Favorites bar, click the Add to Favorites Bar check box. After you create the feed, click the Feeds button on the Favorites bar to display a menu of recent changes, and then click a link in the menu to open the page that contains the actual content. If you do not create a link on the Favorites bar, you can view the feed content by clicking the Favorites button on the Favorites bar, and then clicking the Feeds tab to display the feeds to which you have subscribed.

Tip

Most aggregators and browsers that you can use to read feeds support RSS and Atom.

MSNBC.com page showing syndicated content in Internet Explorer | Figure 6-5

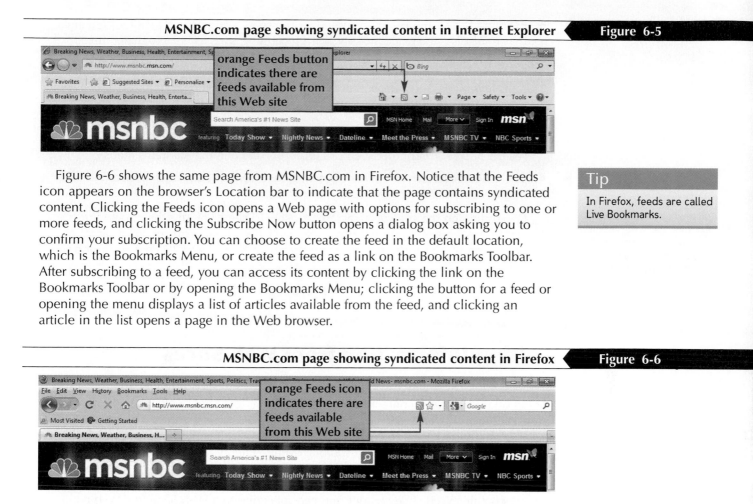

Figure 6-6 shows the same page from MSNBC.com in Firefox. Notice that the Feeds icon appears on the browser's Location bar to indicate that the page contains syndicated content. Clicking the Feeds icon opens a Web page with options for subscribing to one or more feeds, and clicking the Subscribe Now button opens a dialog box asking you to confirm your subscription. You can choose to create the feed in the default location, which is the Bookmarks Menu, or create the feed as a link on the Bookmarks Toolbar. After subscribing to a feed, you can access its content by clicking the link on the Bookmarks Toolbar or by opening the Bookmarks Menu; clicking the button for a feed or opening the menu displays a list of articles available from the feed, and clicking an article in the list opens a page in the Web browser.

> **Tip**
>
> In Firefox, feeds are called Live Bookmarks.

MSNBC.com page showing syndicated content in Firefox | Figure 6-6

Depending on the program you use to subscribe to a feed, you might view the feed's content in different ways. With an aggregator, you might see summaries of the feed's content, similar to how you receive email messages in an Inbox for an email program, with links to the full article. Clicking the link opens a page in a Web browser. Feeds are added using default settings that indicate the frequency with which to download new content from the source. You can change the feed's update schedule by changing its properties.

To cancel a feed, delete the feed from the Feeds tab in Internet Explorer or from the Library in Firefox, or use the accounts feature in an email program or aggregator to delete the feed.

Roberto likes the idea of being able to view news about a specific topic when he has a free minute. He asks you to learn more about finding feeds that might help him with the campaign and provide current information that he can use to connect with voters. The best place to find feeds is to look for the Feeds icon when viewing Web sites that you already use for news and other information. You will use a search engine to find Web sites that include content about Texas politics.

To search for Web sites that contain feeds:

▶ **1.** On the Online Companion page for Session 6.1, click one of the links in the Search Engines section, and then wait while your browser loads the page.

▶ **2.** In the site's search text box, type **Texas politics**, and then run the search.

▶ **3.** Examine the search results returned by the search engine and look for Web sites that might include professionally written content, such as links to major Texas newspapers, Texas political groups, or other political organizations. Click one of the links to open the Web site, and then examine the page to determine if it contains any feeds. You'll know that a site contains feeds when the Feeds icon on the Command bar in Internet Explorer or on the Location bar in Firefox turns orange in color.

Trouble? If the site you opened doesn't include any feeds, return to your search results and select another Web site until you find one that contains feeds.

Tip

Using the links to the syndicated content lets you examine the feed content before you subscribe to it so you can make sure the content is appropriate.

▶ **4.** Click the **Feeds** icon to open a page with feed content, and then click a link that might interest Roberto and scan the content.

Depending on the site you selected, you should see a link to subscribe to feeds from the Web site. If you click this link, you'll see either a dialog box or another Web page that provides options for subscribing to the feed. (Do not subscribe to any feeds at this time.)

▶ **5.** Return to the Online Companion page for Session 6.1.

Getting Information from Web Slices

Tip

Firefox includes an add-on feature called a Webchunk that updates and displays any portion of a Web page's content in a pop-up window, and not just the portion coded by the page's developer.

Internet Explorer 8 includes a new feature that lets the user subscribe to a predefined *portion* of a Web page's contents without subscribing to a feed. A **Web Slice** is part of a Web page that a developer codes so users can subscribe to it. A Web Slice usually displays frequently updated content, such as the price of an item on an auction Web site, a weather forecast, or the score for a sporting event. When you see a green Add Web Slices button on the Command bar in Internet Explorer (as shown in Figure 6-7) or you see the same icon when pointing to specific content on a Web page, the page you are viewing contains Web Slice content. You can subscribe to a Web Slice in a Web page just like you might subscribe to a feed. When you want to subscribe to a Web Slice, click the Add Web Slices button on the Command bar, and then click the Add to Favorites Bar button in the dialog box that opens. The dialog box identifies the Web Slice content and its origin; clicking the Add to Favorites Bar button subscribes to the content and adds it as a button on your Favorites bar. When a Web page contains a feed and Web Slice content, clicking the Add Web Slices button arrow opens a list of the available Web Slices and feeds so you can click the one that you want to subscribe to. When the Web Slice content is updated, the Web Slice button on the Favorites bar will flash briefly, and then the Web Slice button's name will appear in bold text. Clicking the Web Slice button on the Favorites bar displays the Web Slice content in a small window, as shown in Figure 6-7.

Web page that contains Web Slice content ◄ Figure 6-7

When you subscribe to an RSS feed, the content is delivered in an XML file that an aggregator, such as a Web browser or newsreader program, can read and download. A Web Slice enables users to subscribe to the content from the Web page that contains it, without a separate feed file. Web Slice content is coded in HTML, which the browser reads and displays to syndicate the content on the desired schedule.

Roberto wants to see how a Web Slice works, so you will demonstrate it to him next.

To use a Web page that contains Web Slice content:

▶ **1.** On the Online Companion page for Session 6.1, click one of the links in the Web Slices section, and then wait while your browser loads the page.

Trouble? You must use Internet Explorer 8 or higher to complete these steps. Web Slices are not supported in other browsers.

▶ **2.** Click the **Add Web Slices** button arrow on the Command bar. Click any Web Slice in the menu or point to the content in the page to display and click the Add Web Slices icon to open an Internet Explorer dialog box that contains the Web Slice name and URL.

Trouble? If you do not see any Web Slices on this page, return to the Online Companion page for Session 6.1 and click another link in the Web Slices section.

▶ **3.** In the Internet Explorer dialog box, click the **Add to Favorites Bar** button. The Internet Explorer dialog box closes and the Web Slice is added to the Favorites bar.

▶ **4.** Click the **Home** button on the Command bar to load your browser's home page.

▶ **5.** Click the button on the Favorites bar for the Web Slice that you added to display its current content.

▶ **6.** Click the button on the Favorites bar for the Web Slice content again to close the content.

Because Web Slices are portions of frequently updated pages, most users will add and remove sliced content on a regular basis. You'll delete the Web Slice next.

▶ **7.** Right-click the button on the Favorites bar for the Web Slice content to open its shortcut menu, click **Delete**, and then click the **Yes** button. The Web Slice is deleted from the Favorites bar, and the browser will no longer display its content.

▶ **8.** Return to the Online Companion page for Session 6.1.

Roberto thinks that Web Slices might be useful to communicate frequently updated information to the campaign staff. He will consider speaking with the webmaster for his site about implementing this technology in the campaign Web site.

In the course of your research about newsgroups and feeds, you may have noticed a few sites that included links to podcasts. You are curious about podcasting, and how it might help Roberto, so you decide to learn more about it.

Podcasting

As you learned in Tutorial 5, MP3 is a compressed digital audio file format that greatly reduces the file size of an audio file without sacrificing the clarity of its content. When the MP3 file format became popular in the early 1990s, many people began purchasing MP3 players, which are portable devices that play MP3 files. Now, many people use another form of personal entertainment technology from Apple Corporation, the iPod. An **iPod** is a small and lightweight portable media player that was originally designed to store and play hundreds of songs downloaded from the Internet at a minimal cost. As the iPod gained popularity, Apple released other versions capable of storing much more data (and hence, many more songs). Most iPods can display pictures and play video files.

At the same time that these types of devices became affordable and readily accessible, people who knew how to make different types of technology work on these devices found new uses for them. In the early 2000s, a group of programmers created the technical specifications necessary to encode audio recordings in feeds. Soon after, they worked toward the goal of being able to synchronize and encode audio files in feeds, which led to the development of podcasting in 2004. **Podcasting** lets a user subscribe to an audio or video feed, and then listen to it or watch it at the user's convenience on a compatible device, which might include the user's computer or a portable device such as an iPod. A **podcast** is a subscription audio or video broadcast that is created and stored in a digital format on the Internet. (The word podcast is a combination of the words *iPod* and *broadcasting*, but *any* digital audio device or computer with the necessary software can receive a podcast.) Just like with syndicated feeds of text content, an aggregator is necessary to subscribe to the podcast and check for and download new podcasts. The aggregator used for feeds is sometimes called **podcatching software**. Two popular versions of podcatching software are Juice and iTunes, both of which are free downloads from the Internet. Most podcasting software works on any compatible device. Some podcasting software is specifically designed for certain types of audio players, such as Windows Media Player or an iPod, or for specific operating systems, such as Windows Vista, Mac OS, or Linux. Most Web browsers can play content from podcasts and act as an aggregator. When you use a Web browser to play a podcast, you also need a media player such as Windows Media Player or Apple's QuickTime to play the audio or video content on your computer. Figure 6-8 shows the Stanford University Educators Corner page, which contains podcasts from the Stanford Technology Ventures Program. The user can evaluate the available podcasts on this page, and then use one of several methods to access the podcast content: click the iTunes, Zune, or Odeo links near the top of the page to load the podcast content using a browser, use the RSS icon near the top of the page to subscribe to this content, or click the MP3 link for a podcast to save the podcast's file on your device.

Podcasts page for the Stanford Technology Ventures Program Figure 6-8

ⓔcorner
Stanford University's Entrepreneurship Corner

Brought to you by:
Stanford Technology Ventures Program

About | Blog | Sponsors

Popular Videos   **Podcasts**   Speakers   Browse   Subscribe   [Search]

Login | Register

Podcasts

Subscribe to our feed by clicking on your preferred method below:

 iTunes   zune   ODEO   RSS

The Entrepreneurial Thought Leaders lecture series takes place every Wednesday during the academic year.

To learn more about these lectures, visit etl.stanford.edu.

Entrepreneurial Thought Leaders
e corner
Stanford Technology Ventures Program

Tina Seelig (STVP)

Tina Seelig (STVP)
Steve Westly (The Westly Group)
Jeff Hawkins (Numenta)
Steve Ballmer (Microsoft)
Jennifer Scott Fonstad, Steve Perricone (BioFuelBox)
Sheryl Sandberg (Facebook)
Mari Baker (PlayFirst)
Jensen Huang (NVidia)
Elizabeth Holmes (Theranos)

Spring 2009 Podcast

Title	Speaker	Organization	Length	Date	File
The Art of Teaching Entrepreneurship and Innovation	Tina Seelig	STVP	52:00	05-27-09	MP3
Clean Tech Challenges and Solutions	Steve Westly	The Westly Group	57:15	05-20-09	MP3
Inside the Mind of a Reluctant Entrepreneur	Jeff Hawkins	Numenta	57:29	05-13-09	MP3
The Future of Microsoft, The Future of Technology	Steve Ballmer	Microsoft	57:38	05-06-09	MP3
Under the Lid of BioFuelBox	Jennifer Scott Fonstad, Steve Perricone	BioFuelBox	56:02	04-29-09	MP3
Spotlight on Scalability	Sheryl Sandberg	Facebook	57:56	04-22-09	MP3
Building an Organization, Building a Team	Mari Baker	PlayFirst	55:52	04-15-09	MP3
Vision Matters	Jensen Huang	NVidia	01:01:27	04-08-09	MP3

Winter 2009 Podcasts

Title	Speaker	Organization	Length	Date	File
Developing the Future of Home Healthcare	Elizabeth Holmes	Theranos	56:51	03-04-09	MP3
What is the Next Big Thing?	Tim Draper, Tony Perkins, Michael Moe	AlwaysOn	01:10:51	02-25-09	MP3
Innovation as the Crux of Entrepreneurship	John Hennessy	Stanford	01:01:07	02-18-09	MP3
Emerging Opportunities in a Post IT Marketplace	Tom Siebel	First Virtual Group	01:00:05	02-11-09	MP3
A History of Venture Capital	Spencer E. Ante	BusinessWeek	56:45	02-04-09	MP3
Making a Big Company Feel Small	Teresa Briggs	Deloitte	52:51	01-28-09	MP3
The Growth and Bloom of Cooliris	Austin Shoemaker, Soujanya Bhumkar, Josh Schwarzapel	Cooliris	57:56	01-21-09	MP3
13 Mistakes and 13 Brilliant Strokes	Hugh Martin	Pacific Biosciences	54:30	01-14-09	MP3

Podcatching software is RSS-compatible software that downloads feeds from their source to the device on which the software is loaded. The feed contains an **enclosure**, which is similar to a file attachment to an email message. The enclosure is the audio or video file from the server, and this file contains the podcast. For example, if you want to listen to the weekly radio address from the President of the United States, you can use your Web browser to listen to the program as it is being broadcast. If you miss the live broadcast, you can go to the White House Web site and play the recorded program. However, if you always want to listen to the weekly radio address, but you do not want to find the file that you need, you can subscribe to the podcast from the White House. When you subscribe to the podcast, your computer will download the program automatically on the schedule you select from the White House Web site. If you subscribe to the podcast using the podcatching software on your portable media player, it will download and store the radio address when you connect your device to the Internet, and then you can listen to it at your convenience and delete the file when you are finished with it. You can also download and store radio shows from all over the world or programs about different topics or people. After you install the podcatching software on your computer or portable media player, you can use the Internet to find podcasts so you can subscribe to them.

Tip

Many instructors record their lectures and make them available as podcasts for students who miss class.

You suspect that podcasts are used primarily for entertainment purposes but also see other uses for them as well. You want to explore the different categories of podcasts to see if you can find different sources of information that might interest Roberto.

To explore different sources of podcasts:

▶ 1. On the Online Companion page for Session 6.1, click one of the links in the Podcast Directories section, and then wait while your browser loads the home page for the site you selected. Figure 6-9 shows the Podcast Directory page for LearnOutLoud.com, a site that promotes the use of audio and visual podcasts on hundreds of subjects that are geared toward personal and professional education and development.

Figure 6-9 ▶ **Podcast Directory page for LearnOutLoud.com**

▶ 2. Use the links on the site you selected to explore the different categories of podcasts that might interest Roberto. For example, you might look for podcasts about political topics or about issues that you think might be important in a political campaign, such as education and taxes. As you are reviewing the podcasts, also note the dates of the broadcasts. You will probably notice that the broadcast dates are very recent, some occurring on the day of or within a few days of completing this step. Because the podcasts are recent, the information they contain is current. Some sites provide archives of past podcasts that become a source for online research.

▶ **3.** If the site allows you to do so, click a podcast link to play the file. If your computer has the necessary media player to play the podcast, it will start in a new window. Listen to the podcast for a few minutes to get a sense of the content it provides, and then close the window playing the podcast.

   Trouble? If the file does not play on your computer, close the window that opened, and skip this step. You need a plug-in such as QuickTime or Windows Media Player to play a podcast file on a computer.

▶ **4.** Return to the Online Companion for Session 6.1, and then click another link in the Podcast Directories section. Explore the site to search for podcasts that might interest Roberto.

▶ **5.** When you are finished exploring the site, return to the Online Companion page for Session 6.1.

Podcasting's original use was to make it easy for people to create and broadcast their own radio shows, but many other uses soon followed. There are podcasts on many different topics. Podcasts are used by the media to interview politicians and professors on specific subjects, by colleges and universities in distance learning classes, and by movie studios to promote new movie releases. You might find podcasts that contain material that you find controversial, objectionable, or offensive. In these cases, you can simply stop the playback or unsubscribe from the feed.

Because the software that is used to create a podcast is free and easy to download from the Internet, new podcasts are posted on the Internet every day. Some podcasts have different names that further identify the type of content they contain, such as a Godcast to denote a religious broadcast, a vidcast to identify a video feed, or a learncast to identify content that is educational in nature, such as a podcast from a university or other educational institution. When you subscribe to a podcast, you specify how frequently to download files and which files to download. When you connect your computer or compatible device to the Internet, it will automatically download the podcasts to which you have subscribed so you can play them later.

Podcasts might provide important background for Roberto on current campaign topics, and he likes the flexibility they offer to play the content at his convenience. Another technology that you want to demonstrate to him is one in which the content of two or more Web sites are combined into a single site.

Mashups

When you use a computer that runs a certain operating system, such as Windows 7, and install software programs on that computer, the operating system and the software programs you install talk to each other to handle specific tasks such as displaying content on the screen or printing. A software program uses an **Application Programming Interface (API)** as a means of communication with an operating system or some other program. An API is written by a programmer or developer with a specific goal in mind, such as displaying content on a screen or accessing a file system. When a program is developed for a specific operating system, a developer might reference the API used by the operating system to print a documentor display it on the screen, instead of writing the content himself. APIs reduce the amount of coding for third-party software programs and ensure that the programs work together well. For most operating systems, its developers write new APIs and make them available to third-party developers by request. This relationship between developers wasn't always easy because the operating system developers often didn't give third-party developers what they needed to run their own programs. In addition, sometimes the APIs from one developer were not made available to other developers, and vice-versa, so data was not shared between companies.

Instead of keeping data to itself, a company such as eBay or Amazon.com writes an API and makes it available to *any* developer who wants to use it—usually for free. When APIs are shared in this way, the term **Web services** describes the process of organizations communicating through a network to share data, without any required knowledge of each other's systems. As more companies put more APIs on the Internet, developers used them to enhance their own sites by combining content from two or more sites. Amazon.com was the first to make APIs available to other developers, who in turn used them to link to and integrate their content with the Amazon.com Web site. For example, an API called GiftPrompter lets you track gifts that you want to give on a calendar with an interface to Amazon.com to ensure that you get the best selection and prices available on the gifts that you select. Figure 6-10 shows the home page for GiftPrompter.com—a site that an Internet consumer might use to manage the selection and shipment of gifts to family and friends.

Figure 6-10	GiftPrompter.com home page

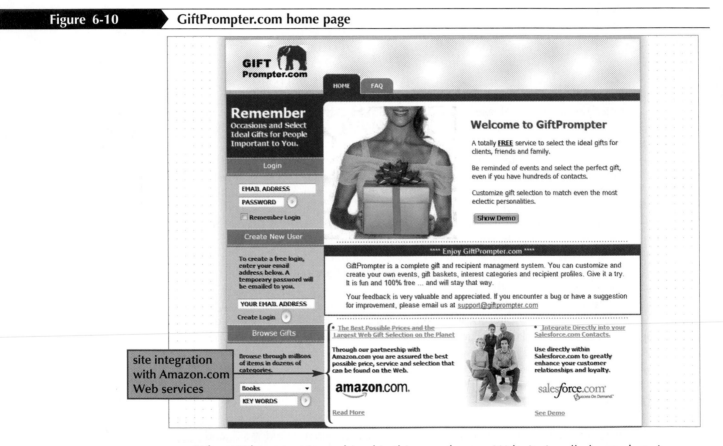

When Web content is combined in this way, the new Web site is called a mashup. In a **mashup**, a developer combines the services from two different sites using the APIs from one or both sites to create a completely new site that uses features from one or both sites. Some examples of mashups are sites that combine the "25 best companies to work for" feature from *Fortune Magazine* with an API from Google Maps that produces a map with locations of the companies; or a list of apartments available on craigslist for rent in a specific city that uses an API from Yahoo! to plot the apartments on a map with details about the apartments such as the square footage, number of bedrooms, and the monthly rent.

Roberto might decide to create a mashup for the campaign. You'll show him a few mashup sites next.

To view a mashup site:

▶ **1.** In the Mashups section on the Online Companion page for Session 6.1, click one of the links to open a Web site that uses mashup technology to combine the data and programming of two or more Web sites. Explore the site and use your understanding of mashups to determine the resources the site uses. For example, Figure 6-11 shows a mashup site that uses crime data from the Houston Police Department's Web site, address data from the U.S. Census Bureau, City Council boundaries from the City of Houston's Public Works & Engineering GIS Web site, Texas House and Senate district boundaries from the Texas Legislature Web site, and interactive maps from Google Maps API. The resulting Web site combines all of this data for the user to report crime activity by address or zip code in the city of Houston.

Houston Crime Maps Web site   **Figure 6-11**

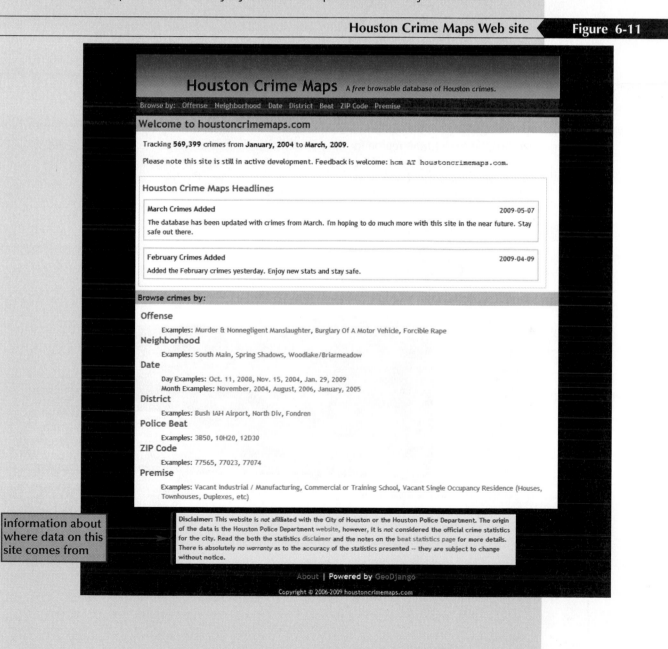

Houston Crime Maps A *free* browsable database of Houston crimes.

Browse by: Offense Neighborhood Date District Beat ZIP Code Premise

Welcome to houstoncrimemaps.com

Tracking **569,399** crimes from **January, 2004** to **March, 2009**.

Please note this site is still in active development. Feedback is welcome: hcm AT houstoncrimemaps.com.

Houston Crime Maps Headlines

March Crimes Added	2009-05-07

The database has been updated with crimes from March. I'm hoping to do much more with this site in the near future. Stay safe out there.

February Crimes Added	2009-04-09

Added the February crimes yesterday. Enjoy new stats and stay safe.

Browse crimes by:

Offense

    Examples: Murder & Nonnegligent Manslaughter, Burglary Of A Motor Vehicle, Forcible Rape

Neighborhood

    Examples: South Main, Spring Shadows, Woodlake/Briarmeadow

Date

    Day Examples: Oct. 11, 2008, Nov. 15, 2004, Jan. 29, 2009
    Month Examples: November, 2004, August, 2006, January, 2005

District

    Examples: Bush IAH Airport, North Div, Fondren

Police Beat

    Examples: 3B50, 10H20, 12D30

ZIP Code

    Examples: 77565, 77023, 77074

Premise

    Examples: Vacant Industrial / Manufacturing, Commercial or Training School, Vacant Single Occupancy Residence (Houses, Townhouses, Duplexes, etc)

information about where data on this site comes from

Disclaimer: This website is *not* affiliated with the City of Houston or the Houston Police Department. The origin of the data is the Houston Police Department website, however, it is *not* considered the official crime statistics for the city. Read the both the statistics disclaimer and the notes on the beat statistics page for more details. There is absolutely *no warranty* as to the accuracy of the statistics presented -- they are subject to change without notice.

About | **Powered by** GeoDjango

Copyright © 2006-2009 houstoncrimemaps.com

▶ **2.** Return to the Online Companion page for Session 6.1, and then click another link in the Mashups section and explore the Web site. Try to determine the resources the site combines, use the site to explore its features, and try to determine the intended consumer use of the site.

▶ **3.** Return to the Online Companion page for Session 6.1.

You might wonder how a mashup is profitable to its developer. The developer usually includes additional APIs on the new site that link to Google AdSense or other content that generates revenue through customized advertising on the site. For example, a mashup might combine information about ski resorts with details about ski conditions, lodging, current weather conditions, and a map of the ski area. When the page is generated, the user sees the ski resorts and conditions she requested along with advertisements to local and other businesses that the user might find interesting. The mashup's developer most likely has an agreement with Google AdSense or another API provider to provide the advertising and to share the income generated by users who click the links to these ads. Other mashups combine useful information, such as the Qlock world map page shown in Figure 6-12. Qlock shows the current daylight conditions around the globe. When a user points to a city on the world map, a box displays the current day and time for the city; in Figure 6-12, the user has displayed the current time information for Melbourne, Australia. Clicking a city on the map zooms the map to the region for the selected city. If satellite imagery exists for the selected region, the user can zoom the image in and out to display topographical data and specific areas, including street and highway names. In some cases, the user can zoom in the map close enough to see individual houses on city streets.

Figure 6-12 ▶ **Qlock World Clock page**

Because mashups rely on Web site data that already exists and APIs that are created by other companies, developers with the necessary programming background find mashups to be relatively easy to create and maintain and profitable for the efforts needed to create them. For this reason, mashups are one of the fastest growing segments of Web sites on the Internet. According to a 2008 study by ProgrammableWeb.com, more than 3,500 mashup Web sites exist and more than three mashups are created each day.

What could Roberto and his campaign staff do with a mashup? They could use the campaign's Web site to combine existing Web resources to display a map of the House district along with data that voters are interested in, such as crime statistics or other information the campaign needs. Roberto wonders where he can get more information about APIs he can use to generate useful content for voters. You tell him that ProgrammableWeb.com has APIs listed by category and includes descriptions of the APIs and links to sites that use them. This combination of information makes it possible to view the kind of data that he can combine, so you'll show Roberto this site next.

To view APIs available on the Web:

▶ 1. On the Online Companion page for Session 6.1, click the **ProgrammableWeb.com** link and wait while your browser opens the home page for this site. See Figure 6-13.

Figure 6-13   **ProgrammableWeb.com home page**

 2. Near the top of the page, click the **APIs** tab, and then after the new page loads, click the **By Category** link below the APIs tab. The page that opens displays APIs available on the Internet by category. For example, Google AdSense is featured in the "Advertising" category.

 3. Scroll down the page and note the other categories of APIs that might interest Roberto and his campaign staff, such as Blogging, Bookmarks, Feeds, Financial, Mapping, and Reference. Because this list is updated daily as new APIs are added by the contributing sites, the list changes all the time.

 4. Click the **Mashups** tab near the top of the page, wait for the new page to load, and then click the **Tag Cloud** link. A new Web page opens and displays a **tag cloud**, with the user-defined keywords shown in a cloud arrangement. Larger words in the cloud indicate more mashups in that category. Pointing the mouse at a keyword displays a screentip that indicates the number of mashups associated with the tag name. This feature gives you an idea of the popularity of each category.

 5. Return to the Online Companion page for Session 6.1.

> **Tip**
>
> When used in the context of APIs or Web sites, a tag is something that a person uses to categorize a Web site, photo, posts, videos, or almost any other form of Web content based on the information it contains.

The last pull technology that you want to show Roberto is social bookmarking, which he might use to categorize Web sites based on the content they contain.

Social Bookmarking Sites

As you learned in Tutorial 1, a bookmark is a feature of a browser that lets you store the URL of a Web page so you can return to the page later. When you use a browser in this way to save Web page URLs, the bookmarks are available only when you open your browser on your computer. **Social bookmarking** is similar to saving a bookmark in your browser, but it refers to the process of saving bookmarks to a public Web site that you can access from any computer connected to the Internet. Because social bookmarking is done on a Web site, you can share your social bookmarks with other users who visit the bookmarking site. To create your social bookmarks, you create **tags**, which are one-word descriptions of the bookmarked content, to assign your favorite Web sites to categories. Many people use social bookmarking to tag content such as recipes, personal health concerns, or technology interests. For example, if you find a useful site on the Internet for information on training for a marathon, you could create a bookmark on a social bookmarking site and tag it using the keywords *training, running, marathon,* or any other keywords that will help you to remember the content on that Web site and find it again when you need it.

To bookmark Web sites and use tags to organize them, you need to register with a social bookmarking site. Because all registered users of a social bookmarking site can share the tagged bookmarks on the site, social bookmarking is a good way to make connections with other users who share your interests or hobbies. As you tag Web sites of interest, other users will tag Web sites they find interesting by using the same keywords or new keywords related to the topic. By bookmarking common sites with tags, these groups of users will develop a structure for organizing the sites that they can access through the bookmarks created by these other users. Thomas Vander Wal, an Internet developer, once called this process of tagging content with keywords a **folksonomy**—combining the word *folks* (meaning "people") and *taxonomy* (meaning "the science or technique of classification")—or a "people's taxonomy."

> **Tip**
>
> You can also tag Web content other than Web pages, such as podcasts.

Roberto is interested in social bookmarking and asks you to explore some sites.

To explore a social bookmarking site:

▶ **1.** On the Online Companion page for Session 6.1, find the **Social Bookmarking** heading and click one of the links to open its home page.

▶ **2.** Examine the site's home page to locate a link named "FAQ," "Learn More," "About," or something similar that provides information about how the site works and provides additional information about social bookmarking. Figure 6-14 shows the Learn More page for Delicious.com, a popular social bookmarking site.

Figure 6-14 | **Learn More page For Delicious.com**

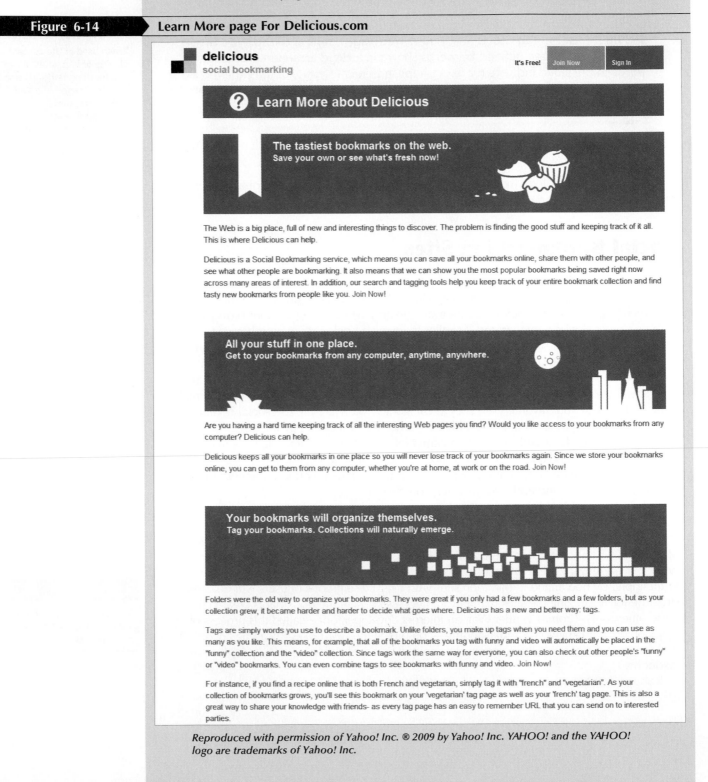

3. Read the information provided, and then return to the Online Companion page for Session 6.1. Click another link listed in the Social Bookmarking section, and then use the "FAQ," "Learn More," or "About" links to learn more about social bookmarking.

4. Return to the site's home page, and then explore the page to determine if the site includes a link to a tag cloud page like the one shown in Figure 6-15 from StumbleUpon. Most social bookmarking sites use a tag cloud to present the tags in a visual way, making more frequently used tags visible to the site's users. Usually, the most popular tags appear in a larger font size, making it possible to see which keywords are being used as tags the most, and as a result, which categories contain the most bookmarks to other sites.

StumbleUpon tag cloud page | Figure 6-15

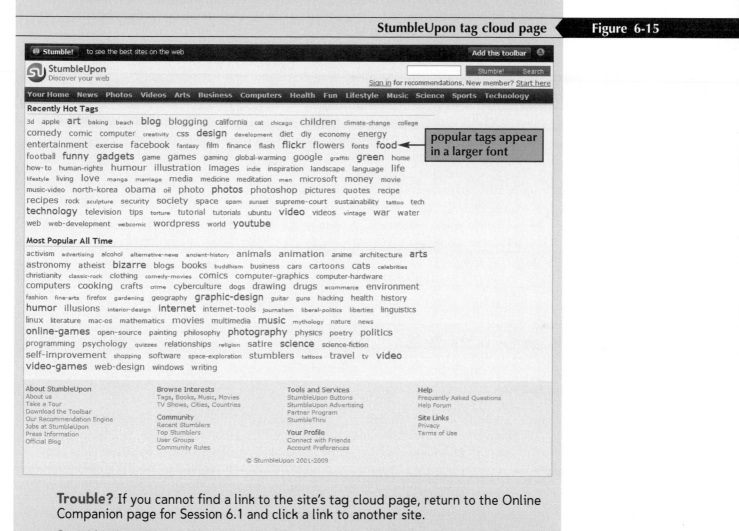

Trouble? If you cannot find a link to the site's tag cloud page, return to the Online Companion page for Session 6.1 and click a link to another site.

Social bookmarking sites use technology that is easy to implement and use by novice users, but this is also one of its potential weaknesses. Inexperienced users might add tags to Web sites using keywords that are uncommon to other users, or they might misspell the keywords, making their resources difficult to find. The inconsistency of keywords for tags by multiple users makes some resources difficult or impossible to find.

Tip

The URL for a tag cloud page usually includes a subfolder with the name of the tag you clicked.

5. Examine the tags in the tag cloud, click one that you think might be of interest to Roberto and his political campaign, and then examine the bookmarked sites for that topic. Each linked site might show the number of people who have tagged the link. Clicking the link to the number of users opens another Web page that shows their user IDs and any comments that they have made about the linked site. It is this community of users that makes a social bookmarking site a "social" activity. Clicking a link to a user opens that user's social bookmarks.

6. Close your browser.

Using tags on a social bookmarking site is a good way to categorize information that Roberto and his campaign staff might need to reference again. They might use a social bookmarking site to gather resources that are important to voters in the upcoming election.

In the next session, you will learn about the next generation of Internet communication, for which users contribute to and manage most of the content.

Review | **Session 6.1 Quick Check**

1. What is the difference between a moderated list and an unmoderated list?
2. Monitoring a mailing list's messages for a sufficient time before posting your first message is called _____ .
3. A series of newsgroup articles that discuss the same subject is collectively called a(n)_____ .
4. What do you need to receive content from a feed?
5. How does podcasting work?
6. What is a mashup?
7. What is a social bookmark?

Session 6.2

Chat

In Session 6.1, you learned about the different Internet communication methods that let users pull information to their computers when they want it. In this session, you will learn about different push technologies that foster online communication. Some of these are older communication methods, but their history is important to the evolution of more current methods.

Chat is a general term for real-time communication that occurs over the Internet using software that is installed on Internet devices. Originally, the term *chat* described the act of users exchanging typed messages, or a **text chat**. Today, however, chats can involve exchanging pictures, videos, sounds, data, and programs. Some chat software lets you give control of your computer to another user so that person can use your programs or troubleshoot a problem that you are having. You can also use chat to collaborate on a file with another user as you talk to each other. Users with a sound card, speakers, and a microphone connected to their computers can participate in a **voice chat**, in which participants speak to each other in real time, much like they would using a telephone. The addition of a Web camera enables users to participate in a **video chat**, in which participants can see and speak to each other. Voice and video chats require a broadband connection to the Internet to handle the data that is transferred during the chat session, but text chats can occur over a dial-up connection.

Chats can be private or public. A **private chat** occurs between individuals who know each other and are invited to participate in the chat. A **public chat** occurs in a public area, sometimes called a **chat room**, in which people come and go by visiting a Web page that hosts the chat. Chats can be continuous, with participants entering and leaving ongoing discussions, or they can be planned for a specific time and duration. Some chats are open to discussions of any topic, whereas others are focused on a specific topic or category of participants. Some chats feature participation by a celebrity or an authority on the chat topic. These chats give worldwide users an opportunity to join discussions with people they would otherwise never have the chance to meet.

Most chat programs include features that allow users to save a transcript of the chat session for future reference, which can be especially valuable for chats that focus on highly technical or detailed topics. You can join public chat sites and simply read the messages sent by other members; you do not need to send messages to the group. The practice of reading messages and not contributing to the discussion is called **lurking**.

Text chat requires participants to type quickly, even in the enhanced graphical environment of the Web. Therefore, chat participants often omit capitalization and do not worry about proper spelling and grammar. Chat participants use the same emoticons that email users find helpful to display humor and emotions in their messages. In addition, chat participants use some of the acronyms shown in Figure 6-16 for common expressions. Because typing in all uppercase letters is usually perceived as shouting, most chat participants type in lowercase letters.

Commonly used acronyms for text-based communication Figure 6-16

Acronym	Meaning
bbl	Be back later
bfn	Bye for now
brb	Be right back
c u l8r	See you later
c ya	See you
eg	Evil grin
f2f	Face to face (meeting in person)
fwiw	For what it's worth
g	Grin
irl	In real life (contrasted with one's online existence)
lol	Laughing out loud
np	No problem
oic	Oh, I see
pmji	Pardon me, jumping in (when interrupting a conversation)
rotfl	Rolling on the floor laughing
ttfn	Ta-ta (goodbye) for now
wb	Welcome back

In addition to avoiding all capital letters, most chat participants frown on **flaming**, in which a participant insults or ridicules another participant. Another unwanted practice is **spamming**, in which someone or an organization sends unsolicited and irrelevant messages to a chat room, just as an organization might send you email spam, or unwanted and unsolicited email messages. Although many chat rooms don't enforce the rules of the Internet (known as Netiquette) when communicating, you should exercise common courtesy and respect as you would when speaking in person with other people.

Different types of chat programs can be used to participate in an Internet chat. The chat program you choose and the type of chat you have (text, voice, or video) depends primarily on the software and hardware that you and other users have installed on your computers, your Internet connection types, and the conversation you plan to have (public or private). Some chat types require specific chat software and a connection to a specific server.

As part of your research for Roberto you want to investigate one of the first chat networks, Internet Relay Chat. Although you don't think that you will advise him to use this chat program, its history is important for understanding the evolving nature of talking on the Internet.

Internet Relay Chat

The early networks that became the Internet included many computers that used the UNIX operating system. Many of these UNIX computers included a program called **Talk** that allowed users to exchange short text messages. In 1988, Jarkko Oikarinen wrote a communications program that extended the capabilities of the Talk program for his employer, the University of Oulu in Finland. He called his multiuser program **Internet Relay Chat** (**IRC**). By 1991, IRC was running on more than 100 servers throughout the world. IRC became popular among scientists and academicians for conducting informal discussions of experiments and theories with colleagues at other universities and research institutes.

Commercial use of IRC soon followed, with firms using it for virtual meetings with clients and employees at worldwide branch offices. Businesses that sell computer software have used IRC to provide customer support and to host user group meetings. News-gathering organizations have used IRC to enhance live coverage of breaking news events. For example, many news reports from the 1991 Gulf War were based on information that came from the war zone through IRC and the Internet. By the mid-1990s, hundreds of IRC servers connected thousands of IRC clients.

IRC uses a client-server network model: IRC servers are connected through the Internet to form an IRC network. Individual chat participants use IRC clients that connect to the servers in the network. Many IRC networks operate independently of each other; usually you select an IRC server based on its proximity to you. The original network was EFNet, which is still one of the largest IRC networks. Other major IRC networks include IRCNet, Undernet, DALnet, and NewNet. Although the servers in each of these IRC networks are connected to each other as part of the Internet, IRC traffic is segregated by network. For example, a person using an EFNet client can chat only with a person who also is using an EFNet client—even though the message packets might travel through DALnet and IRCNet servers that are part of the Internet. Figure 6-17 shows this simultaneous interconnection and segregation of IRC network traffic.

Tip

Using IRC in business saves travel costs and is less expensive than long-distance conference calling.

Independent IRC networks on the Internet Figure 6-17

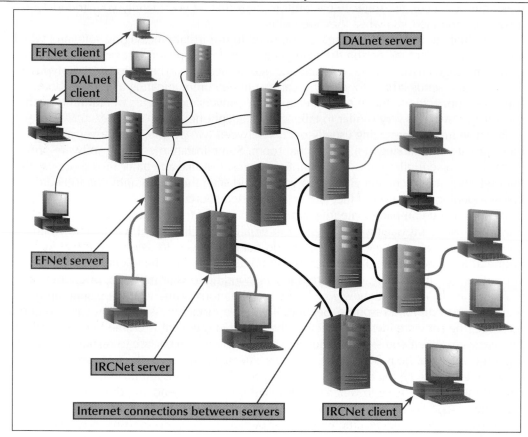

Chat participants run IRC client software on their computers and use it to connect to a local IRC server. After connecting to an IRC server, a user issues commands to join an existing chat or create a new one. IRC networks organize their chats by topic. Each topic area is called a **channel**, and participants who connect to an IRC network join specific channels in which they conduct their chats. Most IRC networks allow participants to join and participate in several chats simultaneously using *one* connection to the IRC server. Users who have joined a channel receive all messages sent to that channel. Each channel has a name, or a **channel heading**, that uses the pound sign (#) to indicate the chat's topic. For example, a channel in which participants discuss current political issues might have a channel heading of #politics.

A participant who creates a new channel becomes responsible for managing the channel and is called the **channel operator**. The channel operator has rights that other participants who join the channel later do not have. For example, a channel operator can change the channel's topic and heading at any time.

Many IRC client software programs are inexpensive shareware programs that you can download from the Web. The Chat Resources section of the Online Companion page for Tutorial 6 contains links to chat programs and Web sites that include information about chatting.

Instant Messaging Software

Instant messaging software lets users chat in real time using software and a device that is connected to the Internet, such as a computer or a cell phone. Instant messaging is a form of chatting that usually occurs between two people who know each other, but it can also occur among a group of people. Instant messaging is especially popular among friends and families separated by geographic distances, but it is also a popular and

Tip

Some people use the term "IM'ing" when using instant messaging. "IM" is also used as a verb, as in "to IM a friend."

efficient form of business communication. Because participants must be online for instant messaging to occur, the software has built-in tools that let you identify your friends and associates and alert you when they are online.

To participate in instant messaging, you need to use instant messaging software, which allows you to select the person that you want to contact, type a message, and then send it. The message arrives on the recipient's device immediately. The recipient then types a response and sends it back to you. You can continue communicating as long as both users are connected to the Internet. Because the conversation occurs in real time, with short responses, it is very similar to talking on a telephone.

Because instant messaging usually occurs between two people, the conversation is more private than talking in a public chat room. Some instant messaging software programs let you send files with your instant messages. Just like any other files sent over the Internet, they might contain viruses, so you should scan them with antivirus software before opening them, even if they are from a trusted source.

Although you can participate in a similar exchange of text messages using an email program, instant messaging is different from email in two important ways. First, when you send an email message to a user, you do not have a way to determine if that user is online at the time you send your message. If the user is online, he might choose to return your message immediately, choose to delay responding to your message, or choose not to read it at all. You don't know which of these situations is true when you send an email message and wait for a response. Second, if you use instant messaging software to send a message, the software identifies whether the intended recipient is online before you send the message. When you send the message, the recipient can choose to respond by sending a message that he is busy at the time your message arrives. Both email and instant messaging involve typing messages at the keyboard, but an instant message occurs faster because you do not have to wait for your email program to send and download messages.

As instant messaging became widely accepted as an easy, inexpensive way to chat with other Web users, different companies used the technology to create their own instant messaging software. The advantage of using instant messaging is that you can communicate with someone in real time, often on many different computer devices and using different Internet connections. However, to use instant messaging to communicate with other Internet users, you need to download an instant messaging software program and you must generally use the program to communicate with people using the *same* software. Some instant messaging software programs offer ways for users to access instant messaging features through a Web page, but in general, users download and use an instant messaging software program to send and receive messages.

ICQ, AIM, Windows Messenger, and Yahoo! Messenger

ICQ (pronounced "I seek you") is an early and very successful instant messaging software program that started in 1996; it now has over 220 million worldwide users. The initial and phenomenal success of ICQ spurred a surge of new ways to communicate using the Internet. Within six months of the introduction of ICQ, AOL created its own instant messaging software called AOL Instant Messenger (AIM). AOL originally created AIM to allow its members to chat with each other, but subsequently made the software available to anyone (even those people without AOL accounts) for use on the Web. Soon Microsoft introduced MSN Messenger (called Windows Messenger in Windows XP and Windows Live Messenger in Windows Vista and Windows 7), Yahoo! introduced Yahoo! Messenger, and other portals and software producers released their own products to capitalize on the continuing success of ICQ.

Although you and Roberto suspect that instant messaging software programs have similar features, you decide to explore some of the more popular instant messaging software programs.

> **Tip**
>
> Even in a private chat, you should protect your identity and privacy by limiting the amount of personal information you provide during your conversation.

To learn more about instant messaging software:

▶ **1.** Start your Web browser, open the Online Companion page at **www.cengage.com/internet/np/internet8** and log on to your account, click the **Tutorial 6** link, and then click the **Session 6.2** link. Click the **AIM** link and wait while your browser loads the page. Figure 6-18 shows the home page for AIM (your page might differ).

AIM home page   Figure 6-18

▶ **2.** Follow some of the links on the page to learn more about AIM. You might start by reading the questions and answers in the FAQ page. Make sure to look for information that Roberto needs, such as how to get started and on what types of devices the software works.

▶ **3.** When you are finished exploring the AIM Web site, return to the Online Companion page for Session 6.2.

▶ **4.** Click the **Windows Live Messenger** link and wait while your browser loads the page. Figure 6-19 shows the home page for Windows Live Messenger (your page might differ).

Figure 6-19 ▶ **Windows Live Messenger home page**

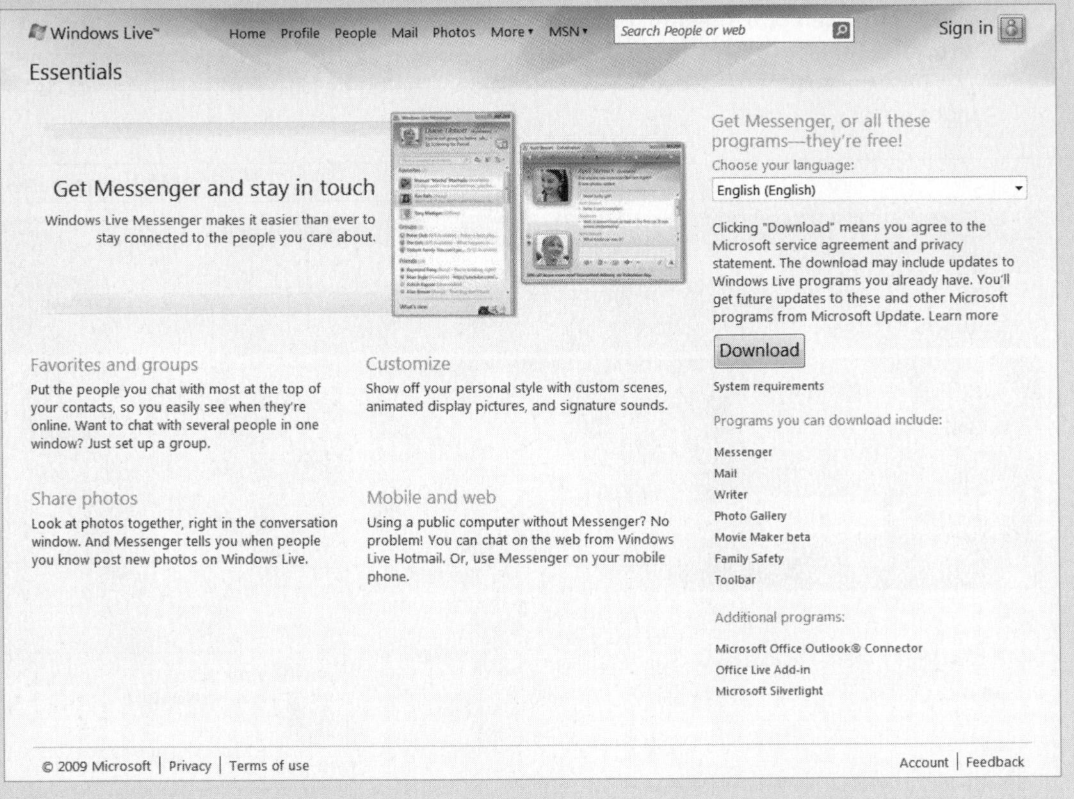

5. Follow some of the links on the page to learn more about Windows Live Messenger. If you see links to videos and other interactive demos that describe the features of Windows Live Messenger and you have the required software to view them, click the links and watch the demos. Make sure to look for information that Roberto needs, such as how to get started, on what types of devices the software runs, and other options.

6. When you are finished exploring the Windows Live Messenger Web site, return to the Online Companion page for Session 6.2.

7. On the Online Companion page for Session 6.2, click the **Yahoo! Messenger** link and wait while your browser loads the page. Figure 6-20 shows the Yahoo! Messenger home page.

Yahoo! Messenger home page < Figure 6-20

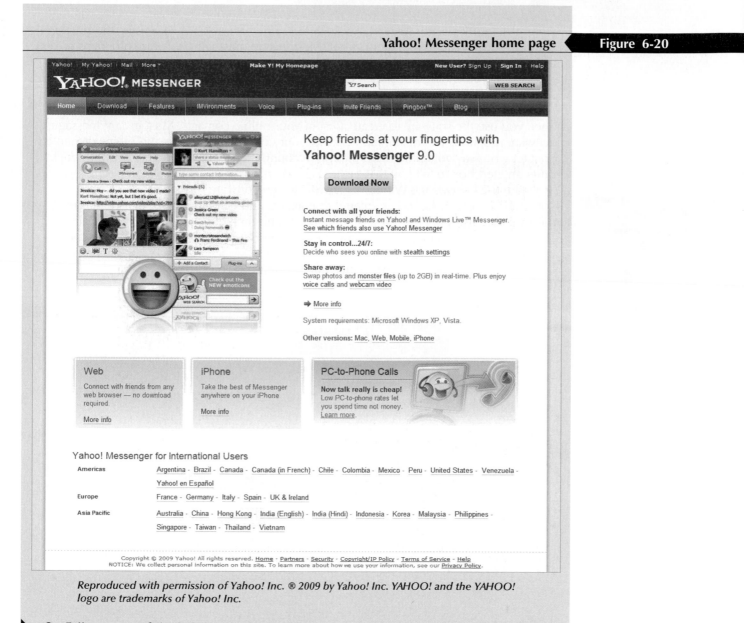

▶ **8.** Follow some of the links on the page to learn more about Yahoo! Messenger. Make sure to look for information that Roberto needs, such as how to get started and on what types of devices the software works.

▶ **9.** When you are finished exploring the Yahoo! Messenger Web site, return to the Online Companion page for Session 6.2.

After viewing the Web sites of several popular instant messaging software programs, you meet with Roberto and the campaign staff to discuss your findings. Some instant messaging software programs have options for logging on to your account using a Web page so you can use the software when you are away from your primary computer; this option could be valuable for people working in neighborhoods. All instant messaging software programs have some features that work on wireless devices, such as cell phones. These options require a Web-enabled cell phone and often also require an account with a specific communications carrier. In all cases, the instant messaging software is free and requires an Internet connection, preferably a broadband connection.

All instant messaging software works in the same basic way. Before using the software, you must download it from the Internet. Most instant messaging software programs are available in different versions for specific computers, operating systems, and handheld devices, so you should select the correct version for the device on which you will use it. After starting the software, you sign on using your user name and password. (If you do not have an account with the instant messaging provider, you will need to create one.) Then you use the software to create a list of your online contacts. Most instant messaging software programs can determine which of your contacts are online and offline. When a contact who was not online signs into his account, the instant messaging software might open an alert box to tell you that he has signed on.

Figure 6-21 shows the Windows Live Messenger software on Roberto's notebook computer. People Roberto has entered as contacts and who are online will appear in the Available list. Roberto can select a contact, and then click the option to send an instant message. After typing his message, it is sent immediately to the person. If one of Roberto's contacts comes online while he is working, an alert box will appear in the lower-right corner of his screen to give him this information.

> ## Tip
>
> Some instant messaging software programs refer to online contacts as "buddies."

Figure 6-21	Windows Live Messenger

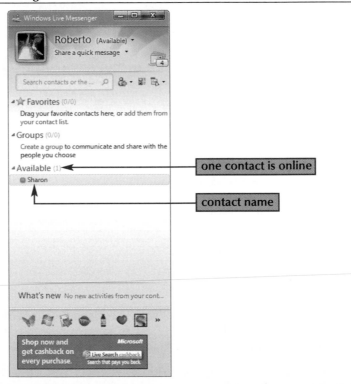

InSight | Protecting Your Privacy When Using IM

When you sign up for an instant messaging service, the provider might send you information via email or provide links to pages about using the service and a list of rules and controls that you can use to protect your online privacy, block specific senders from contacting you, or contact the service to report problems. If you receive email messages from the instant messaging service provider, be sure to read them and file them in a safe place so you can refer to them as necessary as you are learning to use the software.

Using one of the free instant messaging software programs would work well for communication between campaign workers because they could install the software Roberto selects on all of the devices that will use it. However, this solution wouldn't work well for communicating with workers who might not have the instant messaging software that the campaign uses. As you discuss your progress with Roberto, he wonders if there is a chat type that would allow him to keep in touch with his campaign workers and to host "talk to the candidate" sessions to discuss common topics. You decide to investigate the use of Web-based chat sites that do not require specific software to function.

Web-Based Chat Sites

Web-based chat sites offer the same features as text-based chat and instant messaging, but Web-based chat is often easier to use and does not require users to download and install any software. Web-based chats occur at many Web sites on numerous topics, and users can include text, graphics, and hyperlinks in their messages. The primary difference between instant messaging and Web-based chat is the people you contact and talk with during the conversation. For example, with instant messaging, you control the conversation and who participates in it. In a Web-based chat, anyone can join the discussion. The chat room identifies users with their user names as they join the conversation. Some users lurk and others have multiple conversations going at the same time. Although many Web chat sites, such as Yahoo! Chat, have chat rooms designated for specific topics, in practice the conversations are open-ended and rarely follow the designated topic.

When you join a chat room, your user name usually appears in a list so other chat participants can see who is in the room. To lurk in a chat room, you just let the conversation scroll down the screen. To send a message, you type it in a text box designated for sending messages, and then click the Send button. Some Web-based chat sites have a link that lets you report participants who are not following the agreed-upon rules for the chat room. Rules for each site vary, but in general, most Web-based chat sites prohibit spam messages, the use of automated programs to send messages to multiple chat rooms simultaneously, profane and vulgar language, and threats to individuals (flaming). When reported, a chat site has the option of prohibiting the offending participant from entering any chat rooms at the site again.

Just like in email and instant messaging, some chat participants use acronyms to express their thoughts such as using "wb" to "welcome back" a returning chat participant to the room. Some participants insert emoticons into their conversations to express a smile, grin, and other expressions.

Protecting Your Privacy in Chat Rooms | InSight

Most Web chat sites ask you to identify yourself on a registration page before admitting you to the Web chat pages. You should consider carefully whether to provide detailed personal information when you register because most current laws do not require a Web site administrator to maintain the confidentiality of your information. If one Web chat site requires information that you do not want to disclose, simply look for another site with a less intrusive registration page. In addition, although Web sites that provide chat rooms have rules of appropriate conduct, you might encounter conversations taking place that are offensive to you. Fortunately, there are many different Web-based chat rooms available on the Internet, so if your first attempt does not provide a satisfactory experience, simply exit from that chat room and try another one.

Using Social Networks to Share Information

In Session 6.1, you learned how you can interact with Web sites by pulling content to your computer. Some people think of pulling content through mailing lists and newsgroups as the "old" Internet—you had to find the resources and establish how you would pull the information to your computer. In the past several years, the Web has evolved so that connected people *push* information to users who request it or just wander into it. This change is sometimes called the "new Internet" or **Web 2.0**, a term coined during a brainstorming session between representatives of O'Reilly Media and MediaLive International. During the session, Tim O'Reilly and Dale Dougherty were characterizing the change in the way people used and accessed the Web and the change in the technology used on the Web itself. Web 2.0 creates users who actively participate in writing the content that they are viewing; hence the term **user-generated content**. Web 2.0 users not only interact with content, they also are given new and easy ways to create it. In fact, Web 2.0 isn't a "new" Internet at all; the term itself is intended to indicate a change in the way people use the Web, just like a version change in a software program indicates that a new release of the software is better than the old version. Web 2.0 applications enable users to manage and distribute information gathered from online communities to people all over the world, who then take the information and work to improve and expand it.

Web 2.0 applications vary but they all rely in some way on the interactions of communities of people and their data. Web 2.0 includes social networking communities, mashups, video and photo sharing sites, blogs, microblogs, feeds, and podcasts.

In the early days of the Internet, virtual communities were an essential part of the online experience for the small number of people who regularly used the medium. A **virtual community**, now more commonly called an **online social network**, is a place on the Internet where people can gather to discuss issues and share information. As the Internet and Web grew, some of these communities expanded, but others found that their purpose as a place for sharing the new experiences of online communication began to fade. People who use the Internet today no longer see a common bond in the very fact that they are using the Internet. Internet usage has become so widespread that it is no longer anything special in and of itself. Today, multiple common bonds join people who share all kinds of common interests. The Internet is no longer the focus of the community, but has become an important tool that enables communication among members of the community.

Tip

You learned about another Web 2.0 application, wikis, in Tutorial 5.

Online Social Networks

In the past, social networks connected people who had specific common interests. One of the first social networks on the Internet, Classmates.com, started in 1995 as a way to connect people from specific graduating classes at high schools, colleges, and in the military.

Another early online social network, craigslist, which was created in 1995 by WELL member Craig Newmark, started as an information resource for San Francisco area residents. This online community has grown to include information for most major cities in the United States and in several other countries. The company started as a not-for-profit organization but was incorporated as a for-profit company in 1999. According to the site's fact sheet, craigslist retains its .org domain as a way to symbolize the relatively noncommercial nature of the service and its noncorporate culture. This mission is evident in the bare-bones, but highly functional, Web page design characteristic of the site.

The craigslist Web site was an early pioneer, and it is still operated as a community service. Most of the revenue earned by craigslist comes from the 1.5 million job postings it features each month at a cost of $25 to $75 each, depending on the city in which the ad is placed, and brokered apartment listings in New York City. According to craigslist, over 50 million people visit over 550 craigslist sites in all 50 United States and in countries around the world each month.

Connecting with Friends

Another early pioneer of Web 2.0, Friendster, was launched by Jonathan Abrams in 2003 and was an immediate sensation on the Web. In this same year, Google saw the advertising potential for the online social network and offered Abrams a $30 million buyout, which Abrams turned down in favor of obtaining venture capital from another source. Members use Friendster to post profiles with information about themselves and, at their option, to upload their photos and videos. Then, they can ask friends who are already members to link to their profiles so they can interact with each other by chatting and sharing pictures and other information. Friends can invite each other to become Friendster members, which is one reason the site grew so rapidly at first. Although Friendster boasts over 85 million users, it has fallen out of the top ranks of online social networks. Part of the decline of Friendster's initial success and growth occurred when Friendster began deleting **Fakester** profiles that were contrived by members to create fake communities of people, either out of boredom or for deception. Some members who didn't see the harm in creating fake profiles objected to the site's decision to delete them. As a result, some members looked elsewhere for online social networking in which they could still have fun without having to follow rules that they didn't agree with.

With so many online social networks competing for members, it is difficult to determine how many of Friendster's 85 million users return to the site and rely on it to connect with communities. Many other social networking sites have been launched that work in much the same way as Friendster, including LinkedIn, MySpace, Facebook, and Eons. These online social networks have become useful tools for people who want to make new local friends, establish acquaintances before moving to a new location, obtain advice on a variety of topics, or connect with people in specific virtual and geographic communities. Most of these sites provide a directory that lists members' locations, interests, and qualities. On some sites, a member can offer to communicate with any other member, but the communication does not occur until the intended recipient approves the contact (usually after reviewing the sender's directory information). By gradually building up a set of connections, members can develop contacts within the community that can prove valuable later. Although some of these social networking sites are still fairly new, they have proven track records for re-creating (on a much larger scale) the essence of the original Internet communities.

Advertising Revenues

Most, if not all, social networking sites rely heavily on advertising to generate the revenue they need to operate. The social networks that have been successful have catered not only to members' needs, but have also had an open mind with regards to advertising and creativity. In 2003, MySpace, capitalizing on its large membership of people ages 16 to 34 years, allowed Procter & Gamble to create a profile for singer/actress Hilary Duff that included logos and links to free downloads of three of her pop songs. The profile and links were surrounded by a marketing pitch for Procter & Gamble's Secret Sparkle deodorant to a large number of people in the product's target market. MySpace boasts over 70 million users who create profiles and include links to photos, videos, and music. In addition to personal connections and profiles, many corporations, including Ford and Taco Bell, now use MySpace as a way of connecting with consumers by harvesting data in user profiles and displaying relevant advertising.

In 2005, the band Arctic Monkeys made history when its first single was released without an album and climbed to number one on the charts in the United Kingdom. Instead of gathering momentum from an album release or a tour, the band used its MySpace profile to "release" and publicize the single. The band was able to use MySpace to successfully connect with its audience by capitalizing on the power of the Internet, something that had never been done before. Always responsive to its members' innovative ways of using the service, MySpace now includes custom features that let other bands release music.

Facebook, which began in 2004 as a closed network for college students and later was expanded to include high school students, was founded by Mark Zuckerberg, then a student at Harvard University. After gaining new members at a rate three times faster than MySpace, the Facebook network was opened to anyone with an email address but remains a popular online social network for high school and college students, with approximately 85% of its 120 million members being in this age group. With demographics mostly in the young adult category, Facebook is a particularly attractive site for advertisers.

More recently, Facebook has become a communication tool for corporations and even political candidates. For example, Cinemark Theaters, Marble Slab Creamery, and Pepsi use Facebook pages to promote their products and bring users together for marketing and research opportunities through sweepstakes and other promotions. The publisher of this book, Course Technology Cengage Learning, uses the Facebook page shown in Figure 6-22 to provide a way for its employees to celebrate company events and also to connect instructors in different educational areas.

Course Technology Cengage Learning Facebook page ◄ Figure 6-22

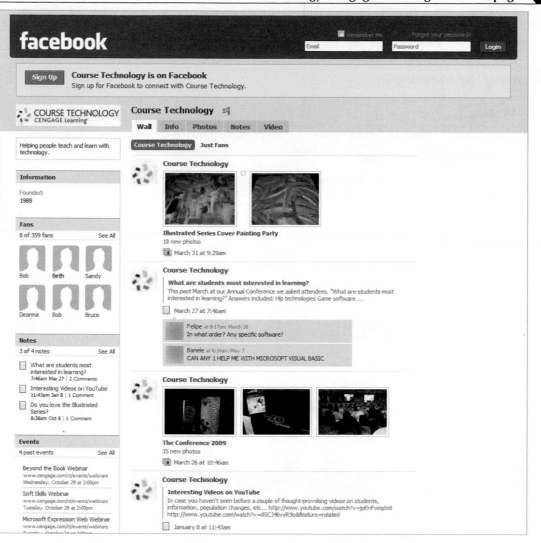

In 2007, Facebook declined purchase offers from Yahoo! and Google; founder and CEO Mark Zuckerberg insisted that the company would remain private to fulfill its mission statement of providing new technologies and innovative ways to connect people in natural ways. In late 2007, Microsoft bought a small interest in Facebook in exchange for an arrangement for online advertising on the Facebook site.

Online Business Networks

Although all social networking sites make it possible for their members to develop business contacts using their services, some of these sites have expressed a desire to focus on business networking. These sites include LinkedIn (41 million members), Ryze (for "rise up," with 500,000 members), and Sermo (a site restricted to credentialed physicians). Users log on to these sites with the intention of seeking jobs, finding potential business partners, recruiting workers, exchanging ideas, and engaging in other business development activities.

The users of these sites are looking for specific business solutions, whether it is a company looking for an employee with specific talents, a business hoping to place its product in a particular retail outlet, or an organization that wants to find a consultant who can provide training on a specific topic. Online business networks tend to use categories that reflect these specific interests and try to make it easy for businesspersons to find the connections they need as quickly and efficiently as possible. The About Us page, which describes the LinkedIn site and the services it provides, appears in Figure 6-23.

Figure 6-23 ▶ **About Us LinkedIn page**

Linked **in**.   Go to LinkedIn.com »

Company Overview
- About Us
- Company History
- Management
- Investors
- Partners
- Contact Us

Press Center
- Press Releases
- Analyst Quotes
- Press Coverage
- Subscribe to Press

Resource Center
- FAQ's & Stats
- Success Stories
- Logo & Screenshots
- LinkedIn for Journalists

Related Links
- LinkedIn Blog
- Learning Center
- LinkedIn Store
- Work for LinkedIn
- Customer Service

Subscribe to Press
Search this site:

[Search]

À propos de LinkedIn | Über LinkedIn | Acerca de LinkedIn

About Us

Latest LinkedIn Facts
- LinkedIn has over 41 million members in over 200 countries and territories around the world.
- A new member joins LinkedIn approximately every second, and about half of our members are outside the U.S.
- Executives from all Fortune 500 companies are LinkedIn members.

Relationships Matter

Your professional network of trusted contacts gives you an advantage in your career, and is one of your most valuable assets. LinkedIn exists to help you make better use of your professional network and help the people you trust in return. Our mission is to connect the world's professionals to accelerate their success. We believe that in a global connected economy, your success as a professional and your competitiveness as a company depends upon faster access to insight and resources you can trust.

What is LinkedIn?

(dot)SUB

It seems like everyone is a member of LinkedIn these days.

▶ |◄◄ 00:00 / 02:28   ⓘ   English [100%]   ▾   ▣ ◀))

LinkedIn is an interconnected network of experienced professionals from around the world, representing 170 industries and 200 countries. You can find, be introduced to, and collaborate with qualified professionals that you need to work with to accomplish your goals.

When you join, you create a profile that summarizes your professional expertise and accomplishments. You can then form enduring connections by inviting trusted contacts to join LinkedIn and connect to you. Your network consists of your connections, your connections' connections, and the people they know, linking you to a vast number of qualified professionals and experts. Through your network you can:

- Manage the information that's publicly available about you as professional
- Find and be introduced to potential clients, service providers, and subject experts who come recommended
- Create and collaborate on projects, gather data, share files and solve problems
- Be found for business opportunities and find potential partners
- Gain new insights from discussions with likeminded professionals in private group settings
- Discover inside connections that can help you land jobs and close deals
- Post and distribute job listings to find the best talent for your company

LinkedIn is free to join. We also offer a premium version of your accounts that give you more tools for finding and reaching the right people, whether or not they are in your network. LinkedIn participates in the EU Safe Harbor Privacy Framework and is certified to meet the strict privacy guidelines of the European Union. All relationships on LinkedIn are mutually confirmed, and no one appears in the LinkedIn Network without knowledge and explicit consent. LinkedIn is located in Mountain View, California and is funded by world-class investors including Sequoia Capital, Greylock, the European Founders Fund, Bessemer Venture Partners, and Bain Capital Ventures.

LinkedIn Corporation © 2008 User Agreement | Privacy Policy | Copyright Policy
Use of this site is subject to express terms of use, which prohibit commercial use of this site. By continuing past this page, you agree to abide by these terms.

Online Political Networks

In the 2004 U.S. elections, political parties and related organizations used blogs and virtual communities in a variety of ways to rally supporters, raise funds, and get their messages out to voters. One new form of virtual community they used was the **online political network**. In previous elections, candidates used Web sites and pull technologies such as sending out email messages to supporters and potential donors, but in the 2004 elections, the strategy changed to focus on push technologies and Web 2.0 applications. Individuals working alone or with established political organizations set up Web sites that provided a place for people interested in a candidate or an issue to communicate with each other. These sites allowed people to discuss issues, plan strategies, and even arrange in-person gatherings called **meetups**.

In the 2008 presidential elections, political candidates running for their party's nomination and in the presidential election made extensive use of Web 2.0 applications in an attempt to make themselves more accessible to voters, to draw people into the campaigns, and to raise money. By using Web 2.0 tools such as online videos and social networks, candidates were collecting extensive campaign contributions that they may not have collected at all or as easily without these tools. Senator Hillary Clinton, for example, raised over $6 million in one day in June 2007 during her campaign for the Democratic nomination for president. Another candidate, Congressman Ron Paul, who was a lesser known candidate in the race, rallied his Internet supporters and raised over $6 million in one day in December 2007 through his Web site during his campaign for the Republican nomination for president.

Roberto is interested in viewing some political Web sites to see how they incorporate push and pull technology and different types of communication with supporters.

To view political Web sites:

▶ **1.** On the Online Companion page for Session 6.2, click a link in the Political Web Sites section, and then wait while your browser opens the home page.

▶ **2.** Explore the site, paying particular attention to the use of online social networks that these political figures use to reach voters and to make them feel personally connected. See if you can find links to join the organization, plan an event, find an event, and join or start a group.

▶ **3.** Return to the Online Companion page for Session 6.2, and then click another link in the Political Web Sites section. Use the information provided in Step 2 to explore the site and its resources.

▶ **4.** Return to the Online Companion page for Session 6.2.

Although online political networks and political campaign Web sites that include Web 2.0 tools have been very successful at rallying voters and creating events to support the campaigns at the local level, they have not been without problems. Then-Senator Barack Obama, running for the 2008 Democratic nomination for president, was the subject of a fan's music video that had millions of viewers almost immediately after being released on the online video sharing site YouTube. (You will learn more about YouTube in the next section.) The Obama campaign declined to comment on the video of a girl pledging her affection and support to the candidate. None of the people involved in producing the video claimed an affiliation to Obama's campaign; there was speculation later that the video was produced to enhance the career of one of the participants, an aspiring songwriter. The video has been played millions of times and although it brought attention to Senator Obama's campaign, the attention was not consistent with the campaign's overall goals for the candidate.

Another popular video on YouTube combined Apple Computer's famous "1984" commercial, which aired during that year's Super Bowl to introduce the Macintosh computer. The original commercial portrayed the IBM personal computer as the evil "Big Brother" and the Mac as a hero. In the YouTube version, the video portrayed Senator Hillary Clinton, who was a candidate for the Democratic presidential nomination at the time, as "Big Brother" and Obama as the hero. There is speculation that the video was created and released as a way to bring conflict to the Democratic campaigns. Regardless of the intent, the video's millions of viewers found it interesting and it is a good example of how online social networks can result in negative publicity for public figures.

Both of these situations involve videos made without the candidates' knowledge, but it's also possible for fans and supporters to create entire Web sites about people without their knowledge or consent. For example, although former Vice President Al Gore denied rumors that he would run for president in 2008, his supporters created a "draft campaign" site to keep voters abreast of important issues. Gore didn't contribute to the site, nor was the site affiliated with him or any specific campaign.

These issues are important examples of how user-generated content on the Web can play a significant role in promoting a person or a message, but also demonstrate how the content can create controversies and false information. The various campaigns make concentrated efforts to monitor the campaign sites and delete or block unwanted or inappropriate content. Also, the investment required to create and maintain a Web site and all of the related links to online social networks is unproven in terms of luring people to the campaign and turning them into voters who support the candidates. Roberto will need to consider the use of online political networks carefully to ensure that they support his campaign effectively and are cost-effective at turning voters into supporters and financial contributors.

Online Social Networks for Sharing Videos

With the explosion in online social networks and Web 2.0 applications, the Internet was ready for its next frontier. At dinner one night, three friends were commiserating on the lack of support for sharing videos on the Web. At the time, photo sharing was relatively easy but Steve Chen, Chad Hurley, and Jawed Karim noted that there were no similar sites for sharing videos. They hatched a plan and in 2005, they launched the video sharing site YouTube. In 2006, Google bought the site for $1.65 billion and by 2007, YouTube's community was viewing over 100 million videos each day.

There were several important changes in technology and on the Internet that made YouTube successful. First, technological advances in digital recording devices, such as Webcams and digital cameras, made it easy and affordable for people to make their own videos. People had videos to share in all sorts of categories—pets and people doing funny things, personal opinions, music videos, political messages, and so on. These movies were of relatively high quality, and users with broadband Internet connections found it easy to upload large files to the YouTube servers.

Second, Web 2.0 was firmly established in 2005 and 2006. When YouTube started, it was immediately picked up by people already participating in well-established online social networks. Word-of-mouth traveled rapidly, and these same Web 2.0 users quickly began uploading and sharing content on YouTube. The site didn't really need to advertise itself—its innovative approach became a social network of its own and the people using YouTube were quick and eager to pass it on.

Finally, instead of fighting YouTube over copyright violations, major networks such as NBC and CBS were the first to drop their objections to copyrighted material being shown on YouTube; they realized the potential advertising opportunities and entered into strategic partnerships with YouTube to broadcast their content. YouTube now has strategic partnerships with many major networks and music labels to broadcast their content. In addition to these partnerships, YouTube relies heavily on display ad placement, brand channels (advertising focused on a specific brand), and contests to generate revenue.

As the popularity of YouTube became well established, other sites, including Yahoo! and Google, added online video sharing services to their sites. You can visit the Web sites for YouTube and other online video sharing sites by using the links in the Video Sharing Sites section on the Online Companion page for Tutorial 6.

Blogs

As you learned in Tutorial 5, a blog is a Web site that is published to express a particular point of view. The blog's author, usually a person or a specific organization, often invites the blog's readers to add comments to the blog's topics. A blog might chronicle a person's life or adventures and become an online personal journal, or it might function as a forum to communicate political, religious, or other opinions of groups of people. Some blogs function much like news organizations by disseminating information about a specific story or from a specific organization. For example, you can find out what's happening at the White House by bookmarking the page for its blog and viewing its frequently updated content, or by subscribing to its feed. A blog might contain only text and comments, or it might also provide photographs, links, and other items such as videos.

Although most historians consider the late 1990s as the date on which the first blogs were published, the content that appears in blogs showed up on the Internet long before this date when webmasters used ordinary Web pages to tell their stories. Some early bloggers started by writing about various topics in Usenet, and then gradually began publishing their commentary on their personal Web sites. These early Web sites contained content that was personal in nature and frequently updated. In 1999, when blogs became easier to create and manage using free blog publishing tools, the number of blogs rapidly increased. Today, there are millions of blogs published on a wide variety of topics. Many blogs are published using free blogging tools available from sites such as Blogger.com, WordPress, or Windows Live, to publish content to the author's own Web site or to a subdomain on the host's Web site. These blogging tools often include simple templates that format the blog's content and provide the blog's overall design, create a form to post comments, and provide code snippets to create hyperlinks and embed photos in the postings. As postings are added to the blog, they appear at the top of the page, with older postings appearing below the newer ones. This chronological method of posting is common to most blogs. Most blogging tools today include features that let the blog's author update the blog's content from a wireless device, making it possible for the blog's content to be updated constantly. You can use the links in the Blogs section on the Online Companion page for Tutorial 6 to visit different blogging sites.

Initially, blogs were used mostly by individuals as a way of communicating with others about personal or other topics. However, blogs were catapulted into the mainstream media when political candidates for president in the 2004 presidential election in the United States started using them as a way to organize their supporters and provide a forum in which candidates could freely discuss campaign issues in an unfiltered way. Democratic presidential candidate Howard Dean was the first person to use a blog to organize a grassroots campaign that included public forums, candidate interviews, and ways to contribute to the campaign. Although Dean eventually lost the presidential nomination, his use of blogs and blog technology gained momentum for the remaining candidates. Both Democratic challenger Senator John Kerry and President George W. Bush used blogs to communicate with their core supporters and respond to stories in the media. Some blogs were not officially sponsored by the candidates themselves but were used as ways to support the candidates. Eventually, there were blogs of all kinds that were used as forums to advance or challenge much of what was being said about the candidates and their policies during the campaign.

Although blogs are a very popular and easy way to disseminate information, it is important to keep in mind that blogs are not subject to the same ethical guidelines of professional reporters, and that the information contained in any blog should always be regarded as personal opinion and not as "hard" news. After the controversy of the 2000 presidential election, in which major television networks proclaimed victory for Vice President Al Gore in the state of Florida before all of the polls were closed in that state, the television networks were careful during election night for the 2004 presidential election to avoid "calling" a state or the election for one candidate until they were certain of the result. However, many bloggers were criticized after the 2004 presidential election for posting exit polls throughout the day and potentially swaying the outcome for the candidate that they supported. Around noon on Election Day 2004, many of the most popular and widely read blogs were forecasting victory for Senator Kerry, but as the actual election results were reported by individual states later that evening, much of the information put forth by the blogs was proved to be inaccurate. Bloggers based their forecasts on exit polls that provided incorrect results because their samples were not representative of all voters. Mainstream media was concerned because the incorrect data provided and widely disseminated by the bloggers hurt the credibility of the media as a whole. Many people read the messages posted on the blogs, believed the information was true, and were unaware of the potential for skewed results due to sampling errors. In addition, many of the blogs were slanted to represent a particular candidate, and they reported stories with that bias.

Although some blogs are blamed for the incorrect polling results during the 2004 presidential election, blogs are an important way of gathering public opinion. Prior to the 2004 presidential election, CBS News reported a story questioning the legitimacy of President Bush's service in the Texas Air National Guard in the 1970s. The story was based on documents that many people believed to be forged. Bloggers responded to the story immediately—some even while the story was airing on CBS—to question the validity of the documents on which the story was based. In this case, the bloggers kept public pressure on the network to prove the validity of the documents, something that CBS News was ultimately unable to do. Although the blogs were extremely active in reporting the story, mainstream media outlets, which were subject to ethical guidelines for professional reporters and were more careful to report only verified facts, eventually picked up the stories being circulated in the blogs and reported them. Eventually, CBS News recanted its allegations. It was widely speculated in the media that blogs led the charge for the withdrawal of the story.

Blogs also make effective use of tagging to categorize information posted by the blogger so it is easy to return to it later. Blogs are now written and used by millions of Internet users to provide unlimited and unrestricted information about any topic. Figure 6-24 shows a page from the Epilepsy Therapy Project blog. The information in the blog is written by registered users at epilepsy.com, a site that provides information about epilepsy and raises money to discover new therapies for this disease. The blog includes articles with hyperlinks to more information, a tag cloud that organizes the blog posts using keywords, and links that readers can use to link to postings and to other blogs.

Figure 6-24

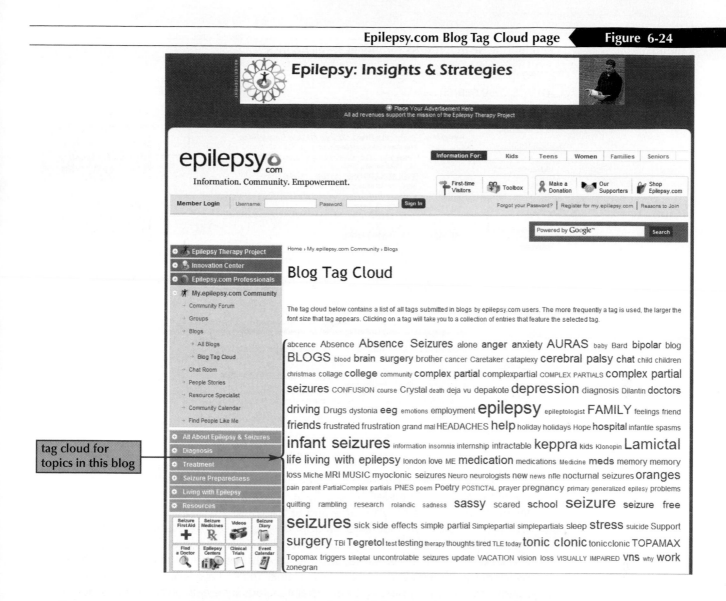

tag cloud for topics in this blog

Because anyone can write a blog, there are millions of them on the Internet. Some are from well-known news organizations such as *The New York Times*, CNN, ZDNet, Reuters, and local newspapers in many U.S. markets. Other blogs are written by individuals who might not claim any affiliation to an organization. When searching for blogs, you should use the skills you learned in Tutorial 5 to evaluate the resources a blog contains and the credentials of its authors. Just like any other Web site, a blog might contain inaccurate or inappropriate information. Fortunately, it is easy to find blogs based on their content and authors. The Google Blog Search is one resource that categorizes blogs and makes it easy to search for them. You'll explore Google Blog Search next.

To use Google Blog Search to search for blogs:

▶ **1.** On the Online Companion page for Session 6.2, click the **Google Blog Search** link in the Blog Search section and wait while your browser loads the home page.

▶ **2.** If necessary, click in the search text box, type **local Texas politics**, and then click the **Search Blogs** button. Google Blog Search opens the page shown in Figure 6-25 (your results will differ).

Figure 6-25 **Google Blog Search results for "local Texas politics"**

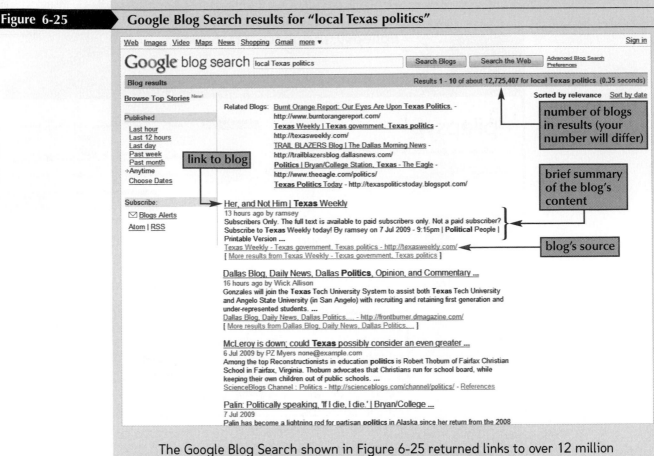

The Google Blog Search shown in Figure 6-25 returned links to over 12 million postings related to the search text, "local Texas politics." Each blog posting includes a link to the blog's source and to the complete posting, a date or time on which the posting was published, a brief description of the posting, and a link to the site. You can use the feature on the left side of the page to fine-tune your search to a specific time period, such as "Last 12 hours" or a custom date that you specify after clicking the "Choose Dates" link. You can also create alerts so you will receive notice of new postings from specific blogs by email, on the Google home page for your browser, or through a feed.

3. Close your browser.

Microblogs

The popularity of using blogs as a way of creating an online personal journal has spawned a new type of blog, called a microblog. A **microblog** is a form of blogging that sends short messages—usually 140 characters or less—on a very frequent schedule. Whereas a blogger might spend hours updating his blog daily, weekly, or monthly with long posts that include text, photos, and links, a microblogger might update his contenthourly or even more frequently using just a few words or a single sentence. The content of a microblog differs from a traditional blog in that it answers the question, "What are you doing?" A microblogger might send one sentence or a few words to describe what's going on in his life at that exact moment, whereas a blogger might take several hours to describe a vacation or express an opinion. Microblog postings are sometimes called **tweets**, and the act of microblogging is sometimes called **tweeting**, which are both references to the popular microblog Web site, Twitter. The About Twitter page is shown in Figure 6-26.

About Twitter page   Figure 6-26

To create a microblog, you set up an account with a microblog Web site, and then search for your friends or people of interest and follow them to receive their updates. In microblogging, a **follower** is a person who is receiving your microblog updates. When you follow a microblog, the updates appear in your microblog account as soon as they are posted. You might receive microblog content through your account on the microblog Web page, or via instant or text messages on a wireless device. Because many people use cell phones to post and receive content on their microblogs and messages are restricted to less than 140 characters, many microbloggers use the same text message acronyms that you find in instant messages. Just like in a blog, as you post content, it might be read by your friends or by people you don't know—it is this act of following people on a microblog that makes it social.

Similar to the evolution of blogs, microblogs have gained popularity beyond the online personal journal and are now widely used for a variety of purposes. In April, 2009, Twitter marked a milestone when actor Ashton Kutcher gained a million followers on his account as part of a challenge with the CNN network to see who could gain one million followers first. The CNN network now blasts news updates to over 1.5 million followers on a regular basis, as well. Many organizations, including well-known retailers and educational institutions, now use microblogs to communicate with customers, students, and other types of followers. Some microblogs, such as Yammer, are used by companies and other organizations to provide a private network for employees to use to communicate about work-related businesses by restricting followers to people with valid email addresses. Other microblogs, such as FriendFeed, let you create private groups that also might be suitable for business communication.

Twitter reached two important new milestones in June 2009. When protests erupted in Iran over allegations of fraud in the country's presidential election, the Iranian government acted to censor all communication, including Internet communication, from leaving Iran by temporarily terminating Internet connectivity and later restoring it at a lower bandwidth, making communication slow to a crawl. Protestors and other people, including journalists,

---

Tip

A **tumblelog** is a microblog that uses short messages, but also includes links, videos, and pictures.

used their cell phones and Twitter accounts to broadcast Iranian news to the world. The information coming from microbloggers at the time was so critical to the outside world that the U.S. State Department requested that executives at Twitter postpone a scheduled network upgrade so that people in Iran could continue to disseminate information about the protests and the election results. Although the information broadcast through Twitter was unverified and chaotic, it proved valuable in many ways because it was one of few uncensored and available forms of communication leaving the country at the time.

Another important milestone for microblogs occurred in late June, when popular entertainer Michael Jackson died in a Los Angeles hospital. Most people will remember *how* they learned the news of Jackson's death instead of *where* they were at the time because most people first learned the news through online social networks instead of mainstream media outlets. Unverified accounts of Jackson's death were sent through millions of tweets, instant and text messages, and email messages, hours before worldwide news and entertainment Web sites were able to confirm and report his death. The number of tweets about Jackson crashed Twitter's servers as millions of people broadcast his death. Similarly, Google reported service interruptions as millions of people bombarded its servers with search requests. Google's servers were so inundated with requests for news about Michael Jackson that the servers interpreted the requests as an automated attack and subsequently responded to requests with an error page for a brief time. Within hours of his death, Wikipedia's page for Michael Jackson was updated over 500 times and accurately reflected the events leading to the entertainer's death.

You can use the links in the Microblogs section on the Online Companion page for Tutorial 6 to visit the Web sites for different microblogging sites.

Protecting Your Privacy and Identity on Social Networks

Online social networks can be powerful tools for keeping in touch with friends and family, communicating with business acquaintances, or making the world seem a little smaller by finding people who share your hobbies and interests. However, the very nature of these open networks can result in problems for users who are not careful about how they use them. When creating a profile on an online social network, consider the following:

- There is a strong likelihood that many people in the world share your same name and maybe even some common life details. When you contact someone as a "friend" through the network, you might not be contacting the correct person—you might just be contacting someone with the same name. Likewise, you could be contacting someone who is pretending to be someone else.

- Some sites have restricted areas for underage users, but with millions of users, it's likely that some of them will be able to access restricted content simply by falsifying their age. Parents need to be especially diligent to monitor the use of online social networking by minors to protect their privacy and the material they view while online. In response to this and other problems associated with minors using social networking sites, some school districts in the United States have blocked access to MySpace, Facebook, and other online social networks on their school computers in an attempt to protect children from inappropriate content and Internet predators. Many corporations and large organizations, such as the Department of Defense, also block their computers from accessing online social networks. Many do so for the sake of "security," but some admit that the blocks occur because employees waste too much time at work visiting these sites.

- **Cyberbullying**—using Internet communication such as email, instant messages, blogs, microblogs, or online social networks to harass, threaten, or intimidate someone—is a problem usually associated with children but can involve adults as well. Most online social networks have codes of conduct that establish penalties for this type of behavior, which should be reported immediately. In addition, the site's Help section usually outlines the steps you can take to prevent cyberbullies from contacting you again.
- Because the nature of an online social network requires you to provide real information about yourself—your name, hometown, education, birth date, picture, and other personal information—and because this information you provide, by design, is public, you might be putting yourself at risk for identity theft and other privacy problems. Most sites include tools that let you hide parts of your profile from other users until you give them permission to access your complete profile. Be sure to read the site's privacy policy and change the default security settings as necessary to protect your privacy in a way that makes you feel comfortable and secure when using the site.

Protecting Your Reputation

In addition to protecting your privacy and identity, it's important to protect your reputation and control the information that you make available to the public. The information you post on a social network is public—and it is often archived even after you delete it. Many employers check MySpace, Facebook, and other online social networks for information that you have posted about yourself. Applicants with exemplary resumes are often passed over for interviews when their MySpace or Facebook pages show them acting in ways that are inappropriate for a corporate culture. Schools are especially careful to monitor online sites—most parents would demand action from school districts if they find that their child's teacher is participating in inappropriate online behavior, even if that behavior is on her "own time." Some universities, including Loyola University of Chicago, Kent State University, and Baylor University, have policies that prevent student athletes from creating profiles on Facebook and other sites. Although the reasons for these bans vary, one stated reason is to protect the privacy of athletes, some of whom travel significantly as part of their involvement in a student athletic program. Another stated reason is to protect the reputation of the school; some universities view student athletes as "ambassadors" of the university and having athletes involved in inappropriate behavior through their online profiles could result in an embarrassment to the school and other athletes.

Another issue related to privacy is the use of your online profile by people in positions of authority. On several college campuses across the United States, students violated code of conduct agreements that they signed when they became tenants of student housing. In one case, students at North Carolina State University took pictures of themselves in a dorm room while consuming alcohol. One of the students posted pictures of the party on his Facebook page. When a university official found the pictures, they became proof of the violation to the student housing contract and proof of the students' underage drinking. In some cases of similar situations on other college campuses, the students were suspended. At some schools, students regarded this lurking by university officials on online sites as an invasion of privacy. Other schools have updated their codes of conduct to specifically authorize the monitoring of student's online profiles as a legal way of taking action against a student when inappropriate or illegal behavior is proven with information students post on their profiles.

Unfortunately, sometimes the online content that is posted about a specific person or a business might not be true, resulting in damage to their online reputation, or the information might be true and cause problems with job applications or required background screenings for different reasons. When the information posted is not true, you might need to employ the services of a reputation management firm to help remove it. These types of businesses are becoming more prevalent on the Internet as a way to help people and organizations monitor their online reputation and, when necessary, work to clear any offensive or negative content from online social networks, blogs, and other sites. The MyReputation page for ReputationDefender.com, a firm that specializes in online reputation management, appears in Figure 6-27. You can explore this site and other online reputation management firms, by clicking the links in the Monitoring Your Online Reputation section of the Online Companion page for Tutorial 6.

Figure 6-27 **MyReputation page at ReputationDefender.com**

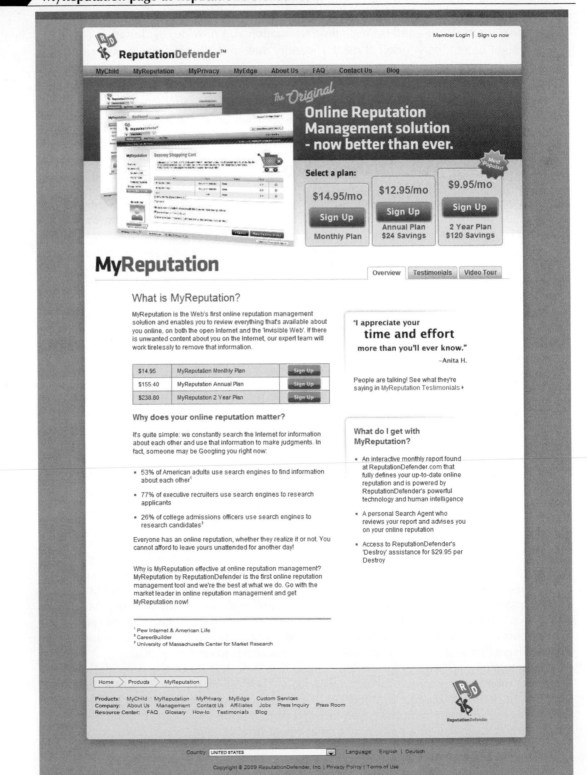

Roberto thinks that instant messaging and microblogging will be important in the final days of the campaign, when everyone is working to get people to the polls to vote. Roberto sees that a blog can be an interesting way to chronicle the efforts of his campaign staff and to connect with voters on important topics. He will investigate using online social networks during the campaign to evaluate their effectiveness at reaching out and disseminating information to voters.

Session 6.2 Quick Check | Review

1. What is lurking?
2. What must instant messaging users have in common to conduct a chat?
3. What are three examples of Web 2.0 applications?
4. How does an online social network earn a profit?
5. What are Ryze and LinkedIn?
6. What is a meetup?
7. What is cyberbullying?

In this tutorial, you learned about the different push and pull communication methods used on the Internet. You explored how to find and use newsgroups, mailing lists, feeds, podcasts, Web Slices, and social bookmarks to pull communication to your computer. You also used a mashup and learned about the technology used to create the site. You explored some push technology, including chat, instant messaging, online social networks, blogs, microblogs, and video sharing sites. Finally, you studied some of the privacy issues involved when using different Internet communications to connect with friends or to hold discussions in a public forum.

As you begin your professional career or just need information about a new hobby, you will find that mailing lists, newsgroups, feeds, blogs, microblogs, and podcasts are an excellent way to gain knowledge and insight from people around the world who share your interests. Social networks are an excellent way to manage connections with friends, family, and future business contacts. The next time you have a question about a specific software program or about building a better mousetrap, check the resources identified in this tutorial to see if you can communicate with an online community to get the information you need.

Key Terms

administrative address	iPhone	public chat
aggregator	iPod	pull technology
Application Programming	list address	push technology
Interface (API)	list administrator	Really Simple
article	list moderator	Syndication (RSS)
Atom	list name	social bookmarking
channel	list server	spamming
channel heading	lurking	subscribe
channel operator	mailing list	tag
chat	mashup	tag cloud
chat room	meetup	Talk
closed list	message	text chat
command	microblog	thread
cyberbullying	moderated list	tweet
discussion group	Network News Transfer	tweeting
distributed database	Protocol (NNTP)	tumblelog
drop	news administrator	unmoderated list
email list software	news server	unsubscribe
enclosure	newsgroup	Usenet
Fakester	newsreader	Usenet News Service
feed	online political network	user-generated content
flaming	online social network	video chat
folksonomy	open list	virtual community
follower	podcast	voice chat
forum	podcasting	Web 2.0
instant messaging software	podcatching software	Web services
Internet discussion group	posting	Web Slice
Internet Relay Chat (IRC)	private chat	

Practice | **Review Assignments**

Practice the skills you learned in the tutorial using the same case scenario.

There are no Data Files needed for the Review Assignments.

After learning about the Internet's communication tools, Roberto is pleased with the work you have done and is interested in learning more about how push and pull communication methods can help get information to voters about his campaign. The first big issue that the campaign needs to research is how to provide affordable or free health insurance for uninsured children. Roberto wants to use the tools you showed him to see what kind of information is available to him. He will use this research to prepare himself for a meetup with supporters next month.

1. Start your Web browser, open the Online Companion page at www.cengage.com/internet/np/internet8 and log on to your account, click the Tutorial 6 link, and then click the Review Assignments link. Click the Google Groups link and wait while your browser loads the page.

2. Click the search text box on the Google Groups home page, and then search for groups using the keywords **uninsured Texas children**.

3. Examine a few of the postings in the search results to get a sense of whether the information might be relevant to Roberto. Remember that he is looking for information about children in Texas who do not have health insurance, and he will use this information to devise a campaign message and plan of action. Be sure to select an article that you believe is from a credible and authoritative source.

4. Follow the links to the article you identified in Step 3, and then print the first page of the article that opens.

5. Return to the Online Companion page for the Review Assignments, and then click a link in the Blogs section and wait while your browser loads the page.

6. Use the resource you selected in Step 5 to search for blogs that contain information about uninsured children in Texas. Be sure to evaluate the blogs and try to select one that is written by a respected news organization or expert. When you find a blog with information that Roberto needs, print the first page of the site's home page.

7. Return to the Online Companion page for the Review Assignments, and then click a link in the Search Engines section and wait while your browser loads the page.

8. Use the search engine to find Web sites related to children's health insurance issues, and then check the Web site to determine if it has any useful feeds. Once again, evaluate the material you find and select one source that you believe will contain useful information. Print the first page of the sponsoring site's home page.

9. Return to the Online Companion page for the Review Assignments, and then click a link in the Podcast Search section and wait while your browser loads the page. Search for podcasts related to your topic. If the podcast has a link to a Web page, click it to learn more about the source. If possible, play the podcast to see what kind of information it provides and evaluate its usefulness for Roberto.

10. Close your browser.

11. In a memo addressed to your instructor, evaluate the information you found. Were the resources you used easy to navigate? What is your opinion of using directories to find relevant newsgroups, blogs, feeds, and podcasts? Did you find the content in each of these areas to be on topic or did you find irrelevant postings? Comment on the effectiveness of each resource and give your advice as to whether Roberto should rely on these tools to prepare campaign materials and to contact voters in his district.

| Apply | **Case Problem 1** |

Find information about mailing lists and newsgroups for a specific topic.

There are no Data Files needed for this Case Problem.

Mustang Bob's Garage   Bob Laucher has driven a Ford Mustang his whole life. When he retired two years ago, he opened a repair shop just outside of Indianapolis, Indiana, specializing in repair and restoration services for "Classic" Mustangs manufactured from 1964 to 1973. Bob's customers frequently ask him about Mustang collectibles, such as key chains, screensavers, toys, and books. He wants to see if he can find an Internet resource for his customers so they can find original Mustang collectibles. In addition, Bob frequently needs rare and difficult-to-find parts for repairs and restorations he makes in his garage; he wonders if the Internet can provide a resource for locating parts, as well.

1. Start your Web browser, open the Online Companion page at www.cengage.com/internet/np/internet8 and log on to your account, click the Tutorial 6 link, and then click the Case Problem 1 link. Click the Google link and wait while the browser loads the page.

⊕ **EXPLORE**   2. Search using the keywords **Ford Mustang mailing list**, and then examine the list of hits returned by Google. Read the descriptions and click links to find a mailing list that includes information about Classic Mustang collectibles. (*Note*: Find a mailing list that Bob can subscribe to and interact with, and not a mailing list that only sends information about product announcements with no interactivity among its participants.)

3. When you find a list that might be of interest to Bob, print the page that includes the subscription information. Do not subscribe to the list, however.

4. Return to the Online Companion page for Case Problem 1, and then click the Google Groups link and wait while the browser loads the page.

⊕ **EXPLORE**   5. Search using the keywords **Classic Mustang**, and then examine the list of hits returned by Google Groups to see if Bob might be able to use some of the newsgroups to locate parts. Based on your review of some articles, note the names of three newsgroups to which Bob might want to subscribe.

⊕ **EXPLORE**   6. In a memo addressed to your instructor, identify the name of the mailing list and the three newsgroups you located, and explain why you think the mailing list and newsgroups will be effective or ineffective for Bob.

7. Close your browser.

| Research | **Case Problem 2** |

Investigate several online business and social networks to learn more about their use in business.

There are no Data Files needed for this Case Problem.

Amelia Bishop   Amelia Bishop just completed her student teaching and graduated from the University of Illinois with a bachelor's degree in elementary education. Amelia wants to find a job in Los Angeles, California teaching at an elementary school. Her goal is to find a school that supports the concept of mentoring so that experienced teachers are encouraged to work closely with new teachers to ensure a smooth transition from student teaching into the classroom. Amelia wants to talk to other teachers who are new to the classroom to get their advice about teaching. She asks you to help her use the Internet to make these contacts and also to expand her job search.

1. Start your Web browser, open the Online Companion page at www.cengage.com/internet/np/internet8 and log on to your account, click the Tutorial 6 link, and then click the Case Problem 2 link.

✛ EXPLORE   2. Choose one of the links to a social network and explore the site to determine if it might help Amelia with finding a job or communicating with other new teachers. Pay particular attention to elementary education jobs and resources in the state of California or the city of Los Angeles. As you explore the site, evaluate the resources it offers and its ease of use. In addition, be on the lookout for other links that might interest Amelia, such as links to housing or local attractions. Finally, evaluate the site's privacy policy and other documentation to see how information in the site is used and what the site does to prevent malicious use.

✛ EXPLORE   3. Return to the Online Companion for Case Problem 2, and then evaluate the resources at another site.

4. In a memo addressed to your instructor, describe your experiences at the sites and the quality of information they provide. In your report, recommend one site to use and give specific reasons for your choice. In addition, evaluate the overall effectiveness of the sites in terms of bringing people together.

5. Close your browser.

| Research | **Case Problem 3** |

Find and evaluate the rules of conduct at several chat sites to learn more about chat etiquette and how to protect your privacy while chatting online.

There are no Data Files needed for this Case Problem.

The Briarcliff School   The Briarcliff School is a college-preparatory secondary school that serves a diverse student body of gifted students. The school's alumni include Fortune 500 CEOs, college football coaches, and a United States senator. The school's computer lab manager recently upgraded all computers on campus to Windows 7 and installed Windows Live Messenger on all computers so they have the software necessary to send instant messages. The school's administrator, Gretchen Nearburg, originally opposed letting students use instant messaging. However, several of the computer science and information technology instructors feel this technology is an important way for students to learn about Internet technology and to keep in touch with family members. Gretchen will reconsider her position, but first she wants to learn more about the rules set forth by a few popular sites that students might use. She wants to make sure that adequate safeguards are in place to protect her students' privacy and to keep them from being exposed to offensive topics. Gretchen asks you to conduct some research and then create a report to disclose your findings and recommendations about the safety of using this application.

1. Start your Web browser, open the Online Companion page at www.cengage.com/internet/np/internet8 and log on to your account, click the Tutorial 6 link, and then click the Case Problem 3 link.

2. Choose one of the sites listed under the Case Problem 3 heading to use in your search, and then click the link to open its home page.

✛ EXPLORE   3. Search the home page for a link that will lead to information about the site's rules of conduct. This link might be titled "Terms of Service," "Code of Conduct," "Rules and Etiquette," "Terms of Use," or a similarly named link. You might also consult the provider's Help menu or a link to a Help system. If you cannot find any rules at the site you choose, return to the Online Companion page for Case Problem 3 and choose another site to use in your search. As you review the site's rules of conduct, search for information about the acceptable rules of use, age limits of participants, language guidelines, banned topics of conversation, and other items that would be of interest to an administrator of a high school with students aged 13 to 19. Make sure to evaluate the resources the site provides for reporting unacceptable behavior and the site's commitment to enforcing its rules.

4. After finding the rules at the first site you selected, return to the Online Companion page for Case Problem 3 and choose another site. Search this site for its rules of conduct.

5. After finding the rules at the second site you selected, return to the Online Companion page for Case Problem 3 and choose another site. Search this site for its rules of conduct.

✦ EXPLORE 6. In a report addressed to your instructor, summarize your findings. Make sure to address Gretchen's concerns about online privacy and other issues. In your opinion, do the rules of conduct at any one particular chat site do more to protect its participants, or are the rules of conduct similar at all three sites you visited? Do the rules of conduct adequately address Gretchen's concerns? Support your recommendations with facts you found at the three chat sites you visited.

7. Close your browser.

Challenge | Case Problem 4

Evaluate mashups to determine the sources they combine and their potential for revenue.

There are no Data Files needed for this Case Problem.

Evaluating Mashup Content and Ad Placement In this tutorial, you learned about the technology that combines content from two or more Web sites to create a mashup. Because the technology that combines mashups is relatively simple and inexpensive or free, new mashups are added to the Web every day. Some mashups are created as public services, others are created for profit. In this Case Problem, you will review two mashup sites and evaluate the content that they contain, the origin of that content, and the advertising included on the site.

1. Start your Web browser, open the Online Companion page at www.cengage.com/internet/np/internet8 and log on to your account, click the Tutorial 6 link, and then click the Case Problem 4 link. Choose a link in the list and then click it and wait while your browser loads the page.

✦ EXPLORE 2. Evaluate the content on the site and try to determine where the data comes from. Your evaluation of the source data can come from information posted on the site or from your analysis of the content.

✦ EXPLORE 3. Note whether the site includes advertising and try to determine its source. How do the ads relate to the content you are viewing on the site? Do you see any ads that are relevant to the city or town in which your computer is connected? If so, how do you think that these ads were generated? If the site doesn't include ads, does it include another way to raise revenue?

4. Return to the Online Companion for Case Problem 4, and then choose another site. Use the information provided in Steps 2 and 3 to evaluate the data and ads featured on the second site.

✦ EXPLORE 5. In a memo addressed to your instructor, answer the questions in Steps 2 and 3 for each Web site. How do the two sites you selected compare in terms of the information provided, the site's ease of use, and the advertising they feature? Use information on the sites to support your responses.

6. Close your browser.

Challenge | **Case Problem 5**

Evaluate the resources available at two news gathering organizations and compare them to the content available through directories.

There are no Data Files needed for this Case Problem.

Evaluating Syndicated Information Resources In this tutorial, you used directories to find information about blogs and podcasts. These types of directories can be good resources for casual users. Almost all major newspapers and news organizations use blogs, podcasts, and feeds to provide information, in addition to their published editions and Web sites. When you are doing more formal research, these news organizations can provide you with a broad range of information written by objective journalists and opinions written by outside contributors and content experts. To see what information is available on the Web, you'll choose a search topic that interests you and then evaluate the information you find.

1. Start your Web browser, open the Online Companion page at www.cengage.com/internet/np/internet8 and log on to your account, click the Tutorial 6 link, and then click the Case Problem 5 link.

⊕ **EXPLORE**

2. Click a link to a feed, podcast, or blog resource and then wait while your browser loads the page. Review the page's contents and find a category of information that interests you. For example, you might choose to explore health, sports, science, or Internet topics. Do not subscribe to anything yet, but use the links to the content to see the articles and postings available for a category. For example, clicking a health category will open a page with articles or postings about health topics. Review the material that you find and evaluate it to see if it fulfills your information needs. Click the individual links to open the postings so you can read them directly. If the content is not what you need, return to the categorical listing and choose another topic until you find one that you like.

⊕ **EXPLORE**

3. Use the Web pages where the content is posted to evaluate the source of the posting. Note the author, the date the content was published, and read a few paragraphs of the article to get a sense of whether the content is written from the author's personal opinion or contains objective reporting.

⊕ **EXPLORE**

4. Return to the Online Companion for Case Problem 5, and then click a link in the Blogs, Feeds, or Podcast Search section. Use the search feature of the site you selected to search for the same category you selected in Step 2. After the search results page loads, use the links to review a few of the sources.

⊕ **EXPLORE**

5. In a memo addressed to your instructor, discuss the content you viewed and evaluate the quality of the information you found at the news organization in using the search directory. What is your impression of the content you viewed at the news organization? What is your impression of the same content you viewed using the search directory? In your opinion, which option provides better information? Why?

6. Close your browser.

Review | Quick Check Answers

Session 6.1

1. A moderated list has a list moderator who is responsible for discarding any messages that are inappropriate for or irrelevant to the list's members. An unmoderated list is one in which no individual is assigned the task of managing the content of the list.
2. lurking
3. thread
4. an aggregator program, a Web browser that supports feeds, an email program that supports feeds, or access to a Web site that includes a built-in aggregator function
5. Podcasting works with podcatching software that is RSS-compatible and that downloads feeds from their source. The feed contains an enclosure, which is an attached audio file that the podcatching software can play on the device on which it is installed.
6. a Web site that combines the services from two different sites using APIs from one or both sites
7. a bookmark that is saved at a Web site using keywords defined by the user

Session 6.2

1. the practice of reading messages and not contributing to a chat or other discussion
2. compatible software and Internet-connected devices, and both users must be online when the communication occurs
3. any three of: social networking communities, video and photo sharing sites, social bookmarking sites, blogs, microblogs, feeds, podcasts, and wikis
4. Most online social networks use advertising as a way of generating income. Other revenue streams come from selling targeted advertising or through brokered apartment listings.
5. examples of online business networks
6. a Web site designed where people can discuss issues, plan strategies, and arrange in-person meetings with political candidates
7. using Internet communication such as email, instant messages, blogs, microblogs, or online social networks to harass, threaten, or intimidate someone

Security on the Internet and the Web

Security Threats and Countermeasures

Case | Remes Video Productions

Remes Video Productions (RVP) is a full-service video production company that specializes in producing training and safety videos. RVP also contracts for smaller jobs, such as producing wedding and family reunion videos and other recreational events. Located near Minneapolis in Eagan, Minnesota, RVP's business has grown steadily since Mark Remes, the company's CEO, founded it in 1997. Over the years, Mark has improved the quality of his work by continually upgrading his equipment and adding services, such as graphics and animated content that he uses in conjunction with videos for clients who request it.

Mark wants to expand his business beyond the Twin Cities and plans to increase sales by 25 percent next year. One of Mark's strategies is to increase RVP's visibility among visitors to the Twin Cities. Mark has used local print advertising successfully in the past, but now he wants to reach a larger audience outside of the Twin Cities. He is especially interested in using the Internet to market RVP to the rest of Minnesota, its surrounding states, and the central provinces of Canada north of Minnesota.

Mark has hired you to help him create a Web site that includes samples of animation, video, and audio content created by RVP that shows off the company's work. The site will allow potential clients to examine RVP's work, and will serve as the only point of contact for many of the company's new clients. Mark wants the Web site to handle credit card transactions for those clients who want to make deposits online to reserve production dates and times.

The proposed Web site will expose RVP to security threats that arise whenever a business is connected to the Internet. To counteract these threats as he plans the content of his Web site, Mark first needs to protect the privacy of his clients. When they use the Web server to purchase services, the server will store their data, including payment information. He needs to secure the transactions between the clients' computers and the RVP Web server and protect the data stored on the Web server from being stolen, altered, or intercepted. Second, because RVP's local area network is connected to the Internet, it needs to be protected against Internet threats that arise when RVP employees use their Web browsers and receive email. Finally, because Mark plans to include sample material for which he owns a copyright on his Web site, he needs to protect it from illegal reproduction.

Starting Data Files

There are no starting Data Files needed for this tutorial.

Session 7.1

Understanding Security Basics: Secrecy, Integrity, and Necessity

As you visit with Mark for the first time, you tell him that security is something that affects a computer *and* its user. **Security** is broadly defined as the protection of assets from unauthorized access, use, alteration, or destruction. There are two general types of security: physical security and logical security. The security provided by an institution, such as a bank, is an example of physical security. **Physical security** includes tangible protection devices, such as locks, alarms, fireproof doors, security fences, safes or vaults, and bombproof buildings. Protection of assets using nonphysical means, such as password protection, is called **logical security**. Protection of the bank's computer assets—both data and procedures to deal with the data—is an example of logical security. The use of logical security techniques to protect data stored on computers is sometimes called **computer security**. Any act or object that endangers an asset is known as a **threat**.

You might protect your computer from the physical security threat of being stolen by locking your house when you leave it. You could also protect the computer's contents using logical security measures such as a password. As technology changes, both Web sites and Internet users fight a constant battle to maintain adequate protection from logical security threats, such as stolen identities, files, programs, and hard drive space; misdirected or intercepted email messages; or illegally obtained and used passwords to access online banking services.

A **countermeasure** is a procedure, either physical or logical, that recognizes, reduces, or eliminates a threat. The importance of an asset at risk determines how a user addresses threats to the asset. A countermeasure can deter a threat (a computer system can require that users use strong passwords that include characters other than numerals and letters), detect a threat (a computer system can maintain a log of access attempts that would show the IP address of an intruder trying many different login/password combinations), or detect and eliminate a threat (a computer system can block attempts to log in after three failed attempts).

Risk Management

An individual or organization usually ignores threats that are low risk and unlikely to occur when the cost to protect against the threats exceeds the value of the protected asset. For example, a tornado is a low-risk threat to a computer network located in Southern California, where tornadoes are rare, but it can be a high-risk threat for a computer network located in Kansas, where tornadoes are fairly common. It would make sense to protect the computer network in Kansas from being damaged by a tornado, but not to protect one from being hit by a tornado in Los Angeles. The risk management model shown in Figure 7-1 illustrates four actions that you could take to manage risks based on the impact (cost) and probability of the physical threat.

Risk management model   Figure 7-1

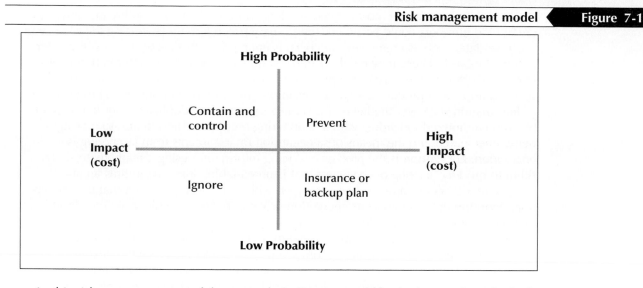

In this risk management model, a tornado in Kansas would be in the quadrant for high probability and high impact, whereas a tornado in Los Angeles would be in the quadrant for low probability and high impact. The appropriate defense for each of these events is dictated by the model. To deal with the risk of a tornado in Kansas, a company would use a "prevent" strategy. Since it is impossible to prevent the tornado itself, the company would take action that would prevent the threat of a tornado from affecting the business. For example, the company might move critical computer equipment into an underground bunker that would survive a tornado. To deal with the risk of a tornado in Los Angeles, a company would use the "insurance or backup plan" strategy. For example, the company could buy insurance that would provide funds to restore the company's assets in the case of a tornado or it could establish a backup plan in which all of its critical information is replicated on computers in another location.

The same sort of risk management model applies to protecting computer assets from logical security threats, such as impostors, eavesdroppers, and thieves. To implement a good security scheme, you identify the risk, determine how you will protect the affected asset, and calculate the cost of the resources you can allocate to protect the asset. Risk management focuses on identifying threats and determining ways to protect the assets from those threats.

Computer security experts generally classify computer security threats into three categories: secrecy, integrity, and necessity. Some threats can be classified into more than one category. A **secrecy** threat permits unauthorized data disclosure and ensures the authenticity of the data's source, an **integrity** threat permits unauthorized data modification, and a **necessity** threat permits data delays (slowing down the transmission of data) or denials (preventing data from getting to its destination). Internet users and Web site operators need to take appropriate countermeasures in each of these three categories to protect themselves and the computers they use to connect to the Internet.

Secrecy Threats and Encryption

Threats to secrecy are the best known of the computer security categories because maintaining the secrecy of communication has been a concern and problem throughout history. To verify a message's secrecy, the recipient needs proof that the message was not altered or intercepted during transit and that the message was sent by the sender who signed it. The sender needs proof that the message was sent without being altered or intercepted and that it was delivered to the intended recipient. These standards apply to all forms of messages, including those exchanged on paper or over the Web.

The secrecy threat that most concerns online shoppers is the possibility that their credit card numbers could be stolen. The primary procedure for protecting the secrecy of sensitive data, such as credit card numbers, is encryption. Businesses face even greater secrecy threats because they regularly transmit all kinds of sensitive information over the Internet. Customer lists, marketing plans, employee identity information, engineering specifications, and product designs are examples of this type of confidential information.

Information sent over the Internet is subject to alteration, duplication, or interception by an unauthorized individual who is monitoring messages. The solution to messages being intercepted and the means of safeguarding their contents from tampering is encryption. **Encryption** is the process of coding information using a mathematical algorithm to produce a string of characters that is unreadable. Some algorithms are a procedure; others use a procedure combined with a key. A **key** is a fact that the encryption algorithm uses as part of its encryption procedure. For example, a simple algorithm that does not use a key would be "reverse the order of the letters" ("time" would become "emit"). An example of an algorithm that uses a key would be "if the key is x, reverse the order of the letters ("time" would become "emit"); if the key is y, use the next letter in the alphabet ("time" would become "ujnf"). The process of using a key to reverse encrypted text is called **decryption**. To decrypt text, you need a key to "unlock" it. Without the key, the program alone cannot reveal the encrypted message's content. Encrypted information is called **cipher text**, whereas unencrypted information is called **plain text**. The study of ways to secure information is called **cryptography**. Encryption is the most common cryptographic process and is the most widely used form of data protection on the Internet.

Two types of encryption are used on the Internet: private-key encryption and public-key encryption. **Private-key encryption** (also called **symmetric encryption**) uses a single key that both the sender and receiver know. The common key might be a password or a number generated by a special device. This method works well in a highly controlled environment in which the sender can safely pass the common key to the receiver using a human courier or other procedure because both sender and receiver must have and use the same key. However, private key encryption can be difficult to implement when the sender and receiver are not physically near each other or when there are a large number of senders or receivers. Figure 7-2 illustrates how private-key encryption works.

Figure 7-2 ▶ **Private-key (symmetric) encryption**

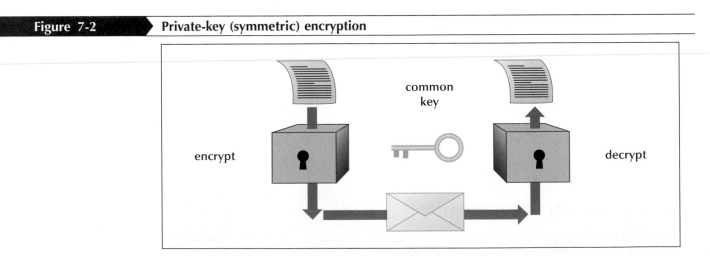

Public-key encryption solves the key distribution problem. With **public-key encryption** (also called **asymmetric encryption**), a person has a private key that is secret and a public key that is shared with other users. Public-key encryption uses a **public key** known to everyone and a **private** or **secret key** known only to one person involved in the exchange. Messages encrypted with a private key must be decrypted with the public key, and vice versa. For example, when an RVP client uses the Web site to submit an order, the client can use RVP's public key to encrypt the transaction—that is the only key any-one outside of RVP knows. The RVP Web site uses RVP's private key to decrypt the message and process the transaction. Figure 7-3 illustrates how public-key encryption works.

Public-key (asymmetric) encryption ◄ Figure 7-3

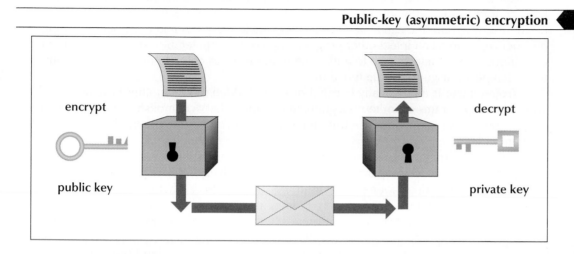

Encryption is considered to be weak or strong based on its algorithm and the number of characters in the encryption key. An **algorithm** is a formula or set of steps to solve a particular problem. The resistance of an encrypted message to attack attempts (its strength) depends on the size (measured in bits) of the key used in the encryption procedure. A 40-bit key is currently considered to provide a minimal level of security. Longer keys provide much more secure encryption. A sufficiently long key can help make the security unbreakable. Keys that are 128 bits or longer are called **strong keys**. Most Web browsers today use 128-bit encryption when they are in secure mode, which is also called **strong encryption**. Some browsers and Web servers are equipped to use 256-bit and even longer keys. As computers become faster and more powerful, the length of keys must be increased to prevent those computers from being used to break encrypted transmissions. You will learn more about how Web browsers use strong encryption to establish a secure communication channel in Session 7.2.

Integrity Threats

Threats to the integrity of data represent the second major category of computer security. Unlike secrecy threats, where someone simply sees or steals information, integrity threats can change the actions a person or organization takes by altering a message's contents. An integrity attack occurs when an unauthorized party alters data while it is being transferred over the Internet or while it is stored on a computer. Integrity threats are reported less frequently and thus the public is less familiar with them.

For example, suppose that a client reserves a date and time with RVP to shoot video for a wedding, but an attacker prevents the company from receiving the reservation so the video is never shot. The integrity of RVP's reservation data is thus compromised. Alternatively, an attacker could use multiple fictitious names to reserve space with RVP in an attempt to prevent RVP from scheduling those dates and times with real clients. In the first case, RVP cannot fill an order that it never received; in the second case, RVP loses income that it would have earned if real clients had been able to make reservations. In both cases, the integrity of RVP's reservation information has been compromised, and this compromise results in a loss of revenue and reputation for RVP.

Another type of integrity violation occurs when an email message is intercepted and its contents are changed before it is forwarded to its intended destination. In this type of integrity violation, which is called a **man-in-the-middle exploit**, the contents of the email are often changed in a way that negates the message's original meaning. For RVP, an attacker could change an event confirmation to a cancellation, causing bad will between the company and its clients.

Viruses, Trojan horses, and worms that attack computers and the programs they run are also forms of integrity threats. You learned earlier in this book that a virus is a destructive program that can attach itself to legitimate programs and files. Besides being destructive, a virus can infect other programs on your computer. Because a virus cannot exist alone, it must attach itself to a file. The term **virus** has come to mean any program that attempts to disguise its true function.

A **Trojan horse** is a potentially harmful program hidden inside another program. Trojan horse programs claim to be legitimate programs that accomplish some task when, in fact, they cause harm when the user accesses or downloads the program in which they are hidden.

Trojan horse programs range from prank programs that display a message and then disappear, to destructive programs that reformat hard drives or delete program and data files. A Trojan horse does not replicate itself, nor does it affect other files or programs. Because most Trojan horse programs are hidden, it is possible to infect a computer by executing a file that you downloaded from a site that offers free software. You can also get a Trojan horse program as an email attachment. The email might even have come from someone you trust but who unknowingly passes along the Trojan horse attachment, thinking it is a useful file or an interesting animation.

When you execute the program you thought you downloaded (or received by email), it secretly launches a separate Trojan horse program, which quietly does its damage. Unfortunately, antivirus software programs and firewalls cannot guarantee that your computer is protected from this type of attack. To protect against this type of threat, you should be careful not to execute a file that you did not request and you should download software only from trusted sources. Some people and companies enforce a general policy of not opening any email attachments, no matter who sent them.

A variation of a virus is a **worm**, a self-replicating program that is usually hidden within another file and then sent as an email attachment. Unlike viruses, a worm can replicate itself on a computer or server, but it cannot infect other files. Some worms arrive as email attachments. When the user opens the attachment, the virus infects the user's computer, and then quickly attempts to send itself to email addresses stored in the address book of the user's email program.

Many viruses can send you an email that includes the name of someone you know in the message's From line, a tactic called **spoofing**. This spoofed From line makes it more likely that you will open the attachment and infect your own computer, because the message appears to have been sent from someone you know. Many of these email attachments have two filename extensions, such as Memo.txt.vbs. The default filename view setting in Windows hides the extension, so the filename appears to be Memo.txt and the .vbs extension (which indicates it is a Visual Basic script, and therefore a likely virus) is hidden. Many computer security experts recommend that users change this default setting in Windows when it is possible to do so (some schools and businesses lock the basic Windows settings on their computers so that users cannot change them).

Tip

If you receive an unexpected email with an attachment, even if it is from someone you know, it is best to check with the sender to confirm that the attachment is not a virus before you open it.

To change the Windows default that hides filename extensions:

▶ 1. Click the **Start** button on the taskbar, and then click **Control Panel**. The Control Panel window opens.

▶ 2. Click **Folder Options**, and then click the **View** tab in the Folder Options dialog box.

Trouble? If you are using a computer at your school or at work, the desktop might be locked to prevent changes. If this is the case, the Folder Options dialog box will not open, or some of the choices might not be operating. You will not be able to complete these steps on this computer.

Trouble? If you are using Windows Vista, click **Appearance and Personalization** to open the Folder Options dialog box.

3. In the Advanced settings pane of the dialog box, scroll down if necessary until the line that includes the option "Hide extensions for known file types" is visible. This option is shown in the Folder Options dialog box in Figure 7-4.

The Windows Folder Options dialog box | Figure 7-4

4. Click the check box in front of the phrase **Hide extensions for known file types** to clear it, if necessary.

5. Click the **OK** button.

6. Close the Control Panel window.

Trouble? If you are using Windows Vista, close the Appearance and Personalization window, then close the Control Panel window.

Antivirus software can prevent the spread of viruses, worms, and Trojan horses by blocking them from being downloaded from the server. Many companies offer antivirus software of different types for individuals, small organizations, and large organizations. An individual or small company might be interested in finding antivirus software that can be used on several computers (a home desktop computer and a notebook computer used when traveling, for example) with one license. A large company would be more interested in software features that let its information technology department update all of the company's computers automatically.

All antivirus software vendors sell their products through Web sites, so you can learn more about the vendors and their products quite easily. Two vendors that provide a full range of antivirus products are Symantec and McAfee.

To learn more about Symantec and McAfee antivirus products:

1. Start your Web browser, go to **www.cengage.com/internet/np/internet8** to open the Online Companion page, log on to your account, click the **Tutorial 7** link, and then click the **Session 7.1** link.

Tip

Different antivirus software products offer different features. Ensure that the features that are important to you or your business are included in the antivirus product you buy.

  2. Click the **Symantec** link in the Understanding Security Basics: Secrecy, Integrity, and Necessity section.

  3. Click the **Norton** link to open the page for that product line, and then click the **Products & Services** link to open that page. The Norton Products page includes links to information about the company's PC security products. Follow the links on this page to learn more about products that RVP might find useful for virus protection.

  4. When you have finished exploring the Symantec site, click your browser's **Close** button to return to the Online Companion page for Tutorial 7.

  5. Click the **McAfee** link. The McAfee home page includes links to pages that provide information about its antivirus and PC security products.

  6. Follow these links to learn more about McAfee products that RVP might find useful.

  7. When you have finished exploring the McAfee site, click your browser's **Close** button to return to the Online Companion page for Tutorial 7.

InSight | **Protecting Against Trojan Horses, Viruses, and Worms**

Being alert to the possibility that an email might contain a Trojan horse, a virus, or a worm is a good first step toward defending against those threats. Setting your Windows Explorer options to display filename extensions lets you determine the type of each file that you download and can help you identify email attachments that contain these threats. Avoid opening attachments that you did not expect (even if they are from senders that you know and trust). Finally, install an antivirus program on your computer. Keep the antivirus program updated and run it on a regular basis.

It is also important to keep antivirus programs updated regularly; most experts recommend daily updates for a company of RVP's size. Based on your research at the Symantec and McAfee Web sites, you should be able to give Mark a good idea of what kinds of antivirus software products are available for companies like RVP.

Necessity Threats

The third category of computer security, necessity, occurs when an attacker disrupts normal computer processing or denies processing entirely. Programs used in necessity attacks use various approaches to reduce processing speed to intolerably low levels. For example, an attack on an ATM network would be successful if it slowed the processing speed of each ATM transaction from its typical speed of two seconds to 30 seconds. At such a slow speed, users would face long lines at the ATM and would soon go looking for another ATM or even another bank. Such an attack would destroy the network's ability to achieve its operating function and would cost the bank the goodwill of its customers.

The most common necessity attack, called a **packet flooding attack** or a **denial of service (DoS) attack**, occurs when an attacker bombards a server or other computer with so many messages that the network's bandwidth resources are consumed. This effectively disables the organization's computer communications. Even if the attack fails to disable the network, the resulting processing delays can render a service unusable or unattractive.

In 2000, an attacker launched a coordinated and simultaneous DoS attack on Amazon.com, Yahoo!, e-Bay, and CNN.com. This attack caused all of these companies' Web sites to shut down completely. The delay lasted for several hours, preventing people from doing business with and accessing these sites. Because the DoS perpetrator does not need to access an organization's server to attack it, Web sites are especially vulnerable to denial of service attacks. Even the Web site for Microsoft was hit by a denial of service attack in 2001.

DoS attacks are a continuing problem on computer networks, but they can create difficulties on other digital networks as well. In 2005, a group of Penn State researchers published a paper that described a technique for creating a DoS attack on a mobile phone network using its text messaging service. Text messages are transmitted on the same channel that mobile phone networks use to initiate regular voice calls. Thus, if the mobile phone network is flooded with enough text messages, voice calls cannot go through. The researchers estimated that it would take fewer than 200 text messages sent per second to shut down a mobile phone operator's Manhattan service completely.

As you learned earlier in this book, a Web browser loads a Web page by sending a message to a Web server that asks for the page. The Web server responds with a message that contains the HTML content of the Web page, along with any accompanying graphics or other files needed to render the Web page in the browser. When a Web browser is used in a DoS attack, it sends a large number of page request messages to the Web server (potentially thousands of requests per minute). Sometimes, that is enough to overload the server. If not, each of the page request messages has a false return address, so the Web server tries to resolve the problem, which takes time. During that time, more page requests come in from the Web browser and, as the efforts to resolve the problem and to process the new requests accumulate, the server becomes overloaded and unavailable to process other, legitimate requests. Ultimately, the server shuts down.

In a **distributed denial of service (DDoS) attack**, the perpetrator uses a large number of computers that each launch a DoS attack on one Web server at the same time. Most DDoS attacks are launched after the attacking computers are infected with Trojan horse programs. Each Trojan horse is coded to open and launch a DoS attack at exactly the same date and time. Other computers are "hijacked" by this type of Trojan horse and, without the knowledge of their owners, are used to help the DDoS attack; such computers are often called bots (short for "robots") or **zombies**. These bots use the same basic automation techniques as the shopping bots you learned about earlier in this book, but for very different purposes.

A company can defend its Web server from DoS and DDoS attacks by adding a computer or program that acts as a filter (called a **denial of service filter**, or **DoS filter**) to its Internet connection between the Web server and the router that connects it to the Internet. DoS and DDoS attacks remain a serious threat today because the attackers continue to develop new ways of getting their messages past Web server filters. In 2009, a large DDoS attack was launched from thousands of zombie computers located around the world. The attack, which began on July 4 and continued for a week, hit dozens of banking and government Web sites in South Korea and the United States.

A denial of service filter, which can be a separate computer or software running on the Web server computer, identifies attacks by watching for patterns of incoming page requests or specific elements of the page request message that repeat. The filter can be configured to block messages automatically if they contain similar elements and arrive in rapid sequence. Of course, attackers try to configure their messages so these filters cannot identify them, but the filter vendors respond by updating their identification criteria frequently. DoS filter functions are often included as part of a network software tool called a **packet sniffer**, which examines the structure of the data elements that flow through a network.

Online Crime, Warfare, and Terrorism

Most people use the Internet for legitimate purposes. Unfortunately, some people use it for all manner of illegal and unethical purposes. Crime on the Web includes online versions of crimes that have been undertaken for years in the physical world, including theft, extortion, distribution of pornography, and illegal gambling. Other crimes are new inventions, such as commandeering one computer to launch attacks on other computers.

Hackers, Crackers, and Script Kiddies

People who write programs or manipulate technologies to obtain unauthorized access to computers and networks are called crackers or hackers. A **cracker** is a technologically skilled person who uses his or her skills to obtain unauthorized entry into computers or networks of computers. A cracker usually intends to steal information, damage the information, damage the system's software, or even do harm to the system's hardware.

Originally, the term **hacker** was used to describe a dedicated programmer who enjoyed writing complex code that tested the limits of technology. The term hacker is still used in this original sense by computer professionals. To them, being called a hacker is a compliment, and they make a strong distinction between the terms hacker and cracker. The media and the general public often use the term hacker to describe those who use their skills for destructive purposes. Some computer professionals use the terms **white hat hacker** and **black hat hacker** to distinguish between those who use their skills for good and those who use their talents to commit illegal acts.

A small number of companies, endorsed by corporations and security organizations, have the unlikely job of breaking into computers. Called **computer forensics experts** or **ethical hackers**, these computer sleuths are hired to probe computers and locate information that can be used in legal proceedings. The field of computer forensics includes the collection, preservation, and analysis of computer-related evidence. Ethical hackers are also hired by companies to test their computer security safeguards.

Most of the stereotypical perceptions of the cracker as an antisocial, destructive programming geek are wrong. Some of them are indeed social misfit malcontents, but most crackers are well-adjusted, gainfully employed individuals who do not intend to damage anyone with the programs they write or the actions they undertake on the Web. Crackers can be almost any age, have almost any socio-economic background, and can be from almost any country. They have a wide range of programming skills and many different motivations for cracking. Although most are male, an increasing number are female.

The appeal of cracking originally was the challenge of creating new attacks that demonstrated programming skills. Today, an increasing number of crackers do it for the money. Companies fear that crackers will infiltrate their computer systems to steal data (and then sell it to their competitors) or create disruptions to their operations.

In the past, one thing that all crackers had in common was a considerable level of skill in programming. However, the emergence of script-writing programs called **virus tool kits**, which allow novices to create their own viruses, worms, and Trojan horses, has changed that. These menu-driven tools give almost anyone the ability to generate troublesome programs without the need to write a single line of code. People who use these script-writing tool kits are often called **script kiddies**, a derisive term coined by crackers who do have programming skills. The Anna Kournikova virus, launched in 2000, was one of the first widely distributed viruses that was created by a person using a virus tool kit.

Online Theft and Identity Theft

The nature and degree of personal information that Web sites can record when collecting information about visitors' page viewing habits, product selections, and demographic information can threaten the privacy of those visitors. An even greater concern arises when information about Web site visitors falls into the wrong hands and is used for criminal purposes. Consumers have become accustomed to providing their credit card and contact information to online vendors, but an increasing amount of personal information is stored on Internet-connected computers at banks, credit card issuers, credit reporting agencies, physician's offices, hospitals, and government agencies. As more and more personal information is stored on these computers, opportunities for theft of that information increase.

In recent years, many companies have made headlines because they released or lost control of confidential information about customers, employees, and vendors without the permission of those individuals. For example, ChoicePoint (a company that compiles information about consumers) sold the names, addresses, Social Security numbers, and credit reports of more than 145,000 persons to thieves who posed as legitimate businesses. More than 1000 fraud cases have been documented as a result of that one privacy violation. Another company that lost control of its customer data is DSW Shoe Warehouse. Hackers broke into its customer databases and stole the credit card numbers, checking account numbers, and driver's license numbers of more than 1.4 million customers. In another hacking case, a computer at Boston College was penetrated, and the addresses and Social Security numbers of 120,000 alumni were exposed.

Not all privacy compromises are the work of external agents. Sometimes, companies just lose things. In recent years an array of well-known companies including Ameritrade, Bank of America, and Time Warner have each reported that they had lost track of shipments containing computer backup tapes that held confidential information for hundreds of thousands of customers or employees.

The kinds of personal information that criminals most want to obtain (listed in the order of their usefulness to the criminal) include:

- Social Security numbers
- Driver's license numbers
- Credit card numbers
- CW2 numbers (the three- or four-digit security code printed on a credit card)
- Passwords (or PINs)
- Credit reports
- Date of birth
- ATM (or debit) card numbers
- Telephone calling card numbers
- Mortgage (or other loan) information

Tip

Most people who have their information revealed by a data security breach do not experience any financial loss from the exposure.

- Telephone numbers
- Home addresses
- Employer addresses

Thieves can use some information (such as customer names, addresses, and credit card numbers) to make unauthorized purchases. Criminals can also use this information to obtain loans from banks, finance companies, or payday loan companies.

If the perpetrator can gather enough information (driver's license numbers and Social Security numbers are important), he or she can steal a person's entire credit record. In this type of crime, called **identity theft**, the perpetrator can use the victim's personal information to open bank accounts, obtain new credit cards, and buy expensive goods on credit, often damaging the victim's credit rating in addition to racking up charges. By the time the victim discovers his or her identity has been stolen, the thief is long gone with the cash and the goods. It can take hundreds of hours of effort for victims of identity theft to clear their credit records of the unpaid charges run up by the perpetrator.

To protect against identity theft, individuals can take some common sense steps that reduce the chances of becoming a victim and that make it easier to recover from an identity theft incident. These steps include:

- Keep credit card, bank account, and investment account information (account numbers, passwords, contact telephone numbers, and so on) together in a safe place that is easy to access should an identity theft incident occur.
- Save credit card receipts and match them to monthly credit card statements; report any unauthorized charges to the credit card issuer immediately.
- Monitor expiration dates on credit cards and contact the issuer if replacement cards do not arrive before the old cards expire.
- Consider placing a preemptive fraud alert on your credit record at all three of the major credit reporting companies (Equifax, Experian, and TransUnion). This requires the reporting company to contact you before releasing your credit report to anyone and can help prevent a perpetrator from opening credit accounts in your name.
- Shred all mail that contains any personal information (such as unsolicited credit card offers) before throwing it into the trash.
- Never use your Social Security number for anything unless it is absolutely required, and do not have it (or your driver's license number) printed on your checks.

If you believe you have become the victim of identity theft, you must act quickly to contact the credit reporting agencies, every financial institution at which you have an account, and the issuer of every credit card you hold. You can learn more about identity theft and what you can do to protect yourself on the Web.

To learn more about identity theft and how to protect yourself:

▶ 1. On the Online Companion page for Tutorial 7, click the **OnGuard Online** link in the Online Crime, Warfare, and Terrorism section.

▶ 2. Click the **Topics** button, and then click the **Identity Theft** button on the left side of the Web page to open the U.S. Federal Government information Web page on the subject, as shown in Figure 7-5.

OnGuard Online Identity Theft information page | Figure 7-5

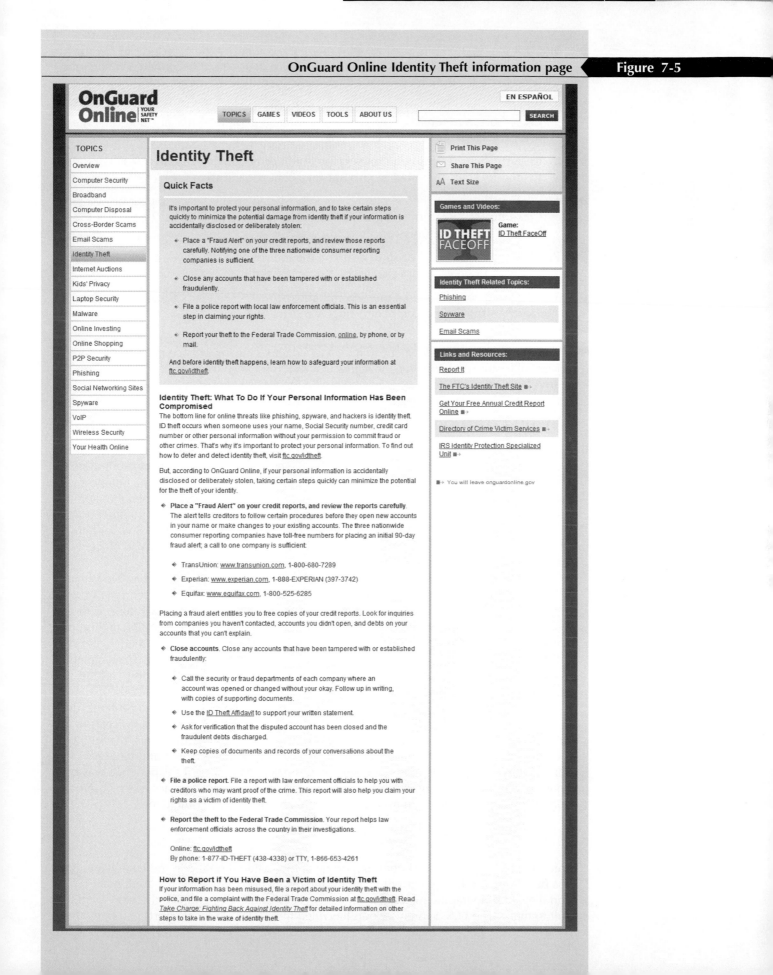

▶ **3.** Click the links on this page to learn more about identity theft, including how the crime can be perpetrated, how you can reduce your risk of becoming a victim, and what to do if you think you have become an identity theft victim.

▶ **4.** When you have finished exploring the resources on this site, use your browser's **Close** button to return to the Online Companion page for Tutorial 7 and click the **Identity Theft Resource Center** link.

▶ **5.** Click the links on this page to examine the information and research results related to identity theft compiled by this not-for-profit organization.

▶ **6.** When you have finished exploring the information on this site, use your browser's **Close** button to return to the Online Companion page for Tutorial 7 and click the **Federal Trade Commission: Identity Theft** link.

▶ **7.** Click the links on this page to examine the information provided, especially regarding what to do if you are the victim of identity theft.

▶ **8.** When you have finished exploring this site, use your browser's **Close** button to return to the Online Companion page for Tutorial 7.

After you report to Mark what you have learned about the importance of protecting the privacy of customer information, he agrees that RVP must keep its customers' information secure. You will learn more about how to secure RVP's Web servers in Session 7.2.

Online Extortion

A company becomes the victim of a criminal extortionist when a perpetrator threatens to launch DoS attacks against a target unless the target pays a "fee." Many smaller companies simply pay the extortionists and do not even report the crime. Other perpetrators break into a company's systems and steal confidential information. They then threaten to release the information unless they are paid. Again, many of these crimes go unreported; the companies pay a fee, and the extortionist moves on to another victim. Smaller companies are easier targets because they generally do not have strong security in place, but larger organizations are not immune to these attacks.

In 2004, lawyer and computer expert Myron Tereshchuk was sentenced to five years in federal prison after pleading guilty to a charge of criminal extortion. Over a period of two years, he threatened a patent and trademark services company, MicroPatent, with disclosure of confidential client information and demanded a payment of $17 million to "go away." He used a variety of means to hide his identity, but after more than a year of investigation by MicroPatent personnel and federal agents, he was identified and caught. When federal agents searched his home, they found firearms, hand grenades, and the ingredients needed to make ricin, a toxic gas used by terrorists.

MicroPatent spent more than $500,000 on outside legal and technical consultants during the investigation and devoted significant internal resources to the effort. MicroPatent's sales managers also had to spend a tremendous amount of time with clients, reassuring them that their confidential information (details of their pending patent and trademark applications, for example) had not been compromised. MicroPatent's experience was not unusual. Several recent surveys have reported that unauthorized data access or information theft costs companies an average of more than $300,000 per incident.

Other Online Crimes

Enforcing laws against distribution of pornographic material online in the United States has been difficult. Under current U.S. law, the distinction between legal adult material and illegal pornographic material is, in many cases, subjective and can therefore be difficult to make. The U.S. Supreme Court has ruled that state and local courts can draw the line based on local community standards. This creates problems for Internet sales because "local community" becomes hard to define. For example, consider a case in which specific photos are sold on a Web site whose server is located in Oregon (where the specific content is considered legal adult material) to a customer who downloads the material in Georgia (where that same content is considered illegal pornography). Producers of adult content and law enforcement agencies both have struggled to determine which community standards apply to the sale. International transactions raise even more difficult questions about which laws should determine the legality of certain kinds of adult content.

A similar issue related to location arises in the case of online gambling. Many gambling sites are located outside the United States. If people in California use their computers to connect to an offshore gambling site, it is unclear where the gambling activity occurs. Several states have passed laws that specifically outlaw Internet gambling, but the ability of those states to enforce laws that limit Internet activities is not yet clear. The U.S. Federal government has outlawed all online gambling activities by its citizens, but enforcement is difficult and the constitutionality of such laws has not yet been tested.

Organized Crime Online

U.S. laws define **organized crime**, also called **racketeering**, as unlawful activities conducted by a highly organized, disciplined association for profit. The associations that engage in organized crime are often differentiated from less organized groups, such as gangs, and from organized groups that conduct unlawful activities for political purposes, such as terrorist organizations.

Organized crime associations have traditionally engaged in criminal activities such as drug trafficking, gambling, money laundering, prostitution, pornography production and distribution, extortion, truck hijacking, fraud, theft, and insider trading. Often these activities are conducted simultaneously with legitimate business activities, which provide cover for the illegal activities.

The Internet has opened new opportunities for organized crime in their traditional types of criminal activities and in new areas such as identity theft, generating spam, and online extortion. Large criminal organizations can be very efficient perpetrators of identity theft because they can exploit large amounts of personal information (obtained, for example, from a cracker who broke into a company's Web server) very quickly and efficiently.

These criminal organizations often sell or trade information that they cannot use immediately to other organized crime entities around the world. Some of these criminal transactions are even conducted online. For example, a cracker who has planted Trojan horses in a number of computers can sell the entire group, called a **bot farm** or a **zombie farm**, online to an organized crime association that wants to launch an attack against a competitor (perhaps a company that competes with one of their legitimate business entities). Most experts believe that the percentage of online crime committed by organized crime associations will continue to increase.

Online Espionage, Warfare, and Terrorism

In recent years, countries have devoted considerable spying efforts to gaining information from private businesses located in other countries. Countries do this type of spying, called **industrial espionage**, to capture intellectual property such as trade secrets, drug formulas, manufacturing process designs, software code, and other information. The government spy agency then gives (or sells) that information to businesses in their home country. When these types of information are stored in computers that are connected to the Internet or when they are transmitted over the Internet, the information can become the target of online espionage efforts.

Many Internet security experts believe that we have entered a new age of terrorism and warfare that could be carried out or coordinated through the Internet. Hate groups and terrorist organizations are gaining a presence on the Web, openly supporting or operating sites that promote their views. Web sites that contain detailed instructions for creating biological weapons and other poisons, discussion boards that help terrorist groups recruit new members online, and sites that offer downloadable terrorist training films now number in the thousands.

The Internet provides an effective communications network on which many people and businesses have become dependent. Although the Internet was designed from its inception to continue operating while under attack, a sustained effort by a well-financed terrorist group or rogue state could slow down the operation of major transaction-processing centers. As more business communications traffic moves to the Internet, the potential damage that could result from this type of attack increases.

Copyright and Intellectual Property Threats and Countermeasures

In previous tutorials you learned about copyright and intellectual property rights. Protecting this property is a security issue, although the methods used to protect copyrights and intellectual property differ from those used to protect other types of data. Threats to intellectual property result from the relative ease with which one can use existing material without the owner's permission. Actual monetary damage resulting from a copyright infringement is more difficult to measure than damage from secrecy, integrity, or necessity violations, but the harm can be just as great. The intellectual property owner loses the earnings (for example, royalties or related consulting fees) from the property and can no longer control its use by others.

The technology of the Internet facilitates copyright infringement in two ways. First, it is very easy to reproduce an exact copy of anything you find on the Internet, regardless of its copyright restrictions. Second, many people are simply naïve or unaware of copyright restrictions that protect intellectual property. Examples of both unwitting and willful Web copyright occur on a daily basis.

Although copyright laws were enacted before the creation of the Internet, the Internet itself has complicated the enforcement of copyrights by publishers. Recognizing the unauthorized reprinting of written text is relatively easy; tracing the path of a photograph that has been used on a Web page without authorization is far more difficult.

Digital Watermarking and Steganography

Some companies that distribute copyrighted art and photographs use digital watermarking and steganography to help protect their ownership interest in those materials. A **digital watermark** is a digital pattern containing copyright information that is inserted into a digital image, animation, or audio or video file. The watermark is inserted into the file using a software program so that it is invisible and undetectable. To view the digital watermark, a software program unlocks the watermark, retrieving the information it stores. Mark might be able to use a digital watermark to add RVP's copyright information to his video and animated clips. If his clips are ever published elsewhere, the digital watermark would prove that they belong to RVP.

Steganography can also protect digital works. **Steganography** is a process that hides encrypted messages within different types of files. Steganography is based on the fact that digital sound, video, image, and animation files contain portions of unused data where secret messages can be hidden. Steganography is generally used as a way to hide messages within different forms of communication, but it can be used to add copyright information to different types of files.

Mark is interested in learning more about digital watermarks and the companies that provide them. He is also interested in learning more about steganography. He wants to ensure that any files he places on the RVP Web site are properly covered by copyright protection.

To learn more about protecting copyrighted works on the Web:

▶ **1.** On the Online Companion page for Tutorial 7, click one of the links in the **Digital Watermarks and Steganography** section.

▶ **2.** Examine the site to learn more about approaches to digital watermarking, steganography, and other protections that Web site owners can use to protect copyrighted property they have made available on their sites.

▶ **3.** When you have finished exploring the site you chose, use your Web browser's **Close** button to return to the Online Companion and select another site. Click the link to that site and examine it for similar information.

▶ **4.** When you have finished exploring these sites, close your Web browser.

You can summarize your findings about how RVP's Web site might use digital watermarks and steganography in a short memo to Mark.

Now that Mark has a better understanding of the main types of online security threats and who perpetrates them, you can provide him with information about specific threats and countermeasures. You will learn about specific Web client, communication channel, and Web server threats and countermeasures in Session 7.2.

Session 7.1 Quick Check | Review

1. What are the three basic categories of computer security threats?
2. What is encryption?
3. What is a Trojan horse program?
4. An attack launched by one or more computers that is designed to overload a Web server and thus reduce or eliminate its ability to respond to legitimate requests for Web pages is called a _____ .
5. What is the difference between a hacker and a cracker?
6. What is identity theft?
7. Why is online extortion a more significant threat to smaller businesses than larger businesses?
8. What are two countermeasures for protecting digitally copyrighted works when they are posted on the Web?

Session 7.2

Web Client Security

Mark is interested in learning how to apply the security principles from Session 7.1 to the specific threats that face RVP. A good place to start is with security on the PCs that RVP has connected to its network and security through that network to the Internet. These computers run Web browsers and, as you learned earlier in this book, are thus called

Web clients. In this session, you will learn about security threats and countermeasures for Web clients, the communication channel that connects Web clients to Web servers, and the Web servers themselves. One of the most important Web client security risks arises from the existence of active content.

Active Content: Java, JavaScript, and ActiveX

One of the most dangerous entry points for denial of service threats come from programs that travel with applications to a browser and execute on the user's computer. These programs, often called **active content**, include Java, JavaScript, and ActiveX components that can run programs on a Web client computer. Active content components can make Web pages more useful by providing interactive elements like shipping calculations or mortgage payment tables. Animated diagrams and instructions can also be created with active content. Unfortunately, these components can also be used for malicious purposes.

For example, a **Java applet**, which is a program written in the Java programming language, could execute and consume a computer's resources. Similarly, a **JavaScript program** can pose a problem because it can run without being compiled (translated into computer-readable codes). A cleverly written JavaScript program could examine your computer's programs and email a file from your computer back to a Web server.

ActiveX components are Microsoft's technology for writing small applications that perform some action in Web pages; these components have access to a computer's file system. For example, a hidden ActiveX component in a Web page could scan a hard drive for PCX and JPEG files and print them on any network printer. Similarly, an ActiveX component could reformat a hard drive.

Because ActiveX controls are so potentially dangerous, Microsoft has built into Internet Explorer a system of identifying ActiveX controls that have been created by known software developers. These controls include a digital certificate (you will learn more about digital certificates later in this session) that identifies the developer; such controls are called **signed ActiveX controls**. Internet Explorer maintains a list of known developers and examines the digital certificate on any ActiveX control before it is downloaded to determine if it is a signed ActiveX control.

ActiveX components only work in Internet Explorer and other browsers that use the Internet Explorer code base in some way. Thus, Firefox, which does not use any part of the Internet Explorer code base, cannot run a beneficial ActiveX component, nor can it be attacked by a malicious ActiveX component.

Although most Java, JavaScript, and ActiveX components are beneficial, you can protect your computer from potential attacks that use them. Perhaps the simplest strategy is to prevent these programs from running by preventing your Web browser from running Java and JavaScript programs.

Note: If you are using Internet Explorer, complete the first set of steps. If you are using Firefox, skip to the next set of steps.

To strengthen security in Internet Explorer:

▶ **1.** Start Internet Explorer.

▶ **2.** Click the **Tools** button in the browser window, and then click **Internet Options**. The Internet Options dialog box opens.

3. Click the **Security** tab to display your security settings. The Internet zone is selected by default and it is appropriate for use when you are viewing most Web sites. The Internet zone's default setting of Medium-high will cause the browser to prompt you before it downloads potentially unsafe content and prevents the browser from downloading unsigned ActiveX controls. The Local intranet zone has a default security level of Medium-low and is appropriate for Web sites that are on an intranet to which you are connected. The Trusted sites zone has a default security level of Medium and is appropriate for Web sites that you know are safe. The Restricted sites zone has a default security level of High and is appropriate for Web sites that you know to be potentially hazardous to your computer.

4. If directed to do so by your instructor, select a different zone by clicking the appropriate icon in the top panel.

5. Click and drag the slider control in the Security level for this zone box to the top position. The security level changes to High, and a short description of the selected security level appears below the bold security setting, as shown in Figure 7-6.

> **Tip**
>
> Advanced users can click the Custom level button and set many individual options for controlling the way ActiveX controls and other commands are executed by the browser.

Changing the security level in Internet Explorer   **Figure 7-6**

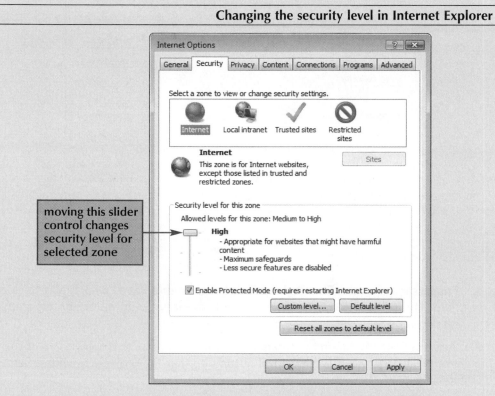

moving this slider control changes security level for selected zone

6. Click the **Default level** button in the Security level for this zone box. The slider control returns to its default setting (Medium-high for the Internet zone).

7. Click the **Cancel** button to close the dialog box without applying any of your changes.

   Trouble? Selecting a higher security level will increase protection for your computer, but it might cause some Web sites that you have visited in the past to stop working properly. Check with your instructor or lab manager before changing any browser's security settings on a school computer.

Note: If you are using Firefox, complete the following set of steps. If you are using Internet Explorer, skip these steps.

To strengthen security in Firefox:

▶ **1.** Start Firefox.

▶ **2.** Click **Tools** on the browser menu bar, and then click **Options** to open the Options dialog box.

▶ **3.** Click **Content** in the top panel of the dialog box to display some of the Firefox settings that affect the level of security that the browser provides. See Figure 7-7.

Figure 7-7 ▶ Firefox Options dialog box, Content tab

▶ **4.** If necessary, click the **Enable JavaScript** and **Enable Java** check boxes to clear them. This will prevent Java programs and JavaScript plug-ins or applets from running automatically.

▶ **5.** Click the **Security** tab in the top panel of the dialog box to display more of the Firefox settings that affect the level of security that the browser provides. See Figure 7-8.

6. If necessary, click the **Warn me when sites try to install add-ons** check box to select it. If selected, Firefox will warn you when a Web site is about to install active content (such as programs, plug-ins, and applets) into your browser.

7. Click the **Cancel** button to close the dialog box without applying any of your changes.

Tip

Advanced users can use the Exceptions button and Advanced tab in the Options dialog box to customize the security warnings and operation of the browser.

Mark appreciates the information about active content security threats and how to customize the settings in Internet Explorer and Firefox to prevent these programs from running without warning you first. There are other threats to the Web client computers on RVP's network; one of the most widely known threats comes from a browser's use of cookies.

Managing Cookies

In most cases, Web sites that use and store cookies do so to enhance your Web browsing experience, and most cookies are safe. However, some cookies can pose security risks. Recall that a cookie is a small text file that a Web server creates and stores on your computer's hard drive. A cookie might store data about the links you click while visiting the Web site (called a **clickstream**), information about the products you purchase, or personal information that you provide to the site. Some cookies are removed automatically when you leave a Web site (a session-only cookie) or on a specific expiration date, such as a year from the date the cookie was written. Other cookies have no expiration date, meaning that they will remain stored on your hard drive until you delete them.

If you have visited a site that asks for your ZIP code so it can provide local weather and entertainment information, that site probably stored a cookie on your hard drive. When you return to that site, the site searches your hard drive for a cookie file it might have written on a previous visit. If the site does not find a cookie, then it loads its default home page. If the site does find a cookie that it wrote, it reads the information stored in the file and displays a customized version of the home page, tailored for you based on the information stored in the file. The site could use information it stored in a cookie to enter your login and password for you. In some cases, the site might display your name and links to products or services that are similar to your previous visit's clickstream. The site might also track your purchases and make recommendations based on products you have purchased in the past.

A cookie is not a program, and it can only store information that you provide to the Web site that creates it. Sometimes you provide this data openly, such as when you enter a value in a field on a form. Other times, the cookie might silently record your behavior (for example, which pages you viewed and in what order you viewed them) at a Web site. Only the Web site that stored the cookie on your hard drive can read it, and it cannot read other cookies on your hard drive or any other file on your computer.

Mark asks about the advisability of having the RVP Web server place cookies on RVP's customers' computers when they visit the Web site. In most cases, cookies are harmless. A cookie might make it easier for a client to find what she needs at the RVP Web site, or it might save her some time in completing an on-screen form. However, cookies can represent a security threat for some users, especially those who access the site from a public computer. For example, if you place an order at Amazon.com (a Web site that uses cookies to help users log in and find products that might appeal to them) using a computer at a public library, the server at Amazon.com will store a cookie on the public computer's hard drive with information about you. When the next user visits Amazon.com, the server might identify the new user as you and could display information based on your previous visits to the Web site. If the cookie stores information about your recent purchases, this new user might be able to place an order using your account, which might include your credit card information and mailing address. Obviously, this problem greatly compromises your ability to keep information about yourself secret, especially if you were looking at products and services at the site that you don't want other users to know that you have viewed. Fortunately, Internet users can control the storage of cookies on their computer's hard drive by changing their browser's settings.

InSight	**How Web Browsers Store Cookies**

Internet Explorer stores cookies on your computer's hard drive in the C:\Windows\Cookies folder (the path to cookie files on your computer might be different depending on how Windows is installed on your computer). Firefox stores all cookies on your computer's hard drive in a file named cookies.txt (the location of this file depends on how Firefox was installed on your computer). To view a cookie's contents, you can open the file in any text editor; in most cases, you will see numbers and codes that will not make sense to you.

Both Internet Explorer and Firefox include commands that let you specify your preferences for accepting, managing, and deleting cookies.

Note: If you are using Internet Explorer, complete the first set of steps. If you are using Firefox, skip to the next set of steps.

Tip
You can delete all of the cookies on the computer, but remember that doing so might delete helpful and time-saving cookies, too.

To learn more about managing cookies in Internet Explorer:

▶ **1.** If you are using Internet Explorer, click the **Tools** button, click **Internet Options**, and then click the **General** tab, if necessary.

▶ **2.** Click the **Delete** button in the Browsing history section of the dialog box to open the Delete Browsing History dialog box, then click the Cookies check box (if it is not already checked) as shown in Figure 7-9. If you click the Delete button in this dialog box, you will delete all of the items selected. Do not click the Delete button unless you are certain you want to delete all cookies (and any other selected categories of items).

Deleting cookies in Internet Explorer ◀ **Figure 7-9**

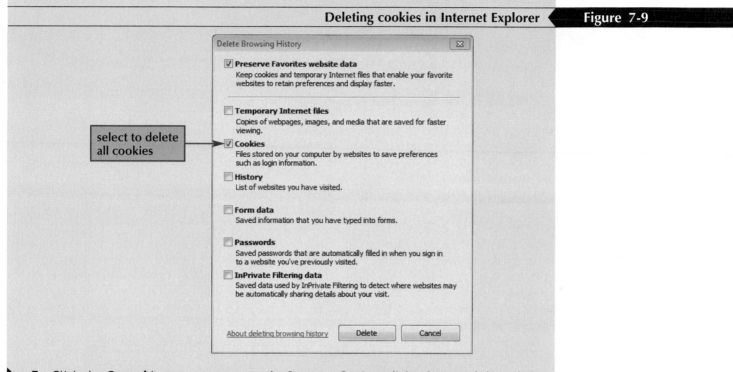

▶ **3.** Click the **Cancel** button to return to the Internet Options dialog box, and then click the **Privacy** tab. The tab shown in Figure 7-10 appears. On this tab you can move the slider up or down to select various combinations of accepting or blocking all cookies or accepting some cookies and blocking others.

Figure 7-10 ▶ Changing cookie settings in Internet Explorer

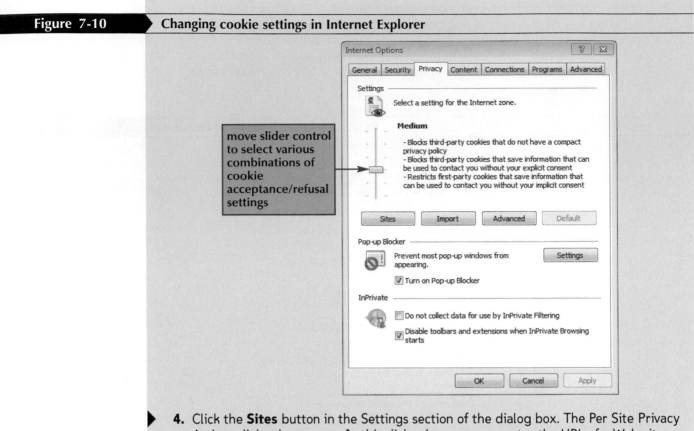

move slider control to select various combinations of cookie acceptance/refusal settings

▶ **4.** Click the **Sites** button in the Settings section of the dialog box. The Per Site Privacy Actions dialog box opens. In this dialog box, you can enter the URL of a Web site and then choose to always allow or always block cookies from that site, regardless of the choice you made for handling cookies in the Cookies section in the Options dialog box.

▶ **5.** Click the **OK** button to close the Per Site Privacy Actions dialog box, and then click the **Cancel** button to close the Internet Options dialog box.

Note: If you are using Firefox, complete the following set of steps. If you are using Internet Explorer, skip this set of steps.

To learn more about managing cookies in Firefox:

▶ **1.** If you are using Firefox, click **Tools** on the menu bar, and then click **Options**. The Options dialog box opens.

▶ **2.** Click the **Privacy** icon in the top panel of the dialog box, if necessary, to open the dialog box that appears in Figure 7-11.

Changing cookie settings in Firefox ◀ Figure 7-11

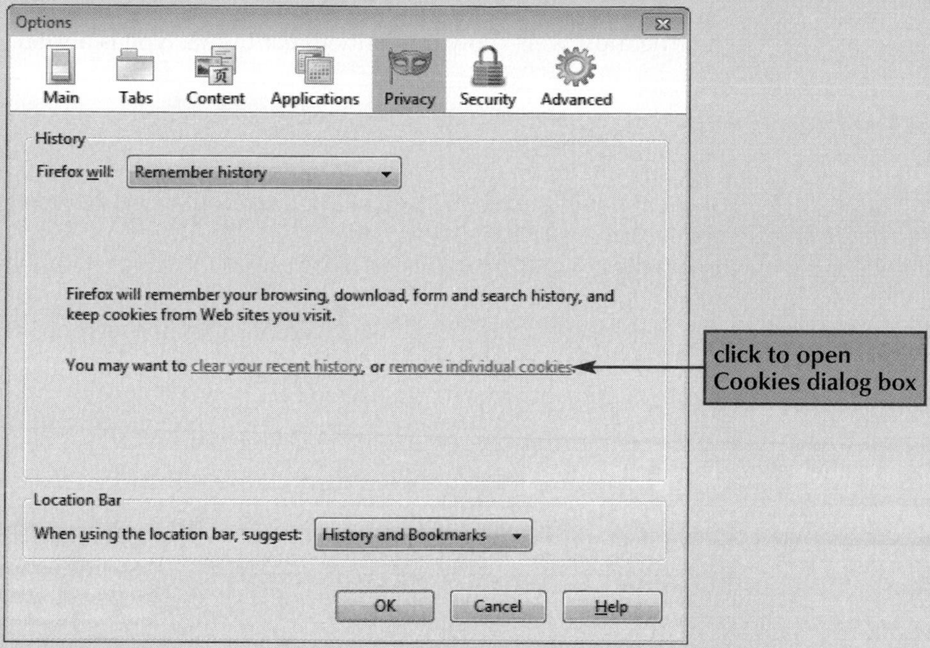

click to open
Cookies dialog box

▶ **3.** Click the **remove individual cookies** link. The Cookies dialog box shown in Figure 7-12 opens. Each cookie is stored in a folder named with the URL of the Web site that issued the cookie. To open a folder and display its cookies, click the arrow icon to the left of the folder. In this dialog box, you can select an individual cookie, examine its content, and remove it if you wish.

The Cookies dialog box in Firefox ◀ Figure 7-12

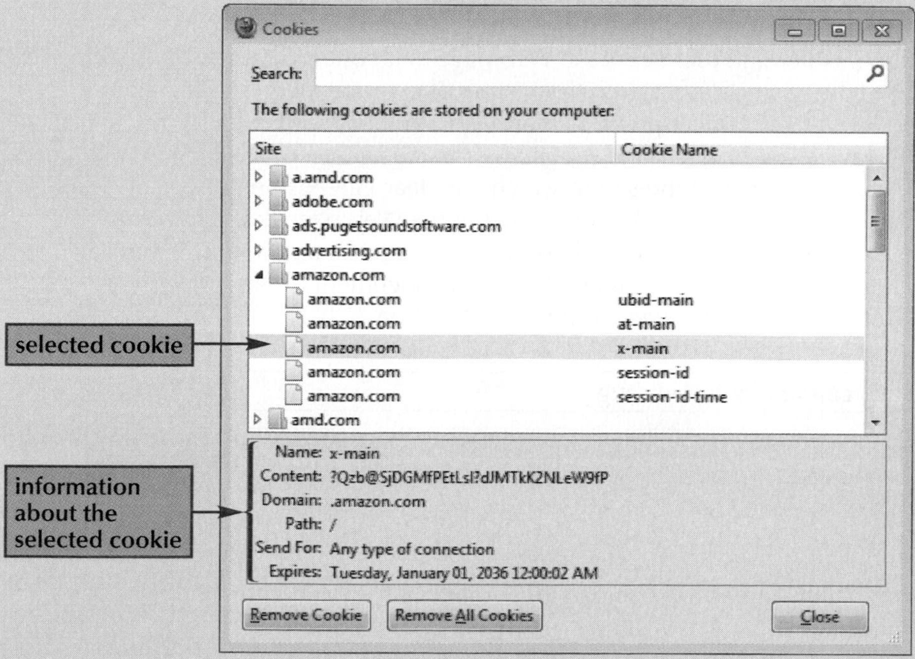

selected cookie

information
about the
selected cookie

▶ **4.** Click the **Close** button to close the Cookies dialog box.

Some sites provide information in their privacy policy to let the user know that the site uses cookies and what type of data it stores in the cookies it writes to the visitor's computer. In addition to potentially revealing private information, cookies can pose a threat in terms of security. The most well-known security threat of this type is a Web bug.

Web Bugs

A **Web bug** is a small, hidden graphic on a Web page or in an email message that is designed to work in conjunction with a cookie to obtain information about the person viewing the page or email message and to send that information to a third party.

The hidden graphic is usually a GIF file with a size of one pixel, which is approximately the same size as the period at the end of this sentence. Because a Web bug is usually created with a GIF file, it is sometimes called a clear GIF or a transparent GIF because it is designed to be hidden on the Web page in which it appears. Figure 7-13 shows a section of an HTML document that creates a Web bug in a Web page.

Figure 7-13   **HTML document containing a Web bug**

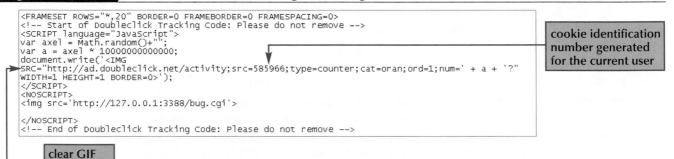

```
<FRAMESET ROWS="*,20" BORDER=0 FRAMEBORDER=0 FRAMESPACING=0>
<!-- Start of Doubleclick Tracking Code: Please do not remove -->
<SCRIPT language="JavaScript">
var axel = Math.random()+"";
var a = axel * 10000000000000;
document.write('<IMG
SRC="http://ad.doubleclick.net/activity;src=585966;type=counter;cat=oran;ord=1;num=' + a + '?"
WIDTH=1 HEIGHT=1 BORDER=0>');
</SCRIPT>
<NOSCRIPT>
<img src='http://127.0.0.1:3388/bug.cgi'>

</NOSCRIPT>
<!-- End of Doubleclick Tracking Code: Please do not remove -->
```

cookie identification number generated for the current user

clear GIF file location

Notice that the location of the clear GIF (in the HTML SRC attribute) is a URL for DoubleClick, a division of Google that develops tools for Internet marketing and advertising. When the user loads the Web page that contains this code, the browser downloads the clear GIF file from the DoubleClick server. DoubleClick has a network of thousands of members that provide information to it. The process of downloading the clear GIF file can identify your IP address, the Web site you last visited, and other information about your use of the site in which the clear GIF has been embedded and record it in the cookie file. Figure 7-14 shows part of the Web page that contains the Web bug. Notice that the GIF file is not visible because it is transparent and therefore hidden. Clearly, you would need to examine the HTML document (in the previous figure) that is the source file of this Web page to find the Web bug.

Figure 7-14   **Web page containing a Web bug**

| computers | software | electronics | cellular | music | games | video | dvd | books | bags | clearance |

clear GIF file location

When you first access a DoubleClick member's Web site, DoubleClick uses a cookie, sometimes called an ad-serving cookie or marketing cookie, to assign you a number and record it. Then, when you visit any DoubleClick member's Web site in the future, DoubleClick reads the ad-serving cookie it wrote on your hard drive and gets your identification number. As you use your browser to visit different Web sites, DoubleClick can use its ad-serving cookie to collect information about the sites you visit and sell this information to its members so they can customize their Web sites with advertising tailored to your interests.

For example, if you have been shopping online for a new computer and you notice that suddenly you are seeing a large number of ads for computers on different Web sites, an ad-serving cookie is likely responsible for the apparent coincidence. An ad-serving cookie might also cause you to receive email messages that contain ads for computers. Some people see this technology as an invasion of privacy; you might not want various computer vendors knowing that you are looking for a new computer, and you might object to receiving email messages from them.

Adware and Spyware: Ethical Issues

Adware is a general category of software that includes advertisements to help pay for the product in which they appear. Many freeware and shareware programs are sold as adware, a practice that provides opportunities for developers to offer software at little or no cost to the user. In itself, adware does not cause any security threats because the user is aware of the ads and the parties responsible for including ads are clearly identified in the programs.

Spyware works much like adware except that the user has no control over or knowledge of the ads and other monitoring features the ads contain. If you use an adware program, the developer tells you that your use of the free software is supported by ads that you will see when you use it, and the developer provides information about how to disable the ads (usually by paying a fee to use the software ad-free). Spyware is just like adware except that the spyware vendor does not inform the user that the software will include ads. Software that gathers personal information about the user's behavior (such as which sites the user visits or what search expressions the user enters on a search engine site) or the user's computer (such as what type of software or hardware is installed on the computer) without the knowledge of the user is also called spyware. Some people find adware to be offensive. Those people can choose not to use adware or can disable the ads by converting the software to a paid version. Spyware is less open about what it does. Many people download and install spyware only to learn about the ads when they start using the software. Worse, people that download spyware that secretly gathers personal information might never learn what the program is doing.

A Web bug is an example of spyware because the clear GIF and its actions are hidden from the user. Spyware is not illegal (unless it is used as part of a criminal activity, such as gathering information to be used in identity theft), but it does create privacy concerns for many Web users, and many people believe that spyware is unethical. The programs you install, especially freeware and shareware programs, might include spyware to track your use of the programs and of the Internet, or they might collect data about you and distribute that data to a third party.

Intuit, the producer of a leading personal income tax program called TurboTax, included a program named SAFECAST/C-Dilla in its software for 2002 tax returns. This program monitors the CD-ROM drives on the machine on which it is installed to prevent duplication of the disk. Although Intuit included this program to protect its copyright and prevent duplication of the program, users were outraged to learn that a program had been installed on their hard drives without warning. Intuit apologized to its users and removed the SAFECAST/C-Dilla program from its products before the end of the 2002 tax filing season. Intuit's actions were not illegal, but by removing the program from its product, Intuit acknowledged the questionable ethics of including a tracking program with a product that its users paid for every year.

Mark is concerned about companies like Google (through its DoubleClick division) collecting data about his employees' use of the Internet, especially if they are free to sell it to other companies that might use that data to send email and other messages to RVP employees. These extra messages might distract employees from doing their jobs, and they would consume network resources at RVP. Mark asks you how to prevent third-party sites from collecting data using ad-serving cookies. He is also concerned about Web bugs and spyware. You explain to Mark that one line of defense is to set Web browsers to block third-party cookie files. In addition, there are many good programs that erase spyware from your computer. These programs, sometimes called **ad blockers**, search for files written by known spyware. The results of a scan by one of these programs, Ad-Aware from Lavasoft, appears in Figure 7-15. You can learn more about ad blockers, spyware, and adware by visiting the links included under the Spyware/Adware heading in the Additional Information section of the Online Companion page for Tutorial 7.

| Figure 7-15 | Results of a scan in Ad-Aware |

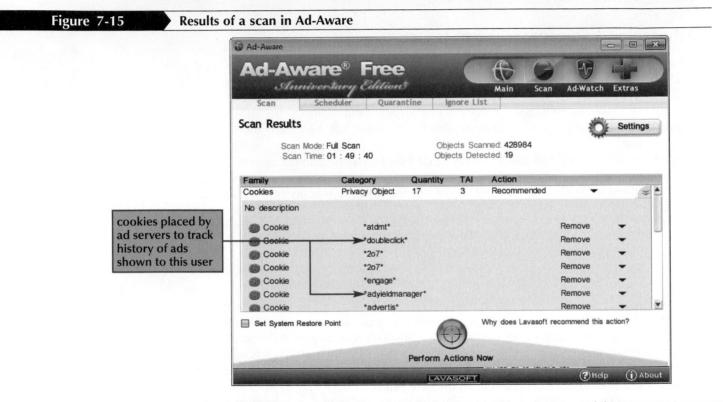

An additional way to defend servers and computers from the types of threats associated with cookies and spyware is a firewall.

Firewalls

Like its counterpart in the physical world, which acts as a barrier to keep a fire from spreading from one area of a building to another, the computer version of a **firewall** is a software program or hardware device that controls access between two networks, such as a local area network and the Internet or the Internet and a computer. Firewalls can be used on both Web servers and Web clients (that is, on both ends of the Internet communication channel). A Web client firewall might be a dedicated hardware device, as shown in Figure 7-16, or it might be a program running on the Web client computer.

Basic Web client firewall architecture   **Figure 7-16**

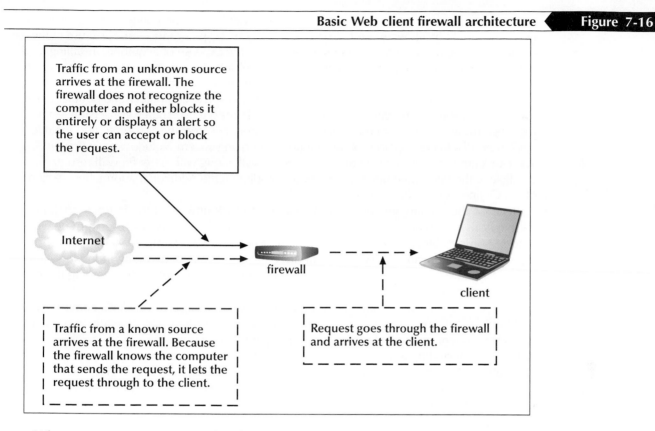

When a computer is connected to the Internet, it receives traffic from other computers without its user even realizing it. Most of this traffic is harmless, but without protection, a cracker can gain access to a computer through a port. A **port** on a computer is like a door; it permits traffic to leave and enter a computer. When the port is closed, traffic can't leave or enter the computer. The port might be a hardware interface, such as a parallel port to which you connect a printer, or it might be a virtual port that handles information.

Virtual ports use numbers to isolate traffic by type; a computer has more than 65,000 virtual ports for different processes such as HTTP/World Wide Web traffic (port 80), FTP traffic (port 21), SMTP email (port 25), POP3 email (port 110), and SSL (port 443). To connect to the Internet, you must open port 80. A cracker can use port 80 or other virtual ports to access your computer if its ports are not properly protected.

A firewall can control incoming traffic by rejecting it unless you have configured it to accept the traffic. For example, some Web sites include features that let you test the security of your computer by asking the site to run a port scan on your computer. During a **port scan**, one computer tests all or some of the ports of another computer to determine whether its ports are open (traffic is not filtered and the port permits entry through it), closed (the port does not accept traffic, but a cracker could use this port to gain entry to and analyze your computer), or stealth (the port might be open or closed, but permits no entry through it). You can run a port scan by visiting a Web site that offers this service. The Additional Information section of the Online Companion page for Tutorial 7 includes links to such sites under the heading Port Scan Sites.

Most firewalls are installed to prevent traffic from *entering* the network, but firewalls can also prevent data from *leaving* the network. This feature is especially useful for controlling the activities of hidden programs that are designed to compromise the security of a computer. When you install a new program on your computer, a firewall that provides this type of outgoing protection will notify you if the new program tries to access the Internet. You can then adjust the firewall settings to allow the program to access the Internet always, only when you approve such access, or never.

Until the recent increase in the number of users with broadband connections to the Internet, hardware firewalls were used almost exclusively by large organizations, because of the number of computers connected to the network and the expense of acquiring, installing, and maintaining the firewall. However, with some firewall software programs available free or at a very low cost, they have become popular with other types of users, including those with home networks or people accessing the Internet using a single computer. One popular personal firewall software program is ZoneAlarm, which offers a free shareware version. Antivirus programs and Internet security suites available from McAfee and Symantec also include basic firewalls. Recent versions of the Windows operating system include a basic firewall. You can learn more about using the Windows firewall, along with other firewall resources, by clicking the links listed under the Firewalls heading in the Additional Information section of the Online Companion page for Tutorial 7.

Because the primary function of a firewall is to block unwanted traffic from reaching the network it protects, each organization that installs a firewall needs to determine what kind of traffic to block and what kind of traffic to permit. For example, Mark might configure the RVP firewall to prevent unauthorized access to the network by individuals and computers outside the network, to prevent programs on the client from accessing the network to initiate data transfers, or both.

By installing a firewall, Mark can control the flow of data between RVP's computers and the Internet. You recommend that Mark seriously consider using firewalls to protect RVP's Web client computers either by installing individual firewall software on the computers or by installing a hardware firewall on RVP's Internet connection for those computers. Now that you have learned about specific security issues for Web client computers, it is time to learn more about security on the communication channel; that is, for information traveling on the Internet itself.

Communication Channel Security

In Session 7.1 you learned how encryption works. Encryption is an important part of maintaining security over information that is sent over the Internet. You explain to Mark that practical uses of encryption require that he know more about two important concepts: authentication and identification. These concepts will be important in ensuring the safe transmission of data sent by RVP employees.

Authentication and Digital Certificates

Authentication is a general term for the process of verifying the identity of a person or a Web site. Authentication countermeasures provide a way for Internet users to confirm the identity of a person from whom they received a message or to confirm the identity and stated security of a Web site with which they will conduct business. The primary countermeasure for authentication is a digital certificate.

A **digital certificate** is an encrypted and password-protected file that contains sufficient information to authenticate and prove a person's or organization's identity. Usually, a digital certificate contains the following information:

- The certificate holder's name, address, and email address
- A key that "unlocks" the digital certificate, thereby verifying the certificate's authenticity
- The certificate's expiration date or validity period
- Verification from a trusted third party, called a **certificate authority (CA)**, that authenticates the certificate holder's identity and issues the digital certificate

A digital certificate is an electronic equivalent of an identification card. For example, by looking at a person's driver's license, you can verify that person's identity by comparing the height, weight, and eye color printed on the license with the person using the driver's license to authenticate his or her identity. You can also compare the picture on the license with the face of the person presenting the license. A digital certificate lets you confirm a person's or an organization's identity using your Web browser or email program. There are two types of digital certificates. Individuals can purchase one type called a **digital ID** (also called a **personal certificate**). Purchasers of digital IDs can use them to identify themselves to other people and to Web sites that are set up to accept digital certificates. The other type of digital certificate is used by Web servers. You will learn about Web server digital certificates later in this session.

A digital ID is an electronic file that you purchase from a certificate authority and install into a program that uses it, such as an email program or a Web browser. Because a digital certificate is difficult to forge or tamper with, an individual can use one in place of a user name and password at some Web sites. The digital ID authenticates the user and protects data transferred online from being altered or stolen. Some email programs include features that send and receive digital IDs with email messages so recipients can use the digital ID to verify the sender's identity.

Digital IDs and Email		InSight

Most people who use digital IDs to protect email messages have a specific reason for doing so, such as lawyers who use email to send and receive messages that contain confidential or sensitive data.

The use of email messages that trick you into revealing personal information, including passwords and your Social Security number, is one of the Internet's most serious security threats. You will learn about this ploy in the next section.

Phishing Attacks

Thousands of consumers have received email messages from banks, online services such as PayPal and eBay, credit card companies, and other businesses indicating that their account data had been lost or must be verified to continue using the service. Many of these consumers knew immediately that the messages were not valid because they did not have an account with the bank or online business identified in the email message.

However, many other consumers did have an account with the apparent sender of the email. These consumers read the messages, clicked a hyperlink to go to a Web site that looked like it belonged to the correct business, and entered the required information into a form. The form illicitly collected the person's name, account number, Social Security number, user name, password, and other sensitive data.

Because the email message seemed genuine and the spoofed site contained the company's correct logos, many people participated in this type of scam without even realizing it. Many well-known organizations, including Visa, eBay, Earthlink, Citibank, and many central processing banks in the United Kingdom, including the Bank of England, have been spoofed in such a scam. Some sites discovered the fraudulent email messages when customers contacted them to verify the information. In some cases, the real sites had to go offline to prevent further attacks on their customers.

This type of attack, called **phishing** because it "fishes" for information, is difficult to prevent because it involves phony email messages that include links to spoofed Web sites. Most email users do not know how to authenticate email messages and Web sites to verify that the sender or site is real.

The basic structure of a phishing attack is fairly simple. The attacker sends email messages (such as the one shown in Figure 7-17) to a large number of recipients who might have an account at the targeted Web site (PayPal is the targeted site in the example shown in the figure).

Figure 7-17 **Phishing e-mail message**

Date: [Date removed] 08:05:42 +0600
From: "Services PayPal" <services@paypal.com>
Subject: PayPal Account sensitive features are access limited!
To: [E-mail addresses removed]

Dear valued **PayPal** member:

PayPal is committed to maintaining a safe environment for its community of
buyers and sellers. To protect the security of your account, PayPal employs
some of the most advanced security systems in the world and our anti-fraud
teams regularly screen the PayPal system for unusual activity.

Recently, our Account Review Team identified some unusual activity in your
account. In accordance with PayPal's User Agreement and to ensure that your
account has not been compromised, access to your account was limited. Your
account access will remain limited until this issue has been resolved. This
is a fraud prevention measure meant to ensure that your account is not compromised.

In order to secure your account and quickly restore full access, we may
require some specific information from you for the following reason:

We would like to ensure that your account was not accessed by an
unauthorized third party. Because protecting the security of your account
is our primary concern, we have limited access to sensitive PayPal account
features. We understand that this may be an inconvenience but please
understand that this temporary limitation is for your protection.

Case ID Number: PP-040-187-541

We encourage you to log in and restore full access as soon as possible.
Should access to your account remain limited for an extended period of
time, it may result in further limitations on the use of your account.

However, failure to restore your records will result in account suspension.
Please update your records within 48 hours. Once you have updated your account
records, your **PayPal** session will not be interrupted and will continue as normal.

To update your **Paypal** records click on the following link:
https://www.paypal.com/cgi-bin/webscr?cmd=_login-run

Thank you for your prompt attention to this matter. Please understand that
this is a security measure meant to help protect you and your account. We
apologize for any inconvenience.

Sincerely,
PayPal Account Review Department

PayPal Email ID PP522

Accounts Management As outlined in our User Agreement, **PayPal** will
periodically send you information about site changes and enhancements.

Visit our Privacy Policy and User Agreement if you have any questions.
http://www.paypal.com/cgi-bin/webscr?cmd=p/gen/ua/policy_privacy-outside

The email message tells the recipient that his or her account has been compromised
and it is necessary for the recipient to log in to the account to correct the matter. The
email message includes a link that appears to be a link to the login page of the Web site.
However, the link actually leads the recipient to the phishing attack perpetrator's Web
site, which is designed to look like the targeted Web site. The unsuspecting recipient

enters his or her login name and password, which the perpetrator captures and then uses to access the recipient's account. Once inside the victim's account, the perpetrator can access personal information, make purchases, or withdraw funds at will.

The links in phishing emails are usually disguised. One common way to disguise the real URL is to use the "@" sign, which causes the Web server to ignore all characters that precede the "@" and use only the characters that follow it. For example, a link that displays:

```
https://paypal.com@218.36.41.188/fl/login.html
```

looks like it is an address at PayPal. However, the "@" sign causes the Web server to ignore the "paypal.com" and instead takes the victim to a Web page at the IP address "218.36.41.188."

In the email shown earlier in Figure 7-17, the link appears in the victim's email client software as:

```
https://paypal.com/cgi-bin/webscr?cmd=_login-run
```

but when the victim clicks the link, the browser opens a completely different URL:

```
http://leasurelandscapes.com/snow/webscr.dll
```

Instead of the URL it shows in the email client, the link in the phishing email actually includes the following JavaScript code:

```
<A onmouseover="window.status='https://www.paypal.com/cgi-bin/
webscr?cmd=_login-run'; return true" onmouseout="window.status='https:
//www.paypal.com/cgi-bin/webscr?cmd=_login-run'"href="http:
//leasurelandscapes.com/snow/webscr.dll">https://www.paypal.com/
cgi-bin/webscr?cmd=_login-run</A>
```

This code was invisible in most email clients that were in use when the first phishing attacks were launched, so many victims never knew that their Web browsers had opened phony sites. An increasing number of email client software products now include a warning whenever a user attempts to open a link in an email message that opens a Web page with an address other than the text that appears in the message. Phishing attack perpetrators today use a variety of other tricks to hide their Web sites' true URLs, including code that creates pop-up windows that look exactly like a browser address bar. The window is programmed to open very quickly and postion itself to precisely cover the browser's address bar. You can learn more about the details of phishing techniques by visiting the Anti-Phishing Working Group's Web site.

To learn more about phishing attacks from the Anti-Phishing Working Group's Web site:

▶ 1. Type **www.cengage.com/internet/np/internet8** in the Address bar or Location bar of your Web browser to open the Online Companion page, log on to your account, click the **Tutorial 7** link, click the **Session 7.2** link, and then click the **APWG (Anti-Phishing Working Group)** link.

▶ 2. Click the links on the page to read articles and news reports on the site to learn more about phishing and what companies are doing to control this security threat.

▶ 3. When you have finished exploring the site, click your browser's **Close** button to return to the Online Companion page for Tutorial 7.

Web Server Security

In Session 7.1, you learned how encryption works, and in this session you have learned how it can be used to enhance the security of messages sent over the Internet communication channel. Mark is interested in learning more about how encryption can be used to help secure the RVP Web site. You explain that just as digital certificates help protect data sent from one individual to another, they can help protect data sent from and received by a Web server as it delivers Web pages to site visitors.

Digital Certificates for Web Servers

Web sites account for the largest percentage of digital certificates in use. A **server certificate** (sometimes called an SSL Web server certificate) authenticates a Web site so site visitors can be confident that the Web site is genuine and not an impostor. A server certificate also ensures that the transfer of data between a user's computer and the server is encrypted so that it is both tamperproof and free from being intercepted. Most Web browsers automatically receive and process digital certificates from Web sites. Figure 7-18 shows a basic representation of how a Web server digital certificate works.

| Figure 7-18 | Processing a Web server digital certificate |

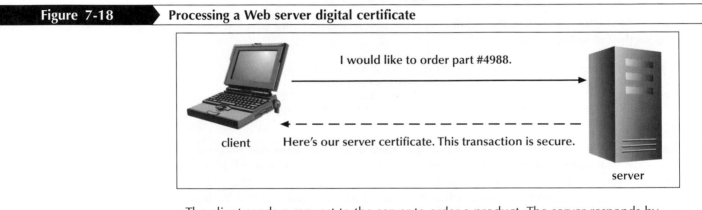

The client sends a request to the server to order a product. The server responds by sending the company's server certificate to the client's browser. The browser responds by confirming the certificate's authenticity. The customer can then continue with the transaction, knowing that the data exchanged with the server is secure.

One of the first certificate authorities to issue server certificates, Thawte, provides digital solutions that protect and secure communication and data on the Internet. Figure 7-19 shows the Thawte Web Server Certificates page.

Thawte SSL Web Server Certificates page ◢ **Figure 7-19**

You decide to visit the Thawte Web site to search for more information about server certificates and learn how they can benefit RVP.

To explore the Thawte Web site and learn about server certificates:

▶ **1.** On the Online Companion page for Tutorial 7, click the **Thawte SSL Facts** link.

▶ **2.** Read the information on the page that opens, paying particular attention to the kind of information a certificate stores, why a company such as RVP needs a certificate, and the benefits Thawte offers to its clients.

▶ **3.** You can click any links on the page that lead to more information about server certificates. Mark needs to know about the benefits he will gain by purchasing a certificate and how to apply for one.

Trouble? The Thawte Web site might change its appearance and content over time. Use the resources and links on the Thawte Web site to learn as much about server certificates as you can.

▶ **4.** When you have obtained the information Mark needs, return to the Online Companion page for Tutorial 7.

User Identification and Authentication

Many online businesses allow customers to create user accounts, which let them check purchase history, create new orders, and perform other personalized tasks. You tell Mark that he might want to let returning customers create and log on to an account that they have created on the RVP Web server to make it easy for them to schedule services and check on their account status. However, if he includes this functionality, Mark needs to ensure the security of user data stored on the server.

User identification is an important countermeasure against different types of secrecy threats. **User identification** is the process of identifying yourself to a computer. Most computer systems implement user identification with user names and passwords; the combination of a user name and password is sometimes called a **login**. Many Web sites require you to establish a user name and password before you can use the site. You can create almost any user name and password you like—these IDs do not have to correspond with your real name. Only you should know your user name and password because the Web site or other computer system assumes that the person who enters the login information is, in fact, the identified user and grants account access to that person.

If you are using a computer that other people can access (for example, a computer in a school lab or at work), you should be careful to log out of Web sites when you are finished using them. If you have multiple browser windows open, your login can remain active even if you close the browser window in which you opened a specific site. One way that Web sites can limit the risk for their customers is to have the Web server log out inactive connections after a period of time. Web sites that allow customers to log in and conduct purchase or sale transactions might log out inactive users after a short period of time, whereas sites that provide information might allow a longer amount of time to elapse before logging out an inactive user. And Web sites that handle financial transactions, such as banks or stock brokerage firms, usually log out inactive users after a very short time—often as little as 60 seconds.

InSight | **Password Effectiveness**

The effectiveness of the user identification system is tied to the strength of the passwords it accepts. Because users create their own passwords, only the user can determine the password's strength. The strongest passwords are those that contain many characters consisting of random strings of letters not found in a dictionary, including numbers and special characters, and combinations of uppercase and lowercase letters. In addition to creating strong passwords, users should avoid using the same password for multiple logins.

To help keep track of their login information for different computers and Web sites, some people use a program called a **password manager**, which stores login information in an encrypted form on their computers. You can learn more about this type of software by clicking the links listed under the Password Managers heading in the Additional Information section of the Online Companion page for Tutorial 7.

Crackers can run programs that create and enter passwords from a dictionary or a list of commonly used passwords to break into a system. A **brute force attack** occurs when a cracker uses a program to enter character combinations until the system accepts a user name and password, thereby gaining access to the system. (Some systems will send a warning to the computer's operator or lock out a user name when someone makes a predetermined number of unsuccessful attempts to log in to a system.) Depending on the system to which the cracker gained access, the damage can range anywhere from reading a person's email messages to gaining access to accounts at financial institutions. Another example of a brute force attack occurs when a cracker submits combinations of numbers to a Web site that accepts credit card payments until the site accepts one. In this case, the cracker can then charge goods and services using the card number that he has discovered and stolen.

When he adds the functionality for creating user accounts to the RVP Web site, Mark will include the information you provided about creating strong passwords so his customers can benefit from it. He asks you how RVP will maintain the secrecy of the user's login information if the user forgets or misplaces it. You tell him that he can include a feature that authenticates the user. **User authentication** is the process of associating a person and his identification with a very high level of assurance. In other words, authentication techniques give a high level of confidence that *you* are correctly identified when *you* log in. Authentication countermeasures include using biometrics, such as a retina scan or fingerprint scan, or asking one or more questions to which only the authentic user could know the correct answers. The system that stores and manages user names and passwords must provide security against threats. Most systems store passwords (and sometimes user names) in an encrypted format to protect them.

The combination of user login plus password is called **single-factor authentication** because it uses one factor; in this case, something the user knows (the password and login). **Multifactor authentication** relies on more than one factor. For example, when you use an ATM, the bank requires that you enter a PIN (one factor, something you know) and insert your ATM card into the card reader (a second factor, something you have). A third factor could be something the user is (for example, a physical characteristic such as a fingerprint or retinal image). Banks use multi-factor authentication for financial transactions because the risk of loss is significant. Another approach that banks and financial institutions use to add security to online transactions is multiple layers of control. **Multiple layers of control** can be implemented by using more than one authentication method. For example, most online banking sites will require you to answer a challenge question (to which you supplied the answer when you set up your account) in addition to supplying the usual login and password when its Web server detects that you are trying to access your account from a different computer than you usually use.

Based on your research, Mark is convinced that a server certificate will help ensure the secrecy of data exchanged by clients and the RVP Web site. One of the terms with which he is unfamiliar is SSL, which appears frequently on the Thawte Web site. He asks you to explain this concept to him so he understands how SSL affects the RVP Web site.

Secure Sockets Layer (SSL) and Transport Layer Security (TSL)

The **Secure Sockets Layer (SSL)** was the first widely used protocol for establishing secure, encrypted connections between Web browsers and Web servers on the Internet. SSL was revised several times and is still used. In 1999, SSL version 3 was improved and reissued by the Internet Engineering Task Force. This improved protocol is called **Transport Layer Security (TSL)**. Both SSL and TSL provide a security "handshake" when a browser and the Web page to which it is connected want to participate in a secure connection. Most Web sites automatically switch to a secure state and encrypt data when it is necessary to do so, such as when the site requests personal or payment information. Web pages secured by SSL or TSL have URLs that begin with *https://* instead of *http://*; the "s" indicates a secure connection. Figure 7-20 shows the Internet Explorer security icon in the browser's address window. Firefox displays a similar padlock icon on the right side of its status bar at the bottom of the browser window. Clicking the padlock in either browser opens a dialog box that provides details about the site's server certificate, expiration date, and the certificate authority that issued it. When the user finishes the transaction and browses to another Web page, the browser and Web server return to a normal (unsecured and not encrypted) state, which is indicated by the disappearance of the padlock icon.

Figure 7-20 Secure state indicator in Internet Explorer

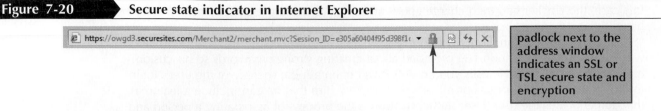

padlock next to the address window indicates an SSL or TSL secure state and encryption

SSL and TSL both use a public key to encrypt a private key and send it from the Web server to the browser. Once the browser decrypts the private key, it uses that private key to encrypt information sent to the Web server during the SSL/TSL connection because private-key encryption is faster than public-key encryption. When the user leaves the secure Web site, the browser terminates the SSL/TSL connection and discards these temporary keys, or **session keys**. Session keys exist only during a single connection (session) between a browser and server.

Although the use of SSL and TSL increased Web users' confidence in online shopping and banking sites, some certification authorities were performing the minimum level of verification of applicants for SSL certificates before issuing them. A growing concern that fraudulent Web sites (including phishing sites) might have obtained SSL certificates led a group of certification authorities to develop a more stringent set of verification steps. In 2008, this development led to the establishment of stricter criteria and an assurance of consistent application of verification procedures. Certification authorities that followed these more extensive verification procedures were permitted to issue a new type of certificate called **Secure Sockets Layer-Extended Validation** (**SSL-EV**). To issue an SSL-EV certificate, a certification authority must confirm the legal existence of the organization by verifying the organization's registered legal name, registration number, registered address, and physical business address. The certification authority must also verify the organization's right to use the domain name and that the organization has authorized the request for an SSL-EV certificate. You can tell if you are visiting a Web site that has an SSL-EV certificate by looking at the address window of your browser. In Internet Explorer, the background of the address window turns green and the verified name of the organization appears to the right of the URL and alternates with the name of the certification authority, as shown in Figure 7-21. In Firefox, the site's verified organization name appears in the address window to the left of the URL, as shown in Figure 7-22.

Figure 7-21 Address of SSL-EV secure site in Internet Explorer

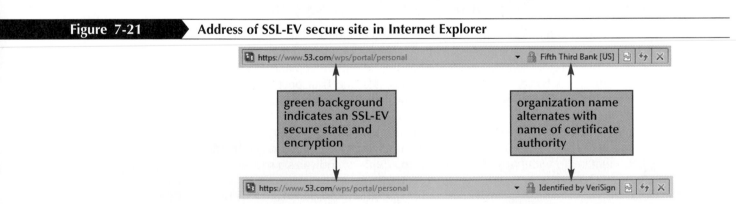

green background indicates an SSL-EV secure state and encryption

organization name alternates with name of certificate authority

Address of SSL-EV secure site in Firefox ◀ **Figure 7-22**

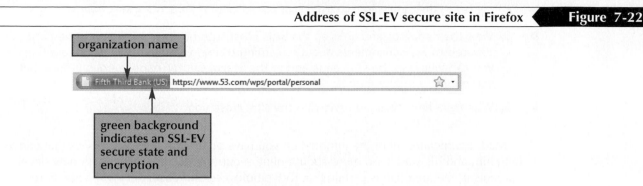

Mark asks if there are any other precautions that he needs to take to protect the RVP Web server, the RVP computers, and his clients' computers. You tell Mark that the firewall protection you discussed earlier would help prevent attacks on the Web server as well as the Web client computers if he installs it at the point where all of RVP's computers connect to the Internet.

The greatest challenge in dealing with online security is staying current with new developments.

Staying Current with Internet and Web Security

Mark is somewhat overwhelmed with the different types of computer security threats and measures. He wonders how he can stay on top of all the information and technologies related to computer security. It seems that each week brings reports of a new virus, a new type of attack, or a new way that criminals are using the Internet to extort money from users of all types.

The CERT Coordination Center is a federally funded research center operated by the Software Engineering Institute at Carnegie Mellon University. (CERT was originally known as the Computer Emergency Response Team, but now goes by just the acronym for its former name.) The primary goal of the CERT Coordination Center is to publish alerts, advisories, and vulnerability reports about current and future Internet security problems it detects and to coordinate communication between software experts. The CERT Coordination Center also works to increase awareness of security problems and issues and to help individuals and organizations improve the security of their computer systems.

Another important security organization is the SANS Institute. Many companies belong to the SANS Institute; it sponsors computer security training and research programs. Its Web site includes the Internet Storm Center and other resources that contain current information on emerging online security issues. You want to show Mark the CERT Coordination Center and the SANS Institute sites so he can use them as resources to stay current and to answer questions about security threats that he might have in the future.

To visit the CERT Coordination Center Web site:

▶ **1.** On the Online Companion Web page for Tutorial 7, click the **CERT Coordination Center** link.

▶ **2.** View the headings and links on the CERT Coordination Center home page. Notice that you can get information about improving and evaluating security, reviewing publications by CERT Coordination Center staff members, or learning more about the CERT Coordination Center.

▶ **3.** Follow some of the links that might interest Mark. When you have reviewed a few pages of content, return to the Online Companion page.

▶ **4.** On the Online Companion Web page for Tutorial 7, click the **SANS Institute** link.

▶ **5.** View the headings and links on the SANS Institute home page. Most of the page is devoted to announcements about upcoming training seminars, but there are links you can follow to the FAQ page and to the Storm Center page, among others that you might find interesting.

▶ **6.** When you have finished reviewing the site, close your Web browser.

Mark appreciates all of the information you have given him about Web sites that can help him and his staff learn more about online security and stay current with new developments in the area. He is certain that RVP employees and customers will have more secure online experiences as a result of your work.

| Review | **Session 7.2 Quick Check** |

1. What is an ActiveX control?
2. True or False: A Web site can read any cookie stored on your computer's hard drive.
3. What is authentication?
4. What information is stored in a digital certificate?
5. How can you tell that a Web page you are viewing with a browser is secure?
6. What are the key elements in a phishing attack?
7. What is a firewall?

| Review | **Tutorial Summary** |

In this tutorial, you learned about the different types of computer security threats and some countermeasures that you can take to prevent them. You also learned about how to protect your copyright interests in your own Web site (or your employer's Web site) and how to respect the copyright interests of others on the Web. You learned about specific security threats that arise on the Internet when it is used as a communication channel and about threats on computers when they are used as Web clients or as Web servers.

If you have your own computer, be sure to use the security information presented in this tutorial to create a safe environment in which to enjoy the Web's many resources. The Online Companion page for Tutorial 7 includes many links that you can follow to learn more about security.

Key Terms

active content
ActiveX component
ad blocker
adware
algorithm
asymmetric encryption
authentication
black hat hacker
bot farm
brute force attack
certificate authority (CA)
cipher text
clickstream
computer forensics experts
computer security
countermeasure
cracker
cryptography
decryption
denial of service (DoS)
    attack
denial of service (DoS)
    filter
digital certificate
digital ID
digital watermark
distributed denial of ser-
    vice (DDoS) attack
encryption
ethical hackers

firewall
hacker
identity theft
industrial espionage
integrity
Java applet
JavaScript program
key
logical security
login
man-in-the-middle exploit
multifactor authentication
multiple layers of control
necessity
organized crime
packet flooding attack
packet sniffer
password manager
personal certificate
phishing
physical security
plain text
port
port scan
private key
private-key encryption
public key
public-key encryption
racketeering
script kiddie

secrecy
secret key
Secure Sockets Layer (SSL)
Secure Sockets Layer-
    Extended Validaton
    (SSL-EV)
security
server certificate
session key
signed ActiveX control
single-factor authentication
spoofing
spyware
steganography
strong encryption
strong key
symmetric encryption
threat
Transport Layer
    Security (TSL)
Trojan horse
user authentication
user identification
virus
virus tool kit
Web bug
white hat hacker
worm
zombie
zombie farm

Practice	**Review Assignments**

Practice the skills you learned in the tutorial using the same case scenario.

There are no Data Files needed for the Review Assignments.

Mark is having trouble with pop-up windows opening as he uses the Internet. Mark plans to install a firewall, which he has learned can help prevent pop-up windows from opening. However, in the meantime, he wonders if there are other countermeasures that can help remove these annoying windows. To find this information for Mark, complete the following steps.

1. Start your Web browser, go to www.cengage.com/internet/np/internet8 to open the Online Companion page, log on to your account, click the Tutorial 7 link, and then click the Review Assignments link. Click a link in the Software Download Sites section to open the download site of your choice.

2. Use the download site's tools to find programs that block pop-up windows and include other desirable features to protect Mark's privacy and enhance his use of the Internet. Find three candidate programs, but do not download any of them. Use your browser's Print dialog box to print one page of information about each of the three programs that you have selected. This page should include the program's name, publisher, license information (freeware, shareware, cost, etc.), and a brief description of the program.

3. Return to the Online Companion page for the Review Assignments, and then click a link in the List of Known Spyware section. Use the page that opens to determine if any of the programs you selected in Step 2 are known to include spyware. If the site includes a search text box, type the name of the first program you found into the text box to search for it. Repeat this process for the other programs you found in Step 2.

4. In a memo addressed to Mark, recommend a pop-up blocker program for him to install based on the program with the best features. Make sure to identify any programs you found that contain known spyware, so Mark can avoid those programs. Finally, in a separate paragraph, evaluate the effectiveness of the Web sites you used to find the pop-up blocker and list of spyware.

5. Close your browser.

Apply	**Case Problem 1**

Apply the skills you learned in the tutorial to learn more about SSL.

There are no Data Files needed for this Case Problem.

Ski-Town Ski and Snowboarding School Jon Sagami is the manager of the Ski-Town Ski and Snowboarding School at Arrowhead Mountain in the Colorado Rocky Mountains. The school offers many full-day and half-day classes to teach children and adults how to downhill ski and snowboard. The school also sells lift tickets, equipment (such as freestyle boards, skis, and ski boots), and clothing (such as snowsuits, insulated gloves, and goggles). Jon wants to expand the school's marketing efforts with a Web site that lets visitors to Arrowhead Mountain learn more about the school and its merchandise and buy tickets and book time with instructors in advance. Because the Web site will accept online orders, Jon asks you to learn more about the Secure Sockets Layer (SSL) protocol. To help Jon plan the Web site, complete the following steps.

1. Start your Web browser, go to www.cengage.com/internet/np/internet8 to open the Online Companion page, log on to your account, click the Tutorial 7 link, and then click the Case Problem 1 link. Click the VeriSign link.

2. Use the information on this site to learn more about the digital certificate products that Verisign offers to businesses who want to use SSL. Jon will need to know how to obtain a digital certificate for the server and how it works.

3. When you have finished gathering information on the Verisign site, return to the Online Companion page and click the Thawte link. Use the information on this site to learn more about the digital certificate products that Thawte offers to businesses who want to use SSL.

✦ EXPLORE

4. In a memo of about 300 words addressed to Jon, outline some basic information about SSL and how to get a digital certificate for Ski-Town. Evaluate the products offered by Verisign and Thawte and recommend one to Jon. Be sure to include the reasons for your recommendation. (*Hint:* The cost of the certificate is a factor, but it should not be the only reason for your recommendation.)

5. Close your browser.

| Research | **Case Problem 2** |

Explore the privacy policies of several Web sites.

There are no Data Files needed for this Case Problem.

Ginger's Golden Kennels   Ginger Gotcher, owner of Ginger's Golden Kennels, is a registered breeder and trainer of Golden Retrievers. Because many of Ginger's dogs have reached champion status, puppies bred on her ranch are in high demand from people across the United States. Ginger receives many calls from potential owners of new puppies and from breeders requesting sire services from her champion male dogs. Because Ginger frequently travels to dog shows across the country, it is inconvenient for her to rely on the telephone to conduct business. Ginger has created a Web site to communicate information and also to let potential owners request and purchase puppies. Ginger is concerned about security—both for her site and also for the protection of her clients' personal information. Ginger has heard that many Web sites post privacy policies so people can examine them and understand how companies collect information about customers and what they do with that information. To help Ginger learn more about privacy policies, you will visit the Web sites of several online stores and report your findings to her by completing the following steps.

1. Start your Web browser, go to www.cengage.com/internet/np/internet8 to open the Online Companion page, log on to your account, click the Tutorial 7 link, and then click the Case Problem 2 link. Click the Amazon.com link and wait while the browser loads the page.

2. Locate and click the link to Amazon.com's privacy notice. Answer the following questions:

   a. What does the policy say about revealing your name and address to other companies?

   b. Does this site use cookies? If so, what type of information does this site store in cookies that it writes on users' hard drives?

3. Return to the Online Companion page for Case Problem 2, and then click the Starbucks link.

4. Locate and click the link to the Starbucks privacy statement. Answer the following questions:

   a. How does Starbucks authenticate users?

   b. How might Starbucks use the information you provide without your permission?

c. Does Starbucks include anything about Web bugs in its privacy policy? If you think it does, is the information clearly described for the average Internet user? Support your answer with language used at the site.

5. Return to the Online Companion page for Case Problem 2, and then click the BBBOnline link.

6. Use the links and pages in the BBBOnline Web site to learn more about the reliability seal program of the Better Business Bureau (BBB). Answer the following questions:

a. What is a reliability seal?

b. How do you obtain a reliability seal?

7. Close your browser.

Challenge | Case Problem 3

Expand your knowledge of public-key encryption and secure email.

There are no Data Files needed for this Case Problem.

Hendricks & Red, P.C.   Ramona Galindo is the office manager of an accounting firm, Hendricks & Red, P.C. Last year, the firm began sending electronic tax organizers by email to clients who requested them. The client installs the tax organizer, uses it to enter his or her tax information, and then returns it to the firm as an email attachment. The tax organizer program encrypts the file the client returns. Although many clients liked organizing their tax returns in this way because it saved them from having to bring materials to the firm, some were worried about returning important information by email. Ramona wants to protect the firm's clients even further by providing a way for clients to encrypt the email messages and the attachment. Ramona asks you to research public-key encryption. To help Ramona, complete the following steps.

1. Start your Web browser, go to www.cengage.com/internet/np/internet8 to open the Online Companion page, log on to your account, click the Tutorial 7 link, and then click the Case Problem 3 link. There are links to several search engines listed here. Use one or more of the links to open the search engine(s) you would like to use for this case.

✛EXPLORE   2. Use the search engine you have chosen to find information about public-key encryption. Locate and read at least three sources of information about public-key encryption. Your focus should be on securing email messages. For each useful Web site that you locate, use your browser's Print dialog box to print the first page of information from that site. (*Hint*: Avoid sites that have a primary purpose of selling you a particular product.)

✛EXPLORE   3. Return to the Online Companion for Case Problem 3 and choose a search engine to use as you search for information about secure email. Find three sources of information about securing email messages. For each Web site that you locate, print the first page of information.

✛EXPLORE   4. In a memo of about 200 words addressed to your instructor, suggest two possible ways that Ramona can secure email messages sent to and from the firm. Support your recommendations with facts you learned from your research. (*Hint*: Return to the Web sites you found in the first three steps if necessary.)

5. Close your browser.

| Create | | **Case Problem 4** |

Create a report on alternatives for securing Web servers.

There are no Data Files needed for this Case Problem.

Bolton Brokerage Services   Les Bolton is a prominent real estate broker in upstate New York. Les provides many of the agents working for him with office space, phone and Internet services, and staff support. Les has had trouble lately securing his Web site. Three times in the last six months, crackers have successfully penetrated his system and defaced the home page in the same way that a person might use spray paint to add graffiti to a highway underpass or public restroom. In addition, someone has copied the company's corporate logo and other copyrighted real-estate pictures and information and posted it on another site that is masquerading as Bolton Brokerage Services. Les has hired you to look into the security measures he should take to prevent the break-ins his business is experiencing. Also, Les would like to see if there is a way to protect the company's logo and real-estate photos by encoding them with an imperceptible mark clearly identifying the rightful owner. To help Les protect his business and clients, complete the following steps.

1. Start your Web browser, go to www.cengage.com/internet/np/internet8 to open the Online Companion page, log on to your account, click the Tutorial 7 link, and then click the Case Problem 4 link. Click the SecurityMetrics Free Port Scan link.

2. If you have permission to do so, click the option to run a free port scan on your computer. It might take several minutes for the port scan results to appear. Use your browser's Print button to print the results page. In a report addressed to Les, answer the following questions.
   a. How secure is your computer?
   b. What actions can you take to protect any open ports?
   c. If you do not have any open ports, what actions have you already taken to protect your computer? (If you are in a public computer lab and do not have access to security information, explain the countermeasures that you believe are in place to secure open ports.)

3. Return to the Online Companion page for Case Problem 4, and then click the VeriSign link. Use the VeriSign Web site to determine the cost of Secure Sockets Layer certificates. When you find this information, use your browser to print it.

⊕ **EXPLORE**

4. Return to the Online Companion page for Case Problem 4, and click the Digimarc link. Use the Digimarc Web site to learn more about protecting copyrighted material and print at least two pages that focus on protecting Les's system and information. (*Hint*: The site includes a wide variety of resources, so you will need to focus on specific techniques that will help protect material that is posted online.)

5. Consider how Les might use digital watermarks or steganography to protect content on his Web site. Return to the Online Companion page for Case Problem 4, and then use the links in the Digital Watermarks and Steganography section to explore a few sites for more information.

6. Write a memo of about 200 words to Les in which you summarize your findings.

7. Close your browser.

Challenge | Case Problem 5

Explore the use of trustmarks and the protection of consumer privacy on the Internet.

There are no Data Files needed for this Case Problem.

Senator Ben Kuenemann During his campaign for the office of state senator, Ben Kuenemann promised to work for consumer's rights. As his first order of business for the upcoming legislative session, Senator Kuenemann wants to draft legislation to strengthen the state's laws so that identity theft and other crimes related to secrecy are punishable by specific fines and criminal penalties. As the senator's chief of staff, you need to research and report on the current standards in place for this. One interesting fact that you have learned is that the Internet has several organizations that encourage online businesses to follow established standards in an effort to become "self-policing" so they can avoid governmental regulation. To get started on your report, complete the following steps.

1. Start your Web browser, go to www.cengage.com/internet/np/internet8 to open the Online Companion page, log on to your account, click the Tutorial 7 link, and then click the Case Problem 5 link. Click the TRUSTe link and wait while the browser loads the page.

⊕ **EXPLORE** 2. Review the contents of the TRUSTe home page to become familiar with the services offered by this site. Then locate a link that describes the TRUSTe program (this link might be named "About TRUSTe" or something similar) and click it. Read the page that opens and use the FAQs link to learn about the TRUSTe trustmark, the organization's objectives, and why this organization believes that self-regulation is important. (*Hint*: Try to determine what businesses or organizations sponsor the site and consider the effects of such sponsors on the reliability of the information contained on the site.)

⊕ **EXPLORE** 3. Return to the Online Companion page for Case Problem 5, and then click the WebTrust link. Follow the links on this page to learn more about the WebTrust seal and what it represents for consumers. (*Hint*: Try to determine what businesses or organizations sponsor the site and consider the effects of such sponsors on the reliability of the information contained on the site.)

⊕ **EXPLORE** 4. Return to the Online Companion page for Case Problem 5, and then click the BBBOnline Privacy Seal link. Use the page that opens to learn about the BBB's privacy seal for businesses so that you understand what this seal represents and the general steps that a business follows to obtain one. (*Hint*: Try to determine what businesses or organizations sponsor the site and consider the effects of such sponsors on the reliability of the information contained on the site.)

⊕ **EXPLORE** 5. Return to the Online Companion page for Case Problem 5, and then click the Network Advertising Initiative link. Use this site to learn about the "opt-out" program for managing consumer participation in Internet advertising and marketing efforts by various firms. If possible, find information about Web bugs and how advertisers are working to disclose information about them to consumers. (*Hint*: This site might refer to a "Web bug" as "anonymous Web usage" or a "marketing cookie.")

6. In a report addressed to Senator Kuenemann, describe the trustmark and privacy seal programs that you explored in Steps 2, 3, and 4. For each program, describe your overall impressions about the site's commitment to privacy. As you summarize your findings, identify whether the program is voluntary, who it affects, and how members obtain the seal or trustmark. From a consumer's perspective, comment on how safe you would feel doing business with a Web site that includes one of these seals or trustmarks on its site. Support your opinions with facts that you gathered at the Web sites you visited.

7. In a new paragraph, summarize your impressions of the opt-out program provided by the Network Advertising Initiative site you visited in Step 5. Do you feel that this opt-out program is sufficient to protect consumer privacy? Do you think that the average consumer has information about this kind of program and how to benefit from it? Does this program satisfy its members' proclamations that governmental regulation of online consumer privacy is unnecessary? Support your opinions with facts you gathered at the site you visited.

8. Close your browser.

Reinforce | **Lab Assignments**

Student Edition Labs

The interactive Student Edition Lab on **Protecting Your Privacy Online** is designed to help you master some of the key concepts and skills presented in this tutorial, including:

- understanding cookies
- deleting cookies in Internet Explorer
- changing how cookies are handled in Internet Explorer

This lab is available online and can be accessed from the Tutorial 7 Web page on the Online Companion at www.cengage.com/internet/np/internet8.

Review | **Quick Check Answers**

Session 7.1

1. secrecy, integrity, necessity
2. the process of coding information using a mathematical-based program and a secret key to produce a string of characters that is unreadable
3. a potentially harmful program hidden inside another program
4. denial of service (DoS) or distributed denial of service (DDoS) attack
5. A hacker is a dedicated programmer who enjoys writing complex code that tests the limits of technology. A cracker does much the same thing as a hacker, but usually intends to steal information, damage the information, damage the system's software, or damage the system's hardware. The media and the general public today often use the terms interchangeably, but computer professionals usually make the distinction between the two terms.
6. A crime in which the perpetrator uses the victim's personal information to open bank accounts, obtain new credit cards, borrow money, or buy expensive goods on credit. By the time the victim finds out that his or her identity has been stolen, the thief is long gone with the cash or the goods.
7. Larger businesses usually have better computer security systems in place. Larger businesses also have more resources to devote to the problem. Smaller businesses often pay the extortion demand rather than report the crime and work with law enforcement officials to catch the perpetrator.
8. digital watermarking and steganography

Session 7.2

1. A technology developed by Microsoft for writing small programs that perform some action in Web pages. ActiveX components have access to a computer's file system and can do damage to that system. ActiveX components only work in Internet Explorer and other browsers that share its code base.

2. False

3. the process of verifying that the source or sender of a message is identified correctly

4. the certificate holder's name, address, and email address; a key that unlocks the digital certificate, thereby verifying the certificate's authenticity; the certificate's expiration date or validity period; and a trusted third party, called a certificate authority (CA), which verifies the certificate holder's identity and issues the digital certificate

5. A padlock icon appears next to the address window (in Firefox, on the status bar), and the URL includes "https" instead of "http." If the site is using SSL-EV, the address window will include the name of the organization and will have a completely green (Internet Explorer) or partially green (Firefox) background.

6. A phishing attack uses phony email messages that include links to spoofed Web sites. Victims who click the email links are asked to enter personal information into a form at the spoofed Web site where that information is stolen and used to access the victims' bank or credit card accounts.

7. a software program or hardware device that controls access between two networks, such as a local area network and the Internet or the Internet and a client

Wireless Networking and Security

Communicating with and Securing Wireless Networks and Devices

Case | Mobile Vet Services

Ruby Wilson began her career as a staff physician at a local veterinary hospital in Broward County, Florida. After 10 years she had gained experience dealing with many different animals, diseases, and conditions. Many of her clients were senior citizens or disabled individuals, and they often commented that getting to the vet hospital was difficult. Because of this burden, Ruby began making house calls for clients with disabilities and senior citizens who had difficulties getting to the vet hospital. When her services quickly became popular, Ruby realized that a mobile vet clinic would help many of her clients.

In 2002, Ruby decided to leave her position at the hospital and started Mobile Vet Services. In her mobile vet clinic, which was a specially outfitted recreational vehicle, Ruby was able to provide routine pet care, such as immunizations, routine surgical procedures such as biopsies and neutering, simple lab services and x-ray procedures, and emergency care. At first she saw animals that belonged to disabled people and senior citizens and provided routine and specialized veterinary care for their pets and service dogs. Her business grew quickly as pet owners without disabilities began relying on her for various veterinary services. She added three more veterinarians and two veterinary technicians to her staff and purchased two additional mobile clinics. In addition, she opened an office in Fort Lauderdale to provide a base location for staff members and facilities for other services, such as pet boarding, advanced surgical procedures, and care for animals requiring long-term care due to illness or recovery.

One of the challenges of working in a mobile vet clinic has been the difficulty in communicating with the main office and staff members. The mobile vets use cell phones to talk to the office, to each other, and to clients throughout the day. However, sometimes a vet needs a lab report or x-ray image and has to drive back to Fort Lauderdale to pick it up. Ruby has hired you as the new office manager. Your first task is to identify ways to improve the clinic's communication, not only among employees, but also between the clinic and its clients. In your previous position as an assistant communications director for a company that sold wireless communication devices, you are already familiar with many ways to expand and enhance mobile communication. You begin your research by examining different ways to improve communication at Mobile Vet Services.

Starting Data Files

There are no starting Data Files needed for this tutorial.

Session 8.1

The Evolution of Wireless Networks

When you connect to your Internet service provider (ISP) using a phone line, cable modem, or DSL modem, you're creating a **wired connection** because the connection between your computer and your ISP uses a cable. A **wireless connection** occurs when data, such as a file or a person's voice, is transferred to another location without the use of any wires. The first wireless technology was used in 1978, when a voice-only network was started in Chicago and operated on an analog cellular network capable of sending data at a rate of up to 9.6 Kbps (kilobits per second). These analog cellular networks and the cell phones connected to them were the first generation of wireless systems. In 1994, carriers created digital networks, or **Personal Communication Service (PCS)**, where data was carried in bits at a rate of up to 14.4 Kbps. In 1999, the first wireless connections were made to the Internet. At first, the technology was expensive and slow, with poor user interfaces and compatibility problems between mobile devices such as personal digital assistants and cellular phones. A **personal digital assistant (PDA)** is a handheld computer that can send and receive wireless telephone and fax calls, act as a personal organizer, perform calculations, store notes, and, in many cases, display Web pages from the Internet. Many PDAs and cell phones perform all of these functions, and they might even have a Global Positioning System (GPS) that displays maps and directions to places around the globe, and a camera and MP3 player. Gradually, the **wireless Internet** has expanded to include different hardware devices, networks, and other options.

Cell phones were one of the first wireless devices to transfer a person's voice. Eventually cell phone manufacturers found a way to support and send text data over the same connection. Most likely your cell phone supports some kind of text messaging service that lets you receive very short, text-only email messages and read them using your phone's display area. This kind of data transfer occurs over **second-generation wireless networks**, or **2G wireless** for short. The 2G standard allows data transfers of up to 14.4 Kbps. As a point of comparison, a dial-up modem might transfer data at a rate of up to 56.6 Kbps, so 2G wireless networks are very slow for transferring the large amounts of data you can receive over the Internet when compared to a wired device. The 2G wireless data transfer rate is adequate for a voice conversation, but it's extremely slow when you're trying to receive formatted information, such as a Web page. At the time, **Short Message Service (SMS)** was the service that let users send text messages of up to 160 characters over a 2G wireless network to a wireless phone.

Around the same time that cell phone carriers were converting their old analog cellular networks to digital networks (in other words, moving from first-generation to second-generation wireless), PDAs and other handheld computers were growing in popularity for business professionals. Some PDAs and other devices use infrared technology to "beam" information from one source to another without the use of wired connections. This infrared technology initially eliminated the need for wired connections to share data between devices, but its limitations in range increased the need for other wireless methods of transferring data.

In the United States, 2G wireless networks still provide digital voice services and SMS. Most major U.S. markets also have **third-generation wireless networks (3G wireless)** in place. The 3G wireless networks offer data transfer rates of up to 2 Mbps (megabits per second) and constant connections. This data transfer rate means that you can display Web pages, play MP3 files, watch a video, make and receive phone calls, and send and receive email and text messages from a single 3G device over a very fast connection.

Tip

SMS is still one of today's most widely used and popular forms of communication methods, with millions of text messages sent each day using wireless devices around the world.

Establishing nationwide 3G wireless networks in the United States has faced and continues to struggle with two major obstacles. The first is bandwidth—3G wireless networks must operate in a spectrum where radio frequencies can carry data, and the U.S. government has to authorize the use of the spectrum on which 3G wireless networks operate. The second obstacle is cost. Carriers of 3G wireless signals must purchase licenses to operate 3G wireless networks, and then they must build cellular transmitters and radio towers to carry the signals. The conversion from 2G to 3G wireless is similar to the conversion from analog to digital cellular networks that occurred in the 1990s—the carriers must invest in technology to make the change. In Europe, the licenses alone have cost carriers more than $95 billion and the estimated cost of building the 3G wireless networks is more than $125 billion. Much like the early days of cell phones, the technology is only as good as the network and its coverage area. Several U.S. carriers, including AT&T Wireless, Sprint, Verizon, and T-Mobile, already offer 3G service in most U.S. markets, and nationwide 3G service might be a reality in a few years. However, the availability of nationwide 3G service depends on the ability of the carriers to build the networks and establish partnerships with the manufacturers of the required devices and hardware.

In the meantime, many carriers have transformed and upgraded their existing networks by creating **2.5G wireless networks** that deliver faster transfer speeds of up to 144 to 384 Kbps. These 2.5G networks also allow you to send files, such as pictures taken with a camera phone, to other users, and to access the Internet.

With the number of wireless Internet users expected to continue increasing in the next several years, more devices are being manufactured to support wireless technology; however, a single network standard on which to transmit information has not yet been developed. It is important for consumers to understand that a wireless device is usually manufactured to work only on a *single* type of network, because different networks use different frequencies on the radio spectrum. If you choose a wireless carrier with a 2.5G network, for example, you might not be able to receive a signal in an area with only a 2G or a 3G network because your device operates on a different frequency. Consumers must be sure to select the wireless device that will pick up a signal in areas of the world where they will use it.

Despite the fact that 3G networks are not yet widely available in some countries, manufacturers are already working on the next generation of networks. **3.5G wireless networks**, also called **mobile broadband**, provide network connections of up to 10 Mbps. In 2009, 3.5G wireless networks already existed in the United States, Hong Kong, Singapore, Japan, China, Israel, Argentina, Brazil, Sweden, Norway, and South Korea, and 3.5G networks were being planned and tested in other countries, as well.

In the next few years, the world might see its first rollout of **fourth-generation wireless networks (4G wireless)**, which are also called **3G wireless and beyond networks**. 4G technology is expected to bring network connection speeds of up to 100 Mbps and deliver high-quality audio and video to wireless devices. 4G networks are also expected to make it possible for a wireless device to move between the different wireless networks without losing the signal.

Cellular was the first industry to create wireless connections that served large geographical areas. Soon after the creation of cellular networks, engineers developed other ways to create wireless networks with different types of devices. Generally, you can classify wireless networking into four categories: wireless local area networking, wireless personal area networking, wireless wide area networking, and metropolitan area networking. It is important to understand each type of network and the technologies used on it, so you can determine the correct wireless devices needed to connect to the network. Some of these wireless options provide opportunities for Mobile Vet Services employees to send and receive important data regardless of the location from which they are conducting business. You decide to investigate how the different wireless networks and devices can help the Mobile Vet Services employees stay in touch with clients, the main office staff, and each other.

Wireless Local Area Networking

A **wireless local area network** (**WLAN**) is a network in which devices use high-frequency radio waves instead of wires to communicate with a base station, which is connected to the Internet. When most people talk about wireless LANs, they are usually referring to the most common type of wireless network, which is created using the Wi-Fi standard. Most likely the new notebook computers Ruby purchased for the mobile clinics and the main office have been equipped with **Wi-Fi**, or **wireless fidelity**, which is the trade-marked name of the Wi-Fi Alliance that specifies the interface between a wireless client and a base station, or between two wireless clients, to create a **hotspot**, or an area of network coverage. The Wi-Fi Alliance is a not-for-profit organization that certifies interoperability of Wi-Fi products and promotes Wi-Fi as a standard for wireless LANs. Wi-Fi is frequently found in restaurants, stores, and other places where people gather and use wireless devices to access the Internet. Wi-Fi is also used to connect users playing electronic games and to connect other types of devices, such as cameras, to the Internet. Many Wi-Fi devices operate in the 2.4 GHz (gigahertz) radio spectrum, which is the same spectrum used by cordless phones, garage door openers, microwave ovens, and other devices. Because this spectrum is unlicensed, it is free; remember that devices operating in the 3G wireless spectrum are required to be licensed. Figure 8-1 compares a traditional wired local area network to a WLAN.

| Figure 8-1 | Comparison of wired and wireless local area networks |

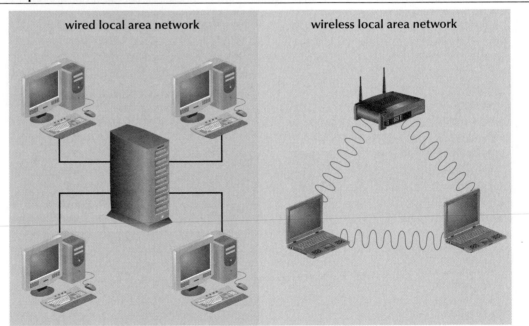

The Institute of Electrical and Electronic Engineers (IEEE) classifies WLANs using different wireless network standards. Four of the most widely used standards are 802.11a, 802.11b, 802.11g, and 802.11n; for this reason, some people call a wireless LAN an 802.11 network because of the network standard on which Wi-Fi operates. The primary difference between these standards is the radio frequency at which they transmit, the transfer rate of data over the network, and the range at which they operate. The **transfer rate** of data is the speed at which data is transmitted from an access point (or base station) to a wireless device. An **access point** is a hardware device with one or more antennae that permits communication between wired and wireless networks so wireless clients can send and receive data. Generally speaking, the closer the wireless device is to the access point, the higher the transfer rate. The **range** is the physical distance between the access point and the wireless device. Most ranges are averages; the range will vary depending on the physical impediments, such as walls, between the access point and the wireless device. In addition, the transfer rate might be reduced when many devices using the same radio frequency are present in close proximity to the access point.

When you see the term *Wi-Fi*, it most often refers to the 802.11b standard, which is the one on which most Wi-Fi devices operate. Devices that use the same wireless network standard are compatible with each other. However, the different standards are generally not interoperable, so a device configured for 802.11a is not necessarily compatible with a device configured for 802.11b. A device called a **dual band access point** makes it possible to connect devices configured for two different Wi-Fi standards to the same access point, and a **multiple band access point** makes it possible to connect any wireless device to the same access point. However, most businesses will invest in devices created for only one wireless network standard because it is less expensive and less technically complicated to do so.

In business settings, Wi-Fi is often used as an alternative in a building or other area in which you might find a traditional wired local area network (LAN); in cases where wiring cannot be installed, wireless networks might be the only way to connect computers to a LAN for Internet access. Wi-Fi is also a popular way to configure wireless devices in homes, especially when rooms in the house where an Internet connection is desired do not have phone or cable outlets. Millions of U.S. households use Wi-Fi to create wireless networks, which represent the largest home market in the world. As wireless technology becomes more affordable, the number of wireless networks in homes is expected to increase dramatically worldwide.

Most new notebook computers and other wireless devices are manufactured with Wi-Fi compatible hardware installed in them and software that locates a Wi-Fi signal and automatically initiates the connection to the wireless network. Because Wi-Fi certified hardware and devices must meet the requirements of the Wi-Fi Alliance for 802.11 wireless standards, any Wi-Fi certified device can connect to any 802.11 certified access point, which is usually mounted on a wall, to send and receive signals. A hardware device or a computer running specialized software serves as a central point for wireless clients and provides a connection to the wireless network. These access points already exist in many hotels, airports, convention centers, restaurants, and other public locations across the United States. As long as you are using Wi-Fi certified technology, you can connect to the WLAN when you are within the range of the network. In most cases, network connections are possible within 200 to 900 feet of the access point, depending on the network standard, surrounding architecture, and other obstacles to the radio waves. Figure 8-2 shows the Wireless Internet page for Mozart's Coffee Roasters, which is one of many businesses in the United States that offers wireless Internet connections to its customers. At Mozart's, you can connect your computer to the Internet using your own wireless device or a rented card from Mozart's; either way, the service is free. Many other businesses, such as McDonald's, Starbucks, Barnes & Noble Booksellers, and Kinko's, also have installed Wi-Fi access points as a way to attract customers and offer new services.

Figure 8-2   **Wireless Internet page at Mozart's Coffee Roasters**

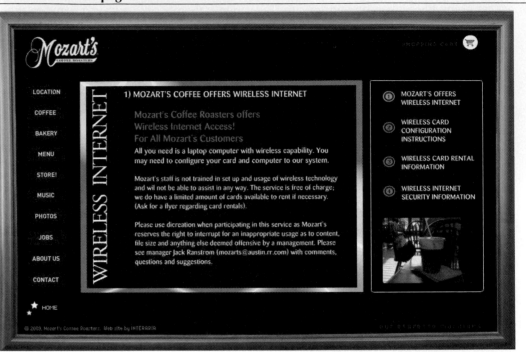

If you position enough access points within the appropriate range of each other, the WLAN can grow to cover an entire office complex or other geographic area. For example, a movement in Seattle in 2001 called for people to put 802.11b access points in their homes and offices, creating a network of access points and an expanded wireless network in Seattle. You could take your wireless device all over town and still connect to the wireless network to access the Internet and your email. But if you traveled outside of Seattle, you would either need to find another access point or use an alternate method to connect to the Internet because you would be out of range of the wireless network in Seattle.

In 2004 and 2005, several U.S. cities, including Grand Haven (MI), Granbury (TX), and St. Cloud (FL), deployed city-wide Wi-Fi networks in an effort to make affordable Internet connections part of the city's basic services. These city-wide wireless networks are often called **municipal broadband**, **Muni Wi-Fi**, or **Muni-Fi** networks to characterize the wireless network coverage area in terms of a city instead of as a hotspot. In 2007, Wireless Philadelphia (which is now known as Digital Impact Group), a not-for-profit organization, made the city of Philadelphia the nation's largest Wi-Fi network by providing wireless services to individuals and businesses in an area of 135 square miles. These services are free to consumers who can access the network. Businesses and institutions are charged fees but eventually will be able to connect to the network for free as well. A unique feature of Digital Impact Group is its Digital Inclusion service, which provides affordable options to families with limited financial resources to help them acquire the hardware and software needed to get online. Figure 8-3 shows the About page for Digital Impact Group.

About Digital Impact Group page   Figure 8-3

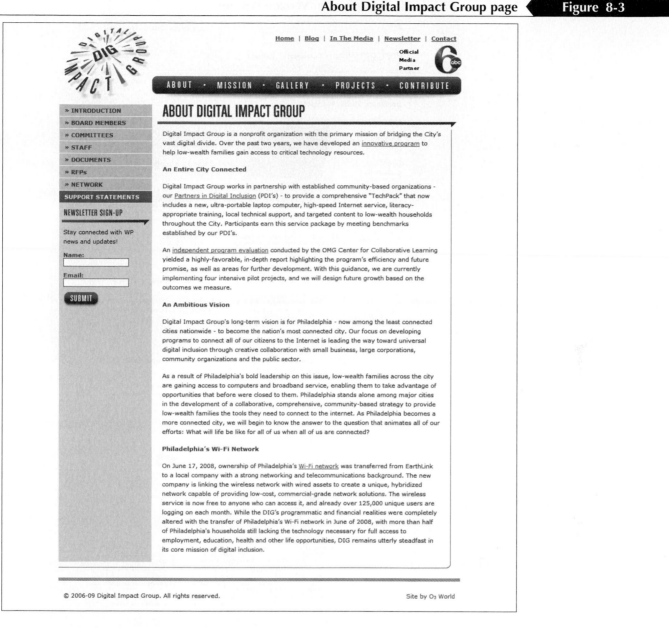

A new type of WLAN that might interest Ruby is **MiFi**, a small wireless device a user keeps in a pocket or briefcase that provides a battery-operated, mobile, personal hotspot for connecting Wi-Fi devices to the Internet. Produced by Novatel and obtaining its 3G signal through a nationwide cellular service, such as Verizon Wireless or Sprint, this device creates a mobile Internet connection for Wi-Fi devices. The MiFi device uses a rechargeable battery that operates for up to four hours or up to 40 hours on standby; it powers off after 30 minutes of inactivity. The hotspot created by MiFi is password protected and can be used to connect up to five Wi-Fi devices located within 30 feet of the MiFi device to the Internet. When you want to provide other Wi-Fi devices with Internet access through your MiFi hotspot, you simply give the user the password for your MiFi hotspot, which is conveniently located on the MiFi device. To create a MiFi hotspot, you must first purchase the Novatel device, and then subscribe to a participating 3G service. MiFi works anywhere in the United States where the carrier's 3G network is available. Because MiFi doesn't use any wires for its power source or 3G signal, it is an excellent option for Internet connectivity on the go. Figure 8-4 shows the Intelligent Mobile Hotspot page for Verizon Wireless.

Figure 8-4   Intelligent Mobile Hotspot page for Verizon Wireless

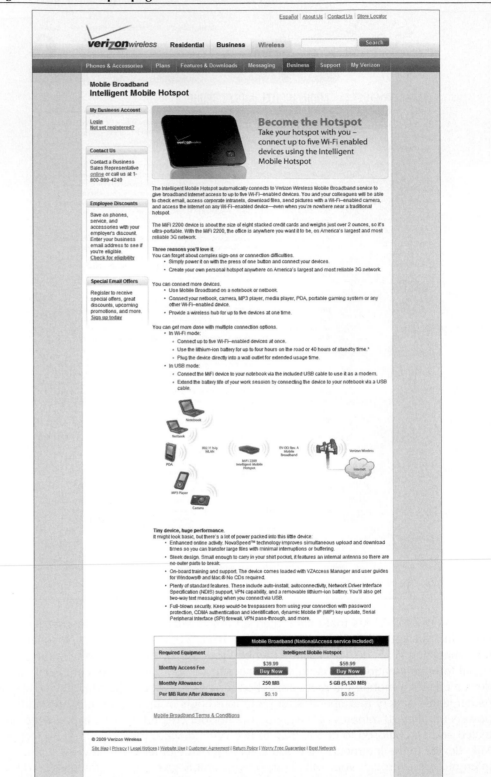

Ruby asks you to provide her with more information about how Mobile Vet Services can use wireless devices to communicate. You tell her that several companies provide information on their Web sites about building a WLAN using Wi-Fi. You will investigate a WLAN option for Mobile Vet Services next by searching for information about WLANs using the Web sites of different companies that produce devices that operate on them.

To find information about WLANs:

▶ **1.** Start your Web browser, open the Online Companion page at **www.cengage.com/internet/np/internet8** and log on to your account, click the **Tutorial 8** link, and then click the **Session 8.1** link.

▶ **2.** Find the heading **Wireless LANs** and then click one of the businesses listed to open its home page.

▶ **3.** Follow some of the links on the home page to learn more about WLAN topics, such as how these networks are configured, the necessary hardware to install them, and other general information that you feel might help you understand the technical requirements, advantages, and disadvantages of installing a WLAN for Mobile Vet Services. You do not need to obtain detailed information about the specific hardware that the business sells; your research should focus on general information about WLANs. If the site provides links to demonstrations and your browser can display them, explore these demos to learn more about wireless technology.

   Trouble? If you try to view a demonstration and your browser tells you that it is missing a required plug-in, cancel the demo and try another link. Do not download any software or browser plug-ins at this time.

▶ **4.** When you are finished exploring the first business's Web site, return to the Online Companion page for Session 8.1, and then click a link to another business in the Wireless LANs section. Follow the links on the home page to continue your research about WLANs.

▶ **5.** Return to the Online Companion page for Session 8.1.

Some of the sites may provide you with specific information about how to set up a WLAN. You tell Ruby what you have learned about the basic requirements of a WLAN that uses Wi-Fi and suggest that using Wi-Fi and MiFi might be good solutions for giving employees some flexibility in where they do their work, either by creating a Wi-Fi network in the main office, by giving them information about where to connect to existing Wi-Fi networks in local businesses, or by purchasing the necessary equipment to create a MiFi hotspot.

Wireless Mesh Networks

Another type of wireless local area network is a **wireless mesh network**, which is commonly used to extend the reach of Wi-Fi hotspots to an enterprise, such as a university campus, hotel, airport terminal, convention center, sports arena, or a large office building. Unlike a traditional WLAN, in which devices connect through the network to a router that is connected to the Internet, a wireless mesh network is a series of wireless nodes (usually, these nodes are access points) that are self-configuring and that talk to each other to relay communication across the network. The advantage of a wireless mesh network is that as new nodes are installed in the vicinity of the mesh network, they automatically configure themselves to work without the use of cables. Similarly, when a node in the mesh network fails, communication is automatically routed around the failed node with little overall loss to the entire network. Perhaps the most important feature of a mesh network is that only one of the nodes needs to be wired to the Internet connection, and then it shares that connection with the other nodes in the network, which talk to each other and automatically figure out the best way to transmit data over the entire network. In other words, communication doesn't always go through the router that is connected to the network like it does in a Wi-Fi network—communication goes through the nodes, which transmit data to the next node and act as an access point in the network. This type of wireless network is generally more expensive to create than Wi-Fi hotspots, but it is more effective and efficient at covering large areas with wireless connections because each node is wirelessly connected to the network—not to the router with cables—and each node requires very little power to operate. Figure 8-5 shows an example of a wireless mesh network.

Figure 8-5 ▶ **Wireless mesh network configuration**

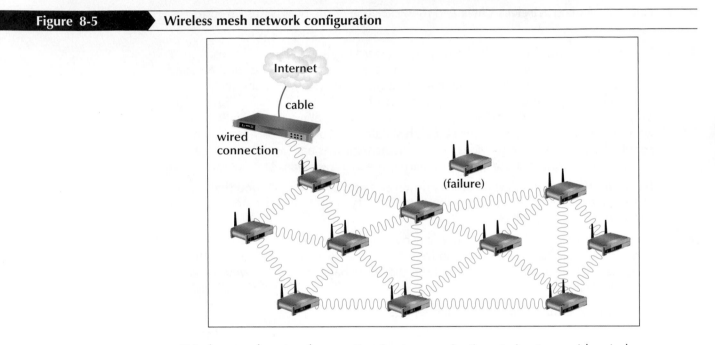

Wireless mesh networks are attractive to organizations trying to provide wireless coverage to a large geographical area. These networks are also frequently found inside buildings, ports, and airport terminals as a method of controlling information from automated services, such as temperature controls, security systems, and fire alarms, all of which use sensors to monitor the operations and status of a large building. In a wireless mesh network, these sensors are linked together through the network and communicate with each other, providing a very reliable and affordable way to monitor the systems in a building or other area.

Ruby wonders if there is a way for staff members to share devices and peripherals without having to install an access point or a wireless mesh network. You decide to research some options for personal area networks to answer her question.

Personal Area Networking

Personal area networking (PAN) refers to the wireless network that you use to connect personal devices to each other, such as a connection between a PDA and a notebook computer or between a notebook computer and a printer. The two major types of personal area networks are infrared and Bluetooth.

Tip

Devices that work in a personal area network are sometimes called **PAN devices**.

Infrared Technology

The **Infrared Data Association** (**IrDA**) is a group dedicated to developing low-cost, high-speed wireless connectivity solutions. Using **infrared** technology, you can wirelessly beam information from one device to another compatible device using infrared light waves. Because infrared uses light waves to carry data, it doesn't interfere with technologies that use radio waves. This technology is popular with PDAs, but you can also find it in use for notebook computers, printers, phones, and other peripheral devices. Infrared provides convenient wireless connections, but there are some limitations. The devices must be compatible and in a direct line of sight with each other for the waves to reach their destinations. In other words, you can't beam information across a room, through a wall, or around a corner. If you want to print an email message you received on your PDA using your infrared-compatible printer, you need to move the PDA within one meter of the infrared port on the printer. Infrared transfers data quickly at up to 4 Mbps. Another disadvantage is the lack of software products that can handle the transfer of data using infrared devices. The software that runs on infrared-compatible devices must also be compatible.

Bluetooth

Another technology in personal area networking lets you connect compatible devices using radio waves instead of wiring devices through a LAN or to each other. **Bluetooth**, named after a 10th century Danish king, is a technology that provides short-range radio links between personal computers, handheld devices, wireless phones, headsets, printers, and other electronic devices. Most of these devices are manufactured with hardware that enables them to receive Bluetooth radio waves; for devices without this hardware you can purchase an adapter to enable them for use with other Bluetooth devices. Thousands of Bluetooth-enabled products are on the market, including built-in Bluetooth support in certain Toyota, Mercedes-Benz, BMW, Lexus, Acura, Land Rover, Audi, and Lincoln automobiles. Unlike a WLAN, Bluetooth doesn't need an access point for communication; compatible devices communicate with each other automatically. If you want to connect a Bluetooth device to the Internet, some manufacturers produce Bluetooth access points that function much like their Wi-Fi counterparts in that they connect Bluetooth devices to a wired network that provides Internet access. Many Bluetooth devices, such as BlackBerry PDAs, also have built-in hardware to pick up a cellular phone network for Internet access.

Bluetooth isn't really "owned" by any specific manufacturer or group; according to the official Bluetooth Web site, the goal of the Bluetooth SIG (Special Interest Group) is to "strengthen the Bluetooth brand by empowering SIG members to collaborate and innovate, creating the preferred wireless technology to connect diverse devices." The Bluetooth SIG promoters include Ericsson, Intel, Lenovo, Microsoft, Motorola, Nokia, and Toshiba, along with more than 10,000 associate and adopter member companies; these companies are actively creating new ways to use Bluetooth technology and manufacturing products that support it. Figure 8-6 shows the home page for the Bluetooth SIG Web site.

Figure 8-6   **Bluetooth Special Interest Group home page**

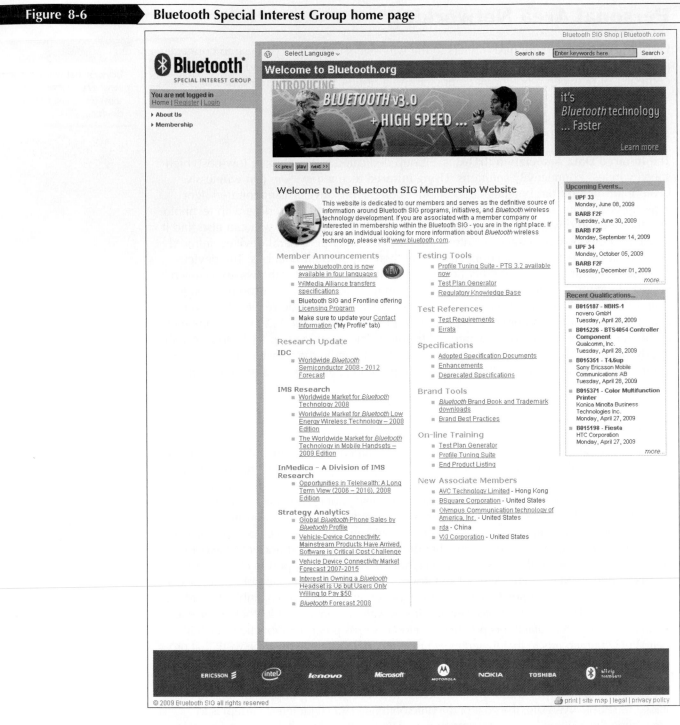

Because all Bluetooth devices must be certified and tested to meet current product specifications, they are compatible with each other regardless of the type of device or manufacturer. Figure 8-7 shows how you might use Bluetooth to create a wireless PAN to connect your electronic devices. When you have visitors to your office, their Bluetooth wireless devices can also connect to your devices. Because some new car models include Bluetooth-compatible cell phones, you can extend your PAN to include the use of some devices while in your car.

Creating a personal area network using Bluetooth ◀ **Figure 8-7**

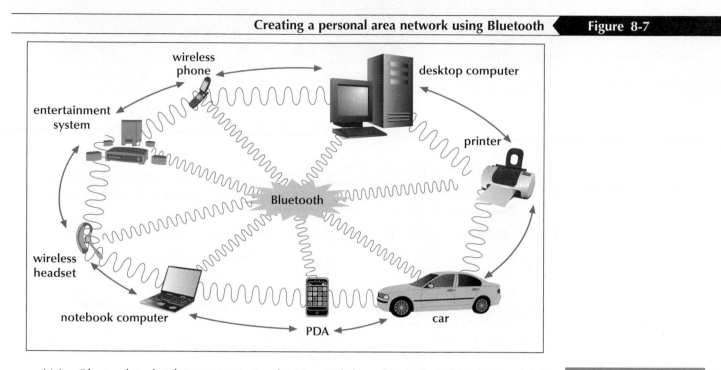

Using Bluetooth technology, you can synchronize and share data among as many as eight Bluetooth-compatible devices within the specified range, usually from 3 to 300 feet, at rates of 1 to 3 Mbps. A collection of devices connected via Bluetooth technology is called a piconet. A **piconet** can connect two to eight devices at a time. However, all devices connected in a piconet must have identical configurations. In a piconet, one device acts as a master during the connection. You can connect piconets with up to eight devices to each other, allowing you to share information between the master devices. You can use Bluetooth-enabled devices to transfer files, listen to music playing on a stereo through a headset, print documents from your office or from another office with a Bluetooth compatible printer, or use a wireless headset to talk on your cell phone or the built-in cell phone in your car. Because Bluetooth uses radio waves, the devices have to be located within the specified range, but the waves can send data around the corner, down the hall, or from your briefcase, without requiring a direct line of sight. Bluetooth might seem similar to Wi-Fi, but it's not. Figure 8-8 compares wireless network standards to Bluetooth.

Tip

Most consumer Bluetooth devices have a range of 30 feet and data transfer rate of 1 Mbps.

Figure 8-8   Comparing Wi-Fi standards with Bluetooth

	802.11a	802.11b	802.11g	802.11n	Bluetooth
Used in	Office	Home or office	Home or office	Home or office	Home or office
Range	Up to 100 feet	Up to 200 feet	Up to 200 feet	Up to 900 feet	Up to 300 feet
Connections	64 devices per access point	128 devices per access point	128 devices per access point	128 devices per access point	8 devices per piconet
Radio spectrum	5 GHz	2.4 GHz	2.4 GHz	5 GHz	2.45 GHz
Data transfer rate	Up to 54 Mbps	Up to 11 Mbps	Up to 54 Mbps	Up to 200 Mbps	Up to 3 Mbps

Ruby is interested in knowing more about Bluetooth to synchronize devices and share resources between the mobile vet clinics and the main office. She asks you to research this technology as part of your investigation of wireless networking options.

To find information about Bluetooth:

▶ **1.** Return to the Online Companion page for Session 8.1, and then find the heading **Bluetooth**.

▶ **2.** Click a link for one of the sites listed, and wait while your browser loads the page.

▶ **3.** Follow some of the links on the page to learn more about Bluetooth topics, such as how these networks are configured, what types of devices use Bluetooth technology, and other general information that might help you understand the technical requirements, advantages, and disadvantages of using Bluetooth at Mobile Vet Services. Your research should focus on general information about Bluetooth, not about the specific companies that manufacture Bluetooth-compatible devices. If the site provides links to demonstrations and your browser can display them, explore the demos to learn more about Bluetooth technology.

    Trouble? If you try to view a demonstration and your browser tells you that it is missing a required plug-in, cancel the demo and try another link. Do not download any software or browser plug-ins at this time.

▶ **4.** When you are finished exploring the first Web site, return to the Online Companion page for Session 8.1, and then click the link to another business in the Bluetooth section. Follow the links on the home page to continue your research about Bluetooth.

▶ **5.** Return to the Online Companion page for Session 8.1.

Many manufacturers create products that are certified for Bluetooth applications. Bluetooth will be a technology that you will carefully consider for the vets.

Wireless Wide Area Networking

Many devices have been capable of making wireless Internet connections since 1999, but they were plagued by slow data-transfer speeds, limited interactivity, poor user interfaces, and reliance on only those networks for which they were manufactured.

Devices connecting to a WLAN based on Wi-Fi or to a wireless mesh network must be within the stated boundary of the WLAN. You can use your notebook computer to make a wireless network connection in your office, the conference room, or any other location within the WLAN's range. However, when you're waiting for a plane at the airport or sitting in a hotel room in another state or country, you must use another network to connect to the Internet. You can connect your notebook computer to a cell phone to connect to the Internet, but this process might require a cable connection between your cell phone and notebook computer.

Wireless wide area networking (**WWAN**) makes it possible to access the Internet from anywhere within the boundaries of the WWAN. As its name implies, a WWAN is a wireless network that provides network coverage to a large geographical area. WWANs provide wireless connections to the Internet using 2.5G and 3G networks created by cellular phone carriers. To access the Internet using a WWAN, you need a WWAN PC card for the device that you want to use and an account with the cellular carrier that owns the network. Once you have a compatible device and an account, you can connect your device to the WWAN and access the Internet from any location where the cellular phone carrier has a signal. For this reason, WWAN is an excellent option for traveling professionals who need Internet access from many different geographical locations and other areas where Wi-Fi service isn't available. Unlike Wi-Fi connectivity, as you travel, your device will remain connected for as long as the device can receive the cellular phone carrier's signal.

Mobile Wireless Connections | InSight

Most major cellular phone carriers offer consumers wireless Internet connectivity service for a daily or monthly rate. This service requires an account with the cellular phone carrier and a WWAN network interface card or modem to pick up the signal. You can purchase a WWAN network interface card or modem separately or have it installed in a new computer from certain manufacturers, such as Dell, Hewlett-Packard, and Toshiba. If you buy the card or modem separately, some cellular carriers call it a PC Card, a Mobile Broadband Card, an Aircard, or a USB modem. These small devices fit into the PC Card slot or USB port on a notebook computer. When you use one of these devices, you will get Internet access when you are within the range of the cellular carrier's network.

Before purchasing a wireless broadband card or modem, check the cellular carrier's network coverage maps for wireless broadband service and make sure that you will be able to pick up the carrier's signal in places where you'll need to connect to the Internet. The coverage area might be identical to where you can get cell phone reception, but this is not always the case, so it's important to check the correct map for wireless service.

Wireless broadband cards and modems are very affordable, but some carriers require a two-year contract for the service when you purchase the device. Be sure to understand the contract terms before purchasing the device; if you purchase the device and sign a contract, you might be subject to fines and other fees if you cancel the agreement before the end of the term. With so many broadband options available, you never know when a more affordable option might present itself, so it's a good idea to look for short-term solutions that match your budget.

You have told Ruby about the different ways to do business wirelessly, including the use of different wireless devices and networks. As the owner of a mobile business, Ruby is very interested in what the future holds for wireless delivery of Internet services.

Metropolitan Area Networking: WiMAX

The last technology that you want to tell Ruby about is **WiMAX (Worldwide Interoperability for Microwave Access)**, which uses the 802.16 standards defined by the IEEE for metropolitan area networks. WiMAX is similar to Wi-Fi because it uses radio waves for communication, but WiMAX transmits at a different radio spectrum and provides a much greater range to create a metropolitan area network. A **metropolitan area network (MAN)** provides wireless broadband Internet access via radio signals in the 2 to 11 GHz and 10 to 66 GHz radio spectrum, with a range of up to 31 miles and speeds of up to 70 Mbps. When multiple WiMAX towers are connected to each other, WiMAX has the potential to solve some of the geographical and speed limitations of wired networks and other wireless networks, including Wi-Fi. For example, the wireless service of many carriers is limited by the coverage area of the network, and Wi-Fi is limited by the number of access points that are connected to each other to form a network. Both of these options provide wireless Internet access, but not at the same speed of a broadband connection such as DSL or a cable modem.

WiMAX provides broadband Internet connections at the same speed as DSL and cable, but through wireless radio connections. In 2005, WiMAX was deployed in several markets, including New York City and a remote part of New Zealand. In New York City, WiMAX provider TowerStream installed WiMAX towers and WiMAX receivers on rooftops and in office windows of a dense part of the city. TowerStream's customers simply plug the WiMAX receiver into their existing local area network, replacing the need for high-speed phone lines or cables. Because the WiMAX signal is so powerful, it can replace up to 60 high-speed T1 lines and serve numerous customers simultaneously. Since its inception, many major U.S. markets, including San Francisco, Chicago, Seattle, Boston, Dallas-Fort Worth, Tampa Bay, Detroit, Atlanta, and Miami, are served by WiMAX service.

In New Zealand, provider Broadcast Communications, Ltd. used WiMAX to bring high-speed Internet connections to remote areas where no cable or telephone lines exist for wired high-speed Internet connections. As early as 2005, nearly half of all New Zealand households, many of which would never benefit from high-speed wired broadband because of geographical limitations, had high-speed wireless Internet connections provided by WiMAX.

WiMAX works by connecting a WiMAX tower to an ISP that provides the Internet service. The WiMAX towers are connected to each other via radio signals. WiMAX transmitters, which can be located up to 31 miles from the towers, send the signal to homes and businesses that have WiMAX receivers. Businesses can plug the WiMAX receiver into their existing local area networks to provide high-speed Internet access to all of their connected devices. Figure 8-9 shows how WiMAX works.

WiMAX network in a metropolitan area Figure 8-9

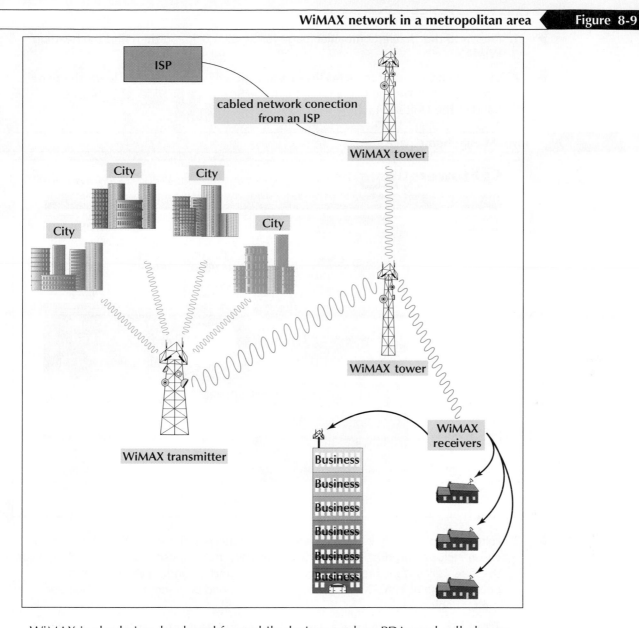

WiMAX is also being developed for mobile devices, such as PDAs and cell phones, making it possible for users to roam between Wi-Fi hotspots and WiMAX coverage areas. Because WiMAX can support many types of data transmissions, it is also used for **VoIP**, or **Voice over Internet Protocol**, which converts audio signals to digital packets so that you can use a broadband wired or wireless Internet connection to make local and long distance telephone calls. In 2008, many manufacturers, including Intel, started producing the necessary hardware for mobile devices to pick up WiMAX signals. Most experts predict that all new desktop and notebook computers and wireless devices will eventually have built-in 802.16 cards, as well. For older computers and devices, consumers can purchase the required equipment and install it, much like what is available now for Wi-Fi devices.

Ruby wants to learn more about WiMAX so you can anticipate the hardware and other considerations necessary for Mobile Vet Services to use it.

To learn more about WiMAX:

▶ **1.** Return to the Online Companion page for Session 8.1, and then find the heading **WiMAX**.

▶ **2.** Click a link for one of the sites listed and wait while your browser loads the page. Figure 8-10 shows the home page for TowerStream, a provider of WiMAX broadband in the United States.

Figure 8-10 ▶ **TowerStream home page**

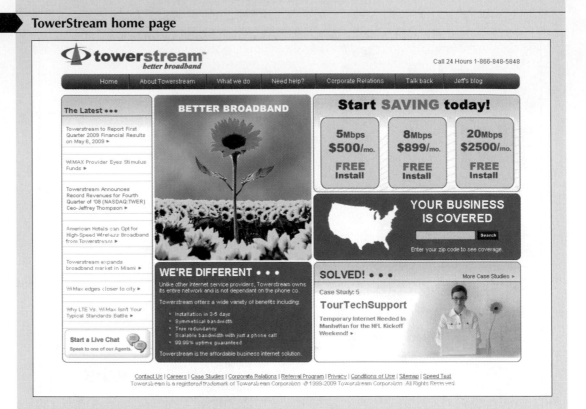

▶ **3.** Follow some of the links on the page to learn more about WiMAX. If the site you chose includes product demonstrations or case studies, use the link provided to run these features. Your research should focus on understanding the current and potential use of WiMAX in a metropolitan area and on general information about the technology.

Trouble? If you try to view a demonstration and your browser tells you that it is missing a required plug-in, cancel the demo and try another link. Do not download any software or browser plug-ins at this time.

▶ **4.** When you are finished exploring the first Web site, return to the Online Companion page for Session 8.1, and then click another link in the WiMAX section. Follow the links on the home page to continue your research about WiMAX.

▶ **5.** Return to the Online Companion page for Session 8.1.

Because all of the vets use wireless devices, you need to know more about the types of tasks that the devices must handle. After speaking with the staff in this morning's meeting, you determine that they are interested in using a PDA or cell phone to make and receive telephone calls, run instant messaging software, and organize their contact data and notes. In addition, several Mobile Vet Services employees expressed an interest in using their wireless devices to view Web pages and to take pictures that they can send back to the main office. Because the vets want to download Web pages and transfer large picture files of photos that they take, you'll need to find an option that has a fast transfer rate and devices that have the desired features. Finally, because the vets travel frequently, you'll need to make sure that the device you recommend and any service provider you select will offer connectivity options for almost anywhere in the United States.

Using Wireless Devices to Access the Internet

The best way to begin your search for wireless solutions for the vets is to begin with an exploration of the network that you plan to use. Because the vets will rely heavily on their devices, your first priority is to explore options that use 3G or 3.5G cellular phone carriers to provide Internet connections through a WWAN. Most cellular phone carriers, such as Verizon Wireless and AT&T Wireless, make it easy to select a device that works on a network and provide other resources such as charts to compare and contrast the different features of the wireless device. Most carriers offer specific products, such as the BlackBerry, wireless USB modem, and MiFi device shown in Figure 8-11, to work on their wireless networks. You'll begin by exploring the Web sites of some of the major cellular phone carriers.

BlackBerry, wireless USB modem, and MiFi device ◀ Figure 8-11

As you are conducting your research, make sure to consider the ways the vets will use their devices so you can select an appropriate device to meet their needs.

To find information about wireless networks and devices:

▶ **1.** On the Online Companion page for Session 8.1, find the heading **Wireless Providers**.

▶ **2.** Click a link to one of the sites listed to open its home page.

3. Locate a link that opens a page describing the plans (or business plans) offered by the cellular phone carrier.

   Trouble? If you are prompted to enter your zip code, enter the zip code for your local or permanent address.

4. Follow some of the links on the page to learn more about the different wireless plans that will support the needs of Mobile Vet Services. If the site provides a link to the wireless devices it sells or manufactures, follow this link to learn about the different devices. If the site provides a link to a map of the wireless network's coverage area, click it and investigate the network's national coverage area. Some sites might provide links to demonstrations; if your browser can display them, explore these demos to learn more about the provider's services.

   Trouble? If you try to view a demonstration and your browser tells you that it is missing a required plug-in, cancel the demo and try another link. Do not download any software or browser plug-ins at this time.

5. When you are finished exploring the first Web site, return to the Online Companion page for Session 8.1, and then click the link to another company in the Wireless Providers section. Repeat Steps 3 and 4 to continue your research about wireless devices and the provider's network plans and coverage.

6. When you are finished exploring the second site, return to the Online Companion page for Session 8.1, and then click the link to another company in the Wireless Providers section. Repeat Steps 3 and 4 to continue your research about wireless devices and the provider's network plans and coverage.

7. Return to the Online Companion page for Session 8.1.

Because the vets indicated a preference for using their devices in places where Wi-Fi is likely to be in use, you also decide to research places that provide Wi-Fi service in the United States. Most places let users connect for free, but others require a subscription to a service or payment for use. Figure 8-12 shows one company that provides subscription-based Wi-Fi service for visitors to the Chicago O'Hare International Airport.

Figure 8-12 **Boingo Wireless page**

Some networks, such as those found in airports and hotels, let you pay a daily fee to use the network. Other networks require a monthly fee for using the network. Fortunately, there are many plans that would work well for Mobile Vet Services.

To find information about Wi-Fi service in the United States:

▶ 1. On the Online Companion page for Session 8.1, find the heading **Wi-Fi Service** and choose one of these sites to use in your search.

▶ 2. Click a link for one of the sites listed to open its home page.

▶ 3. Follow some of the links on the home page to learn more about Wi-Fi service that will support the needs of Mobile Vet Services. Use the site to find information about the type of payment plans and their costs, the coverage area of the network, and other details that you will need to learn more about the service. If the site includes information about single-user pricing and corporate pricing, make sure to investigate both options so you can discuss the different pricing plans with Ruby.

> **Trouble?** If you try to view a demonstration and your browser tells you that it is missing a required plug-in, cancel the demo and try another link. Do not download any software or browser plug-ins at this time.

▶ 4. When you are finished exploring the first Web site, return to the Online Companion page for Session 8.1, and then click the link to another business in the Wi-Fi Service section. Follow the links on the home page to continue your research about the provider's products, services, pricing plans, and the locations they service.

▶ 5. Close your browser.

You will discuss the information you found about wireless services, networks, and devices with Ruby and her staff in your next meeting. You are excited about the possibilities for creating a mobile office to increase the speed at which Mobile Vet Services receives and disseminates information with clients and with the main office. In the next session, you will examine the different methods for securing wireless devices and their transmissions.

Session 8.1 Quick Check | Review

1. What is the transfer rate of data on a 3G wireless network?
2. What is SMS?
3. What are the two primary challenges for installing nationwide 3G wireless networks in the United States?
4. Which Wi-Fi network standard(s) provide the fastest data transfer rate?
5. True or False: You can connect any 802.11b-compatible device to any 802.11b-compliant access point.
6. What is a piconet?
7. What is WiMAX? What is its range and transmission transfer rate?
8. True or False: A PDA will work on any wireless carrier's network.

Session 8.2

Security Concerns for Wireless Networks

In Session 8.1, you learned about the different kinds of wireless connections you can make to the Internet. The kind of connection you make depends on the type of device you have—an Internet device that was manufactured for a certain cellular network won't necessarily work on another cellular network. The type of connection you make also depends on the network that you are connecting to. Being able to pick up a wireless signal doesn't mean that you can automatically use it to connect to the Internet—nor does it always mean that you *should* connect to a wireless signal that you pick up.

Just like in the wired world of networking, ensuring that the data sent over a wireless network is secure presents many challenges. Some of the security challenges are the same between wired and wireless networks, but many of the challenges in protecting a wireless network are complicated by the fact that a wireless network sends its data through the air using radio signals that are easy to intercept. Although there are different kinds of threats to wireless networks—and new threats as hackers get better at figuring out how to manipulate the technology and its signals—the following list of threats are common to all wireless networks:

- Attacks that prevent the use of a device or decrease the network's bandwidth
- Intercepting information sent over a wireless network
- Hacking into a wireless device to gain entry to its data or functions
- Stealing the identity of an access point to gain access to its connected users' devices
- Viruses, spyware, and other security threats sent in the form of files
- Using information entered by the user into a wireless device to steal logins and other sensitive information

Of course, there are also security threats to individual wireless devices, the most notable of which is theft of the device itself. Before you can teach Ruby about securing individual wireless devices, you want to discuss the different kinds of security threats to wireless networks and some of the issues that wireless networks face.

Wireless Encryption Methods

As you learned in Tutorial 7, encryption is the process of coding information so that it is not readable by devices or people who do not have the secret key used to return the information back to its original, readable state. By default, most wireless networks are unsecured, meaning that any compatible wireless device within range of the network can connect to it. Unfortunately, many home and small business networks are never secured and therefore are vulnerable to various kinds of attacks. There are many wireless encryption methods that provide different levels of protection for wireless networks.

Wired Equivalent Privacy

One of the first attempts to secure wireless networks, **Wired Equivalent Privacy (WEP)**, is a security protocol for wireless LANs (using Wi-Fi) that works by encrypting data sent over the network. This protocol is part of the 802.11 standard and has been used since 1999. When WEP is enabled, it encrypts the data sent over the network with a 64-bit or 128-bit key, sometimes also called a **passphrase**, that is entered by the user. These settings—64-bit key and 128-bit key—are standards used in the electronic commerce industry to represent the security level of the key. The key works because both the wireless router or access point and the device connecting to the wireless network have the same key and use it to encrypt and decrypt messages. The encryption slows down the network somewhat because of the time it takes to encrypt and decrypt the messages. The level of encryption provided by the key depends on the key's length; a 128-bit key is said to be more secure than a 64-bit key because it is longer (contains more characters). A 64-bit key contains 10 hexadecimal characters (the digits 0 through 9 and the letters A though F); a 128-bit key contains 26 hexadecimal characters. Figure 8-13 shows examples of randomly generated 64-bit and 128-bit keys and a custom 128-bit key based on a user-entered passphrase.

Security keys in hexadecimal characters ◀ **Figure 8-13**

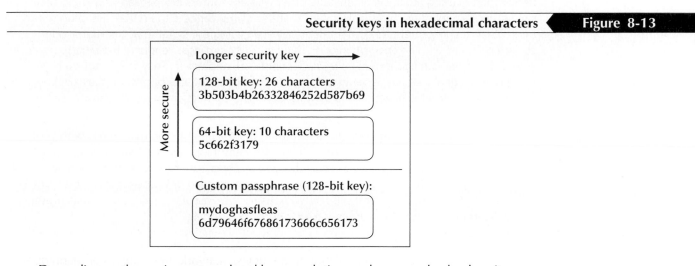

Depending on the equipment used and how much time and money a hacker has, it can take a very long time to decipher an intercepted message encrypted with a 64-bit key, and even longer to decipher an intercepted message encrypted with a 128-bit key. Deciphering a key isn't easy, and it requires a substantial amount of computing power and time. But, for a person who has these resources, it is possible to decipher a WEP-encrypted message. For this reason, and because of the actual way that data is encrypted, many computing experts don't feel that WEP provides sufficient security for wireless networks.

Another vulnerability of WEP encryption is the fact that the key used to encrypt the data you are sending is sent over the network prior to the actual data being encrypted, and this same key is used to encrypt every data packet. This means that you send the key out over the air with no protection before the data you are sending is encrypted. (If you change the key frequently, you'll provide some additional security to the network.) Although this is a simplified explanation of the problem, it does support the consensus of most experts that using WEP is better than nothing, but not ideal, for securing a wireless network.

Wi-Fi Protected Access

Another wireless network security protocol, **Wi-Fi Protected Access (WPA)**, is a standard that was developed by the Wi-Fi Alliance in 2003 to address some of the inherent weaknesses in WEP. WPA provides better encryption than WEP because WPA uses a preshared key to encrypt data (so your key isn't broadcast before your data is encrypted) and individual data packets are encrypted with different keys. This means that a hacker might be able to intercept a data packet, but he won't gain access to the entire message automatically, making the content of the complete message difficult to read. Like WEP, WPA can use a 128-bit key to encrypt data.

Although WPA provides good protection, one drawback is that all devices in the network need to use WPA. Devices manufactured prior to 2003 will still need to use WEP or another protocol to secure data. Some wireless routers and access points let you use a combination of WEP and WPA when your network makes connections to devices that can't manage WPA.

In business settings and in large organizations, networks might carry highly sensitive information such as a person's credit card number or the medical history of a client. These businesses must use advanced methods for securing data.

For home and small business users, however, the choice of which method to use to secure a wireless network is up to the individual user. Most experts agree that some encryption is better than nothing at all. Unfortunately, many wireless routers are packaged with no security settings enabled on them. This means that users who connect the router and plug it into their DSL or cable outlet and then immediately start using the signal that the router puts out are doing so with no encryption or enabled security settings. People in the next room or across the street can also detect your wireless network and use it. They might not do anything to the signal that has negative consequences to you, but at a minimum, they are borrowing your Internet connection and slowing down the connection speed when you use the network.

It's worth taking the time to read and understand the documentation that comes with your wireless router to learn how to secure it. You might need to install some software on your computer to access the router so you can change its configurations. If the router and your computer support WPA, you should use this encryption instead of WEP as it is more secure. However, if your computer won't support WPA, using WEP usually provides sufficient protection to keep casual users from accessing your network's signal.

In addition to adding data encryption to a wireless network, there are other techniques that secure the network by limiting the devices that can actually connect to it.

MAC Address Filtering

Every Internet device has a network interface card that it uses to connect to a network. Each manufacturer of network interface cards adds a unique number, called a **Media Access Control address** (or more commonly called a **MAC address**) to identify the device. Another way to protect a wireless network is to designate the devices that you want to allow to connect to the network. Most routers and access points include software that lets you identify the allowable devices using their MAC addresses. If you enable MAC address filtering for a wireless router or access point, then it will only accept connections from the devices with the MAC addresses that you entered. Other wireless devices still might *detect* your wireless network, but they won't be able to connect to it because their MAC addresses are not specified for access. MAC address filtering adds another layer of security to a wireless network because it doesn't allow unknown devices to make connections.

Ruby asks you where to find a MAC address for a device. You explain that for detachable network interface cards, such as ones that you insert into a notebook computer's PC card slot or USB devices, the MAC address is usually printed on the card or USB device. A MAC address appears in the format 00:00:00:0A:0B:0C, as a combination of digits and letters. When a device contains an internal network interface card, you can see its MAC address by using the Windows Device Manager to view the properties for the network interface card.

Disabling the SSID Broadcast

When a wireless router or access point sends out its signal, it also broadcasts its **service set identifier (SSID)** as a way of identifying the network's name. This feature makes it possible for roaming devices to discover the network and also enables you to log in to the correct network. Most manufacturers of wireless routers and access points use the manufacturer name or the word "default" as the default SSID for the device. When you install a wireless router or access point, you can accept this default name or change it to a name that has up to 32 alphanumeric characters. Most manufacturers strongly recommend that you change the default name as part of its initial configuration. All devices that connect to the wireless network must use the SSID.

For public wireless networks, sending out the SSID is necessary because it provides information that a wireless device needs to be able to connect to the wireless network. However, for home networks, sending out the SSID is not necessary, especially if you have already used MAC address filtering to identify the devices that you want to connect to the wireless network. In other words, after you configure your own devices to connect to your own wireless network, you don't need to broadcast the SSID any longer because you won't need to roam and find the network—you already know the network's name and its settings, and your wireless devices know them once they are configured. Disabling the SSID broadcast of the network makes the network invisible to roaming devices and therefore makes it more difficult for other devices to detect its signal.

If you change the default name of the wireless router or access point, you also prevent unknown users from detecting your network by attempting to randomly connect to a wireless network using a manufacturer name or the word "default" as an SSID. **Wardriving**—driving through a neighborhood with a wireless-enabled notebook computer with the goal of locating houses and businesses that have wireless networks in order to gain access to them—is a common way for hackers to get into unsecured networks. Finding a wireless network that uses "default" or a manufacturer name as its SSID is a good clue to hackers that the wireless network's owner didn't take precautions to secure the wireless network. Used alone and especially with other security precautions, disabling the SSID adds another layer of protection to the network to prevent unknown devices from connecting to it.

You can change the SSID name for your wireless router or access point and disable its signal by logging into the router or access point and changing these settings in the device configuration.

Changing the Default Login

When you install a wireless router or access point for the first time, the device is configured with a default user name and password that is printed in the device's user manual. The default login is provided so you can use your computer to access the device's settings and configure it to work as desired. One of the most serious mistakes that home users make when installing a wireless network is the failure to change the default login for the device. By making this mistake, you make it possible for anyone who already knows the manufacturer's default login to access your wireless network. If you haven't implemented any other security for your device, such as changing the default SSID or disabling its broadcast, your wireless network is visible to intruders and easy to access using the default login. When you install a wireless network, make it a priority to change the default login and password. Be sure to keep your login in a safe place; after you change it, you won't be able to access the device's configuration page again using the default login.

Tip

SSIDs are case-sensitive, so be sure to note the case of the name that you assign and use the same case when configuring attached devices to connect to it.

Tip

Piggybacking is a term used to describe a person who gains access to and uses a wireless network, sometimes by wardriving.

Ruby appreciates the information you provided to her about securing a wireless network. Although she realizes that she can purchase a wireless router or access point and start using it right away, she now understands why it is a good idea to take an hour or so to learn how to configure it properly. To make it easier for her to configure the wireless network in the office, you provide her with the checklist shown in Figure 8-14.

Figure 8-14 ▶	Security checklist for installing a wireless router or access point

☐ Change the default login and password for the wireless router or access point.

☐ Change the default SSID. Be sure to type the name in the desired case, as the SSID is case sensitive.

☐ Obtain the MAC addresses of the wireless devices that will connect to the wireless network, and then enter their MAC addresses using the configuration for the wireless router or device.

☐ Enable MAC address filtering on the wireless router or access point.

☐ Enable the highest level of security that your wireless devices and wireless router or access point can manage. Be sure to use the most secure key the wireless router or access point offers. If you must use WEP, change the passphrase occasionally.

☐ Make sure that all of your wireless devices can connect to the wireless network with the settings you've implemented.

☐ Disable the SSID for your wireless router or access point.

☐ When not using the wireless network for an extended period of time, such as when leaving on vacation, power it off.

Of course, the safest wireless network is one that is turned off. Most experts recommend disconnecting and powering off your wireless network when you won't be using it for an extended period of time, such as when you leave on vacation.

Security Concerns for Wireless Devices

As previously mentioned, the most basic security concern for the owner of a wireless device is theft or loss. In this case, you might just lose a cell phone that you can cancel and replace. If you have a PDA or other device that also stores data such as passwords that you use to connect to online banking or your Internet connection, you might be losing much more than the device itself.

When looking at ways to secure a wireless device, you explain to Ruby that there are some basic precautions that each user must take to secure the actual device and also to secure the connections the device makes. Because these two types of protections involve different security protocols, you'll examine them in detail next.

Protecting the Data on a Wireless Device

Just like on a personal computer, a wireless device is vulnerable to certain kinds of attacks to the data it stores. Unlike a personal computer, the kinds of attacks are different, and they are sometimes different for individual devices. For example, devices enabled with Bluetooth technology are vulnerable to certain kinds of attacks not aimed at devices that do not use Bluetooth.

A wireless device that connects to the Internet needs to have a good antivirus or Internet security software program installed on it. Just like for personal computers, you must configure the antivirus or Internet security suite program to download current virus patterns and other updates on a regular basis.

Wireless devices of all kinds are subject to **over-the-shoulder attacks**, in which an unauthorized person uses his or her physical proximity to your device to attempt to get your login information, passwords, or other sensitive data while you are working. Because some people use wireless notebook computers in public places, such as coffeehouses, they might not question another person standing behind them because they might mistake this person for one who is standing in line or waiting for a friend. When working in public places, it's important to be aware of where other people are located in proximity to you and your device, especially if you are using your wireless device to transmit data that you wouldn't want another person to see. For this reason, most security experts advise against activities such as online banking, checking email, and online shopping in public places. Not only are these activities visible to over-the-shoulder attacks, they are also subject to being intercepted, as you will learn in the next section.

When working in a business facility, such as a convention center, sports arena, or other large building that provides Internet access, or when working in a hotel, opt for a wired Ethernet connection whenever possible. Although your devices are still subject to some basic security threats, connecting to the Internet with a wired connection eliminates the wireless threats to your device.

Setting a password on your device is another way to protect it. If you select a strong password, such as one that contains more than eight characters and a combination of digits and letters, you'll protect the device's data if someone steals it or if you lose it.

Evil Twin Attacks

Because wireless technology makes it possible to work in almost any place with a wireless network connection, many people enjoy the freedom of having a mobile office or the convenience of being able to do work outside of the conventional office or home office environment. As you learned in Session 8.1, many businesses offer Wi-Fi connections as a way of attracting customers and enhancing their experiences. Most customers are glad to be able to enjoy a coffee at a local coffeehouse or restaurant while doing their computer work, especially when they can access the wireless network for free. Some customers are irritated when a business offers Wi-Fi service but requires a fee to make connections because so many businesses offer the same service at no charge. Customers expect Wi-Fi service at certain kinds of businesses and in certain areas, such as airport terminals and retail automotive stores, where customers spend time waiting. Fortunately the technology to build a wireless network is affordable and easy to implement, and businesses such as McDonald's and Panera Bread have many satisfied customers who use their wireless networks.

As with any new technology, the benefits come at a price as hackers have found ways to use the technology that attracts customers to retail outlets as a way to steal data and information from them. In an **evil twin attack**, also sometimes called a **café latte attack** because the attack often occurs at coffeehouses, a hacker gathers information about an access point and then uses that information to set up his own computer to use the real access point's signal to impersonate the access point. To other customers, the hacker looks like a customer who is also enjoying the use of the free access point. As customers use their devices to pick up and connect to the access point, they are unaware that they are actually connecting to the hacker's computer. When you use one of the many free public hotspots for wireless computing, the data you send over the network is not usually encrypted or secure. This data is subject to hackers using **sniffer programs** to illegally monitor activity on the wireless network in order to obtain personal information that you might transmit, such as a login or a credit card number. The hacker uses these connections and a sniffer program to read and store the data that the customers send to his system. For customers who are engaging in online banking, online shopping, or logging on to Web sites that require passwords, the hacker happily collects this sensitive data. Depending on what data the hacker collects, he might later use the customer's credit card numbers to make online purchases or use login information to use the victim's email account. All of this happens without the customer's or the access point's owner knowing about it.

InSight		**Using Public Hotspots Safely**

To protect your device against an evil twin attack, you can refrain from using your wireless device in any public place, but there may be times when you are traveling or working outside of your home or office and need to connect to the Internet. You can take several precautions to protect your wireless device.

First, avoid online banking, online shopping, and visiting Web sites that require you to enter a login or personal information. In other words, don't work in public places where you enter something that a thief would like to steal.

What if you must use email or another service that requires a login? Instead of connecting to any free hotspot that your device picks up, establish a connection to a network that provides some kind of login from the access point's owner. Although you might prefer to get your Wi-Fi service for free, your connection is more secure at places like Starbucks, where the hotspot requires an account with an established service provider such as AT&T WiFi Services. You'll need to pay for your use of the service, but you're more likely to connect to a wireless network that provides some sort of encryption and security.

Ruby is concerned about this information, as she has used public access points in the past while working in the public library and at a local restaurant. Because she is like many other users who enjoy the freedom of working away from the office, she asks if there is any way to protect her wireless devices and her personal data when connecting to a public access point. You tell her that she can protect herself somewhat by limiting the amount of personal information she sends when using the wireless network connection. Another option is to investigate the use of software programs that protect users who connect to public hotspots. You'll examine some of these programs next.

To investigate software that protects wireless connections:

▶ 1. Start your Web browser, open the Online Companion page at **www.cengage.com/internet/np/internet8** and log on to your account, click the **Tutorial 8** link, and then click the **Session 8.2** link. Find the heading **Wireless Intrusion Software** and click a link to one of the businesses listed to open its home page. Figure 8-15 shows the home page for AirMagnet, a service that offers wireless intrusion software for individual users.

AirMagnet home page | Figure 8-15

▶ **2.** Use the links at the site to investigate options Ruby might use to secure wireless devices that connect to public hotspots. Look for products labeled as "personal" products and not as "enterprise" products, which are intended for large organizations. Find out how the software is installed, how it works, and its approximate cost, including trial versions.

▶ **3.** Return to the Online Companion for Session 8.2, and then click a link to another provider. Use the guidelines in Step 2 to investigate the products of the second provider.

▶ **4.** When you are finished, close your Web browser.

Ruby wonders what else she can do to protect her devices. You tell her that disabling the auto connection feature of a wireless device to connect to the strongest network in range or any network in range is a good way to prevent it from connecting to an unknown and unsecured network. The second thing to do is disable file sharing on the device, so if a hacker accesses the device, it will be more difficult to get to the device's files.

Security Concerns for Bluetooth Devices

As you learned in Session 8.1, the usual range of a Bluetooth device is 10 to 30 feet, and up to 300 feet, depending on the device. This range makes it possible to use a wireless headset with a cell phone or print documents without a cable. Because the range of a Bluetooth device is usually smaller than Wi-Fi's range, you might think that Bluetooth devices aren't subject to security problems, but they are. Three security problems of Bluetooth devices are bluejacking, bluesnarfing, and bluebugging. Because Mobile Vet Services already uses Bluetooth-enabled devices, and might purchase new devices that use Bluetooth, Ruby asks you to explain these problems.

Bluejacking

Tip

Some sources state that the word bluejacking is coined from the terms "blue" and "hijacking." During a bluejack, the device is not actually hijacked, so this combination of terms is misleading.

Bluejacking is a term coined from the words "blue" and "ajack." (Ajack is the user name of a person in an Internet forum who claims to have been the first person to bluejack someone else.) The bluejacker sends an anonymous message in the form of a phone contact displayed as a text message to a Bluetooth device to surprise the owner, express an opinion, or make a social connection. In the first documented bluejacking, Ajack sent a message to the owner of a Nokia phone that said "Buy Ericsson!" to express his preference for Sony Ericsson phones.

Bluejacking, although alarming to some people, is mostly harmless because the victim's device is not breached; it is only sent a message. The message is usually sent by a bluejacker who takes advantage of the victim's unprotected device or is interested in the victim. Bluejacking is temporary—when the bluejacker's device or your device move out of range, the messages will stop. Because bluejacking uses a feature of the device designed for legitimate purposes, it does not require special software or equipment. To protect a Bluetooth device from a bluejacking attack, you can disable the device's Bluetooth feature so that its signal is invisible (also called **undiscoverable mode**) to other users.

Bluesnarfing

A more serious security problem of Bluetooth-enabled devices, **bluesnarfing**, occurs when a hacker with special software is able to detect the signal from a Bluetooth device and gain access to its data without the owner's knowledge. The hacker is able to access data stored on the device, such as the contact list, connect to the Internet, listen in on phone calls, and send email messages from the victim's device. Some hackers wait in crowded areas such as shopping malls and set their device to pick up Bluetooth signals. If the hacker can make a connection to an unprotected Bluetooth device, he'll use it for as long as it is in range to access data on the device.

To protect a Bluetooth device from bluesnarfing, you can set the device to undiscoverable mode, making its signal invisible to other users. Since this vulnerability was discovered in 2003, many manufacturers of Bluetooth devices have released software patches to prevent the problem, but many owners did not install them. Newer Bluetooth devices are not subject to bluesnarfing attacks because this vulnerability has been fixed.

Bluebugging

The worst security threat to Bluetooth devices is **bluebugging**, which occurs when a hacker gains access to the device and its functions without the owner's consent. A bluebugging attack lets the hacker use the device to make phone calls, access data, and use the Internet. Some hackers set up phone numbers with per-minute charges to the caller and use bluebugging to dial those numbers while the device is in range. This attack steals from the victim, who is charged for calls he did not make. The hacker can even set callforwarding on the victim's device to send incoming calls to a different number. Most manufacturers of Bluetooth devices have released patches to fix the security flaw that makes bluebugging possible. Newer Bluetooth devices are less vulnerable to these attacks.

The two most serious Bluetooth attacks, bluesnarfing and bluebugging, can only occur within the range of the Bluetooth device and on older devices and those not updated with security patches. Both attacks are less likely when the Bluetooth device is undiscoverable to other users. A good precaution for users of Bluetooth devices is to make sure their devices use the latest software and to turn the Bluetooth feature off when working in crowded areas. Figure 8-16 shows the Device Protection page for the Bluetooth Special Interest Group Web site, which provides information about ways to protect Bluetooth devices from hackers.

Bluetooth Special Interest Group Device Protection page   Figure 8-16

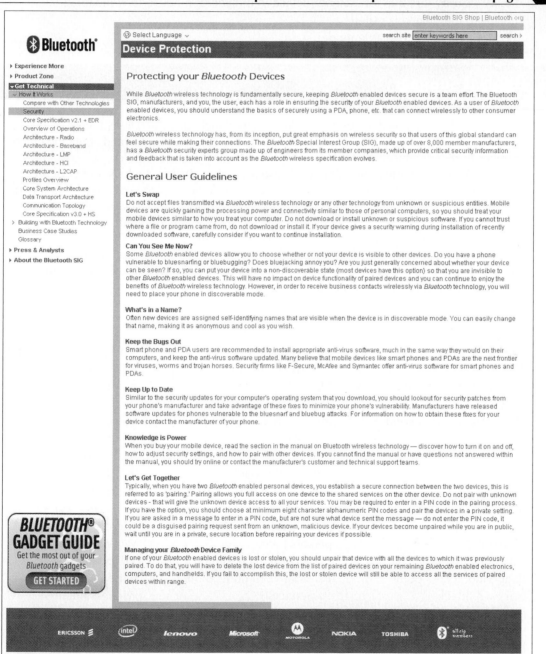

Ruby is satisfied that she can implement appropriate security precautions on any wireless networks that she installs and also on the wireless devices that connect to any wireless networks used by the staff. She will also make sure that Mobile Vet Services staff members who use public hotspots are aware of the precautions you outlined to protect their devices.

Review | Session 8.2 Quick Check

1. What are two types of encryption for wireless networks?
2. What is a MAC address?
3. Why should you disable the SSID on a wireless network?
4. What is an evil twin attack?
5. A security breach that occurs when someone sends a Bluetooth device an unsolicited electronic message with the owner's consent is called _____ .
6. A security threat to a Bluetooth device that involves a hacker downloading data from the device is called _____ .
7. What is undiscoverable mode?

Review | Tutorial Summary

In this tutorial, you learned about the wireless Internet, including the different types of wireless networks, wireless network standards, and wireless devices. You also learned about the different types of security threats and solutions for wireless networks and wireless devices.

Now, or in the future, you might purchase a wireless device, such as a PDA or a cell phone, to avail yourself of the features these wireless devices offer. When selecting a wireless device, make sure that you understand the features of the network on which the device operates. You should carefully examine the network's geographic coverage area, pricing options, and the provider's future expansion plans to ensure that you select the device that most closely matches the functions you need. Whatever option you choose, be sure to protect your wireless network and wireless devices from security threats and to keep abreast of new threats and how to protect yourself from them in the future.

Key Terms

2.5G wireless network
2G wireless
3.5G wireless network
3G wireless
3G wireless and beyond network
4G wireless
access point
bluebugging
bluejacking
bluesnarfing
Bluetooth
café latte attack
dual band access point
evil twin attack
fourth-generation wireless network
hotspot
infrared
Infrared Data Association (IrDA)
Media Access Control address (MAC address)

metropolitan area network (MAN)
MiFi
mobile broadband
multiple band access point
Muni-Fi
Muni WiFi
municipal broadband
over-the-shoulder attack
PAN device
passphrase
personal area networking (PAN)
Personal Communication Service (PCS)
personal digital assistant (PDA)
piconet
piggybacking
range
second-generation wireless network
service set identifier (SSID)
Short Message Service (SMS)
sniffer program

third-generation wireless network
transfer rate
undiscoverable mode
Voice over Internet Protocol (VoIP)
wardriving
Wi-Fi
Wi-Fi Protected Access (WPA)
wired connection
Wired Equivalent Protocol (WEP)
wireless connection
wireless fidelity
wireless Internet
wireless local area network (WLAN)
wireless mesh network
wireless wide area networking (WWAN)
Worldwide Interoperability for Microwave Access (WiMAX)

Practice | Review Assignments

Practice the skills you learned in the tutorial using the same case scenario.

There are no Data Files needed for the Review Assignments.

After carefully reviewing the research you provided, Ruby has decided to implement a wireless network for the main office of Mobile Vet Services. Because the new notebook computers Ruby recently purchased include Wi-Fi and broadband network interface cards, Ruby has decided to create a wireless local area network in the main office and create accounts with a wireless broadband access provider so employees can access the Internet on their wireless devices. She asks for your help to find Wi-Fi hotspots near the office. She is also curious to see which mobile wireless access plan is better—using a Wi-Fi service or a mobile broadband wireless carrier. You conduct your research and summarize its results by completing the following steps.

1. Start your Web browser, open the Online Companion page at www.cengage.com/internet/np/internet8 and log on to your account, click the Tutorial 8 link, and then click the Review Assignments link.
2. Click a link in the Wi-Fi Hotspots section and wait while your browser loads the page.
3. Use the site to find hotspots in the area of Fort Lauderdale, FL, or using the zip codes 33304, 33332, and 33394. Examine the hotspots available in these areas and note the types of businesses that run them. Use the links to two or three Wi-Fi hotspots to learn more about the service provided, including information about the type of network, the security of the network, and the cost of using it.
4. Return to the Online Companion page for the Review Assignments, and then click another link in the Wi-Fi Hotspots section and wait while the browser loads the site's home page. Use the information provided in Step 3 to learn more about the hotspots you find.
5. Return to the Online Companion page for the Review Assignments, and then click a link in the Wi-Fi Service section. Examine the site to learn more about the hotspots in Fort Lauderdale to determine the level of coverage in the city. Use the site to get information about a membership with the Wi-Fi service provider and the equipment needed to use the network. Use the site to learn more about the network's security.
6. Return to the Online Companion page for the Review Assignments, and then click another link in the Wi-Fi Service section. Use the information provided in Step 5 to learn more about creating a Wi-Fi account with this service provider, the cost, the network security, and whether sufficient coverage exists in the city of Fort Lauderdale.
7. Return to the Online Companion page for the Review Assignments, and then click one of the links in the Broadband Wireless section and wait while your browser loads the site's page. Use the links on the page to view a coverage map for the carrier's broadband wireless service. Note whether the service provides broadband wireless service in Fort Lauderdale and the surrounding area. Use the links on the site to find a device that can get wireless Internet and then print the product page for the device. Be sure to find information about the cost of using the service.
8. In a report addressed to your instructor, identify the following information:
   a. The types of businesses that provide Wi-Fi service in Fort Lauderdale, the general cost of using them, and the kind of security they provide.
   b. The Wi-Fi service provider you would recommend that the vets use, and why you feel it is the best choice.
   c. The wireless broadband provider you would recommend that the vets use, and why you feel it is the best choice.

      d. Overall, should the vets use Wi-Fi hotspots, a Wi-Fi service provider, or a broad-band wireless provider to get Internet access when not in the office? Support your recommendation with information you gathered during your research.

   9. Close your browser.

| Apply | **Case Problem 1** |

Evaluate the availability and use of free hotspots in two cities and determine the security issues you might face when using them.

There are no Data Files needed for this Case Problem.

Aspen Hardin   Aspen Hardin is evaluating several colleges that she might like to attend next fall, majoring in business. She will be traveling on day trips to San Francisco and Oakland, California. Because she has a tight budget and needs Internet access while traveling, she wants to determine if there are free hotspots available in these cities that she can connect to with her Wi-Fi certified notebook computer. Aspen asks you to find more information about Wi-Fi hotspots in these areas.

1. Start your Web browser, open the Online Companion page at www.cengage.com/internet/np/internet8 and log on to your account, click the Tutorial 8 link, and then click the Case Problem 1 link. Choose one of the Web sites provided and click it to open the site's home page.

2. Use the links on the home page to find free publicly accessible hotspots in San Francisco, California and Oakland, California. Evaluate the types of businesses that offer free hotspots in each city. Does the site that you are using list hotspots that require fees or a subscription? Print the first page of hotspot locations for each city.

3. Return to the Online Companion page for Case Problem 1, and then click another link to a Wi-Fi service. Use the links on the home page to identify free hotspots in the two cities. Does this site list the same hotspots as the first site that you evaluated? Does the site that you are using list hotspots that require fees or a subscription? Print the first page of hotspot locations for each city.

4. Close your browser.

⊕**EXPLORE** 5. In a report addressed to your instructor, discuss the two sites that you used to find hotspots. As sites that promote "free" hotspots, are these sites easy to use? Do the sites include information about hotspots that require fees or subscriptions? What types of businesses offer hotspots in each city? What advertising supports these sites? Do you feel that the information on these sites is accurate? Why or why not? Be sure to support your answers with information you found at each site.

⊕**EXPLORE** 6. Aspen will be working on a notebook computer. Which types of attacks are her data and her computer subject to when she connects to a free hotspot? Add this information to your report and support your conclusions with information you learned in this tutorial.

| Research | **Case Problem 2** |

Evaluate wireless municipal networks in two major U.S. cities.

There are no Data Files needed for this Case Problem.

Evaluating Wireless Municipalities   Many U.S. cities are implementing city-wide wireless networks in an attempt to attract people and businesses, provide affordable high-speed Internet connections, and improve the quality of the services the city offers. Examples of these cities are Seattle, New York City, and Philadelphia. These cities have chosen different ways to implement the wireless-city concept. In this case problem, you'll evaluate the current status of two cities and report on the progress each city is making toward its goal. Then you will evaluate municipal wireless projects in other areas to see if this trend is occurring nationwide or limited to certain areas.

1. Start your Web browser, open the Online Companion page at www.cengage.com/internet/np/internet8 and log on to your account, click the Tutorial 8 link, and then click the Case Problem 2 link.

✪ EXPLORE 2. Click a link to one of the wireless municipalities listed and wait while your browser loads the site's home page. Use the links on the home page to learn more about the city's attempt to implement a municipal wireless network, including the network's coverage area (not in specific parts of town, but the overall percentage of coverage in general), the technology used (hotspots, wireless mesh network, etc.), the cost to use the network, and methods used by the organization to encourage participation. What type of organization is coordinating the efforts? Is it a not-for-profit organization or a for-profit organization? Are there any business partnerships with other providers to connect the city? If so, who are the partners? Are there any programs geared toward getting low-income residents connected? If so, describe the program.

✪ EXPLORE 3. Return to the Online Companion for Case Problem 2, and then choose a link to another wireless municipality. Use the information provided in Step 2 to evaluate the second municipality's services, coverage, and overall program.

✪ EXPLORE 4. In a report addressed to your instructor, compare and contrast the efforts of the two cities and their progress to create a wireless city. Are they using the same technology, do they offer the same services, and do they have the same goals in terms of connecting people and including low-income residents in the programs? Support your conclusions with specific information you gathered at each site.

5. Close your browser.

Research | Case Problem 3

Learn more about Bluetooth by examining the qualification process and searching for compatible devices.

There are no Data Files needed for this Case Problem.

Jack Campbell, P.C.   Attorney Jack Campbell has practiced criminal law for more than three decades in Montgomery, Alabama. Last year, Jack's assistant, Jillian Hately, purchased a BlackBerry for Jack. She loaded it with Jack's calendar and contact information, and programmed it to send and receive his email. Jack carries the BlackBerry with him to the courthouse, but when working from home, he uses his notebook computer. As a result of his use of different devices, none of them are synchronized and he often misses appointments because they are scheduled on one device but not the others. Jillian thinks the solution for this problem might be to set up a Bluetooth wireless personal area network in Jack's office, so his devices are automatically synchronized when he walks through the door, leaving Jack free to concentrate on his court trials instead of synchronizing his devices. Jack is skeptical about purchasing new compatible devices because he's not convinced that Bluetooth really has universal standards and is easily available for purchase. You will help Jillian convince Jack that Bluetooth might be worth the investment by completing the following steps.

1. Start your Web browser, open the Online Companion page at www.cengage.com/internet/np/internet8 and log on to your account, click the Tutorial 8 link, and then click the Case Problem 3 link. Click the Bluetooth Qualification Program Website link and wait while the browser loads the page.

✪ EXPLORE 2. Follow the links on the home page to answer the following questions in a report addressed to your instructor:
   a. What is a BQTF and what does it do?
   b. What is a BQE and what does it do?

    c. Are all Bluetooth products licensed? If so, who or what licenses the products? Is the license a guarantee of the product's compliance?

    d. What is the current Bluetooth System Specification version?

3. Return to the Online Companion page for Case Problem 3, and then click the Bluetooth.com Connect link. Use the On the Go, On Your Phone, With Your Pictures, With Your Music, At Your Desk, Wacky Applications, and TransSend links on the left side of the page (or similarly named links) to view the suggested usage scenarios for the different types of Bluetooth devices. As you are viewing the scenarios, see if you can find support for how using Bluetooth devices in an office will make things easier for Jack.

⊕ EXPLORE   4. In your report, write an argument for or against using Bluetooth in Jack's office. Remember that Jack is concerned about the compatibility between devices and the cost and availability of new technology. Support your recommendation with information you found on the Web pages you visited.

5. Close your browser.

| Research | **Case Problem 4** |

Expand your knowledge of two other forms of personal area networking—Ultra Wideband and Wireless USB.

There are no Data Files needed for this Case Problem.

Emerging Technologies in High Bandwidth Radio Communications   As you have already learned, personal area networking uses short-range radio signals to create wireless connections between devices located within a short physical distance of each other. The most common personal area network uses Bluetooth devices.

In this case problem, you will research two other technologies that use radio waves—Ultra-Wideband (UWB) technology and Certified Wireless USB (WUSB).

1. Start your Web browser, open the Online Companion page at www.cengage.com/internet/np/internet8 and log on to your account, click the Tutorial 8 link, and then click the Case Problem 4 link.

⊕ EXPLORE   2. Use the links in the Ultra-Wideband Technology section to learn about UWB technology. In addition to the resources on the Online Companion page for Case Problem 4, you can also use a search engine to look for additional resources about UWB. As you conduct your research, answer the following questions:

    a. What is UWB? What is another name given to UWB to represent the type of wireless signal it sends?

    b. What is the normal range of a UWB device? How does this range compare to the range of a Bluetooth device or a Wi-Fi device?

    c. What is noteworthy about the electrical power requirements for UWB devices? Why is power consumption significant?

    d. For what types of devices is UWB suitable?

⊕ EXPLORE   3. Return to the Online Companion page for Case Problem 4, and use the links in the Certified Wireless USB section to learn about WUSB technology. In addition to the resources on the Online Companion page for Case Problem 4, you can also use a search engine to look for additional resources about WUSB. In a report addressed to your instructor, answer the following questions:

    a. What is WUSB?

    b. How does the range of a WUSB device compare to the ranges of other forms of personal area networking, such as UWB or Bluetooth?

c. How does the transfer rate of WUSB devices compare to the rate of other forms of personal area networking, such as UWB or Bluetooth?

d. How can WUSB be used?

⊕ EXPLORE   4. In your report, answer the following questions. How do UWB and WUSB compare to Bluetooth? How are they different? In the future, do you think that UWB, WUSB, and Bluetooth will be competing or complementary standards? Why? What types of products that use UWB and WUSB are currently available? (*Note:* You can use a search engine to identify current products if you want to do so.) What advantages do UWB and WUSB have for consumers over similar devices that use Bluetooth or Wi-Fi technology?

5. Close your Web browser.

Research | Case Problem 5

Explore wireless security issues involved in mobile banking.

There are no Data Files needed for this Case Problem.

Banking on the Run   Jada Snyder, a freshman, is living away from home for the first time while attending college in another state. Just like other college students, she relies on her hometown bank to manage her finances. Jada knows that avoiding the use of a wireless device to conduct activities such as online banking or online shopping is a good way to protect her data from being stolen. However, there are times when she must conduct activities that require the disclosure of personal information such as logins or account numbers. She knows that it is best to work on a wireless network that uses encryption and other security precautions to protect her devices from hackers and to protect the data she sends over the network.

Jada recently read an Internet article about the increase in the number of broadband wireless devices and the increased functionality of basic devices, such as cell phones, that have made it possible for mobile users to connect to online banking sites. Responding to this demand, many banks have implemented secure sites at which mobile users can connect to the bank's site to access account information, make transfers, and even trade stocks. Jada wants to research mobile online banking to investigate the security it offers and the types of devices she can use to access the banking sites.

1. Start your Web browser, open the Online Companion page at www.cengage.com/internet/np/internet8 and log on to your account, click the Tutorial 8 link, and then click the Case Problem 5 link.

⊕ EXPLORE   2. Click one of the links to a bank that uses mobile online banking, and then use the site to answer the following questions about mobile online banking in a report addressed to your instructor:

a. Does the bank require users to preregister to use mobile online banking?

b. What kinds of devices does the mobile online banking service support?

c. What kind of security does the bank offer when mobile devices connect to it? Does the bank offer any additional services to ensure secure transactions, such as additional software? Does the bank guarantee the security of your transactions?

d. What types of transactions can users complete?

⊕ EXPLORE   3. Return to the Online Companion page for Case Problem 5, and then choose another bank and answer the questions provided in Step 2.

⊕ EXPLORE   4. Answer the following questions in your report. Based on the information you found, would you feel secure conducting your banking transactions using mobile online banking? Why or why not? If you feel that the mobile online banking sites are secure, what other risks exist when using one of these services? How can you protect your data and your device from any other risks that you might identify?

5. Close your Web browser.

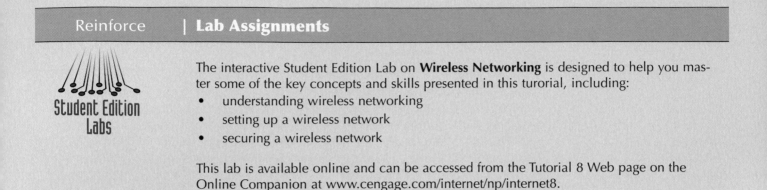

Student Edition Labs

The interactive Student Edition Lab on **Wireless Networking** is designed to help you master some of the key concepts and skills presented in this tutorial, including:

- understanding wireless networking
- setting up a wireless network
- securing a wireless network

This lab is available online and can be accessed from the Tutorial 8 Web page on the Online Companion at www.cengage.com/internet/np/internet8.

Review | **Quick Check Answers**

Session 8.1

1. up to 2 Mbps
2. SMS (Short Message Service) lets you send text messages of up to 160 characters over a 2G wireless network.
3. the costs of purchasing spectrum licenses in which to operate the networks and building cellular transmitters and radio towers to send and receive the signals, and getting the necessary authorization from the U.S. government to use the spectrum
4. 802.11a and 802.11g
5. True
6. a connection of two to eight Bluetooth compatible devices to each other, in which one device acts as a master
7. WiMAX, which stands for Worldwide Interoperability for Microwave Access, is the wireless specification for a metropolitan area network that has a range of up to 31 miles and transfer rates of up to 70 Mbps.
8. False

Session 8.2

1. WEP and WPA are two types of encryption for wireless networks.
2. a unique code assigned by a manufacturer to identify a network interface card on a network
3. Disabling the SSID makes the wireless network invisible to roaming devices and adds a layer of security to the network.
4. an attack that occurs when a hacker gathers information about an access point, and then uses that information to set up his own computer to use the real access point's signal to impersonate the access point in an attempt to garner information that can later be used to steal from victims
5. bluejacking
6. bluesnarfing
7. setting a Bluetooth device so that its signal is not detectable to other Bluetooth devices

Creating Effective Web Pages

Creating HTML Documents and Understanding Browser Extensions

Case | Lakeside Police Department

The Lakeside Police Department employs 18 police officers, six full-time dispatchers, and 10 other full-time employees. The department patrols Lakeside, Illinois, a small suburb outside of Chicago. Many of the officers are residents of the city, and as such they are very well known and highly regarded in the community. Officers provide services not found in most major metropolitan areas, such as serving as school crossing guards, being mentors to children attending the local schools, and providing traffic control at city events such as the annual Fourth of July celebration at the city's lakeside park.

The police chief, Mary Silva, has always believed that community education programs are an important part of providing effective police patrols and service. Chief Silva's latest community education program, which was unanimously approved by the Lakeside City Council, is a series of self-defense classes. These classes are directed at specific groups, including children, elderly residents, women, and people with disabilities. Although the crime rate is low in Lakeside, many residents work in Chicago, where the crime rate is higher, and people in these groups are easier targets for theft and assaults.

Chief Silva wants to create a Web site on which to post information about the police department. She already received approval from the Lakeside City Council, and now she needs your help to understand the issues involved in creating and maintaining a Web site. You will create the pages that describe the self-defense program so Chief Silva can add them to the Web site. Chief Silva has asked you to create the pages for the department and then to provide her with the options for creating a Web site so you can publish it on the Web.

Starting Data Files

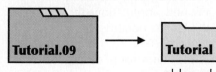

Tutorial.09 →	Tutorial	Review	Cases
	elder_sd.html	elder_sd.html	20.jpg
	logo.jpg	logo.jpg	falcon.txt

Session 9.1

Understanding Markup Languages

As you learned in Tutorial 1, Hypertext Markup Language (HTML) is a nonproprietary markup language that a Web browser interprets and uses to display the content as a Web page. A **markup language** is a general term that indicates the separation of the formatting of a document and the content of a document. Before HTML was created, **Standard Generalized Markup Language (SGML)**—a **metalanguage** that is used to create other languages—was the standard for formatting documents that were not dependent on the operating system or environment on which the documents were created or viewed. Because SGML is very complex, it is used almost exclusively by large organizations.

The first version of HTML was developed using SGML in 1989 by Tim Berners-Lee and Robert Calliau while they were working at CERN—the European Laboratory for Particle Physics—on a project to improve the laboratory's document-handling procedures. Berners-Lee eventually transformed the initial work into the markup language that is now known as HTML. HTML quickly became the language used to create Web pages because of its simplicity and portability, which made it useable with many operating systems and on different types of computers. The creation of HTML resulted in the World Wide Web as we know it today.

HTML quickly evolved through specifications that are the result of the collective work of the organization known as the **World Wide Web Consortium (W3C)**. The W3C establishes **specifications**, or sets of standards, that identify how a browser interprets the HTML code. In turn, the individuals and companies that create browsers attempt to follow these specifications to ensure that the browsers interpret HTML correctly and consistently. The specifications are voluntary, but because the success of a Web site depends on the browser's ability to follow the specifications, most organizations adhere to them as much as possible. The current specification for HTML is 4.01, which is supported by major Web browsers. Since 2004, the W3C has been working on the fifth revision of the HTML specification, tentatively called HTML 5. You can use the resources on the Online Companion page for Tutorial 9 at www.cengage.com/internet/np/internet8 to learn more about the existing HTML 4.01 and draft HTML 5 specifications.

Another popular markup language is **Extensible Markup Language (XML)**, which was a W3C recommendation that began in 1998 to describe the format and structure of data. XML is used to share data across organizations, especially when data is used on the Internet. Most programs, including Microsoft Office, include features that convert data stored in a proprietary format into XML. Although XML is a markup language, it differs from HTML in that XML uses a set of customizable tags to describe data and its relationship to other tags. HTML uses standardized tags but does not allow this kind of flexibility when describing data.

The most recent markup language specification from the W3C combines the formatting features of HTML with a stricter syntax that works to combine HTML and XML so that Web content is more readily and easily delivered to all devices that are connected to the Internet. This specification, recommended by the W3C in 2000, is called **Extensible Hypertext Markup Language (XHTML)**. XHTML, which is currently in version 1.1, is compatible with the HTML 4.01 specification. The main differences between HTML 4.01 and XHTML 1.1 are in the syntax of the language. HTML is somewhat forgiving when it comes to including closing tags and supporting older features of earlier HTML specifications. XHTML is not as forgiving; therefore, many Web developers are using the stricter syntax of XHTML in HTML 4.01 documents so that any new applications that support only XHTML specifications will also be able to use the HTML documents. Figure 9-1 identifies some of the major syntax differences between HTML 4.01 and XHTML 1.1. As a beginning HTML student, it's important to understand some of the differences between the languages that you use to create Web pages as a basis for understanding them. You will learn more about HTML and XHTML syntax as you complete this session.

Tip

When you use Internet Explorer 8 to view a Web page at a site that doesn't comply with the current specifications, click the Compatibility View button to display the page correctly.

Comparison of HTML and XHTML syntax requirements ◄ **Figure 9-1**

HTML	XHTML
No document type declaration is required.	Requires a DOCTYPE declaration at the beginning of the file, such as: `<!DOCTYPE html PUBLIC "-//W3C//DTD XHTML 1.0 transitional//EN" "http://www.w3.org/TR/xhtml1/DTD/ xhtml1-transitional.dtd">`
Tags can be written in uppercase or lowercase letters.	Tags must be written in lowercase letters only.
Attribute values do not need to be enclosed in quotation marks.	Attribute values must be enclosed in quotation marks.
Attributes can be minimized when the attribute name and value are identical, such as `<option selected>` to indicate the status of a selected item in a drop-down list box instead of `<option selected="selected">`.	Attribute minimization is prohibited.
Elements should be closed, although some browsers close elements when the tags are not explicitly included.	All elements must be closed.
One-sided tags are written with the name of the tag only, such as ` ` for a line break.	One-sided tags must be closed by including a space and a forward slash in the tag, such as ` ` for a line break.

HTML specifications that are not included when newer specifications are released or are not included in the XHTML specification are referred to as **deprecated**. In this book, you will use the XHTML syntax as much as possible; deprecated elements are referenced as such but are still covered because some experts agree that the interoperability of the HTML 4.01 and the XHTML 1.1 specifications will result in the continuation of both specifications in the near future.

Understanding Tags and Attributes

A Web page includes different elements, such as headings, paragraphs, and bulleted lists. In an HTML document, these elements are indicated by codes (called tags) that are attached to content. For example, a paragraph is created by typing the opening tag <p> at the beginning of the paragraph and the closing tag </p> at the end of the paragraph. When a Web browser encounters the opening tag for a paragraph, it starts a new paragraph beginning with the text it encounters next. When the browser encounters the closing tag for a paragraph, it ends the paragraph.

Because tags must identify all the elements in a Web page, you frequently need to include one or more sets of tags within other tags. Tags that are included within other tags are called **nested tags**. For example, within a set of tags that identify the beginning and end of a paragraph, you might include tags to change certain words in that paragraph to bold or italic. You might also include tags to identify the font size to use to format the text in the paragraph.

Tags are either two-sided, such as the paragraph tags that indicate the beginning and end of a paragraph, or they are one-sided. An example of a one-sided tag is the HTML <br> tag (or the XHTML <br /> tag), which indicates a line break in a Web page. Generally, one-sided tags cause the browser to take a certain action, without regard to turning a formatting feature "on" and "off," like it does for the beginning and end of a paragraph or when applying bold formatting to a word or phrase. As you learn more about HTML and XHTML, you will use tags and learn which tags represent the various elements in a Web page.

Some tags include **attributes** that specify additional information about the content to be formatted by the tag. For example, the <h1> tag is a two-sided tag that creates a large heading in a Web page. The <h1> and </h1> tags can be used alone to indicate the beginning and end of the heading. However, you can also include one or more optional attributes in the opening tag to describe the heading's content in other ways, such as indicating the alignment of the heading on the page or the font color of its text. For example, the following tag creates a large heading in a Web page that contains red text and is centered on the page:

```
<h1 style="text-align: center; color: red">Heading 1 Content</h1>
```

When a Web browser interprets this tag, it creates a large heading using the text "Heading 1 Content," centers it on the page, and displays it in a red font color. This syntax conforms to XHTML specifications by using quotation marks to enclose the attribute values.

Some attributes are optional; others are not. You might be familiar with a Web page that contains a form with text boxes into which you might type your first name, last name, and phone number; a group of option buttons so you can select your age group, with options such as 18 to 25 or 26 to 35; or a check box that you click to authorize the site to send information to your email address. An HTML document uses the <input /> tag to create the various inputs on the form, such as the text box or option button. In the <input /> tag, the type attribute is required because it is necessary to specify the type of object to create. For example, setting the type attribute to "radio" creates an option button on the page. (An option button was called a radio button a few years ago, and this is where the attribute gets its name.) If you omit the value for the type attribute, the browser doesn't know what kind of object to create. However, assigning a default value of "yes" or "no" to indicate the status of the object when the browser loads the page is optional; if you omit this attribute, the browser will apply the default option, which creates an unselected object (such as an empty check box). For example, the following tag creates a check box named "list" with the initial value of "yes" (indicating a "checked" check box):

```
<input type="checkbox" name="list" value="yes" />
```

When a Web browser interprets this tag, it creates a check box that contains a check mark. The name of the check box in the HTML document is "list." This syntax conforms to XHTML specifications by using quotation marks to enclose the attribute values and a space and a forward slash to close the one-sided tag.

As you work more with HTML, you will learn which attributes you must use with which tags, and which attributes are optional.

Planning an HTML Document

To create a Web page, you can use a simple program called a text editor, or you can use a program that includes multiple features for working with Web pages and Web sites. An example of a text editor is the Notepad program that is installed with Windows. When you use a text editor to create a Web page, you type the content of the Web page and the tags that you need to format the content. In this case, you must have a thorough understanding of HTML and be able to manage the document structure and enter the tags on your own. The second option is to use a program such as Microsoft Expression Web or Adobe Dreamweaver. These programs provide a graphical user interface (GUI) in which you type the content of your Web page and use toolbar buttons and menus to format it. The program creates all of the necessary tags to format the Web page.

No matter which approach you use, it is important to understand some basic HTML before you begin working. You will use Notepad to create the Web page for Chief Silva. Figure 9-2 shows the Web page that she wants you to create.

Women's Self-Defense Class Web page ◀ Figure 9-2

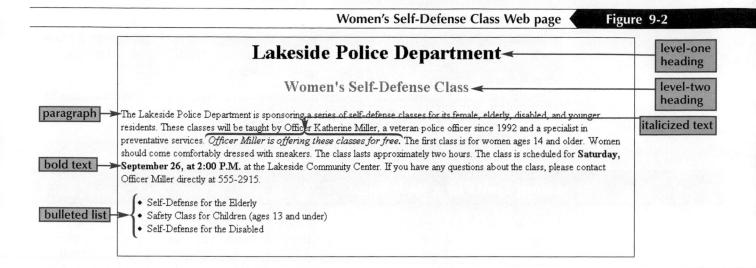

Chief Silva's page includes several elements. The first line of the page contains a heading that is centered and formatted using a larger, bolder font than other text in the page. As you have learned, an HTML document uses tags to format text. The tags that format the headings, such as the document's title, "Lakeside Police Department," are called heading tags. HTML supports six sets of heading tags, numbered <h1> through <h6>, to format text in a Web page. The <h1> tag formats the largest heading text; the <h6> tag formats the smallest heading text. All of the heading tags create bold text. Because this document's title is a level-one heading, you will code it with the <h1> tag.

The subtitle, "Women's Self-Defense Class," is a level-two heading, so it is coded with an <h2> tag. In addition to using the <h2> tag, you will include attributes to change the font color to red. You can create any one of 16 million colors using HTML tags. However, color is an element that depends on the user's computer and browser to render it correctly. Most computers and operating systems will display the colors in the Web-safe color palette correctly. The **Web-safe color palette** is a collection of 216 colors that all computers render in the same way. You can learn more about Web-safe colors by using the resources in the Additional Information section of the Online Companion page for Tutorial 9.

The paragraph below the subtitle is a normal paragraph that uses 12-point Times New Roman font, the default font for Web pages. Fonts are another element that depend on the user's computer. When an operating system is installed on your computer, a certain number of fonts are installed automatically. As you install different programs on your computer, the programs might install new fonts. For example, when you install a Microsoft Office program, you might install 20–30 new fonts on your computer at the same time. You might also install new fonts by downloading them from Web sites or by installing a font program that you purchased. In any case, the fonts that are available on *your* computer are not always the same ones that are available on *other* computers. When you create a Web page on your computer, you can use any one of the installed fonts on your computer to change the font in the Web page. A good rule for beginning Web page developers is to use fonts that are considered to be common on all computers. Figure 9-3 identifies the fonts that are installed on all computers that run the Windows operating system. Computers that run other operating systems have equivalent fonts.

Figure 9-3 | **Commonly installed Windows fonts**

Times New Roman	Arial	Verdana
Georgia	Comic Sans	Trebuchet MS
Impact	**Arial Black**	Courier New

InSight | **Using Fonts in a Web Page**

If you limit the fonts in your Web pages to the basic fonts shown in Figure 9-3, nearly all of the people who view your Web page will see the exact same fonts when they view the page on their computers. If you use other fonts, some of your page's viewers will see the fonts if they are installed on their computers; users without the fonts will see an equivalent font that the browser substitutes. There are ways to include a wider variety of fonts in a Web page; for example, a Web developer can embed fonts in the Web site so that all users can display the specific font the developer used. However, there are tradeoffs when you create a Web page that uses embedded fonts. When pages contain embedded fonts, the files that must be downloaded to each user's computer are much larger. As an HTML beginner, you should use the commonly installed fonts on all computers to ensure that they are displayed correctly when viewed by others.

The paragraph in the Web page that you will create for Chief Silva also includes two nested elements: the italicized sentence and the bold class date and time. Also, the list of items below the paragraph is formatted as a bulleted list. The items in the list in Chief Silva's sketch appear with the default bullet characters for Web pages. After you finish the Web page, Chief Silva will ask you to create other pages and to format the items in this bulleted list as hyperlinks that open the documents describing the self-defense classes for the elderly, children, and the disabled.

Creating an HTML Document

Now that you understand the page that you will create and its elements, Chief Silva asks you to begin work. The first thing you will do is start Notepad, a text editor that is installed with Windows.

To start Notepad and create the HTML document:

▶ **1.** Click the **Start** button on the taskbar, click **All Programs**, click **Accessories**, and then click **Notepad**. Notepad starts and opens a new document, titled "Untitled."

Trouble? If your computer does not have Notepad, you can use any other word-processing program to create an HTML document. If you use a word processor, make sure to save your document with the correct filename extension and not the default filename extension for the word processor, or your Web pages will not work correctly.

Trouble? If you don't have the starting Data Files for this tutorial, you need to get them before you can proceed. Your instructor will either give you the Data Files or ask you to obtain them from a specified location (such as a network drive). In either case, make a backup copy of the Data Files before you start so that you will have the original files available in case you need to start over. If you have any questions about the Data Files, see your instructor or technical support person for assistance.

▶ **2.** If necessary, maximize the Notepad program window.

▶ **3.** Click **File** on the menu bar, and then click **Save**. The Save As dialog box opens.

▶ **4.** Browse to and select the **Tutorial.09\Tutorial** folder included with your Data Files. You will store your HTML document in this location.

▶ **5.** If necessary, select any text in the File name text box, and then type **women_sd.html**.

   Trouble? If you are using a program other than Notepad, make sure that you save your HTML documents with the filename extension .html; otherwise Web browsers will not recognize the file as a Web page.

▶ **6.** Click the **Save** button. The title bar now displays the filename women_sd.html.

You created a text file with the .html filename extension. The filename extensions .htm and .html are associated with Web pages. If you used the default filename extension for text files (.txt) or any other filename extension besides .htm or .html, then a Web browser will not recognize the file as a Web page.

When creating a Web site for the first time, following some common file naming conventions will ensure that your Web site is easy to use and manage. Different organizations might use their own in-house standards to ensure a well-organized site. Some common rules for naming files are as follows:

- When saving HTML documents, use all lowercase letters in the filenames. Although most Web servers process uppercase and lowercase letters as the same characters, it's a good practice to use lowercase letters in filenames in case you ever move your Web site to a UNIX server. Because UNIX servers process uppercase and lowercase letters as different characters, Web sites hosted on UNIX servers consider the files named "About.html" and "about.html" to be different files.
- Avoid using spaces in filenames. Some Web servers don't support filenames that contain spaces, and some browsers don't correctly convert the space character to its URL encoded equivalent, %20, resulting in problems when users attempt to access the page.
- A commonly used option for making filenames easier to read is to separate words with underscore characters. For example, use the filename "about_us.html" instead of "about us.html."
- Save files using names that are based on their contents, to increase the likelihood of search engines correctly indexing the file, and to make it easier for developers and users to find files on the site.
- When the organization that operates a site has specific conventions, be sure to understand and follow them. For example, an organization might store all of a site's images in a folder on the server named "images."
- Use short filenames to make it easier for users to type specific URLs into the browser's address bar, and avoid confusing abbreviated filenames that are difficult to remember.
- Use the filename index or default (and the appropriate filename extension) for a site's home page, so the Web server sends the correct home page for your site when a user accesses the Web site using only the domain name. For example, when a user types the domain name www.cengage.com in the browser's address bar, instead of the domain name and a filename (www.cengage.com/index.html), the server will automatically search for a file named index or default, and then it will display that file in the browser. When the home page is named using a nonstandard filename, such as "cengage_home.html," the Web server will not be able to locate a file named index or default, and the server will display an error page or a directory listing of the Web site's contents, instead of the site's home page.

Creating the HTML Document Structure

In addition to saving the file with the .html filename extension, you must also create the document structure. Every HTML document includes an opening <html> tag to indicate that the file is an HTML document. After this opening tag, you need to define the two sections of the HTML document. The first section, called the **head section**, includes the <head> tag; the head section includes general information about the document, such as keywords that identify the document's content for search engines and comments about the document's creator or the date the document was last updated. The head section also includes the nested <title> tag, which identifies the title of the Web page so the browser can display it in the title bar and on the page tab when the browser uses tabbed browsing. The title is an important part of a Web page because it is used to identify the content of the page; it is also the text that appears as the default name when you use the browser to save the page as a bookmark or favorite. For example, if the title of a page is "Home Page," then users of the page will create a bookmark with this title. A more descriptive title results in a more descriptive bookmark. For example, the title "Lakeside

Police Department Women's Self-Defense Class" is longer, but it is descriptive of the page's contents. Because the <head> tag is a two-sided tag, you must also include the closing </head> tag to close the head section.

The second required section in an HTML document is the **body section**, which includes the content of the Web page along with the tags needed to format the content. The opening <body> tag indicates the beginning of the body section, and the closing </body> tag indicates the end of the body section. Finally, you must include the closing </html> tag as the last item in the HTML document. A good practice is to start your HTML document by creating the head and body sections and typing their opening and closing tags. If you always type your two-sided tags in pairs, you won't make the common mistake of beginners, which is typing the opening tag and then forgetting to type the closing tag.

To create the head and body sections:

► **1.** Make sure the insertion point is on the first line of the new document.

► **2.** Type the content shown in Figure 9-4 in your HTML document, using lowercase letters for the tags and mixed-case for the content. Press the **Enter** key twice at the end of each line to create the blank lines shown in the figure.

Basic HTML document structure in Notepad ◄ **Figure 9-4**

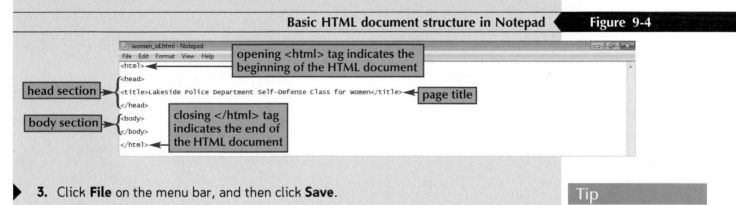

► **3.** Click **File** on the menu bar, and then click **Save**.

Your HTML document has the required head and body sections and a title. The blank lines are not necessary for browsers to interpret the HTML document. In fact, browsers ignore white space in an HTML document, such as the blank spaces between sections. This white space, however, makes your HTML document easier to read.

Tip

If you are working in Windows XP, your Notepad window will look slightly different than the ones shown in the figures.

In the steps and assignments in this tutorial, you won't include a document type declaration at the beginning of your HTML documents because it is beyond the scope of this book. A **document type declaration (DTD)** is a one-sided tag that tells a browser which syntax version of a markup language your document uses. When you omit the document type declaration in an HTML document, the browser renders the page using something called "Quirks" mode. In this mode, a browser will render most basic content correctly. If you later decide to take a course on HTML, XHTML, or XML programming, you will learn that you should *always* include the correct DTD in your documents so browsers will render their elements according to the latest standards.

When you create XHTML documents, the DTD is required; in HTML documents it is strongly recommended but optional. You can learn more about DTDs by clicking the links in the Markup Language Resources section on the Online Companion page for Tutorial 9.

Adding a Comment to an HTML Document

Some organizations request all developers to document their Web pages by identifying the author, purpose, date created or last updated, and other information as required. To add this type of information to an HTML document, you use a comment tag. A **comment tag** is a one-sided tag that the browser ignores and does not display in the Web page; however, the content of the comment tag is visible when you view the HTML document in a text editor. A comment tag has the following syntax, with the word "comment" representing the text included in the comment but not displayed by a browser:

```
<!-- comment -->
```

Just like other tags, a comment can appear on a single line, or it can span multiple lines separated by line breaks. Also, you can place comments anywhere in an HTML document; you do not need to limit comments to the head section. However, identifying information about the HTML document usually appears in the head section because this is where most developers look for and store this type of information. Another use of a comment is to explain a section of the document to indicate its purpose or to provide notes about how the code was developed or is maintained.

Chief Silva asks you to add some information about the HTML document, and you will do so with a comment tag.

To add a comment to the HTML document:

▶ **1.** Click the insertion point at the end of the line that contains the opening <head> tag, and then press the **Enter** key twice.

▶ **2.** Type the following comment, replacing the text "Your Name" with your first and last names, and replacing the text "Date" with today's date in the format MM/DD/YY. Press the **spacebar** five times to indent the second, third, and fourth lines of code.

```
<!-- Women's Self-Defense page
     Content developed by Mary Silva
     Page created by Your Name
     Date
-->
```

Trouble? If the content in your comment doesn't align on the left side as shown, you might need to type an extra space before the word "Women's" on the first line of the comment.

▶ **3.** Save the file.

With the document's structure and documentation in place, you can start adding the document's content.

Inserting and Formatting Headings

The first element in Chief Silva's page is a centered heading that uses the largest font size for headings. You'll type the opening tag for the heading, the content of the heading, and then the closing tag for the heading. To create a level-one heading, you use the <h1> tag. To change its alignment to center, you need to add an attribute to the <h1> tag. In HTML, you add the align attribute with the center value (<h1 align="center">), but the center value is deprecated in XHTML. Therefore, to add a code that is compatible with both HTML and XHTML, you will use the style attribute with the text-align: center value (<h1 style="text-align: center">).

To add headings to the HTML document:

▶ **1.** Click the insertion point after the opening <body> tag, and then press the **Enter** key twice.

▶ **2.** Type the following line of code:

```
<h1>Lakeside Police Department</h1>
```

This code creates the heading in the Web page. Now you need to add the attribute to center the heading.

▶ **3.** Change the opening <h1> tag for the heading as follows:

```
<h1 style="text-align: center">
```

▶ **4.** Press the **End** key, press the **Enter** key twice, and then add the following line of code to the HTML document to create the document subtitle:

```
<h2 style="text-align: center">Women's Self-Defense Class</h2>
```

Now the document includes two headings, both of which are centered. Chief Silva's page shows that the subtitle should be in red font. To make this change, you will need to add another attribute to the <h2> tag to change the color to red. When using the style attribute, you can separate multiple values with a semicolon.

To change font color:

▶ **1.** Click the insertion point between the word "center" and the closing quotation mark in the <h2> tag to position the insertion point between the "r" in "center" and the closing quotation mark.

▶ **2.** Type **; color: red** and then make sure that the opening <h2> tag appears as follows:

```
<h2 style="text-align: center; color: red">
```

Figure 9-5 shows the revised HTML document.

Figure 9-5 **Headings and comment added to the HTML document**

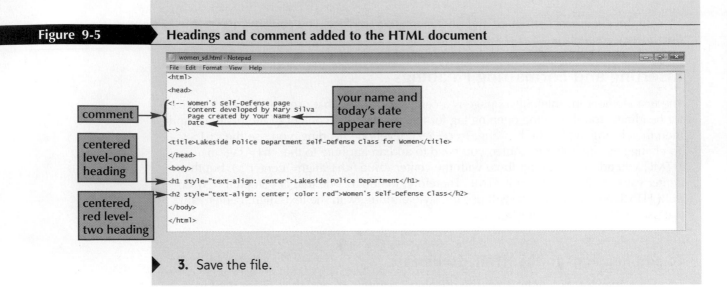

> **3.** Save the file.

As you work in an HTML document, it is a good idea to check your work periodically in a Web browser to look for problems in your coding and also to make sure that the page you are creating looks correct. You can open your HTML document in any Web browser by using the File menu in the browser.

To view the HTML document in a Web browser:

> **1.** Start your Web browser.

> **2.** If you are using Internet Explorer, click **File** on the menu bar, click **Open**, and then click the **Browse** button in the Open dialog box to open the Browse dialog box. If you are using Firefox, click **File** on the menu bar, and then click **Open File**. The Open File dialog box opens.
>
> **Trouble?** If you do not see the menu bar in Internet Explorer, right-click the Command bar to open the shortcut menu, and then click Menu Bar.

> **3.** Open the **Tutorial.09\Tutorial** folder included with your Data Files, and then double-click **women_sd.html**. If you are using Internet Explorer, click the **OK** button in the Open dialog box to open the page.
>
> **Trouble?** If you are using Internet Explorer and a dialog box opens and tells you that the browser needs to open a new window, click the OK button.
>
> Your browser displays the Web page that you created. Notice that the headings are centered, that the level-two heading is red, and the page title appears in the browser's title bar and on the page tab. The path to the file appears in the browser's Address or Location bar. The page does not use the http:// protocol because you are opening the page from a disk and not from a Web server. Figure 9-6 shows the page in Internet Explorer.

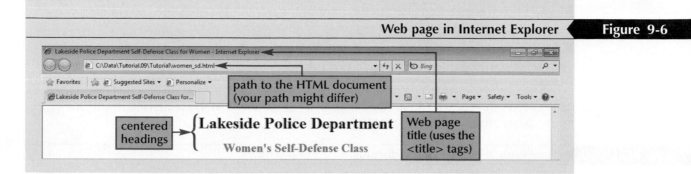

Web page in Internet Explorer **Figure 9-6**

As you are working with your HTML document in your text editor, you can save the page and then refresh it in the browser to see your updates. Note that you must use your text editor to save the HTML document to see all of your changes in the browser when you refresh the page. If you refresh a page in the browser and do not see your changes, return to your text editor, save the page, and then refresh the page again in the browser.

Inserting and Formatting a Paragraph

Next, you will continue adding content to the body of the Web page by typing the paragraph that contains the class description.

To insert a paragraph in the HTML document:

▶ **1.** Use the taskbar to return to Notepad or your text editor.

▶ **2.** Click the insertion point to the right of the closing </h2> tag, and then press the **Enter** key twice.

▶ **3.** Type the following paragraph, exactly as it appears below:

```
<p>The Lakeside Police Department is sponsoring a series of
self-defense classes for its female, elderly, disabled, and younger
residents. These classes will be taught by Officer Katherine
Miller, a veteran police officer since 1992 and a specialist
in preventative services. Officer Miller is offering these classes
for free. The first class is for women ages 14 and older. Women
should come comfortably dressed with sneakers. The class lasts
approximately two hours. The class is scheduled for Saturday,
September 26, at 2:00 P.M. at the Lakeside Community Center. If you
have any questions about the class, please contact Officer Miller
directly at 555-2915.</p>
```

Trouble? If you are using Notepad as your text editor and the text does not wrap to the next line in the program window, click Format on the menu bar, and then click Word Wrap to place a check mark next to it.

Chief Silva's page shows that the sentence, "Officer Miller is offering these classes for free." should be italic, and it shows that the date and time of the class should be bold. To make these changes, you will need to enclose the necessary text in the tags that change text to italics and bold font.

To change font style:

▶ **1.** Click the insertion point to the left of the "O" in the sentence that begins, "Officer Miller is offering…"

▶ **2.** Type the opening tag for italic text, **<i>**.

▶ **3.** Click the insertion point to the right of the period that ends the current sentence, and then type the closing tag for italic text, **</i>**.

▶ **4.** Click the insertion point to the left of the "S" in the word "Saturday," and then type the opening tag for bold text, ****.

▶ **5.** Click the insertion point to the right of the period after the "M" in "P.M." and then type the closing tag for bold text, ****. Figure 9-7 shows the HTML document after making these changes.

Figure 9-7 ▶ **Paragraph added to HTML document**

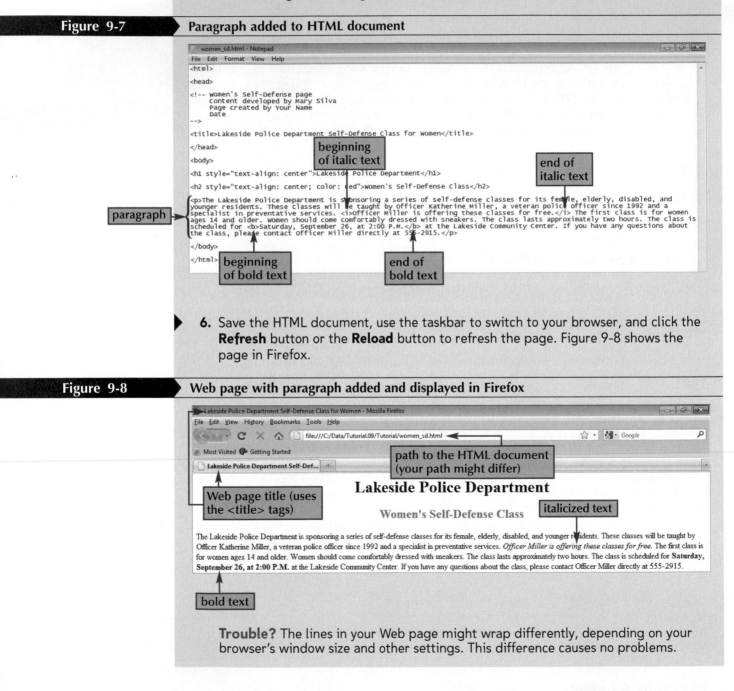

▶ **6.** Save the HTML document, use the taskbar to switch to your browser, and click the **Refresh** button or the **Reload** button to refresh the page. Figure 9-8 shows the page in Firefox.

Figure 9-8 ▶ **Web page with paragraph added and displayed in Firefox**

Trouble? The lines in your Web page might wrap differently, depending on your browser's window size and other settings. This difference causes no problems.

Chief Silva's page contains a bulleted list of the titles to the other self-defense classes that the department will teach. You add the bulleted list next.

Creating a List

HTML supports three kinds of lists: bulleted, numbered, and definition. A **bulleted list** (also called an **unordered list**) contains a list of items with a bullet character to the left of each item in the list. The default bullet character is a black dot or a black square, depending on the browser you are using. A **numbered list** (also called an **ordered list**) creates a list of items with sequential numbering for each item. A **definition list** is usually associated with terms and their definitions. For example, you might use a definition list to create a list of terms and then format each term's description as part of the list. Figure 9-9 shows the syntax and an example for each type of list.

HTML supported lists | Figure 9-9

List Type	HTML Code	Example

Bulleted	```<ul>```
	   ```<li>Item 1</li>```
	   ```<li>Item 2</li>```
	```</ul>```
		(Internet Explorer)
		• Item 1
		• Item 2
		(Firefox)
		♦ Item 1
		♦ Item 2

Numbered	```<ol>```
	   ```<li>Item 1</li>```
	   ```<li>Item 2</li>```
	```</ol>```
		1. Item 1
		2. Item 2

Definition	```<dl>```
	   ```<dt>Item 1</dt>```
	   ```<dd>Definition</dd>```
	   ```<dt>Item 2</dt>```
	   ```<dd>Definition</dd>```
	```</dl>```
		Item 1
		  Definition
		Item 2
		  Definition

Chief Silva's page uses a bulleted list. You will create this list next.

To create a bulleted list:

▶ **1.** Switch to your text editor.

▶ **2.** Click the insertion point to the right of the closing ```</p>``` tag, and then press the **Enter** key twice.

▶ **3.** Type the following lines of code to create the bulleted list, pressing the **spacebar** three times at the beginning of each line that begins with the ```<li>``` tag, so your code is aligned as shown in the figures:

```
<ul>
   <li>Self-Defense for the Elderly</li>
   <li>Safety Class for Children (ages 13 and under)</li>
   <li>Self-Defense for the Disabled</li>
</ul>
```

▶ **4.** Save the file, and then refresh or reload the Web page in your browser. Figure 9-10 shows the page in Internet Explorer.

Tip

If you need to add more items to the bulleted list, you add them using the ```<li>``` and ```</li>``` tags.

| Figure 9-10 | Bulleted list added to Web page |

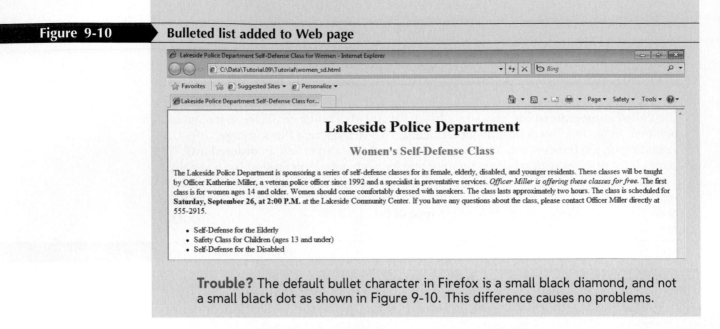

Trouble? The default bullet character in Firefox is a small black diamond, and not a small black dot as shown in Figure 9-10. This difference causes no problems.

Chief Silva is pleased with the appearance of the page. She received a copy of the police department's logo from the city secretary and forwarded it to you as an email attachment. She wants the pages for the Lakeside Police Department to include this logo instead of the typed title, "Lakeside Police Department." She asks you to replace the title with the logo.

Using Images in an HTML Document

You have learned that HTML documents are *text* documents, so how do you display an image in a text document? Most Web pages contain some kind of image, such as a photo or a computer-generated image. In HTML, an **image** is any file that contains a picture, such as a photograph, logo, or computer-generated file. To include an image in a Web page, it must be stored as a file. This file might be a digital picture purchased from a company, a digital picture taken with a digital camera, a scanned copy of an image that exists on paper, or a clip-art image found at a Web site.

Using Pictures in Web Pages | InSight

Pictures can be saved in a variety of file formats, but some formats are commonly used on the Web because they provide high-quality images with small file sizes and fast download times. The most popular formats for pictures on the Web are JPG (or JPEG), GIF, and PNG. Each of these file formats has advantages and disadvantages. Most people use the JPG format for photographs and complex images because JPG files support up to 16 million colors. Because GIF files are limited to 256 colors, they are a good choice for scanned images, line drawings, and simple graphics. The GIF format is licensed by Unisys, and programs that *create* GIF files must have a license to output files in this format. (You do not need a license, however, to *use* a GIF file in a Web page.) PNG files are similar to GIF files, but support up to 16 million colors, and creating PNG files does not require a license. Nearly all Web browsers support JPG, GIF, and PNG files. However, some older versions of browsers do not support PNG files, therefore the PNG format is not as popular on the Web as the JPG and GIF formats.

To use an image in an HTML document, you must create a reference to the file location where the image is stored. If the image is stored in the same folder (directory) as the HTML document, then the browser loads the image from the same folder. If the image is stored anywhere else, the reference to it in the HTML document must include the path to the folder or drive on which the image is stored.

To reference the image in the HTML document, you include the one-sided <img /> tag in the location in which you want to insert the image. When you use the <img /> tag, you must also include the src attribute to define the location (the "source") of the image. You can also use the optional height, width, border, and alt attributes. The height and width attributes describe the image's height and width in pixels; a **pixel** is a single point in an image. The border attribute describes the image's border size (also in pixels). The alt attribute provides alternative text that identifies the image's function or description when it is loaded by a browser that either does not display images or reads Web page content for visually impaired users. Because the alt attribute is required in XHTML, you should always include the alt attribute in your <img /> tag. For example, the code to load the image saved as logo.jpg into a Web page is as follows:

```
<img src="logo.jpg" alt="Lakeside Police Department logo" />
```

This code tells the browser that the file logo.jpg is located in the same directory as the HTML document in which it appears. This type of reference is called a relative path. A **relative path** specifies a file's location *relative* to the location of the current file. If the logo.jpg file is stored in a folder named images on the current drive, then the code to load the image is as follows:

```
<img src="../images/logo.jpg" alt="Lakeside Police Department logo" />
```

This reference is also a relative path because the .. in the file location indicates that the images folder is on the same drive as the current file, but in a different folder. Notice that the slash characters in the path are forward slashes. If the file is stored on a completely different drive than the current file, then the code is as follows:

```
<img src="c:\temp\images\logo.jpg"
alt="Lakeside Police Department logo" />
```

When the browser interprets this code, it will search drive C on the user's computer for a folder named temp, and then within the temp folder, it will search for a folder named images. Within the images folder, it will search for a file named logo.jpg and load it into the Web page. If the user's computer does not have the temp\images folder, or a file named logo.jpg is not saved in that folder, then the browser will display a broken link to the image or the alternate text specified for the image instead of displaying the image itself. Because this path is the sole path in which the browser will search for the file, it is called an absolute path. An **absolute path** specifies a file's location with absolute precision; there is no reference to the current file.

Most Web developers store all of a Web site's images in the same directory as the HTML document or in a folder on the Web site. Usually this folder is named images. By storing all of the images in one place, it is easy to create the references to those images using a relative path.

To change the text "Lakeside Police Department" to an image, you need to select the text and replace it with a tag that inserts the image. The file is stored in the Tutorial.09\Tutorial folder included with your Data Files.

To insert the image in the HTML document:

1. Switch to your text editor, and then select the text **Lakeside Police Department** within the <h1> and </h1> tags.

   Trouble? In Step 1, select only the text, and not the opening and closing <h1> tags; otherwise your page will not display correctly.

2. Type the following tag between the <h1> and </h1> tags to insert the image:

   ```
   <img src="logo.jpg" alt="Lakeside Police Department logo" />
   ```

   The file logo.jpg is a data file saved in the Tutorial.09\Tutorial folder. Figure 9-11 shows the completed HTML document.

Tip

Be sure to type the space and the forward slash before typing the closing angle bracket for the tag so your code is XHTML compatible.

Figure 9-11 Adding an image to the HTML document

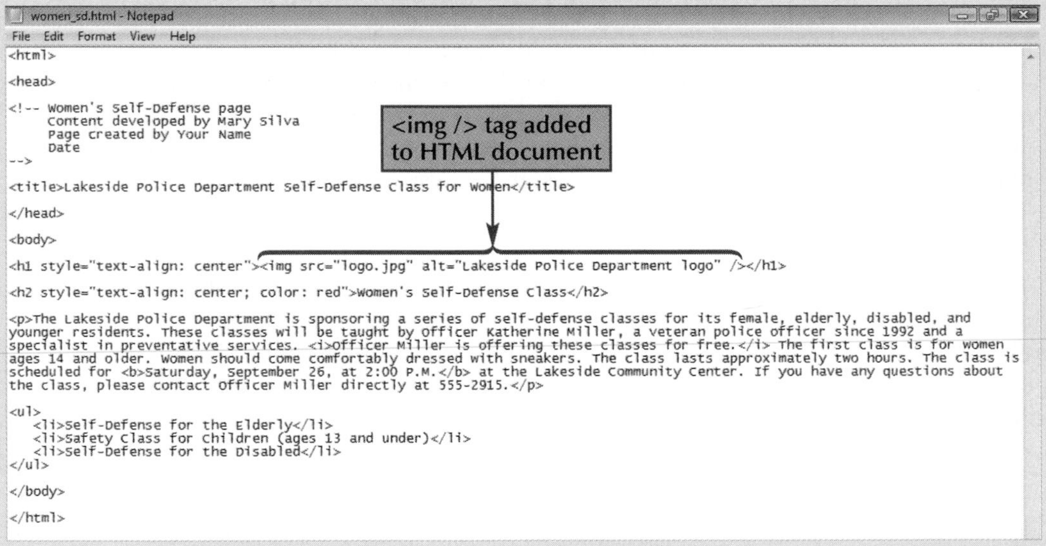


```
<html>

<head>

<!-- Women's Self-Defense page
     Content developed by Mary Silva
     Page created by Your Name
     Date
-->

<title>Lakeside Police Department Self-Defense Class for Women</title>

</head>

<body>

<h1 style="text-align: center"><img src="logo.jpg" alt="Lakeside Police Department logo" /></h1>

<h2 style="text-align: center; color: red">Women's Self-Defense Class</h2>

<p>The Lakeside Police Department is sponsoring a series of self-defense classes for its female, elderly, disabled, and
younger residents. These classes will be taught by Officer Katherine Miller, a veteran police officer since 1992 and a
specialist in preventative services. <i>Officer Miller is offering these classes for free.</i> The first class is for women
ages 14 and older. Women should come comfortably dressed with sneakers. The class lasts approximately two hours. The class is
scheduled for <b>Saturday, September 26, at 2:00 P.M.</b> at the Lakeside Community Center. If you have any questions about
the class, please contact Officer Miller directly at 555-2915.</p>

<ul>
   <li>Self-Defense for the Elderly</li>
   <li>Safety Class for Children (ages 13 and under)</li>
   <li>Self-Defense for the Disabled</li>
</ul>

</body>

</html>
```

3. Save the file, switch to your browser, and refresh the page. Figure 9-12 shows the completed page in Firefox.

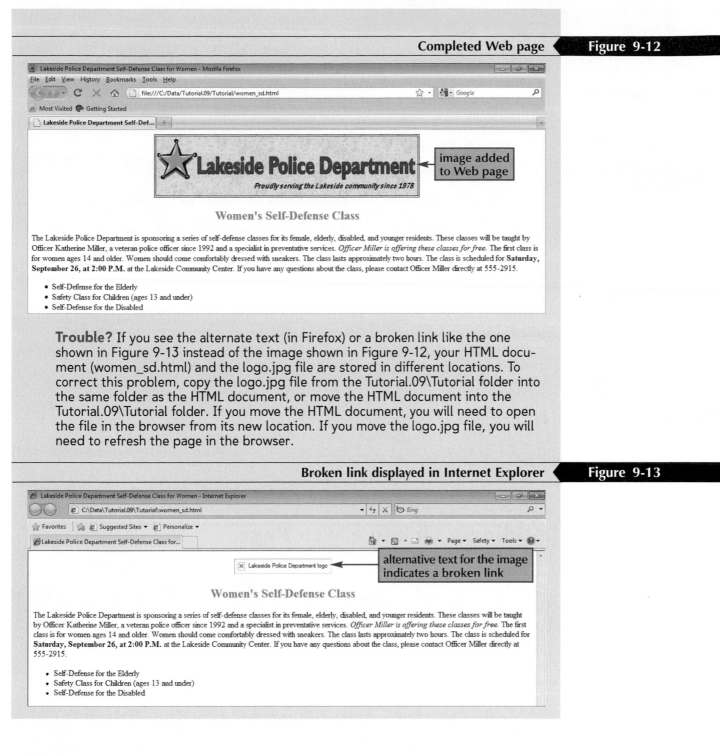

Completed Web page — Figure 9-12

Broken link displayed in Internet Explorer — Figure 9-13

Trouble? If you see the alternate text (in Firefox) or a broken link like the one shown in Figure 9-13 instead of the image shown in Figure 9-12, your HTML document (women_sd.html) and the logo.jpg file are stored in different locations. To correct this problem, copy the logo.jpg file from the Tutorial.09\Tutorial folder into the same folder as the HTML document, or move the HTML document into the Tutorial.09\Tutorial folder. If you move the HTML document, you will need to open the file in the browser from its new location. If you move the logo.jpg file, you will need to refresh the page in the browser.

Using Anchors

Throughout this book, you have used hyperlinks to navigate the pages in a Web site. The HTML tag that creates a hyperlink is the **anchor tag** (<a>). The most common use of a hyperlink is to connect the different Web pages in a Web site together. When connecting Web pages with a hyperlink, the page that opens when the hyperlink is clicked is called the hyperlink's **target** or **target page**. The Web page that contains the hyperlink is called the **source page**. The syntax of a hyperlink that connects a source page with a target page is as follows:

```
<a href="default.html">Home Page</a>
```

The <a> tag is a two-sided tag that includes the href attribute, which specifies the filename of the target page. The text "Home Page" indicates the text that will appear as a link in the source page. Most browsers underline hyperlinks and display them in a blue font so they are easy to identify in a Web page. When you click the "Home Page" link, the browser opens the page named "default.html."

A hyperlink can include a URL to another Web site in the href attribute. When a hyperlink connects to a target page on the Web, the href attribute includes the complete URL, including the HTTP protocol, as follows:

```
<a href="http://www.cengage.com">Cengage Learning</a>
```

In this example, clicking the "Cengage Learning" link on the page causes the browser to open the home page at the URL for that company.

You can also use the <a> tag to include a hyperlink to a location in the same page. When a hyperlink is used in this way, it is sometimes called a **bookmark**. A bookmark uses the id attribute to identify locations in a document so that you can create hyperlinks to those locations. A common use of a bookmark is to provide a way of scrolling a long Web page to a specific location, or to provide a link that scrolls a Web page to the beginning of the page. Creating a bookmark requires two steps. The first step is to use the id attribute to name a section in a Web page. For example, you might name the image at the top of the women_sd.html page so that it becomes the "top" of the page. To accomplish this task, you would change the existing <img /> tag as follows to add the id attribute to it:

```
<img id="top" src="logo.jpg" alt="Lakeside Police Department logo" />
```

To create a hyperlink to the named location, you would insert the following code:

```
<a href="top">Back to top</a>
```

The text for the hyperlink can be anything you choose; in this case it is the text "Back to top."

Adding a Link to a Web Page

You can create a hyperlink at any time when developing a Web page. The trick is to make sure that the page is stored in the correct location. For example, if you include a link to a filename without a path to the file, the browser will look in the current directory for that file. If the file is stored anywhere else, the browser won't be able to open it. This situation represents a common problem when creating hyperlinks. A good way to avoid problems is to test the hyperlink by opening the source page in a browser, and then clicking the hyperlink to make sure that it opens the correct page. After you publish the HTML document to the server, you should do the same testing to make sure that the page still opens correctly.

Chief Silva created the page for the self-defense for the elderly class, and now you want to create a hyperlink from that page to the one you are working on for the women's self-defense class. The file containing the Web page for the self-defense for the elderly class is saved in the Tutorial.09\Tutorial folder.

To create a hyperlink to a file:

1. Switch to your text editor.

2. Click the insertion point to the right of the first opening <li> tag in the bulleted list, and then type the opening tag for the hyperlink, which includes a hyperlink to the file elder_sd.html:

```
<a href="elder_sd.html">
```

3. Click to the right of the word "Elderly" on the same line, and then type the closing tag for the hyperlink, **</a>**. Figure 9-14 shows the HTML document.

Hyperlink added to HTML document ◄ **Figure 9-14**

```
women_sd.html - Notepad
File  Edit  Format  View  Help
<html>

<head>

<!-- Women's Self-Defense page
     Content developed by Mary Silva
     Page created by Your Name
     Date
-->

<title>Lakeside Police Department Self-Defense Class for Women</title>

</head>

<body>

<h1 style="text-align: center"><img src="logo.jpg" alt="Lakeside Police Department logo" /></h1>

<h2 style="text-align: center; color: red">women's Self-Defense Class</h2>

<p>The Lakeside Police Department is sponsoring a series of self-defense classes for its female, elderly, disabled, and
younger residents. These classes will be taught by officer Katherine Miller, a veteran police officer since 1992 and a
specialist in preventative services. <i>officer Miller is offering these classes for free.</i> The first class is for women
ages 14 and older. women should come comfortably dressed with sneakers. The class lasts approximately two hours. The class is
scheduled for <b>Saturday, September 26, at 2:00 P.M.</b> at the Lakeside Community Center. If you have any questions about
the class, please contact officer Miller directly at 555-2915.</p>

<ul>
    <li><a href="elder_sd.html">Self-Defense for the Elderly</a></li>
    <li>Safety Class for Children (ages 13 and under)</li>
    <li>Self-Defense for the Disabled</li>
</ul>

</body>

</html>
```

opening tag for the hyperlink

closing tag for the hyperlink

4. Save the file, switch to your browser, and then refresh the page. The first item in the bulleted list is formatted as a hyperlink. For most browsers, the default formatting for a hyperlink is underlined, blue text.

5. Click the **Self-Defense for the Elderly** link. The Self-Defense for the Elderly page opens in your browser.

Trouble? If the elder_sd.html page does not open, then the files for the target and source pages are not stored in the same folder. Move the files into the same directory, reopen the source page (women_sd.html) in your browser, and then click the hyperlink.

6. Click your browser's **Back** button to return to the women_sd.html page.

7. If you are using Internet Explorer and you enabled the display of the menu bar earlier in this session, right-click the menu bar to open the shortcut menu, and then click **Menu Bar** to hide the menu bar.

8. Close your browser and your text editor.

Figure 9-15 summarizes the tags that you learned in this session.

Figure 9-15

Tag summary

Tag	Description	Syntax
`<!-- -->`	Creates an HTML comment tag	`<-- comment -->`

`<a>`	Creates a hyperlink to a Web page in the same site, to a Web page in another site, or to a named location in the same Web page	`<a href="filename">hyperlink text</a>`
		`<a href="URL">hyperlink text</a>`
		`<a href="named location">bookmark text</a>`

`<b>` or `<strong>`	Creates bold text	`<b>Bold text</b>` `<strong>Bold text</strong>`
`<body>`	Identifies the body section of an HTML document	`<body>...</body>`
` `	Creates a line break in a Web page	` `

`<dl>`	Creates a definition list	`<dl>`
		    `<dt>Item 1</dt>`
		    `<dd>Definition</dd>`
		    `<dt>Item 2</dt>`
		    `<dd>Definition</dd>`
		`</dl>`

`<h1>`	Creates a level-one heading	`<h1>Level-One Heading</h1>`
`<h2>`	Creates a level-two heading	`<h2>Level-Two Heading</h2>`
`<h3>`	Creates a level-three heading	`<h3>Level-Three Heading</h3>`
`<h4>`	Creates a level-four heading	`<h4>Level-Four Heading</h4>`
`<h5>`	Creates a level-five heading	`<h5>Level-Five Heading</h5>`
`<h6>`	Creates a level-six heading	`<h6>Level-Six Heading</h6>`
`<head>`	Identifies the head section of an HTML document	`<head>...</head>`
`<html>`	Identifies the file as an HTML document	`<html>...</html>`
`<i>` or `<em>`	Creates italic text	`<i>Italic text</i>` `<em>Italic text</em>`
`<img />`	Inserts an image	`<img src="filename.ext"` `alt="alternate text" />`

`<input />`	Creates an object (check box, option button, text box, or button) in a form that accepts input from the user in a Web page	`<input type="checkbox" name="check box name"`
		`value="default value" />`
		`<input type="radio" name="option button group name" value="value" />`
		`<input type="text" name="text box name"`
		`size="width in characters" />`
		`<input type="button" name="button name"`
		`value="button label" />`

`<ol>`	Creates a numbered list	`<ol>`
		  `<li>Item 1</li>`
		  `<li>Item 2</li>`
		`</ol>`

`<p style="color: value">`	Changes text color to *value*	`<p style="color:` `color name or value"> ... </p>`

`<p style="text-align: value">`	Changes paragraph alignment to *value* (center, left, right, or justified)	`<p style="text-align: center"> ... </p>`
		`<p style="text-align: left"> ... </p>`
		`<p style="text-align: right"> ... </p>`
		`<p style="text-align: justify"> ... </p>`

`<p>`	Creates a paragraph with the default alignment (left-justified)	`<p> ... </p>`

`<ul>`	Creates a bulleted list	`<ul>`
		  `<li>Item 1</li>`
		  `<li>Item 2</li>`
		`</ul>`

In this session, you learned how to create an HTML document and view it in a browser. The HTML document that you created is very simple; if you are interested in learning more about HTML and XHTML, you can use the resources on the Online Companion page for Tutorial 9 or take a separate class on HTML or XHTML. In the next session, you will learn how to work with Web site management tools and how to determine the best tool for adding content and functionality to a Web page.

Session 9.1 Quick Check | Review

1. What is HTML? How was it developed?
2. What person or organization establishes specifications for HTML?
3. What is XML and how is it used?
4. What is XHTML and how is it used?
5. How are XHTML and HTML similar and how are they different?
6. Define tags and attributes as used in HTML.
7. How do you insert an image in a Web page?
8. How do you link Web pages to each other?

Session 9.2

Using a Web Site Management Tool

You could use a text editor to create all of the pages in a Web site. In this case, you would need to have a thorough understanding of how to write all of the tags and attributes that are required to complete your site. Although it is possible to create an entire Web site, regardless of its complexity, using just Notepad and HTML, most Web developers rely on other options for creating Web sites. Microsoft Expression Web and Adobe Dreamweaver are two Web site creation and management tools. These standalone programs use a graphical user interface (GUI) to generate the HTML documents necessary to produce Web pages. Figure 9-16 shows the Web page that you created in Session 9.1 after creating it in Expression Web. Notice that the page looks the same as it would in a Web browser. The toolbars and panes include tools that let you format text, create hyperlinks, and perform other tasks that are supported by HTML and XHTML.

Figure 9-16   **Web page created using Microsoft Expression Web**

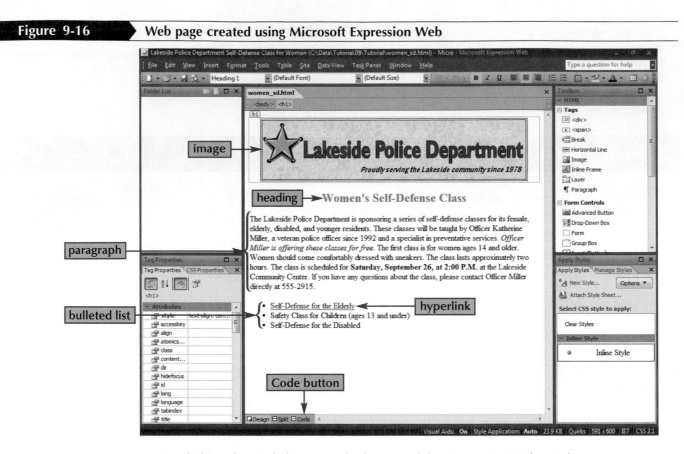

By clicking the Code button at the bottom of the Expression Web window, you can see the HTML document for the current Web page. Figure 9-17 shows the HTML document that Expression Web generated to produce the page shown in Figure 9-16. Notice that Expression Web uses styles to define text formatting, instead of the tags that you used in the HTML document you created in Notepad. The code is different but it produces the same result—the main difference is that the generated code is XHTML compatible.

HTML document generated by Expression Web   Figure 9-17

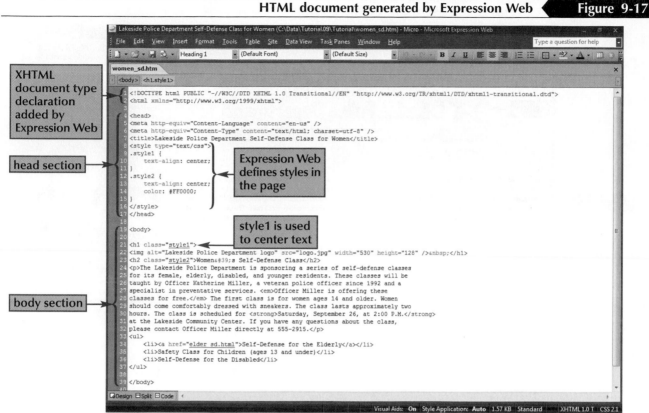

Dreamweaver is another program with a GUI that you can use to create Web pages and then view the HTML documents that the program generated. Figure 9-18 shows the Web page you created in Session 9.1 in Dreamweaver.

Figure 9-18   **Web page created using Adobe Dreamweaver**

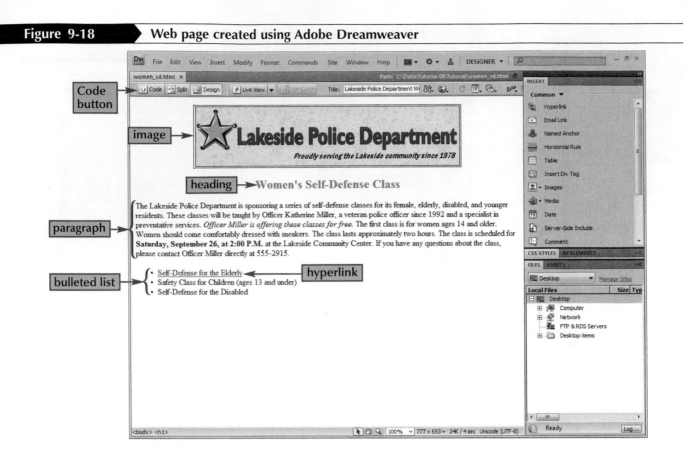

Clicking the Code button at the top of the document window in Dreamweaver shows the HTML document that Dreamweaver generated for the Web page shown in Figure 9-18. Figure 9-19 shows that Dreamweaver also generates code that is compatible with XHTML 1.0—for example, the beginning of the HTML document includes a document type declaration, and one-sided tags are closed with a space and a slash. In addition, notice that the <i> tags are replaced by <em> (for "emphasis") tags and the <b> tags are replaced by <strong> tags. These tags are used in anticipation of the deprecation of the current HTML 4.01 tags for creating italic and bold text.

HTML document generated by Dreamweaver | Figure 9-19

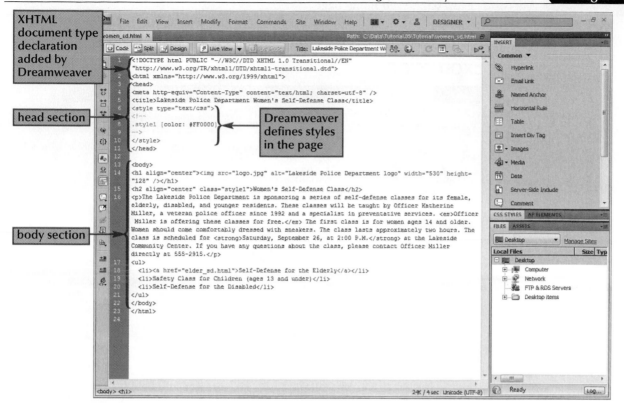

Using a Web site management tool such as Expression Web or Dreamweaver reduces the burden on the developer to understand the syntax of all the HTML tags and attributes that create Web pages. These tools also provide other benefits by simplifying some of the tasks needed to complete a Web site. Both programs simplify the process of adding multimedia, such as animation, movies, and sound, to your Web pages by incorporating drag-and-drop interfaces that let you place the multimedia object in a page and automatically generate the necessary code to support it. These programs also include code snippets that create animations in your Web pages and tools that let you check the entire Web site for broken links and other problems. Next, you'll explore the product pages for Expression Web and Dreamweaver to get a better sense of the features available in these powerful programs.

To learn more about Expression Web and Dreamweaver:

▶ **1.** Start your Web browser, open the Online Companion page at **www.cengage.com/internet/np/internet8** and log on to your account, click the **Tutorial 9** link, and then click the **Session 9.2** link.

▶ **2.** Click the **Microsoft Expression Web** link and wait while the browser opens the Microsoft Expression Web home page, as shown in Figure 9-20.

Figure 9-20 Microsoft Expression Web home page

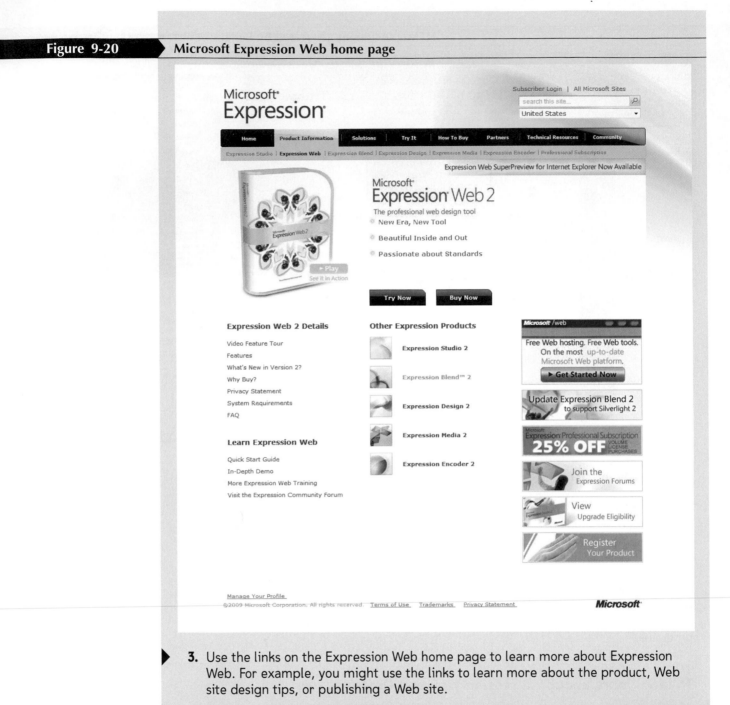

▶ **3.** Use the links on the Expression Web home page to learn more about Expression Web. For example, you might use the links to learn more about the product, Web site design tips, or publishing a Web site.

▶ **4.** Return to the Online Companion page for Session 9.2, and then click the **Adobe Dreamweaver** link and wait while the browser opens the Dreamweaver page shown in Figure 9-21.

Adobe Dreamweaver Features page   **Figure 9-21**

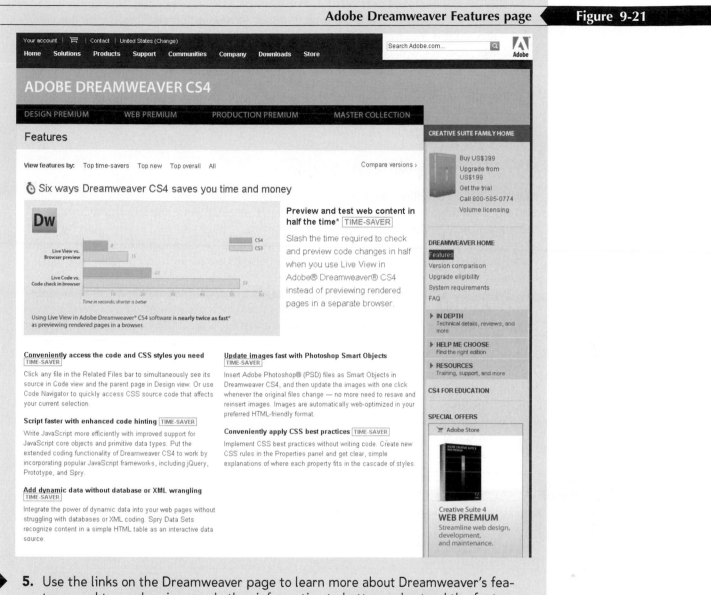

5. Use the links on the Dreamweaver page to learn more about Dreamweaver's features and to read reviews and other information to better understand the features this program offers Web site developers.

6. Return to the Online Companion page for Session 9.2.

Both Expression Web and Dreamweaver offer free trial versions of the software that you can download and use before purchasing a license. These trial programs are a good way to decide which program will best help you manage your Web site and which will be the easiest for you to use.

Choosing Other Development Tools

Some Web pages include content that is beyond the capabilities of HTML. For example, you learned in Session 9.1 that an HTML document cannot store an image, but it can include a reference to an image. In this context, the HTML document identifies the image file so the browser can display it in the Web page. The HTML tag and its attributes identify the location of the image file, and optionally, its height and width dimensions, border size, and alternative text.

Other nontext content that you see in a Web page is called by the browser in a similar way. Some Web pages include dynamic content—content that changes when you view the page—that is also beyond the capabilities of HTML. This dynamic content might be an image that represents the number of times a page has been viewed, an animated graphic, or an interactive product display. This type of Web page content requires more than just HTML to produce. Because Chief Silva might want to include interactive features in the police department's Web pages, you will explore some of the technology required to produce more complicated Web pages, such as those that include programming, image editing, and animation.

Programming with JavaScript

JavaScript is a scripting language that was originally developed as "LiveScript" by Brendan Eich while he was working as a programmer at Netscape Communications Corporation. A **scripting language** is a programming language that is executed by a Web browser. To process the script, the browser must have a feature called a **scripting engine**. The browser's scripting engine translates the code in the script into a format that the browser can execute. JavaScript was originally available as part of the Netscape Navigator browser. At the same time, Microsoft created a compatible language called JScript, and subsequently, the language VBScript, both of which are processed by Internet Explorer. Because JavaScript is interpreted by most browsers, and because only the Internet Explorer browser can process scripts written in VBScript, most developers choose JavaScript to extend the functionality of a Web page.

The most common use of JavaScript is to perform tasks that are not possible in the static world of HTML documents. For example, a Web page might use a very simple JavaScript program to greet the visitor to a Web page depending on the time of day he or she views the page. Figure 9-22 shows the result of a JavaScript program that greets the user. The script uses the page title from the HTML document and a greeting of "Good Morning" because the visitor loaded the page in the morning.

| Figure 9-22 | Web page that contains a script |

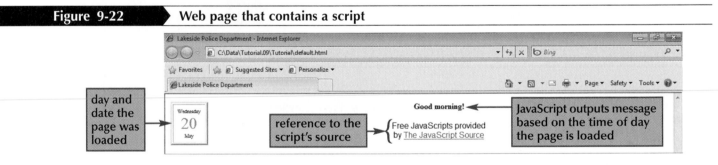

Figure 9-23 shows the HTML document for the page shown in Figure 9-22. The HTML document includes a script that provides the greeting and the date and day of the week. The script itself is embedded in the body section of the HTML document. When you view the HTML document in a Web browser, the browser executes the script and displays the result of the script in the Web page. Most scripts are embedded in an HTML document in this way. When a browser cannot execute the script (because it does not have a scripting engine to process the script), it simply displays the contents of the script as text. To avoid this situation, most scripts are enclosed in HTML comment tags so browsers that cannot execute the script will ignore the script as if it were really a comment. If the browser has a compatible scripting engine, the scripting engine ignores the HTML comment tags and processes the script.

HTML document that contains a script   Figure 9-23

developer's documentation and
instructions for using the script

script

```
default.html - Notepad
File  Edit  Format  View  Help
<html>
<head>
<title>Lakeside Police Department</title>
</head>
<body>
<!-- ONE STEP TO INSTALL DAILY GREETING:
  1.  Copy the coding into the BODY of your HTML document  -->
<!-- STEP ONE: Paste this code into the BODY of your HTML document  -->
<SCRIPT LANGUAGE="JavaScript">
<!-- This script and many more are available free online at -->
<!-- The JavaScript Source!! http://javascript.internet.com -->
<!-- Begin
var Today=new Date();
var ThisDay=Today.getDay();
var ThisDate=Today.getDate();
var ThisMonth=Today.getMonth()+1;
var ThisYear=Today.getFullYear();   //included if you wish to insert the year
function DayTxt (DayNumber) {
var Day=new Array();
Day[0]="Sunday";
Day[1]="Monday";
Day[2]="Tuesday";
Day[3]="Wednesday";
Day[4]="Thursday";
Day[5]="Friday";
Day[6]="Saturday";
return Day[DayNumber];
}
var DayName=DayTxt(ThisDay);
function MonthTxt (MonthNumber) {
var Month=new Array();
Month[1]="January";
Month[2]="February";
Month[3]="March";
Month[4]="April";
Month[5]="May";
Month[6]="June";
Month[7]="July";
Month[8]="August";
Month[9]="September";
Month[10]="October";
Month[11]="November";
Month[12]="December";
return Month[MonthNumber];
}
var MonthName=MonthTxt(ThisMonth);
var d = new Date();
var h = d.getHours();
document.write("<TABLE BORDER=3 BGCOLOR=WHITE  WIDTH=75 HEIGHT=85 align=left>"+"<TD>"+"<p align=center>"+"<font size=-2
>"+DayName+"<br>"+"<font color=orangered size=+3
>"+ThisDate+"</font>"+"<br>"+MonthName+"<br>"+"</b>"+"</font>"+"</p>"+"</TD>"+"</TR>"+"</TABLE>");
if (h < 2) document.write("<P ALIGN=center>"+"<b>"+"Good morning! Yes, it's way past midnight."+"</b>"+"</P>");
else if (h < 3) document.write("<P ALIGN=center>"+"<b>"+"Good morning! Up early or working late?"+"</b>"+"</P>");
else if (h < 7) document.write("<P ALIGN=center>"+"<b>"+"Good morning! Up bright and early!"+"</b>"+"</P>");
else if (h < 12) document.write("<P ALIGN=center>"+"<b>"+"Good morning!"+"</b>"+"</P>");
```

Although you can take courses to learn JavaScript and other programming languages, many Web sites include resources for downloading and using free scripts written in JavaScript in your Web pages. In return for the use of the script, some sites ask you to include a link to the developer's Web site in lieu of payment. Other Web resources that provide more complex scripts require payment for their use. Figure 9-22 includes a link to The JavaScript Source, a resource that includes over 2,500 free scripts that you can use in your Web pages. The Online Companion page for Tutorial 9 includes a link to this and other resources that offer free scripts that you can use in your Web pages. You'll explore these resources next and view some scripts.

To view scripts written in JavaScript that are available on the Web:

▶ 1. On the Online Companion page for Session 9.2, click a link in the JavaScript Resources section to open the home page for that site. Most sites that provide free scripts organize the scripts by topic or category. Figure 9-24 shows the home page for The JavaScript Source.

Figure 9-24 **The JavaScript Source home page**

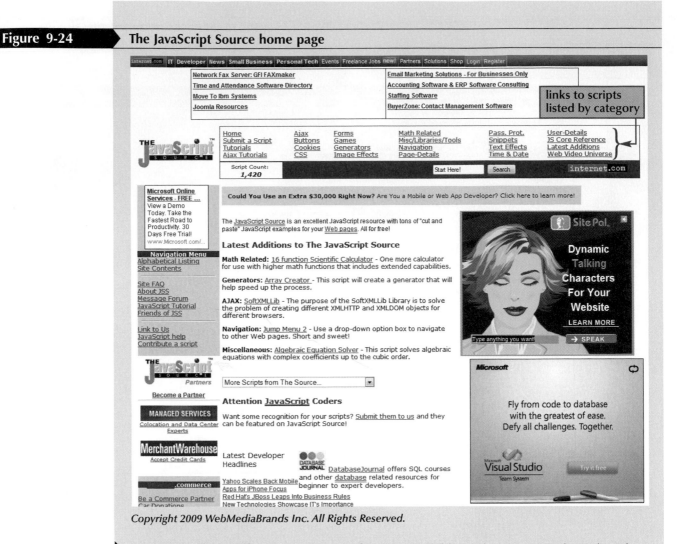

Copyright 2009 WebMediaBrands Inc. All Rights Reserved.

▶ **2.** Explore the different categories of scripts available at the site you selected, and use the Web pages to execute some of the scripts. Figure 9-25 shows the result of a script that computes the number of calories a person burns based on the person's entered weight and number of miles run. The result of the script appears in the "Calories burned" text box with a predefined comment appearing below it. Below the result, the page includes a scrollable window with detailed directions for inserting the script in an HTML document and the actual content of the script. The directions are enclosed in the HTML comment tags so you can insert them in your pages to retain a copy of the script instructions.

Script that computes calories burned ◀ Figure 9-25

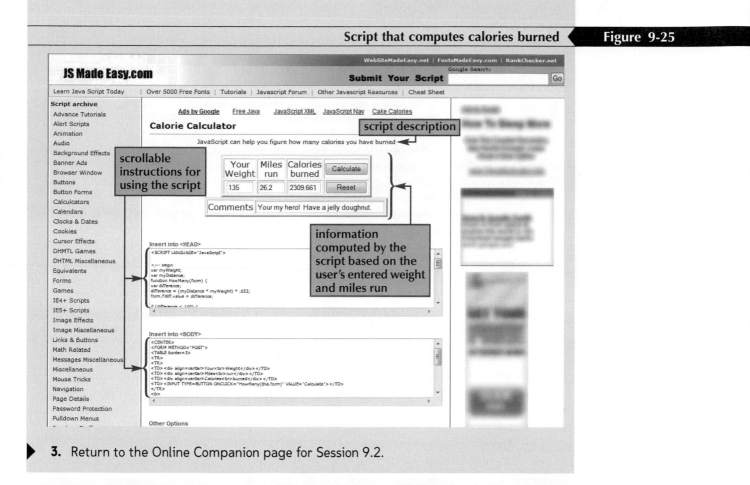

3. Return to the Online Companion page for Session 9.2.

Using JavaScript to Enhance a Web Page | InSight

What can you do with JavaScript without having to learn how to write your own scripts? You can use a script to display a greeting based on the time of the day, the day of the week, or a special occasion. You can display a calendar or an interactive calendar that lets the user pick a date. You can also display the current date and time, or a countdown until a specific day and time, such as a holiday or a grand opening. You can also use JavaScript to display scrolling text, a drop-down menu of selections, or animated buttons that change color or display a message when the user points to or clicks the button. A script might also detect the user's browser version or open a pop-up window with a message. JavaScript adds other functionality to a Web page as well, such as a simple or scientific calculator. Most of the scripts for performing these tasks are available for free on the Web.

If you want to do more with JavaScript, you can take additional courses and learn the JavaScript programming language to write your own scripts.

Creating Animated Content

Although JavaScript can add some interactivity to your Web pages, you might be wondering how some Web sites are able to animate more than just text or buttons. The early versions of Web browsers displayed only text and simple images. As commercial use of the Internet flourished, Web site developers needed a way to include more features, such as sound and animation, in their Web pages. Because of HTML limitations, companies developed their own software to enhance the capabilities of Web browsers. These enhancements, generally called **browser extensions**, allow a Web browser to perform tasks it was not originally designed to perform.

There are three types of browser extensions. One type is called a **plug-in**; in this category you will find integrated browser software that the browser uses to display or play a specific file that you request. Other browser extensions are called **helper applications**, or programs installed on the user's computer that the browser starts and uses to "help" display or play a file. The third category, **add-ons**, includes tools that enhance your browsing experience, such as toolbars that let you access a search engine without opening its Web site or programs that block pop-up ads and other windows from opening when you view a Web site.

Plug-ins differ slightly from helper applications in the way they run. Helper applications are independent programs that are stored on your computer and are useful on their own. They are activated automatically by a browser when needed. For example, when a browser starts a spreadsheet program to display a spreadsheet, the spreadsheet program is functioning as a helper application; when a browser encounters a sound file, the browser might start a media player that acts as a helper application to play the file. Your computer probably has many helper applications already installed on it that your browser uses to display a variety of file formats that you have encountered as you browsed the Web.

Plug-ins, on the other hand, do their work inside the browser and do not activate a standalone program that is stored on your computer. Unlike helper applications, plug-ins are not independent programs; they can start only from within a browser. As Web developers started including different multimedia files in their Web sites, Microsoft and Mozilla began integrating plug-ins with their browsers so users could access and display files without needing a separate program.

Figure 9-26 lists some commonly used browser extensions on the Web.

Figure 9-26 > **Commonly used browser extensions**

Browser Extension	Developer	Description
Adobe Reader	Adobe	Displays formatted document files saved in PDF format
Flash Player	Adobe	Displays simple animations, user interfaces, images, movies, sound, and text
QuickTime Player	Apple, Inc.	Plays audio and video files
RealPlayer	RealNetworks	Plays files in various audio and video media formats
Shockwave Player	Adobe	Displays animated, 3-D interfaces, interactive advertisements and product demonstrations, multiuser games, streaming CD-quality audio, and video
Silverlight	Microsoft Corporation	Delivers high-definition video, high-resolution graphics, and interactive applications to various browsers, platforms, and devices.
Windows Media Player	Microsoft Corporation	Plays files in various audio and video media formats

Two widely used plug-ins for viewing animated content are Flash Player and Shockwave Player. Both players are free from the Adobe Web site, and they work seamlessly with most browsers. **Flash Player** lets your Web browser display simple animations, user interfaces, images, movies, sound, and text that was created using Adobe Flash software. Flash content usually appears in the same browser window as the page you are viewing. According to Adobe, 96% of all desktop computers connected to the Internet have the Flash Player installed and can use the Flash Player to view enhanced content on the Web. Because more than 700 million Internet devices already have the Flash Player, many Web developers regularly use Flash to develop content that is more visually interesting and appealing to their site visitors. In the past, Flash Player was a plug-in, but its popularity has made it essential for viewing content on the Web. Therefore, the latest version of Internet Explorer includes the Flash Player so users do not have to download it.

Shockwave Player is a more fully featured browser plug-in. Shockwave Player lets you view animated, three-dimensional interfaces, interactive advertisements and product demonstrations, multiuser games, streaming CD-quality audio, and video that was created using Adobe Director software. Because Shockwave uses streaming technology, you do not need to wait for an entire file to download before playing it—the animation or sound plays almost immediately. (Remember from Tutorial 5 that streaming is a technology that delivers a continuous flow of information from the server to your browser and allows you to play the information, such as audio or video, before the entire file has been downloaded to your computer. Streaming can reduce the time required to begin playing a file from several minutes to several seconds.) Shockwave content usually appears in a new browser window. Some instructors use Shockwave to deliver audio instruction and interact with students over the Internet just as they would in the classroom. Shockwave is a very popular plug-in; according to Adobe, more than 450 million Internet users enhance their Internet experience using Shockwave Player to play games and view animated content.

You can purchase the Adobe Director program to create Shockwave files and the Adobe Flash program to create Flash files. Chief Silva might want to use animations in the Lakeside Police Department's Web site, so you decide to explore these resources to get a sense of what Flash and Shockwave can do in case she asks you to include them in the site.

To view Flash and Shockwave demos:

1. On the Online Companion page for Session 9.2, click a link in the Flash Demos section, and watch the Flash animation.

   Trouble? If your browser does not have the Flash Player plug-in, follow the on-screen instructions to install it.

2. Return to the Online Companion page for Session 9.2 and explore one or two of the other Flash animations. Notice the use of animated text, sound, and other images and think about how these features make the Web site more inviting and appealing than if the same content appeared as just regular text.

3. Return to the Online Companion page for Session 9.2, and then click one of the links in the Shockwave Demo section. As you explore these demonstrations, notice the kind of interaction that Shockwave creates. You can interact with a product, play a game, or direct some type of action on the screen. Figure 9-27 shows an online game that uses the Shockwave Player plug-in to let the user control the players wearing red sweaters as they throw snowballs at the players wearing green sweaters. Dragging a player causes him to move, holding down the mouse button controls the distance of the throw, and releasing the mouse button throws the snowballs. As snowballs hit the players, they scream out and fall in the snow, until one team wins. Many games that use the Shockwave Player are simple, like Snowcraft, but Shockwave Player is also used for much more complicated online games.

Figure 9-27 ▶ **Snowcraft game that uses Shockwave Player**

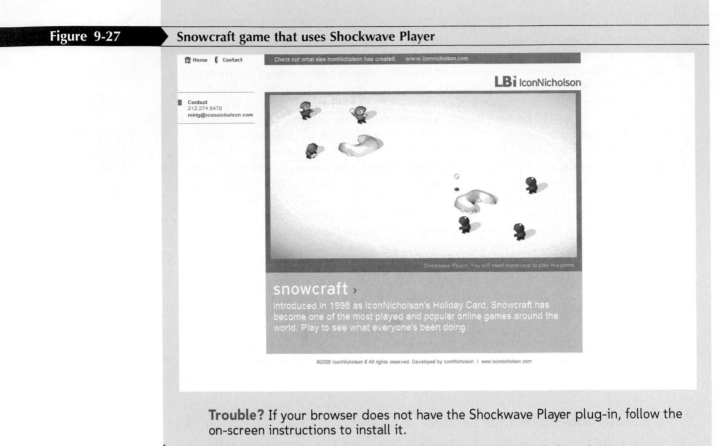

Trouble? If your browser does not have the Shockwave Player plug-in, follow the on-screen instructions to install it.

▶ **4.** Return to the Online Companion page for Session 9.2, and then choose one or two other links to examine some additional Shockwave files.

▶ **5.** Return to the Online Companion page for Session 9.2.

From your exploration of the demos, you probably already noticed a few differences between Flash and Shockwave. The first difference that you might have noticed is that Flash is used on a smaller scale, for items such as simple animations with sound and images. Shockwave is used for more complex applications, such as playing an interactive game. Second, you might have noticed that Flash animations load quickly in a browser, because Flash outputs much smaller files than Director. Several other differences that you might not have seen from the demos are that Flash is a simpler program to learn and use than Director, Flash is much less expensive to purchase than Director, and Flash Player is a much more widely distributed plug-in than Shockwave Player. It is important to note that Flash and Director do have some similarities in the types of features they include and the files they produce. Many of these factors make Flash the more attractive choice for creating animation in a Web page, unless the more robust features of Director are required for creating games and extensive applications. Perhaps the most important feature of the Flash Player is that most Web developers know that 96% of the installed browsers will be able to view animations created using Flash. When choosing an animation program, this is perhaps one of the most important considerations because you want to make sure that people can view your Web site content. Flash is also well delivered to various types of mobile devices, which is an important consideration given the developments and future expansion in wireless Internet devices.

Knowing When to Use Director Instead of Flash | InSight

If Flash is well-suited for many Web applications, when would you need to use Director? Director is the application of choice when you need to create more than just animation with video, sound, and images. Director is a multimedia authoring tool that can be used to create interactive content for the Internet, CDs, DVDs, and kiosks that include photo-quality images, digital video, animation, three-dimensional presentations, text content, hyperlinks, and Flash content. You might use Flash to bring a home page in a Web site to life; you would use Director to create a game for the Internet or to create full-featured product demonstrations that let users control the animation, sound, and video that they are viewing.

Creating content using Flash and Director is both fun and easy. If creating this type of content appeals to you, you might take a course in Flash animation or a general course in Web site animation.

Choosing Image Editing and Illustration Programs

You learned in Session 9.1 that you can insert an image into an HTML document by storing the image in a file and using the <img /> tag to insert the file into the Web page. An image can be any picture, including one you take with a digital camera or create using a drawing or illustration program. Computer-generated graphics come in two basic varieties: raster (also called bitmap) and vector. The main difference between the two graphics types is that **raster graphics** are composed of pixels, and **vector graphics** are composed of paths. Figure 9-28 shows the letter "S" that was created using Paint, a program that is installed with Windows. Paint is an example of a program that creates raster graphics, also called bitmap images.

Graphic created using Paint | Figure 9-28

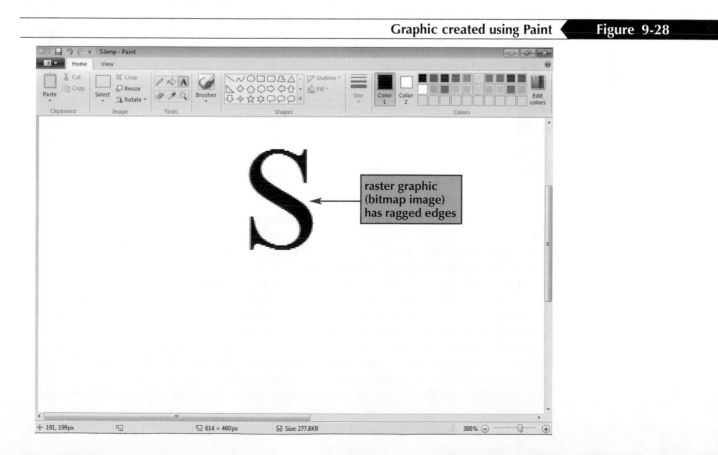

Raster graphics have the following filename extensions: .bmp, .gif, .jpg, .png, and .tif. Graphics with these filename extensions are created using a variety of programs, including Paint, Adobe Photoshop, Adobe Fireworks, and Corel Paint Shop Pro. In addition, any image that you take using a digital camera or make using a scanner is a raster graphic. Because raster graphics are made up of pixels, it is not possible to create layers of content. If you draw a circle using a raster graphics program, and then use a text tool to add a word on top of the circle, the pixels in the text *replace* the ones in the circle. If you later decide to cut the text out of the circle, you'll be left with a hole where the text once was, not the original circle that you drew. In addition, raster graphics are not scalable; if you zoom in on an image created using a raster graphics program, you'll see ragged edges on the image because you cannot change the size of the pixels in the image.

Figure 9-29 shows the letter "S" that was created using Adobe Illustrator. Illustrator is an example of a program that creates vector graphics.

Figure 9-29 ▶ **Graphic created using Adobe Illustrator**

Vector graphics have the following filename extensions: .ai, .wmf, .cdr, and .dxf. Graphics with these filename extensions are created using programs such as Illustrator, CorelDRAW, and AutoCAD programs. Vector graphics are scalable, which means that their edges are smooth at any resolution. In addition, you can layer content in a vector graphic. In the same example using a circle with text on top of it, the text is a *layer* on top of the circle. In other words, the circle exists separately from the text, and vice-versa. Because of this difference, vector graphics are best suited for drawing objects. Each object on a canvas has a certain dimension and color, and the program makes the distinction between the different objects on a canvas for you.

Why is this difference important? Depending on the type of image that you need to create, you might need to select a program specifically designed for that purpose. Raster graphics are the choice for photographs and images with different levels of shading. Vector graphics are the choice when you need to create drawings that require lines and curves to form different shapes. For these reasons, raster graphics require the use of a category of programs called **image editing programs**, and vector graphics require the use of a category of programs called **illustration software**. Some programs, such as Fireworks and Photoshop, do both, but most programs are geared primarily toward one category of graphic or the other.

Most beginning Web page developers can use a simple program such as Paint to draw basic images and create simple logos. An image editing program such as Adobe Photoshop is a good choice for someone who takes a lot of digital pictures and frequently needs to resize, crop, and retouch the images. Most image editing programs include a basic tool palette that lets you perform simple tasks that are common to creating and editing images. Learning how to use illustration software, however, usually requires a more thorough understanding gained from taking a course. The Online Companion page for Session 9.2 includes links to the programs discussed in this section and other resources for working with images.

Choosing a Web Hosting Service

Ideally, you choose a Web hosting service or a Web presence provider to host a Web site *before* you begin work on creating the Web site's pages. Some Web sites are hosted by private (dedicated) Web servers that are managed and maintained by the organization that creates the sites. However, many Web sites are hosted by independent ISPs that sell shared and dedicated server space to small- and medium-sized businesses. The choice of a Web hosting service is more than just one of affordability—it is important to understand what services the company offers and the software it uses to host sites. It is also important to have a thorough understanding of what is involved in upgrading your server space and services in case your initial plan changes over time.

Understanding Your Web Site's Technical Requirements

Searching for a Web host provider can be an overwhelming task, but it is much easier when you know what you're looking for. The best way to begin your search for a company to host your Web site is to evaluate your Web site's content and goals and to understand the tools that you will be using to create your pages. A good place to start is by creating a storyboard of the pages you plan to include. A **storyboard** of a Web site shows the pages that you plan to include, separated into levels that show the relationships of the pages to each other. Figure 9-30 shows a sample storyboard for the community education pages on the Lakeside Police Department Web site. Notice that there is a home page at the top of the storyboard with two levels of pages below it. The pages in the second row include hyperlinks to the home page and to each other, with each page including additional hyperlinks to the pages below it in the storyboard. When a Web site is presented in this way, it is also called the site's navigation structure, because it shows the path of navigation through the site.

Figure 9-30 ▶ Storyboard for community education pages

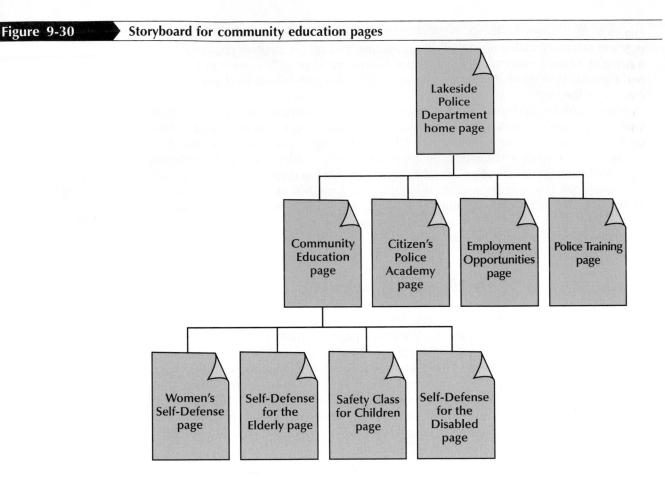

As you evaluate how many pages you'll include and how they are related to each other, you should also examine the planned content for each page. Most pages will contain standard content, such as images, text, and hyperlinks. You might have pages that process information, such as collecting data supplied by the user, which is then stored in a database or a file. The Web page is still an HTML document, but the processing that is required by this type of page requires action by the Web server on which the page is stored. The Web server must collect the data and save it in the specified format (such as comma-delimited, in which the data is stored in a text file and data from individual fields are separated by commas, or in a database table). The Web server must rely on a script to process the data collected by the Web page. You can write these scripts yourself, but a better option is finding a company that provides code snippets to help you process user-entered data.

The type of Web server that the company uses can also be important. Some types of pages that you might want to include in a Web site require a certain kind of server to process them. For example, if your site uses Active Server Pages (ASP), which are dynamic Web pages based on the content stored in a database, you'll need to store the site on a Windows-based Web server because the Unix and Linux Web servers do not support ASP. It is important to identify the technologies that you'll use in your site to make sure that the company's Web server supports them. You don't want to create a Web site and later find out, for example, that your Web hosting company's Linux Web server doesn't support the types of pages you created.

Using a Secure Server

If any of your site's pages require users to supply information that is personal or confidential in nature, then you will need a secure server. A **secure server** encrypts data, which changes it into a format that prevents unauthorized parties from being able to read or use it. Some common situations that require a secure server are credit card transactions and forms that require a user to enter a Social Security number or other private data. When you need a secure server, the Web hosting service will require you to purchase and use a dedicated server. A **dedicated server** is a Web server that hosts only one site, compared to a **shared server**, which hosts several sites. A dedicated server is more expensive to operate. You will also need to install a server certificate to prove to users that the site is actually secure.

Understanding Your Web Site's File Size and Transfer Requirements

Because they are text files, most Web pages are small in terms of file size. However, a Web site can be very large if it contains many digital pictures, images, and supporting files such as a database. For example, if you are a realtor, your site might include hundreds of digital photographs and virtual video tours of the homes that you have listed for sale. These files will require a lot of storage space. You should evaluate this type of information about your site's content before you start looking for a Web hosting service. In addition, you need to consider the amount of traffic your site will receive and the sizes of the files that users will download from the Web server. The HTML document for a property listing might be 1,000 bytes (which is very small). But the pictures of the house and the video files of the main living areas might require five megabytes. When a user downloads the Web page, the user's browser must also download the image and video files, resulting in the transfer of over five megabytes of data. The amount of data that is transferred from the Web server is known as the site's **bandwidth** or **data transfer**. Most companies sell server space based on a file size limit and a daily or monthly data transfer limit. When you exceed either of these limits, you might incur extra fees from the Web hosting service. In addition, your Web hosting service might not be able to increase your Web site's server space or bandwidth, which means that you would need to transfer your Web site to another company that can handle your site's file size and bandwidth requirements. Moving a Web site isn't an easy task, so you'll want to make sure that your Web hosting service can handle not only your current needs, but your anticipated needs for the future, as well.

You might also want to make sure that the company you select to host your site has technical support services available to you when you need them, especially if you are a new Web site developer. When you talk to people at the Web hosting service, try to get a sense of the level of support and service that it provides. For example, you can ask questions about the amount of server downtime it has experienced in the past month, how many hours a day and days a week that technical support personnel answer the phone, and about any online resources that the company provides. When you view the online help resources, you can get a sense of the company's intended audience and whether it will assist you with future questions. If everything is written for advanced programmers, then you'll have to get more outside help than you would if the pages include basic information that is written in a clear and concise way for beginners.

Securing a Domain Name

Another question you need to ask when securing a Web hosting service is about the Web hosting service's policy for securing a domain name for your Web site. You can use a registrar such as Register.com, which is shown in Figure 9-31, or a similar registrar to enter your proposed domain name and check its availability.

Figure 9-31 Register.com home page

If the domain name you want is available, see if the Web hosting service can purchase it as part of your hosting agreement and provide you with the technical assistance you will need to establish the company as the Web site's host. Most larger companies offer domain name services for free with an annual service agreement. When you renew your Web site hosting contract, ask the company if it provides domain name renewal service so it will automatically renew your domain for you. This convenience saves you a step and ensures that your domain name does not expire and become eligible for sale to another entity.

Asking About Other Services Offered by the Web Hosting Service

Finally, you should look at the other services offered by the Web hosting service. Items such as site statistics, email accounts for the domain name you registered, Web site templates, Web site construction tools, and database software are just a few of the items that are "value added" by most companies. You might need to pay an extra service fee to obtain detailed site traffic reports, but this information is helpful when analyzing who is coming to your site and which pages they are viewing. You can use a traffic report to get detailed information, such as how many visitors used the site each day, how many pages the visitors viewed, which pages visitors used to enter and exit the Web site, what search strings were entered into the Web site's search feature, and so on. By analyzing this data, you can see which pages are the most popular and gauge where your site's traffic is coming from. Analyzing a site's traffic is an important way of understanding who is using the site and what information they are seeking. If you use this information correctly, you'll be able to understand the site's visitors and organize and design the site to better serve them.

You'll examine a few Web hosting services next to get a sense of the types of services and plans that they offer so you can report back to Chief Silva and recommend a choice.

To review Web server hosting services:

▶ **1.** On the Online Companion page for Session 9.2, click one of the links in the Choosing a Web Hosting Service section and wait while the browser loads the home page.

▶ **2.** Review the site's home page, and then open a page that lists different Web hosting companies by name.

▶ **3.** Click a link to a company, and then examine the services that the Web hosting service provides. Figure 9-32 shows the home page for ePowHost.com, a company that provides multiple Web hosting accounts. As you are examining the hosting agreements, keep in mind the information you've learned about Web hosting. For example, be alert for different levels of service and whether the company lets you upgrade your server space and data transfer limits. Also, explore the site's technical support pages to see if they are written in a way that is easy for you to understand, so that you can diagnose and correct any problems that you have. Finally, see if the company offers domain name and renewal services for new accounts.

Figure 9-32 ePowHost home page

> **4.** Return to the Online Companion page for Session 9.2, and then use the links pro-
> vided to examine two or three more Web hosting services to review their Web
> hosting agreements. When you are finished, return to the Online Companion page
> for Session 9.2.

By examining a few Web sites, you probably got a feel for the different levels of accounts
that the company offers and the services that it provides. You can also read reviews of different Web hosting services to get a feel for the types of organizations they work with and compare those organizations to your own to get a sense of the company's primary market.

Publishing a Web Site

After you find a Web hosting service to host your Web site, the next step is to move your
files to the company's Web server. Your Web hosting service should give you information
about what user name and password to use and where and how to upload the files. Most
companies will ask you to use FTP to move your files. In some cases, you'll need an FTP
program to make the transfer, but some companies include a built-in FTP interface that
you access as part of your Web site's control panel. (A **control panel** is a Web page that
you access with your Web site's user name and password; it includes all the tools you
need to access and manage your Web site.) If you are using a Web site management program, you might be able to use the program to publish your site by setting up a remote
Web site at the location of your Web server.

When you move your Web site's files to the Web server, be sure to include all of the folders and supporting files to the Web server, and not just the Web site's HTML documents. A common mistake made by many beginning Web site developers is omitting the Web site's supporting files, such as images, backgrounds, custom bullet characters, and multimedia files. If your HTML documents contain hyperlinks to supporting files that use relative paths, be certain to include the supporting files in the same folders as the HTML documents, or the links will be broken in your Web pages. If your HTML documents contain hyperlinks to supporting files that use absolute paths, make sure that the location of the file in the absolute path is available to the Internet user. For example, if a linked file is on your computer's hard drive, you will be able to view the file, but a person accessing the page from a Web server will not because he will not have access to your computer.

The best strategy for maintaining a Web site after you publish it for the first time is to make your changes to the copy of the Web site that you stored on your hard drive or other local drive, and then to move those files to the Web server. It is possible to make changes directly to the pages on the Web sever, but there are two important disadvantages to this approach. First, by having a copy of the Web site on your hard or other local drive (often called a **local Web site**), you have a backup of your Web site. If something happens to the Web site stored on the Web server (often called a **remote Web site**), you will be able to publish the files from your local Web site back to the server to repair any damaged or lost files. Second, if you make changes to pages stored on the server, the potential exists for someone to be viewing the pages—and having problems with broken links and other issues—while you are editing the pages.

Search Engine Submission and Optimization

The last major task in publishing a Web site is promoting it. You could publish your pages and wait for search engines to perform crawls and add your site to their indexes. Or, you can be proactive and use <meta> tags to teach the search engines how to list your site by including the HTML <meta> tag with the appropriate keywords attribute to define your site's primary focus. Figure 9-33 shows the Web page you created in Session 9.1, with <meta> tags for a description of your site and keywords inserted in the head section of the HTML document.

Figure 9-33 ▶ **Meta tags added to Web page**

meta tags in head section

The description <meta> tag is a summary of the page's contents that a search engine might include in its search results. A search engine uses the <meta> tags in an HTML document to index the page by looking at the keywords in the <meta> tag to identify the search expressions that users might type to locate your page. For example, a user who types "Lakeside Police Department community education" into a search engine might hit the page based on the keywords stored in the <meta> tag. Using <meta> tags is a good way to help search engines list your site, but the search engines still need to find the site. To properly promote your site, you can send it to the various search engines on the Web. **Search engine submission** is the process of submitting your site's URL to one or more search engines so they will list your site in their indexes. **Search engine optimization** is the process of fine-tuning your site so that it ranks well in a search engine's results when a user searches the Web using your site's keywords.

Your Web hosting service might include a resource for search engine submission. In this case, you'll need to create the <meta> tags that describe your site. You'll explore some resources for search engine submission and optimization next, because promoting the Web site for the Lakeside Police Department is an important step toward getting people to use it.

To explore resources for search engine submission and optimization:

▶ **1.** On the Online Companion page for Session 9.2, click the **Search Engine Watch** link and wait while the browser loads the Search Engine Watch home page shown in Figure 9-34.

Search Engine Watch home page ◄ Figure 9-34

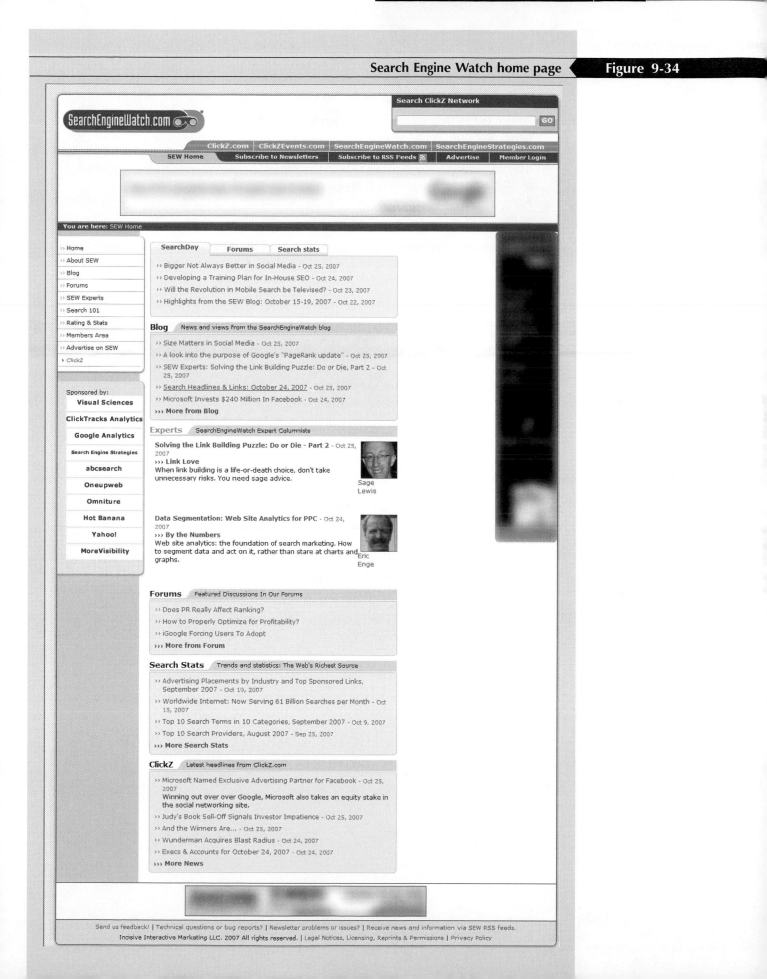

▶ **2.** Explore the links on the Search Engine Watch home page to learn more about search engine submission and optimization. Notice that this site has resources that include search engine submission tips and Web searching tips, in addition to reports about search engines on the Web.

▶ **3.** Return to the Online Companion page for Session 9.2, and then click the **Meta tags generator** link. Read the information in the page to learn more about <meta> tags and examine the page to learn how to use it to generate <meta> tags for a Web site. (Do not generate any <meta> tags at this time.) Look for links to frequently asked questions to learn more about creating <meta> tags for a Web site.

▶ **4.** Close your browser.

You can use the Additional Information section of the Online Companion page for Tutorial 9 to learn more about Web site development. If you have further interest in a specific part of Web page or Web site development, ask your instructor about courses that can help you to increase your understanding and knowledge of specific topics.

Review | Session 9.2 Quick Check

1. What features does a Web site management tool provide?
2. What is JavaScript, and what are some things that it can do?
3. How does a browser display content that is not written in HTML?
4. Which programs would you use to create Flash and Shockwave files for use on the Web? What kinds of files can you create using each program?
5. What is the difference between a raster graphic and a vector graphic? Which type of program would you use to create each type of graphic?
6. Why is it important to create a storyboard of a Web site's content before deciding on the best ISP to host the Web site?
7. What is a secure server?
8. What are some important services that you should look for in an ISP besides Web site hosting plans and domain name and renewal services?
9. What is the difference between search engine submission and search engine optimization?

Tutorial Summary | Review

In this tutorial, you learned about markup languages and the language used to create Web pages. You used a text editor to create a simple Web page that includes an image, heading, paragraph with formatted text, bulleted list, and hyperlink. You also learned about more sophisticated ways to create Web pages and manage a Web site by using programs such as Microsoft Expression Web and Adobe Dreamweaver. You learned about several programs required to create various kinds of dynamic Web page content. You explored how to use JavaScript to display animated content in a Web page, and you examined the use of different image editing programs and illustration software to create images. You also viewed demonstrations that use the Flash Player and the Shockwave Player, two popular programs used for displaying animated content. You explored some of the issues involved in selecting a Web hosting service to host your Web site, and you learned how to move your Web site's files from your local drive to a Web server. Finally, you examined some resources for listing a Web site in search engines and creating <meta> tags to cause your Web site to be ranked high in the search engine results.

Key Terms

absolute path
add-on
anchor tag
attribute
bandwidth
body section
bookmark
browser extension
bulleted list
comment tag
control panel
data transfer
dedicated server
definition list
deprecated
document type
 declaration (DTD)
Extensible Hypertext
 Markup Language
 (XHTML)

Extensible Markup
 Language (XML)
Flash Player
head section
helper application
illustration software
image
image editing program
JavaScript
local Web site
markup language
metalanguage
nested tag
numbered list
ordered list
pixel
plug-in
raster graphic
relative path
remote Web site

scripting engine
scripting language
search engine optimization
search engine submission
secure server
shared server
Shockwave Player
source page
specifications
Standard Generalized
 Markup Language
 (SGML)
storyboard
target
target page
unordered list
vector graphic
Web-safe color palette
World Wide Web
 Consortium (W3C)

Practice	**Review Assignments**

Apply the skills you learned in the tutorial using the same case scenario.

Data Files needed for the Review Assignments: elder_sd.html, logo.jpg, and women_sd.html

After finishing your research about different Web site management tools, technologies, and Web hosting services, Chief Mary Silva of the Lakeside Police Department asks you to finish the self-defense Web pages she requested. She also asks you to prepare a report on your findings, outlining the types of pages that the department should include in its Web site.

1. Start Windows Explorer, and then copy the **women_sd.html** file that you created in this tutorial from the Tutorial.09\Tutorial folder into the Tutorial.09\Review folder included with your Data Files.

2. Start Notepad or your text editor, and then open the **women_sd.html** page from the Tutorial.09\Review folder. (*Note*: Make sure that you open the file from the Tutorial.09\Review folder, and not from the Tutorial.09\Tutorial folder, or your hyperlinks will not work correctly.)

3. Use the Save As command to save the women_sd.html file as **child_sd.html** in the Tutorial.09\Review folder.

4. Make the following changes to the child_sd.html text document to create the Web page for the Safety Class for Children:

   a. Change the level-two heading in the page to **Safety Class for Children (ages 13 and under)**.

   b. Change the font color of the level-two heading from red to blue.

   c. Replace the sentence "The first class is for women ages 14 and older." with the following new sentence: **The third class is for children ages 13 and under and their parents.**

   d. Replace the word "Women" in the next sentence with the word **Children**, and change the class duration from two hours to **one hour**.

   e. Change the bold text to **Saturday, November 7, at 3:00 P.M.**

   f. Change the comment tag to update it for the current page.

   g. Change the HTML page title to **Lakeside Police Department Safety Class for Children**.

   h. Replace the second item in the bulleted list with a link to the **women_sd.html** page in the Tutorial.09\Review folder. Use the link text **Self-Defense for Women**.

5. Save the file and then preview it in a browser. If necessary, return to your text editor and make any changes.

6. After completing and saving the child_sd.html page, use the Save As command in Notepad or your text editor to save the page as **dis_sd.html** in the Tutorial.09\Review folder. Using the guidelines in Step 4, edit the page content to make it appropriate for a class that is taught to disabled individuals. Schedule the class for Saturday, November 14 at 4:00 P.M. for 90 minutes, and change the level-two heading in the page to green. When you are finished making the necessary changes to the HTML document, save it, close your text editor, and then preview the page in a browser.

7. Examine the four pages for the self-defense classes and make sure that each one contains hyperlinks to the other three. A page should not contain a hyperlink to itself. As you update the pages, save each one. When you are finished, open the **women_sd.html** page in a browser and use the hyperlinks to navigate through the pages.

8. Start your Web browser, and then use your favorite search engine or directory to search for police department Web sites in small metropolitan areas. Examine the sites to understand the type of information they contain. Also, review the contents of each page to look for different Web technologies such as scripts, images, and animations so you can develop a plan for the Lakeside Police Department. In your plan, identify the type of content you want to include.

9. Open the Online Companion page at www.cengage.com/internet/np/internet8 and log on to your account, click the Tutorial 9 link, and then click the Review Assignments link. Use the links in the Review Assignments section to conduct sufficient research to recommend a Web hosting service for the Lakeside Police Department. (You should assume that the police department does not have access to a private dedicated sever.) Make sure that the Web hosting service you recommend can process the pages you plan to include in the Web site (Step 8). Print the page that describes the services provided by the Web hosting service and the cost of the plan that you recommend.

10. Write a memo to Chief Silva explaining what technologies you have planned and which Web hosting service you recommend the police department should use to host its Web site. Be sure to support your recommendations with information you obtained through your research.

11. Close your Web browser.

| Apply | **Case Problem 1** |

Apply what you learned to create a Web page that links to a Web site.

Data Files needed for this Case Problem: 20.jpg and falcon.txt

Fighting Falcons High School Reunion   Rebecca Smith is in charge of the 20th reunion committee for Hugo High School. She needs to create a simple Web page that announces the date, time, and location of the reunion, which is scheduled for next summer. She will post the page on the school's Web site and include a link from her Web page to the reunion committee's Web site. All of the pages should be XHTML compatible. To help Rebecca create the Web page, complete the following steps.

1. Start Notepad or your text editor.
2. Type the HTML structure tags in the document to create the HTML document, the head section, and the body section.
3. Add the page title **Fighting Falcons High School Reunion** to the page.
4. Copy the paragraphs stored in the **falcon.txt** document in the Tutorial.09\Cases folder included with your Data Files, and paste them into the body section of the HTML document you are creating.
5. Add the necessary HTML tags to the paragraphs that you pasted in Step 4.
6. Change the text "Can you believe that it has been 20 years already?" in the first paragraph to italic.
7. Change the text "Fighting Falcons Reunion Committee" in the last paragraph to bold and red.
8. Create a new, centered paragraph at the top of the page, and then insert the image saved as **20.jpg** in the Tutorial.09\Cases folder.
9. Format the text "Reunion Web site" as a hyperlink that opens the URL http://www.FightingFalconsReunionCommittee.info. (*Note*: This URL is fictitious, so it will not open a Web site.)
10. Save the file as **reunion.html** in the Tutorial.09\Cases folder.

11. Open the HTML document in a Web browser. If necessary, return to your text editor and make any changes, save the HTML document, and then refresh the page in the browser. Print the Web page.

⊕ EXPLORE   12. Use your browser to view and print the HTML document. (*Hint*: If you are using Internet Explorer, click the Page button on the Command bar, and then click View Source. If you are using Firefox, click View on the menu bar, and then click Page Source.)

13. Close your browser and your text editor.

| Research | **Case Problem 2** |

Determine the best Web site creation and management tool for a local deli to use to create a Web site that accepts online orders.

There are no Data Files needed for this Case Problem.

Shayla's Deli   Shayla Robinson owns and operates a deli that serves breakfast and lunch and caters local events. Because customers who call in their orders and pick them up comprise a large percentage of the deli's business, Shayla's employees spend a lot of time on the phone. Shayla wants to create a Web site on which she can post the menu and daily specials so customers can use it to place orders. Shayla wants to use a Web site creation and management tool to create the Web site. She asks you to conduct some research to determine the best one for the deli to use. The Web site will contain many pages and images, and it will require forms that allow customers to place pick-up orders for breakfast and lunch and to order catering services. She wants to accept credit card orders on the Web site so customers can pay the required deposit for catering orders. To help identify the best Web site creation and management tool for the deli, complete the following steps.

1. Start your Web browser, open the Online Companion page at www.cengage.com/internet/np/internet8 and log on to your account, click the Tutorial 9 link, and then click the Case Problem 2 link. Click the Microsoft Expression Web link and wait while the browser loads the page.

⊕ EXPLORE   2. Use the resources on the Expression Web site to find information about Microsoft Expression Web that will assist you in making a recommendation for using Expression Web to create the Shayla's Deli Web site. Pay particular attention to user interface, online help and tutorials, server issues, cost, and implementation. As you are gathering information, try to get a sense of how easy or difficult it would be for a beginner to use the program. In addition, learn about the tools that Expression Web includes for publishing a Web site and for creating simple images, such as logos.

⊕ EXPLORE   3. Return to the Online Companion page for Case Problem 2, and then click the Adobe Dreamweaver link. Use the guidelines in Step 2 to gather information about Dreamweaver, paying particular attention to what Shayla needs for her Web site.

⊕ EXPLORE   4. When you are finished, write a one-page memo addressed to Shayla Robinson that includes a table identifying the pros and cons of using each program to create the company's Web site. Below this table, write a paragraph in which you recommend the use of one program over the other. Be sure to support your recommendation with specific information.

5. Close your browser.

Create		Case Problem 3

Use JavaScript to enhance a Web page.

There are no Data Files needed for this Case Problem.

Point Blanke Airpark Joe Fehrenbach is the president of the Point Blanke Airpark in Point Blanke, Colorado. The airpark is home to 50 small- and medium-sized aircraft, mostly belonging to retired military officials and pilots. The airpark is a not-for-profit organization and as such, it relies on dues and fundraising efforts to pay for maintenance and renovations to the airpark's small terminal and for other capital expenditures. The board recently voted to conduct a fundraiser in which corporations sponsor the airpark based on mileage their employees travel and based on mileage traveled by the aircraft at the airpark. To help compute the nautical miles and the donations, Joe needs to create a Web page with a mileage calculator and a calculator that computes the donation. To create the page for Joe, complete the following steps.

1. Start your Web browser, open the Online Companion page at www.cengage.com/internet/np/internet8 and log on to your account, click the Tutorial 9 link, and then click the Case Problem 3 link.
2. Use the links to select a site that provides free JavaScript programs.
3. Search the site for a calculator that computes the mileage between airports in the United States. When you find a resource, examine the instructions for using the script and any requirements for its use (such as posting a link to the provider's Web site on your Web page).
4. Start Notepad or your text editor and create an HTML document using the required document structure.
5. Add an appropriate title to the HTML document using the <title> tags.

⊕ **EXPLORE** 6. Create a heading for the Web page and one or two paragraphs about the fundraiser and its objectives. Use your knowledge of HTML to enhance the content you provide to make it visually appealing.
7. Save the page as **airpark.html** in the Tutorial.09\Cases folder included with your Data Files.

⊕ **EXPLORE** 8. Follow the instructions on the Web site you located in Step 2 to insert the script into the HTML document. Make sure that your page contains information required by the provider for your use of the script.
9. Save the HTML document, and then open the file in a browser. Test the script. If necessary, return to the HTML document to make changes.

⊕ **EXPLORE** 10. Return to the Web site you located in Step 2 and search for a script that creates a simple calculator that performs basic calculations. Add the script to your HTML document. In addition, add supporting text to indicate that the donor can use the calculator to compute the per-mile donation based on the mileage computed by the airport calculator. (For example, if the donation is ten cents per mile, the donor would use the calculator to multiply the nautical mileage between airports by 10 cents (or .10).)
11. Save the HTML document, and then refresh the page in your Web browser. Use the airport calculator to compute the mileage between Denver, CO and San Antonio, TX. Then use the calculator to compute the donation based on 10 cents per mile. (*Note*: If you are using Internet Explorer and a warning opens in the Information bar, click the Information bar, and then click Allow Blocked Content on the shortcut menu to display the result of the script. If you are using Firefox and nothing happens when you click the button to calculate the distances, click Tools on the menu bar, click Options, click the Content icon, click the Enable JavaScript check box to select it, click the OK button, and then try again.) Print the page.
12. Close your browser and Notepad.

| Research | **Case Problem 4** |

Review the characteristics of good and bad Web sites using resources on the Web.

There are no Data Files needed for this Case Problem.

The Best and Worst of the Web   You are an editorial assistant for a magazine whose core subscription base consists of Web site developers and programmers. As part of the annual "Best and Worst of the Web" issue, your editor, Chloe Hughes, has asked you to conduct some research to identify Web sites that rank other Web sites based on their content, presentation, and layout. Chloe asks you to use the information you find to write a sidebar feature about what makes a Web site great. Report to Chloe by completing the following steps.

1. Start your Web browser, open the Online Companion page at www.cengage.com/internet/np/internet8 and log on to your account, click the Tutorial 9 link, and then click the Case Problem 4 link. Choose a Web site that lists the "best" sites, and then wait while the browser loads the home page of the site you selected.

    ✦ **EXPLORE**   2. Review the site's information to learn how it is organized and then examine the site's selection of "best" Web sites. As you are viewing the sites, take note of whether you agree with the site's "best" ranking. Print the home pages for at least three sites that you visit.

    ✦ **EXPLORE**   3. Return to the Online Companion page for Case Problem 4, and then choose a link to a site that lists the "worst" Web sites. Review the site's information to learn how it is organized and then examine the site's selection of the "worst" Web sites. As you are viewing the sites, take note of whether you agree with the site's "worst" ranking. Print the home pages for at least three sites that you visit.

    ✦ **EXPLORE**   4. In a report addressed to Chloe Hughes, identify three characteristics of good Web sites and three characteristics of bad Web sites. Be sure to back up your ideas with documentation or examples you found in the Web sites that you reviewed in Steps 2 and 3.

5. Close your browser.

| Challenge | **Case Problem 5** |

Evaluate Web sites in a specific industry to help plan a new Web site.

There are no Data Files needed for this Case Problem.

Hilltop Custom Pools   John Davidson is the owner of Hilltop Custom Pools, a custom residential pool construction company in northern California. John wants you to conduct some research to help him plan the storyboard for his company's Web site. He wants you to look at the Web sites for other custom pool companies and evaluate the resources they use to design their sites and the <meta> tags that they use to increase the effectiveness of their site's ranking in search engines. To help John plan his company's Web site and develop effective <meta> tags, complete the following steps.

1. Start your Web browser and then use your favorite search engine or directory to search for swimming pool contractors in northern California or in any other city, or for custom pool builders that you might already know by name. Evaluate the links and choose one to a specific construction company. Click the link to open the home page to the contractor's Web site, and then print the home page.

    ✦ **EXPLORE**   2. Evaluate the contractor's Web site and take note of any technologies that you can identify, such as information presented in an animation or a script. If you notice the use of any of these technologies, evaluate their effectiveness.

⊕EXPLORE

3. Click the links on the contractor's home page to explore the site and take note of the type of information it contains. Evaluate the Web site as if you were a customer by considering the content of the information provided, the ease with which you can navigate the site, the attractiveness of the layout and design, and any other issues that you deem important to the overall success of the Web site.

4. Look for weaknesses in the Web site's presentation and design. Would you change anything? If so, why? Be specific.

⊕EXPLORE

5. Examine the <meta> tags that the site uses by viewing the source document for the site's home page. (*Hint*: If you are using Internet Explorer, click the Page button on the Command bar, and then click View Source. If you are using Firefox, click View on the menu bar, and then click Page Source.) Evaluate the effectiveness of the <meta> tags used in the home page.

6. Return to your search results and evaluate another contractor's Web site using the guidelines presented in Steps 2 through 5. Print the contractor's home page.

7. When you have finished evaluating the two Web sites, close your browser.

⊕EXPLORE

8. Write a one-page report addressed to your instructor. In your report, provide specific feedback on how you would use the information you found to recommend a presentation, layout, and <meta> tags for the Hilltop Custom Pools Web site.

Reinforce | Lab Assignments

Student Edition Labs

The interactive Student Edition Labs on **Creating Web Pages** and **Web Design Principles** are designed to help you master some of the key concepts and skills presented in this tutorial, including:

- understanding HTML and XHTML
- creating an HTML document
- adding graphics and links to an HTML document
- designing Web site structure
- planning the look and feel of a Web site
- designing a Web site for optimal readability
- using hypertext effectively in a Web site
- using images effectively on Web pages

The labs are available online and can be accessed from the Tutorial 9 Web page on the Online Companion at www.cengage.com/internet/np/internet8.

Review | Quick Check Answers

Session 9.1

1. HTML is a nonproprietary markup language that a Web browser interprets and then displays as a Web page. HTML was developed from SGML in 1989 by Tim Berners-Lee and Robert Calliau as a project to improve research document-handling procedures.

2. The World Wide Web Consortium (W3C) establishes specifications for HTML and other languages used on the Web.

3. XML is a markup language that describes the format and structure of data. XML is used to share data across organizations, especially for data that is used on the Internet.

4. XHTML is a markup language that combines the formatting features of HTML with the stricter syntax of XML so that Web content is more readily and easily delivered to Internet devices.

5. HTML and XHTML are similar in that they are compatible and most browsers render pages written in each format. However, XHTML follows a stricter syntax: tags must be written in lowercase letters only, values for attributes must be enclosed in quotation marks, attribute minimization is prohibited, all elements must be closed, and one-sided tags must be closed.

6. Tags indicate the different elements of a Web page, such as headings, inserting images, and paragraphs. HTML tags can be one-sided or two-sided. Some tags include optional or required attributes to specify additional information about the element.

7. Insert the <img /> tag and the src attribute to indicate the file to insert in the location in which you want to display the image.

8. Use the <a> tag and the href attribute to indicate the location of the hyperlink, the text to format as a hyperlink, and the closing </a> tag.

Session 9.2

1. A Web site management tool generates the HTML code as pages are created, simplifies Web page development by inserting code snippets into Web pages, creates navigation structures, and provides features such as link checking to identify problems in the Web site.

2. JavaScript is a scripting language that is used to add features to a Web page such as displaying a greeting based on the time of day the page is loaded, displaying a calendar, opening a pop-up window, displaying the current date and time or a countdown to a specific day and time, or displaying scrolling text, menus, or animated buttons.

3. A browser uses a program called a browser extension, plug-in, or helper application to display content that it cannot process. The browser calls on the helper application to display the content, which might include animations, spreadsheets, or other non-HTML files.

4. Adobe Flash and Adobe Director create Flash and Shockwave files. Flash is used for simple animations, user interfaces, images, movies, sound, and text. Shockwave is used for more sophisticated animations and movies, including games, three-dimensional interfaces, and kiosk operations.

5. A raster graphic is made up of individual pixels in which "layers" on top of content replace the pixels in the bottom layer. Raster graphics are created by image editing programs, such as Microsoft Paint, Adobe Photoshop, and Adobe Fireworks. A vector graphic is made up of scalable objects that have smooth edges. Vector graphics are created by illustration software, such as Adobe Illustrator, CorelDRAW, and AutoCAD programs.

6. Creating a storyboard lets you estimate the Web site's contents from a technical standpoint so that you are able to select an ISP that can accommodate the technical needs of the pages you'll be including.

7. A secure server encrypts data, which changes it into a format that prevents unauthorized parties from being able to read or use it.

8. Other important features might include email accounts using the domain name, site statistics, Web site templates, Web site construction tools, and online help.

9. Search engine submission is the process of submitting your site's URL to one or more search engines on the Web. Search engine optimization is the process of fine-tuning your Web site so that it ranks well in a search engine's results when a user searches the Web using your site's keywords.

Electronic Commerce

Doing Business on the Internet

Case | Omega Group

Omega Group is a human resources consulting firm that offers a full range of services to midsized and larger companies. Omega's services include recruiting, compensation and benefits, training, and compliance.

Omega's recruiting division specializes in helping companies find good candidates for managerial and executive positions, administrative support positions, and technical professional positions.

The compensation and benefits division helps Omega's clients keep their pay scales and benefits packages in line with their competitors. This group also offers administration services for medical, dental, retirement, and other employee benefit plans.

The training division creates training plans and monitoring systems that let its clients know which employees have completed which training. Omega develops many of its training programs itself, but it also contracts some of the development work to freelance developers. Omega also acts as a reseller of training programs developed by other companies, especially in the more specialized technical fields. Some of Omega's training products are sold on CD as computer-aided training programs. Omega also sells training videos on DVD.

The compliance division helps clients stay aware of human resources-related laws and regulations. These regulations address worker's compensation, health and safety, minimum wage levels, overtime pay requirements, and equal employment opportunity. Sometimes Omega's divisions develop services cooperatively; for example, Omega recently released an equal employment opportunity compliance video produced jointly by the training and compliance divisions.

Omega has a Web site that has information about the firm and its services, but the firm does not sell any products or services on the site. Omega's managing director, Steven Boyce, is interested in extending the firm's Web operations to include selling some of Omega's services and has hired you as his special assistant for online projects. Steven is interested in selling Omega's current services online, using the Internet to reduce operating costs where possible, and perhaps developing new services or products that would make sense to sell online. Steven has asked you to explore these possibilities and analyze their potential for Omega.

Starting Data Files

There are no starting Data Files needed for this tutorial.

Session 10.1

What Is Electronic Commerce?

Although Omega is currently a service business and does not sell products to customers, the company is thinking about doing so. Steven would like you to find out more about electronic commerce and how Omega might use its Web site to increase sales to current clients and to identify new opportunities—new services and products, new clients, or both.

The term electronic commerce is often used to mean different things. Some people use the term "electronic business" (or "e-business") to mean buying and selling products or services on the Web. Others use the term "electronic commerce" when they are talking about buying and selling on the Web and use "electronic business" when they are talking about the more comprehensive idea of using Internet technologies to perform any business process. **Business processes** include all the activities that companies do to achieve their objectives, such as selling goods and services, collecting payments, ordering materials and supplies, hiring personnel, shipping finished goods to customers, identifying new customers, managing the movement of parts and products through manufacturing, conducting quality control and testing, ensuring compliance with laws and regulations, paying bills, and planning for future growth. Some people and businesses use the term electronic business (or e-business) when they are discussing electronic commerce in this broader sense.

Most people today use the terms **electronic business** and **electronic commerce** (and their shorter forms, **e-business** and **e-commerce**) interchangeably to include the broadest definition: any business process, or any collection of business processes, conducted using Internet technologies. Many not-for-profit organizations conduct "business" activities; for example, a museum might sell tickets for an upcoming special exhibition on its Web site. In this book, the term electronic commerce (or e-commerce) is used in its broadest sense; that is, the conduct of selling, buying, logistics, or other organization management activities over the Web.

Industry analysts and researchers usually break electronic commerce activities into four types. Activities undertaken by a company to sell goods or services to individuals is called **business-to-consumer (B2C)** electronic commerce. Activities undertaken by a company to sell goods or services to other business firms or not-for-profit organizations is called **business-to-business (B2B)** electronic commerce. The ordering and purchasing processes conducted by the buyer are also included in the B2B category. Businesses have many dealings with government agencies. For example, all companies must file tax forms and pay taxes and many companies are required to file reports and copies of their financial statements with government agencies. Using Internet technologies in these business processes is often called **business-to-government (B2G)** electronic commerce. Some analysts define a fourth type of electronic commerce, **consumer-to-consumer (C2C)**, to describe the processes that occur when individuals who are not operating formal businesses use the Internet to conduct transactions. One example of C2C electronic commerce occurs in an online auction in which one individual auctions an item to another individual. Most analysts, however, argue that sellers in an online auction are engaging in B2C electronic commerce, even though they might not be operating a formal business. The four types of electronic commerce are shown in Figure 10-1.

Types of electronic commerce | Figure 10-1

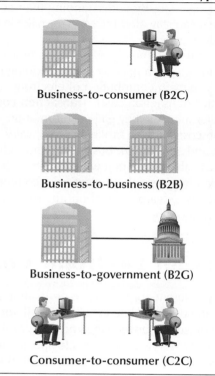

Business-to-consumer (B2C)

Business-to-business (B2B)

Business-to-government (B2G)

Consumer-to-consumer (C2C)

Business Models

The way a company does business, that is, the sum of its business activities and processes, is called the company's **business model**. There are many different kinds of businesses in the world doing many different things; however, all businesses must generate revenues and pay the costs associated with generating those revenues.

In the early days of electronic commerce (during the mid-1990s), many new companies were formed in the hope of developing business models that would work online. These new ventures and their hopeful investors truly believed that if they could identify a good online business model and follow it, they would be very successful. After the speculative bubble fueled largely by this view burst in 2000, companies began looking more closely at electronic commerce initiatives before undertaking them. They started to realize that the idea of creating new online business ventures was not the key to success. Instead, companies looked for ways to use the Internet and the Web to improve the business processes in which they were already engaged.

The business processes that a company uses to find new customers, make sales, and deliver the goods or services that it sells are collectively referred to as the company's **revenue model**. The other business processes in a company, such as purchasing, hiring, receiving, and manufacturing, are sometimes called the company's **operations model**. As companies began to look at their existing business processes, they found that some electronic commerce activities could improve a company's revenue processes, and others could reduce the cost or increase the efficiency of its operations processes.

Competitive Advantage and Transaction Cost Reduction

To stay in business, a company must have a **competitive advantage**; that is, a way of generating more revenues, incurring lower costs, or performing tasks more efficiently than other companies in the same business. Successful companies usually have many competitive advantages over other companies in the same industry. Because the environment in which a business operates changes over time, the way that companies achieve competitive advantages must change, too. By understanding their companies' revenue and operations models, managers can stay alert for ways to make improvements in them and sustain their competitive advantages.

New technologies, such as the Internet, give managers new opportunities for competitive advantages. New technologies can provide ways for doing new things and for doing old things more efficiently. The main contribution of electronic commerce to increased efficiency is that it can reduce transaction costs. **Transaction costs** are the total of all costs that a buyer and a seller incur as they gather information and negotiate a purchase-sale transaction. Transaction costs include brokerage fees, sales commissions, and the costs of information search and acquisition. Businesses and individuals can use the Web to reduce the transaction costs that occur in a wide variety of business processes.

Steven is interested in learning more about electronic commerce and how Omega might use it. A good first step is to learn more about the revenue and operations models that other companies are using on the Web.

Revenue Models for Electronic Commerce

Tip

Even when companies create separate sites for B2B and B2C transactions, they often use the same revenue model for both types of sales.

Businesses today take many different approaches to generating revenue on the Web. These approaches include: the use of online catalogs to sell goods and services, a combination approach that relies on selling advertising and subscriptions for access to information, and charging direct fees for services or access to specific information. Companies use these approaches for both B2C and the selling part of B2B electronic business. Some companies create one Web site to handle both B2C and B2B sales.

Online Catalog Revenue Model

Companies have been selling goods through mail order catalogs for more than 100 years. The first mail order businesses were started in the late 1800s. When the telephone became commonplace, some companies, notably Sears and Montgomery Ward, began accepting telephone orders and eventually grew to become huge retailers. At their peaks in the mid-1900s, these companies had hundreds of retail stores in addition to their catalog businesses. In recent years, both companies have faced declining sales and stiff competition from discount retailers such as Wal-Mart and Target. Montgomery Ward finally succumbed to these pressures and went out of business in 2001. Sears bought Kmart to compete better with the discount retailers.

In much the same way as retailers adopted the technology of the telephone many years ago, they are now adopting the technologies of the Web. In 2002, Sears purchased Lands' End, a company that sold its products exclusively through catalog and online sales. Lands' End was generating more than one-third of its annual sales online. Sears is hopeful that it can use the Lands' End and Kmart acquisitions to help it reestablish its former dominance in retailing.

The online catalog revenue model is based on this time-tested mail order catalog model. In the mail order catalog model, the seller creates a brand image that conveys quality and a specific price point, and then uses the strength of that image to sell through its printed catalogs mailed to prospective buyers. Buyers place orders by mail or by calling the seller's toll-free telephone number. Many retailers have been successful with this business model, including sellers of consumer goods items such as clothes, computers, electronics, housewares, and gifts.

In the online catalog model, a company replaces or supplements its distribution of printed catalogs with a catalog on its Web site. Customers can place orders through the Web site, by telephone, or even by mail. Giving customers this flexibility is important because many consumers are still reluctant to use the Web to purchase goods. In the first few years of consumer electronic business, most shoppers used the Web to obtain information about products and to compare prices and features, but then made the purchase in person or by telephone. These shoppers found early Web sites hard to use and were often afraid to send their credit card numbers over the Internet. Web sites have become easier to use, but many consumers still worry about companies' abilities to maintain the confidentiality of their credit card numbers and other personal information.

Three types of companies use the online catalog model: companies that sell only on the Web, companies that sell through print catalogs and on the Web, and companies that have physical stores and also sell on the Web. The Web-only businesses are sometimes called **dot-com** or **pure dot-com** companies. One of the most famous examples of the Web-only dot-com companies is Amazon.com.

One strategy used frequently by pure dot-com companies is the development of strategic alliances with existing companies. A **strategic alliance** (or **strategic partnership**) is an arrangement in which one company performs some business processes for another company in exchange for money or the sharing of expertise or access to customers. Amazon.com has a number of strategic alliances with companies such as Target and Office Depot. The Amazon.com home page includes links to some of its strategic partners near the bottom of the page.

Strategic Alliances: Not Always a Good Idea | InSight

One of Amazon.com's first strategic partners was Toys R Us. When the two companies signed a 10-year agreement in 2000 that put Toys R Us products on sale on the Amazon.com site, both companies believed it would be a long and beneficial alliance. Amazon.com would earn a percentage of sales for its role in accepting orders on its Web site and shipping the toys out of its warehouses; and Amazon.com agreed not to sell any competing products on its site. By 2004, sales of Toys R Us products on the site exceeded $300 million; however Toys R Us filed a lawsuit against Amazon.com asserting that Amazon.com had broken the agreement by allowing its zShops (now called Amazon Marketplace) vendors to sell competing products. After two years of litigation, which included a countersuit filed by Amazon.com, the court ordered an end to the strategic alliance and denied both parties any monetary damages. Amazon.com filed an appeal of the court's decision, but in 2009 settled out of court, agreeing to pay Toys R Us damages of $51 million and agreeing to the termination of the strategic alliance. Toys R Us now sells through its own Web site.

Most companies doing business on the Web today are not pure dot-com companies, but are established companies that use the Web to extend their existing businesses. Some of these companies run print catalog operations, some have physical retail stores, and some have both print catalog and physical store operations. Companies that have existing sales outlets often worry that their Web sites will take away sales from those outlets. This threat of losing sales from existing stores to the new online catalog is called **channel conflict**. Channel conflict can occur whenever sales activities on a company's Web site might interfere with sales made through existing channels such as physical stores or telephone and mail-order operations. The problem is also called **cannibalization**, because the Web site's sales replace sales that would otherwise have occurred in the company's retail stores.

To learn more about the online catalog revenue model, you decide to visit several online catalog sites operated by different types of companies.

To learn more about Web catalog retailers:

▶ **1.** Open the Online Companion page at **www.cengage.com/internet/np/internet8**, log on to your account, click the **Tutorial 10** link, and then click the **Session 10.1** link.

▶ **2.** Choose one of the links in the Web-Only Retailers section, and then click the link to open the site. Examine the home page and explore the Web site. Identify the types of consumers who would be likely to buy from the site, the types of products sold on the site, and any strategic partners. Repeat this process for one other link in this section.

▶ **3.** Return to the Online Companion page for Session 10.1, choose one of the links in the Print Catalog Retailers section, and then click the link to open the site. Examine the home page and explore the Web site. Identify the types of consumers who would be likely to buy from the site, the types of products sold on the site, and any strategic partners. Identify any potential channel conflicts faced by the company. Repeat this process for one other link in this section.

▶ **4.** Return to the Online Companion page for Session 10.1, choose one of the links in the Retailers with Physical Stores section, and then click the link to open the site. Examine the home page and explore the Web site. Identify the types of consumers who would be likely to buy from the site, the types of products sold on the site, and any strategic partners. Identify any potential channel conflicts faced by the company. Repeat this process for one other link in this section.

After reviewing six Web catalog sites, you discuss your findings with Steven. He is interested in your observations, but he notes that all of the sites you visited were retailers engaged in B2C electronic commerce. Most of Omega's sales would be to other businesses. Steven asks you to visit two more Web sites that use the Web catalog model, but that are engaged in B2B electronic commerce.

▶ **5.** Return to the Online Companion page for Session 10.1, choose one of the links in the B2B Web Catalog Sites section, and then click the link to open the site. Examine the home page and explore the Web site. Identify the types of businesses that would be likely to buy from the site, the types of products sold on the site, and any strategic partners. Identify any potential channel conflicts faced by the company. Repeat this process for one other link in this section.

Based on your research, you realize that the Web sites you visited provide useful information for many different types of businesses that intend to use the Web to make sales to both businesses and consumers.

Advertising and Subscription Revenue Models

Some businesses have relied on advertising as their sole source of revenue for many years. Television networks in the United States use a **pure advertising revenue model.** The networks provide an audience with free programming along with advertising messages. Advertising revenue pays for operations, buys programs, and generates a profit for the networks. In large cities, some newspapers are distributed free of charge. These newspapers earn enough revenue from selling advertising that they can cover the costs of creating, printing, and distributing and still earn a profit.

Other businesses derive their revenue only from subscription fees. For example, some magazines carry no advertising as a matter of policy. This is an example of a **pure subscription revenue model.**

Much more common are magazines that charge a subscription and also carry advertising. These **mixed advertising-subscription revenue model**s are used by many Web sites. In this section, you will learn about a range of advertising only, subscription only, and advertising-subscription mixed revenue models.

In the early years of the Web, many people thought that the potential for Internet advertising was great enough that many Web sites would be able to generate a profit with advertising revenue alone. However, the success of Web advertising has been hampered by two major problems.

First, no consensus has emerged on how to measure and charge for advertising on the Web. Broadcast media advertising rates are based on the size of the audience estimated by rating services such as Nielsen (for television) and Arbitron (for radio). Newspapers and magazines base their ad rates on print circulation and newsstand sales numbers. Web sites can measure their audiences in many different ways, such as number of visitors, number of unique visitors, number of visitors who click an ad to go to the advertiser's site, or other attributes of visitor behavior. Because this great variety of measurements exists, Web advertisers and Web sites have been unable to agree on one standard way to charge for online advertising.

The second problem is that very few Web sites have enough visitors to interest large advertisers. The most successful advertising on the Web is directed at very specific groups. The collection of characteristics that marketers use to group visitors is called **demographic information** and includes such traits as address, age, gender, income, education, hobbies, political affiliation, and religion. Delivering ads to site visitors with specific demographic characteristics is part of a strategy called **target marketing**. It can be difficult to determine whether a given Web site is attracting a specific market segment unless that site collects demographic information from its visitors. Unfortunately for sellers of Web advertising, visitors are becoming increasingly reluctant to provide this type of information because of privacy concerns.

Web portal sites are among the few types of sites that can draw enough visitors (and thus, advertising dollars) to be profitable. A **Web portal** (or simply a **portal**) is a doorway to the Web. Portals are starting points for Web surfers—they usually include general interest information and can help users of the portal find just about anything on the Web. Web portals typically share many common characteristics, including free email, links to search engines, Web directories, membership services, news headlines and articles, discussion groups, chat rooms, links to virtual shopping malls, calendars, and address books. Some portals allow site visitors to customize their entry page contents.

Portals earn most of their revenue by selling advertising. A site with a large audience can charge higher advertising rates than one with a smaller audience. Thus, the audience size (the number of visitors to the Web site) is important. The quality of a portal is a significant factor in attracting visitors and keeping them coming back to a site.

When online advertising volume and rates dropped in the 2001–2003 time period, many Web portal sites increased their reliance on paid services to bring in additional revenue. For example, Yahoo! changed its revenue model to a combination of advertising and subscription revenue. Most of its portal services are still available to members at no charge, but Yahoo! now offers enhanced levels of those services for a monthly or annual subscription fee. For example, a Yahoo! email account is still free, but a member can obtain increased services (for example, the ability to attach larger files to email messages) for a premium account that requires payment of an annual fee. Yahoo! Games are still free, but a member can pay a monthly fee to become an "All-Star" member and obtain access to better games, reserved game areas, and game screens that are free of advertising. The Yahoo! Games All-Star information page appears in Figure 10-2.

Tip

Examples of portals include AOL, Excite, Google, MSN, Refdesk.com, and Yahoo!.

Figure 10-2 | **Yahoo! Games All-Star page**

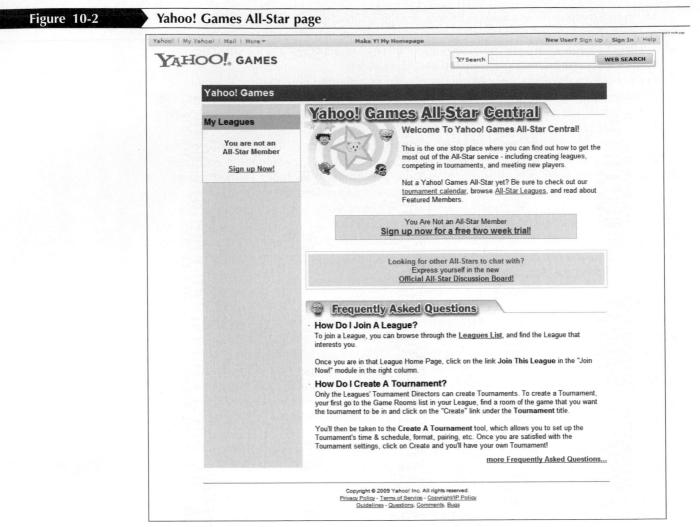

One way that a portal site can increase its advertising revenue is to sell target marketing opportunities to advertisers. A portal site can use it search engine to accomplish this. For example, a user who conducts a search on a portal site using the expression "DVD" can expect to see advertising targeted to people interested in buying DVDs or DVD players. More than one advertiser can purchase the right to show links to their Web sites on the search results pages, so you will often see several ads from different advertisers when you run a search. Portal sites each have their own policies on how they charge advertisers for search results page ads; however, the most common policy is to charge more for adds and links that appear closer to the top of the seach results page.

Newspaper and magazine publishers have also tried to use the advertising-supported model for their sites, but few have been successful in attracting sufficient advertiser interest to operate their sites profitably. Some publishers run their sites at a loss in the hopes that they can attract readers who will subscribe to their print editions. Other publishers are using a combination of advertising and subscription revenue. These sites offer some stories free of charge, but most of the content is available only to subscribers.

The *Wall Street Journal* Web site has been charging a subscription since its inception and is a profitable operation. It does provide some content (including, of course, its classified ads) free of charge. Other newspapers, including the *Washington Post*, *The New York Times*, and the *Los Angeles Times*, use another variation of the combined revenue model. These newspapers do not charge a subscription fee; instead, they offer most of their current stories free of charge on their Web sites but require visitors to pay for articles retrieved from their archives.

From 2005 to 2007, *The New York Times* experimented with a plan that required readers to pay a subscription fee to access some of its more popular columns and features; however, the paper decided that it could earn more revenue by running ads on the Web pages that included those columns and features than it was generating from subscription fees. The *Los Angeles Times* had tried a similar plan in which it reserved some of its content for subscribers, but it stopped doing so when it found that very few readers signed up for the subscription service.

The *Economist* offers yet another combination of revenue models through its Economist.com site. The Economist.com site sells some advertising and offers some free content, but charges a subscription fee for access to the entire site. The *Economist* also publishes content in the subscriber section of its Web site before the printed magazine is delivered to subscribers or sold on newsstands.

Switching Revenue Models | InSight

Some companies have switched revenue models several times as they tried to find the best way to generate revenue online. Encyclopædia Britannica began with two different Web sites. The Britannica Internet Guide was a free Web navigation aid that classified and rated information-laden Web sites. It featured reviews written by Britannica editors who also selected and indexed the sites. The second Web site, Encyclopædia Britannica Online, required a subscription fee but included access to the full content of the Encyclopædia. The free site was designed to sell ads and attract users to the paid subscription site. In 1999, disappointed by low subscription sales, Britannica switched its revenue model and launched a single advertising-supported site. The first day the new site, Britannica.com, became available at no cost to the public, it had more than 15 million visitors, forcing Britannica to shut down for two weeks to upgrade its servers. After two years of trying to generate a profit using this advertising-supported site, Britannica realized it was not earning enough revenue. In 2001, Britannica returned to a mixed model in which it offered free summaries of encyclopedia articles, with the full text of the encyclopedia available for a subscription fee of $50 per year or $5 per month. Britannica has gone from being a print publisher to a seller of information on the Web to an advertising-supported Web site to a mixed advertising subscription model—three major revenue model transitions—in just a few short years. The main value that Britannica has to sell is its reputation and the expertise of its editors, contributors, and advisors. For now, Britannica has decided that the best way to capitalize on that reputation and expertise is through a combined format of subscriptions and advertising support.

Omega's benefits, training, and compliance divisions all publish newsletters and reports of various types. Omega sends some of these publications to clients and potential clients at no charge. Other publications are sold for a flat fee or by subscription. Thus, Steven is interested in having you learn more about how different combinations of subscription and advertising revenue models are used on the Web. Steven asks you to explore the Web sites of some popular newspapers and magazines.

To examine the revenue models of newspaper and magazine sites:

▶ **1.** Return to the Online Companion page for Session 10.1, if necessary.

▶ **2.** Click one of the links in the Newspaper and Magazine Sites section and explore the Web site for that publication. Identify the revenue model (or models) the site is using. Remember, the site might be using several different revenue models for different types of content contained within the site. Identify the types (age, gender, income level, location) of visitors who would find the site appealing.

▶ **3.** Repeat Step 2 for two other sites in the list of links.

Web sites that offer classified advertising have been more successful than magazine and newspaper publishers in their implementations of the pure advertising-supported model. Some of these sites specialize in employment advertising and give employers rapid access to human resources throughout the world. The home page for one of these sites, Monster.com, is shown in Figure 10-3.

| Figure 10-3 | Monster.com home page |

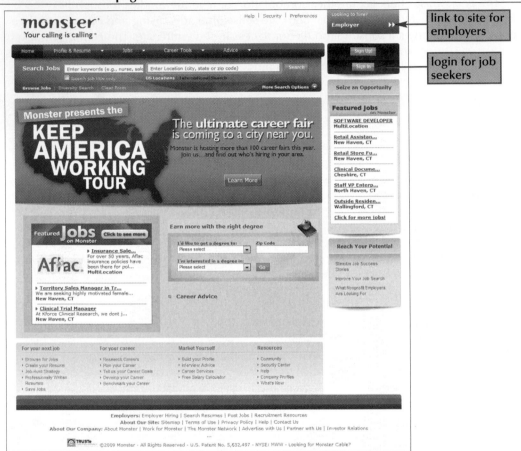

Other sites offer classified ads for autos, boats, motorcycles, houses, apartment rentals, and even airplanes. In addition to charging for the placement of the classified ads, these sites can use the same approach that Web portal and search engine sites use to create target marketing opportunities for advertisers. When a visitor declares an interest in, for example, nursing jobs in Des Moines, the results page can include a targeted banner ad tailored to that individual. The site can charge the employer more for such an ad because it is directed to a narrow market segment.

To examine the revenue models of classified advertising sites:

1. Return to the Online Companion page for Session 10.1, if necessary.

2. Click one of the links in the Classified Advertising Sites section and explore the Web site for that publication. Identify the revenue model the site is using (advertising, subscription, or advertising-subscription mixed). Determine whether the site relies primarily on the sale of classified advertising or some other revenue source.

3. Repeat Step 2 for one other site in the list of links.

In all of the models you learned about in this section, a subscriber or an advertiser (or a combination of the two) pays to allow site visitors to access information on a company's Web site. Steven is interested in the potential for using these revenue models to sell some of Omega's print publications. However, most of Omega's revenue is generated by the services provided to clients by its recruiting and benefits divisions. Steven asks you to investigate Web sites that provide services for which they charge a fee.

Direct Fee Revenue Model

In the direct fee revenue model, businesses offer services for which they charge a fee. The fee can be based on the specific service provided, or it can be based on the number or size of the transactions processed. Some of these direct fee revenue-generating processes work well on the Web. If companies can provide the service over the Internet or give Web site visitors the information they need about the transaction on the Web site, companies can offer a high level of personal service. The cost of providing this type of personal service can, in some cases, be much lower on the Web than in physical store locations.

A wide range of services, from online games to tax-planning advice, is available on the Web today. New services appear regularly as companies find ways to offer their existing services on the Web and create new services just for the Web. As you learned earlier in this tutorial, Web portal sites such as Yahoo! offer free online games to attract visitors. Many of these sites are now offering premium games. Site visitors must pay to play these premium games, either by buying and downloading software to install on their computers or by paying a subscription fee to enter the premium games area on the site.

Now that many consumers have broadband access to the Internet, an increasing number of companies are providing streaming video of concerts and films to paying subscribers. NetFlix, a company that pioneered DVD rental by mail monthly subscription plans, now offers movies that can be viewed online as streaming video. The monthly subscription fee includes a certain number of hours of video access each month (the higher-priced subscriptions include unlimited access). Other companies offer online access to movies on a pay-per-movie basis.

The main technological challenge these companies face is that, unlike broadcast television stations, each additional customer that downloads a video stream requires that the provider purchase additional bandwidth from its ISP. Television broadcasters need only pay the fixed cost of a transmitter because the airwaves are free and carry the transmission to an unlimited number of viewers at no additional cost per viewer. In contrast, as the number of an Internet-based provider's subscribers increases, the cost of the provider's Internet connection increases. Thus, Web entertainment sites must charge a high enough monthly fee to cover the additional bandwidth costs and still make a profit.

Tip

Some sites require visitors to create an account and log in before disclosing subscription fees.

To learn more about direct fee game and entertainment sites:

▶ **1.** Return to the Online Companion page for Session 10.1, if necessary.

▶ **2.** Click one of the links in the Direct Fee Game and Entertainment Sites section and explore the Web site for that service. Identify the revenue model the site is using (advertising, subscription, direct fee per item, or a combination of these models). Examine the breadth of offerings on the site and evaluate the usability of the site, including how difficult it is to determine what products are available and how much the site charges.

▶ **3.** Repeat Step 2 for one other site in the list of links.

Tip

You can often find out what a site's fees are by using a search engine to find reviews of the company's services published on other Web sites.

Services more sophisticated than games or entertainment are also available on the Web. Sites that charge fees for specific professional services are increasingly appearing on the Web. This type of service is more similar to Omega's offerings than the games and entertainment services. Site visitors can prepare their tax returns online at the H&R Block or TurboTax sites. PrePaidLegal.com offers legal services on its Web site.

Individual law and accounting firms also offer various professional services on the Web. The Additional Information section of the Online Companion page for Tutorial 10 includes links under the heading Professional Services Sites that you can use to explore the sites mentioned here.

Another industry that uses the direct fee revenue model for its Web sites is the travel industry. Travel agents earn commissions on each airplane ticket, hotel reservation, auto rental, cruise, or vacation package that they book. In most cases, the transportation or lodging provider pays these commissions to the travel agent. Thus, the travel agency revenue model provides travel advice and then receives a fee from the travel service provider for handling a transaction. The value added by a travel agent is that of information consolidation and filtering. A good travel agent knows many things about the traveler's destination and knows enough about the traveler to select the information elements that will be useful and valuable to the traveler. Computers, particularly computers networked to large databases, are very good at information consolidation and filtering. In fact, travel agents have used networked computers for many years to make reservations for their customers.

When the Internet emerged as a new way to network computers and then became available to commercial users, many new travel agencies began doing business on the Web. Existing travel agencies did not, in general, rush to the new medium. They believed that the key value they added, personal customer service, could not be replaced with a Web site. Therefore, the first Web-based travel agencies were new market entrants such as Travelocity and Expedia. These sites, along with later entrants such as Hotels.com and Orbitz, are among the most visited electronic business sites on the Web. The Orbitz home page appears in Figure 10-4.

Orbitz home page **Figure 10-4**

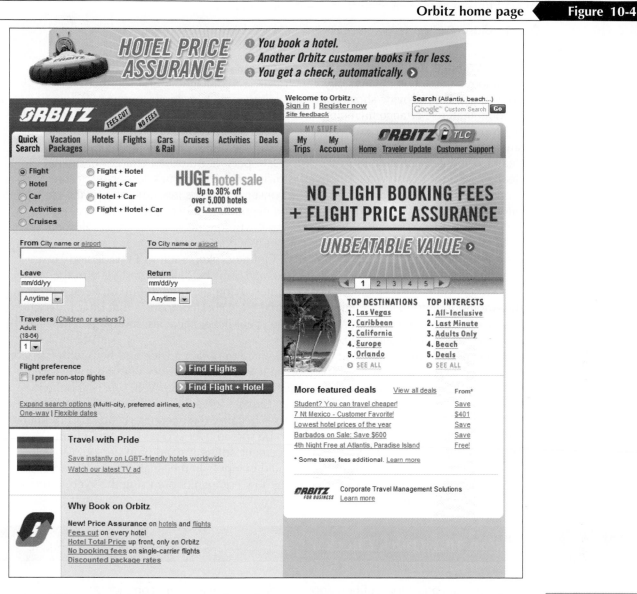

In addition to earning commissions from the transportation and lodging providers, Web-based travel sites generate advertising revenue from ads placed on their travel information pages. These ads let advertisers target customers without obtaining demographic details about them. For example, a customer who is booking a flight to Boston might see an ad for a hotel in Boston on the page that lists airline ticket options. The Additional Information section of the Online Companion page for Tutorial 10 includes links under the heading Online Travel Agencies that you can use to explore the Web sites mentioned here.

Travel agency sites are threatening the existence of many traditional travel agents. The removal of an intermediary from an industry, such as the traditional travel agencies in this case, is called **disintermediation**. The introduction of a new intermediary into an industry, such as the travel agency Web sites in this case, is called **reintermediation**.

To examine the offerings of travel and airline sites:

► **1.** Return to the Online Companion page for Session 10.1, if necessary.

► **2.** Click one of the links in the Travel and Airline Sites section and explore the Web site. Evaluate the usability of the site and the range of travel services offered.

> **3.** Repeat Step 2 for one other site in the list of links.
>
> **4.** Close your browser.

The Web has introduced disintermediation and reintermediation to the business of automotive sales. Auto dealers buy cars from the manufacturer and sell them to consumers. They provide showrooms and salespeople to help customers learn about product features, arrange financing, and make a purchase decision. Autobytel.com and other online firms will locate dealers in the buyer's area who are willing to sell cars for a small premium over the dealer's nominal cost. The buyer can purchase the car from the dealer without negotiating its price with a salesperson. Autobytel charges participating dealers a fee for this service. Autobytel is disintermediating the salesperson and reinter-mediating itself into the value chain. The consumer spends less time buying the car and often pays a lower price while avoiding the negotiation process; the dealer pays a fee to Autobytel that is lower than the commission it would otherwise pay to its salesperson.

Stock brokerage firms also use a fee-for-transaction model. They charge their custom-ers a commission for each trade executed. Online brokers such as E*Trade and TD Ameritrade are threatening traditional brokerage firms by offering trading over the Web. The Online Companion includes links to auto buying sites and online brokerage firms in the Additional Information section for Tutorial 10. Other companies that offer transaction-based services for a fee on the Web include event ticket agencies, mortgage lenders and brokers, banks, and insurance brokers.

Many people find the Web to be a good place to obtain advice and help with transac-tions of various kinds. You suggest to Steven that Omega consider offering some fee-based recruiting and benefit plan management services on the Web. Offering benefit plan management services online might let Omega serve the small business market. The company has never targeted small businesses because the fixed overhead costs of man-aging client accounts are high and need to be spread over several hundred client employees. By offering benefit plan management online instead of in person, Omega could reduce its costs enough so that it could compete in the small business market. In the next session, you will learn more about how companies are using the Web to reduce the cost of operations.

Review | Session 10.1 Quick Check

1. How can a not-for-profit organization engage in electronic commerce?
2. True or False: The business processes that a company uses to find new customers, make sales, and deliver the goods or services that it sells are collectively referred to as the company's business model.
3. The ability of a company to generate more revenues or incur lower costs than other companies in its industry is called a _____ .
4. What steps are followed by a mail-order catalog retailer when it opens a Web site to implement an online catalog revenue model?
5. Companies that sell items online and through other marketing channels (such as physical stores or telephone and mail-order operations) often worry that their online sales take away from their sales in the other channels, which is a problem that is called _____ .
6. True or False: An online magazine must decide either to use the pure advertising revenue model or the pure subscription revenue model.
7. Delivering ads to site visitors with specific demographic characteristics is part of a strategy called _____ .

Session 10.2

Using the Web to Reduce Costs and Increase Efficiency

In Session 10.1, you learned how companies can use electronic commerce to generate revenue. Of course, companies can earn more money by either increasing revenue or reducing costs. The real challenge is using the Internet to reduce costs or increase efficiency. (Increased efficiency makes the amount spent on a particular cost do more work.) The activities that companies undertake to accomplish these goals are sometimes called cost-reduction activities.

Business Cost Reductions Using Electronic Technologies

Although the Internet and the Web have made electronic commerce possible for many businesses and individuals, electronic commerce has existed for many years. For decades, banks have been using **electronic funds transfers** (**EFTs**, also called **wire transfers**), which are electronic transmissions of account exchange information over private networks. Businesses also have engaged in a form of electronic commerce known as electronic data interchange for many years. **Electronic data interchange (EDI)** occurs when one business transmits computer-readable data in a standard format to another business. The standard formats used in EDI have been designed to contain the same information that businesses would include in standard paper forms such as invoices, purchase orders, and shipping documents.

For EDI to work, both parties to the transaction must have compatible computer systems, must have some kind of communications link to connect them, and must agree to follow the same set of EDI standards. When two businesses meet these three criteria, they are called **trading partners**. Figure 10-5 compares the paper flow that occurs in a traditional sale-purchase transaction with the electronic information flow that occurs when two businesses use EDI.

Traditional vs. EDI implementation of sale-purchase transactions ◄ **Figure 10-5**

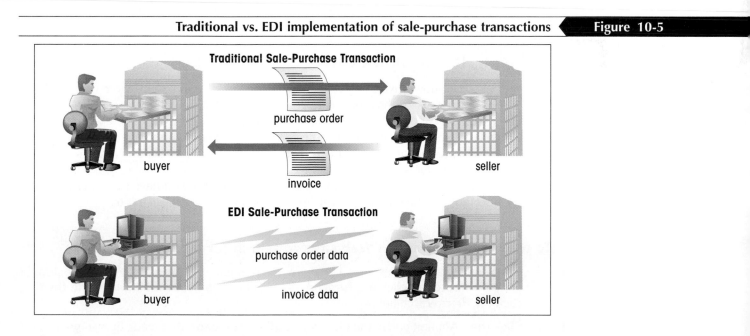

EDI replaces the paper purchase order and invoice with electronic messages. When it was originally introduced, EDI required trading partners to purchase expensive computers and maintain communication links between them; these costs were prohibitive for smaller businesses. However, as large businesses realized cost savings from EDI, they began requiring all of their suppliers to use it. Installing EDI systems presented great difficulties for many smaller firms that wanted to sell products to larger firms but could not afford to implement EDI. However, as the cost of computers decreased and the availability of communications links (including the Internet) increased, many more small firms were able to participate as EDI trading partners.

The transaction shown in Figure 10-5 is not complete; for example, it does not show the buyer's payment for the goods received. To consummate the traditional transaction, the buyer sends a check to the seller in payment for the goods received. Early EDI implementations used electronic transfer for the transaction information but still handled payments by mailing checks. As EDI became more common, trading partners wanted to handle the payments electronically, too. When EDI includes payment information, it is called **financial EDI**.

Although banks use EFTs to transfer funds for their own accounts and for large customer transactions that require immediate settlement, EFTs are too expensive to use for large volumes of ordinary business transactions. Banks settle most of their customers' business transactions through **automated clearinghouses (ACHs)**, which are systems created by banks or groups of banks to electronically clear their accounts with each other. Many individuals have their employers make ACH deposits of their paychecks or use ACH withdrawals to make their monthly car payments.

As the number of businesses using EDI has grown, the demand for efficient networking and payment systems has increased. Businesses called **value-added networks (VANs)** were created to meet the demands imposed by EDI. A VAN accepts EDI transmissions in a variety of formats, converts the formats as needed, ensures that the EDI transmissions are received and acknowledged, and can forward the financial transaction instructions to the trading partners' banks or ACHs. A VAN is a neutral third party that can offer assurances and dispute-resolution services to both EDI trading partners. Some VANs also provide low-cost EDI software to trading partners, which can help small businesses participate in EDI.

Reducing Transaction Costs

As you think about how buyers and sellers might use the Web to reduce the cost of each step, you begin to consider how buyers might use the Web to search for products. The Web can help buyers conduct their information searches more cheaply and efficiently than by making telephone calls, sending faxes, or driving from store to store in hopes of finding the right product at the right price. In fact, some firms have started services that help buyers find products. One of these firms is Pricewatch. You remember that you wanted to upgrade the memory on your desktop computer, but you have been so busy that you have not had time to shop for it. You decide to give Pricewatch a try.

To use price comparison Web sites to search for a specific item:

▶ **1.** Open the Online Companion page at www.cengage.com/internet/np/internet8, log on to your account, click the **Tutorial 10** link, click the **Session 10.2** link, and then click the **Pricewatch** link.

▶ **2.** Click the **RAM** link under the Memory heading. The page that loads lists some memory chips and includes a search box so you can search within the category. Dell manufactured your computer, so you search for memory products that work in Dell computers.

▶ **3.** Type **Dell RAM** in the search for text box, and then click the **Search** button. (Computer memory is often called RAM, or random access memory, to distinguish it from memory that is used in other devices, such as cameras.) The Pricewatch site returns a list of memory chips for Dell computers that are offered for sale by a variety of vendors (who voluntarily supply information to Pricewatch). The products listed include the full range of memory types for all kinds of Dell computers, ranging from laptops to the largest server computers that Dell makes. For each item, the search results page shows the brand, product name, description, price, shipping costs, and information about the dealer offering the item. The results page includes a link to each dealer's site that you can click to make your purchase.

Other comparison shopping sites operate their own Web robots (bots) that search the Web and find price information from vendors' Web sites. DealTime is an example of a bot-based comparison shopping site.

▶ **4.** Return to the Online Companion page for **Session 10.2**, if necessary, and then click the **MySimon** link.

▶ **5.** Type **Dell RAM** in the Search for products box, select **Electronics** from the drop-down list, and then click the **GO** button.

▶ **6.** Examine the search results page and compare your results to those you obtained using the PriceWatch site.

You now begin to think about how sellers can use the Web to reduce costs on their side of the purchase transaction. One of the most expensive components of such transactions can be the provision of after-sale support. After-sale support is especially high for complex technology products such as computers and electronic equipment. For example, many computer printers use software drivers to translate the information a computer sends to them into printing instructions. As computers improve and new software becomes available, printer manufacturers can update their printer driver software to take advantage of new features and capabilities. The traditional method of providing this software on disk to customers who have purchased printers has always been slow, inconvenient, and expensive for printer manufacturers.

Steven's executive assistant, Connie, installed some new software on her computer that is not printing correctly on her Hewlett-Packard printer. You offer to obtain an updated printer driver for her from Hewlett-Packard's Web site.

To find printer driver software for a Hewlett-Packard printer:

▶ **1.** Return to the Online Companion page for **Session 10.2**, if necessary, and then click the **Hewlett-Packard** hyperlink.

▶ **2.** Click the **Support & Drivers** link.

Trouble? Web sites often change the specific names and locations of their links. If you cannot find a link with this name, look for a link with a similar name.

▶ **3.** Navigate the site to find a page that allows you to search for drivers by specific product names. In the search text box on that page, type **P3005** (the model number of Connie's printer), and then click the button or link that activates the search.

▶ **4.** Continue your navigation until you find a page that provides links to the printer drivers for Connie's printer. Note that the page also includes links to other information resources that Hewlett-Packard customers can use to help themselves without needing to call a Hewlett-Packard representative during business hours—which saves Hewlett-Packard a significant amount of money. The Web allows Hewlett-Packard to provide good customer service at a lower cost.

You stop by Connie's office and show her how to use the Hewlett-Packard site to find the printer driver she needs. A short time later, Connie has downloaded and installed the updated printer driver and her new software is working with the printer.

Improving Operational Efficiency with Intranets, Extranets, and Automated Email

All of Omega's divisions have regular training programs for staff members to help them stay current with changing laws and regulations in their areas. Omega's internal training group must let employees know about the training opportunities and schedule them around employees' work schedules. These staffing and training schedules can be difficult to coordinate. Steven suggests that Omega might place a master schedule online that employees can access through Web browsers on their office or home computers. These Web pages could also announce the training programs and allow employees to sign up for them. Omega's training division also would like to offer its programs to clients online. Steven suggests that it might be wise to try online course delivery in-house with Omega employees first, so the mistakes made while learning will involve employees and not clients.

Steven also would like to promote and sell Omega's new services to existing clients. Your job is to investigate using email to send this information.

Using Intranets and Extranets

A set of Web pages or sites that is accessible only to employees of a company is called an **intranet**. Many companies use intranets to reduce operational costs and increase efficiency. As Omega gains experience with its online training activities, it can give clients access to the Web pages with the training program. When an intranet is made available to users outside the company in this way, it is called an **extranet**.

All the major overnight freight companies, including FedEx, UPS, DHL Worldwide Express, and Airborne Express, offer package tracking services on their Web sites. These package tracking services are an example of an extranet. The customers must have either a package tracking number or a shipper's account with the company to obtain the tracking information. The Additional Information section of the Online Companion page for Tutorial 10 includes links under the heading Overnight Freight Companies that you can use to explore these sites.

Many companies use intranets and extranets to coordinate employee, supplier, and customer activities. However, smaller companies that cannot afford to create a dedicated intranet or extranet can obtain some of their benefits by using a Web portal site. As you learned in Session 10.1, Web portals offer services to site visitors so that those visitors will spend time on the site and view advertising for which the portal is paid. The services that Web portals offer vary from site to site, but usually include Web-based email accounts and a customizable personal home page. Some Web portals offer even more comprehensive services, such as online calendars and address books. You will examine these portal sites so you can report back to Steven with information about these portal sites.

To examine the Excite portal site:

► **1.** Return to the Online Companion page for Session 10.2, if necessary.

► **2.** Click the **Excite** link to open the Excite portal home page shown in Figure 10-6.

Excite portal home page ◄ **Figure 10-6**

Join Now link →

search engine →

Web directory →

3. Click the **Join Now** link to display the Excite join now! page shown in Figure 10-7. (Your page might look different.) Excite, like most portals, asks for information about its members. The page also includes a brief statement about the privacy of information you provide.

Tip

You should always consider the terms of a site's privacy policy before you decide to provide personal information.

Figure 10-7   Excite join now! page

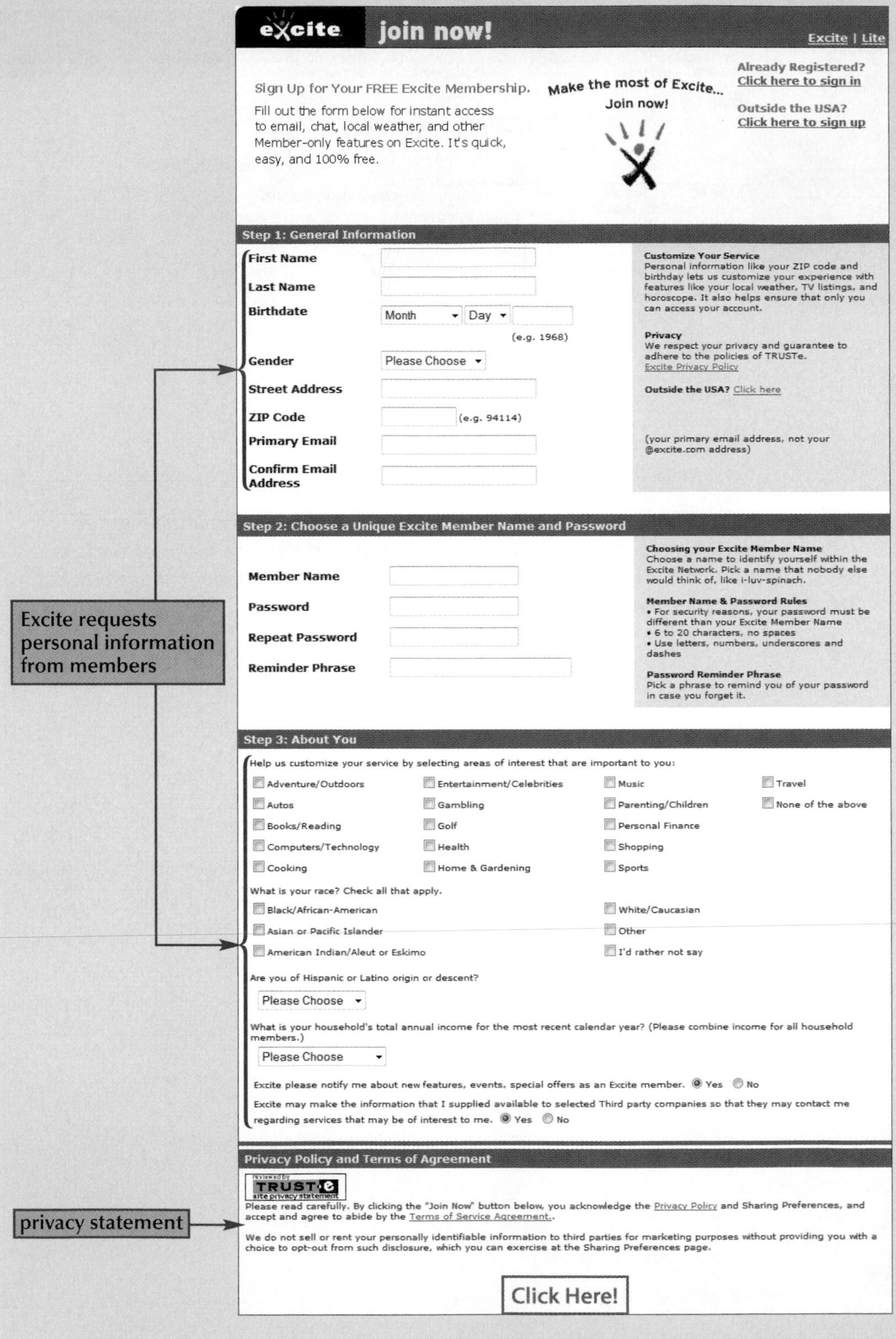

4. Return to the Online Companion page for Session 10.2 and click the link to **Yahoo!**. Examine the site and identify the services offered by the Yahoo! portal.

5. Return to the Online Companion page for Session 10.2.

Using Automated Email Messaging

Steven would like to use extranets to sell new services to existing clients, but is concerned that the managers at Omega's client firms who make the purchase decision might not be the same people who are using the extranet. He asks you about using email messages to send clients information about new products. You agree that email can be a good way to stay in contact with existing customers—but only if they agree to receive it.

Promotional Email Frequency		InSight

Marketing experts recommend that automatically generated email messages with announcements of new products and services not be sent more often than once a week to clients. Messages sent more often than that can cause recipients to leave the mailing list. Another good strategy is to include helpful tips for using products the recipient might have already purchased. Mixing useful content with the sales message can increase the chances that recipients will read the email.

Many companies offer email management services. You can learn more about these companies by exploring the links in the Additional Information section of the Online Companion page for Tutorial 10. Look for the heading Email Marketing Companies.

Online Auctions

One of the more interesting and innovative implementations of electronic commerce is the creation of Web sites that conduct online auctions. Although some of these sites offer merchandise that is the inventory of the Web site owner, most of these sites auction the property of others, much as an auctioneer would at a public auction. Online auctions provide both revenue opportunities and cost-reduction opportunities for businesses.

Each online auction site establishes its own bidding rules. Most auctions remain open for a few days or a week. Some sites provide automated software agents that bidders can instruct to place bids as needed to win the auction, subject to a maximum limit set by the bidder. Because bidders face a significant risk of buying a misrepresented product in a sight-unseen online auction, some auction sites offer mediation or **escrow services** that hold the buyer's payment until he or she is satisfied that the item matches the seller's description. The advantages of conducting online auctions include a large pool of potential bidders, 24-hour access, and the ability to auction hundreds of similar items simultaneously.

In 1995, Pierre Omidyar was working as a software developer and, in his spare time, operating a small Web site that provided updates on the Ebola virus. Omidyar decided to add a small auction function to his Web site to earn some money so he could continue operating it. Interest in the site's auctions grew so rapidly that within a year, he had quit his job to devote his full energies to the Web auction business he had created. By the end of its second year in operation, Omidyar's Web site, which he called eBay, had auctioned more than $95 million worth of goods and was profitable.

Tip

Escrow services fees range from 1 percent to 10 percent of the item's cost, with a minimum fee of between $5 and $10.

Because eBay was one of the first auction Web sites and because it has pursued an aggressive promotion strategy, it has become the first choice for many people who want to participate in auctions. Both buyers and bidders benefit from the large marketplace that eBay has created. eBay's early advantage in the online auction business has been hard for competitors to overcome.

You decide to take a break from your work for Omega and use the Web to pursue one of your hobbies, collecting guitars. You are especially fond of a series of guitars made for many years by the Gibson Company that were originally designed and played by Les Paul. You decide to search for auctions of Les Paul model guitars on eBay.

To search for auctions on eBay:

▶ **1.** Return to the Online Companion page for Session 10.2, if necessary, and then click the **eBay** hyperlink.

▶ **2.** Type **Les Paul** in the search text box near the top of the eBay page, and then click the **Search** button. The page that opens will include a list of auctions that contain the key words "Les Paul."

On the results page that opens, you might see a few auctions of old audio recordings made by Les Paul and Mary Ford, but most of the thousands of auctions listed should be for Gibson guitars. The first auctions listed might be for "featured" items—the seller has paid eBay an extra fee to have the auction listed first. The other auctions are listed in the order of the auction expiration date, with the auctions ending soon listed first. You can change the order in which the auctions are listed, which is helpful for a search, such as this, which returns thousands of listings.

▶ **3.** In the Sort by list box, select **Price + Shipping: highest first** to sort the auctions in descending order of the highest bid made thus far in the auction. If no bids have been made, the price used is the minimum price that the seller has placed on the auction. Any featured items will still be listed at the top of the results page.

Trouble? If a dialog box appears that asks for your location, you can enter a ZIP code (which eBay will use to calculate shipping charges) and click OK or you can click Cancel without entering anything.

▶ **4.** Click the links to several of the auctions. The auction page will show information about the auction, including the eBay ID of the seller, the current bid and the number of bids made in the auction, and the auction's closing date and time. Many of the auctions will include detailed photographs of the guitar.

Sellers and buyers must register with eBay and agree to the site's basic terms of doing business. Sellers pay a listing fee and a sliding percentage of the final selling price. Buyers pay nothing to eBay. In addition to the basic fees, sellers can choose from a variety of enhanced and extra-cost services, including having their auctions listed in bold type or included as featured auctions that appear at the top of bidders' search results pages.

In an attempt to address bidder concerns about seller reliability, eBay has instituted a rating system. Buyers can submit ratings of sellers after doing business with them. These ratings are converted into graphics that appear with the seller's nickname on each auction in which that seller participates. Although this system is not without flaws, many eBay customers feel that it affords them some level of protection from unscrupulous sellers.

Because one of the major determinants of Web auction site success is attracting enough buyers and sellers to create markets for enough items, some Web sites that already have a large number of visitors are entering this business. Sites such as Yahoo! Auctions added auctions similar to those available on eBay. Yahoo! Auctions had some early success in attracting sellers, in part because it offered its auction service to sellers at no charge. Later it began charging sellers, just as eBay has always done.

Yahoo! Auctions was less successful than eBay in attracting buyers in the United States. This resulted in less bidding action than eBay auctions were able to generate. In 2007, Yahoo! Auctions closed its U.S. operations. Yahoo! still runs auctions on a number of its non-U.S. sites. In Japan, for example, Yahoo! Auctions began operations six months before eBay and now holds more than 80 percent of the online auction market in that country.

Amazon.com also operated an auctions site. When it launched in 1999, Amazon Auctions was designed to challenge eBay directly by inducing Amazon's millions of established customers to buy and sell items on Amazon Auctions. Amazon Auctions never developed a sizeable following and has closed.

Although Amazon Auctions never developed into a major competitor for eBay, it did have an impact on the way online auctions are operated. When Amazon entered the online auction business, it announced its "Auctions Guarantee." The guarantee directly addressed concerns raised by eBay customers who had been cheated by unscrupulous sellers. When Amazon opened its auctions site, it agreed to reimburse any buyer for merchandise purchased in an auction that was not delivered or that was "materially different" from the seller's representations. Amazon limited its guarantee to items costing $250 or less. (Buyers of more expensive items generally protect themselves by using an escrow service.) Amazon's advantage was short-lived, however. Before bidders had a chance to move to Amazon auctions, eBay responded by offering its customers a similar guarantee.

Auctions are becoming an efficient way for businesses to improve the process of clearing out old and slow-moving inventory. In the past, most companies would hire a liquidation broker to help dispose of unwanted inventory. A **liquidation broker** is an intermediary who matches sellers of obsolete inventory with purchasers who are looking for bargains. Liquidation brokers and companies that were large enough to arrange their own liquidation sales often found it very expensive to set up a physical auction for obsolete inventory. The greatest expenses were leasing a place to hold the auction and mailing notices of the auction to a sufficient number of people to create a decent-sized bidding pool. It was also difficult to accumulate a wide enough variety of items to attract bidders. Bidders who were interested in only one or two items would be reluctant to attend the auction. As a result, inventory sold this way seldom returned more than 10 percent of its cost.

The Internet changed the economics of liquidation auctions. Today, many liquidation brokers are opening Web auctions to obtain a better range of bids. Auctions are a good way for sellers to obtain the highest possible price if the pool of bidders is large enough. An auction on a Web site can attract bidders from all over the world and these bidders can select the specific item on which they want to bid. The Additional Information section of the Online Companion page for Tutorial 10 includes links to several liquidation broker sites that offer auction services under the heading Liquidation Brokers.

Some companies are too small to operate their own liquidation sites or to attract the interest of liquidation brokers. These companies have found eBay and similar consumer-oriented auction sites to be useful tools for selling their excess inventory and used equipment. The reduction in transaction costs is a powerful force behind all Web auction sites and makes it possible for individuals and small companies to obtain decent prices for unwanted items.

Consumer Concerns

Participants in electronic commerce have two major concerns. The first is for transaction security. Buyers in an electronic marketplace often do not know who is operating a Web site from which they would like to make a purchase. They also desire assurance that the payments they make for goods purchased over the Internet are secure.

Buyers' second major concern is that their privacy not be violated in the course of conducting electronic commerce. Web sites can gather a great deal of information about their customers, even before customers purchase anything from the site. The Web electronic commerce community has made efforts toward ensuring both transaction security and buyer privacy, but these efforts are not yet complete. Many potential consumers are reluctant to make purchases over the Internet because of continuing concerns about these two issues. Several assurance providers have begun operations in recent years. An **assurance provider** is a third party that, for a fee paid by the electronic commerce Web site, will certify that the site meets some criteria for conducting business in a secure and privacy-preserving manner.

Transaction Security and Privacy

Potential customers worry about a number of issues when they consider dealing with a Web-based business. They might wonder whether the firm is a real company that will deliver the merchandise ordered or, if the merchandise is defective, will replace it or refund the purchase price within a reasonable period. Potential customers of any business worry about the same issues; however, the virtual nature of a Web electronic commerce site increases these concerns. In addition, potential customers are concerned about the security of their credit card numbers as those numbers travel over the Internet.

As you learned earlier in this book, the SSL security protocol encrypts information flowing between a Web server and a Web client. Many Web sites involved in electronic commerce use the SSL protocol to protect sensitive information as it travels over the Internet.

A greater concern is how electronic commerce Web sites store their customer information. Many sites store their customers' credit card numbers so that the customers do not have to type the card numbers every time they visit the site to buy something. Of course, the computer that stores these card numbers is connected (directly or indirectly) to the Internet. Any computer that is connected to the Internet is subject to attack from persons outside the company.

There have been a number of widely reported cases in which an intruder has broken into an electronic commerce site's computer and stolen names, addresses, and credit card information. Sometimes, these individuals have even posted the stolen credit card information on the Internet.

Many potential customers of Web-based businesses are also concerned about their privacy. Web sites can collect a great deal of information about customers' preferences, even before they place an order. By recording a user's clickstream, the Web server can gather extensive knowledge about that visitor. Many Web sites use clickstream information to display different ad banners to different visitors.

No general standards currently exist in the United States for maintaining confidentiality regarding clickstream information, much less general identifying information about Web site visitors and customers. Many business Web sites include statements of privacy policy directed at concerned customers, but no U.S. laws exist requiring such statements or policies.

The Electronic Communications Privacy Act of 1986, which was enacted before most people were using the Internet, does not include rules specifically designed to protect the privacy of persons using Web sites to conduct transactions. The Children's Online Privacy Protection Act of 1998 (often referred to as COPPA) does make it illegal for Web sites to collect identifiable information from children under the age of 13 without first obtaining their parents' consent.

Assurance Providers

To fill the need for some kind of assurance over Web site transaction security and privacy policies, several assurance providers have started offering various kinds of certifications. Web sites can purchase these certifications and display the logo or seal of the assurance provider on the Web site for potential customers to examine. Most of these logos are hyperlinks to the assurance provider's site, at which customers can find out more about the nature of the specific assurances given by that provider. Currently, there are five major assurance providers: the Better Business Bureau (BBB), TRUSTe, the International Computer Security Association (ICSA), VeriSign, and WebTrust.

The Better Business Bureau's BBBOnLine certification program grants a Web site the right to use its logo after it has joined the BBB; been in business for at least one year; compiled a satisfactory complaint-handling record; and agreed to follow BBB member guidelines for truthful advertising, prompt response to customer complaints, and binding arbitration of customer disputes. The BBB conducts a site visit during which it verifies the street address, telephone number, and existence of the business. The BBB page for businesses appears in Figure 10-8.

BBBOnLine for Business page   Figure 10-8

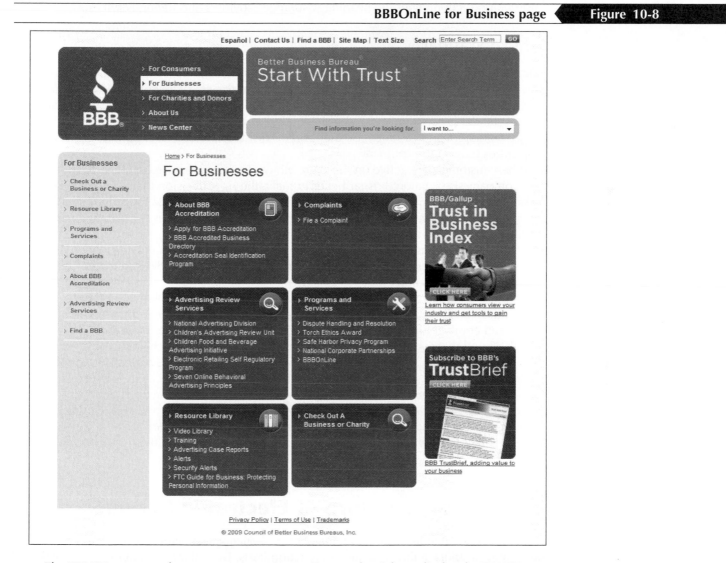

The TRUSTe program focuses on privacy issues. To earn the right to display the TRUSTe logo, a Web site must explain and summarize its information-gathering policies in a disclosure statement on the site. The site must adhere to its stated policies and several other guidelines concerning the privacy of communications. TRUSTe enforces its program by various methods, including surprise audits that it and two independent accounting firms conduct.

The ICSA is an independent association that has developed a series of computer security certifications. The goal of ICSA Web certification is to reduce Web site risks and liability for the site and its customers. ICSA conducts an initial on-site evaluation using its certification field guide and uses subsequent remote testing and random spot-checking of site availability, information-protection measures, and data-integrity provisions.

VeriSign provides a range of services to electronic commerce Web sites, including certification of secure server status and EDI certifications. It is also a partner with the American Institute of Certified Public Accountants (AICPA) in the WebTrust program. The WebTrust program is a comprehensive assurance that requires reviews by a licensed CPA (or Chartered Accountant in Canada) before the site is approved. The review includes examination of Web site performance disclosures, such as delivery times and handling of customer complaints. The site is granted a WebTrust logo only after it satisfies a number of criteria relating to business practices, transaction integrity, and information protection. The WebTrust program requires recertification every 90 days. Links to assurance service provider sites are included in the Online Companion for this tutorial in the Additional Information section under the heading Assurance Providers and Rating Services.

Ethical Standards

Companies that conduct business on the Web should try to follow the ethical standards that they would follow if they were doing business in the physical world. Pursuing business in an ethical manner helps promote a positive image of the business. Although high ethical standards can be more expensive, in the long run they can help establish a company's reputation and can increase the level of trust that customers, suppliers, and employees have in the company.

When customers are active on the Web, ethical lapses can cause immediate damage to a company's reputation. It is far better to make the right decision than to have to repair a damaged reputation after the fact. For example, in early 1999, eBay faced an ethical dilemma. Several newspapers ran stories that described sales of illegal items, such as assault weapons and drugs, on the eBay auction site. At the time, eBay was starting about 250,000 new auctions each day and its policy was to investigate any claims that illegal items were being auctioned on the site. However, eBay did not actively screen or filter listings before the auctions started.

Even though eBay was not obligated by law to screen items auctioned, and even though the screening is fairly expensive to do, eBay managers decided that screening for illegal and copyright-infringing items would be in the best long-run interest of eBay. The team believed that such a decision would send a signal about the character of the company to its customers and the public in general. The eBay managers also chose to refuse auctions of firearms. Many eBay users were unhappy about this decision because the sale of firearms, when done properly, is completely legal. The no-firearms policy also meant that eBay would lose the auction business of gun collectors and gun dealers. However, eBay managers again decided that presenting an overall image of an open and honest marketplace was important to the future success of eBay, and thus was worth the loss of the firearm sales.

International Nature of Electronic Commerce

As you have learned in this session, many of the advantages that electronic commerce offers arise from its ability to reduce transaction costs. By making communication quick and inexpensive, technology makes commerce less expensive for both businesses and individuals. In addition to being inexpensive and easy to use, the Internet and the Web also offer people an unprecedented degree of geographic reach. While allowing companies to do business with customers around the globe, the international reach of the Internet does introduce challenges for sites conducting electronic commerce.

International Culture Issues | InSight

Web sites for international commerce must be designed carefully. Choosing icons, phrasing, and colors can be complicated by cultural conventions that differ from country to country. For example, in the United States, a shopping cart is a good symbol to use on retail sites, but many Europeans use shopping baskets when they go to a store and may never have seen a shopping cart. In Australia, people would recognize a shopping cart icon but would be confused by the text "shopping cart;" they use the term "shopping trolley." In the United States, people use hand signal (the index finger touching the thumb to create a circle) that indicates "OK," but in countries such as Brazil, this hand signal is an obscene gesture. In India, using the image of a cow in a cartoon or other comical setting is inappropriate. Customers in Muslim countries could be offended by an image that shows human arms or legs uncovered. Even colors or Web page design elements can be troublesome. For example, white, which denotes purity in Europe and the Americas, is associated with death and mourning in many Asian countries. A Web page that is divided into four segments could be offensive to a Japanese visitor because the number four is a symbol of death in that culture.

Language Issues

The Internet brings people together from every country in the world because it reduces the distances between people in many ways. The predominant language on the Web is English, although sites in other languages and in multiple languages are appearing with increasing frequency. Once a business overcomes the language barrier, the technology exists for it to conduct electronic commerce with any other business or consumer, anywhere in the world.

To address the language issue, many companies hire a translation firm to translate their existing Web pages into other languages. Although computer-automated translation (often called **machine translation**) can provide rough translations very quickly (up to 400,000 words per hour), human translators must refine these translations before they are accurate. For example, Mexican Spanish is different from the Spanish used in Spain or in South America. Human translators can make adjustments for local versions of a language and can help ensure that the Web site is translated in a way that does not violate local customs. Translation that takes into account the culture and customs of the country is called **localization**.

Human translation can be an expensive proposition, with translation fees ranging from 25 to 90 cents per word; languages that are complex or that are spoken by fewer people are even more expensive. Some companies, such as FreeTranslation.com, offer basic machine translation services on their Web sites at no charge. They offer more refined machine translations and human translation services for a fee to those site visitors who want a better translation. You can learn more about the firms that provide translation services by exploring the links in the Additional Information section of the Online Companion page for Tutorial 10 under the heading Translation Services.

One way to test the quality of a translation technique is to perform a back-translation. A **back-translation** is a procedure in which a phrase or sentence is translated from one language into another, and then translated back into the original language. This result is then compared with the original phrase or sentence to see whether the meaning is consistent. You can use a translation site to perform a back-translation that will help you judge the ability of the site's machine translation algorithms to translate effectively the type of message you are trying to translate.

To perform back-translations on FreeTranslation.com:

▶ **1.** Return to the Online Companion page for Session 10.2, if necessary, and then click the **FreeTranslation.com** link.

▶ **2.** Type **Inventory reduced in price for quick sale** in the text box in the Free Text Translator area of the page, select a translation (from English to your choice of another language), and then click the **FREE Translation** button. The page that opens will include a translation of the phrase into the language you chose.

   Trouble? Before you choose a language, make sure that the Web site allows a translation from that language back to English.

▶ **3.** Select and copy the translated text, and then paste it into the text box in the Translate again area of the page. Select a translation back to English from the language you chose in Step 2, and then click the **FREE Translation** button. The back-translation result will appear in the Web page that opens. As you can see, the result is not grammatically correct, but it often conveys the meaning of the original phrase fairly well (how well depends on which language you chose, because machine translation works better on some language pairs than others).

▶ **4.** Repeat Steps 2 and 3 using the sentence **Cool deals on hot wheels: OEM wheel replacements at fire sale prices, today only!** and use the back-translation to evaluate the effectiveness of the translation algorithm.

Tip

Phrases that include slang, idioms, or industry jargon can be very difficult for a machine translation algorithm to handle correctly.

Legal Issues

Businesses on the Internet must adhere to the same laws that regulate the operation of all businesses. As companies grow, they become subject to many more laws and regulations. Electronic commerce activities can expose even small businesses to a broader range of laws and regulations than they would face if they were not operating on the Internet. As you learned in the previous section, a business on the Web becomes an international business immediately.

In many cases, an e-business can become subject to laws and taxes about which its managers are unaware. Unfortunately, the political and legal structures of the world have not kept up with Internet technology, so doing business internationally presents a number of challenges. Currency conversions, tariffs, import and export restrictions, local business customs, and the laws of each country in which a trading partner resides can each make international electronic commerce difficult. Many of the international issues that arise relate to legal, tax, and privacy concerns. Each country has the right to pass laws and levy taxes on businesses that operate within their jurisdictions. Countries that are members of the European Community (EC), for example, have adopted very strict laws that limit the collection and use of personal information that companies gather in the course of doing business with consumers. U.S. companies that do business in the EC must comply with these laws, which are much more restrictive than the laws in the United States. Within the United States, individual states and counties have the power to levy sales and use taxes on goods and services. In other countries, national sales and value-added taxes are imposed on an even more comprehensive list of business activities.

Complying with all of these laws and regulations can be difficult for small businesses that want to operate electronic commerce Web sites. Therefore, many smaller sites restrict the countries to which they will deliver merchandise or in which they will provide services. These Web sites can place terms of service statements on their sites to protect themselves from laws and regulations of which they might be unaware. A **terms of service (TOS) statement** can include rules for site visitors, a statement of copyright interest in the site design and content, and can restrict the types of business that a visitor can conduct with the site. Most sites place their terms of service statements on a separate Web page and provide a link to it from the site's home page. These links are typically titled "Terms of Service," "Conditions of Use," "User Agreement," or something similar. You can learn more about the legal environment of electronic commerce by exploring the links that are included in the Additional Information section of the Online Companion page for this tutorial under the heading Law and Government Regulation Sites.

Small Business Online

The Internet has given many entrepreneurs the chance to create a business online and turn it into a multi-million (or even billion) dollar company. People like Pierre Omidyar (eBay) and Jeff Bezos (Amazon.com) started with a simple idea and became very successful. In the late 1990s, many people tried to use the Internet to become an overnight success. A few did succeed, but many others failed in their attempt to get rich quickly. In this tutorial, you have learned about some successful online businesses that are now large enterprises. But the Internet today still offers an opportunity for people to start small businesses that are successful.

Online Businesses with No Products

In 2007, software developer Eric Nakagawa had a bad day and asked his friend, Kari Unebasami, to send him something funny to cheer him up. She sent him a picture of a grinning fat cat with the caption "I can has cheezburger?" He posted it and some similar items on a Web site named with the caption and invited others to participate. The site quickly became popular and was receiving dozens of pictures every day. Within a few months, the site was getting more than 100,000 visitors a day. Nakagawa and Unebasami were explaining to Ben Huh, a person they had met through the site, that maintaining the site was becoming a lot of work and they were thinking about just shutting it down. Huh realized that a site with that kind of traffic could charge between $100 and $600 per day for a single ad and that the site's popularity would likely grow. Huh convinced the founders to continue and later bought the site with several other investors for an estimated $2 million. Huh is now CEO of the company running the site, and Nakagawa and Unebasami are pursuing other potentially profitable ideas. The site has more than 2 million visitors (generating substantial advertising revenue) and receives some 8,000 submissions every day.

Other bloggers have also been able to sell enough advertising to turn their blogs into businesses. Jake Dobkins writes about New York City on the blog site Gothamist. Instead of drawing a salary from a newspaper as a food and entertainment reporter, he blogs about the latest in New York night life. Advertising revenue has been sufficient to support Dobkins and the site's co-founder, Jen Chung. Now with a staff of bloggers, editors, and ad salespeople, these entrepreneurs are expanding into other cities.

Michael Arrington began blogging in 2005 about new online business startups. Again, instead of writing a column for a business magazine, he decided to put his research and reporting talents into his own business, which today is operating as TechCrunch, a successful advertising-supported Web site.

Of course, creating an ad-supported blog is not the only way to earn a living online. Anyone who has a skill that can be sold and delivered online can do just that. Many Web designers sell services online. Shirley Kaiser has been online since 1996 with her SKDesigns site. Kristin Zhivago sells her consulting services online at Zhivago Management Partners. John Smith, a Colorado CPA, has been providing accounting and administrative services to small businesses online since 1998 as One Point BPO Services. Ashley Quails started her Web business, Whateverlife.com, when she was a 14-year-old interested in graphic design and found that her friends liked the ideas she had for their MySpace page background designs. The Web site now has more than a million visitors a day and employs three of her friends who help her create new designs. By the age of 17, Ashley was drawing a $3,000 per month salary and had bought a new house for her mother, but she invests most of her profits in the business.

The cost of setting up a Web site and creating an online presence can be far less expensive than renting an office and creating a presence in the physical world. Anyone with a marketable skill that can be delivered online is a candidate to become an online entrepreneur.

Online Businesses with Products

Selling products online is somewhat more complicated than selling a service, since it adds the problem of managing inventory (the products you are selling). Inventory must be purchased or created, stored, and then shipped to customers. Most successful small online businesses that sell products have inventory items with one common characteristic: a high value-to-weight ratio. The **value-to-weight ratio** is the price of the item divided by its weight. Large, heavy products that have a low price (for example, gravel, coal, or lumber) are difficult to sell online because the shipping costs exceed the profit on the item. Items that are small, light, and relatively expensive (such as jewelry, computer chips, or designer shoes) can be shipped at low cost and often have enough profit to cover even next-day shipping costs. Another product characteristic that is good for a small online business is uniqueness. The more unusual a product is, the less likely it is to be sold by a mass-merchandiser, and few small businesses can survive when a large competitor starts selling similar products at very low prices.

Brad and Jera Deal often took their three daughters on walks through the park. During these walks, they would look for letters formed by trees, bushes, or buildings. They took pictures of the best letters they found. When they needed a unique wedding gift for a teacher, they spelled out her name using some of the "letter" photos they had captured on their walks and created a keepsake wall hanging. The gift was so popular that other people wanted similar keepsakes. Today, the Deals sell their keepsake wall hangings through a number of gift stores and their online store, Sticks and Stones. The customer uses the Web site to select the photos for each letter, then the wall hanging is created and shipped. The product has a high value-to-weight ratio and is sufficiently unusual that competitors have been unable to take away many sales.

Jerry Whitlock had been in the industrial machinery business for years. He had even run a company that manufactured seals and gaskets (the parts that keep the oil and other fluids that lubricate machinery from leaking). A seal is a very important item for companies that run machinery, because if the seal leaks, the machine stops working. A machine failure can shut down an assembly line and cost the company thousands of dollars per day. Whitlock had been collecting gaskets and seals for years. Whenever he would hear that a company was going out of business or liquidating inventory, he would buy whatever gaskets and seals they had. Over the years, he build up quite a collection of odd seals. He also learned who made what kinds of seals and how quickly they could manufacture an item. He collected catalogs from these suppliers and stored them in large binders. In 1995, he began a profitable business as a middleman, buying and selling gaskets, seals, and other industrial fittings. As he developed an international reputation as "The Seal Man," business grew. He scanned the catalogs into his laptop computer and took the business online as EPM.com. The products that EPM.com sells have a high value-to-weight ratio and, although they are relatively inexpensive parts, they become quite valuable when a plant is shut down because one of the machines is leaking oil.

Any unique or unusual item is a candidate for sale on the Web. Many small businesses use eBay as a platform for selling items that they have produced or obtained in small quantities. Unlike the customers of a regular online store, eBay visitors do not expect sellers to have unlimited stocks of items they list for sale.

Selling a product does require a larger investment (to purchase inventory), but the right product can be the basis for a successful small online business. One way to avoid the outlay for inventory is to choose a business that combines personalized sales with big companies' established brands. Companies such as Avon, Creative Memories, and Long-aberger rely on individual businesspersons (often called sales consultants) to sell their products. In the past, the sales consultant would hold a gathering to demonstrate products and take orders. Today, sales consultants can set up their own Web pages to accept customer orders. The orders are processed by the company and shipped directly to customers, which reduces or eliminates the sales consultant's need to invest in inventory.

Jerry finds many of these online small businesses to be very interesting. He asks you to review some of the sites to see if there are any ideas that Omega might use in its business.

To learn more about small businesses online:

▶ **1.** Return to the Online Companion page for Session 10.2, if necessary, and then click one of the links under the **Small Businesses Online** header.

▶ **2.** Examine the site to learn more about its revenue model and the background of the site's founder(s).

▶ **3.** Return to the Online Companion page and repeat Step 2 for at least two other sites.

▶ **4.** Compile a brief summary of your findings for Jerry.

▶ **5.** Close your Web browser.

Future of Electronic Commerce

The Internet has allowed far more businesses, organizations, and individuals to become interconnected by their computers than the pioneers of EDI and EFT ever could have imagined. The Web has given the Internet an easy-to-use interface. The combination of the Web's interface and the Internet's extension of computer networking have opened new opportunities for electronic commerce. Businesses that in the past sold retail goods to consumers through catalogs using mail or telephone orders can now use the Internet to make shopping more convenient. Other retailers, such as booksellers, can use large-volume buying power to provide Internet shoppers with low prices and a wide variety of products. Information providers, such as newspapers, magazines, and newsletters, find that the Internet offers new ways to sell existing products and platforms on which to deliver entirely new products. Software manufacturers see that the Internet is an excellent vehicle for distributing new products, delivering upgrades to existing products, and providing low-cost support to users. The immediacy of the medium offers businesses, such as stockbrokers and travel agencies, an attractive way to interact with their customers.

Session 10.2 Quick Check | Review

1. Briefly define the term electronic data interchange (EDI).
2. Banks use electronic funds transfers (EFTs) for large transactions, but for small transactions they use _____ .
3. Email can be a good way for a company to stay in touch with its customers, but only if one important condition is met. Name and explain that condition.
4. What is an intranet?
5. Some companies are disposing of slow-moving or obsolete inventory by selling it on Web auction sites such as eBay instead of selling it through a(n) _____ .
6. Name two concerns that potential customers often have about making a purchase from a Web site.

7. Briefly describe the role that assurance providers play in the conduct of electronic commerce.

8. What are the most important characteristics to have in a product that you want to sell online?

Review | **Tutorial Summary**

In this tutorial, you learned about Web strategies that companies use to generate revenues, increase operational efficiency, and reduce costs. The tutorial described several revenue models and explained how companies use the Web to reduce costs and improve efficiency. You learned about online auctions, which are a type of business that did not exist before the Web, and that companies doing business on the Web have taken steps to assure consumers that their transactions will be secure and that their privacy will be respected. Finally, you learned about the international, legal, and ethical environment in which electronic commerce operates.

Key Terms

assurance provider
automated
   clearinghouse (ACH)
back-translation
business model
business processes
business-to-business (B2B)
business-to-consumer (B2C)
business-to-government (B2G)
cannibalization
channel conflict
competitive advantage
consumer-to-consumer (C2C)
demographic information
disintermediation
dot-com
electronic business
   (e-business)

electronic commerce
   (e-commerce)
electronic data
   interchange (EDI)
electronic funds transfer (EFT)
escrow service
extranet
financial EDI
intranet
liquidation broker
localization
machine translation
mixed advertising-
   subscription
   revenue model
operations model
pure advertising
   revenue model

pure dot-com
pure subscription
   revenue model
reintermediation
revenue model
strategic alliance
strategic partnership
target marketing
terms of service (TOS)
   statement
trading partners
transaction costs
value-added network (VAN)
value-to-weight ratio
Web portal (portal)
wire transfer

| **Review Assignments**

Get hands-on practice of the skills you learned in the tutorial using the same case scenario.

There are no Data Files needed for these Review Assignments.

Steven is intrigued by many of the online business ideas you have identified. He would like you to undertake a competitive analysis in which you visit a few Web sites operated by other firms in Omega's businesses. To summarize your findings, create a table with Omega's four divisions listed across the top. You will add information about each competitor's site in the rows of the table. The format of your results will look like this:

	Recruiting Division	Compensation & Benefits Division	Training Division	Compliance Division
Competitor 1				
Competitor 2				
(And so on)				
-				
-				
-				

1. Start your Web browser, go to www.cengage.com/internet/np/internet8 to open the Online Companion page, log on to your account, click the Tutorial 10 link, and then click the Review Assignments link.
2. Click one of the links to explore the Web site of one of Omega's potential competitors and review its elements. Determine whether the site offers one or more services similar to Omega's offerings. Write a short summary of the key features that the site includes for each of the services it offers that are similar to Omega's. For example, if a site offers recruiting and compliance services, you would make an entry in those two columns for that competitor.
3. Repeat the previous step for at least three other links.
4. Write a report to Steven of about 500 words in which you list at least 10 elements that would be important to include in Omega's new Web site. For each element, explain why you believe it is important and outline any problems you think Omega might face in implementing it. Attach the table you created as an appendix to your report.
5. Close your Web browser.

| **Case Problem 1**

Apply the skills you learned in this tutorial to shop for a new DVD player on the Web.

There are no Data Files needed for this Case Problem.

Dave Baker's New DVD Player Your friend Dave Baker complains that his DVD player has recently started to randomly eject the DVD while he is watching the movie that is on the DVD. You tell Dave that you can show him how to do comparison shopping on the Web for a new DVD player.

1. Start your Web browser, go to www.cengage.com/internet/np/internet8 to open the Online Companion page, log on to your account, click the Tutorial 10 link, and then click the Case Problem 1 link.
2. Click the buy.com link to open the buy.com home page, select Electronics in the drop-down list box near the top of that page, type DVD player in the search box, and then click the Search button. (Alternatively, you can use the links on the left side of the page to open a list of DVD players.)

3. The search results page lists a number of DVD players with their part numbers, prices, and information about their current availability for shipment. Some buyers may make their selection using the brief descriptions that appear on this page, but many buyers want more information. To provide a customized level of product information on this site, buy.com formats the name of each DVD player as a hyperlink that you can click to learn more about that particular model. Click some of these hyperlinks to learn more about at least three DVD players that are currently for sale.

4. Return to the Online Companion page for Case Problem 1, and then click the Amazon.com link to open the Amazon.com home page. Click the Electronics link in the tab near the top of the page, and then select Home Audio & Theater.

5. Find a link on the left side of the page that leads to DVD players, and then click that link. The first page of search results lists a number of DVD players with their part numbers, prices, and current availability for shipment. The name of each DVD player is a hyperlink that you can follow to obtain more details about each DVD player, including customer reviews of the product and ratings of the reviews (each review has an indicator that states how many people found that review to be helpful). Click some of these hyperlinks to learn more about at least three DVD players that are currently for sale.

6. For each site, answer the following questions:
    a. Was the site easy to use? Why or why not?
    b. Did the site offer DVD players in which you would be interested?
    c. Did the site display product information that was easy to understand? Why or why not?
    d. Would you use this site to purchase items online? Why or why not?

7. Print one page of information about a particular DVD player from each site. On each page, indicate one helpful design feature.

8. Close your Web browser.

| Create | **Case Problem 2** |

Research Web portal elements that would be important to include in a Web portal for a community college.

There are no Data Files needed for this Case Problem.

Sagamore Community College Sagamore Community College (SCC) offers two-year associate degree programs in computer technologies. Because of its impressive array of computer laboratories and its state-of-the-art computer infrastructure, the college attracts students from a community that employs many high-tech workers. Unfortunately, SCC does not currently provide timely course and degree information on its Web site. Ernesto Cervantes, SCC's director of Academic Computing, wants to change the SCC home page so students can customize it and use it as a Web portal site. Ernesto wants the portal to offer class lists, information about instructors, and course information. Ernesto would like you to review existing business, government, and general portal sites that might serve as examples for redesigning SCC's home page and make a recommendation regarding the features that would be important to include in the design of SCC's new Web portal.

1. Start your Web browser, go to www.cengage.com/internet/np/internet8 to open the Online Companion page, log on to your account, click the Tutorial 10 link, and then click the Case Problem 2 link.

2. Click one of the links to explore a Web portal site and review its elements. Identify features that would be important to include in the SCC portal design.

3. Repeat the previous step for at least two other links.

4. Write a report to Ernesto of about 500 words in which you list at least six elements that would be important to include in the SCC portal design. For each element, explain why you believe it is important and outline any problems you think SCC might face in implementing it.

5. Close your Web browser.

Research | Case Problem 3

Research the offerings of competing Web assurance service companies for a new small business.

There are no Data Files needed for this Case Problem.

Dorm Lamps, Inc. Your friend Robin has invented a new high-intensity lamp that is an ideal product for college students who share dorm rooms. You and Robin have been selling the lamps for three months through word-of-mouth advertising on your campus. You would like to expand your sales to other college campuses. Robin suggests creating a Web page that will accept orders. The lamps are small and lightweight; therefore, they could be shipped to customers easily using a variety of methods. Because you are both college students with no business experience, you wonder who will trust you or your Web site to deliver quality merchandise. You would like to investigate the terms and conditions of several Web site assurance providers to determine which, if any, you should use for the proposed site.

1. Start your Web browser, go to www.cengage.com/internet/np/internet8 to open the Online Companion page, log on to your account, click the Tutorial 10 link, and then click the Case Problem 3 link.

⊕ **EXPLORE** 2. Click the BBBOnline link to open that page. Examine the Web site assurance criteria presented on this site and determine whether Dorm Lamps, Inc. would qualify. (*Hint*: Estimate the approximate cost of obtaining the assurance.)

⊕ **EXPLORE** 3. Return to the Online Companion page for Case Problem 3, and then examine at least two of the other Web site assurance services listed for this case and evaluate the costs and benefits for Dorm Lamps, Inc. to obtain each service. (*Hint*: The lowest cost is not necessarily the most important consideration; remember to consider both benefits and costs in your evaluation.)

4. Write a three-page summary of your findings. Be sure to recommend a specific assurance service or explain why none of the services you identified would be suitable for Dorm Lamps, Inc. Support your recommendation with facts and logical arguments.

5. Close your Web browser.

Research | Case Problem 4

Research the package tracking services of three major overnight delivery companies.

There are no Data Files needed for this Case Problem.

Battery World You have been using electronic devices such as calculators, cameras, and portable CD players for years. In your job, you use a PDA, a mobile phone, and a laptop computer. One frustration you have experienced using all of these devices is replacing the batteries. You realize that, as more electronic devices need more and different kinds of batteries, a business that offers a wide selection of batteries might be a good idea. Many of these batteries are rather expensive, but the batteries are small, lightweight, and easy to ship. Their high value-to-weight ratio makes batteries ideal products for online sales. After much research, you have decided to open a Web-based business, Battery World, which will stock a wide variety of batteries ready for overnight delivery. You have worked out many of the details of ordering and stocking your batteries, but you have not yet decided on how you might best ship them.

1. Start your Web browser, go to www.cengage.com/internet/np/internet8 to open the Online Companion page, log on to your account, click the Tutorial 10 link, and then click the Case Problem 4 link.

2. Click the FedEx hyperlink to open that page. Examine the services provided on the FedEx Web site for overnight shipments. Include in your study the elements of package tracking, obtaining rate information, and pickup and delivery services information.

3. Return to the Online Companion page for Case Problem 4, and then click the UPS hyperlink. Examine the services provided on the UPS Web site for overnight shipments. Include in your study the elements of package tracking, obtaining rate information, and pickup and delivery services information.

4. Return to the Online Companion page for Case Problem 4, and then click the DHL hyperlink. Examine the services provided on the DHL Web site for overnight shipments. Include in your study the elements of package tracking, obtaining rate information, and pickup and delivery services information.

5. Write a two-page summary that includes a comparison of how easy each company's site was to use as you searched it for the information you needed.

6. Close your Web browser.

Challenge | Case Problem 5

Examine and evaluate the Web revenue and operations models of three online florists.

There are no Data Files needed for this Case Problem.

Web Plants   You have a green thumb and have always enjoyed growing plants, so you have decided to start a company called Web Plants to sell green plants on the Web. But first, you want to learn all you can by studying the revenue and operations models of existing firms that sell flowers and related gift items on the Web. You learn that FTD.com started as the world's first "flowers-by-wire" service in 1910 and moved to the Web in 1994. The 1-800-flowers.com site is an outgrowth of that company's telephone order business. Newer entrants to the online flower industry, such as Proflowers.com, started their businesses on the Web and work with a very different business strategy.

1. Start your Web browser, go to www.cengage.com/internet/np/internet8 to open the Online Companion page, log on to your account, click the Tutorial 10 link, and then click the Case Problem 5 link.

⊕ EXPLORE   2. Click the FTD.com link to open the FTD.com home page. Click the About Us hyperlink near the bottom of that page. The About Us page includes a history of the company and describes many of the details of its operations. Read this page carefully so you understand what FTD.com is, who its customers are, and how it accepts and delivers orders. (*Hint*: You might also want to explore other pages on the site to learn more about how FTD.com does business.)

⊕ EXPLORE   3. Return to the Online Companion page for Case Problem 5, and then click the Spring Hill Nursery link. Click the About Us hyperlink on the left side of the Spring Hill Nursery home page to learn more about the company. (*Hint*: You might also want to explore other pages on the site to learn more about Spring Hill Nursery.)

⊕ EXPLORE   4. Return to the Online Companion page for Case Problem 5, and then click the Proflowers.com hyperlink. When the Proflowers.com home page opens, click the About Us hyperlink near the bottom-left of the page. Explore the links on the About Us page, which lead to more information about the company and its business strategy. (*Hint*: You might also want to explore other pages on the site to learn more about Proflowers.com.)

5. Based on your examination of the three Web sites, create a presentation in which you describe the revenue and operations models you plan to use for your new Web Plants business. In your presentation, be sure to explain which elements of the three Web florists' revenue and operations models you plan to emulate and which you plan to avoid, and explain why. Your instructor might ask you to share your findings with your class in a formal presentation.

6. Close your Web browser.

| Reinforce | **Lab Assignments** |

Student Edition Labs

The interactive Student Edition Lab on **E-Commerce** is designed to help you master some of the key concepts and skills presented in this tutorial, including:

- understanding revenue models
- understanding transaction security

This lab is available online and can be accessed from the Tutorial 10 Web page on the Online Companion page at www.cengage.com/internet/np/internet8.

| Review | **Quick Check Answers** |

Session 10.1

1. By conducting business-like activities; for example, an art museum could sell tickets to an upcoming exhibition.
2. False. This is the definition of a revenue model.
3. competitive advantage
4. The company replaces or supplements its distribution of printed catalogs with a catalog on its Web site, which allows customers to place orders through the Web site.
5. cannibalization
6. False. An online magazine can do both by using a mixed advertising-subscription revenue model.
7. target marketing

Session 10.2

1. EDI occurs when one business transmits computer-readable data in a standard format to another business.
2. automated clearinghouses (also called ACHs)
3. Companies should always ask customers for permission before sending unsolicited promotional or informational emails.
4. a set of Web pages that is accessible only to employees of the company
5. liquidation broker or liquidation auction
6. transaction security and buyer privacy
7. They provide some assurance that a Web site processes transactions in a secure manner and/or follows its stated policies regarding the privacy of customer information.
8. The product should be unusual or unique and should have a high value-to-weight ratio.

Reality Check

The practice of buying and selling personal items online has increased dramatically in recent years, with the growing popularity of consumer-to-consumer (C2C) electronic commerce Web sites such as eBay. For example, when people are planning to move into a new apartment or house, or to another town, they often need to sell or buy belongings to better suit their new living arrangements. Rather than hold a yard sale or head down to the local mall, many people use the Internet to buy and sell personal property. In this exercise, you will use the skills presented in Tutorials 6 through 10 to plan the online sale or purchase of a personal item of your choice. This item could be as small as an audio CD or as large as a refrigerator. For the purposes of this exercise, assume that you need to sell or buy the particular item because you are planning to move to a new town.

Note: Please be sure *not* to include any personal information of a sensitive nature in the documents you create to be submitted to your instructor for this exercise. Later on, you can update the documents with such information for your own personal use.

1. Start your Web browser and review several C2C electronic commerce Web sites, such as Craigslist, Amazon Marketplace, or eBay, that sell items similar to the one you are planning to sell or buy. In an email message to your instructor, identify distinguishing characteristics of the different sites. Discuss the elements that each site emphasizes, and describe how those elements promote sales between individuals.

2. Investigate several B2C Web sites that offer items similar to the one you are planning to sell or buy. In the email message to your instructor, identify the characteristics of the sites that make them effective (or ineffective) at promoting the item. Be specific in describing the features and explain why they help to sell the product or why they detract from selling it effectively.

3. In your email message, describe at least two ways you could use online communications (including email lists, newsgroups, and wireless communication) to stay in touch with potential buyers or sellers of your item.

4. In your email message, describe electronic commerce security features that could help protect the purchase or sale of your item.

5. Use your favorite search tool to identify Web sites that you could use to learn more about the offerings in your new town. These sites could include blogs, online networking sites, or video sharing sites. In the email to your instructor, evaluate the usefulness of at least three of these sites in finding local services, reviewing restaurants, or helping you find a group or club you might like to join.

6. Send the email message to your instructor and close your browser.

Objectives

- Use and expand the skills you learned in Tutorials 4 and 5
- Visit Web sites to find information about a disease or medical condition
- Evaluate the resources you find
- Examine the resources provided by a credentialing site to evaluate health care information on the Web

Locating and Evaluating Health Care Information on the Internet

Many Web sites provide information about medical care, prescription drugs, and related health topics. An increasing number of doctors and other health care professionals have concerns about the quality of medical and health resources available on the Internet because anyone can post anything on the Web—there are no requirements for or restrictions on giving medical advice in this manner. Thus, it is not surprising that recent surveys have shown that a significant number of health information Web sites include information that is incorrect.

When you need information about a specific disease or medical condition, you can use one of the many sites on the Internet to conduct your research. In some cases, you might visit sites with connections to research institutions, medical facilities, and universities. Sites in these categories include the Medical College of Wisconsin HealthLink, WebMD, and the Mayo Clinic. When you visit the sites of these organizations, you can read about the specific disease or medical condition that interests you, and often you will find links to other sites that provide more information. For example, if you are trying to learn about emphysema, a condition commonly associated with smoking cigarettes, one of these sites might provide information about the condition and links to other Web sites, such as the American Lung Association, where you can get more detailed information.

Just like any other Web site, it's up to you to evaluate the quality of the resources and information it provides. Sometimes you can make these determinations easily. For example, the American Lung Association is a well-known health organization that was founded in 1904 to fight tuberculosis and other lung diseases through donations and resources from public and private sources, foundations, and government agencies. Other resources, however, might be more difficult to evaluate because you might not be familiar with them. Fortunately, accrediting agencies that evaluate health information sites have Web sites that provide information about medical sites. Two of these sites are the Health on the Net (HON) Foundation and the URAC Health Web Site Accreditation. You can use the resources at these sites and other credentialing sites to evaluate health resources you find on the Internet. In some cases, the credentialing site might let you search its database to locate sites that it has already deemed credible using its own sets of rules, guidelines, and quality standards.

Starting Data Files

There are no starting Data Files needed for this assignment.

In this assignment, you will select a specific disease or medical condition that interests you (or your instructor might provide one for you to use), find information about it, and then use a credentialing site to evaluate its resources.

1. Visit at least two health information sites to obtain information about the disease or medical condition you selected. You can use your favorite search engine or directory to find the sites. Gather the information and evaluate the quality of the information and the quality of the Web site from which you obtained it.

2. Visit at least one credentialing or accreditation site and review its contents. Write a summary that describes how the site operates and evaluate whether the site accomplishes its goals.

3. Visit a site maintained by the U.S. government that offers health care information, such as the U.S. Centers for Disease Control and Prevention (CDC) or the U.S. National Institutes of Health MedlinePlus. Explore the site you selected and then write a review of the site in which you describe how the government-sponsored site is different from the privately operated sites you already visited.

Additional Research Assignment 2

Objectives

- Use and expand the skills you learned in Tutorials 4, 5, and 6
- Explore the content requirements and processes for published encyclopedia resources
- Examine the content of and quality controls for a collaborative encyclopedia Web site
- Evaluate encyclopedia resources available on the Web and their role in research

Evaluating Encyclopedia Resources on the Internet

In Tutorials 4 through 6, you learned that the Internet contains the largest collection of data on earth. You also learned techniques for evaluating the data you get from the Internet to ensure that it is complete, thorough, unbiased, and free from security threats such as viruses. As you search for information, you must assume responsibility for interpreting and analyzing the information you collect to make sure that it meets these criteria.

When you use Google or another search engine to search for information about a topic, chances are very good that your search results will include links to information that is posted on Wikipedia. Wikipedia, which began in 2001, is a much younger "encyclopedia" than its published counterparts, such as *World Book Encyclopedia* (which is more than 90 years old) or *Encyclopedia Britannica* (which is more than 235 years old). *World Book Encyclopedia* and *Encyclopedia Britannica* have set high standards for research and information for generations by relying on accredited and credentialed authors for content, subject matter experts for thorough reviews of that content, and editorial boards of experts in various fields to set standards for content. This established process of writing and reviewing greatly reduces problems related to bias or inaccuracies.

Wikipedia, on the other hand, does not apply these same types of standards to its content. The content that you find in Wikipedia might be written and reviewed by a casual user or an expert. According to the Wikipedia Web site, since its creation in 2001, over 75,000 people have actively contributed to over 13 million articles in more than 260 languages. As a result of this collaboration, Wikipedia is one of the largest resource sites on the Internet. This collaboration of individuals has resulted in an enormous accumulation of knowledge. However, because material is freely contributed by people who might *not* be subject matter experts, and edited and reviewed by people with their own unique perspectives and biases, Wikipedia's content is subject to different quality standards than you might find in other publications.

Starting Data Files

There are no starting Data Files needed for this assignment.

In this assignment, you will use the Internet to explore some of the pros and cons of using a collaborative site such as Wikipedia as a resource when conducting research.

1. Use your favorite search engine or directory to find the Web site for *World Book Encyclopedia*, and then use the "About Us," "Board," "Reviews," or other similarly named links on the publisher's Web site to learn about its contribution requirements and other quality assurance policies. (You might need to review other pages at each site to get a full picture of the encyclopedia's quality assurance standards.) Pay particular attention to author and reviewer credential requirements, review processes that ensure quality content, and any processes listed for making corrections to the published works.

2. Return to your search engine, and then find the Web site for *Encyclopedia Britannica*. Use the guidelines in Step 1 to evaluate this publisher's Web site for similar information.

3. Return to your search engine, and then search using the term **Wikipedia quality issues** and explore the links to learn about some controversies that have arisen as a result of Wikipedia's collaborative nature. Be sure to review material that details specific problems that have occurred and try to understand, what, if any, measures Wikipedia has taken to resolve these problems.

4. Referring back to the information you gathered in Steps 1 and 2 and the research you did in Step 3, what is your opinion of the use of traditional encyclopedias such as *World Book Encyclopedia* or *Encyclopedia Britannica* when compared to an online collaborative project such as Wikipedia? What role does each encyclopedia play in the field of research? How would you use each of these sources when conducting research? What level of confidence do you place in each source, and why?

Advances in Distance Learning

The Internet has enhanced the way that students in grades kindergarten through 12 learn about and participate in scientific research. The National Aeronautics and Space Administration (NASA) began its historic Mars Exploration Rover Mission, which is a long-term robotic exploration of the planet Mars, in June, 2003 and successfully landed a rover on the planet surface in January, 2004. NASA teamed with the Mars Education Program at Arizona State University to offer students in the United States the opportunity to participate in the Mars Student Imaging Project (MSIP), in which students in grades 5 though college sophomore level work in teams with scientists on the Mars project and choose a site on the Mars planet that they would like to map (photograph) from an orbiting rover. Archived data is also available for students to use in research projects. Students participate in the project through distance learning, which is made possible through video conferencing, chats, and teleconferencing. Students complete their projects by writing and submitting a final scientific report for publication in the online MSIP Science Journal.

Starting Data Files

There are no starting Data Files needed for this assignment.

In this assignment, you will explore the Mars Student Imaging Project site and other distance learning sites that you find on the Internet. Then you will consider the future of using distance learning to enhance the education of grade school and college students.

1. Use your favorite search engine or directory to locate the Mars Student Imaging Project Web site, and then spend some time exploring the site to become more familiar with the project. Which Internet technologies make this project possible for students located in the United States?

2. Use your search engine or directory to explore distance learning opportunities at your own school or at other colleges and universities in your area. How do these programs compare to the Mars Student Imaging Project? Which Internet technologies make these programs possible? Are all students able to participate in distance learning programs? Why or why not?

3. Based on your findings, determine other ways schools can use the Internet to enhance the education of grade school and college students. Are there technological impediments that prevent this method of learning? If so, what are they? What advantages do these types of programs offer students and educators?

Objectives

- Use and expand the skills you learned in Tutorials 1, 4, and 5
- Use a search tool to find Web sites with information about the Semantic Web
- Use the skills you learned in this book to evaluate the resources you find
- Draw conclusions about the future of the Semantic Web based on your research

The Future of the Semantic Web

Tim Berners-Lee, widely regarded as the founding father of the World Wide Web, has been active in promoting and developing a project that blends technologies and information to create a next-generation Web, which he calls the **Semantic Web**. Today, people are the primary users of the Web as a communication medium. An increasing portion of the traffic on the Internet, however, is computers communicating with other computers. The Semantic Web is intended to facilitate automated computer-to-computer communication that can support all types of human activity.

The Semantic Web project, as currently conceived, would result in words on Web pages being tagged with their meanings (the meanings of words are called **semantics**, thus the name "Semantic Web"). These tags would turn the Web into a huge computer-readable database. People could use intelligent programs called **software agents** to read the Web page tags to determine the meaning of the words in their contexts. For example, a software agent could be given an instruction to find an airline ticket with certain terms (such as a specific date, destination city, and a cost limit). The software agent would launch a search on the Web and return an electronic ticket that meets the criteria. Instead of a user having to visit several Web sites to gather information, compare prices and itineraries, and make a decision, the software agent would automatically do the searching, comparing, and purchasing.

The key elements that must be added to Web standards so that software agents can perform these functions (and thus create the Semantic Web) include a well-defined tagging system and a set of standards called an ontology. Many researchers working on the Semantic Web project believe that Extensible Markup Language (XML) could work as a tagging system. Unlike HTML, which has a common set of defined tags (for example, <h1> is the tag for a level-one heading), XML tags are defined by users. Different users can create different definitions for the same XML tag. If a group of users agrees on a common set of definitions, they can all use the same XML tags. For the Semantic Web to work, everyone must agree on a common set of XML tags that will be used on the Web. Semantic Web researchers call this common set of tag definitions a **resource description framework (RDF)**. An **ontology** is a set of standards that defines, in detail, the relationships among RDF standards and specific XML tags within a particular knowledge domain. For example, the ontology for cooking would include concepts such as ingredients, utensils, and ovens; however, it would also include rules and behavioral expectations, such as identifying ingredients that can be mixed using utensils, the resulting product that can be eaten

Starting Data Files

There are no starting Data Files needed for this assignment.

by people, and ovens that generate heat within a confined area. Ontologies and the RDF would provide the intelligence about the knowledge domain so that software agents could make decisions as humans would.

In this assignment, you will search for information about the Semantic Web and evaluate its potential for future use.

1. Use your favorite search engine or Web directory to find sites with information about the Semantic Web, XML, RDF, and the term "ontology" as it is used in this area of research (the term "ontology" is used in philosophy and other disciplines, so you will need to use some of the techniques you learned in Tutorial 4 to narrow your results). Prepare a report of about 800 words that summarizes your findings on each of the four topics. Include citations to at least two Web pages for each of the four topics in your report.

2. For each of the eight (or more) Web pages you cited in the report required by the previous step, evaluate the quality of the information you obtained and evaluate the overall quality of the Web site from which you obtained it. Summarize your evaluations in your report. Be sure to include the reasons for your evaluations and explain how you performed the evaluations.

3. Using the information you have gathered about the Semantic Web, evaluate the likelihood that it will become a useful part of the Web within the next ten years. Include a summary of your evaluation in your report and cite at least four Web sources that support your arguments.

Additional Research Assignment 5

Objectives

- Use and expand the skills you learned in Tutorials 5 and 10
- Use a Web site to translate statements into another language and then back into English
- Evaluate the quality of the translation
- Evaluate the effectiveness of using machine translation in business

Using a Web Site to Translate Business Correspondence

The Internet began as a series of research projects, mostly funded by the U.S. government. As the Internet grew, the citizens of many other countries began using the Internet for research and, eventually, for general information, entertainment, and to conduct online business activity.

As participation in the Internet became global, the number of languages in common use on the Internet grew. Once dominated by English, the Internet today has as many languages as the physical world. Since the underlying function of the Internet is to help people communicate with each other, the global nature of the Internet puts people into contact who do not speak the same language. The need to translate email messages and the content of Web pages from one language to another has become very important.

Having human translators do the work can be expensive. One solution for some applications is machine translation, in which a computer does a rough translation. Some Web sites that offer free machine translation tools are Yahoo! Babel Fish Translation, Free Translation, Mezzofanti Translations, and Reverso Free Online Translator.

The success of machine translation depends greatly on the type of information being translated. One way to check the quality of a translation (human or machine) is to take the result of the translation and translate it back into the original language. This process is called back-translation.

In this assignment, you will evaluate the quality of online machine translation by translating several business-related statements into a foreign language, and then translating them back into English.

1. Use your browser to visit one of the previously mentioned translation services that provides online machine translation or another translation service that you locate using a search engine. Use the site to translate each of the following statements into another language of your choice, and then translate the result back into English.
    a. The scheduled arrival date of your order will be delayed.
    b. The crane operators' union at the port of embarkation has walked out on strike. This will delay the shipment of your order until at least one week after the work stoppage has been resolved. We will keep you apprised of developments.

Starting Data Files

There are no starting Data Files needed for this assignment.

    c.   We appreciate the opportunity to bid on your project. To create a bid, we will need the detailed mechanical drawings by next Thursday, along with the supervising engineer's specifications list for all key parts.

    d.   Our current catalog offers the hottest discounts on all in-stock items. We can meet all of your office furniture needs promptly. With our everyday low pricing, we can beat anybody in the business. Our extended warranties and service plans make us the top dog when it comes to wrapping up the job.

2. Evaluate the success of the machine translations of these four statements. In particular, identify the elements in each statement that were troublesome for the machine translation tool you used, and explain why you believe they were troublesome.

3. Provide an overall evaluation of the usefulness of machine translation technology in business communication on the Internet. Describe one specific situation in which you would use an online machine translation tool, and then describe a second specific situation in which you would be reluctant to use such a tool.

Additional Research Assignment **6**

Objectives

- Use and expand the skills you learned in Tutorials 2, 3, and 8
- Learn more about Short Message Service
- Examine the costs of sending messages
- Consider ways to improve text messaging services

Using Short Message Service

Short Message Service (SMS) is a technology that allows the transmission of text messages between mobile phones (including smart phones) and other devices, such as PDAs and fax machines. Messages can also be sent using SMS to or from any device with an IP address, such as a computer connected to the Internet.

Unlike email messages, SMS messages are limited in size (currently 160 characters) and cannot include graphics or photographic images. Some services allow you to send longer messages, but they automatically break the messages into smaller units (not exceeding the 160-character limit) and send them as separate messages.

SMS use has grown rapidly in recent years. It is useful for sending short messages, such as "Am running late, see you in 30 minutes." On most mobile telephone networks, it is less expensive to send an SMS message than it is to make a phone call. Many wireless companies offer email service using SMS. Users are given email addresses when they subscribe to the wireless telephone service and any message sent to that email address is converted into SMS and delivered to the telephone. Many wireless carriers, including AT&T Wireless, Sprint Nextel, T-Mobile, and Verizon Wireless, offer SMS service as part of their telephone packages. Carriers charge for SMS service by the message, but most carriers offer plans that include a certain number of messages (or unlimited messages) for a fixed monthly fee.

Some wireless service providers also offer separate messaging functions (in addition to SMS) that allow you to send picture and video messages. These picture and video functions usually require an additional cost subscription.

Because SMS messages use much less bandwidth than voice transmissions, they can be useful for communicating when wireless circuits become overloaded with unusually large amounts of traffic, which can happen any time many people want to send a quick communication to others. Thus, SMS messaging can be an important function when a natural disaster strikes and communications systems become overwhelmed. It can also be useful in less pressing circumstances, such as at midnight on New Year's Eve, when many people want to send a greeting at the same time.

In this assignment, you will use your browser to visit two of the Web sites of the carriers mentioned in this assignment that offer SMS to gather information you can use to answer the questions in the following steps.

1. What is the cost to send and receive SMS messages using each of the two services you examined?

Starting Data Files

There are no starting Data Files needed for this assignment.

2. Do the services offer unlimited SMS messaging at a fixed cost per month?
3. Are there any limits on the use of SMS messaging?
4. Do the services provide an email address for SMS messaging?
5. Do the services offer picture or video messaging services?
6. How easy was it to find this information on the two sites you visited?
7. Make at least two recommendations for improving the Web sites' presentations of SMS messaging information.

Additional Research Assignment 7

Objectives

- Use and expand the skills you learned in Tutorial 6
- Visit blogs to evaluate their content
- Consider ways to use blogs in business to enhance communication
- Consider some of the advantages and disadvantages of using blogs

Evaluating the Use of Blogs in Business

In this book, you learned how to use email messages to communicate with another person, a group of people, or a mailing list. You also learned about newsgroups and how to use them to obtain information about a specific topic, and how to use instant messaging, text messaging, blogs, and microblogs to communicate with another person or with groups of people. Each of these methods of communication requires different levels of participation from the user. For example, to use instant messaging software, you must install a program on your computer or wireless device; to join a mailing list or a discussion group, you must use your email program or a newsreader to obtain the messages. To write a blog or microblog, you need access to the Internet and software that publishes and distributes your postings.

Although blogs have been around since 1996, the availability of automated blog publishing systems from Web sites such as Blogger, DiaryLand, and LiveJournal gave them the boost they needed to become commonplace on the Web. Media attention increased their popularity in the 2004 presidential campaign when Howard Dean, who pursued but eventually lost the Democratic nomination for president, was the first presidential candidate to use a blog to rally his supporters across the country, to provide updates from his campaign, and to let people join discussions about current topics. By the 2008 presidential campaign, virtually all of the major candidates used blogs. There are hundreds of thousands of blogs on the Web related to all kinds of topics. Some directories, such as Google, identify blogs based on their category, such as news, arts, or sports.

Users need no technical expertise to create or contribute to a blog, and there is little or no expense associated with the technology. Most sites that offer automated publishing systems offer free or inexpensive accounts that new bloggers can use to set up their own blogs, making it easy for anyone to put their thoughts on the Web. Specific features vary by company, but all automate the process of publishing chronologically arranged postings.

Although individuals maintain most blogs, new bloggers include corporations, attorneys, and educators who have discovered the appeal of this technology for making information available to clients, building a practice, or creating academic knowledge communities.

Starting Data Files

There are no starting Data Files needed for this assignment.

In this assignment, you will learn more about automated blog publishing systems and consider ways to use this technology to enhance communication and develop business relationships.

1. Most blogs are collections of personal musings by an individual, but blogs can also be set up to allow a group of people to engage in a collaborative discussion. Use a directory such as Google to find a categorical listing of blogs. Evaluate a couple of blogs in business-related categories, such as library science, news, or science. How does the information provided in the blog compare to using email, instant messaging, chat discussion groups, or newsgroups as a communication tool? What value does a blog add to the topic? Can you identify any unique advantages of communicating using blogs that you cannot gain from other types of Internet communication?

2. Find a political candidate's blog and evaluate its content. What types of information are included in the blog? How does it differ from information presented elsewhere on the candidate's Web site? What is the impact, if any, on traditional news media outlets of the dissemination of political news through blogs?

3. Find a corporate blog and assess its content. What competitive advantages can blogs offer companies? (If you cannot find a corporate blog, answer based on how you *think* a corporation can gain a competitive advantage by using a blog.)

4. Some blogs that are affiliated with faculty members of colleges and universities, such as a blog associated with a professor at the Indiana University School of Business, are challenging issues of academic freedom. Locate a blog written by a faculty member at a university. Do blogs authored by faculty members differ from other blogs you have found? Do educators have a greater responsibility to control the content of postings at their sites? Do you feel that blogs belong in academic settings? Why or why not?

Additional Research Assignment 8

- Use and expand the skills you learned in Tutorials 5, 9, and 10
- Develop ideas for the design of a surf travel Web site
- Use the skills you learned in this book to design a home page for a travel agency
- Outline the features for a virtual community site that would lead to travel sales
- Choose Web sites that would be good locations on which to place advertising for the travel agency

Reintermediating Travel Services

Ella Cruz has owned and operated the Midtown Travel Agency (MTA) for many years, offering personalized service that keeps her clients coming back year after year. MTA does not have a Web site because Ella feels it is impersonal compared with her practice of staying in touch with clients by phone, fax, or by visiting their homes or offices.

Ella is worried because the travel agency business is facing many challenges these days. At one time, most of MTA's revenues came from commissions on airline tickets. But airlines have reduced or even eliminated commissions to travel agents. Many travel agents (including online travel sites) now charge their customers a flat fee for booking flights; however, many of those customers object to paying such fees. Ella still earns good commissions on cruise ship bookings and hotel reservations because cruise lines and hotels still believe that travel agents are important outlets, but she worries that these commissions might eventually be eliminated. Disintermediation has affected all travel agents, but small travel agencies, such as MTA, that do not have Web sites have been hurt the most.

One way to address MTA's problems would be to explore reintermediation opportunities. Ella is an avid surfer and often books surf vacations for her clients. Her personal experiences surfing in exotic locales has given her extensive knowledge about the best places to surf at various times of the year. One reintermediation strategy for MTA would be creating a Web site that serves as an online meeting area for surf enthusiasts and that also sells surf vacation packages. The stereotypical surfer of the past was a young, unemployed male. Surfers today come from a broader demographic. Many surfers have significant financial resources and enjoy surfing in many worldwide locations. Web sites such as WaveHunters.com and WannaSurf.com have followed a reintermediation strategy and cater to this highly specialized market in ways that general travel agents have not.

Starting Data Files

There are no starting Data Files needed for this assignment.

In this assignment, you will examine surfing Web sites, help Ella plan a Web site for MTA, consider ways to build a virtual community that will draw surfers to MTA's Web site, and identify Web sites that MTA should consider using in its online advertising campaigns.

1. Use your favorite search engine or Web directory to find at least two sites that offer surf vacation packages for sale, such as WaveHunters.com and WannaSurf.com. For each of the two sites you find, list at least four Web site elements that you believe MTA could use on its Web site. Also list at least two Web site elements that MTA should avoid using. For each item on your lists, write a paragraph explaining why you classified it the way you did.

2. Use a sketch to design a home page for MTA that includes the four elements you chose to include in Step 1. After completing your sketch, write a summary of each element that you plan to use and describe the technologies that you need to implement them.

3. In approximately 200 words, describe the specific elements you would include in a virtual community to attract people who are interested in exotic surf vacations to MTA's Web site. Explain how each element would contribute to MTA's goal of reaching people who are likely to buy travel services.

4. Use your favorite search engine or Web directory to find surfing interest Web sites on which MTA could buy advertising space. Choose three specific sites, including at least one online magazine, that you believe are good choices for MTA. For each site you select, explain your rationale for choosing that site.

Appendix A

The Internet and the World Wide Web

History, Structure, and Technologies

The Internet and the World Wide Web: Amazing Developments

The Internet—a large collection of computers all over the world that are connected to one another in various ways—is one of the most amazing technological developments of the 20th century. Using the Internet you can communicate with other people around the world through electronic mail (or email) or instant messaging software; read online versions of newspapers, magazines, academic journals, and books; join discussions on almost any conceivable topic; participate in games and simulations; listen to music or watch videos; and obtain computer software. In recent years, the Internet has allowed companies to connect with customers and each other. Today, all kinds of businesses provide information about their products and services on the Internet. Many of these businesses use the Internet to market and sell their products and services. The part of the Internet known as the World Wide Web (or the Web), is a subset of the computers on the Internet that are connected to each other in a specific way that makes those computers and their contents easily accessible to all computers in that subset. The Web has made Internet resources available to people who are not computer experts. This Appendix explains what the Internet and the Web are, how they came to be, and includes some information about how they work.

Starting Data Files

There are no starting Data Files needed for this appendix.

Uses for the Internet

The Internet and the Web give people around the world a convenient and instantaneous way to communicate with each other, obtain information, conduct business transactions, and find entertainment.

New Ways to Communicate

In the 1970s, email and other messaging systems were developed within large companies and government organizations. These systems let people within an organization send messages to other people in that organization. Very few organizations allowed their computers to be connected to the computers in other organizations, and companies used many different messaging systems, most of which were not compatible with each other.

The Internet provided a common set of rules for email interchange and allowed persons in different organizations (and even persons who were not in any organization at all) to send messages to each other, regardless of the messaging system each person was using. In addition to email, the Web offers other ways to communicate. Electronic discussions are hosted on many Web sites, and many people use instant messaging software to chat with each other over the Internet.

Information Resources

The amount of information that is available online today is staggering. Millions of Web sites, which are collections of HTML documents stored on computers that are connected to the Internet, offer an amazing variety of useful information on almost any imaginable topic. Online versions of newspapers, magazines, government documents, research reports, and books offer a wealth of information greater than the holdings of any library.

Some sites are like encyclopedias; they offer a wide range of information on many different topics. Other Web sites specialize in specific types of information. For example, you can find Web sites that offer DVD player reviews, recipes for Mexican food, or instructions for growing houseplants. Many of the first resources to appear on the Internet were collections of computer software. This is not surprising, because many of the earliest users of the Internet were computer enthusiasts.

Doing Business Online

The Web has made buying and selling products and services easier for companies and their customers. The first major business activity conducted on the Internet was done by large companies who started using the Internet in the mid-1990s to handle the paperwork on purchases and sales of industrial goods. Soon thereafter, individual consumers began buying items such as books, music CDs, and clothing on the Web. Today, billions of dollars in business and consumer transactions occur each year on the Web. Some companies exist only on the Web. Other companies maintain a Web site to supplement sales in their physical stores.

In addition to buying and selling activities, companies use the Internet to coordinate their operations throughout the world, managing supplies, inventories, and factory production operations from thousands of miles away. An increasing number of companies use the Web to recruit employees and find other companies that are potential partners in opening new markets or finding new sources of supplies.

Entertainment

Many Web sites offer reviews of restaurants, movies, theater, musical events, and books. You can download music or play interactive games with people around the world using the Internet.

The Web provides a good way to follow your favorite sports teams, too. All of the major sports organizations have Web sites with current information about the teams in their leagues. In fact, the Web gives you a way to follow sports teams around the world in a variety of languages. The Web has also promoted the growth of fantasy sports gaming by making it easier to collect the statistical results of player performance in real sporting contests and facilitating communication between fantasy gamers as they play their games online.

Computer Networks

As you know, computers that are connected to each other form a network. Each computer on a network has a network interface card installed inside it. A **network interface card** (often called a **NIC** or simply a network card) is a circuit board card or other device used to connect a computer to a network of other computers. Many newer personal computers have a network interface device built into them, so that it is not necessary to add a separate NIC to make the computer networkable. These cards are connected to cables that are, in turn, connected to the company's main computer, called a server. A **server** is a general term for any computer that accepts requests from other computers that are connected to it and shares some or all of its resources, such as printers, files, or programs, with those computers.

Client/Server Local Area Networks

The server runs software that coordinates the information flow among the other computers in the network, which are called **clients**. The software that runs on the server computer is called a **network operating system**. Connecting computers this way, in which one server computer shares its resources with multiple client computers, is called a **client/server network**. Client/server networks commonly are used to connect LANs (the local area networks you learned about in Tutorial 1). Figure A-1 shows a typical client/server LAN.

Client/server LAN ◄ **Figure A-1**

Each computer, printer, or other device attached to a network is called a **node** or **network node**. The server can be a powerful personal computer (PC) or a larger, more expensive computer. Most of these larger computers are called "servers" to distinguish them from desktop or notebook computers. Companies that need large amounts of computing power often connect hundreds or even thousands of large PCs together to act as servers.

Like any personal computer, servers have operating systems; however, they also can run network operating systems software. Although network operating systems software can be more expensive than the operating system software for a standalone computer, having computers connected in a client/server network can provide cost savings. For example, by connecting each client computer to the server, all of the computers can share the server-installed network printer and tape drive for backups.

Most personal computer operating systems, including current versions of Microsoft Windows and Macintosh operating systems, have built-in networking capabilities. Also, some personal computer operating systems that can serve as network operating systems, such as Linux, are available on the Internet and can be downloaded and used at no cost.

Connecting Computers to a Network

Not all LANs use the same kind of cables to connect their computers. The oldest cable type is called **twisted-pair cable**, which telephone companies have used for years to wire residences and businesses. Twisted-pair cable has two or more insulated copper wires that are twisted around each other and enclosed in another layer of plastic insulation. A wire that carries an electric current generates an electromagnetic field around itself. This electromagnetic field can induce a small flow of electricity in nearby objects, including other wires. This induced flow of unwanted electricity is called **electrical interference**. In twisted-pair wiring, the wires are twisted because wrapping the two wires around each other reduces the amount of electrical interference that each wire in the pair might pick up from other nearby current-carrying wires. The type of twisted-pair cable that telephone companies have used for years to transmit voice signals is called **Category 1 cable**. Category 1 cable transmits information more slowly than the other cable types, but it is also much less expensive.

Coaxial cable is an insulated copper wire encased in a metal shield that is enclosed with plastic insulation. The signal-carrying wire is completely surrounded by the metal shield, so it resists electrical interference much better than twisted-pair cable. Coaxial cable also carries signals about 20 times faster than Category 1 twisted-pair; however, it is considerably more expensive. Because coaxial cable is thicker and less flexible than twisted-pair, it is harder for installation workers to handle and thus is more expensive to install. You probably have seen coaxial cable because it is used for most cable television connections. You might hear this type of cable called "coax" (koh-axe) by network technicians.

In the past 20 years, cable manufacturers have developed better versions of twisted-pair cable. The current standards for twisted-pair cable used in computer networks are Category 5, Category 5e, and Category 6 cable. **Category 5 cable** carries signals between 10 and 100 times faster than coaxial cable and is just as easy to install as Category 1 cable. **Category 5e cable** (the "e" stands for "enhanced") and **Category 6 cable** are two newer versions of twisted-pair cable that look exactly like regular Category 5 cable, but are constructed of higher quality materials so they can carry more signals even faster—up to 10 times faster. Many businesses and schools have Category 5 cable installed, but they are replacing it with Category 5e or Category 6 cable as they upgrade their network hardware to handle the highest LAN speeds available today. You might hear these cable types called "Cat-5" or "Cat-6" cable by network technicians.

The most expensive cable type is fiber-optic cable, which does not use an electrical signal at all. **Fiber-optic cable** (also called simply "fiber") transmits information by using lasers to pulse beams of light through very thin strands of glass. Fiber-optic cable transmits signals much faster than either coaxial cable or any category of twisted-pair cable. Because it does not use electricity, fiber-optic cable is completely immune to electrical interference. Fiber-optic cable is lighter and more durable than coaxial cable, but it is harder to work with and more expensive than either coaxial cable or Category 5 twisted-pair cable. The price of fiber-optic cable and the laser sending and receiving equipment needed at each end of the cable has dropped dramatically in recent years. Thus, companies are using fiber-optic cable in more and more networks as the cost becomes more affordable; however, its main use today remains connecting networks to each other rather than as part of the networks themselves. Figure A-2 shows these three types of cable.

Twisted-pair, coaxial, and fiber-optic cables   **Figure A-2**

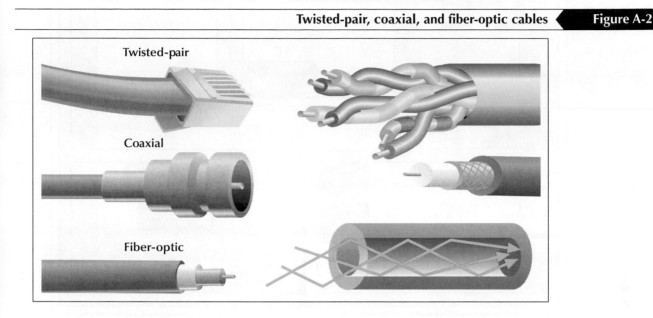

Twisted-pair

Coaxial

Fiber-optic

Perhaps the most liberating way to connect computers in a LAN is to avoid cable completely. **Wireless networks** are becoming more common as the cost of the wireless transmitters and receivers that plug into or replace network cards continues to drop. Wireless LANs are especially welcome in organizations that occupy old buildings. Many cities have structures that were built before electricity and telephones were widely available. These buildings have no provision for running wires through walls or between floors, so a wireless network can be the best option for connecting resources.

Wireless connections are also popular with companies whose employees use laptop computers and take them from meeting to meeting. A wireless network can help workers be more effective and productive in flexible team environments. Many schools have added wireless access points to their networks so that students can use their wireless-equipped laptop computers in classrooms, in libraries, and in study lounges. Some schools have even placed network access points on the outside edges of their buildings so that students can use their computers in patios and other outdoor areas, such as parking lots. The cost of wireless networks is dropping, and many people have installed them in their homes. Figure A-3 shows the physical layout of a small wireless network that might be useful in a small office or a home. The wireless network includes two desktop PCs, two laptop PCs, a shared printer, and no connecting network cables.

Figure A-3 ▶ A small wireless network

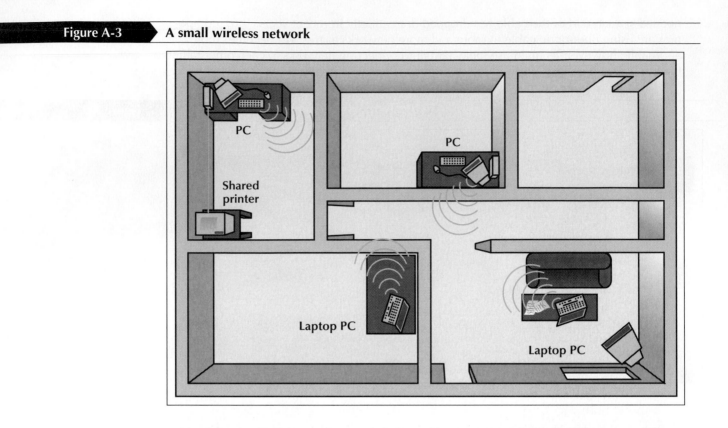

All of these connection types—twisted-pair, Category 1, coaxial, Category 5, Category 5e, Category 6, fiber-optic, and wireless—are options for creating LANs. These LANs can, in turn, be connected to the Internet or to other, larger networks, such as those discussed in the next section.

Origins of the Internet

In the early 1960s, the U.S. Department of Defense undertook a major research project. Because this was a military project and was authorized as a part of national security, the true motivations are not known with certainty, but most people close to the project believe it arose from the government's concerns about the possible effects of nuclear attack on military computing facilities. The Department of Defense realized that the weapons of the future would require powerful computers for coordination and control. The powerful computers of that time were all large mainframe computers, so the Department of Defense began examining ways to connect these computers to each other and to weapons installations that were distributed all over the world.

The agency charged with this task was the **Advanced Research Projects Agency (ARPA)**. During its lifetime, this agency has used two acronyms, ARPA and DARPA; this book uses its current acronym, **DARPA**, for **Defense Advanced Research Projects Agency**. DARPA hired many of the best communications technology researchers and for many years funded research at leading universities and institutes to explore the task of creating a worldwide network of computers. A photo of these dedicated computer networking pioneers appears in Figure A-4.

ARPANET scientists | **Figure A-4**

©1969, BBN Technologies

Courtesy of BBN Technologies

DARPA researchers soon became concerned about computer networks' vulnerability to attack, because networks at that time relied on a single, central control function. If the network's central control point were damaged or attacked, the network would be unusable. Consequently, they worked hard to devise ways to eliminate the need for network communications to rely on a central control function.

Connectivity: Circuit Switching vs. Packet Switching

One of the first networking-related topics to be researched by the DARPA scientists was connectivity, or methods of sending messages over networks. The first computer networks were created in the 1950s. The models for those early networks were the telephone companies, because most early wide area networks (WANs) used leased telephone company lines to connect computers to each other. In telephone company systems of that time, a telephone call established a single connection between sender and receiver. Once the connection was established, all data then traveled along that single path. The telephone company's central switching system selected specific telephone lines, or circuits, that would be connected to create the single path. This centrally controlled, single-connection method is called **circuit switching**. Most local telephone traffic today is still handled using circuit-switching technologies.

Although circuit switching is efficient and economical, it relies on a central point of control and a series of connections that form a single path. This makes circuit-switched communications vulnerable to the destruction of the central control point or any link in the series of connections that make up the single path that carries the signal.

Packet switching is an alternative means for sending messages. In a packet-switching network, files and messages are broken down into packets that are labeled electronically with codes for their origin and destination. The packets travel from computer to computer along the network until they reach their destination. The destination computer collects the packets and reassembles the original data from the pieces in each packet. Each computer that an individual packet encounters on its trip through the network determines the best way to move the packet forward to its destination. Computers and other devices that perform this function on networks are often called routing computers, or **routers**, and the programs they use to determine the best path for packets are called **routing algorithms**. Thus, packet-switched networks are inherently more reliable than circuit-switched networks because they rely on multiple routers instead of a central point of control and because each router can send individual packets along different paths if parts of the network are not operating.

By 1967, DARPA researchers had published their plan for a packet-switching network, and in 1969, they connected the first computer switches at four locations: the University of California at Los Angeles, SRI International, the University of California at Santa Barbara, and the University of Utah. This experimental WAN was called the **ARPANET**. Figure A-5 shows a famous hand-drawn sketch of the Internet as it existed in 1969.

Figure A-5 ▶ **The Internet's humble beginning as the ARPANET, 1969**

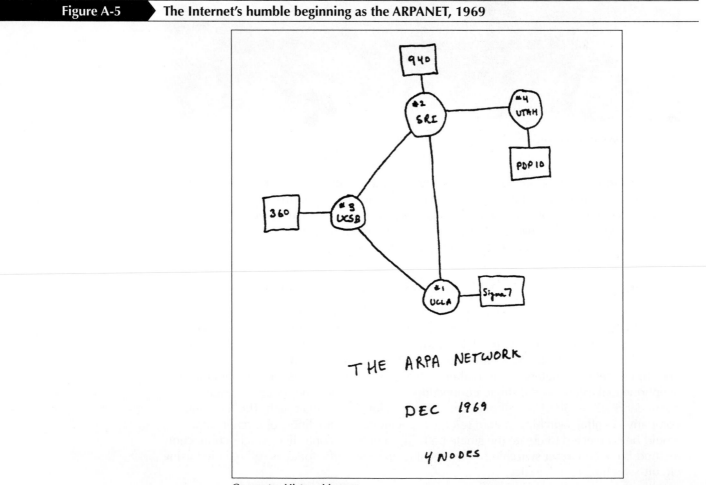

Computer History Museum

The ARPANET grew over the next three years to include more than 20 computers. The ARPANET used the **Network Control Protocol (NCP)** to enable each of those computers to communicate with other computers on the network. A **protocol** is a collection of rules for formatting, ordering, and error-checking data sent across a network.

Open Architecture Philosophy

As more researchers connected their computers and computer networks to the ARPANET, interest in the network grew in the academic community. One reason for increased interest in the project was its adherence to an **open architecture** philosophy; that is, each network could continue using its own protocols and data-transmission methods internally. The open architecture philosophy includes four key points:

- Independent networks should not require any internal changes to be connected to the Internet.
- Packets that do not arrive at their destinations must be retransmitted from their source network.
- Router computers do not retain information about the packets they handle.
- No global control will exist over the network.

This open architecture philosophy was revolutionary at the time. Most companies that built computer networking products at that time, including IBM and Digital Equipment Corporation, put considerable effort into making their networks incompatible with other networks. These manufacturers believed that they could lock out competitors by not making their products easy to connect with products made by other companies. The shift to an open architecture approach is what made the Internet of today possible.

In the early 1970s, Vinton Cerf and Robert Kahn developed a set of protocols that implemented the open architecture philosophy better than the NCP. These new protocols were the **Transmission Control Protocol** and the **Internet Protocol**, which usually are referred to by their combined acronym, **TCP/IP**. TCP includes rules that computers on a network use to establish and break connections; IP includes rules for routing of individual data packets. TCP/IP continues to be used today in LANs and on the Internet. The term "Internet" was first used in a 1974 article about the TCP protocol written by Cerf and Kahn. The importance of the TCP/IP protocol in the history of the Internet is so great that many people consider Vinton Cerf to be the father of the Internet.

A number of TCP/IP-based networks—independent of the ARPANET—were created in the late 1970s and early 1980s. The National Science Foundation (NSF) funded the **Computer Science Network (CSNET)** for educational and research institutions that did not have access to the ARPANET. The City University of New York started a network of IBM mainframes at universities, called the **Because It's Time** (originally, "Because It's There") **Network (BITNET)**.

Birth of Email: A New Use for Networks

Although the goals of ARPANET were still to control weapons systems and transfer research files, other uses for this vast network began to appear in the early 1970s. In 1972, an ARPANET researcher named Ray Tomlinson wrote a program that could send and receive messages over the network. Email had been born and rapidly became widely used in the computer research community. In 1976, the Queen of England sent an email message over the ARPANET. The ARPANET continued to develop faster and more effective network technologies; for example, ARPANET began sending packets by satellite in 1976.

More New Uses for Networks Emerge

By 1981, the ARPANET had expanded to include more than 200 networks. The number of individuals in the military and education research communities that used the network continued to grow. Many of these new participants used the networking technology to transfer files and access computers remotely. The TCP/IP suite included two tools for performing these tasks, which you learned about in Tutorial 1. File Transfer Protocol (FTP) enabled users to transfer files between computers, and Telnet let users log in to their computer accounts from remote sites. Both FTP and Telnet still are widely used on the Internet today for file transfers and remote logins, even though more advanced techniques facilitate multimedia transmissions such as real-time audio and video clips. The first email mailing lists also appeared on these networks. A **mailing list** is an email address that takes any message it receives and forwards it to any user who has subscribed to the list.

Although file transfer and remote login were attractive features of these new TCP/IP networks, their improved email and other communications facilities attracted many users in the education and research communities. Mailing lists (such as BITNET's **LISTSERV**), information posting areas (such as the **User's News Network**, or **Usenet**, **newsgroups**), and adventure games were among the new applications appearing on the ARPANET.

Although the people using these networks were developing many creative applications, relatively few people had access to the networks. Most of these people were members of the research and academic communities. From 1979 to 1989, these new and interesting network applications were improved and tested with an increasing number of users. TCP/IP became more widely used as academic and research institutions realized the benefits of having a common communications network. The explosion of PC use during that time also helped more people become comfortable with computing.

Interconnecting the Networks

The early 1980s saw continued growth in the ARPANET and other networks. The **Joint Academic Network (Janet)** was established in the United Kingdom to link universities there. Traffic increased on all of these networks, and in 1984, the Department of Defense split the ARPANET into two specialized networks: ARPANET would continue its advanced research activities, and **MILNET** (for **Military Network**) would be reserved for military uses that required greater security.

By 1987, congestion on the ARPANET caused by a rapidly increasing number of users on the limited-capacity leased telephone lines was becoming severe. To reduce the traffic load on the ARPANET, a network run by the National Science Foundation, called NSFnet, merged with another NSF network, called CSNet, and with BITNET to form one network that could carry much of the network traffic that had been carried by the ARPANET. The resulting NSFnet awarded a contract to Merit Network, Inc., IBM, Sprint, and the state of Michigan to upgrade and operate the main NSFnet backbone. A **network backbone** includes the long-distance lines and supporting technology that transport large amounts of data between major network nodes. By the late 1980s, many other TCP/IP networks had merged or established interconnections. Figure A-6 summarizes how the individual networks described in this section combined to become the Internet as it is known today.

Networks that became the Internet ◄ **Figure A-6**

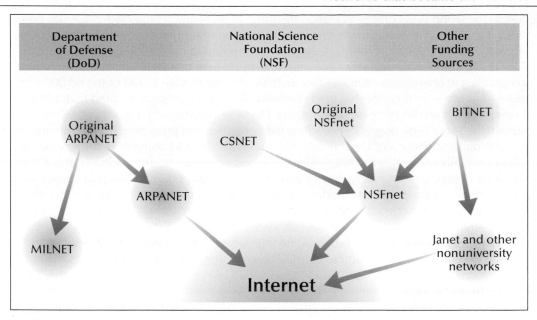

Commercial Interest Increases

As PCs became more powerful, affordable, and readily available during the 1980s, companies increasingly used them to construct LANs. Although these LANs included email software that employees could use to send messages to each other, businesses wanted their employees to be able to communicate with people outside their corporate LANs. The National Science Foundation (NSF) prohibited commercial network traffic on the networks it funded, so businesses turned to commercial email services. Larger firms built their own TCP/IP-based WANs that used leased telephone lines to connect field offices to corporate headquarters. Today, people use the term **intranet** to describe LANs or WANs that use the TCP/IP protocol but do not connect to sites outside a single organization. Although most companies allow only their employees to use the company intranet, some companies give specific outsiders, such as customers, vendors, or business partners, access to their intranets. These outside parties agree to respect the confidentiality of the information on the network. An intranet that allows selected outside parties to connect is often called an **extranet**.

In 1989, the NSF permitted two commercial email services, MCI Mail and CompuServe, to establish limited connections to the Internet that allowed their commercial subscribers to exchange email messages with the members of the academic and research communities who were connected to the Internet. These connections allowed commercial enterprises to send email directly to Internet addresses and allowed members of the research and education communities on the Internet to send email directly to MCI Mail and CompuServe addresses. The NSF justified this limited commercial use of the Internet as a service that would primarily benefit the Internet's noncommercial users.

People from all walks of life—not just scientists or academic researchers—started thinking of these networks as a global resource that we now know as the Internet. Information systems professionals began to form volunteer groups such as the **Internet Engineering Task Force (IETF)**, which first met in 1986. The IETF is a self-organized group that makes technical contributions to the engineering of the Internet and its technologies. IETF is the main body that develops new Internet standards.

Internet Threats

Just as the world was coming to realize the value of these interconnected networks, however, it also became aware of the threats to privacy and computer security posed by these networks. In 1988, Robert Morris, Jr., a graduate student in computer science at Cornell University, launched a program called the **Internet Worm** that used weaknesses in email programs and operating systems to distribute itself to more than 6,000 of the 60,000 computers that were then connected to the Internet. The Worm program created multiple copies of itself on the computers it infected. The large number of program copies consumed the processing power of each infected computer and prevented it from running other programs. This event brought international attention and concern to the Internet. It also eventually brought laws into existence in most countries of the world that make such behavior illegal. Unfortunately, worms and other malicious programs such as viruses still appear regularly on the Internet today; these incidents do considerable damage to individual computers and networks and cost companies millions of dollars in lost productivity.

The Internet is a powerful communications tool for bringing people together over wide distances. Unfortunately, a tool such as the Internet, which can do so much good, can also be used for evil. In addition to causing damage through malicious programs, the Internet makes it easy for criminals and terrorists all over the world to work together more efficiently and effectively.

Although the network of networks that is now known as the Internet had grown from four computers on the ARPANET in 1969 to more than 300,000 computers on many interconnected networks by 1990, the greatest growth in the Internet was yet to come.

Growth of the Internet

A formal definition of Internet, which was adopted in 1995 by the Federal Networking Council (FNC), appears in Figure A-7.

Figure A-7	The FNC's October 1995 resolution to define the term Internet

RESOLUTION: The Federal Networking Council (FNC) agrees that the following language reflects our definition of the term Internet. Internet refers to the global information system that

(i) is logically linked together by a globally unique address space based on the Internet Protocol (IP) or its subsequent extensions/follow-ons;

(ii) is able to support communications using the Transmission Control Protocol/Internet Protocol (TCP/IP) suite or its subsequent extensions/follow-ons, and/or other IP-compatible protocols; and

(iii) provides, uses or makes accessible, either publicly or privately, high level services layered on the communications and related infrastructure described herein.

Source: http://www.nitrd.gov/fnc/Internet_res.html

The researchers who had been so involved in the creation and growth of the Internet accepted it as part of their working environment, but people outside the research community were largely unaware of the potential offered by a large interconnected set of computer networks until the 1990s.

From Research Project to Information Infrastructure

Realizing that the Internet was becoming much more than a scientific research project, the U.S. Department of Defense finally closed the research portion of its network, the ARPANET, in 1995. The NSF also wanted to turn over the Internet to others so it could return its attention and funds to other research projects.

The process of shutting down the ARPANET and privatizing the Internet began in 1991, when the NSF eased its restrictions on Internet commercial activity. Businesses and individuals continued to connect to the Internet in ever-increasing numbers. Although nobody really knows how big the Internet is, one commonly used measure is the number of Internet hosts. An **Internet host** is a computer that connects a LAN or a WAN to the Internet. Each Internet host might have any number of computers connected to it. Figure A-8 shows the rapid growth in the number of Internet host computers. As you can see, the growth has been dramatic.

Growth in the number of Internet hosts ◀ **Figure A-8**

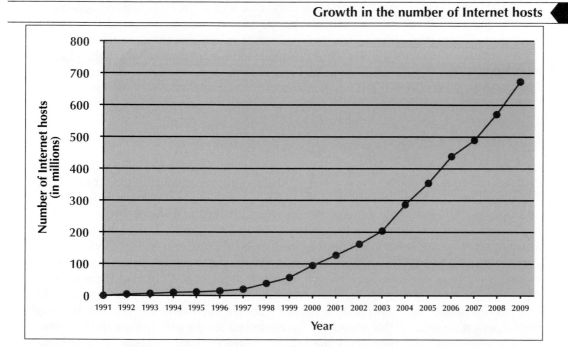

Source: Adapted from Internet Systems Consortium (https://www.isc.org/) and other sources

The numbers in the figure probably understate the true growth of the Internet in recent years for two reasons. First, the number of hosts connected to the Internet includes only those computers that are directly connected to the Internet. In other words, if a LAN with 100 PCs is connected to the Internet through only one host computer, those 100 computers appear as one host in the count. Because the number and size of LANs have increased in recent years, the host count probably understates the growth in the number of all computers that have access to the Internet. Millions of mobile phones have features that allow them to access the Internet. These are connected through a relatively small number of Internet hosts at their wireless service providers, which also understates the number of devices connected to the Internet. Second, the number of computers is only one measure of growth. Internet traffic now carries more files that contain graphics, sound, and video, so Internet files have become larger. A given number of users sending video clips will use much more of the Internet's capacity than the same number of users will use by sending email messages or text files.

The Internet has no central management or coordination, and the routing computers do not retain copies of the packets they handle. Some companies and research organizations estimate the number of regular users of the Internet today to be more than a billion, but no one knows how many individual email messages or files travel on the Internet, and no one really knows how many people use the Internet today.

New Structure for the Internet

As NSFnet converted the main traffic-carrying backbone portion of its network to private firms, it organized the network around four **network access points (NAPs)**, which were operated by four different telecommunications companies. These four companies and their successors sell access to the Internet through their NAPs to organizations and businesses. The NSFnet still exists for government and research use, but it uses these same NAPs for long-range data transmission.

With nearly 700 million connected Internet host computers and more than a billion worldwide Internet users, the Internet faces some challenges. The firms that sell network access continue to invest in the network architecture because they can recoup their investments by selling improved services to existing customers and also attract new Internet users. So the infrastructure of the Internet should continue to be expanded; however, the TCP/IP numbering system that identifies computers and other devices connected to the Internet is running short of numbers. This numbering system is discussed in the next section.

IP Addressing

Each computer on the Internet has a unique identification number, called an **IP (Internet Protocol) address**. IP addressing is a way of identifying each unique computer on the Web, just like your home address is a way of identifying your home in a city. The IP addressing system currently in use on the Internet is **IP version 4 (IPv4)**. IPv4 uses a 32-bit number to label each address on the Internet. The 32-bit IP address is usually written in four 8-bit parts. In most computer applications, an 8-bit number is called a **byte**; however, in networking applications, an 8-bit number is often called an **octet**. In the binary (base 2) numbering system, an octet can have values from 00000000 to 11111111; the decimal equivalents of these binary numbers are 0 and 255, respectively. Each part of a 32-bit IP address is separated from the previous part by a period, such as 106.29.242.17. You might hear a person pronounce this address as "one hundred six dot twenty-nine dot two four two dot seventeen." This notation is often called **dotted decimal notation**. The combination of these four parts provides 4.2 billion possible addresses (256 × 256 × 256 × 256). Because each of the four parts of a dotted decimal number can range from 0 to 255, IP addresses range from 0.0.0.0 (which would be written in binary as 32 zeros) to 255.255.255.255 (which would be written in binary as 32 ones). Although many people find dotted decimal notation to be somewhat confusing at first, most do agree that writing, reading, and remembering a computer address as 216.115.108.245 is easier than 11011000011100110110110011110101 or its full decimal equivalent, which is 3,631,443,189.

In the mid-1990s, the accelerating growth of the Internet created concern that the world could run out of IP addresses within a few years. In the early days of the Internet, the 4 billion addresses provided by the IPv4 rules certainly seemed to be more addresses than an experimental research network would ever need. However, about 2 billion of those addresses today are either in use or unavailable for use because of the way blocks of addresses were assigned to organizations. New kinds of devices that can access the Internet's many networks, such as wireless personal digital assistants and mobile phones, keep the demand for IP addresses high.

Network engineers have devised a number of stop-gap techniques, such as **subnetting**, which is the use of reserved private IP addresses within LANs and WANs to provide additional address space. **Private IP addresses** are series of IP numbers that have been set aside for subnet use and are not permitted on packets that travel on the Internet. In subnetting, a computer called a **network address translation (NAT) device** converts those private IP addresses into normal IP addresses when the packets move from the LAN or WAN onto the Internet.

The IETF worked on several new protocols that could solve the limited addressing capacity of IPv4 and, in 1997, approved **IP version 6 (IPv6)** as the protocol that would replace IPv4. The new IP version is being implemented gradually over a 20-year period because the two protocols are not directly compatible. However, network engineers have devised ways to run both protocols together on interconnected networks. The major advantage of IPv6 is that the number of addresses is more than a billion times larger than the four billion addresses available in IPv4. IPv6 also changes the format of the packet itself.

Improvements in networking technologies over the past 20 years have made many of the fields in the IPv4 packet unnecessary. IPv6 eliminates those fields and adds new fields for security and other optional information.

In just over 30 years, the Internet has become one of the most impressive technological and social accomplishments of the century. Millions of people use a complex, interconnected network of computers that run thousands of different software packages. The computers are located in almost every country in the world. Billions of dollars change hands every year over the Internet in exchange for all kinds of products and services. All of the Internet's activity occurs with no central coordination point or control. Even more interesting is that the Internet began as a way for the military to maintain control while under attack.

The opening of the Internet to business enterprise helped increase its growth dramatically; however, another development worked hand in hand with the commercialization of the Internet to spur its growth. That development was the technological advance known as the World Wide Web.

World Wide Web

The World Wide Web (Web) is more a way of thinking about information storage and retrieval than it is a technology. Many people use "the Web" and "the Internet" terms interchangeably, but they are not the same thing. As you will learn in this section, the Web is software that runs on many of the computers that are connected to each other through the Internet. Two important innovations played key roles in making the Internet easier to use and more accessible to people who were not research scientists: hypertext and graphical user interfaces (GUIs).

Origins of Hypertext

In 1945, Vannevar Bush, who was director of the U.S. Office of Scientific Research and Development, wrote an *Atlantic Monthly* article about ways that scientists could apply to peacetime activities the skills they learned during World War II. The article included a number of visionary ideas about future uses of technology to organize and facilitate efficient access to information. Bush speculated that engineers eventually would build a machine that he called the **Memex**, a memory extension device that would store all of a person's books, records, letters, and research results on microfilm. Bush's Memex would include mechanical aids to help users consult their collected knowledge fast and in a wide variety of ways. In the 1960s, Ted Nelson described a similar system in which text on one page links to text on other pages. Nelson called his page-linking system **hypertext**. Douglas Engelbart, who also invented the computer mouse, created the first experimental hypertext system on one of the large computers of the 1960s. In 1976, Nelson published a book, *Dream Machines,* in which he outlined project Xanadu, a global system for online hypertext publishing and commerce. Figure A-9 includes photos of Bush, Nelson, and Engelbart, three forward-looking thinkers whose ideas laid the foundation for the Web.

Figure A-9 ▶ **Left to right: Vannevar Bush, Ted Nelson, and Douglas Engelbart**

MIT Museum   *Courtesy of Ted Nelson/Project Xanadu*   *Courtesy of the Bootstrap Institute*

Hypertext and the World Wide Web Come to the Internet

In 1989, Tim Berners-Lee and Robert Calliau were working at CERN—the European Laboratory for Particle Physics. (The acronym, CERN, comes from the French name of the laboratory, the *Conseil Européen pour la Recherche Nucléaire*.) Berners-Lee and Calliau were trying to improve the laboratory's research document-handling procedures. CERN had been using the Internet for two years to circulate its scientific papers and data among the high-energy physics research community throughout the world; however, the Internet did not help the agency display the complex graphics that were important parts of its theoretical models. Independently, Berners-Lee and Calliau each proposed a hypertext development project to improve CERN's document-handling capabilities.

Over the next two years, Berners-Lee developed the code for a hypertext server program and made it available on the Internet. A **hypertext server** is a computer that stores files written in the hypertext markup language and lets other computers connect to it and read the files. Berners-Lee, who was familiar with **Standard Generalized Markup Language (SGML)**, a set of rules that organizations have used for many years to manage large document-filing systems, began developing a subset of SGML that he called Hypertext Markup Language (HTML). HTML, like all markup languages, includes a set of codes (or tags) attached to text. These codes describe the relationships among text elements. For example, HTML includes tags that indicate which text is part of a header element, which text is part of a paragraph element, and which text is part of a numbered list element. One important type of tag is the hypertext link tag. A hypertext link, or hyperlink, points to another location in the same or another HTML document. HTML documents can also include links to other types of files, such as word-processing documents, spreadsheets, graphics, audio clips, and video clips.

An HTML document differs from a word-processing document because it does not specify *how* a particular text element will appear. For example, you might use word-processing software to create a document heading by setting the heading text font to Arial, its font size to 14 points, and its position to centered. The document displays and prints these exact settings whenever you open the document in the word processor. In contrast, an HTML document surrounds the text with a pair of **heading tags** to indicate that the text should be considered a heading. Many programs can read HTML documents. The programs recognize the heading tags and display the text in whatever manner that program normally displays headings. Different programs might display the heading text differently.

Like the Internet itself, standards for HTML are not controlled by any central managing organization. Standards for technologies that are used on the Web (including HTML) are developed and promulgated by the World Wide Web Consortium (W3C), an international organization formed in 1994 and sponsored by universities and businesses from around the world. Berners-Lee was appointed director of the W3C when it was formed and continues in that position today.

Web Browsers and Graphical User Interfaces

Several different types of software can read HTML documents, but most people use a Web browser such as Mozilla Firefox or Microsoft Internet Explorer to read HTML documents that are part of the Web. A Web browser is software that lets users read (or browse) HTML documents and move from one HTML document to another through the text formatted with hypertext link tags in each file. If the HTML documents are on computers connected to the Internet, you can use a Web browser to move from an HTML document on one computer to an HTML document on any other computer on the Internet.

The first Web browsers were text-based and lacked the graphical elements, such as buttons, that make today's browsers so easy to use. Figure A-10 shows a Web page displayed in Lynx, a text-based browser that was commonly used in the early days of the Web. As you can see, it does not look very much like the Web pages we are all used to seeing in Web browsers today.

Web page rendered in a text-based browser ◄ Figure A-10

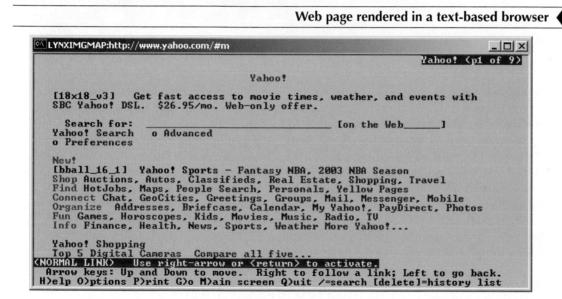

In 1993, a group of students led by Marc Andreessen at the University of Illinois wrote Mosaic, the first GUI program that could read HTML and use HTML documents' hyperlinks to navigate from page to page on computers anywhere on the Internet. Mosaic was the first Web browser that became widely available for PCs. Figure A-11 shows a 1993 Web page displayed in an early version of the Mosaic Web browser.

Figure A-11 ▶ **Mosaic, the first widely available Web browser**

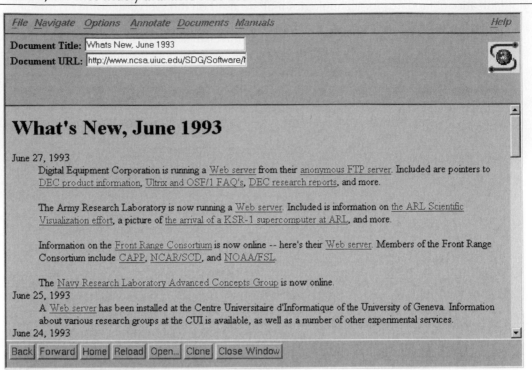

Source: http://www.dejavu.org/emulator.htm

A Web browser presents an HTML document in an easy-to-read format in its graphical user interface. A **graphical user interface** (**GUI**, pronounced "gooey") is a way of presenting program output using pictures, icons, and other graphical elements instead of just displaying text. Almost all PCs today use a GUI such as Microsoft Windows or the Macintosh user interface. Researchers have found that computer users—especially new users—learn new programs more quickly when they have a GUI interface instead of a text interface. Because each Web page has its own set of controls (hyperlinks, buttons to click, and blank text boxes in which to type text), every person who visits a Web site for the first time becomes a "new user" of that site. Thus, the GUI presented in Web browsers has been an important element in the rapid growth of the Web.

Commercialization of the Web and the Internet

Programmers realized that a functional system of pages connected by hyperlinks would provide new Internet users with an easy way to locate information on the Internet. Businesses recognized the profit-making potential of a worldwide network of easy-to-use computers. In 1994, Andreessen and other members of the University of Illinois Mosaic team joined with James Clark of Silicon Graphics to found Netscape Communications. The university was not happy when the team decided to leave the school and develop a commercial product. The university refused to allow the team to use the name "Mosaic." Netscape's first browser was called the "Mosaic Killer" or "Mozilla." Soon after its release, the product was renamed Netscape Navigator. The program was an instant success. Netscape became one of the fastest growing software companies ever.

Microsoft created its Internet Explorer Web browser and entered the market soon after Netscape's success. Microsoft offered its browser at no cost to computer owners using its Windows operating system. Within a few years, most users had switched to Internet Explorer. Netscape was unable to earn enough money to stay in business. Microsoft was accused of wielding its monopoly power to drive Netscape out of business; these accusations led to the trial of Microsoft on charges that it violated U.S. antitrust laws. The charges were settled in a consent decree, but other violations by Microsoft led to a second trial in which the company was found guilty. Parts of Netscape were sold to America Online, but the browser became open-source software. **Open-source software** is created and maintained by volunteer programmers, often hundreds of them, who work together using the Internet to build and refine a program. The program is made available to users at no charge. The open-source release of this browser is called Mozilla, which recalls the name of the original Netscape product. In an interesting turn of Web history, the Netscape Navigator browser available today is based on the Mozilla open-source software.

The proliferation of tools to make the Internet more usable led to an explosion in the amount of information stored online. The number of Web sites has grown more rapidly than the Internet itself. Figure A-12 shows the growth in the Web during its lifetime.

Growth of the World Wide Web ◄ **Figure A-12**

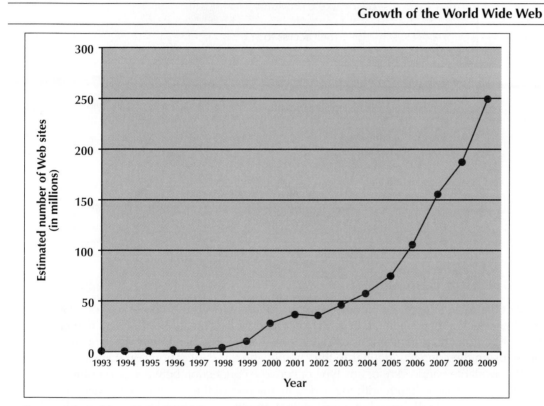

Source: Adapted from Netcraft Web Survey (http://www.netcraft.com/survey/Reports)

After a dip between 2001 and 2002, growth in the number of Web sites resumed at its rapid rate. As individual Web sites become larger, they include many more pages. Experts agree that the number of pages available on the Web today is greater than 1 trillion, and that number is increasing faster than ever. As more people have access to the Web, commercial uses of the Web and the nonbusiness uses will continue to increase.

Business of Providing Internet Access

The NAPs (network access points) that maintain the core operations and long-haul backbone of the Internet do not offer direct connections to individuals or businesses. They offer connections to large organizations and businesses that, in turn, provide Internet access to other businesses and individuals. These firms are called **Internet access providers (IAPs)** or **Internet service providers (ISPs)**. Most of the firms call themselves

ISPs because they offer more than access to the Internet. ISPs usually provide their customers with software to connect to the ISP, browse the Web, send and receive email messages, and perform functions such as file transfer and remote login to other computers. ISPs often provide network consulting and Web design services to their customers. Some ISPs have developed a range of services that include network management, training, and marketing advice. Large ISPs that sell Internet access and other services to businesses are called **commerce service providers (CSPs)** because they help businesses conduct business activities (or commerce) on the Internet. The larger ISPs sell Internet access to smaller ISPs, which then sell access and services to their own business and individual customers. The hierarchy of Internet service providers appears in Figure A-13.

Figure A-13	Hierarchy of Internet service providers

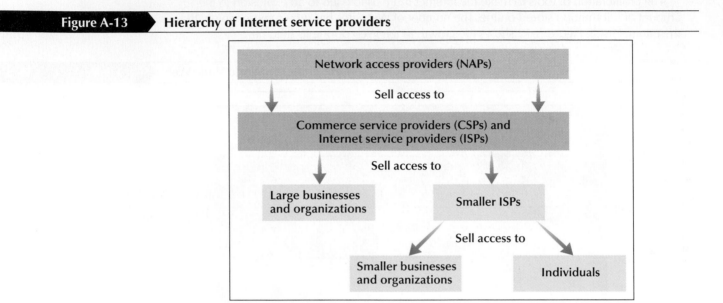

Connection Bandwidth

One of the most important differences among different levels of Internet service providers is the connection bandwidth an ISP can offer. **Bandwidth** is the amount of data that can travel through a communications circuit in one second. The bandwidth an ISP can deliver depends on the connection it has to the Internet and the connection you have to the ISP.

The available bandwidth for any type of network connection between two points is limited to the narrowest bandwidth that exists in any part of the network. For example, if you connect to an ISP through a regular telephone line, your bandwidth is limited to the bandwidth of that telephone line, regardless of the bandwidth connection that the ISP has to the Internet. Bandwidth for Internet connections is measured the same way as bandwidth for connections within networks, in multiples of **bits per second (bps)**. Common terms are **kilobits per second (Kbps)**, which is 1,024 bps; **megabits per second (Mbps)**, which is 1,048,576 bps; and **gigabits per second (Gbps)**, which is 1,073,741,824 bps.

Sometimes computer users are confused by the use of bits to measure bandwidth, because file sizes are measured in bytes. As explained earlier, a byte is eight bits; it is abbreviated with an uppercase "B." A **kilobyte (KB)** is 1,024 bytes, or 8,192 bits. A **megabyte (MB)** is 1,048,576 bytes (or 8,388,608 bits) and a **gigabyte (GB)** is 1,073,741,824 bytes (or 8,589,934,592 bits).

Most LANs today run either Fast Ethernet, which operates at 100 Mbps, or Gigabit Ethernet, which operates at 1 Gbps. Some older LANs use an earlier version of Ethernet that operates at 10 Mbps. The effective bandwidth of wireless LANs depends on the distance between computers and what types of barriers the wireless signals must pass through (for example, wireless signals travel more easily through glass than steel). Most wireless LANs achieve an operating bandwidth of between 2 Mbps and 10 Mbps, although newer wireless devices with more than 100 Mbps are available. Figure A-14 shows examples of typical times required to send different types of files over different types of LANs.

Typical file transmission times for various types of LANs ◀ **Figure A-14**

Type of File	Typical File Size	Wireless (7 Mbps)	Ethernet (10 Mbps)	Fast Ethernet (100 Mbps)	Gigabit Ethernet (1 Gbps)
One-paragraph text message	5 KB	Less than .1 second	Less than .1 second	Less than .1 second	Less than .1 second
Word-processing document, 20 pages	100 KB	.1 second	Less than .1 second	Less than .1 second	Less than .1 second
Web page containing several small graphics	200 KB	.2 second	.2 second	Less than .1 second	Less than .1 second
Presentation file with 20 slides and several large graphics	800 KB	1 second	.7 second	Less than .1 second	Less than .1 second
Color brochure, five pages with several color photos	2 MB	3 seconds	2 seconds	.2 second	Less than .1 second
Compressed music file (MP3 format) containing a four-minute song	5 MB	6 seconds	4 seconds	.4 second	Less than .1 second
Uncompressed music file containing a four-minute song	60 MB	1 minute	50 seconds	5 seconds	.5 second
Compressed video file containing a 10-minute interview	200 MB	4 minutes	4 minutes	17 seconds	2 seconds
Compressed video file containing a feature-length film	4 GB	1.5 hours	1 hour	6 minutes	35 seconds

When you extend your network beyond a local area, either through a WAN or by connecting to the Internet, the speed of the connection depends on the type of connection. One way to connect computers or networks over longer distances is to use regular telephone service (sometimes referred to as **dial-up**, **POTS**, or **plain old telephone service**). Regular telephone service to most U.S. residential and business customers provides a maximum bandwidth of between 28.8 Kbps and 56 Kbps. The rates vary because the United States has different telephone companies that do not all use the same technology. When you connect your computer, which communicates using digital signals, to another computer through a telephone line, which uses analog signals, you must convert the signals from one form to the other. The device that performs this signal conversion is a **modem**, which is short for modulator-demodulator. Converting a digital signal to an analog signal is called **modulation**; converting that analog signal back into digital form is called **demodulation**. A modem performs both functions; it acts as a modulator and demodulator.

Some telephone companies offer a higher grade of service that uses one of a series of protocols called **Digital Subscriber Line (DSL)** or **Digital Subscriber Loop (DSL)**. The first technology that was developed using a DSL protocol is called **Integrated Services Digital Network (ISDN)**. ISDN service has been available in various parts of the United States since 1984. Although considerably more expensive than regular telephone service, ISDN offers bandwidths of up to 256 Kbps. ISDN is much more widely available in Australia, France, Germany, Japan, and Singapore than in the United States because the regulatory structure of the telecommunications industries in those countries encouraged rapid deployment of this new technology.

All technologies based on the DSL protocol require the implementing telephone company to install new equipment at its switching stations, which can be very expensive. New technologies that use the DSL protocol are currently being implemented around the world. One of those, **Asymmetric Digital Subscriber Line (ADSL**, also abbreviated **DSL)**, offers transmission speeds ranging from 16 to 640 Kbps from the user to the telephone company and from 1.5 to 9 Mbps from the telephone company to the user.

Businesses and large organizations often obtain their Internet connection by connecting to an ISP using higher-bandwidth telephone company connections called **T1** (1.544 Mbps) and **T3** (44.736 Mbps) connections. (T1 and T3 were originally acronyms for Telephone 1 and Telephone 3, respectively, but few people use these terms any longer.) Companies with operations in multiple locations sometimes lease T1 and T3 lines from telephone companies to create their own WANs to connect their locations to each other.

T1 and T3 connections are much more expensive than POTS or ISDN connections; however, organizations that must link hundreds or thousands of individual users to WANs or to the Internet require the greater bandwidth of T1 and T3 connections. Smaller firms can save money by renting access to a partial T1 connection from a telephone company. In a partial T1 rental, the connection is shared with other companies.

The NAPs operate the Internet backbone using a variety of connections. In addition to T1 and T3 lines, the NAPs use newer connections with bandwidths of more than 1 Gbps—in some cases exceeding 10 Gbps. These connection options use fiber-optic cables, and are referred to as OC3, OC12, and so forth. **OC** is short for **optical carrier**. NAPs also use high-bandwidth satellite and radio communications links to transfer data over long distances.

A group of research universities and the National Science Foundation (NSF) now operates a network called **Internet2** that has backbone bandwidths greater than 10 Gbps. The Internet2 project continues the tradition of the DARPA scientists by sponsoring research at the frontiers of network technologies.

A connection option available in the United States and some other countries is to connect to the Internet through a cable television company. The cable company transmits data in the same cables used to provide television service. Cable can deliver up to 10 Mbps to a user and can accept up to 768 Kbps from a user. Cable connections usually deliver speeds between 500 Kbps and 3 Mbps, although some cable companies offer guarantees of higher speeds (for higher monthly fees). These speeds far exceed those of existing POTS and ISDN connections and are comparable to speeds provided by the ADSL technologies currently implemented by telephone companies and other companies that rent facilities from the telephone companies.

An option that is particularly appealing to users in remote areas is connecting by satellite. Using a satellite-dish receiver, you can download at a bandwidth of approximately 400 Kbps. In the early days of satellite Internet access, you could not send information to the Internet using a satellite-dish antenna, so you needed to also have an ISP account to send files or email. Today, most satellite ISPs install transmitters on the dish antenna. This allows two-way satellite connections to the Internet.

The actual bandwidth provided by all these Internet connection methods varies from provider to provider and with the amount of traffic on the Internet. During peak operating hours, traffic on the Internet can become congested, resulting in slower data transmission. The bandwidth achieved is limited to the lowest amount of bandwidth available at any point in the network. To picture this, think of water flowing through a set of pipes with varying diameters, or traffic moving through a section of highway with a lane closure. The water (or traffic) slows to the speed it can maintain through the narrowest part of its pathway.

Figure A-15 shows typical file transmission times for various types of Internet connection options. The speeds shown are examples of what a user can expect on average during download operations. Any Internet connection that is faster than POTS is generally called a **broadband** connection.

Of course, faster Internet connections cost significantly more money than slower connections. Figure A-16 summarizes the bandwidths, costs, and typical uses for the most common types of connections currently in use on the Internet. Some companies offer **fixed-point wireless** connections, which use technology similar to wireless LANs. Although fixed-point wireless service is not yet widely available, an increasing number of companies are offering it to both business and residential customers.

Typical file transmission times for various types of Internet connections ◄ Figure A-15

Type of File	Typical File Size	POTS (25 Kbps)	ISDN or Satellite (100 Kbps)	Residential Cable or DSL (300 Kbps)	Business Leased T-1 (1.4 Mbps)
One-paragraph text message	5 KB	2 seconds	.4 second	.2 second	Less than .1 second
Word-processing document, 20 pages	100 KB	33 seconds	8 seconds	3 seconds	Less than .1 second
Web page containing several small graphics	200 KB	1 minute	16 seconds	6 seconds	Less than .1 second
Presentation file with 20 slides and several large graphics	800 KB	4 minutes	1 minute	22 seconds	Less than .1 second
Color brochure, five pages with several color photos	2 MB	11 minutes	3 minutes	1 minute	Less than .1 second
Compressed music file (MP3 format) containing a four-minute song	5 MB	28 minutes	7 minutes	2 minutes	Less than .1 second
Uncompressed music file containing a four-minute song	60 MB	6 hours	1.5 hours	28 minutes	.4 second
Compressed video file containing a 10-minute interview	200 MB	19 hours	5 hours	2 hours	1 second
Compressed video file containing a feature-length film	4 GB	16 days	4 days	30 hours	25 seconds

Types of Internet connections ◄ Figure A-16

Service	Upstream Speed (Kbps)	Downstream Speed (Kbps)	Capacity (Number of Simultaneous Users)	One-Time Startup Costs	Continuing Monthly Costs
Residential-Small Business Services					
POTS	28–56	28–56	1	$0–$20	$9–$20
ISDN	128–256	128–256	1–3	$60–$300	$50–$90
ADSL	100–640	500–9,000	1–20	$50–$100	$40–$500
Cable	300–1,500	500–10,000	1–10	$0–$100	$40–$300
Satellite	125–150	400–500	1–3	$0–$800	$40–$100
Fixed-point wireless	250–1,500	500–3,000	1–4	$0–$350	$50–$150
Business Services					
Leased digital line (DS0)	64	64	1–10	$50–$200	$40–$150
Fixed-point wireless	500–10,000	500–10,000	5–1,000	$0–$500	$300–$5,000
Fractional T1 leased line	128–1,544	128–1,544	5–180	$50–$800	$100–$1,000
T1 leased line	1,544	1,544	100–200	$100–$2,000	$600–$1,600
T3 leased line	44,700	44,700	1,000–10,000	$1,000–$9,000	$5,000–$12,000
Large Business, ISP, NAP, and Internet2 Services					
OC3 leased line	156,000	156,000	1,000–50,000	$3,000–$12,000	$9,000–$22,000
OC12 leased line	622,000	622,000	Backbone	Negotiated	$25,000–$100,000
OC48 leased line	2,500,000	2,500,000	Backbone	Negotiated	Negotiated
OC192 leased line	10,000,000	10,000,000	Backbone	Negotiated	Negotiated

Review | **Appendix Summary**

In this appendix, you learned that the Internet—from its birth as a research project to its role as a global communications network linking more than a billion persons, businesses, and governments—has made information available on a scale never before imagined. You learned how client/server networks work when they are interconnected. You also learned about the people who played important roles in the development and success of the Internet. The Internet grew rapidly, especially after the Web became available. You learned about the business of providing Internet access and the bandwidth and pricing choices for connecting to the Internet.

Key Terms

Advanced Research Projects
    Agency (ARPA)
ARPANET
Asymmetric Digital Subscriber Line
    (ADSL or DSL)
bandwidth
Because It's Time Network (BITNET)
bits per second (bps)
broadband
byte
Category 1 cable
Category 5 cable
Category 5e cable
Category 6 cable
circuit switching
client
client/server network
coaxial cable
commerce service provider (CSP)
Computer Science Network (CSNET)
Defense Advanced Research Projects
    Agency (DARPA)
demodulation
dial-up
Digital Subscriber Line (DSL)
Digital Subscriber Loop (DSL)
dotted decimal notation
electrical interference
extranet
fiber-optic cable
fixed-point wireless

gigabits per second (Gbps)
gigabyte (GB)
graphical user interface (GUI)
heading tag
hypertext
hypertext server
Integrated Services Digital Network
    (ISDN)
Internet access provider (IAP)
Internet Engineering Task Force (IETF)
Internet host
Internet Protocol
Internet service provider (ISP)
Internet Worm
Internet2
intranet
IP (Internet Protocol) address
IP version 4 (IPv4)
IP version 6 (IPv6)
Joint Academic Network (Janet)
kilobits per second (Kbps)
kilobyte (KB)
LISTSERV
mailing list
megabits per second (Mbps)
megabyte (MB)
Memex
MILNET (Military Network)
modem
modulation

network access point (NAP)
network address translation (NAT)
    device
network backbone
Network Control Protocol (NCP)
network interface card (NIC)
network operating system
node (network node)
octet
open architecture
open-source software
optical carrier (OC)
packet switching
plain old telephone service (POTS)
private IP address
protocol
router
routing algorithm
server
Standard Generalized Markup
    Language (SGML)
subnetting
T1
T3
TCP/IP
Transmission Control Protocol
twisted-pair cable
User's News Network (Usenet) news-
    groups
wireless network

Reinforce | **Lab Assignments**

Student Edition Labs

The interactive Student Edition Lab on **Connecting to the Internet** is designed to help you master some key concepts and skills presented in this appendix, including:

- establishing an Internet connection
- using dial-up connections
- installing ISP software
- creating connections manually
- disconnecting

This lab is available online and can be accessed from the Appendix Web page on the Online Companion at www.cengage.com/internet/np/internet8.

Objectives

- Configure and use Outlook Express to send, receive, and print email messages
- Create and maintain an address book in Outlook Express

Using Outlook Express

Case | Kikukawa Air

Since 1994, Sharon and Don Kikukawa have operated an air charter service in Maui, Hawaii. At first, Kikukawa Air employed only Sharon, who managed the office, reservations, and the company's financial records, and her husband Don, who flew their twin-engine, six-passenger plane between Maui and Oahu. After many successful years in business, Sharon and Don expanded their business to include scenic tours and charter service to all of the Hawaiian Islands. As a result of their expansion, Kikukawa Air now has six twin-engine planes, two turboprop planes, and a growing staff of more than 30 people.

Because Kikukawa Air has a ticket counter at airports on all of the Hawaiian Islands, many miles now separate the company's employees. Originally, employees used telephone and conference calling to coordinate the business's day-to-day operations, such as schedule and reservation changes, new airport procedures, and maintenance requests. Sharon soon realized that these forms of communication were difficult to coordinate with the growing number of busy ground-service agents and pilots. Most employees already use email to communicate with each other and with outside vendors and clients, but they are not all using the same email program. Sharon believes that Kikukawa Air could benefit from organizing the company's employees so that everyone uses the same email program, in this case, Outlook Express. This coordination will make it easier to manage the accounts and computers, and will streamline the company's operations.

Sharon has hired you to train the staff members to use Outlook Express to manage their email messages.

Starting Data Files

Appendix.B

Physicals.pdf

Microsoft Outlook Express

Tip

Microsoft Outlook, another email program that you can purchase and use to send and receive email, is part of the Microsoft Office suite.

Microsoft Outlook Express, or simply **Outlook Express**, is an email program that you use to send and receive email. Outlook Express is installed with Internet Explorer on Windows XP computers. Figure B-1 shows the Outlook Express Inbox window. You can customize Outlook Express in many ways by resizing, hiding, and displaying different windows and their individual elements, so your screen might look different.

Figure B-1 ▶ **Outlook Express Inbox window**

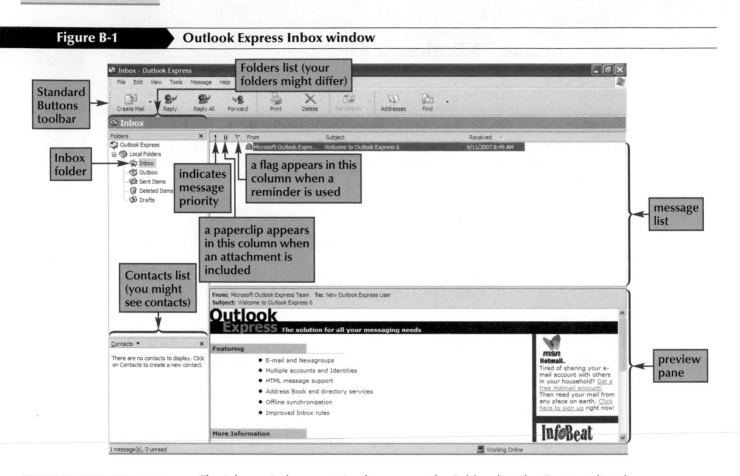

Tip

If this is your first time starting Outlook Express, you might receive a message similar to the one shown from Microsoft in Figure B-1.

The Inbox window contains four panes: the Folders list, the Contacts list, the message list, and the preview pane. The **Folders list** displays a list of folders for receiving, saving, and deleting mail messages. You might see more folders than those shown in Figure B-1, but you should see the five default folders. The **Inbox folder** stores messages you have received, the **Outbox folder** stores outgoing messages that have not been sent, the **Sent Items folder** stores copies of messages you have sent, the **Deleted Items folder** stores messages you have deleted, and the **Drafts folder** stores messages that you have written but have not sent.

The **Contacts list**, which might be hidden, contains information about the addresses stored in your address book. You can click a contact in the Contacts list to address a new message quickly to an individual or group.

The **message list** contains summary information for each message that you receive. The first three columns on the left might display icons indicating information about the email message. The first column indicates the message's priority: You might see an exclamation point to indicate a message with high priority; a blue arrow icon to indicate a message with low priority; or nothing, which indicates normal priority. The sender indicates a message's priority before sending it; most messages have no specified priority, in which case no icon will appear in the column. The second column displays a paperclip icon when a message includes an attachment. Finally, if you click the third column for a message you have received, a red flag will appear. You can use a flag to remind yourself to follow up on the message later.

The message list also displays the sender's name in the From column, the message's subject in the Subject column, and the date and time the message was received in the Received column. You can sort messages by clicking any column in the message list.

The message that is selected in the message list appears in the preview pane. The **preview pane** appears below the message list and displays the content of the selected message in the message list. You can use the horizontal scroll bar to scroll the message.

Creating an Email Account

You are ready to get started using Outlook Express. These steps assume that Outlook Express is already installed on your computer. First, you need to configure Outlook Express so it will retrieve your mail from your ISP.

> **Tip**
>
> Outlook Express is not installed on computers running the Windows Vista or Windows 7 operating systems.

To configure Outlook Express to manage your email:

▶ 1. Click the **Start** button on the Windows taskbar, point to **All Programs**, and then click **Outlook Express** to start the program. Normally, you do not need to be connected to the Internet to configure Outlook Express; however, your system might be configured differently. If necessary, connect to the Internet.

   Trouble? If the Internet Connection Wizard starts, click the Cancel button.

   Trouble? If an Outlook Express dialog box opens and asks to make Outlook Express your default mail client, click the No button.

   Trouble? If an Outlook Express dialog box opens and asks to import information from another email program installed on your computer, click the Cancel button.

▶ 2. If necessary, click the **Inbox** folder in the Folders list to select it.

▶ 3. Click **Tools** on the menu bar, click **Accounts**, and then, if necessary, click the **Mail** tab in the Internet Accounts dialog box so you can set up your mail account settings.

   Trouble? If you have already set up your mail account (or if someone has set up an account for you), click the Close button in the Internet Accounts dialog box and skip this set of steps. If you are unsure about any existing account, ask your instructor or technical support person for help.

▶ 4. Click the **Add** button in the Internet Accounts dialog box, and then click **Mail**. The Internet Connection Wizard starts. You use this wizard to identify yourself, your user name, and the settings for your mail server. See Figure B-2.

5. Type your first and last names in the Display name text box, and then click the **Next** button to open the next dialog box, in which you specify your email address.

6. Type your full email address (such as student@university.edu) in the E-Mail address text box, and then click the **Next** button. The next dialog box asks you for your incoming and outgoing mail server names.

7. Type the names of your incoming and outgoing mail servers in the text boxes where indicated. Your instructor, technical support person, or ISP will provide this information to you. Usually, an incoming mail server name is POP, POP3, or IMAP followed by a domain name. An outgoing mail server name usually is SMTP or MAIL followed by a domain name. When you are finished, click the **Next** button to continue.

8. In the Account name text box, type your Internet mail user name, as supplied by your instructor, technical support person, or ISP. Make sure that you type your user name and not your domain name (some ISPs might require both).

9. Press the **Tab** key to move the insertion point to the Password text box. To protect your password's identity, Outlook Express displays dots or asterisks in this text box instead of the characters you type. To prevent other users from being able to access your mail account, you will clear the Remember password check box. When you access your mail account, Outlook Express will prompt you for your password. If you are working on a computer to which you have sole access, you might want to set Outlook Express to remember your password, so you don't need to type it every time you access your email.

10. If necessary, click the **Remember password** check box to clear it, and then click the **Next** button.

11. Click the **Finish** button to save the mail account information and close the Internet Connection Wizard. The Internet Accounts dialog box reappears, and your account is listed on the Mail tab. Figure B-3 shows Sharon Kikukawa's information.

your account name appears here →

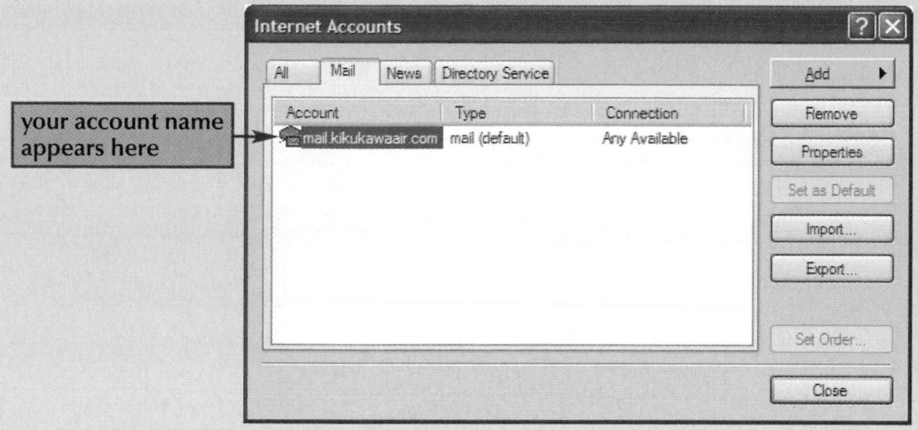

12. Click the **Close** button in the Internet Accounts dialog box to close it.

Now Outlook Express is configured to send and receive messages, so you are ready to send a message to Don Kikukawa.

Sending a Message Using Outlook Express

You will use Outlook Express to send a message with an attached file to Don. You will send a copy of the message to yourself to simulate receiving a message.

To send a message with an attachment:

1. Make sure that the **Inbox** folder is selected in the Folders list, and then click the **Create Mail** button on the toolbar to open the New Message window. If necessary, click the **Maximize** button on the New Message window. See Figure B-4. The New Message window contains its own menu bar, toolbar, message display area, and boxes in which you enter address and subject information. The insertion point is positioned in the To text box when you open a new message.

Trouble? If you do not see the Bcc text box in the message header, click View on the menu bar, and then click All Headers.

Trouble? If you don't have the starting Data Files, you need to get them before you can proceed. Your instructor will either give you the Data Files or ask you to obtain them from a specified location (such as a network drive). In either case, make a backup copy of the Data Files before you start so that you will have the original files available in case you need to start over. If you have any questions about the Data Files, see your instructor or technical support person for assistance.

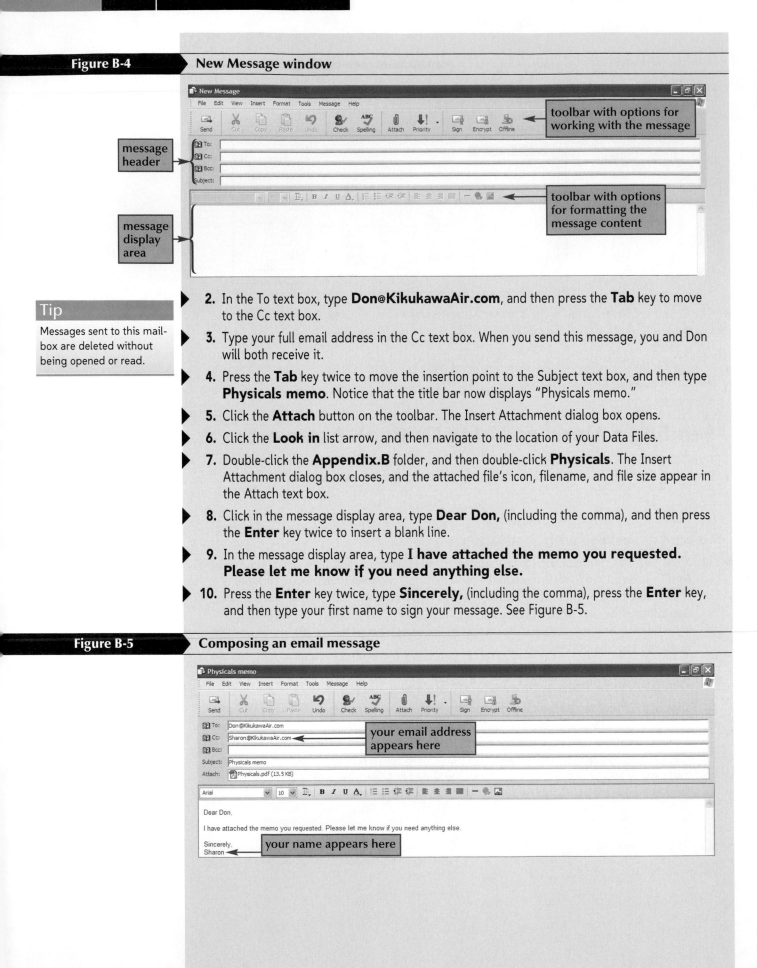

Figure B-4 — New Message window

toolbar with options for working with the message

message header

message display area

toolbar with options for formatting the message content

2. In the To text box, type **Don@KikukawaAir.com**, and then press the **Tab** key to move to the Cc text box.

3. Type your full email address in the Cc text box. When you send this message, you and Don will both receive it.

4. Press the **Tab** key twice to move the insertion point to the Subject text box, and then type **Physicals memo**. Notice that the title bar now displays "Physicals memo."

5. Click the **Attach** button on the toolbar. The Insert Attachment dialog box opens.

6. Click the **Look in** list arrow, and then navigate to the location of your Data Files.

7. Double-click the **Appendix.B** folder, and then double-click **Physicals**. The Insert Attachment dialog box closes, and the attached file's icon, filename, and file size appear in the Attach text box.

8. Click in the message display area, type **Dear Don,** (including the comma), and then press the **Enter** key twice to insert a blank line.

9. In the message display area, type **I have attached the memo you requested. Please let me know if you need anything else.**

10. Press the **Enter** key twice, type **Sincerely,** (including the comma), press the **Enter** key, and then type your first name to sign your message. See Figure B-5.

Figure B-5 — Composing an email message

your email address appears here

your name appears here

▶ **11.** Click the **Spelling** button on the toolbar to check your spelling before sending the message. If necessary, correct any typing errors. When you are finished, click the **OK** button to close the Spelling dialog box.

▶ **12.** Click the **Send** button on the toolbar to mail the message. The Physicals memo window closes and the message is stored in the Outbox folder, as indicated by the "(1)" in the Outbox folder.

Trouble? If a Send Mail dialog box opens and tells you that the message will be sent the next time you click the Send/Recv button, click the OK button to continue.

Trouble? If Outlook Express is configured to send messages when you click the Send button, you won't see the "(1)" in the Outbox folder. This difference causes no problems.

Depending on your system configuration, Outlook Express might not send your messages immediately. It might queue (hold) messages until you connect to your ISP or click the Send/Recv button on the toolbar. If you want to examine the setting and change it, click Tools on the menu bar, click Options, and then click the Send tab in the Options dialog box. If the Send messages immediately check box contains a check mark, then Outlook Express sends messages when you click the Send button on the toolbar. Otherwise, Outlook Express holds messages until you click the Send/Recv button.

Receiving and Reading a Message

When you receive new mail, messages that you haven't opened yet are displayed with a closed envelope icon next to them in the message list; messages that you have opened are displayed with an open envelope icon next to them. You check for new mail next.

To check for incoming mail:

▶ **1.** Click the **Send/Recv** button on the toolbar, type your password in the Password text box of the Logon dialog box (if necessary), and then click the **OK** button. Depending on your system configuration, you might not need to connect to your ISP and type your password to retrieve your messages. Within a few moments, your mail server transfers all new mail to your Inbox. The Physicals memo message was sent to Don and also to your email address, which you typed in the Cc text box. Notice that the Inbox folder in the Folders list is bold, but other folders are not. A bold folder indicates that it contains unread mail; the number in parentheses next to the Inbox folder indicates the number of unread messages in that folder.

Trouble? If an Outlook Express message box opens and indicates that it could not find your host, click the Hide button to close the message box, click Tools on the menu bar, click Accounts, and then click the Properties button. Verify that your incoming and outgoing server names are correct, and then repeat Step 1. If you still have problems, ask your instructor or technical support person for help.

Trouble? If you do not see any messages in your Inbox, then you either did not receive any new mail or you might be looking in the wrong folder. If necessary, click the Inbox folder in the Folders list. If you still don't have any mail messages, wait a few moments, and then repeat Step 1 until you receive a message.

▶ **2.** If necessary, click the **Physicals memo** message in the message list to open the message in the preview pane. See Figure B-6.

Figure B-6 ▶ Receiving an email message

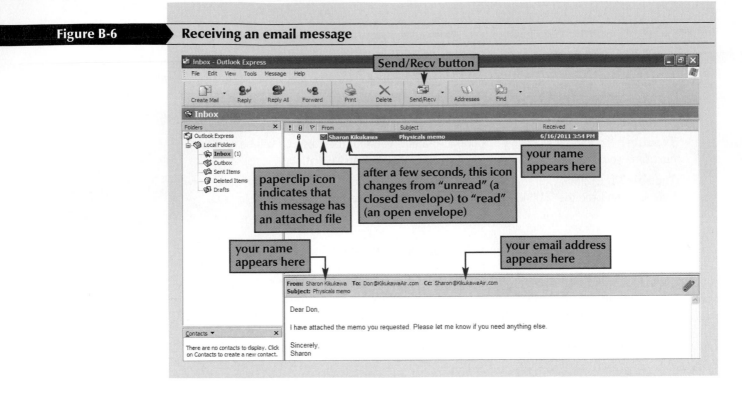

You received a copy of the message that you sent to Don. The paperclip icon indicates the message has an attachment. When you receive a message with one or more attachments, you can open the attachment or save it.

Viewing and Saving an Attached File

You want to make sure that your attached file was sent properly, so you decide to open it. Then you will save the file.

To view and save the attached file:

1. Make sure that the **Physicals memo** message is selected in the message list.

2. Click the **paperclip icon** in the upper-right corner of the preview pane to open the shortcut menu. See Figure B-7.

Viewing an attached file | Figure B-7

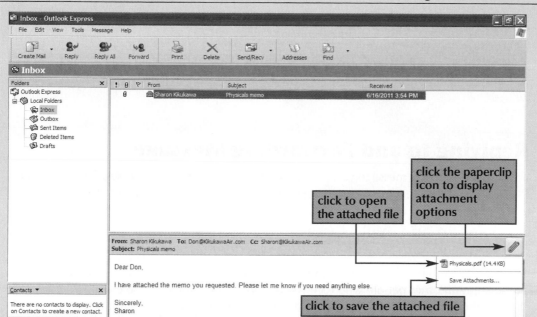

Trouble? If the options on the shortcut menu are dimmed, then Outlook Express is configured to remove all potentially unsafe attachments from messages. Click the paperclip icon to close the menu. If you are working in a public computer lab, ask your instructor or technical support person for help. If you are working on a private computer, click Tools on the menu bar, click Options, click the Security tab in the Options dialog box, and then clear the "Do not allow attachments to be saved or opened that could potentially be a virus." check box. Click the OK button to close the Options dialog box, and then recompose, send, and receive the Test message. It is strongly suggested that you install and configure antivirus software when disabling this option to protect your computer from viruses.

The shortcut menu shows that a file named Physicals.pdf, with a file size of approximately 15 KB, is attached to the message. If this message contained other attachments, they would also appear on the shortcut menu. Clicking Physicals.pdf starts a program on your computer that can open the file. Clicking Save Attachments lets you save the file to the drive and folder that you specify.

3. Click **Physicals.pdf** on the shortcut menu. Adobe Reader or another program on your computer starts and opens the attached file. If necessary, maximize the program window that opens.

   Trouble? If a Mail Attachment dialog box opens warning that the file might contain viruses, click the Open button.

4. Click the **Close** button on the program window displaying the Physicals document. Now that you have viewed the attachment, you can save it.

5. Click the **paperclip icon** in the preview pane, and then click **Save Attachments** on the shortcut menu. The Save Attachments dialog box opens. The Physicals.pdf file is already selected for you.

6. Click the **Browse** button. The Browse for Folder dialog box opens and lists all of the drives on your computer.

7. Scrolling as necessary, open the drive or folder that contains your Data Files, double-click the **Appendix.B** folder to open it, and then click the **OK** button. The Save Attachments dialog box appears again. The Save To location indicates that you will save the attached file to the Appendix.B folder.

8. Click the **Save** button to save the attached file, and then click the **Yes** button to overwrite the file with the same name.

Replying to and Forwarding Messages

You can forward any message you receive to one or more email addresses. Similarly, you can respond to the sender of a message quickly and efficiently by replying to a message.

Replying to an Email Message

To reply to a message, select the message in the message list, and then click the Reply button on the toolbar to reply only to the sender, or click the Reply All button to reply to the sender and other people who received the original message (those email addresses listed in the To and Cc text boxes). Outlook Express will open a new "Re:" message window and place the original sender's address in the To text box; if you click the Reply All button, then other email addresses that received the original message will appear in the To and Cc text boxes as appropriate. You can leave the Subject text box as is or modify it. Most email programs, including Outlook Express, will copy the original message and place it in the message body. Usually, a special mark to the left of the response indicates a quote from the text of the original message. Figure B-8 shows a reply to the message.

Figure B-8 ▶ **Replying to a message**

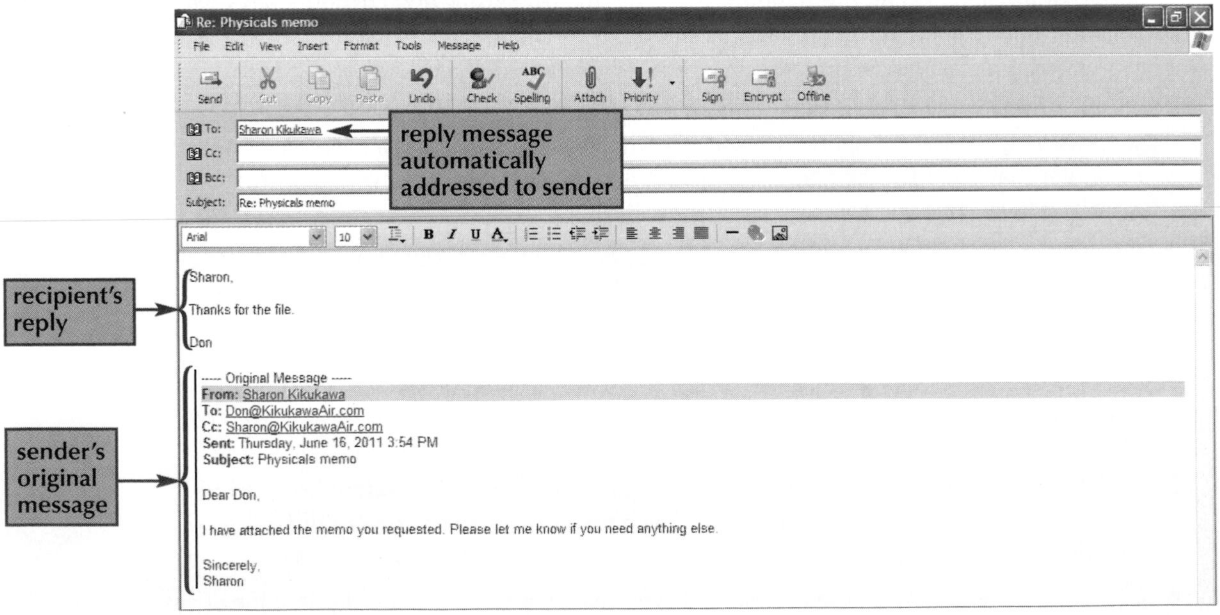

Forwarding an Email Message

When you forward a message, you are sending a copy of the message, including any attachments, to one or more recipients who were not included in the original message. (If you do not want to forward the original sender's attached file to the new recipients, select the attachment filename in the Attach text box, and then press the Delete key.) To forward an existing mail message to another user, open the folder containing the message you want to forward, select it in the message list, and then click the Forward button on the toolbar. The "Fw:" window opens, where you can type the address of the recipient in the To text box. If you want to forward the message to several people, type their addresses, separated by commas (or semicolons), in the To text box (or Cc or Bcc text boxes). Outlook Express inserts a copy of the original message in the message display area (as it does when you reply to a message). However, no special mark appears in the left margin to indicate the original message. Figure B-9 shows a forwarded copy of the message.

Forwarding a message   **Figure B-9**

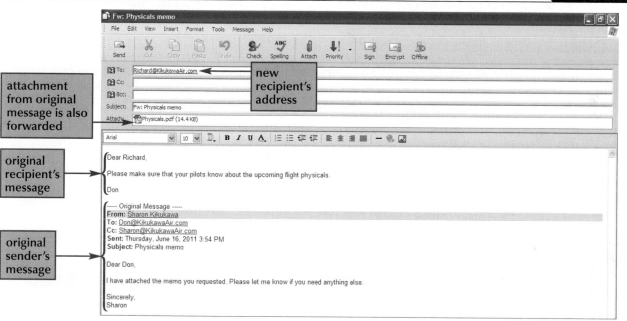

Filing and Printing an Email Message

You can use the Outlook Express mail folders to file your email messages by topic or category. When you file a message, you move it from the Inbox to another folder. You can also make a *copy* of a message in the Inbox and save it in another folder by right-clicking the message in the message list, clicking Copy to Folder on the shortcut menu, and then selecting the folder in which to store the copy. You file your message in a new folder named "FAA" for safekeeping. Later, you can create other folders to suit your needs.

To create a new folder:

▶ 1. Right-click the **Inbox** folder in the Folders list to open the shortcut menu, and then click **New Folder**. The Create Folder dialog box opens. When you create a new folder, first you must select the folder at the level above which to create the new folder. Because the Inbox folder is selected, the new folder that you create is a subfolder of the Inbox folder.

▶ **2.** Type **FAA** in the Folder name text box. See Figure B-10.

Creating a new folder

new folder name

new folder will be a subfolder of the selected folder

Create Folder

Folder name:
FAA

OK
Cancel

Select the folder in which to create the new folder:

Outlook Express
Local Folders
Inbox
Outbox
Sent Items
Deleted Items
Drafts

▶ **3.** Click the **OK** button to create the new folder and close the Create Folder dialog box. The FAA folder appears in the Folders list as a subfolder of the Inbox folder.

After you create the FAA folder, you can transfer messages to it. In addition to copying or transferring mail from the Inbox folder, you can select messages in any other folder and then transfer them to another folder. You can also print a message.

To file and print the Physicals memo message:

▶ **1.** Click the **Physicals memo** message in the message list to select it.

▶ **2.** Click and drag the **Physicals memo** message from the message list to the FAA folder in the Folders list. See Figure B-11.

Filing a message

Inbox - Outlook Express

File   Edit   View   Tools   Message   Help

Create Mail   Reply   Reply All   Forward   Print   Delete   Send/Recv   Addresses   Find

Inbox

Folders
Outlook Express
Local Folders
Inbox
FAA
Outbox
Sent Items
Deleted Items
Drafts

From   Subject   Received
Sharon Kikukawa   Physicals memo   6/16/2011 3:54 PM

selected folder is highlighted and pointer changes shape to indicate a message is being moved

▶ **3.** When the FAA folder is selected, release the mouse button. The Physicals memo message is now stored in the FAA folder.

▶ **4.** Click the **FAA** folder in the Folders list to display its contents in the message list.

▶ **5.** Click the **Physicals memo** message in the message list to select it.

▶ **6.** Click the **Print** button on the toolbar. The Print dialog box opens.

▶ **7.** If necessary, select your printer in the list of printers.

▶ **8.** Click the **Print** button. The message is printed.

Deleting an Email Message and Folder

When you don't need a message any longer, select the message in the message list, and then click the Delete button on the toolbar. You can select multiple messages by pressing and holding the Ctrl key, clicking each message in the message list, and then releasing the Ctrl key. When you click the Delete button on the toolbar, each selected message is deleted. You can select folders and delete them using the same process. When you delete a message or a folder, you are really moving it to the Deleted Items folder. To remove items permanently, use the same process to delete the items from the Deleted Items folder.

To delete the message and the FAA folder:

▶ 1. If necessary, select the **Physicals memo** message in the message list.

▶ 2. Click the **Delete** button on the toolbar. The message is deleted from the FAA folder and is moved to the Deleted Items folder.

▶ 3. Click the **Deleted Items** folder in the Folder list to display its contents.

▶ 4. Click the **Physicals memo** message to select it, and then click the **Delete** button on the toolbar. A dialog box opens and asks you to confirm the deletion.

▶ 5. Click the **Yes** button. The message is deleted from the Deleted Items folder.

▶ 6. Click the **FAA** folder in the Folders list to select it. Because this folder doesn't contain any messages, the message list is empty.

▶ 7. Click the **Delete** button on the toolbar. A dialog box opens and asks you to confirm moving the folder to the Deleted Items folder.

▶ 8. Click the **Yes** button. The FAA folder moves to the Deleted Items folder. The Deleted Items folder has a plus box to its left, indicating that this folder contains another folder.

▶ 9. Click the **plus box** to the left of the Deleted Items folder, and then click the **FAA** folder to select it.

▶ 10. Click the **Delete** button on the toolbar, and then click the **Yes** button in the message box to delete the FAA folder permanently.

▶ 11. Click the **Inbox** folder in the Folders list to return to the Inbox.

Maintaining an Address Book

As you use email to communicate with business associates and friends, you might want to save their addresses in an address book to make it easier to enter addresses into the header of your email messages. To create a new address, open the address book, click the New button on the toolbar, click New Contact from the list, and then enter information into the Properties dialog box for that contact. On the Name tab, you can enter a contact's name and email address; use the other tabs to enter optional address, business, personal, and other information about that contact. If you enter a short name in the Nickname text box, then you can type the nickname instead of a person's full name when you address a new message.

To add a contact to your address book:

▶ 1. Click the **Addresses** button on the toolbar. The Address Book window opens. If necessary, maximize the Address Book window.

▶ 2. Click the **New** button on the toolbar, and then click **New Contact**. The Properties dialog box opens with the insertion point positioned in the First text box on the Name tab.

▶ 3. Type **Jenny** in the First text box. As you type the contact's first name (and eventually the last name), the name of the Properties dialog box changes to indicate that the properties set in this dialog box belong to the specified contact.

▶ 4. Press the **Tab** key twice to move the insertion point to the Last text box, type **Mahala** in the Last text box, and then press the **Tab** key three times to move the insertion point to the Nickname text box.

▶ 5. Type **Jen** in the Nickname text box, and then press the **Tab** key to move the insertion point to the E-Mail Addresses text box.

▶ 6. Type **Jenny@KikukawaAir.com** in the E-Mail Addresses text box, and then click the **Add** button. Jen's contact is complete. See Figure B-12.

Figure B-12	Adding a contact to the address book

▶ 7. Click the **OK** button. The Properties dialog box closes and you return to the Address Book window. Jen's contact now appears in the Address Book window.

▶ 8. Repeat Steps 2 through 7 to create new contacts for the following Kikukawa Air employees:

First	Last	Nickname	Email Address
Zane	Norcia	Zane	Zane@KikukawaAir.com
Richard	Forrester	Rich	Richard@KikukawaAir.com

▶ 9. Click the **Close** button on the Address Book window title bar to close it. Now the Contacts list shows the entries you just added to your address book.

Now that these email addresses are stored in the address book, when you start typing the first few letters of a nickname or first name, Outlook Express will complete the entry for you. Clicking the Check button on the toolbar in the New Message window changes the names you typed to their matching entries in the address book. If you need to change an address, click to select it and then press the Delete key.

When you receive mail from someone who is not in your address book, double-click the message to open it, right-click the "From" name to open the shortcut menu, and then click Add to Address Book. This process adds the sender's name and email address to your address book, where you can open his or her information as a contact and edit and add information as necessary.

You can also use Outlook Express to create a group. Usually you create a group of contacts when you regularly send messages to a group of people. For example, Sharon frequently sends messages to Zane, Jen, and Rich as a group because they have the same positions at the Kikukawa Air ticket counters. She asks you to create a group of contacts in her address book so she can type one nickname for the group of email addresses, instead of having to type each address separately.

To add a group of contacts to your address book and close Outlook Express:

▶ **1.** Click the **Addresses** button on the toolbar, and then, if necessary, maximize the Address Book window.

▶ **2.** Click the **New** button on the toolbar, and then click **New Group**. The Properties dialog box opens and displays tabs related to group settings.

▶ **3.** With the insertion point positioned in the Group Name text box, type **Ticket Agents**. This nickname will represent the individual email addresses for employees working in this position.

▶ **4.** Click the **Select Members** button. The Select Group Members window opens, with existing contacts appearing in a list box on the left side of the window.

▶ **5.** Click **Jenny Mahala** in the left list box, and then click the **Select** button. A copy of Jenny's contact information is added to the Members list box.

▶ **6.** Repeat Step 5 to add the contacts for **Richard Forrester** and **Zane Norcia** to the group. Figure B-13 shows the completed group.

Creating a group of contacts ◀ **Figure B-13**

individual contacts in the address book (your contacts might differ)

contacts added to the Ticket Agents group of contacts

▶ **7.** Click the **OK** button to close the Select Group Members dialog box. The Properties dialog box for the Ticket Agents group contains three group members.

▶ **8.** Click the **OK** button to close the Ticket Agents Properties dialog box. The nickname of the new group, Ticket Agents, appears in the address book in the left pane of the window and the members of the group are listed in the right pane.

▶ **9.** Close the Address Book window by clicking the **Close** button on its title bar.

▶ **10.** Click **File** on the menu bar, and then click **Exit**. Outlook Express closes.

Tip

You can delete one or more members from the group by opening the address book, double-clicking the group name, and then deleting a selected member's name by clicking the Remove button. You can also add members using the group's Properties dialog box.

Review | **Appendix Summary**

In this Appendix, you learned how to use Outlook Express to manage, send, and receive email messages. You also learned how to print, file, save, delete, respond to, and forward email messages. You created an address book into which you stored the name, email address, and other important details about a person or group of people.

Key Terms

Contacts list	Inbox folder	Outlook Express
Deleted Items folder	message list	preview pane
Drafts folder	Microsoft Outlook Express	Sent Items folder
Folders list	Outbox folder	

Objectives

- Configure and use Windows Mail to send, receive, and print email messages
- Create and maintain contacts in Windows Mail

Using Windows Mail

Case | Kikukawa Air

Since 1994, Sharon and Don Kikukawa have operated an air charter service in Maui, Hawaii. At first, Kikukawa Air employed only Sharon, who managed the office, reservations, and the company's financial records, and her husband Don, who flew their twin-engine, six-passenger plane between Maui and Oahu. After many successful years in business, Sharon and Don expanded their business to include scenic tours and charter service to all of the Hawaiian Islands. As a result of their expansion, Kikukawa Air now has six twin-engine planes, two turboprop planes, and a growing staff of more than 30 people.

Because Kikukawa Air has a ticket counter at airports on all of the Hawaiian Islands, many miles now separate the company's employees. Originally, employees used telephone and conference calling to coordinate the business's day-to-day operations, such as schedule and reservation changes, new airport procedures, and maintenance requests. Sharon soon realized that these forms of communication were difficult to coordinate with the growing number of busy ground-service agents and pilots. Most employees already use email to communicate with each other and with outside vendors and clients, but they are not all using the same email program. Sharon believes that Kikukawa Air could benefit from organizing the company's employees so that everyone uses the same email program, in this case, Windows Mail. This coordination will make it easier to manage the accounts and computers, and will streamline the company's operations.

Sharon has hired you to train the staff members to use Windows Mail to manage their email messages.

Starting Data Files

Appendix.C

Physicals.pdf

Microsoft Windows Mail

Microsoft Windows Mail, or simply **Windows Mail**, is an email program that you use to send and receive email. Figure C-1 shows the Windows Mail Inbox window. You can customize Windows Mail in many ways by resizing, hiding, and displaying different windows and their individual elements, so your screen might look different.

Figure C-1 ▶ Windows Mail Inbox window

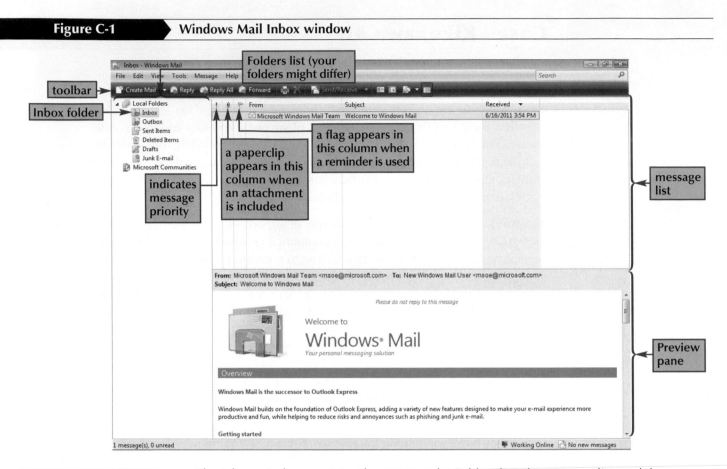

The Inbox window contains three panes: the Folders list, the message list, and the Preview pane. The **Folders list** displays a list of folders for receiving, saving, and deleting mail messages. You might see more folders than those shown in Figure C-1, but you should see the six default folders. The **Inbox folder** stores messages you have received, the **Outbox folder** stores outgoing messages that have not been sent, the **Sent Items folder** stores copies of messages you have sent, the **Deleted Items folder** stores messages you have deleted, the **Drafts folder** stores messages that you have written but have not sent, and the **Junk E-mail folder** stores messages that Windows Mail has tagged as junk and unsolicited mail.

The **message list** contains summary information for each message that you receive. The first three columns on the left might display icons indicating information about the email message. The first column indicates the message's priority: You might see an exclamation point to indicate a message with high priority; a blue arrow icon to indicate a message with low priority; or nothing, which indicates normal priority. The sender indicates a message's priority before sending it; most messages have no specified priority, in which case no icon will appear in the column. The second column displays a paperclip icon when a message includes an attachment. Finally, if you click the third column for a message you have received, a red flag will appear. You can use a flag to remind yourself to follow up on the message later.

The message list also displays the sender's name in the From column, the message's subject in the Subject column, and the date and time the message was received in the Received column. You can sort messages by clicking any column in the message list.

The message that is selected in the message list appears in the Preview pane. The **Preview pane** appears below the message list and displays the content of the selected message in the message list. You can use the horizontal scroll bar to scroll the message.

Creating an Email Account

You are ready to get started using Outlook Express. These steps assume that Outlook Express is already installed on your computer. First, you need to configure Outlook Express so it will retrieve your mail from your ISP.

To configure Windows Mail to manage your email:

▶ 1. Click the **Start button** on the Windows taskbar, click **All Programs**, and then click **Windows Mail** to start the program. Normally, you do not need to be connected to the Internet to configure Windows Mail; however, your system might be configured differently. If necessary, connect to the Internet.

   Trouble? If a Windows Mail dialog box opens and asks to make Windows Mail your default email program, click the No button.

   Trouble? If a Windows Mail dialog box opens and asks to import information from another email program installed on your computer, click the Cancel button.

▶ 2. If necessary, click the **Inbox** folder in the Folders list to select it.

▶ 3. Click **Tools** on the menu bar, and then click **Accounts**. The Internet Accounts dialog box opens so you can set up your mail account settings.

   Trouble? If you have already set up your mail account (or if someone has set up an account for you), click the Close button in the Internet Accounts dialog box and skip this set of steps. If you are unsure about any existing account, ask your instructor or technical support person for help.

▶ 4. Click the **Add** button in the Internet Accounts dialog box, click **E-mail Account**, and then click the **Next** button. The first step in creating an email account is to enter the name that you want to appear in the From line of your messages. See Figure C-2.

5. Type your first and last names in the Display name text box, and then click the **Next** button to open the next dialog box, in which you specify your email address.

6. Type your full email address (such as student@university.edu) in the E-mail address text box, and then click the **Next** button. The next dialog box asks you for your incoming and outgoing mail server names.

7. Type the names of your incoming and outgoing mail servers in the text boxes where indicated. Your instructor, technical support person, or ISP will provide this information to you. Usually, an incoming mail server name is POP, POP3, or IMAP followed by a domain name. An outgoing mail server name usually is SMTP or MAIL followed by a domain name. When you are finished, click the **Next** button to continue.

8. In the Account name text box, type your email user name, as supplied by your instructor, technical support person, or ISP. Make sure that you type your user name and not your domain name (some ISPs require both a user name and a domain name).

9. Press the **Tab** key to move the insertion point to the Password text box. To protect your password's identity, Windows Mail displays dots or asterisks in this text box instead of the characters you type. To prevent other users from being able to access your mail account, you will clear the Remember password check box. When you access your mail account, Windows Mail will prompt you for your password. If you are working on a computer to which you have sole access, you might want to set Windows Mail to remember your password, so you don't need to type it every time you access your email.

10. If necessary, click the **Remember password** check box to clear it, and then click the **Next** button.

11. Click the **Finish** button to save the mail account information and close the dialog box. The Internet Accounts dialog box reappears, and your new mail account is listed. Figure C-3 shows Sharon Kikukawa's information.

Mail account created for Sharon Kikukawa   **Figure C-3**

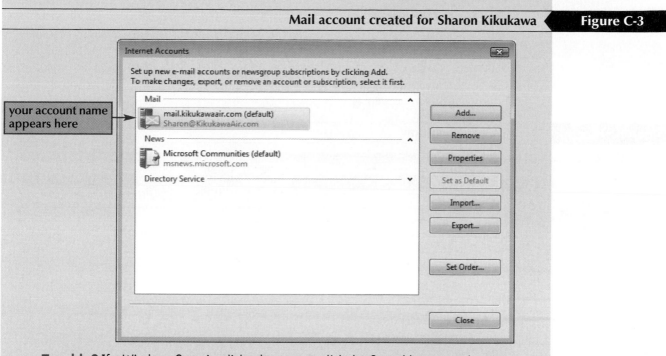

your account name appears here →

Trouble? If a Windows Security dialog box opens, click the Cancel button to close it.

Trouble? If a Windows Mail dialog box opens, click the Close button on the title bar to close it.

▶ **12.** Click the **Close** button in the Internet Accounts dialog box to close it.

Now Windows Mail is configured to send and receive messages, so you are ready to send a message to Don Kikukawa.

Sending a Message Using Windows Mail

You will use Windows Mail to send a message with an attached file to Don. You will send a copy of the message to yourself to simulate receiving a message.

To send a message with an attachment:

▶ **1.** Make sure that the **Inbox** folder is selected in the Folders list, and then click the **Create Mail** button on the toolbar to open the New Message window. If necessary, click the **Maximize** button on the New Message window. See Figure C-4. The New Message window contains a menu bar and toolbar for working with the message options. It also contains the message display area, a toolbar for formatting the message content, and boxes in which you enter address and subject information. The insertion point is positioned in the To text box when you open a new message.

Trouble? If you do not see the Bcc text box in the message header, click View on the menu bar, and then click All Headers.

Trouble? If you don't have the starting Data Files, you need to get them before you can proceed. Your instructor will either give you the Data Files or ask you to obtain them from a specified location (such as a network drive). In either case, make a backup copy of the Data Files before you start so that you will have the original files available in case you need to start over. If you have any questions about the Data Files, see your instructor or technical support person for assistance.

Figure C-4	New Message window

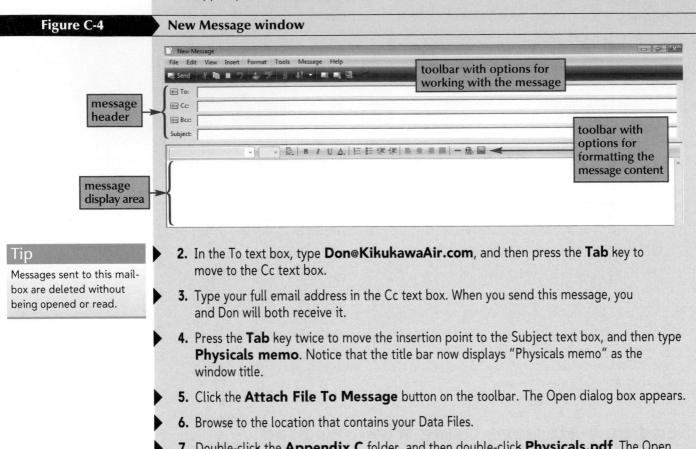

message header

toolbar with options for working with the message

toolbar with options for formatting the message content

message display area

Tip

Messages sent to this mailbox are deleted without being opened or read.

2. In the To text box, type **Don@KikukawaAir.com**, and then press the **Tab** key to move to the Cc text box.

3. Type your full email address in the Cc text box. When you send this message, you and Don will both receive it.

4. Press the **Tab** key twice to move the insertion point to the Subject text box, and then type **Physicals memo**. Notice that the title bar now displays "Physicals memo" as the window title.

5. Click the **Attach File To Message** button on the toolbar. The Open dialog box appears.

6. Browse to the location that contains your Data Files.

7. Double-click the **Appendix.C** folder, and then double-click **Physicals.pdf**. The Open dialog box closes, and the attached file's icon, filename, and file size appear in the Attach text box.

8. Click in the message display area, type **Dear Don,** (including the comma), and then press the **Enter** key twice to insert a blank line.

9. In the message display area, type **I have attached the memo you requested. Please let me know if you need anything else.**

10. Press the **Enter** key twice, type **Sincerely,** (including the comma), press the **Enter** key, and then type your first name to sign your message. See Figure C-5.

Composing an email message | Figure C-5

11. Click the **Spelling** button on the toolbar to check your spelling before sending the message. If necessary, correct any typing errors. When you are finished, click the **OK** button to close the Spelling dialog box.

12. Click the **Send** button on the toolbar to mail the message. The Physicals memo window closes and the message is sent.

   Trouble? If a Send Mail dialog box opens and tells you that the message will be sent the next time you click the Send/Receive button, click the OK button to continue.

   Trouble? If Windows Mail is configured to queue messages, the message will be stored in the Outbox folder, as indicated by a "(1)" in the Outbox folder. This difference causes no problems.

Depending on your system configuration, Windows Mail might not send your messages immediately. It might queue (hold) messages until you connect to your ISP or click the Send/Receive button on the toolbar. If you want to examine the setting and change it, click Tools on the menu bar, click Options, and then click the Send tab in the Options dialog box. If the Send messages immediately check box contains a check mark, then Windows Mail sends messages when you click the Send button on the toolbar. Otherwise, Windows Mail holds messages until you click the Send/Receive button.

Receiving and Reading a Message

When you receive new mail, messages that you haven't opened yet are displayed with a closed envelope icon next to them in the message list; messages that you have opened are displayed with an open envelope icon next to them. You check for new mail next.

To check for incoming mail:

1. Click the **Send/Receive** button on the toolbar, type your password in the Password text box of the Logon dialog box (if necessary), and then click the **OK** button. Depending on your system configuration, you might not need to connect to your ISP and type your password to retrieve your messages. Within a few moments, your mail server transfers all new mail to your Inbox. The Physicals memo message was sent to Don and also to your email address, which you typed in the Cc text box. Notice that the Inbox folder in the Folders list is bold, but other folders are not. A bold folder indicates that it contains unread mail; the number in parentheses next to the Inbox folder indicates the number of unread messages in that folder.

Trouble? If a Windows Mail message box opens and indicates that it could not find your host, click the Hide button to close the message box, click Tools on the menu bar, click Accounts, click your email account, and then click the Properties button. Verify that your incoming and outgoing server names are correct, and then repeat Step 1. If you still have problems, ask your instructor or technical support person for help.

Trouble? If you do not see any messages in your Inbox, then you either did not receive any new mail or you might be looking in the wrong folder. If necessary, click the Inbox folder in the Folders list. If you still don't have any mail messages, wait a few moments, and then repeat Step 1 until you receive a message.

▶ 2. If necessary, click the **Physicals memo** message in the message list to open the message in the Preview pane. See Figure C-6.

Figure C-6	Receiving an email message

Tip

The Search text box on the menu bar searches for text in messages you have sent and received. It is not a way to search the Help system. To access Help, click Help on the menu bar, and then click View Help.

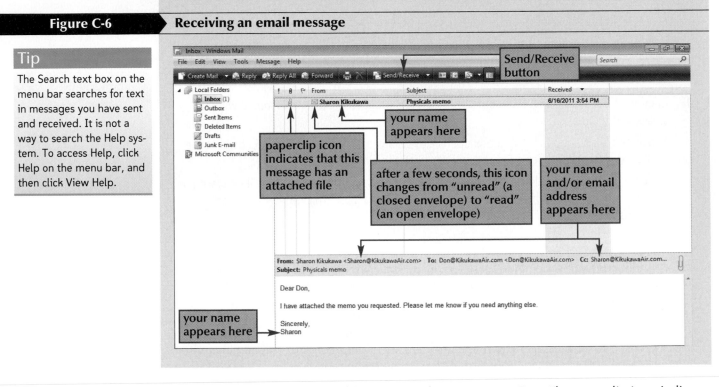

You received your copy of the message that you sent to Don. The paperclip icon indicates the message has an attachment. When you receive a message with one or more attachments, you can open the attachment or save it.

Viewing and Saving an Attached File

You want to make sure that your attached file was sent properly, so you decide to open it. Then you will save the file.

To view and save the attached file:

▶ 1. Make sure that the **Physicals memo** message is selected in the message list.

▶ 2. Click the **paperclip icon** in the upper-right corner of the Preview pane to open the shortcut menu. See Figure C-7.

Viewing an attached file | **Figure C-7**

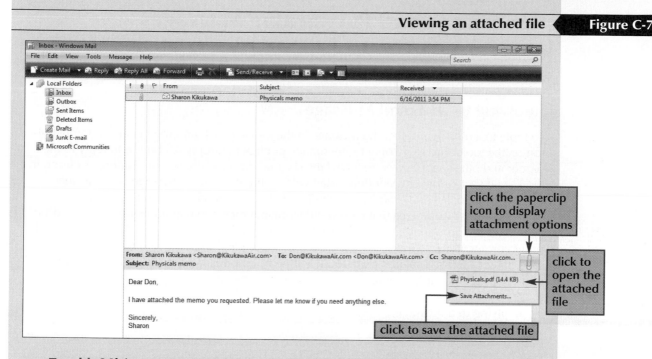

click the paperclip icon to display attachment options

click to open the attached file

click to save the attached file

Trouble? If the options on the shortcut menu are dimmed, then Windows Mail is configured to remove all potentially unsafe attachments from messages. Click the paperclip icon to close the menu. If you are working in a public computer lab, ask your instructor or technical support person for help. If you are working on a private computer, click Tools on the menu bar, click Options, click the Security tab, and then clear the "Do not allow attachments to be saved or opened that could potentially be a virus" check box. Click the OK button to close the Options dialog box, and then recompose, send, and receive the Physicals memo message. It is strongly suggested that you install and configure antivirus software when disabling this option to protect your computer from viruses.

The shortcut menu shows that a file named Physicals.pdf, with a file size of approximately 15 KB, is attached to the message. If this message contained other attachments, they would also appear on the shortcut menu. Clicking Physicals.pdf starts a program on your computer that can open the file. Clicking Save Attachments lets you save the file to the drive and folder that you specify.

▶ **3.** Click **Physicals.pdf** on the shortcut menu, and then, if necessary, click the **Open** button. Adobe Reader or another program on your computer starts and opens the attached file. If necessary, maximize the program window that opens.

▶ **4.** Click the **Close** button on the program window displaying the Physicals memo document. Now that you have viewed the attachment, you can save it.

▶ **5.** Click the **paperclip icon** in the Preview pane, and then click **Save Attachments** on the shortcut menu. The Save Attachments dialog box opens. The Physicals.pdf file is already selected for you.

▶ **6.** Click the **Browse** button. The Browse For Folder dialog box opens and lists all of the drives on your computer.

▶ **7.** Scrolling as necessary, open the drive or folder that contains your Data Files, click the **Appendix.C** folder to open it, and then click the **OK** button. The Save Attachments dialog box appears again. The Save To location indicates that you will save the attached file to the Appendix.C folder.

▶ **8.** Click the **Save** button to save the attached file, and then click the **Yes** button to overwrite the file with the same name.

Replying to and Forwarding Messages

You can forward any message you receive to one or more email addresses. Similarly, you can respond to the sender of a message quickly and efficiently by replying to a message.

Replying to an Email Message

To reply to a message, select the message in the message list, and then click the Reply button on the toolbar to reply only to the sender, or click the Reply All button to reply to the sender and other people who received the original message (those email addresses listed in the To and Cc text boxes). Windows Mail will open a new "Re:" message window and place the original sender's address in the To text box; if you clicked the Reply All button, then other email addresses that received the original message will appear in the To and Cc text boxes as appropriate. You can leave the Subject text box as is or modify it. Most email programs, including Windows Mail, will copy the original message and place it in the message body. Usually, a special mark to the left of the response indicates a quote from the text of the original message. Figure C-8 shows a reply to the message.

Figure C-8	Replying to a message

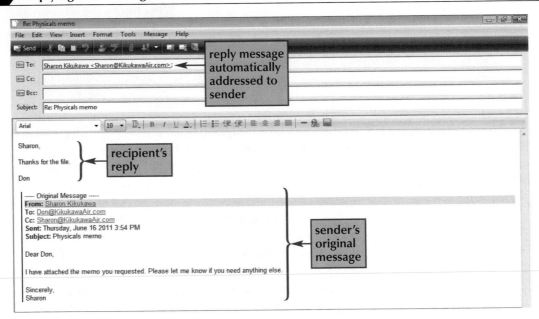

Forwarding an Email Message

When you forward a message, you are sending a copy of your message, including any attachments, to one or more recipients who may not have been included in the original message. (If you do not want to forward the original sender's attached file to the new recipients, select the attachment filename in the Attach text box, and then press the Delete key.) To forward an existing mail message to another user, open the folder containing the message you want to forward, select it in the message list, and then click the Forward button on the toolbar. The "Fw:" window opens, where you can type the address of the recipient in the To text box. If you want to forward the message to several people, type their addresses, separated by commas (or semicolons), in the To text box (or Cc or Bcc text boxes). Windows Mail inserts a copy of the original message in the message display area (as it does when you reply to a message). However, no special mark appears in the left margin to indicate the original message. Figure C-9 shows a forwarded copy of the message.

Forwarding a message ◀ Figure C-9

Often, you receive messages that you need to file and print.

Filing and Printing an Email Message

You can use the Windows Mail folders to file your email messages by topic or category. When you file a message, you move it from the Inbox to another folder. You can also make a copy of a message in the Inbox and save it in another folder by right-clicking the message in the message list, clicking Copy to Folder on the shortcut menu, and then selecting the folder in which to store the copy. You will file your message in a new folder named "FAA" for safekeeping. Later, you can create other folders to suit your needs.

To create a new folder:

▶ 1. Right-click the **Inbox** folder in the Folders list to open the shortcut menu, and then click **New Folder**. The Create Folder dialog box opens. When you create a new folder, first you must select the folder at the level above which to create the new folder. Because the Inbox folder is selected, the new folder that you create is a subfolder of the Inbox folder.

▶ 2. Type **FAA** in the Folder name text box. See Figure C-10.

Figure C-10 ▶ **Creating a new folder**

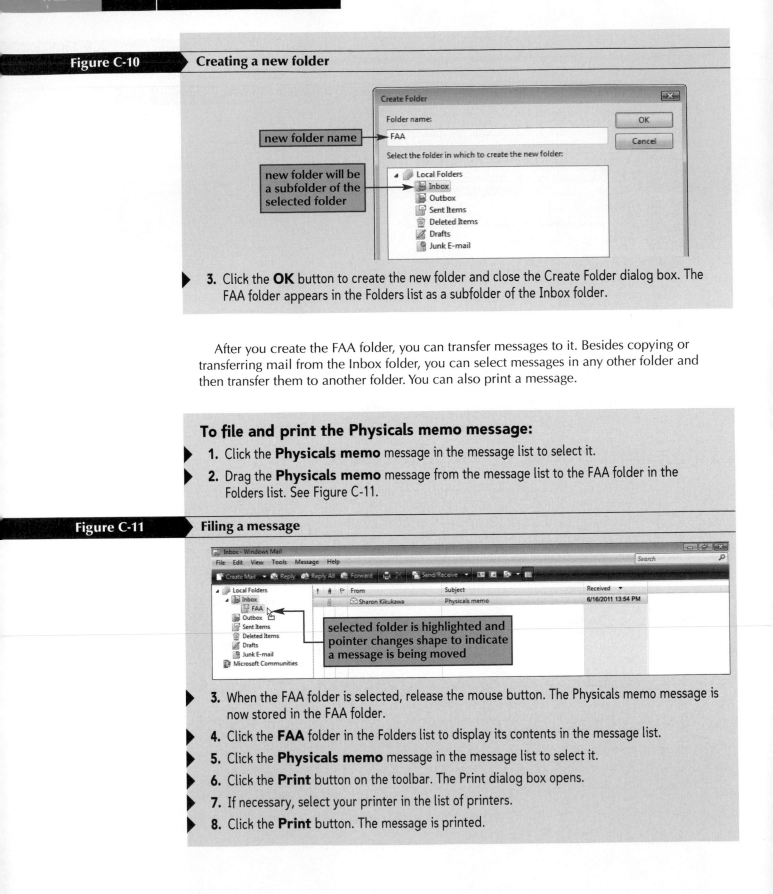

3. Click the **OK** button to create the new folder and close the Create Folder dialog box. The FAA folder appears in the Folders list as a subfolder of the Inbox folder.

After you create the FAA folder, you can transfer messages to it. Besides copying or transferring mail from the Inbox folder, you can select messages in any other folder and then transfer them to another folder. You can also print a message.

To file and print the Physicals memo message:

▶ 1. Click the **Physicals memo** message in the message list to select it.

▶ 2. Drag the **Physicals memo** message from the message list to the FAA folder in the Folders list. See Figure C-11.

Figure C-11 ▶ **Filing a message**

▶ 3. When the FAA folder is selected, release the mouse button. The Physicals memo message is now stored in the FAA folder.

▶ 4. Click the **FAA** folder in the Folders list to display its contents in the message list.

▶ 5. Click the **Physicals memo** message in the message list to select it.

▶ 6. Click the **Print** button on the toolbar. The Print dialog box opens.

▶ 7. If necessary, select your printer in the list of printers.

▶ 8. Click the **Print** button. The message is printed.

Deleting an Email Message and Folder

When you don't need a message any longer, select the message in the message list, and then click the Delete button on the toolbar. You can select multiple messages by pressing and holding the Ctrl key, clicking each message in the message list, and then releasing the Ctrl key. When you click the Delete button on the toolbar, each selected message is deleted. You can select folders and delete them using the same process. When you delete a message or a folder, you are really moving it to the Deleted Items folder. To remove items permanently, use the same process to delete the items from the Deleted Items folder.

To delete the message and the FAA folder:

► 1. If necessary, select the **Physicals memo** message in the message list.

► 2. Click the **Delete** button on the toolbar. The message is deleted from the FAA folder and is moved to the Deleted Items folder.

► 3. Click the **Deleted Items** folder in the Folder list to display its contents.

► 4. Click the **Physicals memo** message to select it, and then click the **Delete** button on the toolbar. A dialog box opens and asks you to confirm the deletion.

► 5. Click the **Yes** button. The Physicals memo message is deleted from the Deleted Items folder.

► 6. Click the **FAA** folder in the Folders list to select it. Because this folder doesn't contain any messages, the message list is empty.

► 7. Click the **Delete** button on the toolbar. A dialog box opens and asks you to confirm moving the folder to the Deleted Items folder.

► 8. Click the **Yes** button. The FAA folder moves to the Deleted Items folder. The Deleted Items folder has an arrow to its left, indicating that this folder contains another folder.

► 9. Click the **arrow** to the left of the Deleted Items folder, and then click the **FAA** folder to select it.

► 10. Click the **Delete** button on the toolbar, and then click the **Yes** button in the message box to delete the FAA folder permanently.

► 11. Click the **Inbox** folder in the Folders list to return to the Inbox.

Maintaining Your Windows Contacts

As you use email to communicate with business associates and friends, you can save their addresses in an address book to make it easier to enter addresses into the header of your email messages. In Windows Mail, the address book is called **Windows Contacts**. To create a new address, click the Contacts button on the toolbar to open the Windows Contacts window, and then click the New Contact button on the toolbar. The Properties dialog box opens, in which you can enter information about the new contact. On the Name and E-mail tab, you can enter a contact's name and email address; you can use the other tabs to enter optional address, business, personal, and other information about that contact. If you enter a short name in the Nickname text box, you can type the nickname instead of a person's full name when you address a new message.

Tip

Windows Mail also includes a calendar, which you can use to enter information about your appointments and reminders. To open Windows Calendar, click the Windows Calendar button on the toolbar.

Tip

As you send messages, Windows Mail might add the addresses of the recipients to your address book automatically. So you might see contacts listed, even if you didn't add them.

To add a contact to Windows Contacts:

▶ 1. Click the **Contacts** button on the toolbar. A window opens and displays your computer's drives and folders in the pane on the left and any existing contacts in the pane on the right. If necessary, maximize the window.

▶ 2. On the toolbar, click the **New Contact** button. The Properties dialog box opens with the insertion point positioned in the First text box on the Name and E-mail tab.

Trouble? If you do not see the New Contact button on the toolbar, right-click a blank area in the pane on the right to open the shortcut menu, click Properties to open the Contacts Properties dialog box, and then click the Customize tab. Click the Use this folder as a template button arrow, click Contacts in the list, and then click the OK button to close the Contacts Properties dialog box. If you still do not see the New Contact button on the toolbar, ask your instructor or technical support person for help.

▶ 3. Type **Jenny** in the First text box. As you type the contact's first name (and eventually their last name), the name of the Properties dialog box changes to indicate that the properties set in this dialog box belong to the specified contact.

▶ 4. Press the **Tab** key twice to move the insertion point to the Last text box, type **Mahala** in the Last text box, and then press the **Tab** key three times to move the insertion point to the Nickname text box.

▶ 5. Type **Jen** in the Nickname text box, and then press the **Tab** key to move the insertion point to the E-mail text box.

▶ 6. Type **Jenny@KikukawaAir.com** in the E-mail text box, and then click the **Add** button. Jenny's contact is complete. See Figure C-12.

Figure C-12 ▶ **Adding a contact to Windows Contacts**

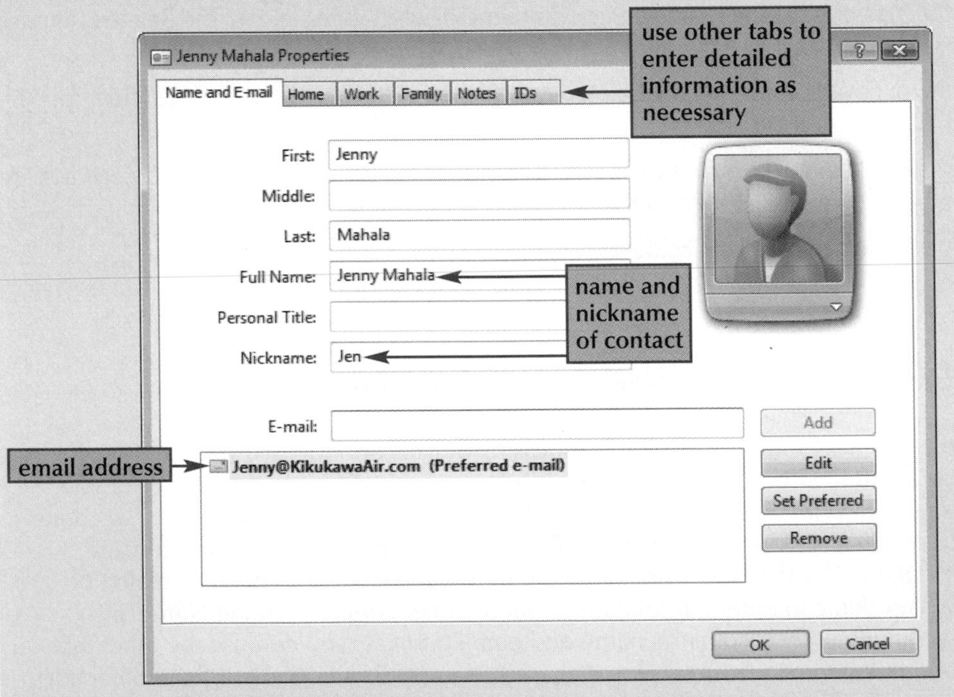

▶ 7. Click the **OK** button. The Properties dialog box closes and you return to the Contacts window. Jenny's contact now appears in the pane on the right.

▶ **8.** Repeat Steps 2 through 7 to create new contacts for the following Kikukawa Air employees:

First	Last	Nickname	Email Address
Zane	Norcia	Zane	Zane@KikukawaAir.com
Richard	Forrester	Rich	Richard@KikukawaAir.com

▶ **9.** Click the **Close** button on the Contacts window title bar to close it.

Now that these email addresses are stored in Windows Contacts, when you create a new message and start typing the first few letters of a nickname or first name in a text box in the message header, Windows Mail will complete the entry for you. Clicking the Check Names button on the toolbar in the New Message window changes the names you typed to their matching entries in Windows Contacts. If you need to change an address, click to select it and then press the Delete key.

When you receive mail from someone who is not in Windows Contacts, double-click the message to open it, right-click the "From" name to open the shortcut menu, and then click Add to Contacts. This process adds the sender's name and email address to Windows Contacts, where you can open his or her information as a contact and edit and add information as necessary.

You can also use Windows Mail to create a group of email addresses. Usually, you create a group of contacts when you regularly send messages to a group of people. For example, Sharon frequently sends messages to Zane, Jen, and Rich as a group because they have the same positions at the Kikukawa Air ticket counters. She asks you to create a group of contacts so she can type one nickname for the group of email addresses, instead of having to type each address separately.

To add a group of contacts to Windows Contacts and close Windows Mail:

▶ **1.** Click the **Contacts** button on the toolbar, and then, if necessary, maximize the Windows Contacts window.

▶ **2.** Click the **New Contact Group** button on the toolbar. The Properties dialog box opens and displays tabs related to group settings.

▶ **3.** With the insertion point positioned in the Group Name text box, type **Ticket Agents**. This nickname will represent the individual email addresses for employees working in this position.

▶ **4.** Click the **Add to Contact Group** button. The Add Members to Contact Group window opens. The pane on the right displays the existing contacts in Windows Contacts.

▶ **5.** Click **Jenny Mahala.contact** in the pane on the right to select her as the first contact in the group.

▶ **6.** Press and hold down the **Ctrl** key, click the contacts for **Richard Forrester** and **Zane Norcia**, and then release the **Ctrl** key.

▶ **7.** Click the **Add** button. Figure C-13 shows the completed group. The Properties dialog box for the Ticket Agents group contains three group members.

Tip

You can modify a group's members or delete one or more members from the group by opening Windows Contacts, double-clicking the group name in the pane on the right, and then deleting a selected member's name by clicking the Remove Selected Contacts button. You add members using the Add to Contact Group button.

Figure C-13   **Creating a group of contacts**

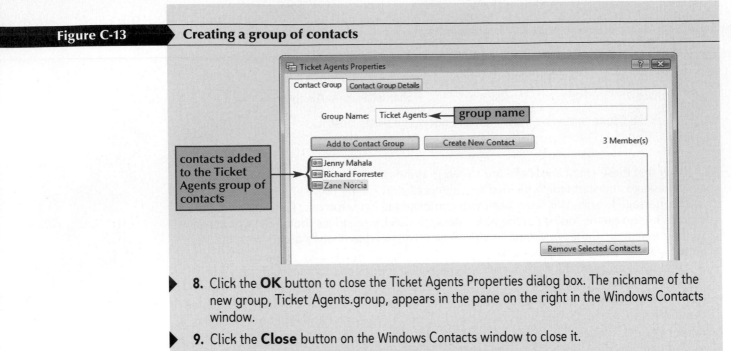

8. Click the **OK** button to close the Ticket Agents Properties dialog box. The nickname of the new group, Ticket Agents.group, appears in the pane on the right in the Windows Contacts window.

9. Click the **Close** button on the Windows Contacts window to close it.

10. Click **File** on the menu bar, and then click **Exit**. Windows Mail closes.

Review | **Appendix Summary**

In this Appendix, you learned how to use Windows Mail to manage, send, and receive email messages. You also learned how to print, file, save, delete, respond to, and forward email messages. You created an address book into which you stored the name, email address, and other important details about a person and a group of people. Now that you have learned these important skills, you can use Windows Mail to send and receive your own email messages.

Key Terms

Deleted Items folder	Junk E-mail folder	Preview pane
Drafts folder	message list	Sent Items folder
Folders list	Microsoft Windows Mail	Windows Contacts
Inbox folder	Outbox folder	Windows Mail

Glossary/Index

Task Reference

TASK	PAGE #	RECOMMENDED METHOD	WHERE USED
FIREFOX TASKS			
Bookmark file, save to a disk	WEB 55	*See* Reference Window: Saving a Bookmark File to a Disk	Firefox
Bookmark, save in a folder	WEB 54	*See* Reference Window: Saving a Bookmark in a Bookmarks Folder	Firefox
Bookmarks folder, create	WEB 53	*See* Reference Window: Creating a New Bookmarks Folder	Firefox
Cookies, delete	WEB 64	Click Tools, click Options, click the Privacy icon, click the remove individual cookies link, select a Web site folder, select a cookie, click the Remove Cookie button	Firefox
Cookies, manage	WEB 64	*See* Reference Window: Managing Cookies in Firefox	Firefox
Firefox, start	WEB 48	Click the Start button, point to All Programs, click Mozilla Firefox, click Mozilla Firefox	Firefox
Help, get	WEB 66	*See* Reference Window: Opening Firefox Help	Firefox
History list, open	WEB 56	Click View, point to Sidebar, click History	Firefox
Home page, change default	WEB 57	*See* Reference Window: Changing the Default Home Page in Firefox	Firefox
Home page, return to	WEB 12	Click the Home button	Firefox
Library window, open	WEB 54	Click Bookmarks, click Organize Bookmarks	Firefox
Page tabs, use for navigation	WEB 59	*See* Reference Window: Using Page Tabs to Navigate in Firefox	Firefox
Print settings, change	WEB 60	*See* Reference Window: Using Page Setup to Create a Custom Format for Printing a Web Page	Firefox
Private browsing mode, enter	WEB 65	*See* Reference Window: Opening Firefox in Private Browsing Mode	Firefox
Security, strengthen in Firefox	WEB 374	Click Tools, click Options, click Content, clear Enable Java and Enable JavaScript check boxes, click Security, click the Warn me when sites try to install add-ons check box, click OK	Firefox
Start page, return to	WEB 12	Click the Home button	Firefox
URL, enter and go to	WEB 50	*See* Reference Window: Entering a URL in the Location Field	Firefox
Web page image, save	WEB 70	*See* Reference Window: Saving an Image from a Web Page	Firefox
Web page, navigate using hyperlinks and the mouse	WEB 51	*See* Reference Window: Navigating Between Web Pages Using Hyperlinks and the Mouse	Firefox
Web page text, copy to a WordPad document	WEB 68	*See* Reference Window: Copying Text from a Web Page to a WordPad document	Firefox
Web page text, save	WEB 68	*See* Reference Window: Copying Text from a Web Page to a WordPad Document	Firefox
Web page, check security	WEB 62	Double-click the security indicator button	Firefox
Web page, move forward in history list	WEB 49	Click the Forward button	Firefox
Web page, print	WEB 60	*See* Reference Window: Printing the Current Web Page	Firefox

TASK	PAGE #	RECOMMENDED METHOD	WHERE USED
Web page, reload	WEB 57	Click the Reload button	Firefox
Web page, return to previous in history list	WEB 49	Click the Back button	Firefox
Web page, save	WEB 67	*See* Reference Window: Saving a Web Page	Firefox
Web page, set a custom format for printing	WEB 60	*See* Reference Window: Using Page Setup to Create a Custom Format for Printing a Web Page	Firefox
Web site, review certificate information	WEB 62	*See* Reference Window: Reviewing a Web Site's Certificate Information	Firefox
GMAIL TASKS			
Attached file, save	WEB 176	*See* Reference Window: Viewing and Downloading an Attached File in Gmail	Gmail
Attached file, view	WEB 176	*See* Reference Window: Viewing and Downloading an Attached File in Gmail	Gmail
Contact Manager, open	WEB 184	Click the Contacts link	Gmail
Contact, add to Contact Manager	WEB 184	*See* Reference Window: Adding a Contact to the Contact Manager	Gmail
File, attach	WEB 171	Click Attach a file, click Browse if using Firefox, locate and click the file, click Open	Gmail
Gmail account, sign in	WEB 164	Go to the Gmail home page, sign in to your account, click Sign in	Gmail
Gmail account, sign out	WEB 190	Click the Sign out link	Gmail
Google account, create	WEB 163	Start your browser, connect to the Internet, go to the Gmail home page, click Create an account, follow the on-screen steps	Gmail
Group, create using Contact Manager	WEB 186	*See* Reference Window: Creating a Group in the Contact Manager	Gmail
Label, apply to message	WEB 181	Click the check box for the message, click Labels, click the check box for the label name, click Apply	Gmail
Label, create	WEB 180	Click Settings, click Labels, click in the Create a new label text box, type label name, click Create	Gmail
Label, delete	WEB 183	*See* Reference Window: Deleting a Label	Gmail
Message, compose	WEB 171	Go to the Gmail home page, sign in to your account, click Compose Mail	Gmail
Message, delete	WEB 183	*See* Reference Window: Deleting an Email Message in Gmail	Gmail
Message, delete permanently	WEB 183	*See* Reference Window: Deleting an Email Message in Gmail	Gmail
Message, forward	WEB 180	*See* Reference Window: Forwarding an Email Message Using Gmail	Gmail
Message, print	WEB 182	Click the message, click Print all, select your printer, click Print or OK	Gmail
Message, read	WEB 174	Sign in to your Gmail account, click the Inbox, click the sender's name for the message in the Inbox	Gmail
Message, receive	WEB 174	Click the Inbox	Gmail

TASK	PAGE #	RECOMMENDED METHOD	WHERE USED
Message, reply to all recipients	WEB 178	*See* Reference Window: Replying to a Message Using Gmail	Gmail
Message, reply to sender	WEB 178	*See* Reference Window: Replying to a Message Using Gmail	Gmail
Message, send	WEB 171	*See* Reference Window: Sending a Message Using Gmail	Gmail
Message, spell check	WEB 173	Click the Check Spelling link	Gmail
HTML TASKS			
Bookmark, create in an HTML document	WEB 460	Add the attribute id="*bookmark name*" to the HTML tag that contains the bookmark text or graphic	Notepad
Bulleted list, create in an HTML document	WEB 455	Type <ul>, type <li>*the first item in the list*</li>, use <li> ... </li> to insert additional lines, type </ul> to end the list	Notepad
Comment, add to an HTML document	WEB 450	Type <!--*content to include in the comment*-->	Notepad
Font, add bold to an HTML document	WEB 454	Type *text to boldface* or *text to boldface*	Notepad
Font, add italic to an HTML document	WEB 454	Type <i>*text to italicize*</i> or *text to italicize*	Notepad
Font color, change	WEB 444, WEB 451	Add the attribute style="color: *color name*" to the HTML tag that contains the text to change	Notepad
Graphic, insert in an HTML document	WEB 457	Type <img src="*filename.ext*" alt="*alternative text*" />	Notepad
Graphic, insert in an HTML document using an absolute path	WEB 458	Type <img src="*drive:\path\filename.ext*" alt="*alternative text*" />	Notepad
Graphic, insert in an HTML document using a relative path	WEB 457	Type <img src="*../path/filename.ext*" alt="*alternative text*" />	Notepad
Heading, add largest to an HTML document	WEB 451	Type <h1>*text to include in the heading*</h1>	Notepad
Heading, add smallest to an HTML document	WEB 462	Type <h6>*text to include in the heading*</h6>	Notepad
Heading, center in an HTML document	WEB 451	Type <h1 style="text-align: center">*text to include in the heading*</h1>	Notepad
HTML document, create	WEB 446	Start Notepad, type the HTML document, save the file with the .htm or .html extension	Notepad
HTML document, view in Firefox	WEB 452	Click File, click Open File, double-click the HTML document	Firefox
HTML document, view in Internet Explorer	WEB 452	Click File, click Open, click Browse, double-click the HTML document, click OK	Internet Explorer
Hyperlink, create to a bookmark	WEB 460	Type <a href="*bookmark name*">*text for the hyperlink*</a>	Notepad

TASK	PAGE #	RECOMMENDED METHOD	WHERE USED
Hyperlink, create to a URL	WEB 460	Type <a href="*URL*">*text for the hyperlink*</a>	Notepad
Hyperlink, create to another file	WEB 460	Type <a href="*filename.ext*">*text for the hyperlink*</a>	Notepad
Line break, create in an HTML document	WEB 462	Type 	Notepad
Numbered list, create in an HTML document	WEB 455	Type <ol>, type <li>*content of the first item in the ist*</li>, use <li> ... </li> to insert additional list items, type </ol> to end the list	Notepad
Paragraph, add to an HTML document	WEB 453	Type <p>*content of the paragraph*</p>	Notepad

MICROSOFT INTERNET EXPLORER TASKS

TASK	PAGE #	RECOMMENDED METHOD	WHERE USED
Cookies, delete all	WEB 40	*See* Reference Window: Deleting All Cookies in Internet Explorer	Internet Explorer
Cookies, set placement options	WEB 40	*See* Reference Window: Setting Internet Explorer Options that Control Placement of Cookies on Your Computer	Internet Explorer
Favorite, move to a new folder	WEB 31	*See* Reference Window: Moving an Existing Favorite into a New Folder	Internet Explorer
Favorites Center, open	WEB 28	Click the Favorites Center button	Internet Explorer
Favorite, create in its own folder	WEB 29	*See* Reference Window: Creating a New Favorite in its Own Folder	Internet Explorer
Full screen, change to	WEB 25	Click the Tools button arrow, click Full Screen	Internet Explorer
Help, get	WEB 42	*See* Reference Window: Opening Internet Explorer Help	Internet Explorer
History list, open	WEB 32	Click the Recent Pages button, click History	Internet Explorer
Home page, change default	WEB 33	*See* Reference Window: Changing the Default Home Page in Internet Explorer	Internet Explorer
Home page, return to	WEB 12	Click the Home button	Internet Explorer
Internet Explorer, start	WEB 21	Click the Start button, point to All Programs, click Internet Explorer	
Page tabs, use for navigation	WEB 35	*See* Reference Window: Using Page Tabs to Navigate in Internet Explorer	Internet Explorer
Private browsing mode, enter	WEB 41	*See* Reference Window: Opening Internet Explorer in Private Browsing Mode	Internet Explorer
Security, strengthen in Internet Explorer	WEB 372	Click Tools, click Internet Options, click the Security tab, adjust security settings, click OK	Internet Explorer
Start page, return to	WEB 12	Click the Home button	Internet Explorer
Toolbar, customize	WEB 25	Click the Tools button arrow, point to Toolbars, click Customize	Internet Explorer

TASK	PAGE #	RECOMMENDED METHOD	WHERE USED
Toolbar, hide or restore	WEB 25	*See* Reference Window: Hiding and Restoring Toolbars in Internet Explorer	Internet Explorer
URL, enter and go to	WEB 25	*See* Reference Window: Entering a URL in the Address Window	Internet Explorer
Web page image, save	WEB 46	*See* Reference Window: Saving an Image from a Web Page	Internet Explorer
Web page, navigate using hyperlinks and the mouse	WEB 27	*See* Reference Window: Navigating Between Web Pages Using Hyperlinks and the Mouse	Internet Explorer
Web page text, copy to a WordPad document	WEB 44	*See* Reference Window: Copying Text from a Web Page to a WordPad Document	Internet Explorer
Web page text, save	WEB 44	*See* Reference Window: Copying Text from a Web Page to a WordPad Document	Internet Explorer
Web page, change print settings	WEB 36	Click the Print button arrow, click Page Setup	Internet Explorer
Web page, review site's certification information	WEB 38	*See* Reference Window: Reviewing a Web Site's Certification Information	Internet Explorer
Web page, move forward in history list	WEB 32	Click the Forward button	Internet Explorer
Web page, preview	WEB 37	Click the Print button arrow, click Print Preview	Internet Explorer
Web page, print	WEB 36	*See* Reference Window: Printing the Current Web Page	Internet Explorer
Web page, refresh	WEB 33	Click the Refresh button	Internet Explorer
Web page, return to previous in history list	WEB 32	Click the Back button	Internet Explorer
Web page, save	WEB 43	*See* Reference Window: Saving a Web Page	Internet Explorer
Web pages, move between using hyperlinks and the mouse	WEB 27	*See* Reference Window: Navigating Between Web Pages Using Hyperlinks and the Mouse	Internet Explorer
Web site, review certificate information	WEB 38	*See* Reference Window: Reviewing a Web Site's Certificate Information	Internet Explorer
WEB TASKS			
Boolean search, conduct using Exalead	WEB 226	*See* Reference Window: Conducting a Boolean Search Using Exalead	Web
Business listings, find	WEB 265	*See* Reference Window: Finding Business Listings on the Web	Web
Clustered search results, obtain using Clusty	WEB 232	*See* Reference Window: Obtaining Clustered Search Results Using Clusty	Web
Current news stories, search	WEB 255	*See* Reference Window: Searching Current News Stories	Web
Filtered search, conduct using Ask.com	WEB 228	*See* Reference Window: Conducting a Filtered Search Using Ask.com	Ask.com
Filtered search, conduct using Google Advanced Search	WEB 229	*See* Reference Window: Conducting a Filtered Search Using Google Advanced Search	Google
Google Groups, search	WEB 305	*See* Reference Window: Searching Google Groups for Newsgroup Articles	Web

TASK	PAGE #	RECOMMENDED METHOD	WHERE USED
Local area map, find	WEB 261	*See* Reference Window: Finding a Local Area Map on the Web	Web
Metasearch engine, use	WEB 219	*See* Reference Window: Using a Metasearch Engine	Web
Travel destination information, find	WEB 263	*See* Reference Window: Obtaining Travel Destination Information	Web
Video clips, find	WEB 284	*See* Reference Window: Finding Video Clips Online	Web
Weather forecast, find	WEB 259	*See* Reference Window: Finding a Weather Forecast	Web
Web research resource, evaluate	WEB 238	*See* Reference Window: Evaluating a Web Research Resource	Web
Web sites that have been modified recently, find	WEB 251	*See* Reference Window: Finding Web Sites that Have Been Modified Recently	Web
White pages listing, search	WEB 267	*See* Reference Window: Searching for Your White Pages Listing	Web
WINDOWS LIVE HOTMAIL TASKS			
Attached file, save	WEB 147	*See* Reference Window: Viewing and Saving an Attached File in Windows Live Hotmail	Windows Live Hotmail
Attached file, view	WEB 147	*See* Reference Window: Viewing and Saving an Attached File in Windows Live Hotmail	Windows Live Hotmail
Category, create using Windows Live Contacts	WEB 155	*See* Reference Window: Creating a Category in Windows Live Contacts	Windows Live Hotmail
Contact, add to Windows Live Contacts	WEB 153	*See* Reference Window: Adding a Contact to Windows Live Contacts	Windows Live Hotmail
File, attach	WEB 144	Click Attach, click File, click Browse if using Firefox, locate and click the file, click Open	Windows Live Hotmail
Mail folder, create	WEB 150	Click the Inbox, click Manage folders, click New, type the folder name, click Save	Windows Live Hotmail
Mail folder, delete	WEB 152	*See* Reference Window: Deleting a Windows Live Hotmail Folder	Windows Live Hotmail
Message, compose	WEB 144	Go to the Windows Live Hotmail home page, sign in to your account, click New	Windows Live Hotmail
Message, delete permanently	WEB 152	*See* Reference Window: Deleting an Email Message in Windows Live Hotmail	Windows Live Hotmail
Message, delete	WEB 152	*See* Reference Window: Deleting an Email Message in Windows Live Hotmail	Windows Live Hotmail
Message, forward	WEB 150	*See* Reference Window: Forwarding an Email Message Using Windows Live Hotmail	Windows Live Hotmail
Message, move to new folder	WEB 151	Click the check box for the message, click Move to, click the folder name	Windows Live Hotmail
Message, print	WEB 151	Click the message, click Print, select your printer, click Print or OK	Windows Live Hotmail
Message, read	WEB 142	Sign in to your Windows Live Hotmail account, click the Inbox, click the sender's name for the message in the Inbox	Windows Live Hotmail
Message, receive	WEB 147	Click the Inbox	Windows Live Hotmail

TASK	PAGE #	RECOMMENDED METHOD	WHERE USED
Message, reply to all recipients	WEB 149	*See* Reference Window: Replying to a Message Using Windows Live Hotmail	Windows Live Hotmail
Message, reply to sender	WEB 149	*See* Reference Window: Replying to a Message Using Windows Live Hotmail	Windows Live Hotmail
Message, send	WEB 144	*See* Reference Window: Sending a Message Using Windows Live Hotmail	Windows Live Hotmail
Message, spell check	WEB 146	Click the Spell check link	Windows Live Hotmail
Windows Live Contacts, open	WEB 153	Click the Contact list link	Windows Live Hotmail
Windows Live Hotmail account, set up	WEB 136	Start your browser, connect to the Internet, go to the Windows Live Hotmail home page, click Sign up, follow the on-screen steps	
Windows Live Hotmail, sign out	WEB 141	Click the sign out link	Windows Live Hotmail
Windows Live Hotmail, start	WEB 142	Go to the Windows Live Hotmail home page, sign in to your account	

WINDOWS LIVE MAIL TASKS

TASK	PAGE #	RECOMMENDED METHOD	WHERE USED
Attached file, save	WEB 113	*See* Reference Window: Viewing and Saving an Attached File in Windows Live Mail	Windows Live Mail
Attached file, view	WEB 113	*See* Reference Window: Viewing and Saving an Attached File in Windows Live Mail	Windows Live Mail
Category, create using Windows Live Contacts	WEB 122	*See* Reference Window: Using Windows Live Contacts to Create a Category	Windows Live Mail
Contact, add to Windows Live Contacts	WEB 120	*See* Reference Window: Adding a Contact to Windows Live Contacts	Windows Live Mail
File, attach in New Message window	WEB 109	Click the Attach button, locate and click the file, click Open	Windows Live Mail
Mail account, set up	WEB 106	Click the Add e-mail account link on the left side of the Windows Live Mail window, follow the on-screen steps	Windows Live Mail
Mail folder, create	WEB 117	Right-click the folder in which to create the new folder, click New folder, type the name of the folder, click OK	Windows Live Mail
Mail folder, delete	WEB 119	*See* Reference Window: Deleting an Email Message or a Folder in Windows Live Mail	Windows Live Mail
Message, compose	WEB 109	Click the New button	Windows Live Mail
Message, delete	WEB 119	*See* Reference Window: Deleting an Email Message or a Folder in Windows Live Mail	Windows Live Mail
Message, delete permanently	WEB 119	Open the Deleted items folder, click the message to delete, click the Delete button, click the Yes button	Windows Live Mail
Message, forward	WEB 117	*See* Reference Window: Forwarding an Email Message Using Windows Live Mail	Windows Live Mail
Message, move to another folder	WEB 118	Drag the message from the message list to a folder in the folders pane	Windows Live Mail

TASK	PAGE #	RECOMMENDED METHOD	WHERE USED
Message, print	WEB 118	Right-click the message in the Inbox, click Print on the shortcut menu, select your printer (if necessary), click the Print button	Windows Live Mail
Message, read	WEB 112	Click the message in the message list	Windows Live Mail
Message, receive	WEB 112	*See* Reference Window: Using Windows Live Mail to Send and Receive Messages	Windows Live Mail
Message, reply to	WEB 116	*See* Reference Window: Replying to a Message Using Windows Live Mail	Windows Live Mail
Message, send	WEB 109	*See* Reference Window: Sending a Message Using Windows Live Mail	Windows Live Mail
Message, send and receive	WEB 112	*See* Reference Window: Using Windows Live Mail to Send and Receive Messages	Windows Live Mail
Message, spell check in New Message window	WEB 111	Click the Check spelling button	Windows Live Mail
Windows Live Contacts, open	WEB 120	Click the Contacts shortcut in the folder pane	Windows Live Mail
Windows Live Mail, start	WEB 106	Click the Start button, click All Programs, click Windows Live, click Windows Live Mail	Windows 7